United States Development Assistance Policy

The Johns Hopkins Studies in Development
Vernon W. Ruttan and T. Paul Schultz, Consulting Editors

United States Development Assistance Policy

The Domestic Politics of Foreign Economic Aid

VERNON W. RUTTAN

The Johns Hopkins University Press *Baltimore and London*

 Published 1996
Printed in the United States of America on acid-free paper
9 8 7 6 5 4 3 2

The Johns Hopkins University Press
2715 North Charles Street
Baltimore, Maryland 21218-4363
The Johns Hopkins Press Ltd., London

Library of Congress Cataloging-in-Publication Data
will be found at the end of this book.
A catalog record for this book is available from the British Library.

ISBN 0-8018-5051-7

To the men and women of the Agency for International Development who practice their professions with skill and dedication, often under exceedingly difficult circumstances, both in Washington and abroad

Contents

Figures, Exhibits, and Tables

Figures

Exhibits

Tables

Abbreviations

ABS	Annual Budget Submission
ACVAFS	American Council of Voluntary Agencies for Foreign Service
ADB	Asian Development Bank
ADF	African Development Foundation
AFBF	American Farm Bureau Federation
AfDB	African Development Bank
AfDF	African Development Fund
AFL	American Federation of Labor
AID	Agency for International Development
AIPAC	American-Israel Public Affairs Committee
AJC	American Jewish Committee
ARENA	National Republican Alliance
AWACS	airborne warning and command system
BHN	basic human needs
BIFAD	Board for International Food and Agricultural Development
BIFADEC	Board for International Food and Agricultural Development and Economic Cooperation
CAME	Conference of Allied Ministers of Education
CARE	Cooperative for American Remittances in Europe [later Relief Everywhere]
CBI	Carribean Basin Initiatives
CBO	Congressional Budget Office
CCC	Commodity Credit Corporation
CFEP	Council on Foreign Economic Policy
CGIAR	Consultative Group on International Agricultural Research
CIA	Central Intelligence Agency
CIO	Congress of Industrial Organizations

CIP	Commercial Import Program
CRS	Congressional Research Service
CRSP	Collaborative Research Support Program
CWS	Church World Service
DCC	Development Coordinating Committee
DLF	Development Loan Fund
EBRD	European Bank for Reconstruction and Development
ECA	Economic Cooperation Administration
ECAFE	Economic Commission for Asia and the Far East
ECOSOC	Economic and Social Council
EEC	European Economic Community
EEP	Export Enhancement Program
EPI	Economic Policy Initiative
EPTA	Expanded Program of Technical Assistance
ERP	European Recovery Program
ESF	Economic Support Fund
Eximbank	Export-Import Bank
FAA	Foreign Assistance Act
FAO	Food and Agriculture Organization
FMLN	Frente Farabunda Marti Tara la Liberación Nacional
FOA	Foreign Operations Administration
FSLN	El Frente Sandinista de Liberación Nacional
FSO	Fund for Special Operations
FVA	Bureau for Food for Peace and Voluntary Assistance
GAO	General Accounting Office
GAP	Group for Alternative Policies
GATT	General Agreement on Tariffs and Trade
GEF	Global Environment Facility
GNP	gross national product
G-R-H	Gramm-Rudman-Hollings Act
GVN	government of Vietnam
IADB	Inter-American Development Bank
IAEA	International Atomic Energy Agency

IAF	Inter-American Foundation
IARC	International Agricultural Research Center
IBRD	International Bank for Reconstruction and Development
ICA	International Cooperation Administration
ICASD	Interagency Committee on Agricultural Surplus Disposal
ICS	in-country service
IDA	International Development Association
IDCA	International Development Cooperation Agency
IDF	International Development Foundation
IFAD	International Fund for Agricultural Development
IFC	International Finance Corporation
IGA	Inspector-General for Foreign Assistance
IIAA	Institute of Inter-American Affairs
ILO	International Labor Organization
IMF	International Monetary Fund
IPVC	Institute for Private Voluntary Cooperation
IRRI	International Rice Research Institute
ISTC	Institute for Scientific and Technical Cooperation
ISTEC	Institute for Scientific, Technical, and Economic Cooperation
ITO	International Trade Organization
LDC	less developed country
MDB	multilateral development bank
MDCA	Mutual Development and Cooperation Act
MIT	Massachusetts Institute of Technology
MSA	Mutual Security Agency
NAC	National Advisory Council on International Monetary and Financial Policies
NARS	national agriculture research system
NATO	North Atlantic Treaty Organization
NGO	nongovernmental organization
NIEO	new international economic order
NSC	National Security Council
NWICO	new world information and communications order

OAS	Organization of American States
ODC	Overseas Development Council
OECD	Organization for Economic Cooperation and Development
OMB	Office of Management and Budget
OPEC	Organization of Petroleum Exporting Countries
OPIC	Overseas Private Investment Corporation
OTA	Office of Technology Assessment
PASB	Pan American Sanitary Bureau (later Board)
PLO	Palestine Liberation Organization
PVO	private voluntary organization
SDF	Sustainable Development Fund
TCA	Technical Cooperation Agency
TCP	Technical Cooperation Programme
TEA	Targeted Export Assistance Program
TFAP	Tropical Forestry Action Plan
UAW	United Automobile Workers
UNAC	United Nations Appeal for Children
UNDP	United Nations Development Programme
UNEP	United Nations Environmental Program
UNESCO	United Nations Educational, Scientific, and Cultural Organization
UNICEF	United Nations Children's Fund
UNIDO	United Nations Industrial Development Organization
UNO	National Opposition Union
UNRRA	United Nations Relief and Rehabilitation Agency
US/AID	U.S. Agency for International Development
USDA	U.S. Department of Agriculture
USOM	U.S. Operations Mission
WFP	World Food Program
WHO	World Health Organization
WIG	Western Information Group

Preface

In the years immediately after World War II, the United States assisted in the economic recoveries of both its allies and its former enemies. Before this task was complete, the United States had committed itself to a program to make "the benefits of our scientific advances and our industrial progress available for the improvement and growth of underdeveloped areas."[1] These commitments were out of character with our own past as well as with the behavior of victors in earlier international conflicts. After World War I we had failed, to the great disappointment of President Woodrow Wilson, to join the League of Nations. After major European wars of the past, the victors typically had insisted on territorial concessions and reparations. And relations with non-Western peoples—after conquest, with colonization, or during trade—had been undertaken with the objective of obtaining economic benefits for the metropolitan country.

This book had its origins in a search for the answers to three questions: (1) Why had the United States engaged in a series of large-scale resource transfers to other countries since World War II? (2) What were the sources of the changes in development assistance policy that followed our initial commitments? and (3) What is the future of U.S. assistance to foreign countries for economic development?

This book is organized in four major sections. In Part One (Chaps. 1 and 2), I outline the conceptual foundations that guide the analysis in the later sections. In Part Two (Chaps. 3–7), I focus on five critical periods in the evolution of U.S. economic assistance policy. These periods each represented important turning points in assistance policy. In Part Three (Chaps. 8–10), I trace the evolution of the several major bilateral assistance efforts. In Part Four (Chaps. 11 and 12), I discuss U.S. policy toward the multilateral assistance programs—the World Bank and other international lending agencies and the specialized agencies and voluntary programs of the United Nations. In Part Five (Chaps. 13 and 14), I trace the history of attempts to reform and redirect U.S. assistance programs and outline my own perspective on the future direction of economic assistance policy.

The Effects of Assistance

Since the late 1940s U.S. assistance activities have often been motivated more by our own security concerns than by the objective needs of the countries we have attempted to assist. At other times we have clearly been motivated by genuine concern for the alleviation of poverty, the development of viable national economies, and the strengthening of democratic political systems in recipient countries. Were these policy changes primarily a response to the external political and economic environment? Or did they reflect changing economic and political forces within the U.S. domestic economy?

These questions were an outgrowth of my involvement in the early 1980s in an assessment of the effects of development assistance. Under a project sponsored by the Bureau for Program and Policy Coordination of the Agency for International Development (AID) and the Intelligence and Research Bureau of the Department of State, Anne O. Krueger and I attempted to assess the effects of economic assistance on economic development.[2] Later I learned that an important motive for the study was interagency rivalry in the area of assistance policy. The Department of the Treasury commissioned a study of assistance policy by Raymond Mikesell of the University of Oregon.[3] The State Department and the Agency for International Development responded by deciding that it would be useful to arm themselves by commissioning their own study.

During the course of our work, Professor Krueger and I discussed the possibility of turning our report into a book. Our report to the AID had been prepared hurriedly. We thought that it could be improved by additional work. Unfortunately, we were diverted by other commitments. Professor Krueger had taken leave from the Department of Economics at the University of Minnesota to assume the position of Vice President for Economics and Research at the World Bank. It was not until 1987, after Krueger left the World Bank, that she and I were able to again turn our attention to reworking the earlier report. We were joined in this effort by Constantine Michalopoulos of the World Bank, who had initially been the project contract officer at the U.S. Agency for International Development (US/AID).[4]

Some findings of the assistance study were particularly significant in turning my attention to the evolution of U.S. assistance policy. One was the frequency with which the pursuit of U.S. strategic interests had weakened the effect of U.S. economic assistance on a recipient country's economic development. This problem was exacerbated during the later years of the Carter administration and the first Reagan administration. After the mid-1970s, the share of assistance accounted for by supporting or security assistance relative to development assistance rose steadily. Indeed, it was the Reagan administration's announced intention to achieve closer linkages between development and security objectives in foreign economic assistance.

Participation in Development Assistance

These findings tended to confirm the impressions I had acquired during my association with development assistance beginning in the early 1960s. During 1963–65 I was on the staff of the Rockefeller Foundation located at the International Rice Research Institute (IRRI) in the Philippines. The IRRI was the first unit in what has since become a system of international agricultural research institutes. The objective set before the staff by Robert Chandler, the director of IRRI, was "to raise rice yields in Asia." This struck me as audacious in the extreme! How could a small research institute with fewer than 20 senior scientists aspire to such an objective? But the objective was attained! IRRI, in collaboration with several national research institutes, developed a series of high-yielding rice varieties that have contributed to a dramatic increase in rice production in some Asian countries.

While I was working at IRRI, I was able to visit the agricultural research systems in almost every country in Asia. I visited Vietnam several times when it was the largest recipient of U.S. assistance. These visits brought me into close contact with the US/AID agency offices and programs. During this period I was impressed many times with the difficulty of bringing effective leverage to bear in achieving economic reform, even in so simple a matter as raising by a few cents the price paid to farmers for rice when host governments pleaded security considerations as an excuse to avoid pursuing economic reform.

I returned to the United States in 1965 to head the Department of Agricultural Economics (1965–70) and later the Economic Development Center (1970–73) at the University of Minnesota. In 1973 I left the University of Minnesota to become president (1973–78) of the Agricultural Development Council. The council was a small foundation established in the 1950s by John D. Rockefeller to work on rural development problems in Asia. I secured US/AID support that enabled the council to expand its fellowship program and to include Nepal and Pakistan in the countries in which it worked. As council president, I was able to observe the operations of AID-sponsored projects throughout Asia.

During the mid-1970s, I also served as co-chairman with Dr. Kazeshi Ohkawa, on a committee established by the Asian Development Bank (ADB) to review the bank's agricultural programs in Asia. I was also a member of the US/AID Research Advisory Committee in 1967–75 and again in 1983–85. In 1986 I withdrew from membership on the Research Advisory Committee because I became convinced that AID had lost the capacity to make effective use of the committee.

Since returning to the University of Minnesota in 1978, I have also continued to be actively involved in research and consultation on issues of economic development and development assistance policy. In 1984–86 I was involved in a study, with John Lewis, of the World Bank in Pakistan.[5] In 1987 I was commissioned to review the program and management review process used by the Consultative Group on International Agricultural Research (CGIAR) to monitor the progress of the international agricultural research institutes.[6] My research, which earlier had been focused primarily on the economic aspects of technical change, became increasingly concerned with problems of the sources and effects of institutional change in the development process.

Questions about AID

When I first became involved in development assistance, I saw no basis for concern about why U.S. private voluntary organizations (e.g., the Ford and Rockefeller foundations) or the U.S. government, through its Agency for International Development, were engaged in foreign assistance. I simply took the involvement as given because the need for technical and economic assistance in the developing world was so obvious. However, I recall commenting to a colleague that Robert Chandler, Director of the IRRI, "is a missionary for science. In an earlier generation, he would have come to Asia as a missionary for the church." I also recall wondering aloud, after one of several trips to Vietnam to advise on rice price policy, whether the role of those of us in the field of technical assistance was not similar to that of the religious who had accompanied the conquistadors to the New World.

In general, however, I embraced the dictum of Daniel Bell that the "age of ideology" had passed. It was not difficult, at the beginning of the Kennedy administration, to accept the view that the primary reason for U.S. economic assistance was a generalized interest in living in a world that was both more prosperous and more democratic. In the late 1960s I viewed the American failure in Vietnam as the consequence of a mistaken effort to contain communism by military means in a part of the world in which the United States had no vital strategic interest.

During the mid-1970s, as the Vietnam War was ending, however, I became increasingly sensitive to the extent that U.S. development assistance policy was dominated by domestic political forces rather than by the objective needs of developing countries. The basic human needs orientation that informed the congressional aid initiatives in the early and mid-1970s seemed to reflect a combination of the same political forces that had given rise to the domestic antipoverty policies of the mid- and late 1960s and to the antitechnology orientation of the environmental movement. These concerns, stemming primarily from domestic political sources, led to a view that the training of agronomists to work in research institutions of less developed countries was too elitist, deeming as appropriate only indigenous technology development and assistance for community or village-level development projects.

I shared the objectives of the proponents of the basic human needs approach to assistance. How could the objectives be questioned? They included "a life expectancy of 65 years or more . . . ; a literacy rate of at least 75 percent . . . ; an infant mortality rate of 50 or less per thousand births . . . ; and a birth rate of 25 or less per thousand population."[7] Nevertheless, I continued to insist that, unless the productive capacity of rural and urban communities and of agricultural and industrial sectors were enhanced, programs directed to meeting basic needs would not be sustained.[8]

One of the problems that faces one who is directly involved in attempting to understand contemporary events is how exceedingly difficult it is to know just what is going on. An example may be useful. During the early and mid-1970s, I visited Bangladesh both as a consultant and in my capacity as president of the Agricultural Development Council. Food aid shipments that were supposed to arrive at the port of Dakka during the period of food shortage in the summer and early fall of 1974 were delayed until late fall, when the harvest was already under way. Inquiries about the reason for the delay suggested that the problem was bureaucratic inefficiency. This was one more example of food aid arriving at the wrong time! Only later did I learn that the United States was deliberately delaying food aid shipments as leverage to force Bangladesh to discontinue its exports of jute bags to Cuba.

Another example was my participation in 1978 on a committee that recommended the establishment of a new Institute for Scientific and Technological Cooperation (ISTC). It was envisaged that ISTC would be separated from the AID agency and function as a foundation-like institution. It would maintain a cooperative relationship with the middle-income countries that had graduated from being eligible for assistance by the US/AID. The ISTC proposal was part of a broader effort proposed by Senator Hubert Humphrey (D-Minn.), shortly before his death, to give AID a stronger role in coordinating the U.S. assistance effort. It was supported by members of the White House staff and the State Department but opposed by the Department of Treasury. By the time the proposal was modified to meet Treasury and congressional objectives, the rationale for a separate technical and scientific cooperation agency had evaporated (see Chap. 13). Yet the bureaucratic and congressional politics that led to the demise of the ISTC idea had been completely obscure to me while I was serving on the ISTC planning committee.

Historians have been more sensitive than social scientists to the ambiguity in the relationship between motives and effects or between means and ends. "History, more than any other discipline, can claim to be a science of unintended consequences."[9] It is possible that assistance rendered for purposes that may be regarded as illegitimate by some—assistance for political or strategic purposes, for example—may contribute to the reduction of poverty or the growth of income in the recipient country. It is also possible that aid rendered for the best of humanitarian or developmental motives may produce results that the supporters of aid would wish to disavow—failed irrigation projects that force more land out of production from waterlogging than is added by irrigation, food aid that renders communities increasingly dependent on external assistance. There is a tendency in both the populist and the professional literature to infer bad motives from bad results and to insist on discovering bad results when the motives for providing assistance are dominated by strategic or economic self-interest. My own view is that the discrepancy between articulated objectives and accomplishments has reflected a combination of continuing ideological obsession with the struggle between liberal and realist views of world order, a constant failure of analysis in relating economic and political objectives to the means required to achieve the objectives, and a frequent misperception of the U.S. national interest.

My concern about the rationale—ethical, political, and economic—for U.S. foreign economic assistance was stimulated further in the fall of 1986 when I participated in a conference, sponsored by the conservative Liberty Fund, on the ethical bases of foreign economic assistance. I was disturbed by the difficulty that many of the conference participants, primarily political philosophers, experienced in finding any ethical bases for foreign economic assistance. There was a strongly held view that American political philosophy does not give our government any right to do good to foreigners at the expense of citizens. After the conference I attempted to work out a response to the question, Why foreign economic assistance? (Chap. 2). My own answer was that the emergence of international political and economic interdependence has extended the moral basis for distributive justice from the national to the international sphere. International interdependence has resulted in an implicit global contract between the citizens of developed and developing countries.

On Method

In an earlier work, Yujiro Hayami and I had outlined a model of induced technical change.[10] This model had enabled us to interpret the process of technical change in both developed and developing countries as largely endogenous. As we worked with the model, we found that it could be generalized to include the process of institutional change. The major gap in our model was the relationships between cultural endowments and the other elements of the model—particularly between cultural endowments and institutional change. Yet it became increasingly clear that neither the economic nor the political relations between the United States and the developing world could possibly be understood unless we tried to understand the role of cultural endowments—particularly the role of doctrine or ideology.

My search for a way to introduce ideological considerations into economic analysis elicited very little assistance from colleagues in the other social sciences.[11] The reason, in part, is the difficulty of recognizing ideology when one sees it. How does one define ideology—theory in action—so that unbiased observers can agree on what they are observing? An even more important reason is that social scientists who have tried to work with the concept of ideology have had great difficulty with what economists term the *identification problem*—whether a variable is appropriately viewed as dependent or independent in a particular analysis.[12]

The role of ideology is particularly important in attempting to interpret political and economic history. Most of us realize, if we reflect back on the history that we were taught in school, that it was largely propaganda. But can political and economic history be more than propaganda? My response, in this book, is to attempt to maintain a continuous dialogue between institutional and intellectual history. Intellectual history is in danger of losing its authority when it is not linked to institutional history. Institutional history can be understood only through the screen of theory. I attempt, throughout this study, to maintain a continuing dialogue between intellectual and institutional history. As a result, this book has more in common with the somewhat outdated politics of policy approach practiced in the 1940s and 1950s by such scholars as my former professor, Charles Hardin of the University of Chicago Department of Political Science, than with the more recent political economy or public choice models employed in political science.

It will be apparent to careful scholars of economic and political history that the book relies to only a limited extent on original sources. The scope of the book precludes the careful sifting of original sources that might have been possible in a more specialized monograph. I and my students have, however, conducted a substantial number of interviews with participants in the events discussed. I have also followed the practice of inviting comments from other scholars and from agency officers and staff.

I have not hesitated to draw policy conclusions and to make policy judgments about the events covered. My interest in doing the book, as noted earlier, derives from my association with economic assistance to developing countries since the early 1960s. I have attempted to make my policy judgments—or biases—as explicit as possible, rather than hiding behind a pretense of academic objectivity.

Part I

Interests and Passions

Chapter 1

The Domestic Sources of Foreign Assistance Policy

The use of foreign aid as an instrument through which the government of one country voluntarily transfers substantial resources to strengthen the economy or institutions of another country is a relatively recent phenomenon.[1] The Marshall Plan, initiated in 1948 to restore the economies of war-ravaged Western Europe, was the first major U.S. public foreign economic assistance program. Since the early 1950s the United States has transferred over $200 billion in economic assistance to the less developed countries of Latin America, Asia, and Africa. From the late 1950s on, the United States has been joined by other developed countries in a global development assistance undertaking.[2]

In subsequent chapters I examine the evolution of U.S. development assistance policy from its initial roots, which extend backward to well before World War II. In this chapter I outline my framework for the analysis of U.S. development assistance policy as it has responded to (*a*) broad themes in American intellectual history, (*b*) the evolution of foreign assistance policy doctrine, and (*c*) the changing interests of the several domestic foreign assistance constituencies.

American Exceptionalism and Foreign Policy

American historical scholarship and political doctrine have, from the nation's earliest years, been ambivalent about the appropriate relation of the United States with the rest of the world. In both historical scholarship and popular culture, the American experience has been interpreted as endowing the nation with unique political virtue. The influence of the frontier in American political life provided a rationale for constructing a view of the New World as innocent, free, and republican in contrast to the oppressive and corrupt Old

World.[3] Although the participation of the United States in two world wars resulted in an erosion of confidence in American exceptionalism among historians and political philosophers, it has remained a powerful theme in popular political culture.

The American exceptionalism perspective has spawned two conflicting doctrines about the appropriate relation of the United States to the rest of the world. The first is the *idealist* (or liberal) doctrine that the American experience represents the perfection of political and economic evolution. An extension of this view is found in the belief that it is the mission of the United States to lead the world—by example, assistance, and cooperation—into a more democratic and prosperous future. The second is the *realist* (or conservative) doctrine that a virtuous America, prosperous and democratic, is continuously threatened with contamination by the antidemocratic and corrupt Old World. An extension of this view is that the United States must continuously be on guard against the corrupting influences of Old World ideology and that we must manage our relations with other countries primarily in the interests of our own security.[4] These two conflicting doctrines have exerted a powerful influence on U.S. assistance policy almost from the beginning.

The basic outline of the policies that have guided U.S. economic assistance to other countries became fully shaped during a 14-week period in the winter and spring of 1947 (see Exhibit 3.1). The 14 weeks began on 24 February 1947, "the day Great Britain informed the Department of State of its inability to maintain its commitments in Greece and Turkey, and ended when General George C. Marshall, the U.S. Secretary of State, presented his famous commencement address at Harvard University on June 5. Out of those hundred days two programs emerged: The Truman Doctrine for aid to Greece and Turkey, and the Marshall Plan of aid to the economic recovery of Europe."[5] Both doctrines, initiated shortly after General Marshall became secretary of state, have often been perceived as reflecting a common theme in response to the threat of Soviet expansionism. However, such perceptive observers as journalist Walter Lippmann immediately noted the difference in the American commitment and the expectations implied by the two programs.[6]

The Truman Doctrine was enunciated in a speech before a joint session of Congress on 12 March 1947. Greece was then involved in bitter civil war, and both Greece and Turkey were facing extremely difficult economic problems. The former under-secretary of state, Dean Acheson, had urged a statement of global policy. President Harry S. Truman insisted that, if Congress was to be convinced that the large funds being sought for military and economic support ($250 million for Greece and $150 million for Turkey) were necessary, the U.S. national interest would have to be defined more broadly than simply as the defense of Greece and Turkey. In his speech Truman, drawing on the theme of George F. Kennan's 1946 "long telegram" and subsequent memorandum, "Psychological Background of Soviet Foreign Policy," identified the Greek Civil War as "part of an ongoing struggle between democracy and dictatorship."[7] He asked Congress not only to appropriate funds to aid Greece and Turkey, but also for support of a commitment to containing the expansionist tendencies of the Soviet Union and providing support to free people who are resisting attempted subjugation "by armed minorities or by outside pressure" along the borders of the Soviet empire.[8]

The Marshall Plan was both more ambitious in its means and less grand in its objectives than the Truman Doctrine. Under-Secretary of State Acheson and President Truman became increasingly concerned, as the Truman Doctrine was taking shape, with the problem of European economic recovery. While in Moscow at the Council of Foreign Ministers in February and March, Secretary Marshall became increasingly concerned about the political future of Western Europe. Assistant Secretary William L. Clayton, returned from a trip to attend the opening of the Economic Commission for Europe, convinced that Western Europe was sliding toward economic disaster. Marshall recognized that only extraordinary measures, involving large amounts of American economic assistance, could avert economic and political chaos. He also was convinced that the American public would not support the level of direct entanglement in European affairs to which the Truman Doctrine seemed to be leading in Greece. In Secretary Marshall's Harvard speech of 5 June, "there was no 'Marshall Plan' for Europe: the essence of his proposal was that only a European plan for Europe could save Europe, or provide a basis on which the American people could prudently and fairly be asked to help Europe save itself."[9]

> Lippmann saw a fundamental difference between the Truman Doctrine and the Marshall Plan. The Truman Doctrine treats those who are supposed to benefit by it as dependencies of the United States, as instruments of the American policy for "containing" Russia. The Marshall speech at Harvard treats the European governments as independent powers, whom we must help but *cannot* presume to govern, or to use as instruments of American policy.[10]

The Economic Cooperation Act, passed by a Republican-controlled Congress on 1 April 1948, authorized a European Recovery program that eventually would expend $13 billion over a four-year time span.

Given that the two stepchildren of American exceptionalism acquired such dominant force in U.S. assistance policy in 1947, consistency obviously is not an excessive burden on political practice. The Truman Doctrine embodied the concerns of realists about America's relation to the rest of the world; the Marshall Plan embodied the idealist premise.

Since 1947 the global political and economic environment has changed dramatically. We have completed what Walt W. Rostow identified as three distinct Cold War periods: 1945–55, 1955–73, and 1973–87. During this period American economic and military hegemony has eroded. Marxist ideology, which seemed so powerful in Western Europe in the early postwar period and so attractive to the intellectual and political elite in the developing world in the 1950s and 1960s, has lost much of its credibility. By the mid-1970s a number of developing countries, among them Taiwan, Korea, Brazil, and Mexico, had achieved levels of educational development and technological sophistication that enabled them to challenge the economic performance of the advanced industrial countries. By the early 1990s, both India and China were emerging as major industrial powers.

But commitment has wavered, in American popular culture and political practice, between the two offspring of American exceptionalism. Infatuation with realist and idealist perspectives has altered over time and in regions of the world. In areas where signs of Soviet involvement could be detected, security concerns often dominated the design of assistance policy. In areas characterized by repressive political and economic regions, the liberal perspective often has led to unrealistic expectations regarding technical, economic, and political development.

It is, perhaps, remarkable that a record of substantial success for U.S. economic assistance has been established, given the domestic and international political environment in which U.S. economic assistance policy has evolved. In collaboration with Anne O. Krueger and Constantine Michalopoulos, I have documented some of these successes.[11] In this book I focus on the domestic forces—economic, political, intellectual, and cultural—that have shaped American economic assistance policy since the days of the Truman Doctrine and the Marshall Plan.

Foreign Policy and Foreign Assistance

The roots of American foreign assistance policy trace back to the interwar period and earlier (Chap. 3). Foreign assistance became institutionalized as a continuing feature of American foreign policy with the enunciation of the Truman Doctrine (1947), the Marshall Plan (1947), and the Point Four Program (1949).

Three objectives—strategic, economic, and humanitarian—have been constant features of U.S. aid programs.[12] The Truman Doctrine established the principle of assistance to strengthen the economic, political, and military viability of countries that were regarded as of strategic importance to the

United States. The Marshall Plan established the principle of massive transfer of resources to sustain the economic and political stability of countries whose commitment to a liberal political and economic order was viewed as in our long-term interest. The Point Four Program committed the United States to using its technical and financial resources to "relieve hunger and misery" through the support of specific projects in agriculture, health, education, and related areas.

These principles were fully established by the early 1950s. They have been pursued by a succession of Democratic and Republican administrations and through very substantial changes in the political leadership and organization of Congress. Much of the debate about policy since the early 1950s has centered on the relative weight given to the several objectives.

The sources of the foreign policy innovations that committed the United States to foreign assistance must, however, be sought not simply in the motives and pronouncements of political leaders or in the debates within and outside Congress but also in the fundamental forces that have induced changes in the perception of the U.S. role in global policy and economy.

A major puzzle is why the United States embraced the role of providing leadership among the developed market economies in the first two decades after World War II. Robert O. Keohane noted that the United States had avoided this role during the interwar period: "What prevented American leadership of a cooperative world political economy in these years was less lack of economic resources than absence of political willingness to make and enforce the rules for the system."[13] Why did the United States decide to commit the political and economic resources to provide hegemonic leadership after World War II?

It is sometimes argued that American economic assistance has been guided by direct economic self-interest. But the evidence to support such an assumption is so weak that it almost precludes seriously considering the assumption as a fruitful hypothesis. Two examples are particularly relevant.[14] Between the early 1960s and the early 1970s, major U.S. attention was focused on Vietnam and Southeast Asia. Yet by no stretch of the imagination could the immense resources devoted to the Vietnam War be justified in terms of economic interest. Trade with and investment in Southeast Asia was and continues to be of marginal economic significance to the United States. The focus of the United States on the Near East from the early 1970s to the early 1980s might, on the surface at least, be interpreted in terms of the economic importance of oil from that region to the U.S. economy. U.S. attention to the Middle East more accurately can be interpreted in terms of commitment to Israel and the effort to keep that commitment from undermining our relations with the oil-providing countries of the region.

When U.S. commercial interests were most strongly supported by foreign economic policy or most favored by assistance policy, as in Latin America during the 1950s and 1960s, it was due more to the unwillingness to challenge business interests than to a considered policy of enhancing U.S. economic interest. During the most active period of the Alliance for Progress, for example, corporate influence on foreign policy weakened. The more relevant puzzle is why the issue of commercial advantage has played such a limited role in both U.S. foreign policy and development assistance policy.[15]

Keohane argued for a more subtle economic or "generalized reciprocity" interpretation, in which apparently unbalanced exchanges can be regarded as balanced by the exchange of tangible for intangible or deferred but unspecified benefits. "It seems best to view the Marshall Plan as a combination of an exchange relationship—material benefits in return for present and future deference—and generalized reciprocity based on situational and empathetic interdependence."[16] Keohane argued that this view is plausible because of the widespread perception that U.S. welfare depended on a prosperous and democratic Europe and because of the close personal ties between American and European statesmen that had been formed during World War II. The generalized reciprocity view is also incomplete. It simply implies a more subtle or sophisticated version of the economic self-interest interpretation.

It seems evident that four additional sources of policy initiative have played an important role in the formation and evolution of economic assistance policy. They are enhanced relative economic and political power, a reactive style of foreign policy formation, a strong popular anticommunist ideology, and a broad sense of obligation to relieving the pervasive poverty in the poor countries of the world.

The events leading to World War II and U.S. participation in the war persuaded the American political and economic elite that it had a greater obligation to shape world events than it had realized in the past. Isolation was not feasible after Britain became incapable of providing a reasonable degree of economic and political stability. Furthermore, the interwar experience convinced the American business and political leadership that American economic and political isolationism had contributed to the global depression of the 1930s and to the rise of militaristic nationalism in Germany, Italy, and Japan.

The decisive role played by American economic and military power in winning the war convinced the foreign policy establishment that America had the capacity and the responsibility to shape the world economic and political system. When disillusion with the possibility of cooperation with the Soviet Union deepened, this perception was rapidly directed into the conviction that it was in the self-interest of the United States, and our allies, to contain the expansionist tendencies of the USSR. It was clear to U.S. policy makers that containment could not be achieved by traditional methods of diplomacy or by military means. Economic assistance was viewed as the way to secure immediate political commitment and, over the long run, to strengthen the capacity of countries on the periphery of the Soviet empire to resist Soviet economic and political penetration.[17]

The unprecedented military and economic resources available to American policy makers in the decades after World War II freed them from specific strategic and economic concerns. These resources freed American policy makers to pursue objectives that did not have to be justified in terms of close calculation of strategic or economic advantage. But it was necessary to convince a reluctant American public and their representatives in Congress of the need to devote the resources necessary for the United States to assume a larger role in the world polity and economy. To achieve this objective, the policy makers drew on the deeply rooted popular anticommunist ideology of the American public.[18]

The people occupying the upper levels of the U.S. foreign policy establishment were not romantic ideologues.[19] By and large, they were conservatives molded by the realist tradition of political thought. But the translation of policy into program required the support or, at least, the acquiescence of the American public and its representatives in Congress. Neither the public nor very many members of Congress, in the early postwar period, were convinced of the benefits to the United States of assuming hegemonic responsibility for the economic and political development of either our World War II allies or the underdeveloped Third World. Acquiescence by the public and Congress to the responsibilities implied by the Truman Doctrine, the Marshall Plan, and the Point Four Program was achieved only by appeals to the deepest political emotions—both the fears and the idealism—of the American people.

The commitment of resources in support of Greece and Turkey was won from Congress by an exaggerated interpretation of the Soviet threat, and that, in turn, required an exaggerated commitment. Acheson insisted to the Senate Committee on Foreign Relations that Soviet advances in the Balkans "might open three continents to Soviet penetration. Like apples in a barrel infected by one rotten one, the corruption of Greece would infect Iran and all to the east. It would also carry infection to Africa through Asia Minor and Egypt, and to Europe through Italy and France, already threatened by the strongest domestic Communist parties in Western Europe."[20] These arguments reached deep into the historic American perception of itself as a virtuous and beleaguered island threatened by the forces of evil and corruption.

The appeals for support of the Marshall Plan and the Point Four Program drew on the perceived threat of Soviet power and Communist ideology. But those appeals also drew on American altruism and on the liberal doctrine that it is the mission of the United States to lead the world into a more democratic and prosperous future. In selling foreign assistance programs to Congress and the public, appeals were made (and continue to be made) to the large reservoir of altruism and sympathy in the American public. Without this continuing concern toward those who suffer from malnutrition and poverty, it would have been impossible to sustain the aid effort toward countries of little strategic importance or during periods when immediate security concerns were not sufficient to mobilize public opinion. But the commitment of American technical knowledge—"American know-how, show-how"—and American economic resources to the solution of the economic problems of poor countries was even less realistic, given the disparity between objectives enunciated and means committed, than was the Truman Doctrine's commitment to containment.

Constituencies and Concerns

Changes in an institution's external environment create pressures and opportunities for internal innovation. But they do not determine the response to new opportunities. It is not enough to argue that new institutions or policy innovations might serve the national interest or contribute to economic or political development. Intellectual resources must be directed to policy design; political resources must be mobilized to translate design into policy and policy into action; and actual human, financial, and material resources must be transferred to recipient countries.

A major premise guiding this study is that changes in U.S. assistance policy respond to and are constrained by domestic political and economic interests and concerns. These include the specific concerns and interests within the government. They also include the ebb and flow of popular concerns reflecting realist or idealist interpretations of (*a*) the appropriate role of the United States in world affairs and (*b*) the implications of external economic or political events for U.S. economic and security interests.

If we are to understand the broad commitment to foreign economic assistance after World War II and the more recent changes in foreign assistance policy, we must identify the major constituencies that influence U.S. foreign assistance policy. In advancing this position I clearly depart from the position of the new realist or strategic interest school in international relations.[21] I also find the interpretation of foreign policy based on bureaucratic politics to be less than fully congenial. I do not deny the role of competition among competing agencies as an important force in selling foreign policy or the development assistance agenda. But during the period covered by this book we have witnessed a democratization of foreign policy making, and of the making of foreign economic assistance policy in particular. Discussions about the implementation of the Marshall Plan could be made by a small foreign policy elite in the administration and the Congress. By the late 1970s, the foreign policy process (assistance policy toward Nicaragua and El Salvador, for example) involved a wide array of official participants and a bewildering assembly of nongovernmental interest groups. Thus, although my approach is somewhat eclectic—drawing on both the strategic interest and the bureaucratic politics models for insight when appropriate, my major focus is on the domestic politics of foreign assistance policy. I view foreign assistance policy as at least as responsive to the ebb and flow of domestic, political, and economic concerns as to changes in the international political and economic environment.

In the following I identify the major constituencies that attempt to influence foreign economic assistance policies and programs. Table 1.1 illustrates the relations among constituencies and concerns. At this stage my assertions about the several concerns and interests should be treated as hypotheses to be tested in the later chapters. At a less formal level they can be regarded as a taxonomy that I use to search my way through the record for understanding of the different agents that have influenced the course of development assistance policy.[22]

I have divided the concerns into two groups. The first is a donor-oriented group. It includes U.S. political and strategic concerns and the economic benefits and costs of foreign assistance to U.S. interest groups, such as industry, shipping, agriculture, and labor. The second group is oriented to the interests of assistance recipients: concerns with the economic development of their countries and humanitarian concerns with their subsistence needs and human rights.

The White House and the State Department

The White House and the State Department were leading actors in the initial design and implementation of foreign assistance policy. The major motive was and has continued to be strategic. Economic development, except for brief periods, has represented a secondary objective viewed in terms of its contribution to political development and stability. Strategic or security considerations tend to dominate economic or political development considerations in the allocation of assistance resources when trade-offs become necessary. Because of the emphasis given to strategic considerations, a high priority has been placed on discretion and flexibility—resistance to earmarking—in the allocation of assistance resources. The White House, particularly the National Security Council, sets the general tone or perspective for assistance policy, while the State Department's role is largely in policy design.

TABLE 1.1
Development Assistance Constituencies and Concerns

Economic constituencies for development	Concerns: Donor oriented; political and strategic	Concerns: Recipient oriented; economic and humanitarian
White House and State Department	++	0
Office of Management and Budget	0	0
Treasury Department	0	+
Agency for International Development	–0	++
Congress		
• Idealist	0	++
• Realist	++	0
Foreign Policy Establishment		
• East-West wing	++	0
• North-South wing	++	+
Suppliers and Contractors	0	++
Ethnic Communities	++	–+
Human Needs	––	++

Symbols: ++, strong positive concern; +, moderate positive concern; 0, neutral; –, moderate negative concern; ––, strong negative concern.

The role of the State Department in the design of assistance policy was most apparent in the early postwar period. The Truman Doctrine of containment and the Marshall Plan for European economic recovery both were formulated in the State Department. The secretaries of state, particularly Acheson and Marshall, played a major role in mobilizing public and congressional support. In recent years the State Department has been assigned responsibility for the country allocation of that portion of the assistance budget designated for strategic assistance (the Economic Support Fund), although the funds are administered by the US/AID. This has at times resulted in considerable friction between the AID administrator and the under-secretary. The importance attached to the Economic Support Fund by the State Department was illustrated by a bitter dispute between Secretary of State Alexander Haig and Office of Management and Budget (OMB) Director David Stockman at the beginning of the Reagan administration. Stockman proposed a 45 percent cut in the 1981 foreign aid budget. By his own description, he was "rolled by Al Haig."[23] The savings that were finally negotiated by Haig and Stockman turned out to be inconsequential. Between 1980 and 1985 the foreign aid budget for economic, strategic, and military assistance more than doubled in spite of OMB concerns.

Office of Management and Budget

The outcome of the disagreement between Secretary Haig and Budget Director Stockman is illustrative of the role of OMB in the policy process. Except for a few years during the early 1960s, OMB has rarely lived up to its promise as a program and policy analysis institution. It has been less concerned with the relationship between budget resources and program outcomes than with simply holding down the growth of expenditures. In the face of opposition from a powerful cabinet officer who is prepared to take his or her case to the White House, the OMB is relatively weak. But on issues that are of somewhat lesser concern, those that are handled at the third or fourth level of a department or agency bureaucracy, the OMB has considerable negotiating power over budget growth and allocation.

The Treasury Department

The Treasury, particularly in the person of Harry Dexter White, was largely responsible for U.S. preparatory work on the design of the Bretton Woods institutions—the International Monetary Fund (IMF) and the International Bank for Reconstruction and Development (World Bank). In more recent years, however, Treasury concerns have centered on the balance-of-payments, domestic capital market, and budget implications of the multilateral and bilateral assistance programs.[24] Since the mid-1960s Treasury has consistently restricted the new borrowings in the United States by the World Bank and the other international financial institutions. Its attitude toward U.S. participation in the refunding of the International Development Association (IDA)—the World Bank's soft loan window—has also reflected its concerns about the influence of the U.S. balance of payments. In spite of these concerns, Treasury has usually been more supportive of multilateral assistance, relative to bilateral assistance, than either the State Department or the Agency for International Development. Treasury has also been concerned about protecting its central role in international lending decisions. Treasury chairs the National Advisory Council on International Monetary and Financial Policies (NAC). Attempts to weaken its role, as in the initial proposals to establish the International Development Cooperation Administration in the late 1970s, have been effectively resisted.

The Agency for International Development

The U.S. Agency for International Development and its predecessor agencies, except for the Economic Cooperation Administration, which administered the Marshall Plan, have been semiautonomous organizations within the State

Department. The agency is motivated, both at home and abroad, by a set of concerns different from that of the rest of the State Department. The agency's bureaucracy has traditionally held a development ideology. It is strongly motivated to measure results in terms of the economic growth or development in the recipient country. Agency staff share with technocrats in the planning agencies of developing countries a view that, when assistance resources are used to achieve political objectives, it is often at the cost of economic growth and viability.[25] Agency staff know that the State Department provides very little protection against congressional abuse when questions are raised about whether assistance funds have effectively contributed to the economic well-being of people in the developing countries or have lined the pockets of the countries' officials. The agency staff views the pressure to ensure that assistance resources provide benefits to U.S. economic interests, such as agriculture and shipping, or that aid resources not be used to generate competition for U.S. exports as reducing the effectiveness of assistance resources. In effect, the AID bureaucracy represents a constituency for efficiency in the use of assistance resources to further economic growth.

The Congress

In the 1950s and 1960s, little attention was given by students of foreign policy to the role of Congress in foreign policy. Congress was viewed as passively responding to the initiatives of an "imperial presidency."[26] In the public choice literature, members of the House of Representatives and the Senate are often viewed as passive reflectors of constituent interests or simple vote maximizers. Both views are too narrow. Many members of Congress, because of the security of their tenure or the lack of well-articulated constituency interests, are quite free to reflect their own biases or studied conclusions on foreign affairs issues. Furthermore, members of the Senate Foreign Relations and the House Foreign Affairs Committees and of the House and Senate Appropriations Committees are often quite zealous in protecting their foreign policy and budget responsibilities against encroachment by the executive. Debates over foreign aid bills have frequently been used as a vehicle by which Congress has attempted to influence a broad range of foreign policy.[27]

Since the procedural reforms of the late 1960s and 1970s, which placed more power in the hands of individual members and subcommittees, Congress has assumed a stronger role in assistance policy initiatives (see Chap. 5).[28] Even during the 1950s and 1960s, however, strong committee chairmen played an important role in influencing administration policy. Representative Otto E. Passman (D-La.), who served on the House Appropriations Committee (and, for many years, was chairman of the Foreign Operations Subcommittee) effectively restrained the growth of the aid budget.[29] In the 1960s Senator J. William Fulbright (D-Ark.) actively supported an increase in the share of American aid flowing through multilateral agencies. Representative Donald Fraser (D-Minn.) played an important role in the late 1960s in developing legislation that directed the aid agency to give greater emphasis to political development and in the early 1970s in legislation that directed the aid agency to allot more resources to meeting the basic needs of the poor in the poorest countries (see Chap. 5). During the 1980s Senator Jesse Helms (R-N.C.) became a consistent embarrassment to his colleagues on the Foreign Relations Committee and a cause of its lack of success in passing foreign aid authorization legislation. The oversight and budget committees expanded their roles in the micromanagement of agency priorities during the 1970s and the 1980s.

Differences between the House and the Senate and between the oversight and appropriation committees have persisted. Frank B. Ballance noted that

> the Senate displayed a persistent tendency to emphasize multilateral assistance more strongly than the House of Representatives. Senate liberals felt that the bilateral aid was inherently politically accented, and the Senate Appropriations Committee supported multilateral aid as a vehicle for funding of infrastructure projects and to counter the interest of the White House and the State Department in diverting economic assistance to strategic purposes. The House Foreign Affairs Committees on the other hand tended to be more preoccupied with bilateral aid, since the more constricted powers of the House on Foreign Affairs placed additional weight on the foreign aid bill as the medium for House debates on foreign policy.[30]

There is also, as has been suggested, a substantial difference among individual members of Congress in the kinds of concerns they bring to their positions on assistance legislation and funding. In the 1950s congressional members with a liberal or international orientation placed strong emphasis on the use of assistance to achieve security and strategic objectives, whereas conservatives attempted to restrain the size of the assistance budget. After the Vietnam War liberals placed greater emphasis on development and humanitarian objectives while conservatives urged that assistance resources be directed more effectively to achieving security and other foreign policy objectives. And both conservatives and liberals continuously have responded to constituency interests for program objectives that will benefit U.S. farmers, manufacturers, and shippers.

The Foreign Policy Establishment

Outside the State Department, the Agency for International Development, and the Congress, there is a shadow foreign policy establishment that has at times played an important role in the formation and support of foreign policy initiatives. It includes former and future secretaries, assistant secretaries, and senior civil servants from the State and Defense Departments. These are the people who often head and serve on presidential commissions and task forces (Chap. 13). Many are members of the Council on Foreign Relations and the regional foreign affairs committees. The foreign policy establishment also includes the directors and several staff members of university and foundation research and public affairs centers, such as Max F. Millikan and Walter W. Rostow of the Massachusetts Institute of Technology Center for International Studies (in the 1950s) and James Grant and John W. Sewell of the Overseas Development Council (in the 1970s).[31]

The foreign policy establishment can be thought of as comprising two overlapping wings—one East-West and the other North-South. The East-West wing generally reflects a realist policy orientation; it is primarily concerned with strategy issues involving relations between the major powers. Interest in the developing countries generally has been derivative of its concerns about managing relations between the United States and the USSR or, more generally, between the developed market economies and the centrally planned economies.

The North-South wing has pressed for a wider perspective. It has insisted that the wide, and widening, disparities in income between the developed and developing countries are a potential source of international political instability. The North-South wing argued that superpower competition, reflected in attempts to exploit economic disparities and political tensions in underdeveloped states, increased global instability. And they insist that the growing economic power of the newly industrialized and energy-rich states in the developing world has created a new reality to global economic and political relations.

The East-West wing dominated foreign policy thought during the first two decades after World War II. The North-South wing achieved a brief ascendancy or, at least, visibility from the end of the Vietnam War until the Soviet invasion of Afghanistan. Since the mid-1970s both wings have tended to fragment as a result of the political disagreements associated with withdrawal from Vietnam and the easing of East-West tensions.[32]

Suppliers and Contractors

Among the direct beneficiaries of U.S. economic assistance programs are a large number of U.S. industries, businesses, and other organizations, such as farm producers, marketing organizations (private firms and cooperatives), and transportation agencies. They supply food for the food aid programs, manufacture the equipment used in assistance projects, transport the commodities to recipient countries, and provide management and advisory services. The maritime interests, in particular, have been notorious in securing legislation that has substantially increased the costs of providing food aid to recipient countries. Private voluntary agencies, universities, and other nonprofit organizations serve as contractors for project design and management, and a large number of academic and nonacademic scholars and consultants are involved in assistance research and evaluation (see Chap. 9).

The direct influence of suppliers is hard to estimate. Relatively little literature has been produced on this issue.[33] It is clear, however, that the senior offices in these organizations have strong incentives to work closely with members of Congress and their staffs and to clarify for them the benefits to their states and districts of the employment and income generated by assistance expenditures (see Chap. 3 for further discussion of the self-interest argument). The influence of suppliers is enhanced by a pro-business orientation in both Congress and the administration, which lends a sense of legitimacy to the pursuit of economic self-interest on the part of the business community.

The Human Needs Constituency

Another American constituency for foreign economic assistance draws on the broad public concern with such issues as basic human needs (food, shelter, health), resource conservation, and civil and human rights. For the most part public support for aid programs has been based primarily on humanitarian concerns rather than strategic or economic self-interest. These concerns tend to be expressed through church groups, civic organizations, and loosely organized coalitions of interest groups, for example, Bread for the World, the League of Women Voters, OXFAM, and other private voluntary organizations (PVOs) (see Chap. 9).

Although these constituencies are only occasionally effective in initiating changes in foreign assistance policy, when they mobilize they can exert substantial influence because they reflect concern with policy issues, such as the basic human needs mandate (in the 1970s) or the preservation of environmental resources and amenities (in the 1980s), that are deeply rooted in American consciousness. These same organizations are uncomfortable with the diversion of assistance resources to overtly political or strategic uses. They often feel used by the political process. They engender a good deal of organized public opposition to economic or military assistance for strategic objectives when it involves supporting authoritarian regimes in developing countries. The general impression that has been drawn from the analysis of public opinion studies is that support for the humanitarian rationale for foreign assistance is widespread but that the commitment is not very intense.[34] In the political marketplace it is difficult for the humanitarian commitment to override the more specific strategic and economic self-interest arguments.

Within the general public there also are several constituencies that are much more highly focused in their concerns. During the first several decades after World War II, a strong China lobby drew on the long history of American foreign missions in China for its emotional support; its leaders, such as Henry Luce, publisher of *Time* and *Life,* and Walter Judd, a Republican congressman from Minnesota, had close personal or family ties to the missionary movement. In recent years the evangelical churches that are active in Latin America have supported the economic, strategic, and military assistance programs in Central America. The members of these constituencies differ strongly on their political orientation. They share with the broader human needs constituency, however, a strong recipient as opposed to donor orientation as the basis for their concern.

Ethnic Communities

The continuing economic assistance to relatively affluent countries such as Greece, Poland, Ireland, and Israel cannot be understood without considering the role of ethnic communities in American political life. Assistance policy toward the Middle East has, in particular, been "subject to the kind of special interest pressure that one applied as a matter of course to domestic politics."[35] The American Jewish community was particularly successful after the 1976 Six Day War and the 1973 October War in escalating U.S. economic and military assistance to Israel. Their success drew on deep emotional capital among the general public arising out of sympathy for the suffering of the Jewish people of Europe during the Holocaust, admiration for the temerity and skill exhibited in building the Israeli state, and a belief among many fundamentalist Christians that the establishment of Israel represented the fulfillment of Biblical prophecy.

The American Jewish community is not the only ethnic community successfully to influence the flow of assistance resources. It is not possible to understand the assistance flows to such relatively affluent countries as Ireland, Poland, and Greece without reference to the significance of the Irish-American, Polish-American, and Greek-American communities in domestic politics. By the 1980s these communities had been joined by the African-American, Arab-American, Asian-American, and Latin-American communities in exerting a measurable influence on assistance policy.[36]

Professional Thought

In addition to the several constituencies discussed in this section, the perception that assistance policy is influenced by professional thought must be considered. During the first two decades after World War II, development research became a growth industry in some social science disciplines: economics, political science, sociology, and anthropology.[37] This growth was induced in part by the government's demand for social science knowledge to rationalize, formulate, and implement foreign assistance policy.

Earlier I referred to the important role played by George F. Kennan's analyses in the formation of containment policy. In the mid- and late 1950s, the savings-investment and foreign exchange gap models, developed at the Massachusetts Institute of Technology Center for International Studies and formalized by Hollis B. Chenery and associates, had a major influence on the conceptualization of assistance needs and the programming of assistance flows. In the 1960s the writings of Theodore Schultz and others at the University of Chicago helped to turn the attention of the assistance community to the importance of new knowledge and new technology as a source of economic development and to the high returns from investment in human capital.[38]

Writers such as Edgar Owens and Robert Shaw were influential in interpreting professional concern with the failure of earlier assistance efforts to successfully address the problems of meeting the basic needs of the poor into language that helped to galvanize action by legislators and assistance program managers (see Chap. 5). As noted earlier, members of this new professional elite, particularly from the field of international relations, moved into official positions in foreign policy and development assistance with each change of administration. The appointment of Clifton R. Wharton, Jr., as deputy secretary of state during the Clinton administration represented the first appointment of a professional with experience in the field of development studies and policy to a senior State Department position (see Chap. 13).

A Framework for Analysis

My basic premise in approaching the study of U.S. foreign economic assistance policy is that domestic sources have been more important in determining the size and direction of assistance than has the international economic and political environment the assistance is intended to influence. In this chapter I have outlined a three-level context in which to test this premise against the history of U.S. development assistance policy.

At the *macropolitical level* I emphasize the persistent aspects of U.S.

political culture: the tendency to vacillate between the two offspring of American exceptionalism—the liberal doctrine, which emphasizes cooperation in international relations, and the realist doctrine, which emphasizes the need for political dominance by the United States. At the *policy formation level,* I emphasize the role of American economic and political power, a reactive style of policy formation, and popular anticommunist ideology. At the *micropolitical level*—the level of program direction and design—I emphasize the role of the several constituencies and interest groups that bring their influence to bear on the process of policy formation program design and project administration. In subsequent chapters I assess the role of these domestic macro- and micropolitical factors as they impinge on the actors or agents involved in assistance policy formation and program design.

Chapter 2

Why Foreign Economic Assistance?

There is general agreement in the economics literature that resource flows among countries in response to market incentives enhance global economic efficiency and welfare in both rich and poor countries.[1] It has also been argued that in the presence of capital market imperfections the transfer of resources from the governments of developed countries to the governments of developing countries on commercial terms, either directly or through multilateral agencies, can normally be expected to be welfare enhancing in both developed and developing countries.[2] These arguments do not apply, however, to official development assistance that involves a substantial grant element.

Two arguments have typically been used in support of transfers that include a grant component. One set is based on the economic and strategic self-interest of the donor country. The second is based on the ethical or moral responsibility of the residents of wealthy countries toward the residents of poor countries. Both sets of arguments have been the subject of continuous challenge.

I argue in this chapter that neither the donor self-interest nor the ethical responsibility argument can be rejected on logical or theoretical grounds. I also assert that the empirical evidence in support of both the economic and the strategic self-interest arguments is exceedingly weak. The ethical responsibility arguments impose less burden on the empirical evidence, but they are subject to continuous challenge by political theorists and moral philosophers.[3]

Donor Self-Interest

Donor self-interest arguments tend to assert that development assistance promotes the economic or political interests of the donor country. This argument is frequently made in official and popular pronouncements in defense of developed country aid budgets.[4] It is also being made by the critics from the Left who assert that aid negatively affects political and economic development in poor countries.[5] The empirical evidence suggests that donor self-interest plays an important role in bilateral assistance, particularly on the part of the larger donors, whereas recipient need plays a larger role in multilateral assistance.[6]

Economic Interest

Most economic self-interest arguments employ some version of the assertion that aid promotes exports from and employment in the donor country. The crude version of this argument simply draws attention to the obvious gains to the U.S. economy from exports of commodities or services subsidized by the assistance program. Producers of food grains in the United States benefit from food assistance, workers in the maritime industry gain from cargo preference provisions, and U.S. engineering firms gain from contracts associated with infrastructure development projects. Programs to protect private overseas investment against economic and political risk have been a prominent component of U.S. and many other national assistance programs.[7]

A somewhat less obvious appeal to specific interests often emphasizes the generalized role of aid in strengthening ties between donor and recipient during the period of assistance. The development of a nation's transportation or communication network can be expected to continue. As the recipient country's infrastructure develops, commercial demand for new and replacement equipment compatible with the aid-assisted investments is expected to widen commercial sales opportunities. Similarly, technical assistance for the development of a grain-milling and feed-processing industry in a less developed country is viewed as enhancing the commercial demand for food and feed grains from the donor country.

A more sophisticated argument often made is that aid is effective in contributing to the economic growth of less developed countries. The effect will be an expansion of demand for goods and services from developed countries. These goods and services are often characterized by high import demand elasticities.[8] Agricultural producers in the United States are urged not to become overly concerned about loss of, for example, oilseed markets to Malaysia and Brazil because, as incomes rise, growth in demand for animal proteins will generate demand for U.S. feed grains. Loss of exports by the mature industrial sectors will be more than compensated for by increase of exports of capital goods and high technology.[9]

The first two arguments rest on relatively weak logical foundations. The use of assistance resources to subsidize domestic suppliers of commodities or services generally reduces the value of a given level of assistance to the recipient country.[10] This concern has generated vigorous discussion about the value and effect of food assistance.[11] Other areas, such as tied procurement of such services as technical assistance, have been subject to much less controversy. But there can be little question that the effect of aid tying is to raise the cost to the donor of providing whatever benefits recipients receive from development assistance.

The growth impact argument rests on stronger logical grounds. It should be technically possible to specify conditions under which government-to-government aid transfers involving a grant element could improve welfare in both donor and recipient countries.[12] The empirical analysis to support this argument is, however, surprisingly limited. It is not sufficient simply to assert that the transfer of assistance resources may be followed by the growth of exports from the donor and the recipients; this growth must be calculated. As yet, neither the contribution of aid recipients' growth to donor trade balances nor the welfare gain and loss calculations have been made.[13]

Political and Strategic Interest

The view that development assistance is a useful complement to other elements of donor political strategy—that its primary rationale is to strengthen the political commitment of the aid recipient to the donor country or to the West—has been a consistent and at times dominant theme in the motivation for development assistance.[14] Political considerations in both donor and recipient countries have, however, often made it advisable to cloak the objectives of short-term political or strategic assistance with the rhetoric of economic assistance—hence terms such as *economic support fund* in the US/AID budget.[15]

The strengthening of the capacity of Western Europe to resist external aggression and the enhancement of the political appeal of centrist political forces were major motivations for the Marshall Plan.[16] Strategic concerns were a prominent feature of the Kennedy administration's Alliance for Progress in the early 1960s.[17] The Carlucci report, commissioned by the Reagan administration, insisted that "the foreign security and economic cooperation programs of the United States are mutually supportive and interrelated and together constitute an integral part of the foreign policy of the United States."[18] The commission urged that efforts be made to enhance the complementarity between U.S. economic and security programs through the creation of a Mutual Development and Security Agency that would bring development, military, and related assistance programs under one agency.

One of the issues that needs to be examined more fully is that of complementarity and conflict between the achievement of short-run political strategic objectives and longer-run political or economic objectives. In some countries short-term donor strategic objectives seem to have been inconsistent with longer-term recipient political development (Vietnam, Nicaragua, Philippines). A common assumption in the earlier literature was that Western style democratization and bureaucratization would be in the interest of both the donor and the recipient. But the study of political development has provided few guidelines for policy makers or practitioners who would guide political development along mutually advantageous lines.[19]

In Summary

There is an interesting dichotomy in the dialogue about the use of foreign assistance in the pursuit of domestic economic and strategic interests. It is clear that self-interest and security arguments have often represented little more than cynical efforts to generate support for the foreign assistance budget. There have been serious efforts to examine the theoretical foundations of the economic self-interest argument. There have also been increasingly serious attempts to evaluate the economic and social effects of economic assistance in developing countries. In addition to a large professional literature, the U.S. Agency for International Development has conducted and published a large body of Project Evaluation Reports. The World Bank has an Operations Evaluation Department that engages in a major program of project completion evaluation studies.

The security rationale has not, however, been subject to nearly as rigorous a theoretical or empirical analysis.[20] The single background paper on the effectiveness of military assistance prepared for the Carlucci Commission asserted a positive linkage between U.S. security assistance expenditures and security interests while admitting that the evidence to support the assertion is "elusive."[21] This is not to suggest that empirical support cannot be provided for the political and strategic self-interest arguments. It is simply to argue that, in spite of Huntington's assertion that the results of security assistance have been at least as successful as efforts to promote economic development,[22] little convincing evidence has appeared in the professional literature on development assistance.

There is an inherent contradiction in both the economic and the security self-interest arguments. The danger is that donor countries may pursue their self-interest under the rubric of aid even if it harms the recipient country. If the donor self-interest argument is used as a primary rationale for development assistance, it imposes on donors some obligation to demonstrate that their assistance does no harm to the recipient.

One effect of the economic and security self-interest arguments has been to clarify that donor governments and assistance constituencies are not indifferent to the form of the resource transfers they make to poor countries. Security assistance draws on a set of ideological concerns that often go beyond a rational calculation of donor self-interest. Food aid taps not only the self-interest of donor commodity producers but also a powerful set of altruistic concerns in donor countries about poverty, hunger, and health in poor countries (Chap. 8). It is doubtful that these forms of assistance are directly competitive—if food aid were reduced, the resources released would not become available to support the security assistance budget.

Ethical Considerations

Efforts to develop an acceptable rationale for development assistance have not been confined to self-interest assertions and rationalizations. There has been an extended argument that assistance is the moral responsibility of rich countries, over and above any considerations of self-interest. But neither the advocates nor the critics of foreign assistance have adhered to careful distinctions between self-interest and moral responsibility.

The typical criticism of foreign assistance starts out with an argument that the resources devoted to foreign assistance are wasted—that assistance has not achieved either its intended economic or its political objective. This tends to be followed by the argument that in any event it is not legitimate, within the framework of Western political philosophy, for government to extract resources forcefully from its citizens to transfer them to foreigners.[23]

Both the popular and the official sponsors of foreign assistance have typically treated the ethical basis for foreign assistance as intuitively obvious.[24] There is, however, a substantial professional literature that attempts to identify a basis in ethical theory or political philosophy for income or resource transfers at the expense of a reduction in welfare in the donor country. In addition, since government-to-government transfers are often involved, there are also attempts to explore the basis for claims for assistance by the recipient country and for the obligation of the donor country to the recipient country.

Entitlement

An argument frequently put forth during the dialogue on the "new economic order" of the 1970s was that there should be compensation by the rich countries to poor countries for past injustices stemming from some combination of political and economic exploitation.[25] A second entitlement argument is based on the uneven distribution of natural resources. It has been argued that natural resources are part of our global heritage and that those areas that are favorably endowed have an obligation to share rents from differential resource endowments with those areas that are less favorably endowed.[26]

The argument based on past injustice, while correct in principle, poses substantial difficulties for translation into contemporary assistance policy. If exploitation occurred and compensation was not made, the effect of compound interest is to magnify the size of the obligation. Much of the development assistance provided by Great Britain and France, the two major colonial powers, has been directed to former colonies and dependencies. Lenin's model of imperialism, in which capital was exported to low-income staple-producing areas under the direct or indirect political control of the major power and earned enormously high rates of return for a narrow class of investors in the metropolitan country, has not held up even to casual examination.[27] It has been difficult to establish the extent to which the imperial relation was, in fact, exploitative.[28] A more relevant argument in a world of both overt and "voluntary" constraints on the movement of commodities, labor, and financial resources is that developed countries have inadequately exploited the human and physical resources of the poor countries.

It is also difficult to decide what weight should be given to the natural resource distribution argument. One can hardly claim that the inhabitants of Kuwait and Somalia deserve the differential resource endowments they have inherited. But natural resource endowment differentials do not represent a very powerful factor in explaining differential growth rates among either developing or developed countries. The difficulty of converting staple exports into a base for sustained national or regional economic development has been a major challenge even in situations that have not been characterized by exploitation.[29] Perhaps the area in which the natural resources distribution issue is of greatest contemporary significance is the debate about the management and distribution of the potential rents associated with the exploitation of the global commons—the ocean and space resources.[30]

Distributive Justice

Most economists have generally felt fairly comfortable—perhaps too comfortable—with a straightforward utilitarian rationale for foreign assistance. If private rates of return to capital investment are higher in developing countries than in developed countries, investment should flow from developed to less developed countries. Because markets are imperfect governments of developed countries should transfer resources to developing countries to assist in the development of physical and institutional infrastructure. But few economists would be willing to embrace the full implications of the utilitarian income-distribution argument—that rich countries ought to give until the point is reached at which, by giving more, there is a loss in utility in the recipient country or countries.

Most political philosophers, and those economists who adhere to a Hobbesian contractarian view of the role of government, have found it difficult to discover any intellectual foundation for development assistance based on considerations of distributive justice. "Justice has meaning only as a rule of human conduct and no conceivable rules for the conduct of individuals supplying each other with goods and services in a market economy would produce a distribution which could be meaningfully described as just or unjust."[31] F. A. Hayek argues, in effect, that justice is a function of the rules or processes that govern individual and group behavior and not of the outcome generated by the rules. The appropriate role of public policy is rule reform.

The Hobbesian contractarian argument with respect to foreign aid has been forcefully articulated by Edward C. Banfield: "Our political philosophy does not give our government any right to do good for foreigners. Since the seventeenth century, Western political thought has maintained that government may use force or threat of force to take the property of some and give it to others only if doing so somehow serves the common good . . . government may take from citizens and give to foreigners when doing so serves the common good of the citizens, but it may not do so if . . . all advantage will accrue to foreigners and none to citizens."[32] This argument reemerged with renewed force in the debate over foreign assistance in the late 1970s and early 1980s.[33] It seems apparent that the emergence of social justice as a significant issue on the political agenda, both within nations and in international relations, is due to lack of confidence that the actual behavior of economic markets and political institutions adequately approaches the conditions specified by Hayek, Nozick, and other libertarian political philosophers.[34]

Attempts have been made to develop a contractarian argument drawing on the Rawlsian difference principle to establish a moral obligation for foreign assistance. A central thrust of John Rawls' theory is that in a just society departures from egalitarian income distribution would be permitted only when differential rewards contribute to the welfare of the least advantaged members of society. Rawls argues that this difference principle would be agreed to by rational individuals attempting to design a constitution—given full general knowledge of the political and economic nature of society except the positions that they would occupy by virtue of social class, individual talent, or political persuasion. The Rawlsian constitution does not imply perfect equalization of incomes. If, for example, inequality calls forth economic activity that benefits the least as well as the more advantaged members of society, it would be permitted.[35]

Rawls made no attempt to explore the implications of the difference principle for international equality. Charles Beitz and C. Ford Runge have argued that an intuitively obvious extension of the difference principle to the international economic order is that justice would imply equal access by citizens of all countries to global resources, except in those cases where departure from inequality could be justified on the basis of benefits to citizens of the least advantaged countries.[36] This argument goes beyond the basis of resource entitlement due to past injustice, discussed above. To the extent that it draws on the Rawls framework, however, it remains vulnerable to the weakness of attempting to derive rules of justice from an "imagined social contract."[37] I would personally prefer a stronger behavioral foundation on which to rest convictions about moral responsibility for assistance to poor countries. This preference reflects a skepticism about both the contractarian approach to political philosophy and the public choice approach to political economy that attempt to derive principles for the design of social and economic institutions from primitive assumptions about human nature.

Others insist that both the moral and the rational arguments apply only to individuals (or families) and not to collectives such as nations.[38] The issue of extending to nations the ethical arguments that have been developed to apply to individuals has been difficult to resolve in spite of the strong popular sentiment that rich nations do have some responsibility for assisting poor nations to achieve adequate levels of nutrition, health, and education.

Richard Cooper asserts that

> much recent discussion on transfer of resources falls uncritically into the practice of . . . anthropomorphizing nations, of treating nations as though they are individuals and extrapolating to them on the basis of average per capita income the various ethical arguments that have been developed to apply to individuals. This is not legitimate. If ethical arguments are to be used as a rationale for transferring resources, either a new set of ethical principles applicable to nations must be developed, or the link between resource transfers must be made back to the individuals who are the ultimate subjects of standard ethical reasoning.[39]

An Implicit Global Contract

A contractarian argument that limits the responsibility of the rich toward the poor to only national populations has great difficulty in confronting a world where citizens hold multiple loyalties, where national identity may be wider or more narrow than state boundaries, and where policy interventions as well as market forces guide the flow of labor and capital and the trade in commodities and intellectual property across state boundaries.[40] In this world a state moralist or political realist approach to international relations that would limit the expression of the moral concerns of individual citizens to national governments about the basic political rights or subsistence needs of people in other countries seems highly archaic.

Increased interdependence among nations results in a rise in both political tension and concern about lack of equity in economic transactions. The ethical foundation for a system of development assistance rests on the premise that the emergence of international economic and political interdependence has resulted in an implicit extension of Kenneth J. Arrow's argument for redistribution to include the international sphere: "There are significant gains to social interaction above and beyond what individuals can achieve on their own. The owners of scarce personal assets do not have substantial private use of these assets; it is only their value in a large system which makes these assets valuable. Hence, there is a surplus created by the existence of society which is available for redistribution."[41]

The growth of global and political interdependence implies a decline in the significance of national boundaries. Because boundaries are not co-extensive with the scope of economic and political interdependence, they do not mark the limits of social obligation in the sharing of the benefits and burdens associated with interdependence.[42] A functioning international economy increases the value of the natural, human, and institutional resources of the developed countries and makes part of this surplus available for redistribution.

Some Questions

Acceptance of an ethical responsibility by the citizens and the governments of rich countries does not resolve the question of what level of assistance is appropriate. It was noted earlier that the utilitarian or consequentialist argument seems to be based on equating marginal utilities—the rich countries ought to give until the point is reached at which, by giving more, the loss in utility in the donor country would exceed the gain in utility in the recipient country or countries.[43] However, the actual level of aid allocations by donor countries seems to reflect the much weaker moral premise that, if it is possible to contribute to welfare in poor countries without sacrificing anything of moral or economic significance in the donor country, it should be done.[44] There seems to be an implicit moral judgment among the citizens and governments of the rich countries that the moral obligation to feed the poor in Ethiopia is stronger than a moral obligation to assure a rate of growth of the Ethiopian gross national product (GNP) of 6 percent rather than 5 percent per year.[45]

Neither the commitment to development assistance nor the commitment to a particular level of development assistance provides guidance about who should receive aid. The ethical considerations that support the distributive justice argument imply that assistance should be directed to improving the welfare of the poorest individuals in the poorest countries. But there is also an ethical argument that aid should be directed into uses that produce the largest increments of income from each dollar of assistance—the argument that assistance resources are limited and should not be wasted.

The empirical evidence does not offer any clear inferences concerning the effect of aid on savings, investment, and rate of growth. There is, however, evidence that assistance resources have generated relatively high marginal rates of return—rates of return that are high relative to what the same resources would have earned in the donor countries.[46] What little empirical evidence there is also suggests that donor governments are willing to trade off some efficiency for equity in their aid allocations—that recipient income levels do carry modest weight in the allocation of aid resources.[47] But there is little more than anecdotal evidence on the distributive effects of development assistance in recipient countries.[48]

Acceptance of responsibility for assistance does not resolve the question of what form of assistance to offer. The goals of assistance range from attempting to assure immediate "subsistence rights" or basic needs,[49] to giving assistance designed to strengthen the capacity of a nation to meet the subsistence requirements of its own people, to modifying the institutions that influence the resource flows among nations. On some grounds it would seem obligatory to secure some minimum level of subsistence before allocating resources to the other two objectives. But this conclusion is not at all obvious if the effect is to preclude either (*a*) expansion of the capacity needed to assure future subsistence or (*b*) reform of the rules of conduct that govern economic and political relationships among nations (i.e., reform of the rules on agricultural trade of the General Agreement on Tariffs and Trade [GATT]).

Another issue is the extent to which development assistance policy and administration should be directed to bringing about institutional reform in the recipient country. The way in which development assistance is directed toward meeting basic needs and to strengthening the capacity for economic growth of the recipient country will depend on the institutions that influence relations among individual citizens, economic and social organizations, and the government. Different institutional arrangements will influence how different socioeconomic classes, different ethnic groups, and residents of rural and urban areas participate in programs designed to meet basic subsistence, health, and educational objectives. Institutional arrangements with respect to the organization and stability of property rights and the system by which the public revenue is generated and spent will affect the production decisions of farmers and the investment decisions of industrial entrepreneurs.

If a donor government's ethical concern extends to an obligation to assure the citizens of the donor country that resources devoted to assistance are used effectively, either for immediate relief of subsistence needs or to generate longer-term economic growth, it will also be necessary to enter into a dialogue with the recipient country about institutional reform when it enters into negotiations about resource transfers.[50] A dialogue on issues of institutional reform requires the donor country to invest in enhancing its own cultural and social science disciplines. Such a dialogue should be guided more by pragmatic considerations about the potential effects of policy reform in the recipient country than by ideological considerations based on the donor's own internal political processes or its economic or political self-interest.

In Conclusion

The first conclusion that emerges from this review is the weakness of the self-interest argument for foreign assistance. The individual (or group) self-interest arguments, after careful examination, often represent a hidden agenda for domestic rather than international resource transfers. The political realists have not been able or have not thought it worthwhile to demonstrate the presumed political and security benefits from the strategic assistance component of the aid budget. Rawlsian contractarian theory does provide a basis for ethical responsibility toward the poor in poor countries that goes beyond the traditional religious and moral obligations of charity. It also provides a basis for making judgments about the degree of inequality that is ethically acceptable.

But the contractarian argument cannot stand by itself. Its credibility is weakened if, in fact, the transfers do not achieve the desired consequences. Failures of analysis or design can produce worse consequences than if no assistance had been undertaken.[51] There is no obligation to transfer resources that do not generate either immediate welfare gains or growth in the capacity of poor states to meet the needs of their citizens. It becomes important, therefore, to evaluate the consequences of development assistance and to consider the policy interventions that can lead to more effective development assistance programs.

Since the 1950s our understanding of the development process has made major advances. But we can never fully understand the consequences of any assistance activity or of intervention into complex and interdependent social systems. Our limited knowledge about how to give and use aid to contribute most effectively to development does not, however, protect us from an obligation to attempt to assess the consequences of our strategic or development assistance and to advance our capacity to understand the role of external assistance in the development process.

Part II

The Evolution of Policy

Chapter 3
Before Point Four

Official commitment by the United States to assistance for the economic development of poor countries can be traced to the fourth point of President Harry S. Truman's inaugural address of 20 January 1949.[1] In this speech, Truman proposed "a bold new program for making the benefits of our scientific advances and industrial progress available for the improvement and growth of underdeveloped areas."[2] The speech marked a major shift in American foreign assistance from almost exclusive emphasis on postwar relief and reconstruction policy to a focus on economic development.

The commitment expressed in President Truman's address was new, but assistance to developing countries by the United States was not. The assistance policies and programs that emerged out of President Truman's commitment were preceded by a broad range of government and nongovernment experience with cultural interchange and technical missions by philanthropic organizations and government agencies in such areas as agriculture, health, education, and financial reform that extended back to the nineteenth century.[3] The policies and programs also drew on the more recent assistance for the rehabilitation of our World War II Western European allies under the Marshall Plan beginning in 1948. Other government experience included assistance to Latin America before and during World War II and assistance to China, to other East Asian countries, and to Greece and Turkey immediately after the war.

No attempt is made in this chapter to provide an exhaustive survey of the motives or effects of these earlier activities. Rather, I try to assess how these earlier programs contributed to the shaping of U.S. assistance doctrine and programs that have been pursued since the Truman commitment.[4]

I write from the perspective that historical experience and tradition are of continuing significance in attempting to understand both U.S. aid flows among countries and regions and the particular form of aid program activities.[5] One cannot understand, for example, the very large aid flows to the Republic of China, after its establishment on Taiwan, without referring to the history of

U.S. support for China during World War II and the long history of U.S. economic, religious, and cultural involvement in China during the nineteenth century. Similarly, one cannot understand the continuing commitment of assistance resources to Israel without reference to the events leading up to the Holocaust and the exodus of Jewish people from Eastern and Western Europe or to ethnic politics in the United States.

Interwar Isolation

The deterioration in international economic and political relations during the 1930s left the United States, on the eve of World War II, with very little flexibility to provide either economic or security assistance to other countries.[6] During the nineteenth century suggestions that funds be appropriated to meet foreign disasters, the Irish famine of 1845 and the Russian famine of 1881, were rejected on the grounds that appropriation of funds by Congress for such purposes would be unconstitutional. During the 1920s European governments had been able to maintain World War I reparation and debt repayment schedules only by new private borrowing in the United States. The response of President Calvin Coolidge to suggestions that the United States renegotiate the terms of the war loans was "They hired the money, didn't they?"[7]

This system collapsed with the financial panic of 1929 and the depression of the early 1930s. The United States responded by attempting to isolate itself from international political and economic forces.[8] The Johnson Act of 1934 required that any debtor government that did not maintain its debt repayment schedule be considered in default and denied access to the American private capital market. The act had the effect of denying to the European governments being threatened by aggression all access to American private sources of credit. The Johnson Act was followed by a series of neutrality acts (1935, 1936, and 1937) that placed an embargo on the export of arms to countries at war, prohibited American ships from carrying arms to belligerent ports, and subjected the private export of arms to government regulation. The 1936 act gave the president the discretionary power to determine when a state of war existed and, thus, to bring the arms embargo into effect. It also introduced the principle of "cash and carry," which denied private sources of credit to governments subject to the embargo. Latin American countries at war with non-American states were exempted from the limitations imposed by the act.

The United States did not free itself from the limitations imposed on international economic cooperation until passage of the Lend-Lease Act of 1941. German military success in Europe and Japanese military success in

China finally swept away the commitment to isolation. The act permitted the United States to provide financial assistance to any country in which resistance to the Axis powers was deemed essential to the defense of the United States.

Several institutional innovations of the 1930s facilitated a more active assistance effort when the political environment began to change in the early 1940s. An Export-Import Bank was established in 1934 to provide loans in support of United States foreign trade expansion. Two other institutions, the Reconstruction Finance Corporation and the Stabilization Fund of the U.S. Treasury, were also available, but their use was limited by congressional authority. The experience with the post–World War I debt issue was important for the design of post–World War II international financial institutions. Opponents to the Johnson Act argued that attempts to bring about a resumption of debt payments during the 1930s had retarded world economic recovery and should not be repeated.

Wartime Assistance to Latin America

During World War II the United States made large grants and extended credits to support its allies in Europe and Asia.[9] The wartime assistance programs most relevant to postwar development assistance policy and design were three programs directed to Latin America. These included the activities of the Interdepartmental Committee on Scientific and Cultural Cooperation, the Institute of Inter-American Affairs, and the Export-Import Bank.

The Interdepartmental Committee on Scientific and Cultural Cooperation

The establishment of the Interdepartmental Committee on Scientific and Cultural Cooperation was an attempt to institutionalize the capacity to respond to requests from Latin American governments for scientific, technical, and economic assistance from the United States. These requests gradually had expanded since the organization of the Pan-American Union in 1890. A series of inter-American conferences had adopted resolutions urging technical cooperation and cultural interchange. In 1939 Congress passed legislation authorizing the president to detail employees of U.S. federal agencies to provide advice and assistance on the request of the government of any American nation.

An Interdepartmental Committee with membership drawn from 25 bureaus in 18 departments was established to administer the program; the Assistant Secretary of State for Public Affairs acted as chairman. Budget requests were developed by the committee, and funds were allocated to individual agencies with the assistance of a small staff in the office of the chairman. Each agency was responsible for administering its own activities. Between 1940 and 1948 the member agencies sent a large number of short-term technical missions to the field. Funds were also allocated for study and training grants, the establishment of cultural centers and libraries, support for translation and other information services, and support for U.S.-sponsored schools.

In his review of the activities sponsored by the Interdepartmental Committee, Philip M. Glick noted that the program was not conceived as an organized effort to promote economic development in Latin America. Most of the missions were small, consisting of one or two experts sent to the host countries for less than a year—often for only a few months. Most were consultative or advisory rather than operational. Program funds were spent primarily on the salaries and expenses of the technicians. During the late 1940s it was generally conceded, in both Washington and the host countries, that the committee's decentralized approach was an obstacle to planning and managing the program in a manner that would give greater priority to the strategic development needs of the host countries. In 1950 the committee was abolished and its projects were transferred to the New Technical Cooperation Agency.

The Institute of Inter-American Affairs

In 1940 President Franklin D. Roosevelt established, by executive order, an Office of Commercial and Cultural Relations among the American republics in the Council on National Defense. In 1941 the organization was moved to the Executive Office of the President and renamed the Office of the Coordinator of Inter-American Affairs. Nelson Rockefeller was appointed coordinator. The establishment of the office reflected the same concerns with strengthening technical and economic cooperation with Latin American countries that had led earlier to the establishment of the Interdepartmental Committee. It also reflected President Roosevelt's impatience with the State Department's lack of enthusiasm for programs of technical and economic assistance and his penchant for avoiding direct confrontation over program jurisdiction.

To avoid the problem of the State Department's assuming management of the program, Rockefeller established in 1942 two separate public corporations to cooperate with Latin American governments. They were the Institute of Inter-American Affairs (IIAA), which was directed to the fields of public health and agricultural development, and the Inter-American Educational Foundation, which was directed to the areas of elementary and vocational education. The two corporations were merged by congressional action in 1947.

Programs were initiated rapidly in all three areas—health, food supply, and education—but no attempt was made to develop all three programs in each country. Each program operated independently; in fact, little effort was made to coordinate their activities either in Washington or at the country level.

The operating approach adopted by the IIAA had an important influence on the organization of technical assistance or cooperation under later programs. The work was managed by establishing a country-level joint organization, termed *servicio* (Spanish for service), for the separate fields of agriculture, health, and education. "In the course of its work IIAA came to distinguish between a 'program' and a 'project'. The whole of the work of a given *servicio* came to be considered its 'program'; the separate works included in the program were called 'projects'."[10] The work of each *servicio* was formalized under a program agreement with the host country.

The *servicio* functioned as a semiautonomous bureau in a host country ministry. The director typically was the chief of the IIAA technical mission. He was responsible to the head of the ministry in which the *servicio* was located and to the IIAA; his staff consisted of both national and expatriate technicians. The program of the *servicio* was financed by a joint fund made up of a contribution from IIAA and an appropriation by the country's national legislature.

Between 1942 and 1950, when the IIAA program was integrated into the Technical Cooperation Agency (see Figure 13.1), which had been set up to administer the global Point Four Program, the IIAA spent $163.2 million on salaries of U.S. personnel and on contributions to *servicio* programs.

The Export-Import Bank

A proposal for an inter-American development bank was suggested at a meeting of the Inter-American Conference of Foreign Ministers in 1940. Although the idea was not implemented, President Roosevelt proposed and Congress enacted an amendment to the Export-Import Bank Act which increased the bank's lending power from $200 to $700 million. The increase was earmarked "to assist in the orderly marketing of the products of the countries of the Western Hemisphere."[11]

One of the first loans under the Export-Import Bank's new authority was $20 million toward the construction of a steel mill in Brazil that had been planned initially in cooperation with Germany. William Adams Brown, Jr., and Redvers Opie regard this loan as a prototype for the project-financing procedures adopted in financing the Marshall Plan European Recovery Program. By the early 1950s the Export-Import Bank was also making development and emergency food relief loans in Asia. After the outbreak of conflict in Korea during 1951, lending authority was again raised and the focus was shifted to financing projects for the development of strategic materials (Chap. 11).

During these early years American embassies in host countries reacted to the three programs with a range "from coolness to hostility." When the war ended, opinion among State Department administrators ranged between those who looked forward to the termination of programs with which they were uncomfortable and those who viewed the programs as useful instruments through which to pursue foreign policy objectives; by the late 1940s the position taken was that the programs should be continued but located within the Department of State.

The experience in Latin America during the 1940s was productive of several lessons and several unresolved issues. Experiences with the Interdepartmental Committee and the Institute of Inter-American Affairs provided an important guide for the organization of technical assistance, and the Export-Import Bank provided experience with large-scale lending for industrial and infrastructure projects. However, experience in Latin America did not offer a resolution of the issue of whether foreign technical and economic assistance is most effectively managed by an independent agency or by the State Department. The inability to resolve this issue reflected, and continues to reflect, a deeper tension over the objective of foreign economic assistance: its role (*a*) in advancing short-term U.S. political and strategic objectives and (*b*) in advancing longer-term U.S. interest in the development of the host country.

Assistance for European Recovery

At the end of World War II, it was optimistically assumed by American officials that assistance to the countries of Europe would involve an orderly settlement of the Lend-Lease accounts and a short transition period of relief and reconstruction. During 1946 and 1947 relief to maintain basic subsistence levels was made available by the Government and Relief in Occupied Areas (GARIOA) program and the United Nations Relief and Rehabilitation Agency (UNRRA). By 1946 it was becoming increasingly apparent that Roosevelt's "Grand Design" for economic and political cooperation between the United States and the USSR was breaking down (Exhibit 3.1). By the spring of 1947, it had become apparent that neither economic recovery nor political stability in Europe could be assured without massive resource transfers. I noted in Chapter 1 that both the Truman Doctrine and the Marshall Plan were articulated within a span of 14 weeks that began when Great Britain informed the

United States that it could no longer maintain its economic and security commitments to Greece and Turkey.

The Greek-Turkish Aid Program

On 12 March 1947, President Truman requested that Congress appropriate $400 million for assistance to Greece and Turkey for the period ending 30 June 1948. The request was for $250 million for Greece to restore the economy and regain control of the country and $150 million for Turkey to modernize its economy and its military. Truman also requested the authority to send American civilian and military personnel to the two countries to supervise the use of the financial and material assistance provided by the United States and to train Greek and Turkish personnel. Despite the urgency of Truman's request, Congress did not act on it until mid-May.[12]

The significance of the Greek-Turkish Aid Program for the purpose of this study is that it involved the United States directly in the management of the countries' economic and military affairs much more deeply than had been initially intended.[13] The main objective of the assistance to Greece—the pacification of the countryside and the containment of Communist penetration—was achieved. However, by the time the Marshall Plan was being considered by Congress it was apparent that neither the American electorate nor their representatives in Congress were willing to expand commitments to direct intervention to the extent that had been involved in the assistance to Greece.

The Marshall Plan

The Marshall Plan was a second response to the heightened concern with the political consequences of economic collapse in Western Europe. By the time Secretary Marshall returned from the Foreign Ministers' Conference in Moscow (April 1947), a broad consensus was emerging in Washington that both the economic and the security environments in Western Europe were deteriorating.

It was increasingly clear that economic recovery, internal political security, and resistance to external aggression were intimately linked. The dominating circumstance determining the timing of the shift in policy (from assistance for reconstruction to assistance for development) was the perceived threat of communistic political ascendancy in Western Europe.[14] The Marshall Plan, enunciated in Secretary Marshall's commencement speech at Harvard on 5 June 1947, reflected both heightened concern with the potential economic and political collapse of Western Europe and a recogni-

Exhibit 3.1
Chronology of Critical Events Leading to the Truman Doctrine, Marshall Plan, and Point Four

22 February 1946—Kennan sent his long telegram.

5 March 1946—Churchill gave his iron curtain speech at Westminster College, Fulton, Missouri.

24 February 1947—Great Britain informed the U.S. State Department of its inability to maintain its commitments in Greece and Turkey.

12 March 1947—President Truman went before Congress to request $400 million in military and economic aid for Greece and Turkey.

5 June 1947—Secretary of State Marshall gave his Harvard commencement address.

17 December 1947—The Foreign Aid Act of 1947 to provide interim emergency aid to France, Austria, Italy, and China was passed by Congress. It included primarily commodity aid to support consumption.

3 April 1948—The Foreign Assistance Act of 1948 was passed by Congress. Title IV was the China Aid Act.

16 April 1948—The recipients of Marshall Plan aid signed the convention establishing the Organization for European Economic Cooperation.

20 January 1949—President Truman proposed the Point Four Program in his inaugural address.

5 June 1950—The Act for International Development was passed by Congress as part of the Foreign Economic Assistance Act of 1950.

---

tion that an alternative to the Truman doctrine of containment must be sought (Chap. 1).

On 27 June 1947, a tripartite conference (among France, Great Britain, and the USSR) opened in Paris. Britain and France reluctantly agreed to the American condition that funding would be provided only for a comprehensive scheme based on joint planning and resource sharing. This condition was not acceptable to the USSR; thereupon Molotov, the USSR foreign minister, withdrew from the conference. On 12 July 1947, the British and French convened a second conference, attended by 16 nations, to survey necessary needs and to draft a comprehensive recovery program. The conferees established the Committee for European Economic Cooperation (CEEC) to plan and direct the recovery program.[15]

Moving the European Recovery Program (ERP) through Congress was not easily achieved. Passage in the Senate was assured by the support of Senator Arthur H. Vandenberg (R-Mich.). In the House, the administration's relations with the Republican leadership were more antagonistic. In retrospect, it seems that the war scare of mid-March 1948 was manufactured by the Truman administration to assure passage of the ERP.[16]

In its conception and execution, the Marshall Plan had both economic and political objectives. It was an attempt to secure the foreign policy objectives of a liberal political and economic order by strengthening the economies of Western Europe. The objectives of the Economic Cooperation Act were to be (1) strengthening agricultural and industrial production, (2) expanding foreign trade, (3) creating and maintaining internal financial stability, and (4) encouraging and developing European economic cooperation.[17]

Several aspects of the ERP were particularly significant in the formulation of assistance policy for the developing countries. The first was the establishment of an independent agency to manage the recovery program. The State Department and the Bureau of the Budget pressed for an office of foreign programs to be headed by a new assistant secretary of state. The Congress, and Senator Vanderberg in particular, insisted that the program be administered by an independent agency. This position was supported by the business community. It became clear to the administration that passage of the European Recovery Act would not be possible without yielding on the issue of administration. When the European Economic Cooperative Act of 1948 was passed, it included provisions for making the Economic Cooperation Administration (ECA) an independent agency with a single administrator, who was to have cabinet status and direct access to the president. On Vanderberg's recommendation Paul G. Hoffman, president of the Studebaker Corporation and a leader within the liberal business community, was selected as administrator of the Economic Cooperation Administration. W. Averill Harriman moved from his position as Secretary of Commerce to that of U.S. Special Representative in Europe.

The second important feature of the European recovery program, which was significant for future assistance programs, was its emphasis on planning. The allocation of ECA resources was to be based on the preparation of detailed program plans in each country. Hoffman and Harriman insisted, over strong European—particularly British—opposition, that the Organization for European Economic Cooperation (OEEC) review program plans and make decisions regarding allocation of ECA resources to each country.

Two other aspects of the program were also important for future assistance policy. One was U.S. control of the counterpart funds, the local currency counterpart of American grants. Another was the important role of technical assistance for the modernization of European production facilities and management.

Assistance Programs in Asia

American assistance to Asia after World War II was initially limited to China, Japan, Korea, and the Philippines. The general presumption was that the European metropolitan powers would resume their prewar roles in much of South and Southeast Asia. The focus of assistance efforts in these areas was to sustain consumption, support raw material inputs, and repair and rehabilitate wartime damage to plants and equipment. Expenditures under the several relief programs amounted to about $2.5 billion—somewhere in the $12.5 billion range in 1985 dollars.

Assistance to China and Southeast Asia

Modest amounts of commodity import assistance were provided to Indonesia in 1948–50 through European Recovery Program grants to the Netherlands. French military and civil expenditures in Indochina also were indirectly supported by ERP aid to France. But the China Aid Program, enacted in 1948 as part of the ERP authorization, was more significant as a source of U.S. policy on economic assistance to the developing countries of Asia.

The China Aid Program was included in the Economic Cooperation Act of 1948 (the act authorizing the Marshall Plan), despite some reluctance by the Truman administration, because of pressure by the Asian-oriented members of Congress. The disagreement between Congress and the administration over aid to China is of particular interest in that it represents an early discussion of the relative merits of economic and military assistance. Charles Wolf, Jr., described the disagreement.

> In the initial discussion of China Aid in Congress, military reverses suffered by the Nationalist forces led to strong advocacy of military aid and of the prospective gains to be derived from it. The argument was not for military aid *instead* of economic aid, but rather for military aid as a *complement* to economic aid . . . By contributing to internal security, military aid was . . . considered likely to increase the gains from economic aid . . . By contrast, the official stand of the Administration was that deterioration of the situation in China was not due to military causes, nor could it be reversed by military aid. The inability of the Nationalist government to halt the communist advances . . . were due instead to the governments' lack of administrative capacity and integrity.[18]

Although the China Aid Program must be judged a failure in terms of its primary objective—strengthening the capacity of the Nationalist government to resist the deteriorating military and political situation—it did contribute important lessons for future assistance programs. In several provinces (particularly Kwangsi, Saechwan, and Kwontung), the Joint Commission on Rural

Reconstruction, initiated with U.S. economic assistance and patterned after the Latin American *servicio,* began a moderately effective rural development program. In several coastal cities, such as Canton and Swatow, the ECA also achieved some success stimulating economic activity.[19]

The experience with military and economic assistance to China strongly influenced the Truman administration position that it should rely primarily on economic rather than military assistance west of the Aleutians-Japan-Philippine perimeter. The extension of economic and technical assistance to South and Southeast Asia under the China Area Aid Act—passed by Congress on 5 June 1950, the same day that it approved the Act for International Development (the Point Four Program)—reflected both the administration's position on economic assistance and congressional commitment to continued support for the Nationalist government after it moved to Taiwan. The resources transferred from the China Aid Program were substantially larger than the resources made available to support the Technical Cooperation (Point Four) Program.[20]

Economic and Military Assistance to Korea

From the end of World War II until 1 January 1949, when the United States extended diplomatic recognition to Korea, assistance to Korea was administered by the military through the Government and Relief in Occupied Areas program. Beginning in 1949 responsibility for economic assistance to Korea was transferred to the Economic Cooperation Administration. The emphasis of assistance shifted from relief to recovery and development. The funding of economic assistance to Korea in 1949 became entangled in a bitter debate in Congress over responsibility for the "loss" of China. After the North Korean invasion of 25 June 1950, the primary objective of assistance reverted to sustaining civilian consumption and the provision of basic inputs, such as fertilizer and cotton, to maintain commodity production.

The economic assistance to Korea before the outbreak of the Korean War supported an initial recovery. Both agricultural and industrial production rose to well above prewar levels. Nevertheless, the inference that was drawn from the Korean experience was that the United States invited the North Korean attack by not including Korea within the U.S. defense perimeter and by limiting military assistance. It seemed to confirm a perspective that economic assistance was not enough to assure the political and economic viability of the new states that were emerging in the postcolonial, post–World War II world.[21]

New Multilateral Institutions

An important objective of U.S. postwar foreign economic policy, enunciated even before entry into World War II, was to bring about a liberal international economic order. The United States was also committed to the emergence of a more democratic and stable international political order. The major institutional expressions of this concern with a more liberal economic order were the creation of the International Bank for Reconstruction and Development (World Bank) and the International Monetary Fund and the attempt to create an international trade organization.[22] The major institutional expression of concern with a more democratic and stable international political system was the establishment of the United Nations and its specialized agencies.[23]

The Fund and the Bank

Preliminary thinking about a postwar stabilization fund and an international bank was under way in Washington and London as early as 1941.[24] The preliminary ideas were influenced by earlier initiatives, particularly the 1940 proposal for an inter-American bank. After a series of meetings in 1943, a meeting to prepare an agenda was held in June 1944 at Atlantic City. It was followed in July by a 44-nation conference at Bretton Woods, New Hampshire.

The initial discussion at Bretton Woods was dedicated almost entirely to the stabilization fund. As a result of pressure from the nations interested in reconstruction and from several developing countries, a group was set up to work on a proposal for an international bank.

The articles of agreement for the fund and the bank were sent to Congress by President Roosevelt in January 1945. The Agreements Act was passed by Congress and signed by President Truman on 31 July 1945. Britain delayed parliamentary approval until negotiations with the United States over Lend-Lease settlement were concluded. On 31 December 1945, the Articles of Agreement for the fund and the bank went into effect. The first meeting of the governors of the fund and the bank was held in Savannah, Georgia, in March 1946, and the World Bank opened for business on 25 June 1946. The International Monetary Fund commenced commercial financing on 1 March 1947. The first loan was $220 million to France in May 1947.

The three main functions assigned to the IMF by participants at the Bretton Woods Conference were (1) to administer a code of conduct with respect to exchange rate policies and restrictions on convertability, (2) to provide member governments with financial resources when it became necessary to correct payment imbalances, and (3) to provide a mechanism for members to consult and collaborate on international monetary matters. The fund had the authority to finance temporary deficits. Resources were made available by members' subscriptions. Access to IMF resources to meet balance of payment problems was established in relation to members' subscriptions.

The fund's influence on policies and practices was limited during the late 1940s. There was little interest in issues of getting exchange rates "right." In general it was held that exchange rate adjustments would not have much effect on exports and imports because of the limited capacity of postwar economies to respond to changes in incentives and because of the widespread use of import and exchange controls. Restrictions on access to fund resources by countries that had access to U.S. economic assistance under ERP and the relatively strong export position of many developing countries also limited the use of IMF facilities.

The World Bank got off to a slow start (Chap. 11). It was plagued by managerial instability and poor relationships between its president and executive directors until the appointment of Eugene Black as president in May 1949. The development of the bank's program to finance reconstruction was overtaken by events. Economic conditions in Europe deteriorated more rapidly than anticipated, and the resources required for reconstruction far exceeded the bank's capacity. When the European Recovery Act was passed, the bank withdrew from the reconstruction field after making initial loans to France, Netherlands, Denmark, and Luxembourg.

It is hard to disagree with Mason and Asher's conclusion that "the early years of the Bank have to be characterized as inauspicious" (p. 36). The same conclusion could have been drawn about the IMF.

The United Nations

The second major initiative to establish an institutional framework for postwar political and economic cooperation was the United Nations Organization.[25] The preparatory work that would lead to a postwar international organization began even before the United States entered World War II. In May 1944 the United States acted as host to the meeting at Hot Springs, Virginia, that led to the formation of an interim Commission on Food and Agriculture, which later became the United Nations Food and Agriculture Organization (FAO). It was agreed at the Bretton Woods Conference in 1944 that the International Bank and the Monetary Fund should cooperate with any general international organization that might be established.

The basic structure of the United Nations Organization was established at a four-power conference at Dumbarton Oaks in the summer of 1944, was further amplified later that year at the Yalta meeting of Churchill, Roosevelt, and Stalin, and was formalized at the San Francisco conference in April and May of 1945. The charter agreed to at the June 1945 organizing conference in San Francisco bound member states to take joint and separate action in cooperation with the organization for the achievement of higher standards of living, full employment, and conditions of social and economic progress and development; for the solution of international economic and social problems in general; and for international cultural and educational cooperation. Specialized agencies such as the financial institutions were to be "brought into relationship with the United Nations" in carrying out programs in the social and economic spheres (Chap. 12).[26]

The United States also played a major role in establishing and funding a cooperative postwar relief and rehabilitation agency. After consultations during 1942 and 1943 and a four-power (United States, Great Britain, Soviet Union, and France) agreement in 1944, the United Nations Relief and Rehabilitation Agency was established to provide both relief and rehabilitation in liberated areas. At U.S. insistence it was agreed that each member government (except those that had been occupied) would contribute 1 percent of its national income. The UNRRA was a departure from post–World War I policy in its emphasis on rehabilitation, involving both financial and technical assistance, rather than simply relief. Between 1944 and 1947 the United States contributed approximately $3 billion to the UNRRA. The UNRRA program was terminated at the end of 1947, in part because of rising tension between the United States and the Soviet Union over administration of the program and the decision by the United States to administer the Marshall Plan as a bilateral program.[27]

The approach adopted by the United Nations for the provision of technical and other services has been through the establishment of a complex of separate and autonomous specialized agencies. This pattern was already established at the time of the 1945 organizing conference. In addition to the prior establishment of the two Bretton Woods financial institutions, the new organization inherited the International Labor Organization (ILO), an incipient Food and Agriculture Organization, and several former autonomous agencies, such as the Universal Postal Union (UPU) and the International Telecommunication Union (ITU). The structure that emerged by the early 1950s has continued almost unchanged (Chap. 12).

Some U.N. agencies had made substantial progress in program development by the late 1940s. The FAO, for example, had provided staffing for much of the technical assistance carried on under the UNRRA.[28] But it was well into the 1950s before it was possible to begin to extract development assistance "lessons" from the work of the specialized agencies and commissions.

The mid-1940s were a remarkably creative period of institutional innovation. These innovations were initiated and carried out by a group of bureaucratic entrepreneurs and technicians who were associated with the foreign affairs and treasury departments (ministries) in the United States and the United Kingdom. The wartime and early postwar environment was conducive to the emergence of a foreign policy establishment whose experience in both the private and public sectors had convinced them of the importance of resolution of, and the capacity of government to resolve, the problems that had led to international economic and political stagnation and collapse during the interwar period. The structure of the new international institutions was largely the product of intense and often difficult collaboration between the United States and the United Kingdom. The ability of these two countries to resolve their own difficulties when they were confronted with the need to respond to initiatives from other powers, particularly the Soviet Union and France, was critical for the emergence of the postwar economic and political system.

Lessons from Experience

Some of the lessons, often mutually inconsistent, that were drawn from experience with assistance to Europe, Latin America, South Asia, and East Asia have been described in this chapter. These lessons had an important influence on the design of subsequent assistance programs.

The lesson drawn from the Latin American experience was that well-designed and relatively low-cost programs of education, technical assistance, and cultural interchange could generate relatively high economic dividends for the recipient and high political dividends for the donor.

The lesson drawn from attempts to prevent the collapse of the Nationalist regime in China was that security assistance, in the absence of a viable economy and an effective government, was ineffective. The inference was drawn that assistance should be directed to governments that are sufficiently committed to political reform and economic development to make effective use of assistance.

The lesson drawn from experience in Greece and in Korea was that security assistance could be effective in enabling governments with limited administrative capacity to resist the threat of external aggression and internal subversion if the United States was prepared to involve itself deeply in the management and support of a country's economic and security systems.

The lesson drawn from the Marshall Plan was that careful economic planning by recipient governments and donors was a prerequisite to the effective use of large resource transfers.

These lessons were learned selectively. The lessons from experience in Greece and Turkey were embraced by the more conservative elements in the American political spectrum. The lessons from Europe—from the Marshall Plan—were embraced by the economists and planners in the new assistance bureaucracy, while the lessons from Latin America were embraced by the technical and scientific staffs of the assistance agency. The lessons from China and Latin America were embraced by the more liberal elements of the political spectrum.

The lessons were not fully integrated into a coherent foreign assistance doctrine. Assistance policies and priorities have shifted in response to trends and fluctuations in domestic political forces at least as much as or perhaps more than they have shifted in response to objective economic and political changes in the developing world. In the next several chapters, I examine how these domestic political forces have interacted to generate change in U.S. development assistance policy.

Chapter 4

Technical Assistance for Economic Development

In this chapter I seek to examine the expectations and motives behind early post–World War II U.S. aid to developing countries.[1] As a starting point I take the Act for International Development of 1950, first proposed as the fourth point of President Harry S. Truman's inaugural address of 20 January 1949 (Chap. 3). This program was to consist of two parts. The first was a technical assistance program that would help transfer modern techniques and know-how to the less developed areas. "The United States is preeminent among nations in the development of industrial and scientific techniques. The material resources which we can afford to use for the assistance of other peoples are limited. But our imponderable resources in technical knowledge are constantly growing and are inexhaustible."[2] The second part of the program authorized the Export-Import Bank to issue guarantees to private investors in developing countries against certain risks peculiar to foreign investment.

The Point Four program, as it came to be called, marks a distinct break in American development assistance policy. Earlier, U.S. aid to developing areas had been sporadic, with the limited objectives of winning political support, relieving exceptional disasters in specific countries, or assisting in post–World War II reconstruction (Chap. 3). With the significant exceptions of aid to East Asia and Latin America, previous aid had not focused on development as an issue. The Point Four Program was thus the first attempt by the United States at a global program to attack the root causes of development on a long-term basis.

Today's conventional wisdom is that the Point Four Program was a sincere but misguided attempt by the United States to extend the success of the Marshall Plan to the developing world.[3] It is popularly believed that during the 1950s experts thought that underdevelopment stemmed from a lack of infrastructure that made private investment unprofitable. By transferring large amounts of financial capital to the developing areas, the government would make possible the construction of large infrastructure projects. This would establish the proper climate for private investment in the industrial sector. Since the Marshall Plan had resulted in dramatic improvement in the gross national product of Europe, a similar program would succeed in other regions as well.

The Point Four Legislation

The Point Four Program first surfaced as a major part of President Truman's inaugural address. The basic idea was developed by Benjamin Hardy of the State Department. Clark Clifford, Truman's Special Counsel, had made a request to the State Department for material to be utilized in preparing the president's inaugural address. The memorandum stimulated a memorandum from Benjamin Hardy, a young public affairs officer, but his memorandum was never forwarded to the White House by his superiors at the State Department. Hardy then bypassed official channels by phoning George Elsey, who worked for Clark Clifford on the White House staff. Clifford, who was searching for a new initiative to present to the American public, took the proposal to President Truman. Truman was enthusiastic about the idea and authorized its inclusion in the inaugural address. The draft of the address was not circulated to the State Department for comment to avoid diluting the effect of the speech. After the address, an unenthusiastic State Department was left in the awkward position of trying to determine what the president had in mind.[4]

Congress began considering Point Four legislation shortly after President Truman's inaugural address. The first bill, supported by the administration, was sponsored by the chairman of the Foreign Affairs Committee, John Kee.[5] It found that the United States had a common interest in the material progress of all peoples and advanced proposals to promote the development of economically underdeveloped areas of the world. To achieve this, the president was authorized to enter into technical cooperation programs, with funds to be appropriated in the future. This bill also authorized the creation of an Institute of International Technical Cooperation within the State Department. The Kee bill sought the participation of the United Nations and other international organizations wherever practicable and encouraged the involvement of private agencies and persons.

Congressman Christian A. Herter of Massachusetts introduced a Republican alternative.[6] It placed much greater emphasis on the role of private investment in the process of development. The Herter bill sought to establish a Foreign Economic Development Administration within the State Department. The United States would enter into bilateral treaties and agreements with other nations as a condition to their participation in the program. These agreements would protect private investment from uncompensated expropriation, foreign exchange restrictions, and double taxation. They would also create joint commissions to oversee each nation's economic progress.

The Herter bill also directed the administration to support Export-Import Bank loans to participating nations. Under the Herter bill, the administration would also sponsor technical missions in the fields of health, sanitation, agriculture, and education and provide assistance to increase economic efficiency.

On 5 June 1950, 16 months after it had been proposed by President Truman, Congress passed into law a compromise bill known as the Act for International Development.[7] Like the Kee bill, it recognized a common interest in the freedom and in the economic social progress of all peoples, progress that could be furthered through a cooperative endeavor to exchange technical knowledge and skills and to encourage the flow of investment capital to less developed areas. Congress placed several restrictions on the scope of the program. The administration could authorize assistance only where the recipient nation (1) paid a fair share of the program's cost, (2) provided all necessary information concerning the program and gave it full publicity, (3) sought to integrate the program fully into its overall technical cooperation policy, (4) made effective use of the program's results, and (5) cooperated with other nations in the mutual exchange of technical knowledge and skills. Finally, the act directed the termination of any program that was inconsistent with American foreign policy. Congress also retained oversight powers by providing that it could terminate any program by a joint resolution of both houses. It also directed the president to prepare an annual report of all operations under the act.

The act sought the greatest practicable participation of private agencies and persons. Partly to ensure this, it established an advisory board of up to 13 private individuals drawn from voluntary agencies, business, labor, agriculture, health, and education to advise and consult with the program's administrator concerning the general policy of technical assistance. Where desirable, a joint commission composed of nationals of both the United States and the recipient nation would oversee assistance to each nation. As part of their duties, these joint commissions could prepare studies recommending specific projects contributing to economic development. The act also authorized the president to participate in and contribute to multilateral programs of technical assistance wherever possible. A total of $35 million was authorized to establish such a program.

Development Thought

The literature on economic development from academic, official, and popular sources expanded rapidly as the United States began to assume a more active role in economic assistance. In 1949, President Truman appointed Gordon Gray to prepare a report on America's international economic policy. A year later the president commissioned another study prepared by a specially created board under the chairmanship of Nelson A. Rockefeller. The United Nations also commissioned a group of experts that included future Nobel awardees W. Arthur Lewis and Theodore Schultz to prepare a study on economic development.[8] There was also an outpouring of books and other professional literature.

Taken as a whole, these writings indicate a broad intellectual consensus on the nature of economic underdevelopment and on the general policies that would help alleviate it.[9] There was widespread recognition that any program to promote economic development would have to be coordinated and comprehensive. It would need to focus on a number of interrelated fields at once, such as health, education, infrastructure, and agriculture. Fragmentary assistance limited to certain fields or of short duration was unlikely to accomplish much.

There was also general agreement that economic development required a balanced pattern of growth within less developed areas.[10] Industrialization would have to extend beyond the extractive industries into processing, manufacturing, and import substitution. More importantly, countries would have to devote attention to their agricultural sectors, focusing on expanding agricultural productivity and establishing small-scale rural industries. Contrary to later perceptions, writers of the time stressed rural development as a prerequisite to broader economic growth.

There was also agreement on the nature of development programs.[11] Modest but well-designed projects were more likely to succeed than were large, ambitious ones. There was a limit to the ability of less developed countries (LDCs) to absorb capital and technology. Ignoring this constraint was likely to result in waste and inefficiency. To facilitate effective use of aid, much of the initial finances would go into surveys of national needs and resources to match technical skills to the conditions within each nation. Economic and technical assistance programs of the West, if attempted at all, should be conducted on a generous scale. Excessive concern with cost and rates of return would only slow the pace of development and create friction between donors and recipients, as would unnecessary conditions on receiving such aid. Partly to alleviate this concern about cost, the involvement of international agencies in the development process received wide support. Finally, donors would have to avoid pursuing economic or trade policies that conflicted with the broader results of their technical assistance program. This meant opening up domestic markets to increased LDC production and eliminating disincentives to the flow of capital abroad.

One of the primary targets of development efforts would have to be the improvement of a nation's human capital through expanded health and education services.[12] Although some writers were strongly concerned about the degree to which population growth impeded economic development, all recognized that improved public health was crucial to increases in human productivity.

There was also a great deal of agreement on the nature of economic underdevelopment. The primary characteristic of such a system was low labor productivity caused by lack of accompanying factors of production.[13] To eliminate this shortage, the less developed countries needed a higher rate of saving. Unlike the situation in Europe, however, low productivity in LDCs was compounded by absolute poverty, making it difficult to accumulate a surplus of production over consumption that could be used for reinvestment. Part of the solution thus lay in private transfers of capital from the West to the less developed areas. There was great doubt, however, as to whether such flows, channeled through capital markets, would be sufficient.[14] In many cases, developing areas lacked the physical and human capital necessary to attract private investment. As a prerequisite to private capital flows, public economic and technical assistance would have to finance the creation of a climate in which future investments could be profitable.[15]

Most disagreement took place over the nature and extent of government attempts to finance capital movement overseas. Many experts believed that, for developing areas to obtain the capital needed to finance economic growth, the United States would have to begin a program of large loans and grants.[16] Others felt strongly that the government should confine its efforts to sponsoring technical exchange programs and encouraging developing countries to establish favorable climates for private investment.[17]

Congressional Hearings

Both houses of Congress held annual authorization and appropriation hearings on the technical assistance program from its inception. The first authorization hearings, held in 1949–50, dealt exclusively with the new Point Four Program. From then on, however, testimony on technical assistance was incorporated within hearings on the overall foreign aid bill. In this section I review the original authorization and appropriation hearings for technical assistance, the first hearings on authorizing Export-Import Bank investment guarantees, and the 1952 authorization hearings.[18]

The testimony at each hearing reflected different views on the nature of economic development. Over half of the testimony came from administration officials justifying budget requests. Congress did allow some opportunity for the expression of public views, although it often confined this to short, 10-minute statements and the reprinting of written statements in the record. Almost all of the speakers from outside the administration were affiliated with business, labor, agricultural, or charitable organizations. There were no unaffiliated representatives of the academic community at the hearings.

The Administration's Viewpoint

Most of the administration's testimony came from officials within the State Department. The statements of other departments dealt largely with their perceived role in the new program. The basic premise behind the administration's policy was that underdevelopment stemmed from two shortages: a shortage of knowledge and a shortage of capital. The Point Four Program would limit itself to meeting the first shortage by projects designed to transfer technical information and know-how. Most of the external capital needed for investment would have to come from the private sector. In those areas, such as infrastructure and social services, where private business could not capture enough of the benefits to make investment profitable, the Export-Import Bank and the International Bank for Reconstruction and Development would extend loans.

The administration strongly supported the concept of Point Four embodied in the Kee bill. It based this support on economic, political, social, and humanitarian grounds.[19] Of these, economic and political (security) justifications received the most emphasis. Purely humanitarian concerns rarely appeared as a major point in the administration's testimony. Economic effects received the most emphasis. The Point Four effort of technical assistance and investment guarantees would go far toward eliminating poverty and improving living standards. It would also benefit the United States. Since extractive industries accounted for much of the developing world's economic power, their expansion would increase the supply of raw materials available to the West. In addition, the program would help expand American exports.[20] The United States had most of the physical capital and consumer goods desired by other nations. One of the chief obstacles to expanded trade with less developed countries was their lack of purchasing power in dollars, the so-called dollar shortage. By helping developing nations to expand their exports and earn dollars, the United States would build up the market for its own exports and expand the world economy. Supporters of the bill often pointed out that there was a positive correlation between a nation's GNP and the amount of American imports it purchased.

The administration also focused on the political security benefits of the program. The first hearings were held shortly after the Communist victory in China.[21] There was a popular perception that Soviet-style communism was threatening to spread to other areas of the world, using as one weapon the appeal to traditionally downtrodden groups with false promises of economic growth and equality.[22]

The Point Four Program, by dealing with the underlying causes of poverty in key areas such as agriculture, forestry, and fisheries, would directly counter this propaganda with positive action.[23] It would show people everywhere that freedom, not communism, held the key to economic prosperity. By stressing areas such as health, education, and other social services, the technical exchange program would concentrate directly on improving the way people lived.

The administration also spent a great deal of time laying out the proposed structure of the program. The first part of Point Four would consist of a technical assistance program that concentrated on small-scale projects with the purpose of transferring useful knowledge and techniques to developing countries.[24] Because of its limited scope, the program's cost could be kept down. In most cases, the recipient nation would provide most of the capital, paying for all local costs and a share of the total exchange costs.[25] The program would concentrate its efforts on the exchange of knowledge rather than capital, thus helping less developed countries to overcome their critical shortage of skilled personnel.[26] The program would not be involved in either the funding or the construction of large capital projects. Administration officials repeatedly assured skeptical congressmen that the program would not involve the large capital expenditures of the Marshall Plan.[27] Because of its emphasis on the transfer of knowledge between individuals, the availability of adequately trained, competent personnel seemed to be the main bottleneck to the program's expansion.[28]

Coordination of the program would come under a newly established Technical Cooperation Agency (TCA) within the State Department. This agency would supervise each nation's participation in the program; specific technical assistance projects, however, would be handled by the government agency best equipped to work in the area. Under an agreement between the TCA and the Economic Cooperation Administration, there would be no duplication of efforts.[29] The Point Four Program would not undertake bilateral programs in Europe, with the exception of Turkey. The ECA would continue to handle technical assistance to colonies until its authorization expired in 1952. This assistance would be integrated with existing programs in Europe dealing with agriculture, forestry, industry, mining, and transportation.

Many speakers viewed the program as merely a natural extension of successful programs in other areas. In particular, they stressed previous efforts in China and Latin America, often by private agencies. Administration officials emphasized the need for a sustained commitment toward development. Progress would be slow and often intangible. One speaker saw the possibility of a 50-year program. The Point Four Program was not like the Marshall Plan, which had a life expectancy of four years; Congress was warned not to expect quick or dramatic results.[30]

The administration recognized that technical assistance alone would not produce economic development. To take advantage of new techniques, less developed countries would need investment capital, which, to the extent possible, would have to come from within the LDCs themselves. The degree of their poverty would prevent this from being enough, however, and would necessitate a flow of external capital. Most of the outside capital would have to come from the private sector, which could transfer with it the managerial and business skills necessary to make investments profitable.[31]

One of the main reasons that private funds were not moving abroad was the negative climate that existed in most developing areas.[32] The principal deterrents included unstable political conditions, balance-of-payments problems, and government interference with private foreign investment. These, together with the high rate of return available at home, made foreign investment unattractive.

To reverse this situation, the government proposed a series of initiatives aimed at making foreign investment more secure. One of these was the negotiation of bilateral treaties of friendship, commerce, and navigation with other countries.[33] These treaties sought to establish a better climate for foreign investment by ensuring adequate compensation for expropriation and by guaranteeing, among other things, a reasonable opportunity to remit earnings and withdraw capital and reasonable freedom to manage, operate, and control enterprises; they also provided for the personal security and nondiscriminatory treatment of foreign investors.

A second initiative was an investment guarantee program under the direction of the Export-Import Bank. The administration recognized that, however comprehensive, treaties and information programs would not eliminate all of the risks associated with foreign investment. To reduce these risks ever further and thus increase private investment, it proposed a self-funding guarantee program that would insure qualifying investments against risks peculiar to foreign investment. In evaluating these risks, the bank would consider each nation separately, extending guarantees only if the host nation demonstrated a willingness to cooperate in establishing a proper climate.[34]

One major issue was over the proper risks such a program should insure. The major risk that guarantees would cover was inconvertibility. Bilateral treaties could not totally eliminate this risk because no nation would surrender sovereign control over its economy and because the dollar shortage was not entirely the fault of the less developed countries. Other risks that the bill might cover were expropriation without compensation and loss due to war. Only the former was included in the administration's bill. The program would not guarantee that an investment would be profitable or insure against ordinary business risks. As proposed, the bank would offer guarantees to certain investors for a fee. These fees would go into a reserve fund from which claims would be paid. The government would be subrogated to the investor's claims once it paid off on a guarantee. The bank promised not to seek priority status for its claims, however, in order to avoid creating further currency shortages. The main purpose was to attract new, productive capital to the less developed countries. The program would not require appropriation of any new funds. Because of the experimental nature of this program, great flexibility was vital to its success.[35]

Underlying the entire discussion was the assumption that increased foreign investment would benefit the United States through greater security and goodwill, increased exports, and greater global prosperity. The administration also recognized that certain investments, owing to their nature, would be unable to obtain private funding. In such cases less developed countries could obtain loans from the Export-Import Bank and the World Bank.[36] These loans could take place only where adequate private financing was not available. Although the terms were not specified, the loans were to be near the market rate; grant assistance was not an option except in certain situations where Congress authorized emergency assistance to meet extreme disasters.

The State Department also proposed to make maximum use of the United Nations, its specialized agencies, and other multilateral organizations.[37] Drawing upon these institutions would multiply the financial and human resources available to development projects, would serve to strengthen the ability of these organizations to act as constructive forces in international affairs, and, finally, by easing the suspicions of the recipients, would help to eliminate some of the conflict that could arise between the donor and host in bilateral assistance.

The Department of Labor stressed that the program's success depended upon its ability to benefit the workers of the Third World. To ensure this, it cited programs in the field of labor aimed at upgrading the level of skills. More importantly, the department mentioned the need to develop adequate working standards and to improve living conditions. The department supported extending the principles of collective bargaining, unionization, and minimum working conditions to the Third World. In addition, the United States would support programs to provide services such as unemployment insurance, employment agencies, and retraining centers.[38] These programs would be run both bilaterally and through the International Labor Organization.

Business Interests

Most of the testimony on the perception of economic development by the business community came from established organizations such as the U.S. Chamber of Commerce and the Detroit Board of Commerce and from individuals sympathetic to its cause, such as Norman M. Littell and Congressman Herter. Few individual businesses engaged in foreign investment spoke before the committees.

The business community stressed that the greatest opportunity for development in LDCs lay in attracting private investment.[39] Only private sources could provide the large amounts of capital needed for investment without threatening the economic health of the United States and could bring the managerial and business skills needed to make industry efficient. In the view of the business community, the central problem of underdevelopment was low productivity resulting from inferior capitalization, management, and supervision.[40] The main reason that private investment was not meeting the needs of LDCs lay in the failure of developing nations to establish business climates competitive with those in the West. If LDCs followed the proper policies, the private sector would respond favorably.[41]

According to this view, the government's role in development should consist largely of encouraging positive initiatives on the part of less developed countries. Negotiating bilateral treaties was a major part of this.[42] These treaties should commit LDCs to giving private investment the same treatment received by public enterprises, eliminating double taxation, providing prompt and adequate compensation for expropriation, and otherwise creating an atmosphere suitable for private investment. Many thought that the successful negotiation of these treaties should be a prerequisite for participation in the technical assistance program.

The business community was divided over the issue of investment guarantees. Many enterprises already committed to ventures abroad felt that any guarantee program should cover old investments as well. To do otherwise would put them at a competitive disadvantage against newer activities. A few companies even opposed the issuance of any guarantees, arguing that guarantees merely encouraged uncompetitive investment abroad at the expense of the American capital market. Most representatives of the business community favored some form of guarantee program, however. A major disagreement with the administration came over which risks the programs would cover. The business community wanted guarantees to cover inconvertibility, expropriation, and all other government acts. Repayment should not be limited to sunk capital but should cover lost earnings and profits as well.[43]

The business community was especially concerned that the government avoid competing with the private sector in providing capital to the developing world. Such a program would quickly bankrupt the U.S. economy while accomplishing little. The United States should not undertake equity investments. Loans by the Export-Import Bank and the World Bank should be available only in cases where private funds were not. Above all, the United States should impress less developed countries with the need to follow appropriate policies to attract private investment. If they did, the business community would respond with new investments. If LDCs failed to do so, they should not be able to appeal to government programs with the argument that the private sector was not doing its job.[44] To help ensure this neutrality, the business community pressed for legislation mandating the fullest use of private enterprise and establishing a board of businessmen to oversee compliance with the requirement.[45]

Labor's Viewpoint

Labor organizations tended to show strong support for the Point Four initiative. They equated success with tangible improvements in the living standards of the working and peasant classes. Projects should be geared toward meeting the needs of their intended beneficiaries, since American prosperity was directly linked to the purchasing power of the world's poor.[46]

In relation to private investment, this meant that Congress must ensure that effort went into protecting and improving local living standards as well as ensuring the security of foreign investments. The program should not serve as a cover for exploitation and excessive profits for business.[47] Instead, Congress should make sure that workers shared in the benefits of increased production through higher wages and better working conditions. One way to do this was to promote free trade unions that could engage in collective bargaining with business groups.

The labor community showed strong support for opening up trade with the rest of the world. It specifically discounted the threat of increased LDC production competing with American jobs.[48]

Agriculture

Organizations representing American agriculture voiced strong support for a comprehensive Point Four Program. Although they stressed the need to expand industrial production in both rural and urban areas, most of their comments focused on rural development. Although the United States could not by itself create development abroad, it could promote proper self-help policies within LDCs and encourage private investment. Because of its success in the United States, the farm community strongly advocated an active role for the government in sponsoring agricultural extension services, cooperatives, land-grant colleges, and experiment stations.[49] These methods had already proven successful in Latin America.

Like labor, the agricultural producers were not concerned with the threat of competition from less developed countries. They saw increased food production as a necessary prerequisite to development and expected that most of it would be consumed internally rather than exported. These organizations also supported heavy involvement by the United Nations.[50]

Charitable Groups

A large variety of religious and civic groups urged a more humanitarian approach in the proposed program. These groups tended to be less concerned with the political or strategic advantage.[51] Instead, they found their main rationale in the moral implications of conditions overseas.[52] For them, the primary purpose of the program was to meet local needs by raising low productivity and low living standards. As such, it would strengthen the moral underpinning of American foreign policy.[53]

These groups urged that the program's success be measured largely in terms of its effect on poverty. They stressed the need to isolate the program from political considerations.[54] To ensure this, all groups gave strong support to heavy involvement of the United Nations and other multilateral agencies.[55] This would reduce the suspicion of less developed countries toward the new initiatives of the West and lessen the friction between donor and recipient nations. It would also give the United States access to a wider body of technical expertise in the field.[56]

There was strong support for a role by the government in creating the economic and physical infrastructure necessary to make private investment possible and considerable skepticism that private investment would arrive in sufficient amounts once it received proper guarantees. As a result of this skepticism, charitable groups were more concerned that the benefits of development go to local citizens and not to foreign capitalists.[57] Many sought assurances that the government would not use the program to underwrite excessive profits due to exploitation.[58] Private investment should be tailored to the needs and priorities of the host nation and not vice versa. They also stressed the role that private organizations such as their own should play in the program.[59]

This group of speakers also tended to stress successful programs of the past, especially those in China and Latin America.[60] These programs demonstrated what a few dedicated people could do when provided with the proper support and funding. The new effort should be an extension of previous efforts with greater official support.[61] Although a few groups desired increased capital expenditures in the future, most were content with limiting the program to technical as opposed to economic assistance.[62]

Congress

Although many senators and congressmen on both the authorization and appropriations committees expressed skepticism about various parts of the program, few opposed the principle behind it. According to party lines, their views generally followed one of two main philosophies.

The liberal view, supported by most Democrats, favored the administration's proposal. They viewed it as a significant extension of previous efforts and as a bold new foreign policy initiative. If properly run, it would become a major cornerstone of U.S. policy overseas.[63] This side tended to be skeptical about the willingness of the private sector to move large sums of capital overseas. Although they supported the idea of encouraging such investment through guarantees and the elimination of double taxation, they questioned the degree to which this would eliminate the need for public funds. Many were concerned that, left to themselves, American firms would exploit the developing countries through low pay and sweatshop conditions. To counteract this, the law should require private investment to raise the living standards in less developed countries and to reward increased production with higher wages.[64]

The conservative side, whose main proponent was Congressman Herter of Massachusetts, favored his alternative bill that placed greater emphasis on the need to attract private investment as a prerequisite to successful development. Conservatives supported the view of the business community that the main reason greater investment was not occurring was the hostile business environment overseas.[65] This view favored making the improvement of investment climates a condition to participation in the technical assistance program. It discounted the threat of corporate exploitation and concentrated instead on the dangers of excessive government involvement.[66] In particular, the government should be careful that its activities did not compete with the public sector. Conservatives tended to favor explicit restrictions on the agency's scope of power and discretion.[67]

A few congressmen were skeptical about the need for any program at all. Although they supported the general idea of technical assistance, they questioned the need for new legislation, arguing that the proposed program was authorized under existing legislation. One member, in particular, viewed the new proposals as little more than a politically motivated giveaway program.[68]

None of the committee members supported large public expenditures in connection with the program. Many were concerned about the risk of creating a new program that could later grow to require large appropriations.[69] Although some recognized the need for greater public funding to compensate for insufficient private investment, many feared that the United States would be forced to supply large amounts of capital to save face when proposed projects failed to obtain adequate funding elsewhere. This possibility raised real concerns about the effect of the program on the American economy, especially at a time of high deficits.[70]

There was also general agreement on working with U.N. agencies as part of the program.[71] There was a serious disagreement over the method of providing these agencies with funds, however. Many members of the Senate Appropriations Committee were incensed that the administration had pledged $10 million to a new development program within the United Nations before Congress had authorized it.[72] They felt that in doing so the administration had usurped Congress' power by forcing its hand.

In retrospect, the original Point Four Program was an enlightened, if modest, attempt to address the causes of underdevelopment overseas. The government's role was not to extend beyond organizing technical assistance projects to correct the gaps of knowledge and health existing between the Third World and the West. Somewhat naively, public officials believed that it would be possible to rely almost exclusively on private industry to provide the necessary capital to ensure success. Had this reliance proved justified, U.S. assistance need not have gone beyond the modest amounts required for technical assistance. Private capital flows, however, never approached the amounts required by the less developed countries. This unsatisfied demand, together with new political considerations, resulted in a movement of U.S. aid from the original small-scale projects.

Toward Security

By 1952 the program's emphasis had changed noticeably. The Korean War added new momentum to the growing Cold War, leading to a remilitarization campaign in both the United States and Europe. As a result, aid under the Marshall Plan continued beyond its scheduled termination date of 1952. Its rationale shifted, however, from financing the reconstruction of war-torn economies to underwriting the procurement of necessary commodities, which, but for U.S. aid, would lead to a diversion of necessary funds from the Allies' remilitarization efforts.[73]

Security concerns easily spilled over to discussions of economic and technical aid. A basic premise of U.S. foreign policy was that Russia would take advantage of weakness or disintegration wherever it found it. To combat this, the United States sought to build up collective defense capabilities as quickly as possible on the basis of self-help and mutual aid.[74] Development assistance thus was increasingly linked to the overall foreign policy concerns of the United States, including its military assistance programs. By this time, the administration was telling Congress that recent Communist advances threatened the national security and that the United States was in danger of losing Asia and the Middle East to Russia. Economic and technical assistance programs were necessary to ensure military security abroad. As a result, the political and security aspects of technical assistance quickly became its main selling point.[75]

These concerns affected the technical assistance program. Beginning in 1951, hearings on development aid were incorporated into those on the broader foreign aid bill, with the better part of the time devoted to the European remilitarization program. Also in that year, Congress amended the assistance act to read "no economic or technical assistance shall be supplied to any other nation unless the President finds that the supplying of such assistance will strengthen the security of the United States and promote world peace, and unless the recipient country has agreed to join in promoting international understanding and good will and in maintaining world peace, and to take such action as may be mutually agreed upon to eliminate causes of international tension."[76]

Another manifestation of this linkage was the Mutual Security Act of 1951, which combined both economic and military assistance in the same bill. This legislation placed the Technical Cooperation Agency under the supervision of the Mutual Security Agency (MSA).[77] Under this arrangement the TCA was to have wide autonomy and remain insulated from security programs. Not all technical assistance came from the TCA, however. In Southeast Asia, where the Communist threat was most immediate, technical assistance programs came directly under the MSA, which integrated them into a broader program including military aid. The MSA also continued to handle technical assistance to the African colonies. In spite of this large responsibility, technical assistance still comprised less than 10 percent of the total MSA budget.[78]

Another major difference between the 1952 bill and its predecessors was the dramatic increase in capital requests. The administration targeted most of this aid for three countries: India, Pakistan, and Iran. Because of the immediacy of the Communist threat to these nations, highlighted by recent Communist victories in local Indian elections, the assistance programs were to be qualitatively different from those elsewhere. The TCA would supervise the transfer of large amounts of capital to this region in an attempt to accelerate the process of development and telescope 20 or more years of development into 4 or 5.[79]

Even in areas where the basic characteristics of technical assistance did not change, budget requests increased, with greater emphasis being placed on financial transfers.[80]

Officials justified these expenditures as necessary complements to the exchange of knowledge. If pilot programs were to succeed, field personnel had to have the equipment needed to demonstrate the worth of new techniques. Only when less developed countries had seen physical evidence that a new idea was better would they invest their own resources into expanding its use. This was true even in nations enjoying positive foreign exchange flows.

Administration officials dismissed fears about the program's effect on the national deficit.[81] They viewed the deficit's size as negligible compared to the nation's GNP, characterizing it as a temporary imbalance rather than a structural problem. Its significance paled in comparison to the threat to national security posed by communism.

Officials also dismissed charges that the program was moving along too slowly. Many opponents of Point Four had argued that no new appropriations were needed because the previous year's funds were not yet all committed, but administration officials countered that, because of the lateness of the congressional appropriation, the TCA had not had time to expend the funds properly. It was expected that by the end of the fiscal year almost all of the funds would be gone. Another factor inhibiting the program's expansion continued to be the serious lack of skilled technicians available for service overseas.[82]

By 1952, much of the official development network was already in place. It was thus possible to begin to evaluate agency programs. The World Bank had already shifted its emphasis from the reconstruction of Europe to the development of Latin America, the Middle East, and Southeast Asia (Chap. 11).[83] It expected to lend approximately $300 million in 1953, mostly for capital development projects. In addition to its loan activities, the bank was engaged in technical assistance activities in LDCs, principally in the form of background surveys. Its activity was limited, however, by the need to raise money in U.S. capital markets. In light of this, the bank claimed that it had made as many loans as it appropriately could. Although there was some support for the establishment of an International Finance Corporation within the bank to help finance private investments, opinion on its merits was mixed. A bank official pointed out that private foreign investment was decreasing primarily because of poor local climates and not because of the lack of capital.[84]

The International Monetary Fund also received criticism for sitting on its resources. The U.S. director of the fund defended its record by stating that, in accordance with U.S. wishes, the IMF limited its operations to temporary stabilization operations and did not finance relief or reconstruction efforts or the large and sustained outflows of capital needed for economic development. Its primary purpose was to help nations solve temporary financial and monetary problems and to encourage free exchange and trade policies.[85]

In spite of the increased emphasis on the capital investments needed to accompany technical assistance, the main focus of American efforts was still on small-scale pilot projects.[86] The central idea was that these projects would serve as means of pump priming, stimulating a larger flow of both domestic and foreign private investment. Projects would continue to concentrate on teaching new methods. Although technical experts working on these programs were exclusively American, efforts were under way to train local officials to replace them.

The administration defended the placement of technical assistance on a grant rather than a loan basis. Loans still financed the majority of development efforts; the TCA was providing grant aid to fund only technical assistance, not project capital costs, and then only where the less developed country was truly unable to pay for technical services itself.[87] Projects that were fundable with loans were refused and referred instead to the Export-Import Bank. Officials thus requested that Congress repeal a requirement passed the year before that it make at least 10 percent of its expenditures on a loan, rather than a grant, basis.[88]

Grant aid was also justified by the feeling that it was more productive to have less developed countries increase their contribution to current projects than repay the United States for past expenditures. As a result, the TCA expected LDCs gradually to assume a larger role in financing development programs.[89] The United States was currently funding African projects on a one-to-one basis. In Latin America, where similar efforts had a longer history, the ratio was three to one, with every U.S. dollar matched by three local ones.

The emphasis of these projects was on getting benefits directly to the people. Assistance was concentrated on increasing food production, education, and health services as opposed to industrial production.[90] To be effective in combating communism, there must be equitable distribution of the benefits of increased production.[91] Although there was a limit to the administration's power overseas, officials recognized the need to press for appropriate structural changes in the areas of labor and manpower. At the same time, the administration warned Congress against placing excessive political constraints on economic aid, such as conditioning assistance to Africa on progress toward decolonization.[92]

The programs in Asia reflected many of these concerns. To American eyes, Asia was characterized by (1) a critical shortage of trained administrators and technicians, (2) the existence of a growing economic and social revolution brought about by rising expectations that provided a breeding ground for communism, and (3) the existence of valuable raw materials vital to U.S. security interests.[93] This combination made American technical assistance advisable. Although the initiative of such programs was supposed to rest with the recipient government, U.S. goals sought to build strong, stable governments, support the buildup of military and internal security forces to combat communism, further economic progress, and advance the development of raw materials for export.

The business community stepped up its opposition to large government expenditures. Business leaders testified about the effect of large foreign aid programs on an economy already suffering from high tax rates and a growing deficit.[94] They feared that the foreign aid program was fast becoming a self-perpetuating program with its own bureaucracy. Such programs served only to underwrite unwise LDC economic policies based on socialism.[95] This in turn reduced the flow of private investment into these areas. To prevent this, foreign aid funds should be scaled down and conditioned on recipient governments pursuing strict policies leading to balanced budgets, the elimination of overly ambitious welfare or public works projects, and the removal of unwise restrictions on commerce and currency. In addition, there should be more capital flow between businesses rather than between governments.[96] There was also widespread questioning of the belief that foreign aid led to improved international relations.[97]

The labor community accused the U.S. Chamber of Commerce of distorting the nature of economic aid. Although the unions agreed with the administration on the need to respond to Communist threats overseas, they placed more importance on economic as opposed to military aid. Only the former would address the underlying economic dissatisfaction that imperiled the security of friendly governments. Union leaders urged Congress to place heavier reliance on the role of economic assistance in guaranteeing security. To do this, economic funds should be increased and should result in tangible improvements in standards of living abroad.[98] The United States should not rely solely on private enterprise and the "trickle down" theory. In addition to increases in the amounts of foreign aid, two other reforms were needed.[99] The first was to increase the economic power of workers through the establishment of free trade unions. The second was to condition aid to both LDC governments and private industry on the pursuance of policies that would distribute the benefits of increased production among the masses.

The farm community also urged Congress to place more emphasis on economic as opposed to military assistance.[100] Although it mentioned the dangers of overappropriation and the establishment of a permanent staff in charge of the program, it supported the administration's request and believed that any budget cuts should come out of military assistance.[101] Like labor, it also stressed aid's positive effects on the U.S. economy. Like most other groups, it supported making aid conditional on the pursuance of appropriate development policies.[102]

Charitable groups expressed degrees of opposition to the growing polarization of foreign aid. Some completely opposed the Mutual Security Program as a plan for escalating the Cold War.[103] Most, while agreeing with the administration on the increased security threat, opposed its obsession with military as opposed to economic assistance.[104] In their eyes, current expenditures were yielding large dividends and increasing America's prosperity.[105] More than any other group, they supported maintaining, or even increasing, the levels of aid.[106]

Additional issues arose in congressional remarks on the new proposal. Although support for technical assistance remained strong, many congressmen expressed concern about the increase in capital expenditures. They were concerned that Point Four was expanding beyond its original mandate by providing too much material assistance. These growing costs adversely affected the nation's economic health and undercut the dollar.[107] Some congressmen saw the program as a wise investment, however, and stressed the positive effects that development would have on U.S. trade and world stability.[108]

The source of threats to stability was also in dispute. Conservative members of Congress stressed the military threat posed by communism.[109] Their liberal counterparts tended to see this as a symptom of more fundamental sources of unrest, such as economic poverty and colonialism. The latter thus placed greater emphasis on the role of economic assistance and support for independence in addressing the problem.[110] They backed the administration's request for increased funds.[111] A few went further, criticizing the IMF for being too conservative in its loans to less developed countries.[112]

There was reaffirmation that Congress had intended to encourage development of the basic agricultural and raw material sectors rather than industrial development. Even strong supporters of the program emphasized that its size must be limited by the availability of skilled technicians to transfer knowledge and the ability of host countries to implement changes. Administrators should refrain from using hard-sell tactics to rush projects by recipient governments.[113]

A few congressmen questioned the belief that economic development would bring political stability. They foresaw that in many cases such development would undercut the established order, creating a political vacuum. Some members viewed this as a positive development, at least where the old government had opposed changes necessary to economic progress. Others, however, worried about the consequences to U.S. security.[114]

Beyond 1952

By 1952 the foreign aid program had changed considerably. The effort to transfer knowledge to the LDCs through relatively small-scale technical assistance and pilot-project efforts was being increasingly complemented by large-scale capital transfers. The early experience under the program, as well as the experience of the Technical Cooperation Agency in Asia, had shown that attempts to transfer technical skills or technology without the transfer of complementary resources were ineffective. Since the early 1950s both technical and capital assistance have represented essential elements in American development assistance doctrine—although the weight given to each element has varied over time.

A second issue that emerged during the early 1950s was a more rigorous dialogue over the use of assistance resources to achieve short-term political or security objectives, as compared to longer-term economic and humanitarian objectives. This has remained a continuous source of tension.

Chapter 5
Development Policy from Eisenhower to Kennedy

In this chapter I seek to examine the trends in political and professional thinking and the political driving forces that led to the launching of the "development decade" of the 1960s.[1] In 1961, President John F. Kennedy took office, ushering in a new era of assistance for the economic advancement of developing countries. Kennedy consolidated aid programs into one new organization, the Agency for International Development, and initiated the Peace Corps and the Alliance for Progress. Foreign aid appropriations increased substantially, and Congress passed a multiyear aid authorization. The United States became a member of the Organization for Economic Cooperation and Development (OECD). The most notable feature of the new program, however, would be its emphasis on the long-range economic development of the recipient nations rather than on short-term security concerns.

These foreign aid initiatives were more the culmination of a decade of political and academic thinking than the beginning of a new aid philosophy (Chap. 4). The *New York Times* of 4 June 1961 editorialized, "It should be noted at the outset that the overhaul [of the foreign aid program] is not quite so drastic as the headlines suggested . . . In short, the Kennedy Administration has re-embraced the concept on which the old Point Four program was based."[2]

As fear of the spread of communism grew during the 1950s, so did interest in the foreign aid program. The U.S. program expanded largely as a response to a growing Soviet aid program and to a fear that the citizens of many developing countries would turn to the Soviet camp for relief from their poverty. This fear may have reached a height in 1960–61, when all doubt was removed that Cuba (just 90 miles from the U.S. mainland) was in the Communist camp.

While the economic contest between communism and capitalism became a major component of the Cold War, the importance of the Third World countries to the general well-being of the United States became increasingly evident, even outside the context of the Cold War. The developing countries' prosperity and stability could significantly affect the prosperity and stability of the United States. Commerce with them could be vital for the supply of both strategic and nonstrategic goods to the United States.

The aid program received further support from lobbies for labor, business, and agriculture. Money spent on aid was often viewed as a jobs program from which many workers and employers could benefit. These groups tended to be less interested in helping other countries develop than in creating employment opportunities at home and market opportunities abroad. They did not themselves urge new aid initiatives but tended to support initiatives advanced by the administration. Certainly there were many who were opposed to aid because of its inevitable effect on taxes. There was also considerable controversy concerning the net effect on the United States of newly developed countries becoming competitors as well as markets for U.S. goods. Economic interests were often advanced as security measures through the argument that a strong domestic economy is critical to the defense of the country.

Many church and volunteer organizations supported aid for humanitarian purposes, and their politically active members added strength to the pro-aid lobby. In terms of political debate, however, the humanitarian issue could only be regarded as peripheral.

The academic literature of the 1950s was dominated by capital-intensive, "big push" and "take-off" theories and models. As dollar allocations reached a peak in 1961 and began to decline, disappointments in the aid program's results were accompanied by a return to an emphasis on long-term social and political reform in the development process.

Security Concerns and Development Assistance

In the period 1952–61, the security objective of development assistance was by far the most compelling when compared with humanitarian and economic objectives. The expansion of the aid program leading up to and including the 1961 initiatives paralleled an increase in the perceived security threat of spreading communism. Aid was intended as a weapon to address that threat. In this section I examine the evolution of the aid program during this period from a security perspective.

The Development Assistance Program Annexed by the Security Effort, 1952–1954

Economic aid (as embodied in the Marshall Plan) was scheduled to be phased out in 1952. The plan, however, was extended. Mutual Security Agency

Director Averell Harriman explained that the start of the Korean War prevented the plan's earlier demise.[3] The MSA had been created in 1951, bringing military and economic aid under one umbrella organization that increasingly saw its mission as the relatively short-term one of containing communism in countries on the periphery of the Eurasian Communist bloc (Chap. 4). The use of development aid as a short-term security measure and the simultaneous attempt to reduce its expense dominated the aid program through the mid-1950s.

The distinction between military and economic aid became very clouded after the Korean War began. General Alfred M. Guenther, noted in 1952 that "the economic and military aspects of defense . . . defy separation [in modern warfare]."[4] The demise of development assistance was forestalled by its use in the security arsenal, although its usefulness, combined with the perceived security threat at that time, was not convincing enough to prevent an overall reduction in foreign aid spending. The original intentions of technical and other long-term assistance programs had their advocates, but the future of the aid program was assured primarily by the security lobby of the administration and Congress.

A growing conservatism was confirmed in 1953, when General Eisenhower became president and the Republicans won slight majorities in both houses of Congress. The conservative ideology was supportive of the policy of containing communism with a ring of military alliances, nuclear deterrence, and the strengthening of foreign forces in strategic areas. Neutral countries in the Cold War were regarded negatively. Budgetary restraint was paramount, and economic development of less developed countries was thought to be best handled by the private sector. Eisenhower's final MSA budget request for fiscal year 1954 was $5.5 billion, down from President Harry S. Truman's $7.6 billion request for the same period. Secretary of State John Foster Dulles described the budget reduction as the minimum that could be "reconciled with the essential security of the U.S."[5] Congress appropriated $1.0 billion less than the administration request. In 1955 the administration requested only $3.5 billion and suggested that 10 percent be authorized in the form of loans rather than grants. Congress raised the loan ratio to 30 percent.

Harold Stassen began his two-year directorship of the foreign aid program in 1953 in the awkward position of having to carry out the dismantling of the program at the same time that he was warning the Senate Appropriations Committee that the United States would have to continue giving aid to free nations for the 10 years that he expected the Soviet threat to last. When asked to discuss the administration's $2 billion cut from Truman's aid budget request in this light, Stassen said, "We are seeking more defense, more rapidly, with less dollars, lasting longer."[6]

There was a growing response to perceived threats to U.S. security in the

Asian theater. House Appropriations Committee Chairman John Taber (R-N.Y.) asserted that recent events demonstrated the need for the United States to "do whatever [it could] to build up support for the defense of the Far East, Southeast Asia, and the Western Pacific." Senator Styles Bridges (R-N.H.) seemed to have revised his attitude when, speaking in support of the foreign aid bill, he declared that it would "assist our Free World partners to raise and support the forces required for collective defense." Senator Walter George (D-Ga.) announced a revision in his outlook (which had been for sharp cuts in aid) "in view of the conditions existing in the world."[7]

The conflict in Indochina was intensifying. Stassen warned that cutting aid to India would "make it more likely that the Communists would take over that country."[8] The "loss" of the world's largest democracy (India) to communism was regarded by many as unacceptable, especially given Communist China's apparent economic success.

Although Congress was continuing its effort to phase out the development aid program, at the same time it was beginning to appreciate the value of aid as a partial response to the problem of Communist expansionism in Asia. Criticism became focused more on the administration of aid than on its existence. A 6 February 1954 staff report to the Senate Appropriations Committee noted that technical assistance was losing its identity in the program of large-scale grants for economic assistance. The report said that poor use of funds indicated that funding cutbacks could be endured without resultant reductions in activity.[9]

Stassen hinted acknowledgment that the administration had been preoccupied with military (over economic) solutions to world tensions when he remarked that, "on the basis of the ending of the hostilities in . . . [Korea and Indochina] . . . the administration [will be] moving more extensively in the economic and ideological and technical field in this part of the world."[10] He also announced increased support of free labor union activity in developing countries because the Communists were moving in on labor's side in these areas. Senate Foreign Relations Committee Chairman Alexander Wiley (R-Wis.) described foreign aid in positive terms as "probably the single most anticommunist program," but at the same time he took pride in the great budget reductions made in the program.[11]

Toward Long-Term Development Assistance

Initiatives by the Soviet Union on the economic aid front had a profound effect on U.S. policy. One of these initiatives was a 1955 tour of Asia by Premier Nikolai A. Bulganin and Communist party head Nikita Khrushchev. Their visit included India, Burma, and Afghanistan and resulted in an offer of

Soviet technical assistance in the construction of a steel mill in India, among other projects. In response to Western critics, Khrushchev challenged: "Perhaps you wish to compete with us in establishing friendship with the Indians?"[12] Soviet economic assistance was regarded as increasing sharply in the name of economic development programs, and there was a popular belief that Soviet aid had fewer strings attached to it than did U.S. aid.[13] U.S. policy makers took the Soviet challenge to heart but were very uncertain of where else to take it.

The economic aid contest with the Soviet Union began to dominate U.S. foreign policy. Dulles, himself, seemed to accept this new Cold War philosophy when he commented in 1956 that Soviet tactics now had "more guile and less force . . . The second round [was] now beginning." The administration reversed its trend of aid cuts, citing "immediate threats to security and stability . . . now centered in Asia." Dulles asserted that foreign aid was an "essential part of our overall foreign policy" needed to persuade the Communists that "world conquest is futile" and that Communism was "pressing hard." The aid program would be "needed for a considerable period of time," he continued.[14] Stassen repeated the argument that military aid would "obtain more defense for the U.S." than the same amount spent on U.S. military forces. John McCloy, former U.S. High Commissioner in Germany, issued a report saying that, even with military superiority, the United States could "lose the struggle for freedom." He argued that it must address the USSR's economic, social, and political challenge.[15]

This apparent reversal on the part of the administration added to the confusion over foreign aid in Congress. Dulles was criticized not only for these apparent contradictions, but also for oversimplifying and underestimating the Soviet strategy in international affairs. Aid activists criticized the lack of coordination and comprehensiveness in the aid program.[16] In his call for the gradual reduction of economic and military aid, Senator Russell Long (D-La.) noted that "there [was] no war going on." Senator George Malone (R-Nev.), observing the then-annual trend to "give away more millions," complained, "We hardly understand what the legislation is about." However, Representative D. R. Matthews (D-Fla.) may have summed up the mood of Congress when, in acknowledging his misgivings about aid, he declared, "If someone were to say to me: 'You are voting for a giveaway program to foreign nations,' I would say . . . 'It is a gamble with money rather than with the precious lives of our boys.'" The Foreign Relations Committee, now headed by Senator George, going on record in support of aid, affirmed that its continuation was essential to free world security.[17]

The containment of Soviet influence was seen to require more than strategic defense pacts on the Communist periphery. A sharing of economic largess would be an increasingly important weapon in preventing alliances between the Soviet Union and developing countries. Thus, economic assistance was becoming a regular feature of the overall security package of the United States, although there was confusion as to what its exact role would be.

In his 1956 State of the Union message, Eisenhower asked Congress for limited authority to make longer-term commitments on aid projects in order to give "assurance of continuity in economic assistance" programs. Noting that one and one-half years earlier a similar program suggested by Stassen had been overruled by the State Department, a questioner asked Dulles if the State Department had changed its position. Dulles surprisingly replied, "No, the State Department has been in favor of something of this sort for some time." Lacking confidence in the State Department, Congress showed bipartisan opposition to the proposal for long-term funding, and the proposal did not move forward. Senator George remarked, "I honestly don't know how or why this long term commitment business arose."[18]

Amidst the confusion over the direction of the aid program, Eisenhower announced on 4 May 1956 his intention of forming a commission to study the issue. Ultimately, six different administration and congressional studies were conducted, but the 1956 Mutual Security Act became something of a stopgap measure pending their findings. Congress's final aid appropriation was (as usual) less than the president's request, but it was more than $1 billion greater than the previous year's appropriation.

The president's Citizen Advisers on the Mutual Security Program (the Fairless Commission) concluded that economic development should be continued as a long-range endeavor and that congressional funding approval should be on a two-year rather than a one-year basis. The assistance program was considered one of "collective security."[19]

On 7 July 1956, the Senate formed a special committee to study foreign aid. It consisted of the members of the Foreign Relations Committee and the chairmen and ranking minority members of the Appropriations and Armed Services committees. The committee's report recommended a continuation of foreign aid and called for clear distinctions to be made among military, technical, and development assistance.[20] Proposing a revolving fund for development loans, the committee cautioned that it should not be "set up in haste." Repayable loans were to be emphasized over grants.

Despite the conclusion that technical assistance "would serve [U.S.] interests for many years to come," it should be subject to annual authorization review for at least two or three years, according to the report. The report also suggested that efforts be made to reduce military and supporting aid. Military aid should be administered by the Department of Defense with policy direction by the secretary of state. Foreign aid policies and other activities abroad would be better coordinated by the president and the Senate, but private contractors, universities, and personnel from other government departments should be used wherever possible in carrying out the work of the program. Major witnesses before the committee included H. Christian Sonne, chairman of the board of trustees of the National Planning Association, who called for a five-year economic development program based primarily on loans, and Max D. Millikan, director of the Center for International Studies at the Massachusetts Institute of Technology (MIT), who warned that abandonment of the aid program would cause underdeveloped countries to turn "increasingly to the Soviet bloc." He recommended a 10-year, $10 billion program of economic aid, of which 80 percent would be loans.[21]

A draft of the House Foreign Affairs Committee report was issued on 23 December 1956; it called for a reduction, rather than an increase, in foreign aid, with nonmilitary aid based primarily on loans. It said that countries receiving Soviet aid should also be eligible to receive U.S. aid. The report concluded that "foreign aid appears to be the most useful nonmilitary device available to the United States for influencing other nations." In another study, the International Development Advisory Board called for a fund to put the program of economic development on a flexible and long-term basis, with congressional funding for periods of at least three years.[22]

As these study reports were coming in, another factor arose in the Soviet-U.S. contest to demonstrate to the developing world which system (capitalist or free market) showed the greater promise: the Soviet Union succeeded in putting into orbit the first manmade satellite, Sputnik.

Long-term Development Assistance

A conference initiated by President Eisenhower to promote the importance of development assistance was held in February 1958. One of the speakers was former President Truman, who asserted: "The only thing we can do with armaments is to buy time. One of our best hopes [for obtaining peace] is economic assistance for other nations."[23] Eisenhower's support of economic development aid, however, was still in a formative stage.

In 1958, the trend toward assistance in long-term development began to be put into action. The first loan from the Development Loan Fund was announced for India's Five-Year Plan. More importantly, Under-Secretary of State Douglas Dillon declared support for an Inter-American bank in a reversal of longstanding U.S. policy.[24] That overture to Latin America was probably inspired by Vice President Richard Nixon's disastrous South American tour, during which he was assaulted by angry mobs. Rising concerns over unemployment, the federal deficit, and the balance of payments prevented significant increases in the aid budget, however. Another 1958 event of note was a resolution endorsed by the administration and passed by the Senate calling for an "international development association" to be created as a soft loan division of the World Bank.[25]

The year 1959 began with the New Year's Eve victory of the Cuban revolution led by Fidel Castro. With unusual unanimity, the administration and Congress approved U.S. participation in the new Inter-American Development Bank (Chap. 11). Responding to concern that India might choose a future under communism, the Senate passed (with administration endorsement) the Kennedy-Cooper Resolution for long-term development assistance in South Asia. Senator John F. Kennedy (D-Mass.) argued that 1959 must be "our round" after the Communist "round" of 1958. In an open letter to the president, Senator Mike Mansfield (D-Mont.) observed that "we are now at the beginning of a shift back to an era of economic emphasis."[26]

In 1959 the president's Draper Committee issued its report making several suggestions for improvements, which included recommendations for a single agency to administer the program, long-range (rather than year-to-year) financing of the Development Loan Fund, and increased emphasis on self-help efforts by the aid recipients as a condition of the aid. Calling for long-term development assistance, Representative Charles Brown (D-Mont.) remarked that "we should strive to prevent trouble rather than wait until trouble is fomented and then try to bribe our way out." Under-Secretary of State Dillon stated that another year would be needed to observe the program and that a longer-range program would be requested for fiscal year 1961.[27] Later in 1960, the Act of Bogota was initiated by the administration and passed by Congress as the first effort in what would later be dubbed the Alliance for Progress. The act signaled a new direction for the program by emphasizing the social aspects of reform in the developing countries. A House Foreign Affairs Committee Special Study Mission reported that there was a "strikingly dangerous gap between such grandiose projects at the top and the millions of human beings still starving."[28] In one response to that finding, Congress directed the president to consider instituting a Point Four Youth Corps, a concept similar to that embodied in the Peace Corps the following year.

Bipartisan support for foreign aid still derived primarily from perceived security threats. Vice President Nixon said that "recent events" mandated the "absolute need for keeping our mutual security operating at an efficient level." Twenty-eight House Democrats wrote to President Eisenhower expressing criticism of his handling of foreign policy but promising to resist "unwise cuts" in the Mutual Security Act appropriation because they viewed it as an "indispensable part of our foreign policy."[29] By 1960, economic aid was a permanent fixture of foreign policy.[30]

A Culmination in Development Assistance Trends

The year 1961 was a landmark in the sense that much of the aid philosophy that had been evolving during the preceding years was formalized into law. The administration of the program was overhauled as Congress authorized further separation of economic from military aid, and the economic program was centralized in a new Agency for International Development. Congress advanced several more steps in the direction of long-term commitments by giving the Development Loan Fund a five-year authorization, if not appropriation. The Act of Bogota was dressed up and given permanence as the Alliance for Progress. The dollars authorized and appropriated for economic development assistance reached a post–Marshall Plan high. The United States ratified the convention establishing the Organization for Economic Cooperation and Development and set up the Peace Corps as a permanent organization. Aid rhetoric increased in volume from both security and humanitarian perspectives.

Kennedy often referred to the security that his aid program was intended to address. During the Berlin crisis he asserted that the "Soviet threat is worldwide . . . We face a challenge in Berlin, but there is also . . . a challenge in Southeast Asia . . . in our own hemisphere and wherever else the freedom of human beings is at stake." In an appeal for support for his aid program, he declared that it involved "very importantly the security" of the United States and deserved the backing "of every American who recognizes the real nature of the struggle in which we are engaged."[31]

U.N. Ambassador Adlai Stevenson noted that "aid and strong argument would be needed to reverse Latin American support for Castro." Secretary of State Dean Rusk warned that the "Western world must recapture the leadership of the revolution of political freedom . . . and not yield its leadership to those who would seize it and use it to destroy us." Defense Secretary Robert S. McNamara described military and economic aid as complementary (a message heard several times during the Eisenhower administration).[32]

By 1961, it was evident that Cuba's new revolutionary government was clearly "in the enemy camp," and this a mere 90 miles from the U.S. mainland. Che Guevara promised that Cuba would not "export revolution" to other American countries if it received a pledge of "nonintervention to go ahead with [its] work." His words were probably heard as more of a threat than a comfort. Soviet Premier Khrushchev proclaimed that the Soviet Union was about to "touch the heels" of the United States (economically) and "other peoples [would] follow . . . our example." Pakistani President Ayub Khan addressed a joint session of Congress in an appeal for passage of Kennedy's aid program. He announced that, "unless Pakistan is able to meet the economic needs of its people, in another 15–20 years, we shall be overtaken by communism . . . If we go under communism, then we shall still press against you; but not as friends." Eliminating any doubt that security was a most serious issue in 1961, Kennedy advised that "any prudent family" should provide itself with a fallout shelter.[33]

Much of the congressional debate in 1961 concerned the president's request for long-term financing of development loans. He asked for five years of authority to borrow from the Treasury with a provision that the eventual loan repayments be fed into a fund for future loans. The main objection to this course was that it would enable future expenditures without congressional appropriation, a device labeled "back-door spending." A lesser objection was that assurance of continued aid would reduce the recipients' incentives to help themselves.[34] The law that was actually enacted provided for a five-year authorization with annual appropriations. It was an approach endorsed by New York Governor Nelson Rockefeller and former Vice President Nixon. Kennedy called it "wholly satisfactory."[35]

The inertia of the previous few years' congressional thinking combined with suitable negative world circumstances to make 1961 a big year in development assistance history. Another important factor was a very determined president. Representative Otto Passman (D-La.) described Kennedy's efforts as "absolutely unprecedented" during Passman's 15 years in Congress. In addition to strong testimony by Secretary of the Treasury Dillon and Secretary of State Rusk, Peace Corps Director Sergeant Shriver personally visited every congressional office in support of the aid program. The Citizens Committee for International Development was organized to exert more pressure, and businessmen nationwide were contacted by the White House to exert still further pressure. Passman also charged that patronage threats were used in the campaign.[36]

The centerpiece of the 1961 economic assistance program was the Foreign Assistance Act (Senate Bill 1983, PL 87–195), which was passed by a vote of 69 to 24 in the Senate and 260 to 132 in the House. Intended as a bold new initiative and as an answer to many of the charges of poor administration of the aid program, the bill was enacted only after considerable debate.

As in the past, the matter of attaching strings to aid was especially troublesome. Secretary of State Rusk remarked that recipients would not be coerced into alliances or special commitments to the United States; however, aid would be conditional on the adequacy of their performance in the process of development. When Senator Homer Capehart (R-Ind.) asked if we would have no concern whether a country that we help goes Communistic, Rusk replied negatively, asserting, "We affirm the world of choice . . . and I know of no country which has on its own volition, by the vote of its people, deliberately accepted a Communist regime."[37]

Senator J. William Fulbright (D-Ark.) asked Frank M. Coffin of the president's Task Force on Economic Assistance why we continued to give aid to Haiti, perpetuating the "highly unsatisfactory regime" there. Coffin responded: "For the short run we face the alternative of giving up Haiti and having another instance where elements that are against the philosophy which we all believe in take over. This is too big a risk." Senator Wayne Morse (D-Oreg.) later declared that "we should not be in a position of preventing revolution if that was the will of the people." Senator Hubert H. Humphrey (D-Minn.) questioned the whole premise of aid's role in the structural reform of the recipient. Regarding Iran, he observed, "I have a hard time bringing myself to a sincere belief that those aristocrats . . . who have lived on privilege, and who are literally wallowing in luxury, are going to design a program of self-destruction."[38]

Regardless of whether the aid program would be successful or not, there seemed to be a consensus that the economic development of less developed countries would help forestall the expansion of communism. Senator Capehart expressed it in almost those words, and Lloyd Neidlinger, executive director of the U.S. Council, International Chamber of Commerce, commented, "A strong private economy is a powerful assurance against the possibility of Communist domination or influence." A variation on that theme was offered by Jerry Voorhis, executive director of the Cooperative League of the United States, who entered into testimony an article stating that "the only major rebuffs Italian Communists suffered in the last election were where democratic cooperatives are strong."[39]

After a summer of lively debate, there were probably no congressmen convinced that the foreign economic assistance problem was solved, but the new aid program did pass, and with more money behind it than at any time since the Marshall Plan. Senator Humphrey may have spoken for a good many of his colleagues when he announced: "As far as I am concerned I am probably going to support the foreign aid program. However, I do it just like I go to see the dentist; I am just not happy about it."[40]

Development Assistance and Economic Self-Interest

Economic self-interest arguments did not provide the impetus for the aid program, but they did contribute importantly to the program's base of support. When the aid program was passed in 1961, the sentiments shared in testimony by representatives of business, labor, and agriculture were little changed from those expressed during the previous few years.

It is perhaps obvious that economic self-interest concerns are not entirely distinct from security ones. On the one hand a strong U.S. economy is arguably the best defense on the security front. On the other hand, economically strong allies can be viewed as being superior allies in respect to security.

The Position of Agriculture

Throughout the period under consideration, there was general support in the agricultural sector for an economic aid program. In 1952, the National Farmers Union advocated increased aid.[41] Agricultural products stored by the federal government under the farm support program had been used previously for famine relief (e.g., in India in 1951), and in 1953 Congress passed a law authorizing the president to use up to $100 million worth of surplus farm products for relief abroad. Also that year, the Mutual Security Act specified that between $100 million and $250 million of foreign aid funds were to be used for purchase of U.S. farm goods.

Most importantly, a bill was introduced in the Senate that year for a foreign aid/surplus disposal program that ultimately was enacted as Public Law 480 in July 1954 (see Chap. 8). PL 480 was initially a three-year program that authorized the president to sell up to $700 million of agricultural surplus to friendly nations for foreign currencies. The foreign currencies acquired would be primarily directed to develop new foreign markets for U.S. agriculture, to purchase materials needed for national security, and to make loans to promote multilateral trade and economic development. The act also authorized $300 million of surplus donations for needy people in friendly countries or for "friendly" but needy populations without regard to the friendliness of their government.

With a Commodity Credit Corporation (CCC) stockpile of $5.5 billion of surplus commodities, the program was designed to dispose of some of the surplus and to promote foreign trade in farm products. The bill was generally supported by farm organizations,[42] although the National Council of Farmer Cooperatives warned that the price support program had enabled other countries to "undersell and absorb our foreign markets" and that the United States should emphasize private industry rather than state trading.[43]

Proponents saw the program primarily as a specific market expansion program that would alleviate the CCC's surplus problem. Any effect on development abroad was secondary. The fear of creating foreign competition was a consideration in changing the wording of the law so that foreign currencies would be used not to encourage "production" (in the recipient countries), but rather to promote "economic development and trade."[44] Some congressmen thought it was a wasteful giveaway program, while others viewed it as a goodwill program to fight communism.[45]

The PL 480 program expanded, and in 1958 it was continued for an additional 18 months with a $6.25 billion appropriation. Also that year, the administration's Davis Committee recommended putting the program on a five-year basis and calling it "Food for Peace." The committee also emphasized the program's use as a foreign policy tool with a stated goal of helping recipients to become independent of foreign aid. Nevertheless, the program was widely recognized by the State Department, as well as by most other observers, as a surplus disposal program. PL 480 had become a very important agricultural program, accounting for 27 percent of all wheat exports, 22 percent of all cotton exports, and 47 percent of all vegetable oil exports in 1956.[46]

As concerns the Mutual Security Act, the American Farm Bureau Federation (AFBF) consistently supported the program but often called for cuts in the expenditures. The National Farmers Union supported the administration's program and called for increased technical aid in 1959.[47] There was no discernible shift in the agriculture lobby's position on aid between 1952 and 1961. Their congressional testimony did not expound on the pros or cons of helping other countries to develop.

Organized Labor

Organized labor consistently supported a foreign economic assistance program throughout the period under consideration. In 1953, the American Federation of Labor (AFL) testified in favor of a two-year extension of the aid program and an expanded Point Four Program. The AFL also called for encouragement of labor unions and international competition.[48] The Mutual Security Act that year did make it a policy to encourage other countries to strengthen free trade unions.

In 1956, AFL–Congress of Industrial Organizations (CIO) President George Meany declared that "labor will support a program of substantial military and economic aid to other free nations to protect them from being forced to yield to communism." Both the AFL-CIO and the United Automobile Workers (UAW) were members of the Point Four Information Service, which held conferences in 1952, 1955, and 1956 to promote foreign economic assistance.[49]

The UAW and AFL-CIO also advocated an expansion of the Development Loan Fund in 1959. In 1960 the AFL-CIO's legislative director, Andrew J. Biemiller (formerly a congressman, D-Wis.), joined with others calling for long-term aid commitments when he urged that the Development Loan Fund be put on a "strong continuing basis" with at least $1 billion for fiscal year 1960. He also called for no cuts in the Mutual Security Program.[50]

The AFL-CIO's Biemiller again gave a strong endorsement to the foreign aid bill in 1961. In Foreign Affairs Committee testimony, he said that labor supported the aid program because of the threat of communism and because "it is right." Then he went on to describe its benefits for labor. "[Labor has] a tremendous interest in the foreign market. If we were to cut off foreign trade, then you would really have an unemployment problem in the United States." Unemployment would "probably amount to a couple hundred thousand more" if not for the aid program. Biemiller agreed with Representative Robert R. Barry (R-N.Y.), who commented that, "from the standpoint of jobs, there are more jobs created by our entire foreign aid program than there are lost by the imports we receive." His somewhat disingenuous rationale was in part that "cheap labor is not as productive as American labor, on comparable jobs."[51]

Victor Reuther testified as the assistant to the president of the Industrial Union Department of the AFL-CIO, a department representing seven million members. He agreed that foreign aid programs generated jobs. "With 5.5 million [Americans] unemployed," he announced, "it takes a deliberate policy to invest." Committee Chairman Thomas Morgan (D-Penn.) was especially concerned that the aid program was creating an ability for other countries to compete with the United States, with resulting loss of U.S. jobs. Biemiller acknowledged the concern and said that his union had proposed an international minimum wage. Reuther asserted that "we have introduced, I think to a large extent on the initiative of American trade unions, the whole concept of the escalator clause, the protection against inflation, of an automatic adjustment to reflect the increase in productivity."[52] The unions seemed to view the aid program as a jobs program for their members. Additionally, they felt that it was building up new markets faster than it was promoting new competition. Organized labor also had a direct stake in the aid program through its involvement with groups such as the American Institute of Free Labor Development, which received appropriations to facilitate the organization of non-Communist trade unions in developing countries.

Business Interests

The shipping industry has long been a beneficiary of aid. The Mutual Security Act of 1953 specified that at least 50 percent of commodity tonnage shipped abroad as aid had to be shipped on U.S. flag vessels. When PL 480 was initiated in 1954, the same rule applied to shipments on that program. Despite the fact that several members of the Foreign Affairs Committee argued that a shipping subsidy should be handled someplace other than in a foreign aid bill, Representative Thor Tollefson (R-Wash.) was able to secure passage of the amendment. The mining industry was successful in having eliminated from the bill a provision that authorized the president to encourage the production of strategic materials in friendly nations. This was an amendment sponsored by Senator George Malone (R-Nev.).[53]

Industry had mixed feelings on the subject of development assistance. The National Foreign Trade Council "was strongly opposed" to the diversion of public funds (intended for technical assistance) to the direct promotion of the industrial development of underdeveloped countries. At the same time Ford Motor Company President Henry Ford II and James T. Duce, president of the Arabian-American Oil Company, both gave favorable testimony for foreign aid in general and technical assistance in particular.[54] In 1956, 80 percent of 100,000 independent businessmen polled reportedly responded that they were opposed to the continuance of foreign aid "as a permanent feature of our nation's foreign policy." In 1957, J. Peter Grace, president of W. R. Grace and Company, recommended loans, investments, and technical assistance to Latin America, an area in which his company had sustantial interests.[55]

In the 1958 congressional debate, several congressmen voiced concern that the aid program was setting up competition against American business. Representative Gordon Canfield (R-N.J.) sought unsuccessfully to prohibit the use of aid funds to establish textile-processing plants in any foreign country, and Representative Robert Griffin (R-Mich.) moved to prohibit funds for the establishment of any kind of plant that might compete with U.S. industries. Both motions were rejected, but Representative George W. Andrews (D-Ala.) warned that "these programs will wreck the economy of our country."[56]

The Chamber of Commerce of the United States was generally supportive of aid but at a reduced level of spending. In 1959, chamber spokesman William C. Foster (who was administrator of the ECA in 1950–51) recommended that the administration do a better job of selling the aid program to the American public and that Congress cut the administration's budget request for military and economic aid. The chamber's 1961 testimony was also rather unenthusiastic. J. Warren Nystrom, manager of the chamber's International Relations Department, said that the chamber had "no policy on these expanded [foreign investment] guaranties . . . In general we would favor anything that might be done to encourage private enterprise to move overseas, but we want to take a careful look at this and find out whether this is the correct approach."[57] Nystrom supported multiyear authorizations but with appropriations for just two years (rather than for five or more). He also wanted cuts in virtually every category of aid. Another representative of the chamber, Forrest D. Murden, associate government relations counsel for the Standard Oil Company of New Jersey, agreed with Emilio G. Collado, director of Standard Oil, who stated: "[I do] not think there is any evidence that, in the aggregate, U.S. investment abroad has affected adversely the level of investment and employment in the United States. On the other hand, U.S. foreign investment helps protect our share of the world market and creates substantial employment opportunities in the U.S. by helping to maintain and increase foreign demand for U.S. goods."[58]

The U.S. Council of the International Chamber of Commerce is a separate organization from the Chamber of Commerce of the United States. In 1961 testimony, its executive director, Lloyd Neidlinger, called for "maximum use of private foreign investment in economic development programs" and liberalization of the investment guarantee system.[59] The chamber organizations did not so much address the concept of foreign aid (in their testimony over the years), but rather their concern that, for as long as an aid program existed, it would be carried out by private enterprise as much as possible.

The Citizens Foreign Aid Committee (represented by an insurance executive, the head of a financial analysis firm, and a retired U.S. army brigadier general) testified before the Foreign Affairs Committee in 1961. The spokesmen seemed to support Third World development and technical assistance, but they were opposed to the overall aid program. They objected to the notion that foreign aid (as a spending program) is good for the U.S. economy. The fact that aid money is spent on American goods and services is not of benefit to the U.S. economy, they argued, since the American people are then deprived of those goods and services and "an economic amount of purchasing power is not removed, with the result that the total effect is inflationary." Regarding the development of broader markets, they said that the United States never should have built up its competition overseas.[60] Walter Harnischfeger, national chairman of the Citizens Foreign Aid Committee, gave highly spirited anti-aid testimony before the Senate Foreign Relations Committee. He submitted a statement from A. G. Heinsohn, the manager of two cotton mills employing over one thousand workers, who blamed foreign aid for a substantial loss of business in the textile industry to foreign competition. Heinsohn quoted Robert T. Stevens, president of J. P. Stevens and Co., as protesting that "textiles have . . . been called upon to carry far too much of the load of our foreign policy."[61]

The Council for International Progress in Management, a group funded partly by the International Cooperation Administration, was represented by a team of businessmen who had taken leaves of absence from their companies to teach management techniques and to extol the virtues of free enterprise to developing countries. They generally did not address the aid bill under consideration, but they did speak most enthusiastically about the good that technical assistance can do. A. C. Nielson, Jr., president of the A. C. Nielsen Corporation of Chicago, gave three reasons for helping the developing countries: "If they can use our techniques [and] produce more, they can sell these products [raw materials] to us for less money, . . . they will be good potential customers for our exports, . . . [and] technical assistance strengthens their industrial capacity which in turn strengthens their military capacity." When asked what he thought about foreign investment guarantees, Austin S. Igleheart, retired chairman of the board of General Foods Corporation, declared, "If we are not smart enough to handle our own funds, we certainly don't want Uncle Sam to stand behind us."[62]

Humanitarian Concerns

Referring to the period around 1961 when the development decade was launched, John Montgomery observed that "liberal idealism was considered good politics; candidates could appeal to altruistic aspirations without sounding hypocritical."[63] That may well have been the case, but altruism seems to have been the weakest motivating factor in the aid effort. Although President Kennedy became the inspirational center of this trend to idealism, he himself gave security concerns as the primary purpose of an expanded aid program.[64] In this section, I consider just what role (however minimal) altruism did play in the formulation of aid policy.

Representative Barratt O'Hara (D-Ill.), alluding to the days of his youth, observed: "People didn't have very much money, but they contributed cheerfully for the foreign missions . . . That money was used in the foreign lands not only to promote religion but as well to fight disease, to fight illiteracy, and do a lot of things that broadened life . . . What the government is doing now is merely following the pattern that the churches have set for us." Some religious groups seemed to share this view.[65]

The very word *aid* implies an altruistic motivation. Authors Ian Little and Juliet Clifford have noted the confusion surrounding the word in commenting, "Buying something from a man may help him, but one does not speak of 'aiding' him if it is something one wants."[66] They went on to argue that democratically elected government is mandated to serve the interests of its constituency and, if *aid* precludes self-interest, then the government would be violating its duty in giving the aid. By common usage, the government calls its program of giving an *aid* program, although the program is clearly intended to serve the interests of the United States. The churches are not necessarily acting out of this kind of self-interest, so it is a rather dubious position to say that government is following the pattern set by the churches. The motivations for giving may be very different (Chap. 2).

Presbyterian leader Clifford Earle attempted to bridge the gap between church motives and government motives when he stated, "We recognize . . .

that a government and the Congress have to act in terms of national interest, and we would remind ourselves and the American people in whatever way we can that American interest is served when we help others to help themselves in the way this program is designed to do." Baptist leader W. G. Mather had trouble seeing things the way Earle did. He confessed himself "a little disturbed by the beginning statement of the [aid] bill that it is to 'promote the foreign policy, security, and general welfare of the U.S. [by] assisting peoples of the world.'"[67] Nevertheless, he did support the bill. Although different church leaders may have had different levels of comfort with foreign aid, throughout the decade from 1951 to 1961 all of the representatives of religious organizations who were called upon to testify did so in favor of expanded aid programs.

The Americans for Democratic Action (ADA) and the American Association of University Women were consistent aid supporters. The League of Women Voters had also had a long history of support for economic assistance. It was part of the organization's agenda to work "for community understanding and support of economic development assistance" and to make this a vital issue in the forthcoming election.[68] League Director Barbara Stuhler testified, "There is probably no single subject of league concern about which there is greater unanimity than the importance of our foreign aid program." When asked point blank whether the league was supporting this program on its merits without regard to communism, Stuhler rejoined: "I wouldn't want the league to appear that unrealistic, if you don't mind, I think you can argue for the program on its own merits, but we live in a bipolar world where the struggle is between communism and democracy and you simply can't overlook the impact of a foreign aid program without considering this background of the struggle between the U.S. and the U.S.S.R." Roberta Cox of the National Congress of Parents and Teachers, speaking in favor of the aid program, testified that members of her organization "consider[ed] communism a very unhealthy ideal."[69]

Although otherwise humanitarian organizations supported the aid program, selfless humanitarianism did not seem to play a major role in the debate during 1961 or the decade preceding it. Even Congressman O'Hara, who compared foreign aid to church welfare activity, was very much involved in the debate in terms of how the United States would fare economically under the program. He clearly thought that the country would come out ahead.[70]

Academic Thought

In the 1950s economists and political scientists wrote prolifically about economic development.[71] Two basic questions were: (1) Do the economically advanced countries have an interest in the economic development of the less developed countries? and (2) If so, how should this assistance be made? By considering some of the seemingly more significant writings of the period, I attempt to show that academic thinking changed from support of development motivated by economic, humanitarian, and security interests in the early 1950s to support resulting from security (specifically anti-Communist) concerns in the late 1950s and early 1960s.

The answer to the second question concerning how best to assist in development also evolved during this period. At first, development was envisioned as a long process requiring many social and political changes and a balanced growth of agriculture and industry.[72] In the mid-1950s the emphasis turned from balance to a "big push" theory calling for rapid advancement on all fronts with an accent on industry rather than agriculture. Import substitution became a high priority. By the early 1960s there was a return to stressing the importance of long-term planning and a greater appreciation for agriculture and other primary industries.

Whether Third World Development Is Beneficial to the United States

In the early 1950s, as reconstruction of Europe was nearing an end and Truman had recently announced his Point Four initiative, the United Nations launched a study of how full employment might be accomplished throughout the world. The West had an expanded appreciation for the extent to which the countries of the world were interdependent. The developed countries' prosperity was seen as hinging in part on that of the developing countries. Nelson Rockefeller wrote that Truman's Point Four pronouncement placed this interest in the well-being of the world "squarely on economic considerations."[73] There was concern that, in order to have increasing supplies of raw materials to feed economic prosperity, the developing countries that supplied those materials would have to share in the prosperity.

An ill-defined sense of moral duty appeared in some of these writings as the advanced countries were said to have an obligation to help their disadvantaged neighbors. The desirability of economic development was largely unquestioned. Gunnar Myrdal had described foreign aid as a type of international welfare system for redistributing wealth and equalizing opportunity. The Randall Commission declared in 1954 that the United States recognized no "right of underdeveloped areas to economic aid." Myrdal characterized that statement as "harsh." Nurkse, in describing U.S. foreign aid programs, noted that "it may be that we've seen the beginnings of a system of international income transfers." Blelloch tied welfare and economic considerations together when he asserted that the development of the advanced countries "depends on the extension of the concept of the welfare state to cover all the economically significant portions of the earth's surface."[74] The existence of a moral obligation to help other countries to develop was an issue that would be debated well into the 1960s and probably into the indefinite future (see Chap. 2).

Although security concerns had long been present in the foreign aid debate, they reached a new height with the Korean War.[75] Max Millikan's and Walt Rostow's famous *Proposal* was based on discussions held during a 1954 meeting called to consider how the United States might facilitate a more stable world and enhance U.S. security against aggression. By 1957, Howard Ellis asserted that the economic benefits to the United States of the aid program were nearly insignificant; political considerations were the justification. In that same year, Edward Mason affirmed that security interests were the prime motivation behind aid. Writing in 1959 and 1960, John Montgomery found that "the indefinite necessity for American aid occasioned by the continued dynamic of Communist expansionism and the revolutionary drive of the economically underprivileged nations has revealed itself only gradually."[76]

The theme underlying the security argument for economic development is that economic development enables underdeveloped countries to choose the democratic rather than the totalitarian way of life; this choice is then said to be inherently in the U.S. interest.[77] In George Liska's words: "In giving aid to other countries, the objective of the United States is to promote its short-range and long-range security within the evolving structure of international relations and to help preserve recipient countries from other than peaceful change." According to Charles Wolf, economic growth would most greatly reduce the less developed countries' vulnerability to extremist political behavior (defined as communism). Preventing the expansion of communism was almost universally accepted as being in the U.S. interest. Edward Banfield was one notable exception to that consensus, since he regarded the friendship of other countries as relatively unimportant to U.S. security.[78]

In 1962 Howard Wiggins challenged the alleged connection between development and stability when he observed, "It is by no means assured . . . that an increase in living standards will bring with it a political stability favorable to American interests." Bert Hoselitz and Myron Weiner suggested that development can lead to more violence; they used India, Asia, Africa, and Latin America as examples of their position.[79] These reservations concerning the security argument for economic development were for the most part made in the early 1960s; from the time of the Millikan-Rostow proposal through 1961, however, the security argument had prevailed. It might be noted that during that period the Cold War and McCarthyist anticommunism were dominant forces. Therefore, it may have been prudent for anyone favoring foreign economic assistance for whatever reason to have emphasized the anti-Communist argument.[80]

How Best To Help the Less Advanced Countries To Develop

From Point Four (1949) to the Foreign Assistance Act of 1961, there was a body of literature that did not specifically take a position on the advisability of development but rather offered suggestions on how to bring it about or speed it up. As observed in Chapter 4, some of the earliest literature of the period called for unified, balanced programs; heavy emphasis on human resources; modest steps (rather than ambitious ones); and well-thought-out development plans. Special emphasis was given to the need for "strenuous domestic efforts" for any development plan to succeed.[81]

Blelloch noted a general agreement that development should be based on the extraction of primary materials. Industrialization was only secondarily encouraged in order to diversify the economy, create a consumer class, and facilitate urbanization (leading, it was hoped, to a fall in the birth rate). At the same time John Adler took a stance that later seemed to dominate aid programs for years to come. Arguing for a modification of the extractive-industry approach, he asserted the need to emphasize balanced growth. Hollis Chenery would later argue that development programs taking a longer view tended to stress comparative advantage over balance.[82] As security motivations began to dominate the aid discussion, the view did become shorter and the push for balance came to overshadow comparative advantage. The Point Four message clearly emphasized technical assistance over capital assistance.

In 1951, a United Nations expert panel (on which Theodore W. Schultz and W. Arthur Lewis served) issued a report proposing massive capital transfers, along with other measures. The report asserted that more than $10 billion of imported capital would be needed annually to achieve a 2 percent per capita income growth rate in the developing countries. Another report, *Partners in Progress,* also came out in favor of economic aid for long-term development.[83] The question of appropriate levels of capital contributions largely dominated the aid debate from that point forward. Another big question concerned how long capital infusions would be needed. Although Hans Singer acknowledged that the success of the Marshall Plan meant very little for development prospects, he did allow that "the injection of foreign capital [into developing economies] could be sufficiently short lived to be discussed in terms of 'Marshall Plan time.'" The 1951 U.N. report assumed a high degree of disguised unemployment that required industrialization for its elimination—industrialization dependent on external capital. Mason contended that the theory behind large, capital-intensive development projects resulted from the fact that they were the easiest to carry out; the theory was effectively devised to justify the practice.[84]

After the mid-1950s the assumption of disguised unemployment was challenged increasingly. Having directed technical assistance studies for three years in Latin America, Theodore Schultz in 1956 maintained that "economic thinking based on the two central ideas—disguised unemployment and industrialization—does not give us even the beginning of a theory for the purposes at hand." Then, in 1964, he protested that the theory of zero marginal productivity in agricultural labor was wrong. He declared, "There is no longer any room for doubt [that] agriculture can be a powerful engine for growth."[85] This seems to be a significant shift in emphasis from his position as co-author of the 1951 U.N. report.

Once the U.N. report opened up the possibilities of massive capital transfers, a test of the "big push" theories became possible. Paul Rosenstein-Rodan had illustrated the theory in 1943 by positing a hypothetical isolated economy of 20,000 workers that would achieve wealth by launching a full range of industries simultaneously. Such a plan for instantaneous growth fitted well with the notion espoused by Singer and Prebisch, among others, that the terms of trade were going against primary producers and that import substitution was needed.[86] Kindleberger and Morgan further supported the import-substitution approach in light of the adverse prices and income elasticities associated with primary products.[87]

Rosenstein-Rodan was a collaborator on the Millikan/Rostow theory that described three stages through which developing countries must pass: (1) a "precondition stage," in which technical assistance and some grants should be given; (2) a "transition stage," wherein such countries would be given as much capital as they could absorb on favorable loan terms; and (3) the stage of self-sustaining growth, in which the country's access to capital would be on the open market. Technical assistance programs would be offered where needed to give the recipient countries the necessary capital-absorptive capacity. This theory was the most prominent of the various aid theories proposed during the latter half of the 1950s and was refined to consist of five stages in Rostow's *Stages of Economic Growth,* published in 1960.[88] The felicitous choice of terminology—the traditional society, the preconditions for take-off, the take-off, the drive to maturity, and the age of high mass consumption—contributed to rapid acceptance of the stage framework in both popular and professional discussion. But some academic critics challenged the assertion that the two- or three-decade-long transition (take-off) stage could be identified at all.[89] The "take-off" and "big push" theories were very similar in their requirement for large infusions of capital.

Another argument for emphasizing capital projects came from Albert Hirschman, who argued the educational value for capital-intensive techniques through their introduction of technical knowledge and skills. Hirschman was very critical of the big push, since he feared that, without the necessary social and political development, a massive infrastructure of social overhead projects would be built with little resultant output. Walter Galenson and Harvey Leibenstein regarded the most profitable projects to be those with the highest capital/labor ratios, an indication, in their opinion, that capital-intensive efforts should be preferred.[90]

Beyond the Issues of Capital

By 1961, with the massive capital expenditure programs finally under way, attention turned again to the social, political, and economic causes of underdevelopment. J. P. Lewis asserted in 1962 that lack of outside capital was not the principal impediment to rapid expansion in production. In 1961 John Kenneth Galbraith said that it was "doubtful that many of us, if pressed, would insist that economic development was simply a matter of external aid. But nothing could be more convenient than to believe this, for once we admit that it is not the case, we become entrapped in a succession of grievously complex problems." He noted a contemporary view that sufficient capital was the primary missing ingredient in economic development but then went on to say that literacy, social justice, reliable government, and a clear understanding of the development process were crucial requirements that must be considered.[91]

Raul Prebisch acknowledged a "growing conviction in Latin America that . . . development ha[d] to be brought about by [their] own efforts and [their] own determination to introduce fundamental changes in the economic and social structures of [their] countries." Also softening his view on import substitution, Prebisch wrote that the need for it "would not be quite so acute if [Latin American] countries could add industrial exports to the traditional primary ones which tend to grow slowly." According to Paul Hoffman, "We have acquired experience during the 1950s and can profit from past mistakes." He thought that inadequate attention had been given to "investment in education, technical training, and survey resources."[92]

In Conclusion

Development theory, academic thought, humanitarian sentiment, economic self-interest, and the Cold War were highly interrelated in the years leading up to 1961. The political process was the medium in which these forces interacted to produce the economic assistance policies that emerged out of Washington that year.

Development assistance, as an academic discipline, grew in popularity at a time when technology was effectively shrinking the world, colonialism was ending, and many changes in the Third World seemed inevitable. When this enthusiasm combined with the many political calls for anti-Communist strategies, it is not surprising that academia produced blueprints for security-related development assistance.

The government's development assistance initiatives from the mid-1950s up to 1961 drew largely from academia. Congress and the various administrations repeatedly called on the Center for International Studies (CENIS), the National Planning Association, and other research and academic institutions for policy recommendations.

By 1961 the foreign aid program had become an accepted element of U.S. foreign policy. Congressional acceptance, however, was always less than enthusiastic and was not achieved without a great deal of continuous debate over specific programs and dollar amounts. Increases in aid funds or in administration control over those funds required an extra measure of argument, and in 1961 the program's proponents elicited or inspired backing not just from the security lobby, but also from humanitarian, public interest, labor, and even some business organizations. President Kennedy engaged in a major public relations campaign to win support for the aid program among the people of the United States. In retrospect, Kennedy made his greatest contribution to development assistance doctrine both during the last year of his tenure in the Senate and in the first year of his presidency by translating the security concerns of the 1950s into greater support for economic development assistance.

The program that became law in 1961 was mostly contained in the Foreign Assistance Act of 1961, Senate Bill 1983. The act authorized the president to replace the International Cooperation Administration with a new agency, the Agency for International Development, which would be directed by an administrator with rank equivalent to that of an under-secretary. According to its mandate, the program was to emphasize long-range assistance to promote economic and social development. Recipients would be required to take self-help measures to reform and develop social and economic institutions.

A new Development Loan Fund was initiated, and the president was authorized to commit to development loans (subject to appropriation) $1.2 billion in fiscal year 1962 and $1.5 billion per year for the following four years. The authority to commit for future years was very significant; it had not previously been made available for foreign aid. The president was further empowered to make development grants of $380 million in fiscal 1962.

Congress approved guarantees of up to $1 billion for investments by U.S.

citizens or business entities that would promote social improvements in underdeveloped areas. A $62 billion subscription payment was made to the International Development Association, and $110 million was invested in the relatively new Inter-American Development Bank.

There were also initiatives not embodied in the Foreign Assistance Act. The Senate ratified U.S. participation in the Organization for Economic Cooperation and Development. The president used an executive order to establish the Peace Corps, which was then given permanent status by Congress. Its first-year appropriation was $30 million.

The Alliance for Progress was formally inaugurated on 17 August 1961, when the United States signed in Uruguay the Charter of Punta del Este, in which it agreed to help finance a 10-year, $20 billion development program throughout Latin America. The PL 480 agricultural surplus program was expanded to authorize 1961 foreign currency sales to increase by $2 billion, and the program was extended for three years at the rate of $1.5 billion in sales and $300 million in gifts each year.

A New Charter

The Foreign Assistance Act of 1961, although substantially amended, has remained the basic authorizing legislation for U.S. foreign assistance. After years of attempting to identify a philosophy for the foreign aid program, Congress spelled one out with uncharacteristic clarity. Development assistance would be designed to support improvement in the lives of poor in developing countries so that they would then be less likely to look to communism for relief. Military and security assistance would occupy a secondary role.

For the program to work, it would have to be substantial, be consistent over a long term, and have few strings attached except that the recipient governments would need to carry out the social, political, and economic reforms necessary for self-sustaining growth. By assisting the recipients to develop into nations of self-determined and self-supporting people, the United States could enjoy the kind of world neighborhood that would afford the greatest security and wealth for all of its members.

This philosophy was untested, it clearly lacked unanimous support, and it was fully expected to be very difficult to practice. In this light, 1961 could be viewed, not so much as a year of culmination in economic development assistance, but rather as a new base on which to conduct the next round of debate. The intent of the new charter would soon be subverted by escalation of hostilities in Vietnam. Its vision would be captured again in the 1970s and in the 1990s.

Chapter 6

The Basic Human Needs Mandate

In 1973 Congress initiated a significant departure in U.S. foreign development assistance policy. These changes were referred to in government as *New Directions.* In popular and professional discussion, they were increasingly referred to as the *basic human needs* (BHN) mandate. My aim in this chapter is to attempt to understand the sources of the BHN mandate. This will involve examining the evolution of U.S. development assistance policy from the mid-1960s to the early 1970s.[1]

New Directions was addressed to meeting the basic needs of the poor majority in the poorest countries. It was to involve them directly in the development process. The most distinctive feature of New Directions was that it proposed to concentrate economic assistance into five functional budget categories: Food and Nutrition, Population Planning and Health, Education and Human Resources Development, Selected Development Problems, and Selected Countries and Organizations. This marked a departure from the development assistance programs of the 1960s, which had emphasized general purpose resource transfers.[2]

An important feature of New Directions was that it was primarily a response to congressional initiative. Earlier shifts in development assistance policy had emerged largely from sources within the Truman, Eisenhower, and Kennedy administrations. This transition to a larger role for Congress in foreign economic assistance policy was a reflection of the more active role that Congress began to play in the entire foreign policy arena during the latter years of the Vietnam War. This emerging role of Congress as a major force in foreign policy represented a new challenge to traditional realist doctrine in foreign policy.

In this chapter, I examine the roles of both Congress and broader popular sources of change in foreign assistance policy during the early 1970s.[3] I first review the administration sources and then turn to the congressional and popular forces that induced a more activist foreign policy role by Congress. I give separate attention to sources of policy change within the administration and the Agency for International Development because of the independent role played by AID Administrator John R. Hannah in responding to congressional concerns.

Administration Sources

The foreign policy of the Kennedy and Johnson administrations has been referred to as "flexible response." According to historian John Lewis Gaddis, this was an expansive foreign policy supported by a rationale advocating that the economy could sustain or even benefit from an increase in domestic and defense spending. In this view, the main objective of flexible response was to increase the range of available options before resorting to nuclear war. This included placing a new emphasis on economic assistance to the Third World.[4] Walt Rostow viewed this era as a second Cold War cycle during which communist versus noncommunist methods of modernization in the developing world were tested.[5]

The stage for New Directions may have been set as early as 1961, when President Kennedy pledged to help the poor countries of the world "not because the communists are doing it, but because it is right." The 1961 Foreign Assistance Act (FAA) reflected this view in its reduced expression of concern over communism and Communist activity in the Third World as compared to the aid legislation of the Mutual Security Act of 1957.[6] AID's mandate was to place greater emphasis on transfer of capital and technical assistance relative to military aid. The major reorientation of the 1961 FAA was that it sought to base economic aid on long-range plans related to social as well as economic aspects of development.

In 1968, in what might be seen as a move to head off mounting congressional criticism of the foreign aid program, President Johnson appointed the Perkins Committee to examine the role of development assistance in the new administration. The Perkins report, which was heavily influenced by US/AID views, recommended the continuation of the foreign aid program in its then-current form.[7] Among its chief recommendations, the report suggested an increase in official development assistance levels and a stress on food production, family planning, science and technology transfer, education, and popular participation.[8]

In 1969 a new administration brought with it a significant departure in foreign policy.[9] Although detente had earlier origins, the policy had been reformulated by Nixon and Kissinger to reflect their belief in the need to redefine the U.S. role in a fundamentally changed international system. Rostow sees this period (1969–73) as one of relative political equilibrium between the United States and the Soviet Union.[10] As detente began to take shape, it seems to have laid the strategic foundation for New Directions.

Some analysts have viewed detente as a "new means to the old end of containment" or as "self-containment on the part of the Russians."[11] Gaddis has characterized the policy as consisting of five main elements: (1) to engage the Soviets in serious negotiations on substantive issues, (2) to "link" negotiations in substantive areas in order to modify Soviet behavior, (3) to pressure Moscow by establishing links between the United States and China, (4) to phase down American commitments in the world, and (5) to isolate the bureaucracy from the policy-making process.[12]

The fourth element seems to have been particularly influential in shaping New Directions. It was spelled out for the first time in some detail in July 1969, when President Nixon enunciated the Nixon Doctrine on Guam. In 1970, the president generalized what he termed the "central thesis" of the doctrine: "The United States will participate in the defense and development of allies and friends, but cannot and—will not—conceive all the plans, design all the programs, execute all the decisions, and undertake all the defense of the free nations of the world. We will help when it makes a real difference and is considered in our interest" (see Chap. 10).[13]

In August 1969, the Presidential Mission for the Western Hemisphere, led by Nelson Rockefeller, issued its report on the foreign aid program. The study can be viewed as an early attempt to define the role of economic assistance within the context of the Nixon Doctrine. The *Rockefeller Report* advised that the United States move to a system of tariff preferences for imports from developing countries, support regional markets, and participate in regional development banks. The report also recommended the establishment of an Economic and Social Development Agency to supersede US/AID.[14]

In his 1970 Foreign Policy Report to Congress, Nixon's discussion of economic assistance focused on the partnership approach to aid and urged a greater role for multilateral institutions. The president indicated that the developing countries must assume a larger role in defining their own development strategies and that trade and private investment should play a larger role in development.[15]

In March 1970, the Peterson Task Force on International Development reported its findings to the president. The task force had been commissioned in 1969 when the president first publicly embraced the need to restyle the aid program.[16] It was headed by Rudolph Peterson, chairman of the Bank of America. The report may be viewed as an official study that was sensitive to the moods of Congress, the executive, and the public.[17]

The Peterson report recommended that (1) foreign aid policy should be redesigned so that developing countries could establish their own priorities and receive assistance in proportion to their own self-help efforts, (2) multilateral lending institutions should become the major channel for development assistance, (3) development and military assistance programs should be completely separated, (4) the use of private sector initiative and resources should be expanded, (5) foreign aid policy should seek popular participation and dispersion of benefits, and (6) the downward trend in U.S. Official Development Assistance (ODA) should be reversed.[18]

The programmatic recommendations of the report included abolishing US/AID and channeling development assistance through three new institutions: (1) an International Development Bank for development loans, (2) an International Development Institute for technical assistance and research, and (3) an International Development Council to coordinate U.S. trade, investment, and financial policy.

In September 1970, Nixon issued a special message to Congress proposing reform of the foreign assistance program based directly on the Peterson proposals. The intent was to initiate a complete overhaul of the foreign assistance program to "make it fit with a new foreign policy." The president indicated that he planned to submit a revised version of the proposals to Congress as draft legislation during 1971.[19]

In a February 1971 report to Congress, Nixon reiterated support for the Peterson proposals. In April 1971, Nixon sent two draft bills, the International Development and Humanitarian Assistance Act and the International Security Assistance Act, to Congress, where they died in House committee. The bills had drawn heavily from the Peterson recommendations and to a lesser extent from the *Rockefeller Report.*[20]

Several reasons for the demise of the bills have been suggested.[21] In the winter of 1970–71, when there should have been consultations among US/AID officials, commission members, and congressmen, there were none. This may have been because the president was not really interested in reshaping foreign aid during his first term in office or because US/AID officials had no incentive to lobby for a bill that would have eliminated their agency. More likely still, Congress simply may not have been enthusiastic about the aid program.

The president's 1972 Report to Congress voiced his concern over the rejection of the Peterson proposals, and he termed 1971 "a year of crisis for foreign assistance." The president's May 1973 Report to Congress emphasized the continued progress of the Nixon Doctrine and contained a new section on U.S. political and economic interests in the developing world. The president asserted that development was tied not only to humanitarian needs, but also to the stability of developing nations and regions. The United States would receive needed energy resources and raw materials in exchange for machinery and products needed by the developing countries.[22]

In contrast to the 1972 report, the 1973 report discussed only improvements in the foreign aid program. Improvements cited by the president included (1) focusing bilateral aid on the key problem areas of health, education, agriculture, and population planning; (2) dealing with recipient countries as partners more able to plan their own development; (3) coordinating U.S. bilateral assistance more effectively with other donor countries and agencies; and (4) providing substantial support for multilateral assistance programs.[23]

The Nixon-Kissinger foreign policy had sought to "phase down" American commitments abroad. This was in sharp contrast to the expansive foreign policy of Kennedy and Johnson. Nixon and Kissinger seem to have reached a satisfactory definition of the role of development assistance (with the Peterson report) only when the Nixon Doctrine had begun to mature. Although Congress rejected the Peterson proposals in 1973, it was to introduce its own foreign assistance legislation, which seemed remarkably consistent with the Nixon Doctrine's low-key approach to U.S. involvement in world affairs.

AID Sources

During 1971 US/AID initiated a number of program and administrative reforms designed to respond to the president's Special Message to Congress of September 1970 and his legislative proposals of April 1971. In the fall of 1971, when it became clear that Congress would delay action on Nixon's foreign aid proposals, US/AID accelerated its internal reform process.[24] Out of this process came US/AID's primary contribution to New Directions—the proposal to divide the US/AID budget along functional lines.[25]

In the fall of 1971, US/AID Administrator John Hannah appointed Ernest Stern, who was then at the World Bank, to chair a task force on agency reorganization.[26] The Stern Committee began its work in the fall of 1971 and filed its report in December. The report acknowledged the press of human needs but did not suggest a new strategy for alleviating them. It did, however, strongly recommend a sectoral approach for US/AID authorizations. US/AID saw the sectoral approach as a way to refocus congressional attention on the program.[27] It was thought that the tactic of targeting assistance to areas such as food, education, and health would appeal to certain members of Congress and be less subject to attack.[28]

Maurice J. Williams, who was then deputy administrator of US/AID, recalls that at the end of 1971 Hannah took his senior staff to a retreat and brainstorming session at Arlie House in Virginia. Over the Christmas holiday, Williams had the assignment to pull together the conclusions from that session, which he admits had been "a bit all over the place."[29]

Williams noted that Hannah had a strong "people-oriented" approach to development. He was well respected in Congress and politically very astute. By January 1972, Hannah had sorted out the results of the brainstorming and began to announce a series of internal reforms, including a major reorganization of the agency.[30] The upshot of these changes was the centralization of decision making and a program focus that emphasized a more equitable distribution of development benefits. The changes called for an increased concentration of US/AID resources on agriculture and food production, with an emphasis on human nutrition, population control, health care, and low-cost education.[31]

Additional changes within US/AID included separation of the administration of the security and the development assistance programs and a reduction of US/AID's staff by roughly 30 percent. Testifying before the House on 20 March 1972, Maurice Williams stated that "in addition [to the above changes] we are now directing programs to focus more directly on basic human needs."[32]

In July 1972, Hannah spoke with the president about the possibility of reforming US/AID during the next administration. Having what he believed to be consent on the matter, Hannah approved major "Policy Determination" and "Policy Background" papers by October. Both spelled out a new US/AID policy for encouraging employment generation and more equitable income distribution in discussions with developing nations.[33]

During the fall of 1972, Hannah had two bills prepared: one a continuation of the existing budget mechanism and the other with functional categories. The draft functional bill was informally presented to the two authorizing and appropriating committees at the same time that it was circulated within the executive branch.[34] Although the committees apparently liked the legislation, it was not well received at the White House.[35] The proposals languished at the Office of Management and Budget partly because there were so many of them and no one was quite sure who should handle them.[36]

In May 1973, the administration sent the Foreign Assistance Act to Congress unamended. Anticipating this, Hannah and his staff had established an effective liaison with researchers from the Overseas Development Council (ODC) and staff from the House Foreign Affairs Committee to consider ways to secure passage of the bill. Historian Robert A. Pastor indicates that, by the time the OMB rejected the proposals, they had already been accepted by the House. He notes that at this point US/AID disclaimed responsibility for them. In summarizing the process, Pastor says that it was "AID's initiative, congressional redrafting with the help of the ODC, and OMB acceptance of a *fait accompli*."[37]

During 1974, US/AID cautiously responded to New Directions by shifting its accounting practices. The shift was from a budget broken down into capital and technical assistance accounts to one divided by functional accounts reflecting the outlines of the new legislation.[38]

Congressional Sources

During the 1960s, there were a series of amendments to the 1961 FAA that were, in effect, precursors to the 1973 basic human needs mandate. As noted in Chapter 5, Senator Hubert H. Humphrey (D-Minn.) succeeded in inserting an amendment in the 1961 FAA that declared that the purpose of U.S. policy was "to encourage the development and use of cooperatives, credit unions, and savings and loan associations."[39] The 1962 FAA added amendments declaring, in effect, that the highest priority should be given to programs providing loans or guarantees to institutions that would supply low-interest loans for the purchase of small farms, for small business, or for vocational training. Additional language authorized the president to support agrarian and land-tenure reform.[40] Congressman Clement Zablocki (D-Wis.) introduced an amendment providing that in recipient countries "emphasis shall be placed also upon programs of community development which will promote stable and responsible governmental institutions at the local level."[41]

The 1963 FAA added a subsection that declared that no assistance would be provided to a project from the Development Loan Fund unless the president determined that the project would promote economic development. Moreover, the project had to provide for "appropriate participation" of private enterprise. The 1964 FAA moved further in this direction by including a provision to the effect that US/AID should make use of U.S. firms in financing its capital projects.[42]

Title IX of the 1966 FAA represents another forerunner to the 1973 New Directions legislation. The amendment was introduced by Congressman Donald Fraser (D-Minn.) and co-sponsored by Congressman Zablocki. The original text of the amendment consisted of a single sentence: "In carrying out programs authorized in this chapter, emphasis shall be placed on assuring maximum participation in the task of economic development on the part of people in the developing countries, through the encouragement of democratic, private, and local government institutions."[43] Marian Czarnecki, who was chief of staff for the Foreign Affairs Committee, seems to have taken the lead in drafting the first unofficial version of Title IX. Title IX received considerable support from Congressman Bradford Morse (R-Mass.) and 25 other House Republicans. From both sides its justification drew heavily upon the political development literature.[44] Fraser mentioned that he saw Title IX as encouraging the "building blocks" of participatory governance. Similarly, the House noted that "there is a close relationship between popular participation in the process of development and the effectiveness of that process."[45]

Programs authorized under Title IX covered nearly the full range of foreign assistance activities. These included development assistance, the Development Loan Fund, technical cooperation programs, development grants, the Alliance for Progress, and multilateral and regional programs in Southeast Asia. The aim and scope of Title IX led Braibanti to term it "the most important element of doctrine in U.S. foreign assistance policy."[46]

The 1967 FAA expanded and strengthened the mandate by adding provisions that recognized the problem of implementing and evaluating popular participation. A new section on the objectives of development assistance was appended. This section included language that emphasized the building of economic, political, and social institutions in the developing countries in order to protect U.S. security and the interests of developing countries. To meet these objectives, the 1967 FAA provided that development was primarily the responsibility of the developing countries themselves, that self-help efforts were essential to successful development, and that assistance would be concentrated in those countries that took positive steps to help themselves and to encourage the democratic participation of their peoples.[47]

The 1967 FAA also stipulated that the president should take into account the extent to which the receiving country was implementing measures to increase production, storage, and distribution of food. Additional criteria included the extent to which the recipient country was targeting expenditures to key areas, including agriculture, health, and education.[48]

Section 102 of the 1967 act included the following provisions: "The first objectives of assistance shall be to support the efforts of less-developed countries to meet the developmental needs of their peoples for sufficient food, good health, home ownership, and decent housing, and the opportunity to gain basic knowledge and skills required to make their own way forward to a brighter future. In supporting these objectives, particular emphasis shall be placed on utilization of resources for food production and family planning."[49]

During 1968, Title X further strengthened the commitment to population planning by instructing US/AID missions abroad to take "all practicable steps" to facilitate the development of population projects and programs.[50]

The foreign aid bills of the early 1970s became hostage to legislative battles to end the Vietnam War. During this period, US/AID usually functioned on the basis of continuing resolutions at existing levels of appropriations. In 1971, the foreign aid bill suffered a serious setback when, for the first time, on October 29 the Senate voted down its funding, 41 to 27. It was attacked by conservatives for its failure to gain allies in the developing world and by liberals who objected to its large military component.[51] The objectives of Senator William Fulbright (D-Ark.), chairman of the Senate Foreign Relations Committee, were more complex. Fulbright and others were increasingly concerned that economic assistance had a tendency to lead to political commitments that in turn could lead to military involvement (Chapter 10). Pastor argues that Congress was also negatively affected by the U.N. decision to expel Taiwan on 25 October 1971. This prompted congressional resolutions calling for U.S. withdrawal from the United Nations or a reduction of the U.S. contribution to it.[52]

In early November, a Senate-passed bill that separated economic and military assistance was sent to Congress, which remained deadlocked over the Mansfield amendment requiring the withdrawal of all troops from Southeast Asia within six months. In 1972, a large number of Senate votes against the bill indicated continued dissatisfaction both with the foreign aid program and with the administration's policy in Southeast Asia.[53]

The House Initiatives of 1973

On 10 April 1973, a group of Foreign Affairs Committee members—14 Democrats and 1 Republican—sent a letter to President Nixon urging him to reform the foreign aid program on the basis of six principles. The six New Directions principles were as follows: (1) the Foreign Assistance Act of 1961 was to be amended by the Mutual Development and Cooperation Act of 1973 and the name of US/AID was to be changed to the Mutual Development and Cooperation Agency; (2) future U.S. bilateral aid should be focused on the functional categories of food production, rural development, and nutrition; population planning and health; and education and human resource development; (3) recipient countries should do more to design and implement their own developmental priorities, and the United States should favor those countries that sought to improve the lives of their poorest majority through popular participation; (4) bilateral aid should be increasingly channeled through the private sector; (5) an Export Development Credit Fund should be created to expand U.S. exports to advance the development of the lowest-income countries; and (6) a single government agency should coordinate all official development-related activities.[54]

When the administration responded with the unamended version of the bill on May 3, a bipartisan group of 26 House Foreign Affairs Committee members responded in turn with assistance legislation entitled the Mutual Development and Cooperation Act (MDCA) of 1973.[55] The MDCA, as well as the letter that had been sent to the administration, had been loosely patterned on Hannah's original US/AID proposals.[56] The title of the MDCA was meant to reflect the increasing economic and political interdependence between the United States and the developing countries, and it was premised upon the idea that the process of development was mutually beneficial to both the United States and the Third World.[57]

In addition to the New Directions provisions, the 1973 FAA included the earlier legislation linking human rights and foreign aid. This was a relatively inconspicuous Senate initiative stating that "it is the sense of Congress that the President should deny any economic or military assistance to the government of any foreign country which practices the internment or imprisonment of that country's citizens for political purposes." Historian Lars Schoultz notes that major credit for raising the level of congressional concern for human rights is given to an extended set of hearings before Fraser's Subcommittee on International Organizations and Movements during 1973.[58]

During the summer of 1973, when the MDCA was debated by the House and Senate committees, the provision for the Export Development Credit Fund received considerable support. It was, however, deleted when the bill came to the House floor. This was because it was thought to duplicate services provided by the Export-Import Bank, the World Bank, and US/AID's Development Loan Fund. On 26 July 1973, the House version of the bill was passed by five votes, 188 to 183. The Senate version was passed on October 3, by a vote of 54 to 42. In conference committee, the House provision to change the name of the Foreign Assistance Act to the Mutual Development and Cooperation Act and to change the name of US/AID to the MDCA was deleted. The remaining provisions were signed into law on 17 December 1973.[59]

Congressional Reforms

Congress clearly began to play a more central role in the formulation of assistance strategy in the early 1970s. A brief review of the reforms in committee rules and procedures and in congressional-executive relations is necessary to understand the basis for the more active congressional role.

Martin Sampson indicates that, although there is agreement that Congress became more active in foreign affairs during the 1970s, there is less agreement as to exactly why this occurred. He identifies four explanations: (1) congressional assertiveness occurs in cycles, with war tending to end the swing to Congress; (2) inept presidents allow Congress to become more involved in foreign policy; (3) the Vietnam War created congressional distrust of the executive and thus changed the content and the process of U.S. foreign policy; and (4) new interdomestic issues (ones that cut across domestic and foreign politics) have created incentives for Congress to become and to stay involved in foreign affairs.[60]

Former House member Charles Whalen offers an interpretation of the procedural changes that tends to emphasize the third explanation. He says that procedural reforms, well under way by the mid-1960s, were supported by anti–Vietnam War members who saw them as the only means of obtaining a vote on the war. Whalen maintains that the reforms were adopted in piecemeal fashion between 1970 and 1974 with the mutually reinforcing aims of decentralizing power within the House, creating greater openness in House procedures, and strengthening the House's capacity to deal with the executive branch.[61]

Intellectual Sources

During the 1960s and early 1970s, a closer relationship emerged between development thought and official assistance policy. Many ideas were conveyed to decision makers in Congress and in US/AID through the academic literature, congressional hearings, official and unofficial aid reports, conferences, professional staffs, and a variety of informal channels.

Development thought in the 1960s shifted in two directions. First, shortages in domestic savings and foreign exchange earnings were identified as potentially limiting factors on growth. The counterpart in official policy was to extend program-type lending to fill the foreign exchange gaps in the less developed countries. A second focus of the 1960s, influenced by the emergence of the dual-economy literature, was on sectoral development and, in the late 1960s, on sector lending for agriculture. As sectoral development processes began to be better understood, the importance of investment in human capital and of policies designed to overcome resource scarcities through technical assistance began to be appreciated.[62]

The 1960s also saw the multidisciplinary broadening of development theory.[63] Studies by sociologists and political scientists viewed the transition from a traditional state to "modernity" as involving changes in attitudes, as well as in social and political institutions.[64] Many of these studies implied that development in the less developed countries should replicate the transition to modernity undertaken by the industrialized countries.

Some analysts saw political development as part of the wider process of modernization marked by three criteria: structural differentiation, subsystem autonomy, and cultural secularization. Samuel Huntington maintained that the problem of political development was measurable and essentially one of economic growth outstripping the pace of institutional development. He argued that the most effective way to prevent "political decay" was to broaden the degree to which people participated in the political process.[65] These sorts of ideas had provided the conceptual basis for Title IX.

Support for the Vietnam effort by the liberal "Cold War intellectuals" was an important factor contributing to the decline of the field of political development. In a retrospective assessment, John O. Montgomery argued that the experiments with political modernization and administrative reform were responsible for substantial disillusionment as the expected results failed to materialize. In his view, an important outcome was public mistrust of bureaucracy and the emergence of a populist front stressing rural development and popular participation.[66]

The Pearson report (1969) was an important mainstream study that had been commissioned by the World Bank and headed by Lester Pearson, former prime minister of Canada (Chap. 12). The report recommended (1) the removal of barriers to the exports of less developed countries and the promotion of more favorable conditions for foreign direct investment; (2) a volume of aid equal to 0.7 percent of the GNP of the developed countries to sustain a growth rate of 6 percent per annum in the less developed countries; (3) redirection of technical assistance to the problem areas of agriculture, education, and population growth; and (4) strengthening and expanding of the multilateral aid system through the use of international organizations. The Pearson report merited particular attention in Nixon's special message to Congress for its description of recent changes that had been occurring in the Third World. The report generated a negative response from many development specialists who thought its recommendations were too modest and conventional.[67]

There was also an escalation of idealogical criticism from both the left and the right. On the left, some analysts viewed development assistance as an imperialist conspiracy designed to exploit Third World resources and cheap labor through ties of vested interest with Third World political and economic elites.[68] The criticism from the right emphasized the role of foreign aid in expanding the public sector and in concentrating political power in the less developed countries.[69] P. T. Bauer argued these and other deleterious effects of foreign aid: it increased the recipient country's debt burden, raised inflation, discouraged investment in agriculture, and generally destroyed motivation and market efficiency.[70] A neo-Malthusian critique maintained that a "population-food collision" in the Third World was inevitable, with no hope for technological solutions.[71] William and Paul Paddock argued that aid programs should be opposed because there was no evidence of their effectiveness. In contrast, Anne and Paul Ehrlich called for massive "unprecedented aid" and suggested a policy of "triage" for some of the very poorest nations.[72] A populist critique focused on the technocratic biases in the administration of aid resources. This view held that development assistance had minimal influence or tended to increase income disparities and strengthen the privileged position of large farmers in the developing countries.[73] An important critique was offered by the International Labor Organization and the United Nations, which began to implement a basic-needs or employment-oriented strategy. The new ILO strategy resembled, in many respects, the living standards movement of the 1930s.[74]

In 1969, the ILO launched the World Employment Program; its primary objective was to raise the living standards of the poor and to provide them with more productive work opportunities. Early ILO studies were focused on such issues as the relationship between population growth and employment, the possibility of adopting more labor-intensive technologies, the effect of trade expansion on employment, the links between educational systems and the labor market, urban employment problems, and the relationship between income distribution and employment (Chap. 12).[75]

In 1970, the Organization for Economic Cooperation and Development issued one of the first general surveys on the scope and nature of the employment problem in less developed countries.[76] The basic human needs approach was also foreshadowed in United Nations studies of the early 1970s.[77] Similarly, the World Bank became involved in 1973, when its president, Robert McNamara, pledged his organization to direct its resources toward improving the productivity and welfare of the rural poor in the poorest countries.[78]

By May 1973, a summary analysis of some of the major proposals for the reorganization of U.S. development aid had been transmitted to the House Committee on Foreign Affairs by the Congressional Research Service (CRS). The summary included the Perkins, Rockefeller, and Peterson reports, as well as nine additional studies.[79] The CRS summary identified several common themes:

1. Development assistance serves the national interest of the United States and is recognized as an instrument of national security policy.
2. Economic development is a good thing in its own right, and that fact should merit U.S. participation in the process.
3. Multilateral aid is more disinterested than is bilateral aid and should play a larger role in development.
4. Trade policy should be assigned a greater part, and barriers to entry of the products of developing countries should be reduced.
5. Private investment should be assigned a greater part in development.
6. Developing countries must play a greater part in formulating their own programs, and they must become more responsible for the consequences.
7. The requirements of social justice (i.e., ensuring that there would be

popular participation in decisions and that the benefits of development would reach the neediest) should be taken into greater account.

8. Security assistance should be administered separately from development assistance.[80]

Other key studies of the early 1970s seemed to show that not only had there been a relative decline in the living standards of the lowest income groups in the developing countries during the 1960s, but also there had been an absolute decline in some cases.[81] In a statistical study of 74 developing countries, Adelman and Morris concluded that "economic growth itself not only tends to be accompanied by actual declines in political participation but is one of the prime causes of income inequality."[82]

An influential study by Edgar Owens and Robert Shaw advocated a "new" development strategy based on the participation of the rural poor.[83] The strategy had been distilled from the "relatively successful experience of post-war Japan, Taiwan, Korea, Egypt, Yugoslavia, Puerto Rico, and Israel," and it was a reaction against the 1960s policies of focusing investment on "capital-intensive endeavors in the big cities and on large farms." The populist tone of the book seems to have contributed to the effect it had on some members of Congress. Fraser says that he saw Owens as one of the true "practitioners" of political development and the book as a kind of "natural evolution of participatory thinking."[84]

James P. Grant, who was president of the Overseas Development Council, says that the ODC became the principal advocate for the argument that "you could get growth with trickle-up."[85] He notes that it was a very conscious effort on his part to bring Owens and Shaw together to write the book.[86] These types of ideas, concerning the necessity of growth with equity, provided the intellectual basis for New Directions.[87]

External Sources

If intellectual thought informed the decisions of policy makers, so too did events in the international environment. The House Committee on Foreign Affairs intended New Directions to better reflect the emerging interdependence between the United States and the Third World. We now look to certain external changes that made that interdependence more evident.

The Legacy of Vietnam

U.S. involvement in Vietnam produced the most profound consequences affecting the timing and direction of the basic human needs mandate. We have seen that the war was a factor contributing to the increasing assertiveness of the House, but it also gave rise to the Nixon Doctrine and to new foreign aid strategies (Chap. 10).

Opposition to the war within both the administration and Congress was increasing by 1966. In Congress, Senator Fulbright argued that the United States had fallen victim to the "arrogance of power" and was courting disaster. In an interview Fraser indicated that Vietnam was clearly a watershed in his thinking on foreign aid. During 1965–67 he and some of his associates felt compelled to rethink the assumptions and goals of U.S. foreign policy.[88]

The Tet offensive in January 1968 precipitated a full-blown revaluation of U.S. policy in Vietnam. By March 1968, the new secretary of defense, Clark Clifford, recommended the scaling down of American objectives to a negotiated settlement instead of military victory. In so doing the administration accepted the principle that South Vietnam should do more to defend itself—a concept already familiar to Congress and one that formed the central basis of the Nixon Doctrine of 1969.[89]

The chronology of events demonstrated to Congress the apparent failure of what was in essence America's most protracted and costly foreign aid endeavor. To some officials, current military and economic aid strategies seemed no longer viable as instruments of containment, and thus new strategies were required.

The Decline of Bipolarity

The decline of bipolarity was a second factor pointing in this direction. *Bipolarity* refers to the global distribution of power between the United States and the Soviet Union during the period from roughly the late 1940s until the Cuban missile crisis of 1962. According to Charles W. Kegley and Eugene R. Wittkopf, the bipolar system was characterized by the primacy placed upon alliance systems, most notably the North Atlantic Treaty Organization (NATO) and the Warsaw Pact, used to link each superpower and its allies for defensive and offensive purposes. A main feature of the system was that each superpower's allies provided forward strategic bases in exchange for protection. John Spanier maintains that, by the mid-1960s, the erosion of the major Cold War ties led to a system, apparent by the early 1970s, more accurately described as *bipolycentric*. *Bipolycentrism* refers to a system characterized by many centers of power, diverse relationships among lesser powers, and attempts by superpowers to establish alignments with the lesser powers.[90]

Kegley and Wittkopf maintain that one of the major reasons for the decline of the bipolar system was the fact that rapid changes in intercontinental ballistic missile (ICBM) technology decreased the usefulness of cohesive alliance systems. A second reason was that, as the military capabilities of the superpowers became more evenly matched, the European NATO members began to doubt whether the United States would actually be willing to trade New York City for Bonn or Paris in the advent of nuclear war.[91] Thus, the decline of bipolarity suggested the need for the United States to adopt new forms of cooperation with the Third World for reasons of national security.

The Economic Rise of the Third World

A third factor may be seen in the increasingly larger role of the Third World in international political and economic affairs. To some officials these changes constituted a perceived threat to the United States. An alternative view, found in the Pearson report, was that these changes had enabled Third World nations to do more to determine its own development priorities. C. Fred Bergsten, senior economist on the National Security Council from 1969 to 1971, voiced the more extreme view when he warned that

> present U.S. policy neglects the Third World almost entirely, with the exception of our few remaining military clients (mainly in Southeast Asia). This policy is a serious mistake. New U.S. economic interests, which flow from the dramatic changes in the position of the United States in the world economy and the nature of the new international economic order, require renewed U.S. cooperation with the Third World. New policy instruments, including but going beyond foreign aid, are needed to promote such cooperation.[92]

In this view, as the capabilities of the Third World grew stronger and became more self-confident, it seemed to pose a threat to the United States in three main economic areas: (1) in natural resources, many Third World countries had great potential for strategic market control and for exerting political and economic leverage against the United States; (2) in investment, the Third World countries could exercise leverage by threatening confiscation of foreign-owned assets or massive repudiation of their debts; (3) in trade, developing countries could threaten U.S. exports by cutting their own export prices or by becoming cheap "pollution havens." Moreover, the United States seemed to need positive help from the Third World to expand U.S. trade, maintain the international monetary system, and stem the flow of narcotics.[93]

The legacy of Vietnam, the decline of bipolarity, and the rising economic power of the Third World seemed to point to the fading of the absolute dominance of the United States in world affairs. This was made evident, even in the early 1960s, by the recovery of Western Europe and Japan from the effects of World War II and, in the early 1970s, by the collapse of the United

States–led international monetary system. These factors demonstrated the need to adopt new strategies for gaining the allegiance and cooperation of the Third World.

Societal Sources and Public Opinion

In 1964, President Johnson launched the Great Society program, which, with its emphasis on relieving urban poverty, was a domestic precursor to New Directions. As the decade progressed, the expansionist policies were constrained by a perception of resource scarcities. During these years foreign policy began to reflect interdomestic political concerns, and foreign aid budgets were cut back by the late 1960s.

The political science literature of the 1960s and 1970s generally held that public opinion seldom has a direct effect on foreign policy.[94] Surveys of public attitudes toward development assistance issues suggest that public interest and knowledge are limited and that domestic issues are of primary concern. These surveys generally indicate a continuity in the level of public support for development aid. A late 1960s study showed that "small, quite constant, majorities of between 51 and 58 percent have on successive occasions from 1958 to 1966 said they were in favor of foreign aid." The Chicago Council on Foreign Relations reported similar findings concerning public support for foreign aid during the 1960s. An early 1966 Gallup poll found that 53 percent of the American public was in favor of foreign aid.[95]

A detailed survey on developmental issues by the Overseas Development Council concluded that a historically high level of 68 percent of Americans favored foreign aid in 1972.[96] This high figure was not supported, however, by the 1974 Chicago Council on Foreign Relations poll, which showed only 52 percent in favor of aid. A 1986 survey sponsored by the ODC and the American Council for Voluntary International Action (InterAction) found that the level of public backing for foreign economic aid had remained fairly steady over the past four decades. The survey found that 54 percent of the public approved of foreign aid in 1986 and that 39 percent were opposed. Both the 1972 and 1987 surveys found that the major reasons given by Americans for favoring economic assistance reflected a humanitarian concern, with economic and political concerns "being far less important."[97]

Since public opinion toward foreign aid was characterized by continuity rather than change during the study period, we would expect it to have had little effect on New Directions. Several analysts have concluded, however, that the "internationalist" mood of the American public began to erode during the late 1960s to mid-1970s, owing to differing perceptions of the meaning of the

Vietnam War.[98] This erosion of internationalism may have had an indirect influence on New Directions because some key members of Congress saw it as pointing to diminishing support for foreign aid and the need to adopt new approaches. Senator Fulbright evidenced this view in June 1973. "There is, I believe, general agreement that the traditional foreign economic aid program does not command the support of Congress or the public. What is needed, in my opinion, is not a cosmetic job to make foreign aid a more salable package to the public and Congress, but a thorough study of the entire spectrum of our Nation's economic relationships with the developing countries, of which foreign aid is only a small factor."[99]

The evidence suggests that public opinion played a supporting role in the transition to the New Directions orientation in foreign assistance. Congress responded to an increased public skepticism concerning the foreign commitments that led to Vietnam, rather than to declining support for foreign aid. The effect of Vietnam was to discredit traditional assistance policy and encourage the development of the the equity and human needs orientation of the New Directions mandate.

The Coalition of 1972

Several analysts have concluded that the influence of special interest groups on American foreign policy began to increase in the 1960s as U.S. involvement in Vietnam expanded. They maintain that the antiwar lobby of the late 1960s, through its access in Congress, built a base for future interest group activism. A related view is that the congressional reforms of the early 1970s facilitated interest-group access.[100] It is of interest, therefore, to examine the role played by the Overseas Development Council in affecting New Directions.

On 20 April 1973, after the House had sent its foreign aid letter to the president without receiving a reply, Congressman Fraser met with James P. Grant at the ODC to discuss what the next step should be. This encounter led to a series of breakfast meetings to discuss the content and strategy of a new foreign aid bill. The meetings were hosted by Representatives Zablocki and Fraser and were attended by a group of 7 to 10 congressmen. James P. Grant spoke at three of these meetings and brought with him the outlines of what was to become the New Directions legislation.[101]

Charles Paolillo, a lawyer from US/AID, was asked to draft the bill. According to Grant, Paolillo was entirely responsible for the original draft of the legislation, which was then handed over to the House. The ODC strategy centered on how to "get equity with growth." It was also aimed to mobilize an additional constituency. The ODC lined up and assisted in writing the testimony of witnesses who appeared before the House during June.[102] Later in

June many of the same witnesses also testified in favor of the new foreign aid bill before the Senate.

In his appearance before the House committee, Orville Freeman, former secretary of agriculture and president of Business International, addressed only the Export Credit Fund portion of the bill.[103] He endorsed the fund on the grounds that it would repair America's noncompetitive export position in the low-income markets and pointed to the success of a "parallel program"—Public Law 480.

Edward Mason, professor emeritus, Harvard University, and member of the Board of Trustees of the Overseas Development Council, was the first person to deal directly with the New Directions proposals.[104] Mason endorsed the bill's purpose to redirect aid to the poorest sectors and also its emphasis on private initiative. He also supported the bill's aim to separate development assistance from military and political objectives and its "most novel" aspect—the U.S. Export Development Credit Fund. Mason maintained that the fund would have a pronounced effect on the geographic allocation of aid because it intended to limit potential borrowers to countries having per capita incomes of less than U.S. $200.

Tony T. Dechant, who was the chairman of the Advisory Committee on Overseas Cooperative Development and president of the National Farmers Union, was accompanied by representatives of the cooperative movement, who added their support to the House proposals.[105] Dechant said that cooperatives could continue to help large numbers of the rural and urban poor, unlike large capital projects, which relied on "trickle down" approaches. He also said that cooperatives strengthened local-level institutions and encouraged participation of the poor.[106]

Grant was the first person to deal with the proposed New Directions changes in detail. His testimony is the clearest and most extensive public articulation of the bill's six main proposals. Grant maintained that development ought to "encompass minimum human needs of man for food, health, and education, and for a job which can give him both the means to acquire these basic needs as well as a psychological sense of participating usefully in the world around him." Citing *Development Reconsidered,* he said that the recent experience of a number of poor countries demonstrated that these goals could be met through an effective combination of domestic and international policies.[107]

The largest portion of Grant's testimony was devoted to a discussion of the Export Development Credit Fund, the purpose of which was to make credits available for financing U.S. exports—primarily electrical products, heavy construction equipment, and fertilizers—to countries with less than $200 per capita annual GNP. According to Grant, the fund seemed "an ingenious idea" to increase exports "by some $1 billion a year at no additional cost to the taxpayer." Grant also justified the bill on the grounds that "international politics and power relationship are changing, with security concerns giving way to economic issues among nations." These changes "require the U.S. and other rich nations to pay greater attention to the needs and desires of many developing countries."[108]

In a letter that appeared on the House record, Vice President Edward E. Hood of General Electric wrote that his company strongly endorsed the proposed legislation because it would "substantially serve to stimulate U.S. exports to underdeveloped nations, contribute very significantly to an improved U.S. balance of payments, and generate thousands of new jobs."

In another letter, Leonard Woodcock, president of the United Auto, Aerospace, and Agricultural Implement Workers of America, endorsed the aim to redirect development assistance to the poorest people and noted that aid met only a small part of the need for foreign exchange earnings in the poor countries. He emphasized the importance the UAW attached to an open trading system and supported the Export Fund as a way of both increasing U.S. exports and assisting Third World development.[109]

In his letter for the House record, David Rockefeller, president of the Chase Manhattan Bank, backed the bill on the grounds that it directed assistance to the neediest people in the poor countries. He also approved the Export Fund on the grounds that it would make the financing of U.S. exports more competitive with that of other rich countries.[110]

Edgar Owens, an official in the US/AID and the senior author of *Development Reconsidered,* did not testify before the House but prepared a lengthy statement for the record, which repeated the central thesis of his book.

James MacCracken, chairman of the American Council of Voluntary Agencies (ACVA), testified together with the executive directors of the major religious relief agencies.[111] He said that in ACVA, which represented a constituency of 41 voluntary agencies working in foreign service, there was general consensus for support of the bill because it brought aid "down to the level of the people." Lucy Wilson Benson, president of the League of Women Voters, provided a letter for the House record that endorsed each of the bill's main provisions.[112]

Primary criticism of the proposed legislation was furnished by William C. Paddock, author and consultant in tropical agriculture. He repeated his earlier thesis (see note 72) that the U.S. foreign aid program should be discontinued because its effectiveness could not be determined.[113]

Liberal interest groups played a strong supportive role in promoting New Directions. This seems to have been mainly because Congress recruited interest group backing, but it was also because "basic needs" enjoyed a broad-based appeal, particularly among some of the liberal organizations and private voluntary organizations that had gained increased access to Congress as a result of the Vietnam War. Thus, in 1973 an effective coalition was formed among liberal congressmen, some members of US/AID, the ODC, the international cooperative movement, some members of big business, and those representing humanitarian concerns.

Beyond New Directions

During the mid-1970s changes effected in US/AID policies reflected the thrust of the New Directions legislation. Country Development Strategy Analyses were required to give special attention to the analysis of the extent and sources of poverty. Agriculture, rural development, health, nutrition, and family planning received increased emphasis in the development assistance budget. The basic needs orientation of US/AID was complemented by the efforts of the World Bank and a number of bilateral donors, including Canada, Britain, the Netherlands, and the Nordic countries.[114]

Changes in the regional allocation of development assistance also reflected a shift away from the less developed countries with a relatively high per capita income and toward the poorest countries. In Latin America, programs in Uruguay, Brazil, and Venezuela were phased out. In Asia there was increased focus of mission activity in Bangladesh, Indonesia, and the Philippines; assistance to Korea was terminated. There was a rise in the number of US/AID missions in Africa from 8 in 1973 to 28 in 1980, and there was growing support for the programs of private voluntary organizations.

Schoultz maintains that, by adopting human rights as the soul of his foreign policy, President Carter legitimized a humanitarian concern in much the same way that John Kennedy had legitimized economic aid through the Alliance for Progress.[115] Similarly, the Nixon Doctrine and detente provided a window in which the strategic and humanitarian objectives of economic assistance were in relative harmony. By the end of the decade, however, the New Directions thrust had begun to falter. Security concerns, particularly in the Middle East, began to receive a higher priority. The supporting (i.e., strategic) assistance share of the economic assistance budget rose relative to development assistance. Israel and Egypt became the two largest recipients of aid from the United States.

Chapter 7

Lost Directions

U.S. Foreign Assistance Policy since New Directions

When Jimmy Carter was elected in 1976, he was committed to the restoration of moral purpose in American foreign policy.[1] His administration enthusiastically embraced the principles of the basic human needs mandate (Chap. 6). But by the last year of his administration, events in East Asia and Central America had induced a new emphasis on economic assistance for security purposes (Chap. 11). This trend was extended through the first Reagan administration. The easing of tension between the United States and the USSR during the second Reagan administration was accompanied by a decline in the resources devoted to foreign economic assistance. This trend was continued through the Bush administration.

Throughout most of the Bush administration, the U.S. development assistance program was in disarray. It was plagued by lack of leadership. Both its critics and its advocates called for reorganization, reform, and redirection (Chap. 13). But the problems that plagued U.S. assistance efforts during the Bush administration were, to a substantial degree, inherited from the Reagan administration. The objective of this chapter is to show how domestic political considerations, interacting with the inflated Cold War concerns of the first Reagan administration and the dramatic easing of tensions with the USSR during the second Reagan administration, acted to weaken U.S. commitment to economic assistance for economic development. As a first step, I review the budget trends for the years 1988–93. I then review administration policy toward development assistance during the Carter and Reagan administrations. Third, I turn to the roles of the Congress, the US/AID, and professional thought in shaping development assistance policy during the 1980s.

Trends in Economic Assistance

Total foreign economic assistance, although relatively stable in current dollars from the latter years of the Carter administration through the Reagan and Bush administrations, declined substantially in real terms (in inflation-adjusted 1987 dollars) during the Reagan and Bush administrations (Figures 7.1 and 7.2). There were substantial changes in the relative trends in the several economic assistance accounts. Multilateral assistance rose from 15 to 20 percent while food aid declined from 18 to 14 percent of economic assistance between the last Carter budget (1980) and the last Reagan budget (1989). During this same period, development assistance declined from 40 percent to 24 percent while aid channeled through the Economic Support Fund (ESF) rose from 26 percent to 42 percent.

There were also substantial changes in the flow of economic assistance resources. Although the Middle East consistently received approximately half, Africa and Asia each received a smaller share of bilateral economic assistance. The most dramatic change, however, was an increase from 14 to 23 percent in the economic assistance to Latin America—primarily to Central America.

The Budget Process

The U.S. government establishes annual budgets for foreign assistance; the issues of how much to allocate and to whom are largely political and vary little from year to year (e.g., Israel has received approximately $3 billion per year in total economic assistance since 1987). What varies from year to year is the purposes for which foreign assistance is channeled to recipients. This issue generates the most intense debates and rifts between executive and legislative branches in the budget process.

The budget process is exceedingly complex and time consuming.[2] It begins in Washington with programming guidelines that are sent to U.S. field missions and then are returned to Washington in the form of proposals written by the US/AID missions and U.S. embassies. Mission staff develop Country Development Strategy Statements (CDSSs) that lay out recommendations for development assistance. The recommendations are reviewed in Washington, along with the input from ambassadors, consultants, and State Department officials. This process leads to the preparation of Project Identification Documents (PIDs). These, in turn, give rise to an Annual Budget Submission (ABS) that justifies the funding needed to carry out the CDSS objectives. The ABS levels are established by State Department–US/AID consultation based on a mix of perceived security and development needs. Regional bureaus con-

FIGURE 7.1
U.S. Foreign Economic Assistance by Major Program: 1980–1993, Current Dollars

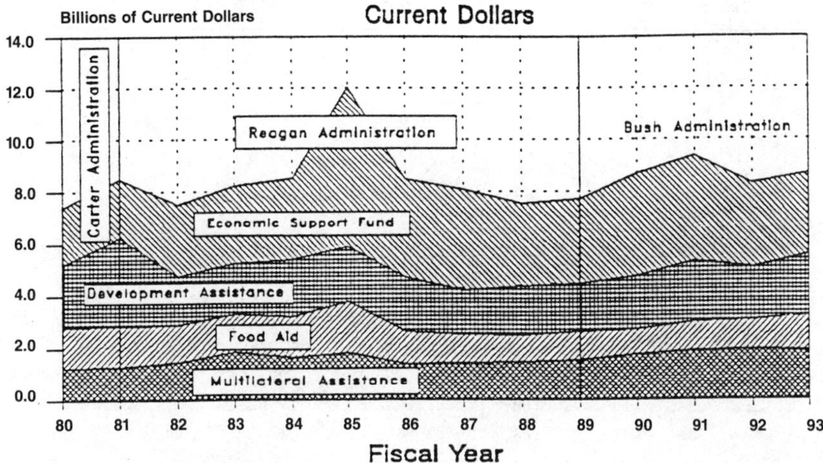

Assistance includes obligations and loan authorizations. Disbursements may lag authorizations. For example, disbursements were somewhat lower than obligations in 1985 and somewhat higher in 1986 and 1987.

Source: U.S. Agency for International Development, Congressional Presentations (Washington: Agency for International Development, various years).

solidate the data into an overall US/AID ABS that is integrated, in turn, with State Department recommendations for an overall package.

At the State Department the mission proposals and recommendations are routed to the Interagency Review Group, chaired by the under-secretary for security assistance, science and technology, and final budget recommendations are sent to the Office of Management and Budget. The OMB reviews the budget and submits it to the president for review and recommendations. When the president gives approval, the budget is printed and sent to Congress.

Traditionally, Congress first passes an authorization and then an appropriation for foreign assistance. However, during its first years, the Reagan administration bypassed the usual process to move foreign assistance directly through the appropriations process, thus forcing aid into a continuing resolution.[3] "The executive branch achieved its major objectives, mainly sharply increased spending in selected areas, especially security assistance programs, through continuing resolutions, while avoiding many congressional conditions and limitations that would likely have been attached to regular foreign assistance statutes, particularly authorization measures."[4]

This strategy was very effective during the first administration owing largely to William Schneider, under-secretary for security assistance, science

FIGURE 7.2
U.S. Foreign Economic Assistance by Major Program: 1980–1993, 1987 Dollars

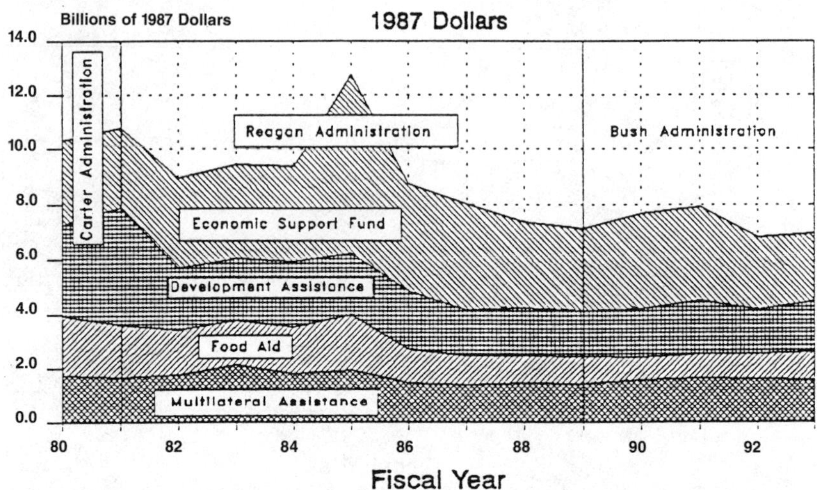

Assistance includes obligations and loan authorizations. Disbursements may lag authorizations. For example, disbursements were somewhat lower than obligations in 1985 and somewhat higher in 1986 and 1987.

Source: U.S. Agency for International Development, Congressional Presentations (Washington: Agency for International Development, various years).

and technology. He was the State Department's top foreign aid official and point man on the Hill for foreign assistance.[5] He was skillful in working the system to bypass the authorization process and achieve the administration's objectives. He had to "lobby" only the current power base in appropriations: Clarence D. Long (D-Md.) and Jack K. Kemp (R-N.Y.) in the House and Robert W. Kasten (R-Wis.) and Daniel K. Inouye (D-Hawaii) in the Senate.[6]

Kasten and Kemp supported the administration's objectives for the most part. Inouye and Long would finally agree to the proposals when the administration gave in on continued funding for development assistance, principally the International Development Association, the World Bank agency specializing in low-interest loans. Inouye was a strong supporter of the IDA. Long was perceived as a weaker person and, thus, not a major obstacle to Schneider and the political pressure of the administration.[7] This system effectively increased spending and changed priorities during the first administration but was not conducive to new programs or initiatives. Nevertheless, it suited the needs of the administration. More important, the priority changes were achieved without modifications to the structure of the foreign assistance act.[8]

During the second Reagan administration, the imposition of budget restrictions and the election of a new chairman of the Foreign Operations Subcommittee for House Appropriations (David Obey [D-Wis.]), in conjunction with the lack of a new initiative and policy design, severely hampered administration initiatives. Congress was critical of security assistance and tried to maintain the development assistance budget. The administration, however, continued to stress short-term political and security needs over developmental needs. The result was a series of executive-legislative confrontations that essentially stymied the entire foreign assistance program (see "Congressional Sources," below).

Administration Sources

The White House and State Department, which are part of a president's administration, establish foreign policy goals that affect the flow of assistance. In this section, I present an analysis of administrative sources in terms of the Carter administration and the two subsequent Reagan administrations.

The Carter Administration

The Carter administration entered office committed to the objectives of the basic human needs mandate. AID administrator John Gilligan called for a commitment to improve conditions in poor countries through economic and technical assistance, multilateral lending, and attention to basic human needs.[9]

The administration also attempted to respond to a concern of Congress, particularly Senator Hubert H. Humphrey (D-Minn.), for more effective aid coordination. It proposed to reorganize the foreign assistance program under a single umbrella organization, the International Development Cooperation Agency (IDCA). IDCA would incorporate all economic assistance programs scattered throughout the various departments—State, Treasury, Agriculture, and others—into an independent agency that would be able to achieve more effective coordination of assistance programs and give foreign aid more political and bureaucratic clout. The proposal to establish IDCA also included an Institute for Scientific and Technological Cooperation. The latter was to be set up to manage technical assistance in agricultural production, population planning, health, and energy (Chap. 13).[10]

However well-intentioned the motivation to establish IDCA and ISTC, the effort foundered on interagency bureaucratic politics. US/AID lobbied heavily for more autonomy, while Henry Owen, White House special assistant for economic matters and an ally of US/AID, led the administration drive to push IDCA through Congress. IDCA, however, lacked the necessary power base to change the foreign assistance bureaucracy. The role the director of IDCA relative to the role of the administrator of US/AID was unclear, as was the chain of command: who was to report to whom and who had the final say on budget matters. Many congresspersons saw both IDCA and ISTC as just another layer of bureaucracy surrounding the foreign assistance program. When the Reagan administration assumed office, it effectively disestablished IDCA by appointing Peter McPherson as both director of IDCA and administrator for US/AID.[11]

The Carter administration's major foreign policy initiatives that influenced the foreign assistance program most were human rights and North-South dialogue. Critics argue that the human rights initiatives were flawed, given that some countries received preferential treatment. Foreign aid became a tool to enforce human rights in countries of little strategic importance, whereas countries of greater political and strategic significance to the United States were not subjected to the same sanctions. Also, many policy makers viewed the North-South dialogue as counterproductive in the pursuit of a global balance of power.[12]

The completion of negotiations and the signing of the Panama Canal Treaty (1977) were a consistent reflection of Carter's foreign policy perspective. The Panama Canal Treaty was initiated during Henry Kissinger's term as secretary of state. The treaty was a reflection of the Carter administration's commitment to more positive relations with the countries of Latin America. This commitment was also reflected in the administration's response to the Nicaraguan revolution (1979) and in the support for El Salvador after civil war broke out there in 1980. The administration clashed with Congress over support for the newly formed Sandinista government and resorted to executive powers to assist El Salvador.

During the initial years of the Carter administration, there was an attempt to increase the flow of economic assistance in the form of Development Assistance relative to the Economic Support Fund (ESF). This reflected Carter's view that the United States should free itself from "that inordinate fear of communism which once led us to embrace any dictator who joined us in that fear."[13] After the Soviet invasion of Afghanistan, there was a major shift in attitude. In his January 1980 State of the Union address, President Carter enunciated what came to be known as the Carter Doctrine: "An attempt by any outside force to gain control of the Persian Gulf region will be regarded as an assault on the vital interests of the United States, and such an assault will be repelled by any means necessary, including military force."[14]

The shift was symbolic of the Carter relation with Congress in the twilight of his administration (Chap. 10). Carter's foreign policy was beleaguered by rising Soviet expansionism and economic crises (both global and domestic);

he gave lip service to healthy and productive relations with the Third World, but Congress was more concerned with inflation, the Soviet Union, and fiscal restraint. These concerns were behind the foreign assistance program shift toward a more security-dominated, bilateral program and the decline of the entire foreign assistance budget. "What was most distinctive about the foreign policy of the Carter administration—idealist objectives, tolerance of leftist revolutionary nationalism, and relatively open decision making—eroded as conflicts with traditional security and economic concerns emerged and as the domestic political salience of those traditional concerns became manifest."[15]

The First Reagan Administration

The Republican platform set the tone for the Reagan approach to foreign assistance when it urged a shift from multilateral to bilateral programs and from economic to military and security accounts. Robert Berg, then-director of evaluation at US/AID, described the Reagan administration as knowing exactly what foreign assistance policies to pursue before it occupied the White House.[16] The transition team for US/AID was headed by Edward J. Feulner, Jr., president of the Heritage Foundation, who opposed government-to-government assistance and favored a bilateral assistance program in which U.S. economic interests and foreign policy objectives would be dominant.[17] He believed that foreign assistance programs created inefficient bureaucracies that hindered economic development. Feulner worked with the administration and M. Peter McPherson, general counsel for the transition and subsequently US/AID administrator (1981 to 1986), to adopt policies and programs consistent with this view.[18]

Unlike the Carter administration, which publicly espoused basic human needs in foreign assistance but actually shifted to security concerns, the Reagan administration sought to restore foreign economic assistance to what it regarded as its traditional role as an instrument of national security policy. The administration denounced the Soviet Union's expansionist tendencies and labeled the Soviet presence as the underlying factor in the "turmoil which disturbs mankind around the world." It responded to Soviet expansionism with a massive buildup of defense programs and a "declared intent to respond firmly to any Soviet move."[19]

The Reagan administration sharply distinguished those who were friends of the United States from those who were not. Unlike the Carter administration, it elected not to work with cumbersome international bureaucracies (multilateral development banks [MDBs] and United Nations agencies) but favored the more manageable bilateral initiatives.[20] The administration channeled funds, for example, to friendly nations regarded as threatened by internal (El Salvador,

Sudan) or external forces (Honduras, Pakistan) and cut aid to governments considered unfriendly, uncooperative, or mismanaged (Nicaragua, Tanzania).[21]

The Reagan administration immediately embraced the ruling junta in El Salvador. The aid given for military purposes—"to repulse leftists"—and economic purposes—"to help relieve social unrest"—was administered by military advisers.[22] In the case of Pakistan, Reagan sought warmer relations with President Mohammed Zia Ul-Haq in hopes of countering the influence of the Soviet Union after the 1979 invasion of Afghanistan.[23] By targeting strategically important countries with ESF funds and policy reform measures conducive to privatization, the administration was able to dampen conservative opposition to foreign assistance. With an overall increase in the entire budget and policy guidelines that became known as the *four pillars,* the administration could pursue programs that fell under either the basic human needs mandate or its own "four pillars" guidelines.

The four pillars of development assistance were based on a memo submitted by M. Peter McPherson during the presidential campaign; the memo outlined Reagan's ideas for foreign assistance. The four pillars were designed to "achieve the kind of foreign assistance program envisioned by the President—one which seeks to foster self-sustaining development by using initiative and creativity to help people help themselves while at the same time stimulating international trade and aiding the truly needy."[24]

The four pillars were (1) *policy dialogue and reform,* seeking to agree with host country governments on the policy constraints to development and practical improvements that could be made; (2) *institutional development,* focusing on decentralizing institutions and encouraging reliance on private and voluntary, rather than public, institutions; (3) *technology transfer,* seeking breakthroughs in such areas as biomedical research, agriculture, and family planning; and (4) *private sector development,* enhancing the role of the private sector in solving development problems.[25]

The administration's second secretary of state, George Schultz, expanded on the notion of foreign and U.S. national interests by setting forth two basic premises for U.S. involvement in the Third World: (1) there will be no enduring economic prosperity for our country without economic growth in the Third World, and (2) there will not be security and peace for our citizens without stability and peace in developing countries. Schultz went on to say that "our security and economic assistance programs are essential instruments of our foreign policy and are directly linked to the national security and economic well-being of the United States."[26] The challenge to the Reagan foreign assistance policy was how to fit the rhetoric of the four pillars into a foreign policy design that secured U.S. national interests. Critics denigrated the significance of the four pillars.[27]

In February 1983, the Commission on Security and Economic Assistance (the Carlucci Commission) was appointed to define the role of security assistance vis-à-vis that of development assistance in U.S. foreign policy. The most prominent of its many recommendations was the establishment of a Mutual Development and Security Administration. The new organization would be responsible for integrating the economic and security assistance programs. The commission argued that "the most effective means to achieve program integration, a country approach to program development, an improved evaluation system and increased public support is to consolidate certain aspects of current programs under a new agency, reporting to the Secretary of State."[28]

The ultimate goal of the commission was not only to show that foreign assistance is indeed an important foreign policy tool, but also to demonstrate "that in the absence of an effective security framework and a sound macroeconomic policy environment, economic cooperation has substantially reduced potential for positive long-term development impact." The commission concluded that all of the instruments of foreign cooperation must be combined in "sound, well-managed and integrated programs, with consistent, coherent policy goals, or all interests may suffer."[29]

Critics argue that the "sound" advice of the commission did not have a major effect on policy implementation and that the commission was only a "rubber stamp" for a policy approach already under way in the administration.[30] Throughout the entire first Reagan administration, economic and security assistance, at least at the rhetorical level, were being used to achieve the same ends: growth and stability. This attempt to forge a stronger link between economic and security assistance was the major reason for the sharp increase in the ESF account.[31] Its programs were relatively free of restrictions (compared to other aid categories), funds could be disbursed very rapidly to countries strapped by the world recession and rising debt crisis, and base-right commitments could be expanded. The administration's emphasis on economic reform and security lent itself nicely to the cash and budget support transfers of ESF.

Two other studies were commissioned during the first Reagan administration. At Treasury, Donald Regan and Barry Sprinkle, both exceedingly skeptical of a continuing U.S. commitment to foreign assistance, arranged for Raymond F. Mikesell of the University of Oregon to study how developing countries might make the transition to self-sustained development. The narrow terms of the study's reference disturbed US/AID and the State Department officials. When Treasury was unwilling to widen the scope, US/AID and State commissioned its own study by Anne O. Krueger and Vernon W. Ruttan of the University of Minnesota to examine the development effects of economic assistance.[32]

The Mikesell study was more supportive of the aid effort than Regan and Sprinkle had hoped. The Krueger-Ruttan study, however, was more critical, particularly of some efforts of the New Directions program, than US/AID and the State Department had anticipated. It is doubtful that either study had a major influence on assistance policy. Nevertheless, some agency personnel argue that the studies contributed to a more informed and rational interagency discussion of assistance policy.[33]

The following outline of four program initiatives illustrates the ideological, political, and strategic emphasis of the Reagan administration.

Private Sector Initiative

This initiative was the clearest reflection of the Reagan administration policy orientation: "finding practical means of enhancing the private sector's role in assistance programs and in LDC development." The initiative reflected a concern that developing countries were overly hostile to reliance on market forces to guide investment and consumption decisions and, hence, were not using their resources efficiently. "LDCs which have overextended the role of the public sector and restricted the operation of the private sector have experienced slow growth, heavy budget deficits and rising debt burdens."[34] The resulting US/AID policy was to engage in program actions to eliminate legal, regulatory, and other constraints to private enterprise development and to assist and promote private enterprises. With multilateral assistance, US/AID could not target specific enterprises or political institutions; furthermore, the administration wanted to influence the direction of assistance by MDBs and international organizations at every opportunity. Development assistance, ESF, and PL 480 loans or grants were seen as "appropriate" devices to support private enterprise development.[35]

In 1983, the president formed a task force to develop guidelines for this private sector focus. The task force, made up of prominent business persons or "private sector leaders," was commissioned "to determine how U.S. resources, particularly foreign assistance, could increase trade, investment, and private enterprise in developing nations."[36] The recommendations included the formation of an Economic Security Council to coordinate domestic and international policy and increased emphasis on channeling resources to the private sectors of developing nations and not to governments.

Population Assistance

The Reagan administration ideology was also reflected in its policy on population assistance. Since the late 1960s, the United States and some Western

European and Asian nations had been trying to unify efforts to limit fertility in the developing nations. The United States supported the belief that rapid population growth had an adverse effect on economic development, health, and individual potential, particularly among women. U.S. policy favored family planning programs to reduce fertility and promote economic growth.[37]

At the first World Population Conference in Bucharest (August 1974), the United States prompted the participants to confront the issues of population and its relation to development, as well as to consider population policies and action.[38] The nations of the Third World, however, did not concur with U.S. views. They were committed to a new international economic order to alleviate the problems of population growth and argued that "development is the best contraceptive."

Nevertheless, by the 1980s the Third World nations were accepting the view that population growth threatened economic development while donor countries were increasing assistance for population control. By this time the United States had altered its view. At the Second International Conference on Population in Mexico City (1984), the official U.S. position held that population has a neutral effect on economic growth; where the effects were detrimental, they could be alleviated by rapid economic growth.[39]

James L. Buckley, head of the U.S. delegation to the conference in Mexico, defined population growth as "neither good nor bad. It becomes an asset or problem in conjunction with other factors, such as economic policy, social constraints, and the ability to put additional men and women to useful work." The new U.S. strategy as outlined by Buckley was to remove subsidies and controls and rely "on the creativity of private individuals working within a free economy."[40] Julian Simon, an economist at the University of Maryland and an intellectual standard-bearer in the delegation, gained notoriety with his work *The Ultimate Resource,* in which he argued for population growth: "The most important economic effect . . . is the contribution by additional people to our stock of useful knowledge."[41]

Further emphasizing the break in policy was the fact that the preparation for the Mexico conference did not follow standard procedure. Instead of the State Department carrying out the planning and preparation, the White House acted unilaterally to issue a position paper and form a delegation, which became a source of conflict with State and US/AID.[42]

Before 1984 the United States had channeled money for population programs through many international organizations. Owing to criticisms from the New Right and other antiabortion pressure groups, support was suspended for organizations that funded abortions (e.g., the International Planned Parenthood Federation [IPPF] and the United Nations Fund for Population Activities [UNFPA]).[43] The administration began withholding funds from UNFPA and IPPF in 1985 while at the same time maintaining rhetorical support for the population program—albeit in the context of its position at the Mexico Conference and of the view from the New Right. Congress expressed its disagreement by appropriating additional funds.[44] US/AID Administrator M. Peter McPherson mediated between the administration and Congress to maintain a steady flow of funds to the population assistance programs.

Regional Emphasis

Three regions were designated as priority areas for economic assistance by the Reagan administration—Central America and the Caribbean, the Middle East, and Africa.

CENTRAL AMERICA AND THE CARIBBEAN

The Reagan administration assumed office determined to reverse what it regarded as Soviet-generated instability in Central America and the Caribbean (Chap. 10). Both economic and military assistance to the region expanded rapidly. AID mission staffs were increased and became in some countries what amounted to shadow governments. The goal was to "reestablish uncontested U.S. political and economic hegemony in our own backyard."[45]

The administration's initial economic response to instability in the region was the Caribbean Basin Initiatives (CBI). The initiatives, announced at an address before the Organization of American States in February 1982, would provide eligible countries with preferential duty-free access to the U.S. market, tax incentives for U.S. foreign investment, and increased foreign aid—conditioned on policy reforms that would encourage private enterprise.[46]

Congress passed the foreign aid component ($350 million) of the CBI in September 1982, after cutting $75 million from the amount earmarked for El Salvador. But it delayed action on the trade provisions. In July 1983, after the Grenada invasion focused public attention on the region, Congress passed the Caribbean Basin Recovery Act. The act gave the administration far less than it had requested. Some traditional Caribbean exports, most importantly sugar and textiles, were excluded from the provisions that assured preferential access. The proposed incentives for direct foreign investment, with the exception of some tourism incentives, were never passed.

For some countries, the effect of reduced earnings from export of sugar more than offset the increases in economic assistance. Nontraditional exports, particularly apparel and fruits and vegetables, did expand rapidly. Whether there was any net benefit to the region from the CBI, at least prior to the revisions that were included in the Customs and Trade Act of 1992, remains questionable.

In hopes of generating a broad consensus of support for his program, particularly in Central America, the Reagan administration appointed, in July 1983, a National Bipartisan Commission on Central America (the Kissinger commission). The commission found that the roots of Central American problems of poverty, injustice, and stagnant economic growth were both "indigenous and foreign. Discontents are real, and for much of the population conditions of life are miserable." Hence, the region was "ripe for revolution."[47]

The Kissinger commission endorsed the Reagan view of the turmoil in Central America and of what should be done: "substantial" increases in military aid for El Salvador and "covert" aid to the Contras in Nicaragua. Recommendations included long-term military and economic aid for the entire region and a meeting between Reagan and Central American leaders to plan the long-term economic development of the region.

The Kissinger commission had little effect on aid policy, but it demonstrates the importance placed by the administration on the region. After all, it was the Reagan Doctrine of supporting resistance movements around the world that justified support for the Contras. Congress, concerned about a second Vietnam, was reluctant to respond to the administration's policy of providing largely cash transfers.[48] The issues involved in economic support for security purposes in Central America are discussed in greater detail in Chapter 10.

AFRICA

The Reagan administration's foreign assistance objectives in Africa were remarkable for their lack of clarity.[49] The objectives included promoting the U.S. global geostrategic position, supporting U.S. positions in multilateral fora, ensuring the access of U.S. diplomats to the many governments in Southern Africa, fostering economic development through financing projects or balance-of-payments support conditioned on policy reforms, and providing humanitarian relief.

During the first years of the Reagan administration, Africa benefited from the overall increase in foreign assistance. The program utilized the ESF to address the perceived policy reform needs of many African countries. ESF offered the necessary flexibility, the kind not provided under the development assistance budget. However, when foreign assistance was decreased in 1986, funding for Africa was retrenched.[50] The short-term ESF transfers generated little measurable effect on development.

Many administration initiatives in Africa were criticized as reactive—simply responding to crises—and as ignoring long-range planning. The Sahel Development Program, for example, which originated in President Ford's FY1978 foreign aid request, was designed to institutionalize the U.S. commitment to a coordinated, long-term, multinational project to support severely drought-affected West African states; it was never fully supported by the Reagan administration and thus was stalled because of lack of funding.[51]

The Reagan administration opposed most multilateral lending to Africa. The administration believed that U.S. funds should be used for bilateral programs directed to policy objectives, such as promoting market-oriented activities and rewarding friendly nations. The United States could not control programs within the MDBs (see "Multilateral Assistance," below). U.S. contributions to such organizations as IDA, a major lender to Africa; the International Fund for Agricultural Development (IFAD); and the African Development Fund were consistently lower than those of several other donor countries.[52]

The World Bank and other donors (including many private voluntary organizations in the United States) took special interest in African development. The consensus was that Africa needed "plenty of aid."[53] In 1984, participants in the World Bank and the International Monetary Fund proposed a "special assistance facility" for the region, but the administration opposed the special fund in favor of bilateral activities.[54]

Other administration initiatives, such as the Economic Policy Initiative (EPI), a plan to provide aid to countries that were willing to promote changes in their economic systems or to countries that were willing to promote growth through more capitalist-oriented free market policies, met with little success in Congress. One Democratic House aide expressed concern in Congress that EPI "had become a slush fund to reward political allies."[55]

Most development experts agree that the many aid programs for Africa have not been very successful. "The basic reason for the failure of these projects is their inappropriateness to African conditions. They were too complex, requiring a degree of coordination by African bureaucracies that would be difficult for any government." An additional problem faced by the United States was how to impose restrictions on the assistance when its funds were but a fraction of official development assistance for Africa.[56]

THE MIDDLE EAST

U.S. assistance in the Middle East escalated rapidly after the 1973 October (Yom Kippur) War between Israel and Egypt and Syria. Aid to Israel exceeded $500 million at the beginning of the Carter administration and rose to close to $2.0 billion by the end of the first Reagan administration. In September 1977, President Carter succeeded in bringing Prime Minister Menachem Begin and President Anwar Sadat together at Camp David. An intensive diplomatic effort over a year and a half that included a visit to Israel by Carter resulted in a set of awards and a peace treaty in March 1979. As part of the peace process, Carter found it necessary to make a commitment that Egypt would receive parity with Israel in assistance flows. Congress has interpreted parity as 70 percent (Chap. 10).

Without Carter's personal commitment, there would have been no peace treaty. But in Israel some members of the Kenneset regarded the peace treaty as a sell-out. *New York Times* columnist William Safire insisted that Carter had deliberately betrayed the Israelis. In the 1980 election, Carter received only 45 percent of the Jewish vote—the weakest support from the Jewish community of a Democratic candidate in recent history.[57]

The Reagan administration came into office with a view that the Soviet Union was the major source of tension in the Middle East. Israel was viewed as a strategic asset. But realization of Israel's value as a strategic asset required a reduction of tension in the region. It also required a strengthening of the defense capacity of Saudi Arabia and the other moderate Arab states in the region. A proposed sale of military aircraft to Saudi Arabia aroused intense opposition from the Jewish community in the United States. Thomas Dine, executive director of the American-Israel Public Affairs Committee (AIPAC) warned the administration that the American Jewish community was prepared to fight the sale "all the way."[58] Faced with the possibility of defeat in the arms sale, the administration insisted that Congress must chose either "Reagan or Begin." Although the administration was successful in winning Senate approval for the sale, the victory cost the president large political resources. Senator Charles Percy (D-Ill.), chairman of the Senate Foreign Relations Committee, was defeated in his subsequent bid for reelection—a defeat for which AIPAC took credit.

In spite of continued tension between the United States and Israel generated by Begin's Greater Israel policy and its opposition to the administration's efforts to strengthen relationships with the Arab countries of the region, Reagan continued to view Israel as a strategic asset.[59] Military and economic assistance to Israel continued to grow. In 1981, Economic Support Fund transfers were placed on a grant basis. In 1985 and 1986, a special ESF "emergency transfer," initiated in Congress, was made to compensate Israel for costs incurred in its invasion of southern Lebanon.

Multilateral Assistance

The Reagan administration was very skeptical of multilateral assistance. This skepticism is best exemplified by the cuts in the foreign aid program proposed by David Stockman, director of OMB, in 1981; he labeled them "deep cuts in foreign economic aid on the basis of pure ideological principle." The principle was to give bilateral assistance precedence over multilateral assistance and security assistance precedence over development assistance. Only ESF received "lenient treatment."[60]

Stockman and others, particularly Donald Regan and Barry Sprinkle at

Treasury, believed the many international organizations, as well as US/AID, to be "infested with socialist error . . . The international aid bureaucracy was turning Third World countries into quagmires of self-imposed inefficiency and burying them beneath mountainous external debts they would never be able to pay."[61]

In the spring of 1981, the administration commissioned an interagency review of the MDBs, chaired by the Treasury Department (Chap. 11). The purpose was to provide a "comprehensive and dispassionate examination of the [MDBs], and by applying the administration's basic policy preferences and priorities to the findings, to establish a policy and budgetary framework for U.S. participation in these institutions in the 1980s." Although the study listed 19 criticisms of the MDBs, ranging from staff salaries to systems of project evaluation, it supported MDB lending in general and advocated political impartiality by lending institutions.[62]

Much of the administration's anti-MDB sentiment centered on the approach to meeting basic human needs espoused by World Bank President Robert McNamara. McNamara, president of the World Bank from 1968 to 1981, had used basic human needs to advance a reform agenda at the bank designed to channel larger assistance flows to the poor majority in the poorest countries. Opponents on the right criticized the bank for promoting socialism.[63]

Robert Clausen, a Carter appointee, succeeded McNamara as president of the World Bank in 1981 and attempted to change bank policy—or at least its rhetoric. He insisted that bank programs should favor the private sector and political and institutional reform. This was interpreted as an attempt to gain congressional support, given the similarity to the rhetoric of the Reagan administration.[64]

The administration, however, "successfully" cut funds to the World Bank and other multilateral lending institutions; the only multilateral program that escaped major cuts was the controversial IDA.[65] Earlier we noted that the IDA commitment was necessary to the administration to satisfy liberal calls for a more BHN-oriented approach to assistance. Criticisms of IDA centered on low-interest loans as basically gifts and their ineffectiveness as an instrument of U.S. influence abroad.[66] By the end of the first Reagan term, the initial U.S. pledges to MDBs had been cut by more than 30 percent. All of the banks—the Asian Development Bank, the Inter-American Development Bank, and the African Development Bank—were affected.

In the development community the belief is widespread that the banks provided much of the intellectual force behind development assistance strategies in the 1980s. Critics of the administration contend that the policies of alleviating poverty were "sacrificed to the Washington ideology."[67]

The Reagan administration also assumed a position critical of multilateral assistance channeled through U.N. specialized agencies and voluntary programs (Chap. 12).[68] The administration habitually proposed cutting contributions to most U.N. specialized agencies; the most drastic cut was made in funds for the United Nations Educational, Scientific, and Cultural Organization (UNESCO).[69]

The administration announced its intention to withdraw from UNESCO in December 1983. A State Department document accused UNESCO of not adequately reflecting the view of the free market, developed countries. UNESCO was accused of "endemic hostility" toward the institutions of free society—a free press, open markets, and human rights—and of displaying widespread mismanagement and "excessive budget growth."[70]

The administration appointed a commission to study UNESCO and its response to the administration's criticisms. When no satisfactory change in UNESCO operations was found, the United States withdrew in 1984. However, the United States retained "observer status" at UNESCO and made voluntary contributions to "selected international scientific or cultural activities in UNESCO's field of competence considered important to U.S. interests."[71]

These Reagan administration initiatives were clearly consistent with the administration's intent to shift away from the basic human needs philosophy and toward macroeconomic reform and a short-term security orientation in its economic assistance. The shift generated considerable controversy among traditional aid constituencies.[72] Perhaps Larry Nowels, a specialist in foreign affairs at the Congressional Research Service, said it best: "The new directions legislation, which calls for aid directly to the poor, remains on the books, but the thrust of the Reagan administration's four pillars is toward macroeconomic growth. The question of the extent to which aid resources should focus on promoting growth through reliance on the private sector and market mechanisms as opposed to strengthening the resources of the poorest population remains a key issue for debate."[73]

The Second Reagan Administration

During the second Reagan administration, the central focus of foreign assistance shifted again. Where the first Reagan administration had been characterized by increased bilateral economic and security assistance, the second Reagan administration was characterized by an increased sense of international cooperation and lower levels of assistance.[74]

A major shift, at least at the rhetorical level, moved U.S. policy from security to economic stabilization and growth. United States–Soviet relations were improving dramatically, and the outlook for future cooperation was good. The U.S. economy could no longer support—in a political sense—the increases of earlier foreign assistance budgets; both policy officials and critics questioned the efficacy of an assistance program "dominated by military and short-term security concerns."[75]

John Sewell and Christine Contee (Overseas Development Council) argued that four major factors were involved in this shift: (1) The United States has been transformed from a creditor nation to a debtor nation; (2) the U.S. global trading position shifted (the United States experienced unprecedented trade deficits); (3) the commercial banking system became internationalized, and the health of the U.S. banking community was dependent on the ability of foreign banks to repay loans; and (4) the political stake of the United States in broad-based growth and development in key countries such as Mexico, Brazil, Argentina, and the Philippines increased as these countries liberalized both their economic and their political systems.[76]

During Reagan's second term, James Baker III traded jobs with Donald Regan and became secretary of the treasury; he set out to work with international lending institutions to provide the impetus for developing countries to "grow" their way out of their economic crises. Baker understood the urgency of resolving the deteriorating world economic situation, which was being attributed to the domestic policies of the Reagan administration.[77]

Just as Kennedy had turned the Cold War security concerns of the Eisenhower administration to increased concerns about development, so James Baker turned the concerns about global debt into support for international cooperation. The argument was that the United States could assist developing countries to restore growth and resolve debt problems, which, in turn, would benefit the economic and political interests of the United States. In an address at the annual meeting of the World Bank and the IMF in South Korea in the fall of 1985, Baker acknowledged for the first time the need for new money to support the process of policy reform in the most deeply indebted countries (the Baker 15). He announced a "Program for Sustained Growth" (the Baker plan) consisting of three elements: policy reform, a central role for the IMF, and increased lending by private banks.[78] Baker suggested that $20 billion in new commercial bank lending would be required over the next three years and called on the banking community to respond. Commercial banks were, however, unwilling to provide the necessary capital and the economic "reforms" were too ambitious for many politicians in the borrowing countries. In addition, critics claimed that the World Bank mandate was never specified and that the United States remained hostile to reducing or forgiving debt.

This sense of international cooperation during the second Reagan administration intensified with reduction in tension between the United States and the USSR.[79] The warming in East-West relations brought about an atmosphere of optimism. One result was closer scrutiny of the security assistance budget and a greater emphasis on development assistance. No longer could massive defense buildups be justified solely on the basis of countering Soviet-backed insurgency. The effect was a slowing of the increase in security assistance and greater reliance on private sector initiatives, market mechanisms, and private voluntary organizations. Smaller budgets gave Congress greater leverage on the flow of assistance (via earmarks) and on the administration's flexibility in pursuing foreign policy goals. As a result of earmarks and the lack of funds, the Middle East, Central America, and base-right countries had a virtual monopoly on ESF resources.[80]

Nevertheless, other programs were not completely neglected. For example, in 1987 the administration proposed—and Congress supported—the initiation of the Development Fund for Africa, a fund within the development assistance program that provided a flexible source of aid for policy reform and balance-of-payments support. Congress earmarked $500 million for the fund under a continuing resolution (HJ Resolution 395).[81] With the easing of tension between the USSR and the United States and the disintegration of the Soviet empire, the stage was set for the United States, during the Bush administration, to begin to channel substantial assistance to the formerly centrally planned economies of Eastern Europe and the former USSR.[82]

The United States' relationship with the United Nations also changed. In September 1988, the Reagan administration reversed its eight-year feud and authorized the release of $44 million in outstanding U.N. dues, signaling "a willingness to release an additional $144 million in dues to be appropriated by Congress for the next fiscal year." This was an apparent reaction to the decline in anti-Western sentiment in the United Nations under Secretary Perez de Cuellar. In addition, the administration asked the State Department to work out a multiyear plan to repay the $520 million in past debts to the United Nations and its specialized agencies, such as the World Health Organization ($28 million) and the Food and Agriculture Organization ($82 million).[83]

US/AID Sources

US/AID underwent three major changes between the early 1970s and the mid-1980s. The first change occurred during Daniel Parker's period as administrator. New Directions legislation altered US/AID objectives and led to a stronger project orientation as opposed to the centralized programming procedures of the 1960s. At the same time, Congress became more active in directing the use of AID resources. Functional budgeting, earmarking, and additional reporting requirements subjected US/AID to closer congressional micromanagement (Chap. 6).

The second change came in 1978 under the direction of John Gilligan. He appointed a commission (the Babb commission) in 1977 to study US/AID's organizational structure. The commission's recommendations led Gilligan to modify the centralized agency format in favor of a more decentralized structure; the latter was seen as a more effective means of implementing New Directions legislation.[84]

Decentralization entailed increasing the number of people in the field, placing more authority in the hands of regional bureaus, and organizing smaller central bureaus. Inasmuch as New Directions was targeted at poor and small—mostly rural—projects, the Babb commission also recommended the formation of a Rural Support Bureau and a new Bureau for Private and Development Cooperation with responsibility for "encouraging increased participation of private and nongovernmental institutions."[85]

Because of the nature of the basic human needs mandate, US/AID shifted away from operational responsibilities to planning and financing projects that other groups implemented while US/AID monitored and evaluated. The arguments for this shift were based on the lack, in many recipient countries, of skilled middle-level managers who were capable of carrying out development projects. The BHN projects often were technical in nature and outside the expertise of US/AID staff members and country management. This change led to recipient countries and US/AID staff members working together to identify the contractors needed to carry out projects.[86]

The effect of this situation was that the administration and US/AID cooperated with special interest groups, particularly AID contractors and private voluntary organizations, and key members of Congress to pass legislation. This dependence on interest groups and Congress led to many restrictions on amendments to US/AID funding and shifts in regional focus and policy; more importantly, it reinforced congressional mistrust of US/AID and the administration's intentions.[87]

The third reorganization came in 1979 when William Bennett succeeded Gilligan as administrator. Bennett continued the decentralization policies of Gilligan but commenced the necessary procedures to move US/AID from the State Department to the International Development Cooperation Agency.[88] Bennett also is credited with strengthening the Office of Evaluation.

Toward the end of the Carter administration, there was more concern with the limitations of the BHN approach to development assistance. Critics argued that BHN was interpreted too narrowly and did not allow for the changing needs of recipient countries arising from the changing global economic environment and that the success of individual developmental efforts is as much a function of the overall set of economic policies that induce individual decisions as it is of the sound design of individual projects. Critics also were quick to point out that the slow-moving US/AID bureaucracy was ineffective in implementing the BHN mandate.[89]

The Reagan administration was strongly committed to moving away from the BHN orientation and streamlining the aid process. The ideological standard-bearer for US/AID and the administration was John Bolton, deputy for program and policy coordination. He moved rapidly to develop a set of new policy papers outlining rather specifically, sector by sector and program by program, the new US/AID approach to economic development. The policy papers, the blueprint for US/AID, codified systematically a broad range of decisions. They were designed to make a lasting impression on the US/AID decision-making apparatus and to institutionalize the change in direction proposed by the Reagan administration.[90]

Peter McPherson, US/AID administrator and, simultaneously, director of IDCA, was more sympathetic to the BHN objectives than was the administration. Although he coordinated the US/AID program with the programs of the State Department, he was willing to resist administration pressures and to blur the difference between development assistance and strategic concerns. He also was able to "hold the center" against pressures from proponents of the "social agenda" to cripple US/AID's contribution to, for example, family planning.[91]

McPherson had acquired development experience as a Peace Corps volunteer in Peru. Later, he became a lawyer and served on the White House legal staffs during the Nixon and Ford administrations. Before the 1980 election he was deputy to E. Pendleton James, personnel director for the White House; later, both men became members of the Reagan transition team.[92] McPherson believed that the enunciation of the four pillars of development assistance represented a major contribution by US/AID to development assistance thought.[93]

In efforts to increase agency efficiency, McPherson continued the decentralization measures begun by Bennett and strengthened the system of evaluation and information gathering. US/AID was given the authority to "deobligate" funds from projects that were "lagging" and to "reobligate" them to other projects. In addition, McPherson emphasized project implementation as opposed to the more bureaucracy-laden project design. He accomplished this emphasis largely by increasing reliance on nonproject-type assistance in which assistance was linked to policy reforms and structural adjustment.[94]

In keeping with the four pillars and the use of nonproject assistance, US/AID established the new Bureau for Private Enterprise. It was headed by Elise R. W. du Pont, a lawyer and wife of then-governor of Delaware, Pierre S. (Pete) du Pont. She had very little development experience. The bureau defined its policy as fostering "the growth of productive, self-sustaining income and job-producing private sectors in developing countries using the financial, technological and management expertise of the U.S. private sector, indigenous resources, multilateral institutions and agency resources where appropriate."[95]

The bureau retained historic US/AID priorities by focusing most of its efforts on agricultural projects. It was willing to "go one step further," however, to finance agribusiness projects as well as intermediate financial institutions, "such as private development funds and venture capital firms, that will operate in the developing world."[96]

By 1986, McPherson commented, "the concept of private-enterprise development . . . permeated our entire program," as in, for example, private sector delivery of health services. In Bangladesh, "contraceptives reached the people much faster through the private sector than they would have done through the government. The same is true with a variety of other health programs, such as the distribution of packets for oral-rehydration therapy."[97]

Other areas that were emphasized by the Bureau for Private Enterprise were privatization (through the AID-funded Center for Privatization) and financial market and institutional development, which provided credit for people and organizations previously unable to obtain credit. The bureau also worked through the International Executive Service Corps (IESC) to provide technical assistance to the private sectors of recipient countries. The US/AID participant training programs added an emphasis on private sector assistance, especially business management training.[98] Concurrently, US/AID placed increased emphasis on "transitional assistance"—assistance to reform economic and political institutions that were regarded as a hindrance to development.[99]

US/AID also gave increasing responsibility to the private voluntary organizations; they became more active participants in development and relief activities overseas and are associated with grassroots, people-to-people programs. In the policy paper on PVOs, the first objective listed is "to increase the economic development impact of PVO programs through increased program integration and focusing resources on field programs."[100]

A major preoccupation of the administration continued to be using US/AID programming effectively to achieve foreign policy objectives, but success was limited because McPherson was committed to maintaining the humanitarian and development objectives of the agency. The work of McPherson, along with some members of Congress and special interest groups, especially the humanitarian PVOs, enabled the agency to resist many of the more radical reforms on the Reagan agenda.

Despite attempts to create a more efficient and focused agency, US/AID was subjected to many diverse and often conflicting pressures by the administration, Congress, and special interest groups. AID experienced great difficulty in its attempts to balance the needs of the administration and Congress with those of developing countries.[101]

Congressional Sources

During the Carter administration, the major congressional initiative was the creation of the International Development Cooperation Agency; however, as noted earlier, it collapsed of its own political weight. Congress subjected the Carter assistance packages to many across-the-board spending cuts. Indeed, Carter often complained of being unable to administer his aid program effectively because of intense congressional oversight. When Carter took office he had pledged to double foreign aid by 1982, but he was balked by the rise of Soviet expansionism, the Iran affair, the Nicaraguan revolution, and the domestic economic crisis.[102]

What the Carter administration lacked in executive power, the Reagan administration made up for in popularity and the ability to push legislation through Congress. The major congressional role during the first Reagan administration was to influence policy via amendments and earmarks. The role is most evident in the dialogue between Congress and the executive over priorities. The administration dramatically increased resources channeled through the ESF, whereas Congress favored more economic-oriented programs but initiated no major foreign assistance strategies. Aid was funded under continuing resolutions rather than new authorization. According to Representative David R. Obey (D-Wis.), chairman of the Foreign Operations and Export Financing Subcommittee of the House Appropriations Committee, it was "the lack of support for aid and the lack of consensus on how foreign aid should be used [that] prevented Congress from passing a freestanding appropriations bill."[103]

Congress made some efforts to remedy its lack of input in foreign assistance and to take more initiative in legislation. In a major policy shift, the House and Senate, in 1981, agreed to a proposal by Clement Zablocki (D-Wis.), chairman of the House Foreign Affairs Committee, to make aid authorizations for two years. Zablocki argued that it would be beneficial not to have to debate and vote on politically unpopular foreign assistance programs every year, especially during election years.[104] The response of Congress to the Reagan administration's Private Enterprise Initiative was somewhat passive. The House Foreign Affairs Committee was primarily concerned with protecting the BHN mandate. In an interview, a staff member commented that "we more or less went along with it. We felt that the greater stake the administration had in the program, the more support there would be for the overall authorization."

Both the House and Senate Foreign Relations committees initiated major legislative provisions to maintain oversight of the foreign assistance programs. The Reagan administration, in turn, sought to bypass the congressional restrictions by the use of reprogramming and "emergency powers" (e.g., providing military assistance to El Salvador).[105] The Senate committee's response was to earmark the entire ESF account. Both the House and Senate committees also rejected the administration's efforts to limit congressional earmarks, and they voted to give themselves reprogramming veto power, power previously limited to appropriations committees.[106]

In 1983, an amendment (presented by Senator Paul Sarbanes [D-Md.], Senate Foreign Relations Committee) was enacted to shift funds from the Military Assistance Program (MAP) and ESF accounts into development aid programs; the United Nations Development Program was a direct beneficiary. Sarbanes said that it was "important for the committee to establish the proposition that we ought to be moving in this direction."[107]

Nevertheless, the first Reagan administration was able to increase the foreign assistance budget and to pursue its policy of a security-dominated assistance effort in spite of the fact that no new authorization legislation was passed between 1981 and 1985.[108] During the second administration, however, budget constraints and ensuing disagreements between Congress and the administration over foreign assistance priorities brought about major decreases in overall spending. The most serious funding cut resulted from the Balanced Budget and Emergency Deficit Control Act, written by Senators Phil Gramm (R-Tex.), Warren Rudman (R-N.H.), and Ernest Hollings (D-S.C.).[109]

The Gramm-Rudman-Hollings Act (G-R-H) proposed balancing the budget by 1993. It set annual ceilings on the budget deficit. In the event of a deficit exceeding the set limit, the act mandated automatic reductions—sequestration—in federal spending. According to Obey, the act has had a "major influence on congressional spending decisions."[110]

Obey became chairman of the Foreign Operations and Export Financing Subcommittee of the House Appropriations Committee in 1985. This committee, which controls foreign aid spending, had accumulated much power in the absence of congressional authorization bills by the Foreign Affairs Committee. An outspoken critic of the Reagan administration and its emphasis on security over development assistance, Obey believed that under Reagan the aid program was a "short-term put-out-the-fire program."[111]

Obey was critical not only of the administration's approach to assistance but also of G-R-H. When the bill passed despite his efforts, Obey made a commitment to its principles and tried to hold the administration to the budget limits. The administration, however, continued to ask for large increases in the foreign assistance budget as if G-R-H had never happened. A political battle ensued between Obey and the administration in which the foreign assistance budget was a pawn.

Larry Nowels referred to one interesting example as the "Manila Meltdown." Just months after passage of G-R-H, the administration requested a 15 percent increase in the FY1987 foreign assistance budget. Instead, Obey cut the budget by the required G-R-H guidelines. Secretary of State Schultz, who was in Manila at the time, returned as soon as he heard that his budget was slashed and began a massive campaign to generate public support for foreign assistance, but to no avail. Nowels pointed out that, had the administration's request been more reasonable, perhaps the budget would not have been decreased so dramatically.[112]

According to Nowels, Obey held foreign assistance hostage to lower defense spending and increase revenues (i.e., increased taxes). Carol Lancaster argued that Obey, probably the most influential person on the Hill in terms of foreign assistance, used his political acumen and ability to build coalitions to hold the administration's security efforts in check. He called for a broad-based approach to foreign assistance and more attention to international debt, environmental concerns, and basic human needs.[113]

Since the first year of G-R-H and the hotly contested foreign assistance funding debate, foreign assistance has been part of the overall Budget Summit arrangement, which sets ceilings for all categories of the U.S. government. The foreign assistance budget has been maintained at levels even higher than expected because of compromises reached with federal spending, taxes, and deficit reduction.[114]

The budget austerity measures extended to funds for U.N. agencies. The most important measure was the Kassebaum amendment (Section 143 of Public Law 99-93). It went into effect in fiscal year 1987 and restricts U.S. funding of U.N. organizations to under 20 percent of their annual budgets until these organizations "adopt voting rights on budgetary matters proportionate to the contributions of each member state."[115] Funds are also withheld from U.N. activities benefiting the Palestine Liberation Organization (PLO) or the South West Africa Peoples' Organization (SWAPO). The estimated total effect of these reductions is only around $1 million (see Chap. 12).[116]

Foreign assistance funding shortfalls, combined with congressional earmarks and oversight, greatly hinder the flexibility of the foreign assistance program.[117] Even when Congress brings bills to fruition, however, partisan differences and declining funds create difficulties. Earmarking and micromanagement are products of a policy that is not well defined in objectives or goals. In January 1988 the chairman of the House Committee on Foreign Affairs, Dante B. Fascell (D-Fla.) appointed a task force, headed by Representatives Lee Hamilton (D-Ind.) and Benjamin Gilman (R-N.Y.), to study foreign assistance and to provide direction for rewriting the act (Chap. 13). The purpose was to find workable solutions to the many problems complicating the foreign assistance legislation of the last decade. The task force concluded that "foreign assistance is vital to promoting U.S. foreign policy and domestic interests, but . . . the program is hamstrung by too many conflicting objectives, legislative conditions, earmarks, and bureaucratic red tape."[118]

External and Societal Sources

The rise of global interdependence increased the sensitivity of both the government and the public to changes in the international economic and political environment. The 1970s also witnessed the emergence of a new class of conservative intellectuals who had an important effect on assistance policy at the beginning of the first Reagan administration.

Changes in the external environment associated with the U.S. war in Vietnam were an important factor in the congressional initiatives that led to the New Directions legislation of the early and mid-1970s (Chap. 6). In the early 1980s these concerns were reinforced by an international debt crisis and the growth of conservative constituencies.

The economic forces that led to the debt crisis began in the early 1970s when the Oil and Petroleum Exporting Countries (OPEC) quadrupled oil prices. This rise, in conjunction with many other factors, culminated in Mexico's devaluating its currency in 1982 and the "official" commencement of the global debt crisis.[119] The debt crisis resulted in a sharp decline of private financial flows to developing countries. Doubtful credit worthiness and sound fiscal management revised the flow of private funds to debtor nations and severely hampered their prospects for growth.[120]

Because of the sharp decrease in private flows, the second Reagan administration abandoned some of its private sector rhetoric and supported public sector involvement in financial markets. Specifically, the Reagan administration (1) contained much of its hostility toward MDBs, (2) intervened in the management prerogatives of commercial banks on how much they should lend to developing countries, and (3) worked with Congress to increase the authority of regulatory agencies that oversee international banking.[121]

The global economic crisis pushed the United States into closer international economic cooperation, which foreign assistance translated into a new focus on structural adjustment and policy dialogue. This focus also played a role in warming United States–Soviet relations and led to the Soviet withdrawal from overtly expansionist policies and to the articulation of Glasnost and Perestroika.

Public Opinion

During the late 1980s several polls were conducted examining public perceptions of U.S. foreign assistance programs.[122] Americans in general believed that development issues and relations with less developed countries are less important than are domestic issues. A majority, however, supported U.S. assistance programs that focused directly on humanitarian concerns.[123] Another interesting finding is that public opinion and U.S. policy showed major differences in key areas; for example, in the area of economic assistance, the public showed a preference for development assistance. During the Reagan administration, however, the ESF account received the largest funding increases. In response to a question on whether the United States is a world leader that "should set an example for other wealthy nations by helping other poor nations," 78 percent agreed. Yet the United States ranked last among the members of the Organization for Economic Cooperation and Development [the Development Assistance Committee (DAC)]—the rich countries—in official development assistance as a percentage of GNP.[124]

In general, the several public opinion studies came to the same conclusion: that for most Americans domestic concerns should take precedence over international concerns. The studies also indicated the presence of great differences among the views of political leaders, the administration, and the public. Beginning in 1982, however, the respondents showed increased support for a more active role for the nation in world affairs.[125] Thus, it seems that public opinion supported the administration's rising concern with global economic cooperation at the outset of the international debt crisis. However, public opinion seems to have had little effect on the flow of financial assistance; in fact, "people-to-people, poverty-oriented aid was considered more effective by the public." The administration's focus, nevertheless, was on security and growth.[126]

The Community of Private Voluntary Organizations

The rise in public awareness and sentiment toward humanitarian assistance, coupled with the administration's emphasis on macroeconomic concerns, may have been at the heart of increased involvement of the PVOs. It can also be argued that the BHN initiatives of the 1970s created their own special interest groups; the emphasis on the rural poor strengthened the commitment of many church and service-oriented PVOs to support for Third World development (Chap. 9).

As AID sought a closer relation with the PVOs, the PVOs reciprocated with increased support of the development assistance effort. They formed networks that reached millions of Americans to inform them of the assistance effort. Leaders of PVOs testified before congressional committees, met with US/AID officials, and were able to mobilize widespread support. However, given the increased demands for charitable contributions, the roles of AID and the PVOs began moving closer and closer together.[127]

Many members of the PVO community see this movement as a threat to their autonomy. Bishop Broderick of Albany, then executive director of Catholic Relief Services, commented in 1983, "we do not want to look like the tool or fool of the United States Government." Some PVOs—notably OXFAM—refused government funding for the very reason that they do not want to be associated with the administration's policies.[128]

Larry Minear labeled the relation between US/AID and the PVOs as "politicized." He cited the increased amount of funding available to the PVOs and the ESF resources that were "provided within a more explicitly political context." Minear claimed that, even though PVOs were able to extend the reach of U.S. development assistance, because the United States had become "less guided by humanitarian imperatives, . . . the independence of PVO collaborators is at a greater risk."[129]

Interest Groups

Other interest groups playing a significant role in shaping the administration's assistance policy were the environmental groups, the agricultural interests, including BIFAD and the universities, and the ethnic lobbies, especially the American-Israel Public Affairs Committee.

Historically, universities have been heavily involved in agricultural research on behalf of developing countries, but their influence seems to have undergone a decline (Chap. 9). The Board for International Food and Agricultural Development (BIFAD) institutionalized the program, giving strong support to US/AID and a voice to the university system. The conservative voice of the administration tended to circumvent the role of universities in developing its approach to assistance.[130]

The Jewish lobby, particularly the American-Israel Public Affairs Committee, was very effective during the 1980s. Some attribute the strategic partnership of the United States and Israel to the effectiveness of AIPAC. It claims large, sustained levels of funding. Other ethnic interest groups have followed the AIPAC model in garnering support for foreign assistance (Chap. 10).

Environmental and agricultural groups were also effective in influencing assistance policy. Historically, agriculture lobbies worked to sustain the level of subsidies, to protect the United States's "competitive advantage" in agriculture, and to maintain food aid (Chap. 8).[131] Although some agricultural organizations prefer that the United States not engage in the transfer of agricultural technology and support, many agricultural groups have taken the position that accelerated growth in the developing countries—fostered through the transfer of technologies, training, and research—could pay off in terms of increased demand for U.S. agricultural commodities.[132]

Environmentalists have insisted that "poverty itself pollutes the environment. Those who are poor and hungry will often destroy their immediate environment in order to survive."[133] Such groups as the Natural Resources Defense Fund and the Sierra Club actively lobby Congress and publish material on environmental degradation and development. They also have successfully generated grassroots support.

Both environmental and agricultural groups have found that, by coordinating their efforts, they can generate support for development assistance programs that are environmentally sound, sustainable, and directed toward poverty alleviation and resource management. John W. Mellor referred to this goal as "breaking the cycle" of a cause-and-effect relation of poverty and environmental degradation.[134]

Intellectual Sources

The ideological perspective of the Reagan administration created a fertile environment for conservative critics of the foreign assistance program. In the view of the Right, economic assistance distorts the free operation of the market and impedes private-sector development. "Conservative thinking," wrote Gregg Easterbrook in the *Atlantic,* "has not only claimed the presidency; it has spread throughout our political and intellectual life and stands poised to become the dominant strain in American public policy." He cited the growing number of conservative think tanks and other "noteworthy" public policy groups.[135]

Several of the more conservative critics of foreign assistance in the Reagan administration were products of (or were destined for) the Heritage Foundation. In 1981, Edward Feulner, president of the foundation, argued that "aid is neither a necessary or a sufficient condition for economic development. Foreign assistance too often encourages wrong attitudes and wrong development. It tends to be from government to government: the most able, skilled individuals in Third World countries generally end up working for government instead of the private sector. It ends up reinforcing government as opposed to private structures."[136]

The Heritage Foundation was strongly opposed to the mainstream of "post World War II internationalism."[137] Feulner, who headed the US/AID transition team for the Reagan administration, believed that IDCA should be abolished, Food for Peace cut back substantially, and MDBs deemphasized. He supported the trade and development program, the Overseas Private Investment Corporation (OPIC), and the increased use of PVOs in the delivery of assistance.[138]

The most frequently quoted critics of foreign assistance were two English economists, Peter Bauer and Basil Yamey, associated with the Hoover Institute. They saw foreign aid as the source of the North-South conflict, not its solution.[139] They insist that "economic achievement has depended, and it still does depend, on people's own faculties, motivations, and ways of life, on their institutions and on their rulers. In short, economic achievement depends on the conduct of people, including governments. External donations have not been necessary for the development of any country anywhere."[140]

The Right also enthusiastically embraced the writings of the iconoclastic Peruvian writer, Hernando de Soto. De Soto advanced the idea that the problem in Third World countries is the state, not the informal economy or black market. Inefficient government bureaucracies stymie peasants' creativity and entrepreneurial genius, leaving the poor majority at the mercy of the established upper class minority.[141]

The Right has often been supported in its anti-aid view by the Left; both are antistatist. Where de Soto emphasized the peasant entrepreneur, the Left emphasizes the peasant community leader who organizes people to fight against the ruling class. In its purest sense, the Left holds that, in a donor-recipient relationship, "the interplay of power and economic interests prevents them [the recipient governments] from utilizing the aid provided in a manner conducive to poverty alleviation in their countries."[142] In this view the rich countries use poor countries only to further their own objectives.

Among the better-known critics on the Left were such writers as Frances Moore Lappé and Teresa Hayter and such organizations as the Development GAP.[143] The critics from the Left fall into two categories: the institutional pessimists and the structural theorists. Both concentrate on the interplay between economics and power and on how institutions impede the effectiveness of assistance; the structural theorists, however, are more global in their analysis.[144]

Critics from the Left generate support for their ideas through grassroots and community-based lobby groups. GAP is very influential in, for example, Bread for the World and Results, and Frances Moore Lappé is co-founder of the Institute for Food and Development Policy, a not-for-profit research and educational center that promotes food and justice issues around the world.

Riddell pointed in his study to the weakness in the theoretical structure of both right and left arguments and to the need for "retaking the middle ground." He argued for the middle ground, not on the basis that assistance is necessary or sufficient for development but on the basis that assistance is an effective tool in the development process.[145] Support for retaking the center was also advanced in studies by Mikesell, Krueger and Ruttan, Cassan, and others. Krueger and Ruttan argued that "official flows on commercial terms could hardly reduce world welfare." These arguments, however, are contingent on the need for institutional development and policy reform to sustain investment and productivity. Other proponents of the middle argue for a more balanced approach to development assistance.[146]

The critics from the Right were most successful at the beginning of the first Reagan administration. By the second Reagan administration, Congress was again taking a more active role in assistance policy. The ideologically driven administration policies in Central America, southern Africa, and the Middle East served to strengthen the force of the criticisms from the middle and left.[147]

In Conclusion

Some of the many influences that shaped U.S. foreign assistance debate during the late Carter and both Reagan administrations have been outlined in this chapter. Two distinct shifts in assistance policy were identified: (1) the move away from basic human needs and toward more security domination and (2) the move away from security toward a policy of greater economic cooperation.

The sources of influence have been both foreign and domestic. The shift away from BHN, for example, reflects the changing needs of developing countries and the failure of the BHN approach to successfully address many elements essential to the development process: the growth of economic capacity and the policy environment needed to assure economic growth. This shift was strengthened by the Cold War rhetoric of the Reagan administration and its determination to achieve closer linkages between economic and security objectives.

The shift toward global economic cooperation was motivated by the international debt crisis and the recognition of the need for increased economic interdependence. The domestic economy's slow growth and the burden of exceptionally high budget deficits resulted in Congress's increased reluctance to sustain foreign economic assistance. Both Congress and the development community were increasingly critical of a policy that allocated assistance resources primarily to meet short-term political and strategic objectives rather than long-term development needs.

During the 1980s, US/AID lost much of its capacity to influence the direction of the foreign assistance program because its initiatives were more administrative than substantive. By the early 1980s, intellectual leadership on development issues, particularly policy reform, had been assumed by the World Bank, and leadership in the resolution of the world debt crisis shifted to Treasury and the International Monetary Fund. The State Department became more active and more influential in the allocation of assistance resources and in determining the size of the economic support fund relative to the development assistance budget. US/AID was forced into a running battle with its domestic critics on the Right and into a rearguard battle to protect its budgetary discretion against contractors and clients.

The evolution of program assistance has been more a product of bureaucratic and congressional politics than of administrative initiatives. What is perhaps most surprising is that AID and the U.S. assistance program were not more badly damaged. The reason, in substantial measure, is the fact that the idealogues of the Right were unable to follow up on their initial successes in reordering agency policy with a new policy focus capable of capturing the imagination of Congress and the aid bureaucracy.

Part III

Bilateral Assistance

Chapter 8

The Politics of Food Aid Policy

Food aid has been one of the most popular and most controversial of U.S. assistance programs.[1] The feeding of hungry people appeals to the most fundamental humanitarian instincts of the American people. It represents a natural expression of generosity on the part of a nation blessed—or burdened—with surplus food production capacity. While appearing to do good for others, we also are doing good for ourselves—or at least for the producers and handlers of the surplus agricultural commodities.

In contrast to other foreign assistance programs, alternative legislative and administrative channels are involved in both the authorization and the administration of food aid programs. The Senate rules provide equal status to the Foreign Relations and the Agriculture, Nutrition, and Forestry committees in authorization. In practice, membership of the two committees has overlapped. In the House of Representatives, food aid legislation is considered by the House Agriculture Committee, the Foreign Affairs Committee, and the Select Committees on Hunger. Administration of food aid is even more complex. The Department of Agriculture (USDA) determines what commodities and quantities are available, the Treasury Department sets the terms of the loans, the Office of Management and Budget determines whether funding is available, the Department of State assesses the political ramifications, and the Agency for International Development implements the programs in the field. Interagency disagreements are worked out in the Food Aid Subcommittee of the Development Coordinating Committee (DCC).

The division of program responsibility has led to continuing tension among the several agencies and their patrons, clients, and constituencies in Congress, in the farm organizations, and in the development assistance interest groups. These tensions have been driven, since the beginning, by the need to dispose abroad the agricultural commodities generated by failure to resolve the contradictions in domestic farm policy. This division of responsibility, in both the legislative and the executive sector, has contributed to a lack of coherence among program objectives—surplus disposal, market development, humanitarian relief, and strategic and development assistance.

The evolution of the U.S. food aid program can most conveniently be discussed under four headings: (1) surplus disposal and market development, (2) food for peace, (3) food power, and (4) food aid for basic needs. In this chapter I review and interpret the events and forces that led to the initial design and subsequent modifications or reform of the U.S. food aid program.[2] Although I do not attempt to evaluate the substantive accomplishment of the U.S. food aid programs, the relationship between program effects and support for food assistance is discussed in the final section of the chapter.

The reader is urged to keep in mind that the motives of the donor in giving food aid, or any other form of aid, do not directly determine the benefits realized by the recipient. The best intentions of the donor for the recipient do not assure that aid will be used effectively, and aid given with little concern by the donor for the recipient's welfare may be used to great effect by the recipient.

Surplus Disposal and Market Development

The passage of the Trade Development and Assistance Act in the summer of 1954 (Public Law 480) committed the United States to a program of food assistance to poor countries. The passage of the act was precipitated by the collapse of agricultural commodity prices after the Korean war. It was preceded by a number of less comprehensive humanitarian assistance and surplus disposal activities.

The resort to an enlarged program of food aid reflected the continuing inconsistency between the economic views held by the dominant policy officials in the Eisenhower administration and the economic and political environment with which they were forced to come to terms. The Eisenhower administration was committed to a liberal international trading order based on trade expansion for the United States and "trade, not aid" for developing countries. Its commitment to a liberal international economic order was, however, confronted by a domestic agricultural policy that, in spite of deeper intervention in agricultural commodity markets, generated mounting surpluses of agricultural commodities. Congress and the administration, at cross purposes over how to resolve the contradictions of the agricultural commodity programs, turned to subsidized disposal of agricultural surpluses in the international market as a partial solution. The export subsidies took several forms—

direct cash subsidies, payment-in-kind subsidies, competitive bid sales, sales for foreign currencies, and direct grants justified by mutual security and humanitarian assistance criteria. The passage of the Trade Development and Assistance Act in 1954 and the evolution of food assistance policies and programs can only be understood in the context of the broader debate over farm and trade policy that occurred during the 1950s.[3]

Before PL 480

The PL 480 legislation was preceded by a long history of humanitarian assistance and surplus disposal; the provisions of the act incorporated both the objectives and the instruments used in these earlier programs. The United States provided emergency food aid for the relief of survivors of an earthquake in Venezuela in 1812 and to Ireland in response to the famine of the mid-1800s. During and immediately after World War I, food aid was provided to Western Europe and the USSR under a succession of agencies culminating in the American Relief Administration.[4] During the interwar period, the Export-Import Bank, established in 1934, had been used to promote American exports by providing loans, at concessional rates, to foreign governments and businesses for the purchase of commodities from the United States. The Agricultural Adjustment Act Amendment of 1935 (Section 32) authorized the use of up to 30 percent of yearly custom revenue by the secretary of agriculture to subsidize exports of agricultural commodities. The Surplus Property Act of 1944 and the Agricultural Act of 1949 authorized the Commodity Credit Corporation to sell stockpiled surplus commodities on the international market at below the market price. A 1949 amendment to its charter authorized the CCC to barter agricultural products for strategic materials to be added to the national stockpile. Surplus supplies were also made available for disaster relief under special legislation such as the Indian Emergency Food Act of 1951 and the Pakistan Relief Act of 1953; such measures included the sale of surplus agricultural commodities for local currencies. The Mutual Security Act of 1951 (PL 82-165) contained a new budget category, "defense-supporting assistance," under which food aid was programmed.

The American Relief Administration, which was set up after World War I to provide assistance to Western Europe and Russia, had utilized private voluntary agencies to distribute food and other supplies. Before and during World War II, the President's Committee on War Relief Activities and the President's War Relief Control Board acted to support and coordinate (and sometimes to limit) the efforts of private voluntary agencies. After World War II these two supervisory entities were replaced by the Advisory Committee on Voluntary Foreign Aid, whose function was to assure that activities of the private voluntary agencies receiving government assistance were consistent with official policy (Chap. 9). The agencies registered with the Advisory Committee played an expanded role in the implementation of the Marshall Plan (1949–51).

In 1948 the role of private voluntary organizations was further institutionalized when Congress passed legislation authorizing the government to pay transport costs for the delivery of voluntary relief supplies. The Agricultural Act of 1949 contained a provision (Section 416) authorizing the secretary of agriculture to donate surplus agricultural commodities in danger of spoilage to voluntary agencies registered with the Advisory Committee. This was the beginning of the channeling of large-scale surplus commodities through the PVOs for disposal. During the Korean War, however, the government curtailed food aid and reduced its cooperation with the PVOs. When farm prices collapsed after the Korean War, the stage had already been set for the development of a more comprehensive food assistance program. A political constituency for food aid, consisting of farm commodity groups, shippers and handlers, and private relief agencies, was already in place, and its members had considerable bureaucratic experience with program design and administration.

Packaging Food Aid

The main impediment to the passage of a larger and more comprehensive program was a presidential administration that had little sympathy for the commodity programs that had resulted in surplus accumulation as markets weakened. The economic philosophy of Secretary of Agriculture Ezra Taft Benson reflected his training as an agricultural economist, his service as an elder of the Church of Jesus Christ of Latter-day Saints (Mormons), and his role as a former secretary of the National Council of Farm Cooperatives. He "held conflicting ideals of individualist competition, cooperation, and humanitarianism . . . The desire to assist the farmer tempered the belief that the government must leave him the 'freedom to farm.' The humanitarian impulse to share America's agricultural technology with other nations contradicted the fear that increasing foreign production would decrease American exports. The conviction that the hungry must be fed confounded the conviction that it was morally preferable to sell rather than to donate."[5]

Even so, Secretary Benson and his colleagues in the Department of Agriculture, particularly Assistant Secretary Earl L. Butz and economic advisor Don Paarlberg, were more ready to use food aid to resolve the food surplus problem than were most members of the Eisenhower cabinet. Secretary of the Treasury George Humphrey had adopted a strong "trade, not aid" posture. Secretary of State John Foster Dulles viewed a larger aid program as a useful instrument of foreign policy, but he was troubled by the foreign relations implications of subsidized exports of agricultural commodities.[6]

During 1953 the administration initiated a series of studies designed to examine how the surplus disposal problems might be resolved. This effort included the creation of the Presidential Commission on Foreign Economic Policy (the Randall commission) and the subcabinet-level Interagency Committee on Agricultural Surplus Disposal (ICASD), chaired by Under-Secretary of Agriculture True D. Morse. Simultaneously, at Secretary Benson's urging, the major farm organizations—the Farm Bureau, the Grange, and the National Farmers Union—were holding local discussions with their memberships on the direction of farm policy. The Randall commission report urged elimination of "inflexible price-support programs which result in fixed prices, open or concealed export subsidies, import quotas at home and abroad, exchange restrictions, and state trading." In the meanwhile, Secretary Benson had outflanked the Randall commission by securing a commitment, in the president's 1954 agricultural message to Congress, to propose a set-aside of $2.5 billion in Commodity Credit Corporation stocks to be "insulated" from commercial markets and used for disaster relief, foreign aid, domestic school lunch programs, and stockpile reserves.[7]

The ICASD was experiencing a good deal of internal stress because of its attempts to resolve how food aid would be administered.

> Agriculture and the Foreign Operations Administration each believed it was the correct agency to administer the program, Agriculture because it held the commodities; and FOA because of its Mutual Security Administration experience; State wanted to regain its authority over foreign policy and to be in a position to safeguard established trade relations; Treasury hoped to ensure that at least part of the funds derived from sales were earmarked for the account of the United States, and the Office of Defense Mobilization was interested in using the commodities in its defense stockpile barter program.[8]

By March it seemed that the administration was losing control over the food aid agenda. Political pressure had been building in the agricultural community since 1952 for a program of sales for foreign currencies.[9] Congress was critical of the State Department's failure to make full use of the provisions of Section 550 of the 1953 Mutual Security Act, which authorized "not less than $100 million and not more than $350 million for the export and sale of surplus commodities to be paid for by foreign currencies." During 1953 numerous bills containing proposals relating to surplus disposal were introduced in both the Senate and the House. Senator Hubert H. Humphrey (D-Minn.) proposed a comprehensive program of food aid that included donations, sales at world market prices, sales at concessional prices, long-term loans, sales for local currencies, trade for strategic materials, and grants to voluntary agencies. At the urging of the Bureau of the Budget, the White House brought Charles Francis, chairman of General Foods, into the White House to serve as surplus disposal coordinator. The incredibly naive Francis assured the president that, if he was given a free hand to "get rid of surpluses," the burdensome stocks could be reduced in about 90 days.[10] Francis attempted to move aggressively to dump surpluses on the world market with little of Humphrey's sensibilities about trading with the Soviet bloc or Dulles's concerns about relations with our trading partners.

The threat that the House Agriculture Committee might draft its own legislation spurred the administration to paper over its internal differences. In May a draft bill was presented to Congress. A slightly revised bill was introduced in the House in early June. The congressional debate reflected considerable disagreement over two issues. One was whether the program was in the general interest or in only the interest of agriculture. The second issue was whether the costs of the program should appropriately be charged against the agricultural budgets or foreign aid budgets. Both issues are reflected in an exchange in which House Agriculture Committee Chairman Harold Cooley (D-N.C.) insisted that he did "not think that foreign aid should be saddled on the back of agriculture." Congressman Walter Judd (D-Minn.) responded that "neither should agricultural losses be saddled on the back of foreign aid."[11] This would not be the last time these two issues would be debated.

The Agricultural Trade and Development Assistance Act of 1954 (PL 480) was passed by both the House and the Senate in mid-June. When President Dwight D. Eisenhower signed the bill on July 10, he commented that the legislation would "lay the bases for a permanent expansion of our exports of agricultural products, with lasting benefits to ourselves and peoples of other lands."[12] The act had three titles: Title I authorized sales of surplus agricultural commodities for foreign currencies to "friendly" nations. Title II authorized government-to-government donations of food for famine and other urgent relief programs for both friendly nations and "friendly but needy populations without regard to the friendliness of their government." Title III provided authority for donation abroad through nonprofit voluntary agencies and the barter of surplus agricultural commodities for strategic materials. It also provided the donation of commodities to several domestic assistance programs, such as school lunch and disaster relief.[13]

Managing Food Aid

After a period of intense bureaucratic infighting among the Agriculture and State departments and the Foreign Operations Administration (FOA), an executive order was issued, on September 9, establishing the responsibility of the several agencies. The Department of Agriculture was given primary responsibility for the administration of Title I—the sale of surplus commodities for foreign currency. The Foreign Operations Administration was given responsibility for foreign famine and related relief programs. The State Department was given the responsibility for negotiating agreements with foreign countries. Budget and Treasury were responsible for allocation and management of foreign currencies. The Interagency Committee on Agricultural Surplus Disposal, now chaired by Charles Francis, would deal with policy issues. Actual program direction would be handled by an Interagency Staff Committee on Agricultural Surplus Disposal (ISC), to be composed of one representative from each agency on ICASD and chaired by William Lodwick of the USDA Foreign Agricultural Service.

Among the issues that remained unresolved by the enacting of PL 480 were what commodities would be programmed, what nations would receive the commodities, and how the foreign currencies accumulated under the program would be used. The departments of State, Treasury, and Budget preferred to restrict the eligible commodities to those already in surplus. Agriculture wanted to include not only those commodities currently held in CCC stocks but also other commodities judged to be in surplus supply. The Foreign Operations Administration preferred as broad a menu as possible to meet the diverse food needs of the recipient countries. The political reality that programming non-CCC commodities strengthened support for the program both at home and abroad assured that Agriculture's position would prevail.[14]

The issue of which nations would receive PL 480 commodities became the focus of the efforts by Treasury and State to limit the size of the program and of Agriculture and Congress to move increasingly large quantities of commodities. The pressure to move commodities dominated policy—even to the extent that some recipient countries were pressured into taking commodities that they did not want—tobacco for Greece and cotton for India—in order to obtain commodities that they could use. The concern by Agriculture that food aid not displace commercial sales and by State that it facilitate a more liberal international economic order gave way to pressure from Congress and its agricultural constituencies. "The major farm and commodity interests made it clear that as long as surpluses disappeared, they were largely uninterested in the political ends they served."[15]

The issue of how to use the foreign currencies obtained as payment for Title I sales emerged as an unexpectedly difficult problem. Proposals were made to finance agricultural development projects with the soft currencies. Many of the proposed uses ran into objection from the host country. Other projects were excessively cumbersome to administer. In the 1957 extension of the 1954 act, an amendment introduced by House Agriculture Committee Chairman Cooley authorized up to 25 percent of the proceeds from PL 480 Title I sales to be made available as loans to domestic and foreign enterprises for market development and facilities investments in recipient countries. (These came to be called *Cooley loans*). Soft currencies continued to accumulate to the point where concern was expressed that the United States had control over too much of the money supply in recipient countries.[16]

By the late 1950s the PL 480 program accounted for approximately one-third of U.S. grain exports and over one-fifth of foreign aid commitments. Yet it was apparent that the disposal programs were not going to resolve the problem of domestic agricultural surpluses. The short-run effect on export demand, whether by inducing changes in consumer preferences (from rice to wheat, for example) or by assisting American agribusiness to establish a foreign presence (livestock feed in Korea, for example), was relatively small. The stocks of agricultural commodities being accumulated by the Commodity Credit Corporation continued to grow. Bureaucratic battles over program objectives and size remained unresolved, and farm organizations and Congress were increasingly critical of what they perceived as excessive bureaucratic delays in program administration. It also seemed to the administration that Congress, prodded by Senator Humphrey, was prepared to extend the program on a long-term basis.

Food for Peace

Beginning in the late 1950s, a serious effort was made to move the PL 480 program from its limited surplus disposal and market development objectives and to make U.S. agricultural surpluses into a more effective instrument of foreign policy.[17] This transition was consistent with a trend away from the narrow security orientation that had dominated foreign assistance in the early and mid-1950s to a greater emphasis on development assistance. Both the late Eisenhower and the early Kennedy administrations attempted to transform narrow security concerns into support for development assistance by urging the view that a more prosperous and democratic world would also be a more secure world (Chap. 5).

New Clothes

The effort to reform food aid was set in motion when, in 1957, Senator Humphrey secured authorization from the chairman of the Senate Committee on Agriculture and Forestry, Allen J. Ellender, to initiate a study of PL 480 operations and policy. The study lasted more than a year and included 10 days of public hearings. The committee report, titled *Food and Fiber as a Force for Freedom,* was issued in February 1958. Its major criticisms of the existing program were that (*a*) it was administered as a surplus disposal program with little attention to humanitarian and foreign policy goals, (*b*) friendly countries often thought they were doing the United States a favor by taking surplus commodities, (*c*) the program was viewed as a temporary effort because of the annual authorization process, and (*d*) the machinery for administering the program was inadequate and the administrators uninterested.[18]

On 16 April 1959, Senator Humphrey introduced a bill (S. 1711), titled *International Food for Peace Act of 1959,* that was designed to reflect the results of his studies. The Humphrey bill called for a revision of PL 480 to emphasize its humanitarian aspects, including the establishment of a long-term credit sales program, grants of food for building reserves in developing countries, grants of local currencies to foundations to be used for social development in developing countries, and the initiation of administrative reforms. In retrospect, the Humphrey proposals shaped the future of the U.S. food aid program, but they were not warmly received by either the administration or Congress.

Somewhat similar reforms had been proposed in 1958 by former Assistant Secretary of Agriculture John H. Davis in a study commissioned by the State Department. Davis had urged a five-year "comprehensive food-fiber program, which might be called the *Food for Peace Program,* to be announced by the President and designed to utilize and adapt our agricultural productive capacity for the . . . advancement of peace in the free world." The Davis plan encountered numerous objections within the administration, particularly within the cabinet-level Council on Foreign Economic Policy (CFEP) and the ICASD. The CFEP chairman, Clarence R. Randall, was worried that Davis's plan would provide an excuse to postpone reforms in the domestic agricultural commodity programs. Perhaps the most damaging criticism, from the administration's perspective, was reflected in a comment by Secretary Benson; if the administration adopted the Food for Peace idea, he said, "it might be accused of embracing a proposal favored by Senator Humphrey."[19]

By late 1958, however, Benson was shifting his position. He managed again to outflank both Randall and the ICASD by arranging for President Eisenhower to announce, in his 29 January 1959 message to Congress on agricultural policy, that he was setting in motion steps to explore anew with other surplus-producing nations all practical means of utilizing the various agricultural surpluses in each country in the interest of reinforcing peace and the well-being of friendly peoples throughout the world—in short, using food for peace.[20] Benson's efforts were supported by the State Department and the International Cooperation Administration (ICA),[21] but Randall was so incensed that he had not been consulted in advance that he considered resigning.[22]

The Humphrey bill provided for an extension of Titles I and II for five years, long-term credits, grants of CCC stocks to establish food reserves abroad, and a White House post of Food for Peace administrator. Benson, again working around the objections of Randall and the Council on Foreign Economic Policy, arranged for the president's legislative office to forward to Congress on May 20 a bill providing for a three-year renewal of PL 480. When the CFEP met on June 4, it recognized the inevitable. After some minor modifications, the White House forwarded to the Hill a revised bill (introduced as S. 1748).

The reactions in Congress to the Humphrey proposals were not much more enthusiastic than those in the White House. Congressional support for PL 480 was split among those members of congress interested primarily in surplus disposal and those (led by Humphrey) hoping to transform the program into a major instrument of foreign policy. The first group was led by Senate Agriculture Committee Chairman Ellender and by House Agriculture and Forestry Committee Chairman Cooley. Cooley made his position abundantly clear when he responded to testimony by the State Department: "We are primarily interested in getting rid of these surpluses and we don't care how you do it and under what authority. We have told you we want the commodities sold for dollars first and then for foreign currencies, or then donate them."[23]

The Senate Agriculture Committee effectively killed Senator Humphrey's proposal by taking up the administration proposal. Anticipating a negative reaction from the committee, Humphrey arranged for hearings to be held by the Senate Foreign Relations Committee, of which he was also a member. The Foreign Relations Committee reported the bill (S. 1711) favorably to the Senate in early August. Humphrey then adopted a strategy of introducing his proposals a section at a time, both at the Agricultural Committee hearings and on the floor of the Senate.

The Food for Peace bill that was finally passed and sent to the president was the result of a long series of compromises both within the Senate Committee and between the Senate and House members of the conference committee. The new bill, the 1959 Agricultural Trade Development and Assistance Extension Act (PL 86-341), extended Titles I and II for two years—less than the three years recommended by the CFEP or the five proposed by Senator Humphrey. The provisions for a more aggressive barter program, the food reserve proposals, and the food for development grants were eliminated. Humphrey was successful in getting a new Title IV provision, which incorporated a large grant element in dollar sales (10-year supply contracts with dollar payments spread over 20 years). At the White House the job of Food for Peace coordinator was added to Don Paarlberg's other responsibilities. Humphrey succeeded in having the short title of the new bill changed to the Food for Peace Act of 1959.

What inferences can we draw from the efforts made between 1957 and 1959 to amend PL 480? There was growing acknowledgment, first at Agriculture and later at State, that food assistance could no longer be viewed as a short-term program that would be phased out as surpluses disappeared. As this view began to prevail, there was recognition that the program's image as little more than a surplus disposal activity should be repaired. With foreign assistance becoming increasingly subject to more careful congressional oversight, the State Department (and its ICA) began, at first grudgingly and later with more enthusiasm, to welcome its access to resources of food aid that were less subject to legislative restrictions.[24] There remained, however, a large gap in perception between, on the one hand, some members of Congress and the Department of Agriculture, who saw the Food for Peace label as a convenient public relations device to paper over the reality of surplus disposal, and, on the other hand, other members of Congress, and the ICA and the State Department, who were concerned that food aid make a genuine contribution to development.

New Directions

President John F. Kennedy entered office with a much more activist orientation toward the role of economic assistance in foreign policy and the role of food aid as an instrument of foreign policy. He appointed a committee of distinguished citizens, including Senator Humphrey and CARE President Murray D. Lincoln, to advise him on food aid. During the campaign, Kennedy had committed himself to greater aid efforts in both Latin America and South Asia. He was strongly committed to both enhancing aid and changing the objectives of food aid. The administration also embraced a determined "supply management" perspective in its approach to domestic farm policy and viewed the availability of food surpluses as an opportunity to relieve domestic poverty and malnutrition.

The first executive order signed by President Kennedy after his inauguration directed the secretary of agriculture to initiate a pilot food stamp plan and expand the school lunch program. His second executive order created the Office of Food for Peace. Former Congressman George S. McGovern (D-S.Dak.) was appointed director of the Food for Peace Program. In their study of the legislative history of PL 480, David McLellan and Donald Clare assert, in a burst of excessive enthusiasm, that the establishment of a Food for Peace agency attached to the White House in the early weeks of the Kennedy administration marked the formal transition of PL 480 from an instrument of farm policy into an instrument of foreign policy.[25]

Secretary of Agriculture Orville L. Freeman and his chief economic advisor Willard W. Cochrane were even more committed to reducing farm surpluses and to the humanitarian and developmental objectives of food aid than was the president.[26] In 1962 the administration, anticipating the reduction of surplus stocks, attempted to obtain authorization to purchase in the open market commodities that were not in the federal stockpile. Freeman urged that food aid policy be restructured and geared to meeting recipient needs rather than to surplus availability.[27] The administration's commitment was reinforced when, in cooperation with the United Nations Food and Agriculture Organization, it convened a world food congress to commemorate the twentieth anniversary of the founding of the FAO. The congress was designed to mobilize support from the public and voluntary agencies for the U.S. Food for Peace Program and the U.N. Freedom from Hunger Campaign. The Kennedy administration also moved to broaden the domestic constituency for its foreign assistance policy by engaging the private voluntary agencies in a more active dialogue over food aid policy and their role in the Food for Peace Program. When McGovern resigned his position as Food for Peace director to run for the Senate, he was replaced by the president of CARE, Richard Reuter.

One consequence of the changes in foreign assistance policy during the Kennedy administration was that leadership in food aid policy and administration was beginning to shift away from the Department of Agriculture—with State assuming greater responsibility for determining the direction and amount of food aid flows and Agriculture managing food aid financing and logistics.[28] It was not until the first year of Lyndon B. Johnson's presidency, however, that major changes were made in food aid legislation. As the Kennedy administration's agricultural policies began to achieve some initial success in slowing the growth of agricultural production, concern about commodity surpluses began to recede. The agricultural interests in Congress became increasingly critical of the shift toward institutionalizing the humanitarian, development assistance, and strategic uses of food aid.

In 1964 the Johnson administration, in the hope of obtaining a quick passage, asked only for a simple extension of the Food for Peace legislation, with relatively few amendments.[29] In retrospect, the administration seems to have been less than fully sensitive to the criticisms that were emerging in Congress. When the administration transmitted the proposed extension of PL 480 to the House Committee on Agriculture on 18 February 1964, it clearly did not anticipate the serious difficulties the proposal would face in both the House and the Senate. The criticism in the House focused on three issues. One was what was viewed as an excessively strong orientation toward foreign assistance and too large a role for the Agency for International Development in PL 480 programming and operations. A second object of criticism was food aid to the Soviet Union, to the centrally planned economies of Eastern Europe, and to countries considered to be within the Soviet sphere of influence, such as Egypt (Chap. 10).[30] The third concern, closely related to the first, was that excessive foreign currency sales were having the effect of depressing world prices for agricultural commodities. The House first voted to eliminate presidential authority to use soft currencies for economic development grants and then a day later reversed itself when Congressman John J. Rooney (D-N.Y.) reported that 90 percent of the soft currencies held by the United States in Vietnam were used to support the war effort.

Discussion on the Senate side was complicated by the fact that the chairman of the Senate Committee on Agriculture and Forestry showed many of the concerns expressed in the House. There was on the Senate side, however, strong support, particularly from Humphrey and McGovern, for giving even stronger weight to the humanitarian, developmental, and strategic objectives of food assistance. The debates on the floors of both the House and the Senate were emotional and acrimonious. Humphrey, sensing a shift in the political tide, played a less active role than he had in earlier PL 480 debates. The chairman of the Senate Foreign Relations Committee, William Fulbright, was so incensed about the use of food aid to support administration policy in Vietnam that he attempted to have the bill that emerged from the conference committee referred to his committee to consider its foreign policy implications.

The bill that emerged from Congress differed very substantially from the legislation proposed by the administration. Among the most significant changes were a requirement that PL 480 expenditures be classified under international affairs and finance rather than under agriculture in the president's budget, restrictions on Title I sales to Communist countries, and authorization of the use of Title I currencies in support of counterinsurgency programs.

The 1964 legislation was particularly important, not only in terms of the changes in the legislation, but also in terms of the relationship among interest groups, Congress, and the administration. The Farm Bureau and the Grange, both supportive of food aid in the 1950s, opposed the extension of food aid. Although the National Farmers Union and four commodity groups did support the program, the strongest support was from the private voluntary organizations. In the 1950s an aggressive Congress had been pressing a disposal program on a reluctant administration. The 1964 legislation clearly reflected a determination by Congress, particularly the House, to exercise greater congressional control and supervision of Public Law 480 operations.[31]

On 20 October 1965 President Lyndon B. Johnson transferred the Food for Peace office and Director Reuter from the White House to the State Department, where they were placed under the Agency for International Development.[32] This set in motion a period of bureaucratic infighting during which Secretary Freeman attempted to recapture greater control over Food for Peace. In December 1966 Reuter resigned for "personal reasons." The position of director was left vacant, and on 16 March 1967 President Johnson signed an executive order that confirmed the role of the State Department as the lead agency for Food for Peace. Reuter's departure reflected a tendency that had begun two years earlier to dampen the role of the private voluntary organizations in both food aid policy and administration. The allocation of Title III resources would, in the future, bear a closer relationship to foreign policy objectives.

Self-Help

In a 10 February 1966 message to Congress, President Johnson proposed additional changes as part of the legislation to extend PL 480. The proposal included changing the name of the program to "Food for Freedom" and adding several new features: "(1) to make self-help an integral part of the food aid program; (2) to eliminate the 'surplus' requirement for food aid; (3) to expand the magnitude of food aid shipments; and (4) to authorize the CCC to enrich nutritionally the food shipped under the program."[33] These proposals represented an attempt to obtain the authorization needed to strengthen the foreign economic assistance purposes of the program during a period of declining food surpluses. They also reflected President Johnson's intense concern with food shortages in South Asia. The self-help concept was particularly important to President Johnson and his advisors. It signaled an attempt to end earlier congressional constraints on assistance for expansion of agricultural production in recipient countries. It served, in particular, to legitimize the pressure that the Johnson administration was putting on India to increase its investments in agricultural research, in irrigation, and in the fertilizer industry and to liberalize its controls over investment and prices. In addition to the administration's bill, other proposals were introduced in both the House and the Senate. The House Agriculture Committee merged the several proposals into a single bill (H.R. 14-929), which was substantially amended by the Senate. After being twice considered by the conference committee, it was passed by both houses on October 21, with considerably less tension and recrimination than the extension of the 1964 act had caused.

The 1966 act was the most significant food aid legislation since the original PL 480 of 1954. It contained a number of provisions that were the culmination of almost a decade of effort to transform food aid from an instrument of surplus disposal to an instrument of development assistance.[34] The most significant change was the authorization to utilize commodities that were not in surplus. The act also limited Food for Peace shipments to commodities that recipient countries could not obtain with their own resources. Another major change made continuation of Food for Peace assistance conditional on the recipient nation's progress toward self-sufficient agricultural production. The president was also directed to conduct the program so as to assure a progressive transition from foreign currency sales to sales in dollars or other convertible currencies by the end of 1971. The authority of the secretary of agriculture to designate recipient countries was withdrawn. In addition, Title I combined the old Titles I and IV by allowing sales for both foreign currencies and dollars. The new Title II program included the foreign donation programs not previously authorized under Titles II and III. The new Title III provided for barter transactions, and the new Title IV contained the general provisions and definitions.

Multilateral Food Aid

In addition to legislative efforts, the Kennedy and Johnson administrations also undertook two major initiatives to institutionalize multilateral food assistance.[35] Interest in multilateral approaches to food aid had been building since the mid-1950s. An FAO consultative subcommittee on surplus disposal was formed in 1954 to attempt to deal with complaints by grain exporters in developed and developing countries that the United States was dumping surplus commodities on them under the cover of food aid. The subcommittee also attempted to formulate acceptable rules governing surplus disposal. In 1958, the FAO Committee on Commodity Policies conducted a staff study on multilateral uses of food surpluses.

There was little interest on the part of the United States in multilateral approaches until, in the 1960 presidential campaign, Richard M. Nixon urged that the United States support the creation of a multilateral surplus food aid mechanism. In spite of opposition by the Department of Agriculture, President Eisenhower proposed, in an address to the U.N. General Assembly on September 22, that the United Nations study the possibility of multilateral food assistance. The Nixon and Eisenhower initiatives were made in part to counter Kennedy's campaign proposals to strengthen the U.S. foreign assistance effort. In October 1960 the General Assembly authorized its Food and Agriculture Organization to initiate a study of possible multilateral arrangements for the mobilization of available foodstuffs and their distribution in areas of greatest need. FAO Director General B. R. Sen appointed an expert group, chaired by Hans W. Singer, to study the proposal.

Although the incoming Kennedy administration found it somewhat awkward to support the Nixon proposal, their embarrassment was lessened by the fact that neither the State nor the Agriculture Department had made any effort to "staff out" or translate the proposals into policy. At the April 1961 Rome meeting called to consider the findings of the FAO expert group that had been set up to study Eisenhower's proposal, the U.S. delegation, headed by Food for Peace Director McGovern, attempted to move the negotiations forward by proposing a multilateral fund of $100 million, with the United States to contribute 40 percent. This proposal had not been included in the terms of reference of the U.S. delegation but was cleared with the White House in a series of telephone conversations.

Later in 1961, the proposals were debated by the U.N. Economic and Social Council. In December 1961 the General Assembly approved a resolution authorizing a three-year experimental program. After further discussion by the Economic and Social Council and the FAO, policies and a structure of governance were agreed on. Pledging sessions were held in 1962, and the World Food Program (WFP) got under way in 1963 with initial pledges of $91 million out of an indicative target of $100 million for the three-year program.[36]

A second U.S. initiative was made during the Kennedy round of negotiations (1962–67) of the General Agreement on Tariffs and Trade. As the negotiations were being completed, Under-Secretary of Agriculture John A. Schnittker introduced, as the U.S. price for agreeing to a new international wheat agreement, a proposal for wider sharing of the burdens of food aid. As a result of these negotiations, the 1967 International Wheat Agreement included the Food Aid Convention (FAC), which committed the United States and 11 other developed exporting and importing countries (including the European Economic Community [EEC]) to an annual program of 4.5 million tons of wheat. The U.S. pledge of 1.9 million metric tons represented food aid that it would have provided in any case. The convention provided that the donor countries that did not export wheat could fulfill their commitments with another cereal grain or with the cash equivalent in wheat purchases from one of the exporters. This had the effect of removing grain from the international market at European expense, thus opening up the market for increased commercial sales by the United States. The Food Aid Convention was renewed in 1971, 1974, 1980, and 1986. In 1980 the minimal annual contribution was increased to approximately 7.8 million tons of wheat, with the U.S. commitment set at about 4.5 million tons.

Although the United States played an important role in the development of the multilateral food aid institutions, its commitment to them has always been somewhat conditional. The strength of the U.S. commitment has depended to a substantial degree on the extent to which the WFP and the Food Aid Convention could be viewed as extensions of the U.S. bilateral program. The U.S. interest in burden sharing stopped short of letting multilateral programs become large enough to interfere with the political leverage of the bilateral program. At that point, U.S. interest has tended to shift from burden sharing to the use of country-specific consortia of bilateral donors. The United States has, however, at times found it useful to channel food aid through the WFP when assisting refugee groups or providing emergency assistance to countries that were difficult to assist directly because of domestic political pressures. The United States has also used its leverage to weaken the role of the FAO in WFP policy making and to provide the WFP greater autonomy in program management.[37]

The success of the Kennedy administration in its effort to achieve multilateral burden sharing and to incorporate greater emphasis on self-help in meeting food needs must be read against the changes in the world food situation in the mid-1960s. Massive transfers of food grains were made to India in response to the food deficiencies that resulted from the South Asian droughts of 1965 and 1966. Concern over global food shortages was beginning to replace concern about the burden of food surpluses. Lower prices and rising incomes, combined with the closer links between production of and demand for commodities achieved by the Food and Agriculture Act of 1965, stimulated rapid growth of commercial exports. Growth of commercial exports combined with more effective supply control created confidence that the period of uncontrolled domestic food surpluses had ended. Secretary Freeman stressed that it was dangerous to the developing countries to continue to rely on U.S. food surpluses to meet food deficiencies.[38] From the mid-1960s until the end of the Johnson administration, the self-help provisions of the 1966 act were used as a short tether to encourage developing countries to devote a larger share of assistance and domestic resources to agricultural development.

Food Power

President Kennedy did not hesitate, during his campaign or his tenure as president, to draw attention to the threat of Soviet expansion in the Third World. During the 1950s food aid had been used in an attempt to weaken the dependence of Poland and Yugoslavia on the Soviet Union and to strengthen the governments of Korea and Taiwan. The Eisenhower and Kennedy administrations, when justifying the massive amounts of food aid to India beginning in the mid-1950s, had emphasized the strategic role of India and the importance of food aid as a guarantee of political stability. In retrospect it is clear that the Kennedy administration's positive attitude toward food aid was due more to the flexibility it gave the administration in pursuing foreign policy objectives than to its value as an instrument of humanitarian assistance and economic development. The use of food aid as an instrument for political and strategic leverage would be refined and intensified during the Johnson and Nixon administrations.[39]

An initial opportunity to use food aid to counter Soviet influence occurred when Algeria faced a major famine immediately after gaining independence, in the winter of 1962–63. The Kennedy administration responded rapidly with the largest infusion of food aid that had yet been given to any country. In 1962 the administration also attempted, with rather limited success, to use the Food for Peace Program to blunt Egyptian antagonism toward Israel. A troubled program of food assistance to Egypt continued during the Johnson administration until 1967. When Egypt went to war against Israel in June 1967, the flow of PL 480 grain stopped. It was not resumed until 1974, when Secretary of State Henry A. Kissinger saw an opportunity to again use food aid as a bargaining chip to advance his peace proposals (Chap. 10).[40]

The Short Tether

By the mid-1960s, the Johnson administration's "short tether" policy was rapidly evolving from an instrument for inducing greater agricultural development efforts into one for inducing closer adherence to U.S. political objectives.[41] During the 1965 Kashmir border conflict, President Johnson suspended financial assistance to India and Pakistan but did not stop the flow of food aid. He did order that food aid be placed on a month-to-month basis and that all program loans of over $5 million and project loans of over $40 million be submitted to him for personal review and approval. Johnson and Freeman used the short tether policy as an effective inducement to the government of India to reallocate both foreign and domestic resources toward the agricultural sector. The Indian minister of agriculture, Chidambaram Subramanian, welcomed the external pressure, since it provided him with the leverage he needed to convince his colleagues in the cabinet and Prime Minister Shastri to shift development resources to use in agriculture. During 1966 and 1967, relations between the United States and India, and between President Johnson and Prime Minister Indira Ghandi, worsened as Ghandi, attempting to blunt domestic criticism of excessive dependence on the United States, established closer relations with the USSR and criticized U.S. policy in Vietnam. The United States delayed and reduced food shipments—even during the tight food supply situation that prevailed in India in 1967. During this period Johnson was, in effect, his own Food for Peace officer.[42]

Security Assistance

Small amounts of food aid had been provided to South Vietnam since the mid-1950s. In the early 1960s both military and food assistance to Vietnam began to escalate. Public Law 480 shipments were used to evade the ceilings in the dollar amount of aid to Vietnam that had been agreed to in Geneva in 1954 (Chap. 10). By the mid 1960s something in the neighborhood of 80–90 percent of the soft currency generated by food aid was utilized to support the counterinsurgency effort. The 1964 extension of the Trade Development and Assistance Act, as noted above, contained an explicit provision to permit the use of Title I currencies to support counterinsurgency efforts. Under the "common defense" interpretations of Title I, proceeds from the sale of the commodities by the Vietnamese (and Cambodian) governments "could be used *as foreign exchange* to purchase war material. For a number of years this new food for war strategy went virtually unnoticed—or at least, unchallenged—by Congress and by the citizen antiwar movement."[43] The only significant change in the 1968 act to extend the PL 480 program was a provision that 5 percent of Title I local currencies be made available for voluntary population control programs. Such programs became one of the self-help programs to be considered in Title I programming.

Although President Nixon had promised, during the 1968 election campaign, that he had a "secret plan" to end U.S. involvement in the war in Vietnam, he was not able to conclude negotiations before the 1972 election. Under Nixon, a shell game designed to evade congressional oversight replaced Johnson's short tether. As Congress began to impose more severe restrictions on aid to Vietnam, the administration's attraction to food aid was enhanced. Congress had no direct means of controlling either the choice of recipients or the specific value of food aid for any given country. If Congress chose to cut back the dollar levels budgeted for PL 480, the dollar resources under the control of the Commodity Credit Corporation were large enough that the effect on flexibility of presidential action would not be felt for some time.[44]

The situation remained unchanged in the extensions of the PL 480 program in the Agricultural Act of 1970 and in the Agricultural and Consumer Protection Act of 1973. However, a provision inserted in the Foreign Assistance Act of 1973 prohibited the use of foreign currency funds for common defense and internal security unless Congress explicitly authorized such use.[45]

Although this provision was a clear reflection of congressional intent, it had little practical significance, since the proceeds from sales of PL 480 commodities are fungible. In the Foreign Assistance Act of 1974, a more meaningful restraint was added, limiting to not more than 30 percent the U.S. concessional food assistance that could be allocated to countries not appearing on the U.N. "most seriously affected" list. The Nixon administration attempted to evade this provision by increasing the total level of funds budgeted for PL 480 for 1975.

During the late 1960s, relations had steadily worsened between the Johnson administration and the private voluntary organizations involved in the distribution of humanitarian assistance under (new) Title II. The resignation of Food for Peace Coordinator Reuter reflected his concern that, as the strategic uses of food assistance expanded, the voluntary agencies were being arbitrarily excluded from the dialogue on food policy that they had enjoyed during the Kennedy administration. At the same time, the PVOs were being pressured by the administration to expand their activities in Vietnam. The relationship deteriorated further during the first Nixon administration (1969–73). The volume of PL 480 grain available for distribution declined by almost half between 1969 and 1973, and an increasing share of both Title I and Title II shipments were directed toward Vietnam. While cooperating with the government, the PVOs voiced their dissatisfaction with the increasing politicization of their programs. In spite of their reservations, they allowed themselves to be used because they were dependent on government money and supplies; most were willing to do whatever was necessary—including distributing food in situations that were at best questionable and at worst harmful to recipients.[46]

Declining Surpluses

During the 1950s and well into the 1960s, there was little difficulty in simultaneously pursuing the surplus disposal, development assistance, humanitarian assistance, and foreign policy objectives of food aid. The existence of the surpluses obviated the need to make difficult choices. As the burden of surplus commodities began to decline, the weight that had been placed on the disposal objectives could be shifted without serious offense to the agricultural constituency.

Then the situation began to reverse. By the beginning of the first Nixon administration, surpluses had been substantially reduced. The Johnson administration's aggressive reduction of food and feed grain acreage at home, an active food aid program in South and Southeast Asia, and steady growth of commercial sales during the 1960s had sharply reduced domestic food stocks. Beginning in 1966 food aid came under increasing criticism from the same congressional, commercial agriculture, and agribusiness constituencies that had welcomed it in the 1950s.

In the early 1970s a series of events severely tested the commitment of the United States to the economic development and humanitarian objectives of Food for Peace.[47] The U.S. dollar had become increasingly overvalued. The overvalued exchange rates had contributed to the dampening of external demand for U.S. commodity exports since at least the mid-1950s. It was in effect a tax on exports and a subsidy to imports, which resulted in a widening deficit in the U.S. balance of payments.[48] The Nixon administration devalued the dollar in 1971 and then let it "float" in 1973. In 1972 there was a sharp decline in world wheat production, due largely to poor harvests in the Soviet Union and a drought-induced decline in wheat and rice production in South Asia. The Organization of Petroleum Exporting Countries quadrupled the price of petroleum in late 1973 and early 1974. The combination of rising agricultural, fuel, and other commodity prices triggered a worldwide concern about impending resource scarcities and precipitated a period of great instability in U.S. food policy.

One effect of the devaluation of the U.S. dollar and the decline in food grain production was stimulation of the commercial demand for U.S. agricultural commodities. The USSR entered the world market on a massive scale in the winter of 1972–73, and the influence of this event on commodity stocks and prices was dramatic. The price of wheat more than doubled between the end of 1972 and 1973. The carryover of U.S. stocks of wheat, which stood at 209 million bushels at the end of 1972 (down from over one billion bushels a decade earlier), fell to less than 20 million bushels by the end of 1973. Land diverted from wheat production dropped from the all-time high of 20.1 million acres in 1972 to 7.2 million acres in 1973.[49]

The response of Nixon administration officials to these events has been characterized as inept. "In the summer of 1972 the Nixon administration pursued food policies that seemed almost calculated to fuel the price inflation that followed. Massive wheat sales were encouraged both through direct intergovernmental negotiations and through export subsidies. And even after the magnitude of the Russian purchases were known, the administration persevered with a wheat program aimed at reducing production in 1973, a program developed before it was known that Russia would buy one-fourth of the 1972 crop."[50] The effect was to stabilize the Russian food economy and destabilize the U.S. and world grain and livestock economies.

Within a matter of months, food aid had become severely competitive with commercial sales—at a time of intensive concern about the U.S. balance of payments. Thus, "at the very time when the global demand for U.S. food aid had reached its highest point since the Second World War, a combination of Butz-dominated farm policy and Kissinger-dominated foreign policy resulted in both a substantial reduction in the size of the overall food assistance program and a growing tendency to allocate such supplies as were available on the basis of immediate U.S. political interests."[51] A freeze on U.S. food aid shipments in the spring and summer of 1974 contributed to a decline from 7.3 to 3.3 million metric tons between 1973 and 1974 (down from approximately 10 million metric tons in the early 1970s and the over 15 million metric tons shipped annually in the early 1960s). From 1957 through 1971 India had received the largest food aid grant. By fiscal 1973 South Vietnam, Cambodia, and South Korea accounted for 67 percent of Title I food aid. This percentage rose to over 70 in fiscal 1974. During the height of the 1974 famine, when world food grain prices were at an all-time peak, Bangladesh was forced to cut back on commercial imports because of foreign exchange constraints. At the same time, U.S. food aid to Bangladesh was delayed, under PL 480 prohibitions against "trading with the enemy," in an attempt to force Bangladesh to discontinue its exports of jute bags to Cuba.[52]

While Kissinger, in his role as national security advisor, was attempting to direct the flow of Food for Peace commodities to support the administration's strategic objectives, Secretary Butz was somewhat belatedly attempting to respond to the opportunities for commercial sales of food and feed grains by dismantling the constraints on agricultural production and reducing food aid. Under the Agriculture and Consumer Protection Act of 1973, intervention to influence commodity price levels was authorized only when prices fell below target levels. Butz sent the annual USDA budget request to the Office of Management and Budget with a zero figure for PL 480. Butz took the position that, with commercial agricultural exports at an all-time high, he no longer needed the food aid outlet, saying, "If Henry needs it, let the money come out of his budget!"[53]

By this time the coalition of Cold War liberals in Congress was disintegrating. As noted earlier, the Foreign Assistance Act of 1973 prohibited the use of foreign currency funds for common defense and internal security as of 1 July 1974. The 1973 act also contained what came to be known as the basic human needs mandate. It directed the president to focus U.S. assistance efforts on the functional categories of food production, rural development, health and nutrition, population planning, and human resource development (Chap. 6). This orientation was reinforced in the Foreign Assistance Act of 1974, which directed that in fiscal 1975 not more than 30 percent of concessional food aid could be allocated to countries other than those designated by the United Nations as "most seriously affected" by food shortages, unless the president certified that the use of such food assistance was solely for humanitarian purposes.

The World Food Conference

The tensions that had been building between the agriculture and state departments, between the administration and Congress, and between the government and the food assistance constituencies were exacerbated at the 1974 World Food Conference. In his first major address after becoming secretary of state, Kissinger proposed before the U.N. General Assembly on 23 September 1973 that a world food conference be convened in 1974 under U.N. auspices, to coordinate global action on the food needs of the developing countries (Chap. 6).[54] At the same time that plans for a world food conference were going forward, Kissinger was engaged in shuttle diplomacy aimed at ending the October 1973 war between Egypt and Israel. As a sweetener to the negotiations, he made commitments that substantial increases in food aid would become available on their successful completion. These commitments were particularly compelling because grain was bringing a high price in the commercial markets during the 1973–75 food shortage. The negotiations were completed during the World Food Conference.[55]

In the summer of 1974, the United States suffered a major drought, which resulted in a further decline of grain production and stocks.

> By the time of the opening of the World Food Conference, the United States was caught in an awkward conflict among four competing factors: (1) the absolute supply of grain available for export either in trade or aid was limited by the reduced size of the U.S. crop and depleted government-owned reserves; (2) a World Hunger Action Coalition, composed of church groups, voluntary agencies, and congressional leaders, had coalesced around the American Freedom from Hunger Foundation demanding that the United States increase its food aid contributions; (3) the poor world harvests had placed a tremendous demand on U.S. wheat and soybean crops and forced the temporary and controversial imposition of export controls on soybeans in 1973, causing growers and exporters alike to exert heavy pressure on the Administration to avoid at all costs any further restrictions on free market trade; and (4) inflation had continued to increase in the United States causing consumers to be vocal in their demands that the Administration hold the line on further food price increases.[56]

These circumstances intensified the conflicts between domestic and foreign policy considerations in food policy. Failure to resolve these conflicts resulted in considerable tension among members of the U.S. delegation at the World Food Conference. Butz was designated chairman of the U.S. delegation, but Kissinger was scheduled to deliver the keynote address. The Kissinger speech was prepared in the State Department, with no input from the Department of Agriculture, and was cleared directly with the president. In spite of opposition by a coalition of the OMB, the Council of Economic

Advisers, the Council for International Economic Policy, and Treasury, Kissinger had succeeded, on the basis of expectations that commodity prices would decline, to obtain a commitment from President Ford in the spring of 1974 that the United States would maintain its financial commitments and increase the volume of food aid shipments. Commitments of food aid to Egypt, Syria, and Jordan were an important component of Kissinger's Middle East peace strategy. By midsummer, during the worst drought since the 1930s, commodity supplies were down and prices were sharply up. The spring commitment was reversed. Dollar commitments would be retained, but the volume of food aid shipments would be reduced. As a result, Kissinger was unable, in his address to the conference, to go beyond acknowledging that "an expanded flow of food aid will clearly be necessary," without making an explicit U.S. commitment.[57]

At the conference itself delegates from developing countries took turns blistering the U.S. government and the Soviet Union for "rationing" the world's food supply. The U.S. delegation, including members of the World Hunger Action Coalition and the Inter-religious Task Force on U.S. Food Policy and Senators Richard Clark (D-Iowa) and Humphrey, pressured Secretary Butz to cable the president to approve a minimum volume increase in food aid of one million tons for 1975. Bolstered by his budget and treasury officials, Ford again refused. Of the disorganization of the U.S. delegation, conference Secretary-General Sayed A. Marei, speaker of the Egyptian parliament, commented, in a classic diplomatic understatement, "I must say the Americans did their part to make the world aware of food problems."[58]

Events soon overtook both ideology and policy. During the winter of 1974–75, grain prices began to decline. In February 1975 Secretary Butz was able to announce a fiscal 1975 U.S. food aid budget of $1.6 billion—the largest (in current dollar terms) since the late 1960s. Although both Butz and Kissinger continued to refer, somewhat loosely, to the use of "food power," more sober considerations suggested that the longer-term political costs of such a policy, both at home and abroad, would outweigh any short-term benefits. American agricultural interests, in particular, were vociferous in their objections to any actions based on strategic and political considerations that would interfere with commercial sales.[59]

The major outcomes of the World Food Conference were a commitment to an annual food aid target of 10 million tons, the establishment of the Committee on Food Aid Policies and Programs to develop guidelines for bilateral food aid within the World Food Program, the organization of the U.N. World Food Council, and the creation of the International Fund for Agricultural Development.[60]

The World Food Council was conceived as an institution that would function as a political forum in which global food issues, including food aid, could be resolved and action implemented and coordinated. It was established over the active opposition of the FAO leadership and was, in effect, a vote of no confidence in the FAO and its secretary general, A. H. Boerma.[61] The council has clearly not lived up to the expectations held by its sponsors. The issues that it was intended to address became less immediate as the world food crises of the early and mid-1970s receded, and it has been subject to continuing guerrilla warfare from the FAO secretary general's office. The stature of its leadership has declined. The World Food Council has been unable to command either the political or the bureaucratic resources necessary to fulfill its mandate—to inform and coordinate international efforts to alleviate world hunger.

The organization of the IFAD as a specialized agency of the United Nations in December 1977, after three years of painful negotiations, represented a successful effort by the countries of the Organization for Economic Cooperation and Development to tap the resources of the Organization of Petroleum Exporting Countries (OPEC). The United States, which took the position "we give through the AID and the World Bank," was coerced into participation. In 1977 an agreement was reached under which, over a three-year period (1978–80), OECD members would pledge $566 million, OPEC members $435 million, and several less developed countries $16 million in voluntary contributions. The IFAD rapidly established a reputation for operational efficiency. Its projects, largely co-financed with the multilateral banks and the FAO, were selected with a strong emphasis on relief of rural poverty. In spite of the generally high regard in which its efforts were held, the IFAD experienced increasing difficulty replenishing its funds. The decline of world petroleum prices reduced OPEC enthusiasm for the projects. The Reagan administration was hostile to multinational initiatives. The IFAD has continued to function, at somewhat lower levels of funding, largely because of the enthusiastic support of other OECD countries and an increasingly favorable reputation in the U.S. Congress.[62]

Redesigning Food Aid

The same public and congressional pressure that led to the U.S. withdrawal from Vietnam also led to both popular and congressional pressure for reform of U.S. assistance policy. There was strong criticism of assistance for large infrastructure and industrial development projects—condemned as a "trickle down" policy—and support for programs of direct poverty alleviation. The Foreign Assistance Act of 1973 directed that the development assistance component of the AID program place greater emphasis on meeting the basic needs of the poorest people in the poorest countries (Chap. 6). The 1974 act directed that during 1974 at least 70 percent of Title I concessional sales be allocated to those countries most seriously affected by the current economic crisis. In his 1976 campaign and in his inaugural address, President Jimmy Carter stressed the assurance of human rights as a major foreign policy objective.

The congressional perspective was not shared by the Nixon and Ford administrations. As noted above, Secretaries Butz and Kissinger were involved in aggressive interagency rivalry over the objectives, the size, and the budgeting of food aid. With Congress continually escalating its micromanagement of the security-supporting component of the AID budget, Kissinger, in line with his policy that nations that voted against the United States in the United Nations could expect to experience cutbacks in American aid, continued to seek ways of using food power as a policy instrument. Aid to Tanzania and Guyana was suspended in 1976 because of their votes against U.S. policy toward Israel and Korea.

A sense that the Food for Peace Program was being abused—being devoted to ends that were not appropriate—led Congress to press for program reform. To obtain greater leverage, Senator Humphrey directed the staff of the Committee on Agriculture and Forestry to initiate a comprehensive review of the Food for Peace Program. The review involved extensive field inspections, consultation with experts, and committee hearings. In May 1975 Humphrey introduced a bill (S. 1654) that provided for a comprehensive restructuring of PL 480.

Food Aid for Basic Needs

This time Humphrey was more successful in his legislative efforts than he had been in the mid- and late 1950s. Some of the proposals contained in S. 1654, as well as several other reforms designed to direct a higher proportion of food aid to the poorest countries, were included in the International Development and Food Assistance Act of 1975 (PL 94-161):[63]

—A minimum requirement of 1.3 million tons of commodities distributed through Title II donations was established. Of this, 1.0 million tons were reserved for distribution through the World Food Program and voluntary agencies.

—It was provided that not more than 25 percent of Title I aid could be allocated to countries having a per capita income of more than $300.

—Authorization was given for the president to waive repayment of up to 15 percent of annual Title I concessional credit loans in cases where the recipient agreed to use the funds generated for population control or food self-sufficiency programs.

—The president was directed to seek an international agreement, subject to congressional approval, for an international system of nationally held food grain reserves.

—The President was urged to maintain a significant U.S. contribution toward the annual 10-million-ton food aid target established by the World Food Conference.

The 1977 International Development and Food Assistance Act (PL 95-88) strengthened the provisions of the 1975 act, added a requirement that Title I food aid be denied to any country that engaged in gross violation of human rights (unless such aid would directly benefit needy people), increased the minimum tonnage of commodities available to the World Food Program and the voluntary agencies, and extended the act for four years. A provision was added that food aid should not be authorized until it was determined that it would not act as a disincentive to local production (the Bellman amendment). The 1977 act also amended the Food for Peace Program by adding a new Title III labeled the "Food for Development Program." The objective of the new title was to encourage food-deficient countries to undertake development projects and policy reforms that would stimulate agricultural production. The "debts-to-grants" conversion mechanism provided to achieve this objective consisted of multiyear agreements in which a "relatively least-developed" country could receive forgiveness of debts incurred under PL 480 if it implemented the reforms specified in the Title III agreement.[64]

The 1977 act also required the secretary of agriculture to appoint a task force to review and report on the administration of Food for Peace. The House and the Senate also passed resolutions (H. Res. 784 and S. Res. 271) calling on the president to establish a commission to study how the United States should deal with domestic and international hunger and malnutrition. The USDA study provided an excellent review of the history of U.S. food aid policy and administration. The report of the Presidential Commission on World Hunger, chaired by Ambassador Sol M. Linowitz and directed by Daniel E. Shaughnessy, included a comprehensive analysis of hunger both at home and abroad and of the U.S. efforts to combat it.[65] The reports, coming in the last years of the Carter administration, had no significant effect on the U.S. food assistance program. They were more a reflection of the poverty-oriented basic needs perspective of the previous decade than a guide to the future. During the last two years of the Carter administration, foreign policy moved toward a stronger security orientation—a direction that would be reinforced during the first Reagan administration (Chap. 7).

The Return to Surplus Disposal

During the 1970s, American farmers rapidly expanded their productive capacity, encouraged by favorable prices and the expectation that the world would need and would be able to pay for the commodities that could be made available from North America. The developing countries had become the major source of growth in demand for American agricultural commodities. In the early 1980s, however, a combination of debt crisis in the developing world and a heavily overvalued American dollar resulted in a sharp decline in agricultural exports from the United States.[66]

The restrictions that Congress had placed on the share of PL 480 Title I commodities that could be shipped to middle-income and centrally planned economies had begun to reduce the number of countries eligible to receive food aid. As resources declined, allocations were limited primarily to lower-income countries that had the institutional support of AID missions. By the late 1970s, the supporters of export enhancement and surplus disposal programs were finding other disposal alternatives more attractive than PL 480. The PL 480 Title I and Title II programs had been supplemented by AID grants and loans for the purchase of agricultural commodities. These loans, primarily to countries such as Israel, Egypt, and Sudan, were rationalized in terms of mutual security interests.[67]

The Agriculture and Food Act of 1981 (PL 97-98) was developed before the implications of the changes in agricultural commodity prices and exports of the early and mid-1980s were fully anticipated. The price support provisions of the bill reflected continued optimism about the future fueled by the food shortages and inflationary prices of the 1970s. The high price targets established in the act encouraged the production of surpluses, left the United States as a residual supplier in world markets, and contributed to subsequent accumulation of surpluses. The Food for Peace provisions of the act were extended through 1985 with very few amendments. The 1980 act did authorize use of PL 480 commodities to support health and literacy programs for the rural poor. The Foreign Assistance Act of 1981 (PL 97-113) reduced the minimum Title II volume requirements for commodities allocated to PVOs and the World Food Program.[68]

As exports declined and surpluses mounted in the early 1980s in response to the overvaluation of the dollar and a worldwide recession induced by U.S. monetary policy, the agricultural constituencies responded by again putting pressure on Congress to develop other export enhancement programs that would offset the export-depressing effects of the declining demand for U.S. commodities in world markets. The agricultural constituencies also became increasingly critical of efforts by the U.S. bilateral assistance program and by the multilateral assistance agencies to stimulate agricultural production in developing countries that might compete with U.S. agricultural exports. The Bumpers amendment to the Foreign Assistance Act of 1986 instructed the US/AID to avoid supporting agricultural development that would expand competition with U.S. agricultural exports.[69]

These pressures resulted in the most significant changes in food aid policy since the Food for Peace Act of 1966.[70] In the 1985 farm bill (euphemistically titled the Food Security Act of 1985), Title I was amended to again permit sales of commodities for nonconvertible foreign currencies.[71] The local currencies were to be used to promote private sector agribusiness, particularly credit, input, and marketing organizations, in the recipient country (Sections 106 and 108).[72] At the initiative of the White House, a new provision—"Food for Progress" (Section 1110)—was added, which provided for grants of either PL 480 or Section 416 commodities to countries that had made commitments to introduce or expand free enterprise–oriented policy reforms in their agricultural economies through changes in commodity pricing, marketing, input availability, distribution, and private sector involvement. The minimum tonnage to be programmed under Title II was raised to 1.9 million, with the requirement that at least 1.425 million tons be programmed through PVOs, cooperatives, and the World Food Program. The 1985 act also authorized both private voluntary organizations and cooperatives to monetize (i.e., sell or barter) not less than 5 percent of donated commodities in recipient countries. The foreign currency acquired by the PVO or cooperative would be used to carry out food distribution activities or development projects. In authorizing monetization, Congress was apparently seeking ways to enable the PVOs to serve as more effective channels for the disposal of surplus commodities. Critics view monetization as a further step toward complete dependency, or even corruption, of the PVOs resulting from government patronage. Shippers and suppliers succeeded, over the objections of the agricultural interests, in obtaining a requirement that 75 percent of nonemergency minimum tonnage be bagged, processed, or fortified commodities and that the portion of food aid shipped on U.S. vessels (cargo preference) be raised from 50 to 75 percent.

Other export enhancement programs were also included in the 1985 act. In 1982, under pressure from the dairy industry to expand surplus disposal, Congress had resurrected Section 416 of the Agricultural Act of 1949 and authorized the USDA to make available for donation to foreign countries dairy products acquired by the CCC through price support operations. This reopened a door to CCC that had been closed since Congress had tightened control of food aid during the Vietnam War. The Food Security Act of 1985 extended the program to include grains and oilseeds and directed that, although the Section 416 program should be managed as part of Title II of the

PL 480 program, its costs should be charged to the CCC rather than PL 480 and not considered as part of the international affairs budget (the 150 account). By 1988 more than 40 countries were receiving food aid under the Section 416 program.

The 1985 act also included several forms of nonconcessional export assistance: the Export Enhancement Program (EEP), the Targeted Export Assistance Program (TEA), and short-term (GSM-102) and intermediate-term (GSM-103) credit guarantee programs from the Commodity Credit Corporation.[73] Under the EEP the Department of Agriculture makes government-owned commodities available to U.S. exporters. Combining commodities obtained from the government with commercially purchased commodities enables U.S. exporters to offer lower prices to buyers in countries that are being offered commodities at subsidized prices by other exporting countries. The EEP has been used extensively to counter heavily subsidized wheat exports from the European Economic Community. It has been targeted largely toward North Africa, the Middle East, and the centrally planned economies. Under the TEA, the USDA uses surplus stocks from the Commodity Credit Corporation to provide partial reimbursement for export promotion activities undertaken to offset the adverse effects of "unfair" trade practices by exporters from other countries.[74] Under the CCC program, exporting firms are assisted in making sales to foreign buyers who have difficulty obtaining commercial credit. Private lending institutions provide short- or intermediate-term credit for purchases of U.S. farm commodities. The CCC guarantees repayment. Major recipients of these credit guarantees have been South Korea and countries in Latin America, the Middle East, and Eastern Europe.[75]

The most important legislation of the 1980s affecting the future of food aid was the Balanced Budget and Emergency Deficit Control Act (the Gramm-Rudman-Hollings Act), also passed in 1985. The effect of the Gramm-Rudman-Hollings Act has been to make food aid less of a "free good" to the Agency for International Development. Before 1985, authorization and oversight of PL 480 was the province of the Senate and House agriculture committees and PL 480 appropriations were the province of the agricultural appropriation subcommittees of the House and Senate committees. This meant that there was almost no trade-off between the volume of food aid and the amount of financial aid—they came out of different pockets. Even if food aid was less valuable than financial aid, in terms of U.S. foreign policy and economic assistance objectives and to the recipient country, one could argue that it added significantly to the general foreign affairs budget (the 150 account). The total aid package was larger than if there had been no food aid. Since the passage of G-R-H, this has been somewhat less true. By setting a ceiling on the total budget, G-R-H forces a trade-off among food aid, financial aid, and other budget components.

The pressure by the agricultural community for export enhancement programs beyond the PL 480 umbrella represented, first, an effort to get around the program restrictions that Congress had imposed on PL 480 in 1966 in order to push the program toward development and humanitarian objectives and, second, an attempt to avoid the financial constraints of the foreign assistance budget (the 150 account). In hearings before the House Subcommittee on Government Operations, a wheat producers' representative commented: "During the 1970s and early 1980s, the PL 480 and Export Credit programs were looked upon by most of the industry as important but not terribly significant factors in total wheat marketing. However . . . all of the export programs have become more and more important in terms of total export marketing. During the 1985–86 marketing year, more than 50 percent of all wheat exported from the United States was sold under PL-480, GSM credit, or the Export Enhancement Program."[76]

The evolution of U.S. food aid policy in the late 1980s was also beginning to reflect the effects of several changes in the international economic and political environment. By the late 1980s large amounts of food aid were going to Egypt and other strategically important countries. In contrast, the countries that suffered most severely during the African food crisis of the mid-1980s received relatively small amounts. The African food crisis of the mid-1980s was the first severe test of the international food aid system that had emerged after the food crises of the 1960s and 1970s. In 1980 the International Food Aid Convention was renegotiated. It contained provisions designed to avoid the sharp declines in food aid that had occurred in 1972 and 1974 and strengthened the provisions for burden sharing. Yet the response to the 1980s African crisis was hardly more effective than responses to the earlier crises had been. Early warning systems were slow in triggering food aid, the flow of commodities lagged behind the crisis situations, and delivery was plagued by logistical problems. It now seems "fortuitous that the African food crisis coincided with a period of overhanging surpluses. The response might have been more limited and possibly even more tardy if there had been a tighter market situation than prevailed during 1983–86."[77] Although the African crisis was very severe, it affected a relatively small number of people. This meant that undue pressure was not placed on the capacity of the United States and other developed countries to respond. The capacity simply did not exist to respond to an emergency of the magnitude of the South Asian food crisis of the mid-1960s.

Several other trends that have influenced the future of U.S. food assistance have also become apparent since the mid-1980s. One has been a somewhat surprising rise in project food aid relative to emergency and program food aid. A second has been the rise in the share of multilateral food aid relative to food aid by the United States. This has been accompanied by a decline in the grains and a rise in dairy products as a share of total food aid—a reflection of massive dairy surpluses in the EEC.[78] By the end of the decade, food surpluses were becoming a less important source of food aid commodities. Triangular food aid transactions, in which a donor provides food aid from another country, had risen substantially. A positive consequence of the triangular transactions has been a rise in donor acquisition of commodities from developing countries—rising to 8–10 percent of total food aid—to meet food aid commitments.[79]

Reforming Food Aid—Once Again!

During the fall of 1989 and into the spring of 1990, the economic environment for reform of farm legislation, including food aid legislation, was sharply different from that in 1985.[80] Growth in U.S. agricultural production had been slowed as a result of the very expensive acreage reductions provided for in the 1985 Food Security Act and a severe drought in 1988. Stocks had been further reduced by a resurgence of agricultural exports in response to decline in the value of the dollar relative to other major currencies. By the fall of 1989, U.S. and world wheat and feed grain stocks had declined to levels that had not been seen since the mid-1970s.

The political environment for food aid, and foreign economic assistance more generally, had also changed. Farm commodity organizations had developed an almost paranoid, obsessive belief that the self-help provisions of PL 480 were contributing to the growth of grain and oilseed production in countries that were potential competitors with the United States. An exceedingly critical review of U.S. foreign assistance programs was issued by the administrator of the Agency for International Development during the last weeks of the Reagan administration (the Woods report), and proposals for reform issued by the Task Force on Foreign Assistance of the House Foreign Affairs committee (the Hamilton Committee report) also helped create a general atmosphere favorable to the reexamination of food aid policies.

Senator Patrick J. Leahy (D-Vt.) had a longstanding interest in both domestic and international hunger issues. When he assumed chairmanship of the Senate Committee on Agriculture, Nutrition, and Forestry, he assigned a staff person to begin looking into the possibility of reforming the U.S. aid program. Leahy's initiative was strongly supported by the ranking minority member, Richard G. Lugar (R-Ind.).

Between late summer of 1988 and early fall of 1990, the AID Bureau for Food for Peace and Voluntary Assistance (FVA) sponsored a series of workshops, in association with various university and think tank organizations, to examine food aid accomplishments, needs, and policy reforms. By the summer of 1989, memoranda outlining the weaknesses of the existing programs and the reforms that should be considered were circulating furiously among the members of the Interagency Food Aid Subcommittee and staff members of the several House and Senate committees. Staff at the State Department were, as usual, nervous about any changes.

Among the proposed changes that attracted a good deal of support in the Senate Agriculture Committee, particularly at the staff level and among some members of the Food Aid Subcommittee, was a proposed revision that would organize the activities under the several titles by objective rather than by form of assistance (loans or grants). Under this proposal Title I would include export promotion, Title II would include humanitarian and development assistance, and Title III would include grants for development assistance.

The situation in the House was somewhat more complicated than that in the Senate. The chairman of the House Agriculture Committee, E. (Kiki) de la Garza (D-Tex.), was more cautious in supporting reform than was his Senate counterpart. He was concerned that the clarification of objectives within the several titles would weaken the coalition of farm organizations, private voluntary organizations, and food activists that had traditionally supported food aid, and he resisted pressure from the commodity organizations to make market development the only objective of Title I. But when the chairman of the House Foreign Affairs Subcommittee on International Trade, Sam Gejdenson (D-Conn.), initiated legislation similar to the Senate proposal, de la Garza moved reluctantly to work out compromise language. In the end the compromise was forced by instructions from the House Rules Committee, among whose members was Tony P. Hall (D-Ohio), chairman of the House Select Committee on Hunger and a strong supporter of food aid reform.

Within the administration, the OMB staff initially supported the Senate committee reforms. At the beginning of the process, administration leadership on both the USDA and AID were too inexperienced or preoccupied with other issues and unable to resolve interagency disagreements or to exercise leadership in reform. In general, the staff at the Department of Agriculture adopted a "don't fix it if it ain't broke" approach, while some AID staff were active in criticizing the existing program and advancing policy changes. As the 1980 legislative session progressed, it became clear that the USDA was lined up strongly behind the House version. The OMB then backed away from its initial support for reform.

The State Department, particularly Deputy Secretary Lawrence S. Eagleberger, interpreted the proposed changes as a power play designed to limit the president's flexibility in the management of food aid. Eagleberger's argument was summarily rejected by Senators Leahy and Lugar, who responded that "flexibility is not the problem, a lack of accountability is!" The legislation that eventually emerged from the conference committee in Subtitle A of Title XV of the Omnibus Food, Agricultural, Conservation, and Trade Act of 1990 (PL 101-624, 28 November 1990) was remarkably close to the version that had been advanced by the staff of the Senate Agriculture Committee. The major features of the new legislation were as follows.

—*Title I* was rewritten to give USDA primary responsibility for concessional sales and was retitled "Trade and Development Assistance." Title I authorizes a concessional loan program to finance the sale and export of commodities to developing countries that are experiencing a shortage of foreign exchange and having difficulties meeting their food needs through normal commercial export channels. The loans may be repaid with local currency, and the currencies may be used to carry out market development, agricultural business development, and agricultural research. These local currencies would be exempt from the appropriation process.

—*Title II* was rewritten to give AID primary responsibility for direct food grant or donation activities and was retitled "Emergency and Private Assistance." Title II authorizes the donation of commodities for use in emergency relief, to combat malnutrition, to promote economic development, and to encourage sound environmental policies. Food provided for emergency relief may be distributed through public or private agencies; food provided for nonemergency assistance may be distributed through PVOs, cooperatives, and intergovernmental organizations. The PVOs and cooperatives that distribute the commodities are required to work with indigenous organizations in making the assistance available at the local level. The new law raises the minimum requirements for shipments under Title II to 1.925 million metric tons in fiscal year 1991 (and to 2.025 by fiscal year 1995) and provides that 75 percent of the commodities programmed under Title II be in the form of processed, fortified, or bagged commodities. Cash grants will be made to PVOs and cooperatives to strengthen their capacity to manage the grant programs. The Food Aid Consultative Group (to be chaired by the US/AID administrator and consisting of the under-secretary of agriculture for International and Commodity Programs, representatives of U.S. and LDC PVOs and of cooperatives participating in Title II activities, and the US/AID inspector-general) was established.

—*Title III,* Food for Development, was completely rewritten. The old language was deleted and replaced by a bilateral food aid grant program to be administered by AID. It provides for the donation of commodities to the "least developed" countries for direct feeding programs, emergency food reserves, and economic development. The commodities donated under this title may be provided through the Commodity Credit Corporation or through private trade channels. If the commodities are sold in the recipient countries, the local currencies generated by the sales are to be jointly programmed for economic development purposes by the recipient country and AID.

—*Title IV,* General Authorities and Requirements, includes provision for continuation of the Bellman amendment, which requires that food aid not result in substantial disincentives or disruption in domestic production or marketing in the recipient countries. It also continues the requirement that the local currencies generated under the act not be used to finance the production for export of agricultural commodities that would compete in the world market with similar items produced in the United States if such competition would cause "substantial injury" to U.S. producers. Programming on a multiyear basis, with some exceptions, is mandated for all food aid programs (Titles I, II, and III). The "docket" authority of the secretary of agriculture was modified to require determination of commodity availability before the beginning of the fiscal year for the programs.

—*The Food for Progress Act* was amended to make middle-income countries and "newly emerging democracies" eligible to receive food aid. The commodities can be channeled through PVOs and cooperatives in addition to recipient governments. There had been some interest on the part of the State Department and the administration in bringing the Food for Progress title under PL 480, but some technical issues were not worked out in time.

When the reform effort was begun, it was not obvious that it could be brought off successfully. Early in the process there were predictions that the commodity groups would kill the reforms. The senior staff of the Senate committee were, however, exceedingly skilled in building a consensus among the commodity groups, the development interests, and the food activists. But the strong backing of Senator Leahy was essential in maintaining the momentum of the reform effort.

What significance should one attach to the changes in the 1990 act? Perhaps the most important is that program responsibility is more clearly identified and the need for interagency coordination is sharply reduced. Under the previous arrangements the de facto authority to decide on food aid shipments rested in the Interagency Food Aid Subcommittee of the Development Coordinating Committee. If the new legislation operates as intended, the Food Aid Subcommittee will be abolished or its functions sharply reduced. But it is hard to imagine, given the traditions of the federal bureaucracy, that a new committee will not emerge to coordinate programming and resolve disagreements among USDA, AID, and OMB.

What does this new assignment of responsibility mean for the USDA and AID? The USDA now has even greater flexibility in pursuing market development objectives. It can use commodities programmed under Title I, along with Commodity Credit Corporation commodities programmed under 416(b) and the Market Promotion Program (formerly the Targeted Export Enhancement Program), to defend existing markets and to pursue surplus disposal and market development objectives.

The advantages to AID of the new program are less clear. A larger share of the food aid budget will now be programmed directly by US/AID as food aid grants under Titles II and III. The cash grants to PVOs may induce them to continue programming food aid in areas where logistical problems or civil unrest impose high costs on their operations. It remains to be seen whether the establishment of the new Food Aid Consultative Group will strengthen or weaken AID's Title II programming role, which has already been substantially eroded by its PVO and cooperative constituencies. Depending on the size of budgetary support, Title III might be able to open up new possibilities for achieving greater consistency between food aid and the other development assistance activities of AID.

It is somewhat surprising, given the very large amount of political energy devoted to the 1980 revisions of the food aid legislation, that the revisions seem to have greater significance for process rather than for program. It seems clear that USDA and AID now have greater freedom to pursue the program objectives in which they are primarily interested with less bureaucratic interference from other agencies. It is less clear whether the reforms will do very much to resolve the continuing contradictions among the various objectives of the U.S. food aid program.

Professionals, Clients, and Interests

The United States food aid program has been a source of considerable self-congratulation by the interest groups, politicians, and bureaucrats involved in program development and management. It has been denounced by populist critics from both the Left and the Right. Development scholars and policy analysts have been skeptical of the blurring of program objectives. Among the several objectives, only emergency food aid has received general approval—but critics have been highly vocal about blunders and inefficiency in program management and operation.

Professionals and Populists

Agricultural and other development economists have been particularly active in the debates about food assistance. In 1954, the same year that PL 480 was passed, the FAO initiated a series of studies of the potential effects of FAO under the direction of Mordecai Ezekial. The study used an early vision of what later became known as "the two-gap model"—in this case a foreign exchange gap and a food gap—to simulate the effects of food aid. The study concluded that, if food was used to put underemployed labor to work building infrastructure, it could contribute as much as one-fourth of the investment cost. It could also ease the foreign exchange gap resulting from the responsiveness of domestic supply to rising demand during the initial stages of development. The FAO study was influential, or at least useful, since it provided a rationalization for the marriage of convenience between disposal and development.[81]

An argument also made by some agricultural economists was that the imperatives of rapid technical change and slow growth of demand in the U.S. economy, which virtually guaranteed that surplus disposal programs would continue, created an opportunity to employ the surpluses to achieve development objectives. The argument was made in its most sophisticated form by Willard W. Cochrane of the University of Minnesota in a presidential address to the American Farm Economic Association in 1959. "Advancing technology in American agriculture is forcing, first, the acceptance of foreign surplus disposal, and second, the acceptance of comprehensive supply control. The logical result must be the integration or the marriage of these seemingly opposing lines of action into a unified policy. And it is [my] purpose . . . to record—to legitimize—this marriage of foreign surplus disposal and comprehensive supply control, however distasteful it may be to some friends and relations."[82] Cochrane went on to argue and illustrate the potential uses of food aid in human and physical capital formation.

The Ezekiel-Cochrane "marriage of convenience" argument was the target of an iconoclastic argument by Professor Theodore W. Schultz of the University of Chicago at the following year's meeting of the American Farm Economic Association. Schultz was sharply critical of the gap between the potential effects outlined in the Ezekiel study and program operations—"what has been happening bears little or no resemblance to the assumptions on which the study was based."[83] The Schultz critique can be capsuled in four points:

1. The financial cost to the Commodity Credit Corporation of the commodities distributed by the PL 480 program have been in the neighbor-

hood of twice the value of these products had they been sold on world markets. Thus, it is a serious error to treat the costs to the CCC as a valid measure of our food aid efforts. Approximately 50 percent of the cost should be charged against the costs of the agricultural commodity programs.

2. The value of the PL 480 commodities to the countries receiving them was in the neighborhood of 37 cents for each dollar of CCC costs in the mid- and late 1950s. Thus, even charging 50 percent of the costs to the foreign aid program would overstate the value of the assistance to the receiving countries except in times of severe food shortages.
3. The cost to the United States of the commodities distributed abroad under the PL 480 program, measured in terms of the marginal revenue forgone from foreign sales, is probably close to zero—but only if it is assumed that the programs that generate the surpluses must be taken as a fact of life.
4. The receipt of PL 480 commodities can be expected, except during periods of food emergency, to have a negative effect on the incentives of the governments of recipient countries to invest in agricultural development and on the incentives of individual farmers to expand agricultural production.

The tone and the agenda for much of the academic debate and the research on food aid over the next decade was set by the Cochrane-Schultz argument.

Professional dialogue over the costs and the effects of food aid in the 1950s and early 1960s was heavily conditioned by the disposal orientation of the food assistance programs. A good deal of effort went into attempts to test the disincentive hypothesis with largely inconclusive results. It is almost impossible at this stage to know whether the professional dialogue had any influence on food aid policy or program. By the early 1960s, however, there had been attempts to both target food aid to have a more direct effect on the poor and to design projects in which the food aid made a direct impact on development.[84] Although an extensive specialized literature emerged, development economists tended to avoid the issue largely because of a presumption that it was a disposal program rather than a development assistance program. A casual reference to the Schultz critique was usually adequate to sustain their distaste for the topic.

In retrospect, it is surprising how much effort was devoted to attempting to identify the direct price and agricultural production effects of food aid. This was a relatively minor theme in the Schultz critique. Much less attention was devoted to attempts to evaluate the more important effects of food aid on government decisions to make the investments in land and water development, fertilizer production capacity, and the capacity of the agricultural research and extension systems to invent and diffuse more productive agricultural technology. By the mid-1970s the evidence that had been assembled was being interpreted to imply that, under conditions of food scarcity or effective program management, the direct disincentive effects on agricultural production could be quite small.[85] In India, for example, distribution of food aid through "fair price" shops was highly effective in reaching the poor. The income effect of the lower prices at the fair price shops also contributed to higher consumption. As a result the food aid was almost entirely absorbed by additional consumption, with the result that any effect on prices received by Indian producers was negligible. It should be noted, however, that very few other countries either attempted or were able to realize the effectiveness in directing food aid to the poor that was achieved by India.

The simultaneous threat of energy and food crises in the early and mid-1970s widened the professional dialogue about food aid and agricultural development. The agricultural and development economists who had dominated the debates since the 1950s were forced into the background. There was a burgeoning professional and populist literature on the world food problem by new participants in the policy debate—many of whom did not think it important to become more than superficially familiar with the technical or institutional aspects of food production, distribution, or policy. Philosophers asserted a moral responsibility by those who were blessed with abundance for food aid to the poor—both at home and abroad.[86] Metaphors such as "spaceship earth," "tragedy of the commons," "lifeboat ethics," and "triage" were introduced into the popular vocabulary to capture concerns about resource scarcity, environmental degradation, and food scarcity.[87]

The contradictions, which Paul O. Isenman and Hans W. Singer have noted in the economics literature on food aid, also apply to much of the other professional and populist literature of this period.

> Many economists appear to view food aid and non-food aid from remarkably different perspectives. Most economists believe that aid recipients should use (non-food) aid receipts to increase investment, employment, and output in accord with a well-thought-out development plan and/or the signals provided by market forces; they would be terrified if the aid were used instead for short-term consumption increases or for low priority development projects with an uncertain impact . . . While it is inconsistent to insist that food aid not be used for investment and to criticize food aid for not contributing to investment, both of these views are well established in the "conventional wisdom" of food aid.[88]

An additional disturbing aspect of the "food crisis" literature of the 1970s was its revelation of the poverty of much of the formal economic analysis of resource scarcity and food security. In the 1970s, the analysts who were responsible for the construction and interpretation of futures trends and models were unable to insulate themselves from the short-run trends and events that dominated the intellectual and policy environment. They were dominated by the pervasive climate of "technology pessimism" and "food pessimism." It seems quite clear that the model builders and futures simulators were strongly influenced by an intellectual environment that would have regarded a more optimistic view of the future as "out of touch with reality."[89]

The favor with which food aid was regarded during the food crisis of the early 1970s was relatively short lived. During the late 1970s and early 1980s, a newly emerging populist and frequently polemical criticism focused on the regressive distributional effects of program food aid (under Title I) and the continuing failure of project food aid (under Title II) to achieve program objectives.[90] This new criticism was quite different, in both its rhetorical style and its concern, from that of the development and agricultural economists of the 1950s and 1960s, who had focused primarily on production disincentives and trade displacement. The populist critics of both the Left and the Right have confronted the proponents of food aid with the challenge of demonstrating uses of project food aid that have had a positive influence on families or communities that has extended beyond the period when the assistance was rendered. The response, like the criticism, has typically relied on case studies of selected projects, some of which have demonstrated moderately high internal rates of return, rather than a comprehensive evaluation of the bilateral and multilateral food aid system.

The most serious effort to assess the populist literature has been a series of studies by Hans Singer, Edward J. Clay, and several collaborators.[91] They addressed the three major criticisms of food aid: (1) food aid is inferior to financial aid, (2) food aid acts as a disincentive to recipient-country food producers, and (3) food aid provides an incentive for recipient governments to slacken effort to promote domestic food production. Their response is that the distinction between the incentive and disincentive effects of food and financial aid has been overdrawn. Effective program management can avoid the problems stressed by the critics. Furthermore, efforts to use food aid as a development tool have been with us now for the last 30 years and are likely to be with us for another 30. "It is time to stop debating whether food aid is better or worse than other forms of aid or income transfer and . . . to make it more effective."[92]

During the middle and late 1980s, some trade and development economists were attempting to counter the criticism by farm commodity groups, noted earlier, that aid—including food aid—in support of agricultural production was taking markets away from American farmers. They argued that, because a high proportion of the total population in the poorest developing countries is dependent on agriculture, growth in agricultural productivity and in rural incomes is necessary to sustain growth in the total economy. Once the growth process gets under way, high income elasticity of demand for the preferred food grains, for cooking oil, and for animal protein produces an explosive growth in agricultural demand. The result is rising demand for agricultural imports, particularly the feed grains needed to sustain rapid growth in animal production. Thus, the long-term effect of technical assistance and other aid to "get agriculture moving" is an expansion in demand for imports of U.S. agricultural products.[93]

There were some creative suggestions for the reform of food aid programs in the late 1980s. John W. Mellor proposed the use of food aid to mitigate the unfavorable effects of structural adjustment programs on the poor.[94] He noted that the restrictive monetary and fiscal policies associated with the structural adjustment process are both likely to reduce the employment and purchasing power of the poor. Efforts to remedy government budget imbalances and trade deficits during the initial stages of the adjustment are likely to limit commercial food imports and force domestic food prices upward. As the adjustment process proceeds, the growth of income and employment will contribute to rapid growth in food demand. If food aid is targeted to low-income people, through food-for-work and food subsidies, it can both ameliorate some of the regressive effects of the structural adjustment program and contribute directly to rural development. Since bilateral food aid is "inherently unstable," Mellor urged that an international device such as the cereal import facility of the International Monetary Fund be activated for the purpose.

Another creative suggestion for reform of the food aid program was a proposed design for an international food stamp program by Willis L. Peterson of the University of Minnesota.[95] Peterson showed that it would be possible to design a food stamp program that would avoid disincentive effects on agricultural production in recipient countries while simultaneously expanding the demand for agricultural exports from donor countries. The objective would be achieved as a result of the demand enhancement aspects of the program.

Aid donors would, in effect, issue food stamp coupon books to poor people through the auspices of the recipient government. Food vendors in the recipient nations could redeem the coupons from the donor country aid agency for convertible currency. The recipient country would be required to maintain freely convertible currency and free trade in food commodities. The recipients of the food stamps would, therefore, be indifferent when purchasing food with the stamps as to whether the food was produced domestically or imported. Food would be imported only if it was available at lower cost than were domestic supplies. Peterson estimated that the effect of the food stamp program on consumption, by lowering the cost of food to the poor, would increase world demand for food on the order of 16 percent and demand for exports by over 50 percent. His calculations suggest that the cost of the program to the developed countries would be no more than was currently being spent by the OECD countries on food aid and farm price support programs. Peterson suggested initiating the program in a few countries on a pilot basis to gain experience with operational aspects of the program.

But it would be hard to demonstrate that the large literature generated by the professional scholars and the populist critics has exerted more than a marginal effect on food aid policies and programs. If there has been one constant in the professional debates about food aid, it has been the failure of the proponents and the critics to confront each other on common ground. The proponents have focused on the modeling of schemes that, if properly managed, could have a positive influence on recipient welfare and economic development. The critics have used case studies of projects that were unsuccessful or positively harmful to attempt to discredit the arguments of the proponents. Even an exceedingly attractive proposal, such as the international food stamp program, has only a slight chance of receiving serious consideration. Program change is an evolutionary rather than a revolutionary process.

Perhaps the major effect of the professional literature on food aid has been to narrow the range of controversy about the influence of food aid. It is difficult for anyone who has even limited familiarity with the literature to continue to argue that food aid has a pervasive negative impact on the growth of agricultural production, or that supplementary feeding programs have had a widespread and measurable positive impact on the nutritional status of children, or that economic growth has been significantly advanced by food-for-work programs, or that food aid does not displace commercial exports. The literature is also clear that food aid has been important in meeting emergency food needs, in meeting the subsistence needs of poor people, and in providing budgetary support for fragile governments.

Interests and Clients

Support for food aid has moved through three phases.[96] In the 1950s and into the mid-1960s, major support came from the agricultural constituencies and their congressional patrons. The 1950s and 1960s were years of large U.S. grain stocks. From the 1950s into the 1970s, Senator Hubert H. Humphrey (D-Minn.) led the congressional effort to initiate and expand food aid. Indeed, it is difficult to write a history of food aid without its becoming in part a biography of Hubert Humphrey (see the preface).

During the 1960s and 1970s, when food aid was heavily oriented toward political and security objectives, the administration itself became a major constituency for food aid. Food aid, for example, was used to make large financial resources available to the government of Vietnam. As the Vietnam War wound down, Israel and Egypt became large recipients of food aid.

During the late 1970s, the humanitarian assistance community, operating through the private voluntary organizations, became a strong constituency for food aid. The use of food aid as an instrument of development has, from the beginning, received strong rhetorical support, but it has never been able to generate substantial constituency support.

Since 1980, funding for the promotion of agricultural exports through subsidies has increased substantially but principally through programs other than those created by Public Law 480. As a result, constituencies interested in market development and trade expansion have shifted much of their attention from food aid to other export enhancement programs.

The interest groups discussed in this section include the four major clients of the PL 480 programs—the farm commodity groups that benefit from market development, the agribusiness firms that handle the commodities, the maritime interests that are involved in the overseas shipment of farm commodities, and the private voluntary organizations and cooperatives involved in the distribution of Title II commodities.

Farm Groups

During its initial years, the general farm organizations were strong supporters of food aid. The initial proposals for the sale of agricultural commodities for foreign currencies were made at the 1952 American Farm Bureau convention. The interest of the general farm organizations in food aid has never strayed far from their concern with surplus disposal. This has meant that their interest tended to weaken or even evaporate whenever surpluses became less burdensome. The general farm organizations have represented neither consistent nor effective support or opposition to food aid since surplus stocks began to decline in the late 1960s.

During the 1970s and 1980s, the commodity organizations have acquired increasing political strength relative to the general farm organizations. This has been due, at least in part, to the emergence of strong subcommittees, organized along commodity lines, in the House Agriculture Committee. This helped create the symbiotic relationship between interest groups and subcommittees that enabled commodity organizations, such as the National Corn Growers Association, the National Association of Wheat Growers, and the

American Soybean Association, to use their political resources successfully to pursue limited but highly focused political agendas.

The commodity organizations have been both supporters and participants in the market development activities supported with PL 480 funding. Except during the period of high prices in the 1970s, they have opposed the use of U.S. foreign assistance resources, including projects funded with PL 480 resources, to enhance the production in developing countries of commodities that might compete with U.S.-produced commodities.[97] And they, along with the general farm organizations and the voluntary organizations, have vigorously opposed the use of food aid as a bargaining chip for U.S. political or strategic advantage. While typically conservative in their domestic politics, farm organizations have seen no inconsistency in pressing for sales on concessional terms to either the centrally planned economies or countries ruled by right-wing authoritarian or totalitarian regimes.

Agribusiness

The role of the agribusiness industry in support of or in opposition to food aid has been difficult to document. Their representatives do not play an active role in House and Senate hearings. However, the leading firms in the industry, several of them with headquarters in Minnesota, had relatively easy access to Senator Humphrey. Dwayne Andreas, chairman of Archer-Daniels-Midland, a major soybean- and corn-processing firm and a close friend and financial supporter of Humphrey, has commented to reporters about his ability to influence the regulations governing the administration of the PL 480 program. Representatives of Cargill, working through Senator Humphrey, were effective in persuading the Agriculture Department to put surplus government grain up for sale at inland as well as at port locations. This helped Cargill offer more for the U.S. grain and still make money because of its superior transportation facilities.[98] The populist and radical critics have been particularly energetic in criticizing what they have interpreted as incestuous relationships among the grain trade, the U.S. Department of Agriculture, and congressional interests that have supported the use of local currency sales proceeds to support the market development objectives of U.S. exporters.[99]

The agribusiness sector, however, has generally opposed farm programs that have been responsible for surplus accumulation. They have been more favorable to programs that partially or fully "delink" commodity prices and payments to farmers. Cargill was, for example, particularly active in the mid-1960s and again in the 1980s in proposals to delink prices and payments and reduce the role of the government in international trade. The agribusiness sector has also, during the several rounds of GATT negotiations, supported a more liberal international trading regime. It seems apparent that the agribusiness sector, and the grain trade in particular, has been more effective in influencing program than policy.

The Maritime Industry

The maritime industry, including related shipping, port, and labor organizations, has been among the more successful interest groups in bending the food aid program to its own advantage. It may have been a historical accident that both cargo preference (PL 664) and food aid (PL 480) legislation was enacted in 1954,[100] but the survival of this youthful liaison has not been an accident. The shipping industry was successful, in the Food Security Act of 1985, in forcing an increase in the portion of food aid shipped on U.S. vessels from 50 to 75 percent. Shipping interests have also pressed for a provision that would bring commercial grain shipments and other bulk commodities funded under the Agency for International Development's Economic Support Fund under the cargo preference provisions.

The maritime industry has been able to maintain and even strengthen the cargo preference provisions (in addition to ship building and operating subsidies) over the opposition of the Department of Agriculture, agricultural producers, and the exporters of other bulk commodities, as well as the Great Lakes maritime unions. There are several reasons. One is that the direct cargo preference subsidy, reflected in higher shipping costs on PL 480 commodities, is relatively small—running in the $150 million range—in contrast to subsidies to agricultural producers—running in the $10 billion to $20 billion range since the early 1980s. Others point to the strength of labor support for cargo preference and to the secondary employment benefits in the congressional jurisdictions represented on the Senate Merchant Marine Subcommittee and House Merchant Marine and Fisheries Committee. Senator Paul Sarbanes (D-Md.) is a vigorous supporter of cargo preference—the port of Baltimore is in his state. But several members of Congress from the Midwest, who are also strong supporters of PL 480, have failed to support the elimination of cargo preference. The flow of political action committee contributions from the Seafarers International Union, the Transport Institute, the Maritime Research and Development Institute, and related front organizations helps explain this seeming contradiction. The single focus of the maritime interests has apparently given the industry greater leverage on this particular issue than that wielded by its opponents, whose legislative agendas tend to be more diffuse.

Voluntary Organizations

The participation of the private voluntary organizations in food aid predates the passage of PL 480. Their interests have been represented primarily through the Surplus Commodities Policy Committee of the American Council of Voluntary Agencies and the Inter-religious Task Force on U.S. Food Policy (more recently Interfaith Action for Economic Justice). From the Marshall Plan era to the present, the most active agencies have been CARE, Catholic Relief, Lutheran World Relief, Church World Services, and the American Jewish Joint Distribution Committee.[101]

The commitment to broad humanitarian objectives on the part of the voluntary agencies has led to continuing tension with the government agencies responsible for food aid (Chap. 9). The agencies with the strongest humanitarian commitments tend to view governments as the source of unfortunate barriers to richer and more productive relationships among peoples. From the point of view of the voluntary agencies, the primary objective of foreign aid should be the elimination of hunger, disease, and injustice. They view the use of food aid in the interest of political or strategic advantage as subversive of the basic humanitarian impulse of a society based on moral purpose.

There has, however, been considerable stress within the PVO community on how to achieve consistency between their basic humanitarian concerns and their client relationship to the government food aid program. CARE, which has limited private financial support, has been driven by both bureaucratic ambition and financial imperatives to suppress whatever misgivings it might have about the surplus disposal and security objectives its distribution programs have served. Catholic Relief Services, mindful of the worldwide evangelical mission of the church, has typically taken the view that more is better, whatever the objectives of its patron—the U.S. government. Lutheran World Relief and Church World Service have both experienced greater internal tension in attempting to resolve their client role with their convictions about church-state relationships. Lutheran World Relief has resolved the problem in a manner reminiscent of Solomon—by limiting government support to less than 50 percent of its level of program activity. It has also occasionally opposed efforts by CARE and Catholic Relief to broaden government financial support for PVO programs. Several other voluntary relief organizations, such as the American Friends Service Committee, have viewed any government support as a corruption of the concept of volunteerism.

The voluntary agencies have not, until fairly recently, shared the qualms about the effects of food aid on agricultural development or the efficiency of commodity aid relative to financial aid that have been the focus of so much debate among economists and populists. It has been enough that food was available to meet the needs of poor people. The view was expressed rather dramatically during the first year of the PL 480 program in testimony before the House Agriculture Committee: "Just as there is no surplus person in the world, so there is really no surplus food in the world in relation to the needs of people . . . The challenge presented by the mountain of surplus food is a moral one which, if met dynamically, can help immeasurably to capture the sympathy and imagination of the world."[102]

The voluntary agencies did, however, pressure the reluctant departments of State and Agriculture in the late 1950s to allow them to initiate programs that would involve the exchange of food for work. But it was not until the early 1960s, during the Kennedy administration, that such proposals were adopted.

During the 1950s, Senator Humphrey, who shared the sense of mission of the voluntary agencies, praised their work and drew on their support in his efforts to reform and expand food aid. The government became more open to the PVOs during the Kennedy administration, when George McGovern and later William Reuter, one of their own, served as Food for Peace coordinator. President Kennedy held a White House reception for the representatives of the voluntary agencies, but his support was more symbolic than substantial.

The limited influence exerted by voluntary agencies on food aid policy and programming was, at least until the mid-1970s, a function of the size of food surpluses. During periods of burdensome surpluses, they were welcomed as partners in food aid; when surpluses receded, however, their role as clients was again made clear to them. The political victories of the voluntary agencies were small triumphs and were more often in the area of program administration than food aid policy—government funding of transport costs, diversifying the commodities available for voluntary agency distribution, maintaining the flow of dried milk for the donation programs.

Since the mid-1970s, the voluntary agencies have achieved somewhat greater political success. Congressional reaction against the security orientation of food assistance during the Vietnam War and the publicity associated with the world food crises of the mid-1970s created a more favorable political environment for the pursuit of humanitarian objectives. As noted earlier, the 1975 International Development and Food Assistance Act, as well as subsequent legislation, specified minimum levels of commodity distribution through Title II donations. The share of food aid distributed under Title II, largely through nongovernmental organizations (NGOs), has risen substantially since the mid-1970s. And the 1987 act contained provisions for monetizing not less than 10 percent of donated commodities to be used for program support.[103]

The political significance of the voluntary agencies should also be seen in a broader context than their activities in support of their particular interests in greater resources for their own programs. They share with the agricultural commodity organizations an intense aversion to the use of food aid to advance U.S. political or strategic objectives. They have contributed to a broad and pervasive support for a basic needs orientation in development assistance. They have very substantial capacity to mobilize public opinion and to draw attention to problems that are difficult for governments to address. And NGO field staff have often been an effective source of criticism of the corruption and ineffectiveness of official aid.[104] They and their constituencies have often been the only source of broad-based support for development assistance. They have successfully pursued a "camel's nose in the door" strategy. The revision of the Food for Peace Act contains a provision that creates the Food Aid Consultative Group, which includes representatives of the PVOs.

One conclusion stands out rather clearly. There is a congruence between the geographic location of interest groups and the regional distribution of congressional support for food aid. Legislators from the corn and wheat belts have been the most consistent supporters of food aid. During and after World War II, earlier isolationist and protectionist sentiment among rural constituencies gave way to aggressive pursuit of government support for market development, surplus disposal, and humanitarian relief. It is no accident that both Democrats and Republicans from the Midwest found a basis for supporting food aid, regardless of their committee assignments. Lee Egerstrom of the *St. Paul Pioneer Press Dispatch* has commented that, if "Senator Humphrey had been assigned to the Public Works Committee, the Food for Peace Program would have been attached to the Maritime Administration!"

Why Food Aid?

It has been difficult to find a principled answer to the question, Why food aid? There has been a continuing effort among some proponents of food aid to show that food aid is, at least for some purposes, a more effective instrument of economic assistance than financial aid. This has not been an easy task.

Food aid is no longer an effective method for dealing with agricultural surpluses. The dominant objective of food aid in the 1950s and into the early 1960s was to dispose of U.S. agricultural surplus. Yet the program was, even then, unable, within the constraints in which it was forced to operate, to move sufficient commodities to have much more than a marginal effect on U.S. surplus stocks. The program found it difficult to avoid substituting concessional credit sales for commercial sales. It has been argued that in some sense the program could be viewed as an offset to the increasing overvaluation of the dollar during the 1950s and 1960s.[105] But an earlier devaluation or more rapid transition to a floating exchange rate would have been more effective. In the absence of devaluation, a straightforward two-price "domestic allotment" program to hold domestic prices above world market levels and permit exports to move into world markets at border prices would have been more effective in disposing of surpluses.

A second important objective of U.S. food aid from the very beginning has been its use as an instrument of market development for U.S. producers. There have been three elements in this effort. The most direct of these was the Cooley loan program of the late 1950s and 1960s, which offered subsidies to agribusiness for facility investments in recipient countries. The second has been support for commodity organizations for technical assistance, consumer education, and food promotion programs in recipient countries. The third has been the more subtle effect of large-volume commodity imports in changing the tastes of consumers in favor of wheat or rice and away from "inferior" domestic carbohydrates. The facilities subsidies have at times been important in the development of a recipient's national capacity to produce the inputs needed to sustain agricultural production—fertilizer in India, for example. The latter two programs have been credited with some success in situations where the growth of consumer income was consistent with the changes in consumption patterns being promoted—higher consumption of wheat products in Japan and the use of U.S. feed grains in pork and poultry production in Taiwan and Korea.

There has, however, been a lack of clarity in discussions of market development. It is quite appropriate to include technical assistance, consumer education, and food promotion campaigns under the rubric of market development, but it stretches the concept too far to include large-volume concessional sales, on the grounds that they will contribute to change in consumer tastes, as market development. It seems doubtful that a program justified primarily on market development criteria would have been able to claim more than a small fraction of the resources allocated under PL 480 Title I.[106]

What about food aid as an instrument of leverage in support of U.S. political or economic objectives? The history of efforts to employ food aid to induce other governments to initiate economic or political reforms or to support the U.S. global political agenda indicates that it is an exceedingly blunt instrument. The limited successes against India in the 1960s and against Bangladesh and Egypt in the 1970s, for example, suggest that success has been achieved only when there was substantial political support for the reform in the recipient country or the recipient country was in an exceedingly weak bargaining position. As an instrument to create generalized goodwill toward the United States, food aid has, when sensitively administered, been somewhat more effective. But it would be difficult today to find serious advocates of the "food power" perspective that briefly captured the imagination of populists and politicians in the early and mid-1970s.

If there is any area in which food aid might be expected to have a substantial influence, it is on recipient-country economic development. A very high share of the commodities transferred under Title I have been used by the recipient governments to generate revenues that could be used to support their development budgets. It is generally agreed that the potential release of other resources for development is greatest where food aid replaces commercial imports because it then frees foreign exchange for other purposes. But donors, particularly the United States, have insisted that agricultural commodity aid be additional—that it not displace commercial imports. Substantial quantities of the food transferred under Title II have been used to support food-for-work or other local development projects. In spite of efforts to direct the resources generated by food aid into development-related investment, it is generally conceded that there continues to be very substantial leakage into routine budget support, current consumption, and the pockets of public officials and their clients. No one (except perhaps Hans Singer and John Mellor) argues that PL 480 commodity transfers are as efficient as financial transfers when measured against development objectives. It is somewhat discouraging, after more than 30 years of effort, to find program designers, managers, and advocates claiming little more than that agricultural commodity assistance can become an effective instrument for development—but that radical changes in the way it is programmed and administered will be necessary.[107]

The strongest support for the view that food aid is a superior instrument of assistance has been put forward by the basic needs constituency for food aid.[108] It has been argued that food aid for disaster relief and for meeting the needs of the nutritionally deprived is a superior form of assistance. It can, in principle, be mobilized quickly for disaster relief, and it can be targeted to the nutritionally deprived. If targeted to improve nutrition and as an incentive to participation in formal schooling and training programs, food aid can, it is argued, contribute effectively to human capital formation without having significant disincentive effects on agricultural production. But evaluations of school feeding programs in developing countries have found it difficult to document the effects on school attendance or academic achievement that seemed so intuitively obvious to feeding program advocates. Experience during the 1980s and into the 1990s suggests that the lessons that should have been drawn from past mistakes, particularly when food aid transfers were made primarily for security reasons, have had almost no effect on food aid practice.[109]

Multiple Constituencies for Multiple Objectives

In the past it has been this diversity of objectives that has accounted for the continuing political viability of food aid as a component of U.S. development assistance. There has been a constituency for food aid in times of food surpluses and in times of food scarcity. The commodity interests and the human needs constituency have not been able to agree on the objectives of food aid, but they have been able to cooperate in support of PL 480 appropriations. Those in the administration who have been concerned with foreign policy and development assistance have seldom believed that food was as useful as money—but they have welcomed it because it was accessible and fungible.

The importance of the multiple objectives of the program for its continued political viability was recognized and insisted upon by Senator Humphrey. This point was stressed by a former staff member of the Senate Committee on Agriculture and Forestry, Thomas R. Saylor, in a discussion of the 1975 revision of the PL 480 legislation: "The multiple objectives and accompanying multiple constituencies provide a much broader base of support than other foreign assistance programs provide. To undermine this would be to severely weaken PL 480 and leave it much more vulnerable to the budget cutting process."[110]

It is hard to disagree that, until at least the late 1960s, the food aid program was larger than it would have been if it had been targeted to more specific—and less inconsistent—objectives. And the total aid effort was also larger than it would otherwise have been in the absence of food aid. But it is doubtful whether this argument can be made to carry as much weight in the 1990s. The coalition of commodity groups, shippers, and PVOs was ineffective in preventing a substantial decline in food aid shipments in the 1970s. During the 1980s, when surpluses reappeared, the agricultural interests chose to support disposal efforts largely outside of the PL 480 framework. As a result, there is some evidence of a closer relationship between the PL 480 titles and the flow of food aid transfers.[111] One effect of the 1990 legislation should be to further reduce the fungibility of food aid.

The Future of Food Aid

There are now clear signs that the old congressional-agency-interest group coalition has been eroding. Several USDA studies have found that export subsidy programs, including PL 480, were a less cost-effective method of enhancing exports than were either export credits or consumption-oriented market development programs.[112] As personnel ceilings have continued to erode AID staff capacity, both in Washington and in the field, the agency has found that the administrative requirements necessary to make food aid an effective instrument for development have become excessively burdensome. Conflicts also emerged between some members of the PVO community and AID over the use of food aid monetization to support the development of indigenous PVOs in recipient countries. Yet the PVOs themselves were finding it increasingly burdensome to respond to emergency food aid needs, particularly in African countries characterized by high delivery costs and weak institutional infrastructure.

Forecasts of program levels in areas as highly politicized as food aid are notoriously hazardous. A National Academy of Sciences workshop suggested that an increase in food aid to between 20 and 50 million metric tons from the current level of about 10 million metric tons would be needed by the end of the 1990s.[113] This forecast was included in the boilerplate of both the House and Senate 1990 bills. Yet it seems unlikely that the economic and political forces that have contributed to the increasing separation of the supply management and market development objectives from the economic development and humanitarian assistance aspects of U.S. food aid will become weaker in the immediate future. If U.S. food stocks should continue to decline in response to the reform of domestic commodity policies, budget constraints will force a more difficult trade-off between food aid and financial assistance. An implication is that the agricultural commodities distributed under PL 480 auspices will continue to decline relative to commercial exports, to assisted exports, and to other forms of bilateral aid. This implies that it may be difficult to sustain even the present World Food Program target of 10 million tons of bilateral and multilateral food aid.

The positive perspective on PL 480 is that it has generated substantial benefits to each of its major domestic clientele groups and some benefits to recipient countries that would not otherwise have been available. It was useful not because it was superior to other forms of aid but because the commodities were available! A minimalist defense might be that it was the least bad use that could be made given the surpluses that were available. This defense cannot, however, avoid confronting the argument that better use could have been made of the same resources.

The food aid provisions of the 1990 Agricultural Development and Trade Act allow the Department of Agriculture, under special circumstances, to purchase food not included in the docket determined by the secretary as available for use under the Food for Peace Act. This presents the department a modest opportunity to design a program in which commodities can be more directly programmed to meet planned emergency food aid and to combat chronic malnutrition and hunger. Food security could be more effectively assured by further broadening the mix of commodities that might be made available to poor countries. The definition of food aid should, for example, be broadened to include the technical inputs—fertilizer, pesticides, and animal feeds—that are necessary if farmers in recipient countries are to contribute effectively to their countries' food needs. All food aid should be placed on a grant basis. The United States now provides development and economic support for assistance primarily on a grant basis to deeply indebted recipient countries. As of 1994, however, we were continuing to provide concessional food aid loans with a 7- to 10-year grace period and up to 30 years to repay the loan (down from 40 years in previous legislation). This anomaly should be corrected. Creative suggestions for more radical reform of food aid have come from outside the official food aid agencies. G. Edward Schuh has proposed that food aid support of school feeding programs be reorganized to reinforce incentives for school participation.[114] John W. Mellor has proposed the use of an expanded food aid effort to mitigate the unfavorable effects of structural adjustment programs on the poor. Willis Peterson has outlined the elements of an international food stamp program that would avoid disincentive effects on agriculture in recipient countries while simultaneously expanding the demand for agricultural exports from donor countries. Bound by continuing large budget deficits and by competition between Eastern Europe and the Third World for assistance resources, it is unlikely that the political resources needed to bring about dramatic institutional innovation in food aid policy will be mobilized in the 1990s.

Food Aid and Food Security

Food aid represents a very limited component of a much larger issue. That issue is how to eliminate or, at the very least, how to reduce hunger among the poor in the poorest countries. There continues to be much confusion about this issue. Some argue that supply-side constraints imposed by resource endowments and lack of appropriate technology are the primary sources of poverty and hunger. Others argue that the primary constraints are on the demand side—that hunger could be overcome by more equitable distribution of income or other forms of entitlements.

But, of course, both arguments are half right and half wrong. It is true that global food supplies, if entitlements were more equally distributed, would be adequate to more than meet the needs of the world's poor. Greater equity in the distribution of income could not, however, prevent future shortages in a world in which the supply of food remained at or even near present levels. To meet future demand arising out of population and income growth, technical advances to facilitate more intensive use of agricultural resources will be necessary. Furthermore, the only reliable source of entitlements for the majority of families in poor countries must come from more productive work. And, for the poor majority in the poorest countries, this means enhancing their capacity to produce marketable surpluses of agricultural commodities.

There are sources of hunger in addition to those arising from supply-side constraints or inadequate distribution of entitlements. The most serious of these is caused by political instability. War and civil strife, associated with ideological, ethnic, or religious conflict, has resulted in a continuous growth in refugee populations over the last several decades. As long as such conflicts give rise to the displacement of peoples, there will be need for direct transfer of food and other resources.

The fundamental issue that confronts national societies and bilateral and multilateral assistance agencies is not food aid. Rather, it is how to create opportunities for the poor to make productive contributions to the development of their societies and how to reward the contributions made by the poor in a manner that will give them equitable entitlements to the dividends from economic growth.

It is much more important that research efforts be directed to the broader issues of how to enable the people who live in poor countries to become more productive and how to create the economic and political institutions that release and reward productivity than to continue to turn out more studies of food aid policy and programming.

Chapter 9

Universities, Voluntary Organizations, and Public Foundations

Interests, Clients, and Constituencies

Since its very beginning the United States aid program has turned to nongovernmental institutions for inspiration and assistance. The assistance policies and programs that emerged out of President Truman's 1949 commitments to make the benefits of scientific and industrial progress available to underdeveloped areas were preceded by a broad range of both government and nongovernment experience with cultural interchange and technical assistance in areas such as agriculture, health, education, and financial reform that extended back into the nineteenth century (Chap. 3).

By the early 1950s the Technical Cooperation Agency and the Mutual Security Agency were drawing on the resources of American universities to support assistance efforts in areas such as agriculture, health, and planning. By the mid-1950s the universities had become heavily involved, with U.S. assistance agency and private foundation support, in major institution building efforts in the Third World countries.

The private voluntary organizations that had assisted in the postwar relief and rehabilitation efforts became more closely linked to official efforts to provide humanitarian assistance in developing countries. In a policy statement issued in 1982, the AID identified five PVO "functional sub-categories" that were recipients of AID support: (1) traditional voluntary organizations, (2) cooperatives and credit unions, (3) AFL-CIO labor institutes, (4) family planning organizations, and (5) nonprofit consulting firms.[1] In addition to drawing on the resources of existing institutions, Congress has acted to establish several autonomous foundation-like agencies to implement assistance programs. These include the Asia Foundation, the Inter-American Foundation (IAF), and the African Development Foundation.

The relationship between AID and these three sets of institutions (universities, PVOs, and foundations) has always been somewhat uneasy. "Public and private objectives and programmatic interests frequently do not coincide. AID is accountable to Congress and the U.S. public; PVO's must account to their contributors."[2] From one perspective it is appropriate to view these institutions as clients of AID—dependent on the resources provided by the agency to carry out their developmental and humanitarian activities. From another perspective it is more appropriate to view them as constituencies that have substantial capacity to influence assistance policy. In this chapter I discuss the origins and the evolution of assistance policy toward the three constituencies: universities, PVOs, and "official" foundations.

The University Partnership

Two weeks after President Truman's "Point Four" speech, in which he pledged to "make the benefits of our scientific advances and industrial progress available for the growth of developing areas," Truman received a letter from Dr. John A. Hannah, president of Michigan State University and president of the Association of Land-Grant Colleges and State Universities, pledging support for the program: "This is to offer the full cooperation of the members of the Association of Land-Grant Colleges and Universities in carrying out the fourth point of your inaugural address . . . One of the greatest contributions America can make to the improvement of living standards, elimination of hunger, and fostering of peace . . . is by encouraging education in food production, food handling, food utilization, and better homemaking and family life among rural and urban people."[3]

The focus of this section is to understand the forces that have molded the relationship between the universities and the U.S. assistance agencies: those that have aided its success and those that at times have threatened its continuation.[4] In tracing assistance agency–university relationships, I give major attention to cooperation in the area of agricultural research and education. This focus reflects both my own familiarity with collaboration in the field of agriculture and the larger resources devoted to agriculture, relative to such areas as development planning, health and population, human and natural resources, and science and engineering, by the Agency for International Development and predecessor agencies.[5]

Point Four and the Early Years, 1949–1960

The involvement of universities in international development assistance began as part of the American missionary effort in the nineteenth century. Effective institutionalization of this effort was not accomplished, however, until after the appointment of Harold Stassen as administrator of the Foreign Operations Administration in 1953 (Chap. 5). Although a few university projects were begun before 1954, the majority of agency projects were implemented by the in-house technicians of the Mutual Security Agency and the Technical Cooperation Agency, predecessors to the FOA (see Figure 13.1).[6]

The Stassen Era

The Mutual Security Act of 1953 instructed FOA Director Harold Stassen to eliminate 25 percent of the agency's personnel by 1 January 1954.[7] During hearings on the act, Secretary of State John Foster Dulles noted that private sector initiatives might implement U.S. technical assistance as well as or better than government assistance. The reduction of technical capacity within the agency as a result of the reorganization later emerged as a source of disharmony in university-agency relationships. On 11 September 1953 Stassen announced a plan to reduce MSA technical assistance staff and rely more heavily on private voluntary agencies and colleges and universities to carry out technical assistance. In October he presented the plan to the annual meeting of the National Association of State Universities and Land-Grant Colleges. The technical assistance budget, he announced, would be increased by 20–30 percent to facilitate greater participation by the universities.[8]

By expanding university participation Stassen hoped to generate greater political support in Congress for a stronger commitment to foreign aid. Stassen's directive did not draw on any policy analysis of university capacities and involved little consultation with the agency's missions. The agency staff, in response to Stassen's habit of issuing policy directives without prior consultation, referred to his directive as "SSS" (Stassen Says So). Twenty new university projects were initiated during Stassen's 18-month tenure, including major programs in Brazil, India, Korea, Thailand, and Peru. The rapid expansion helped to institutionalize the program by creating a critical mass of university projects. But Stassen's leadership style also "created a legacy of hostility in the agency toward university participation and led to a substantial increase in negative incidents following his departure."[9]

The merger of MSA and TCA into the FOA also generated considerable concern about the focus of the U.S. assistance effort. A presidential advisory board warned Stassen that "lumping our Point Four program with military or economic programs abroad would amount to a 'major mistake.'"[10] The smaller TCA would be engulfed by the larger MSA, changing the character of the program and reducing broad popular support for Point Four. Other nations would read into this change new evidence of U.S. imperialistic tendencies. The administration used a speech by Walter M. Ringer, director of the Point Four Program for Europe, at the Women's National Republican Club to deny the charge that technical assistance was being tied to military assistance. At the same time, more and more technical assistance was being linked with military assistance and targeted to the nations on the periphery of the Soviet empire.

The motivation for the Point Four Program was strategic—the containment of Soviet expansion—as well as economic and humanitarian. Among policy makers this distinction was clearly understood. But among the general public and technicians working in the field, Point Four was primarily perceived as a response by the U.S. government to the material deprivation of Third World nations. This perception began to change with the merger of the two agencies (TCA and MSA) into the Foreign Operations Administration. In 1951, the *New York Times* had declared that the Point Four Program represented "a systematic attack on the vicious circle that keeps two-thirds of the world's population too poor, too enfeebled, and too backward to produce adequately, and too unproductive to overcome without help the poverty, sickness, and ignorance that hold them down. To these people the crude propaganda and drastic techniques of the communists must come with the shock of religious revelation." Two years later the *New York Times* announced that Point Four had become "an instrument of America's 'cold war' policy."[11]

The Hollister Era

Foreign aid programs were reorganized again in 1955 under the rubric of the International Cooperation Administration (see Figure 13.1). The new agency director, John B. Hollister, had little interest in technical assistance. He had been executive director of the Hoover commission task force that had studied the foreign assistance program and determined "that 'mistakes and waste' had characterized the U.S. foreign aid program and that 'important savings' could be made through more efficient administration."[12] In contrast to the rapid growth of university projects during the Stassen administration, Hollister's administration challenged the continuation of existing projects and limited the initiation of new projects. His administration eventually terminated five university projects (two in Jordan, two in Chile, and one in Ecuador) and began only three (in Indonesia, Japan, and Guatemala).[13]

In Hollister's view expenditures for technical assistance personnel were overhead rather than part of the direct cost of transferring knowledge. He believed that foreign assistance could be made more efficient by supplying the capital to finance development projects rather than by transferring personnel to advance technology and enhance human resources. This was in contrast to the university perspective, which viewed investment in human resources as central to the development process. The Hollister era clearly was a low point in relations between the agency and the universities. Long-term agency staff members referred to that period as the "Dark Ages."[14]

Hollister's administrative philosophy was reflected in a directive stating that new project goals needed to be quantifiable, that detailed documentation was a prerequisite for the consideration of any proposal, and that a detailed review process was required before a proposal could be submitted to the director. Since the achievements of university projects were difficult to measure, Hollister's new administrative policies worked against university contract programs. In 1955, during a Conference on University Contracts Abroad, Hannah noted that he planned to "investigate objectively with Mr. Dulles, Mr. Hollister, and the White House, if necessary, to determine what their feelings are . . . I haven't seen anything he [Hollister] has said or written that indicates he has any awareness at all of this university program."[15]

Tensions between the agency and the universities increased to the point that the American Association of Land-Grant Colleges and Universities warned that many universities might withdraw their participation in the program because of "the lack of major concern for and support of institutions at the top ICA administrative levels."[16] Tensions were diffused only when Hollister personally addressed the meeting of the association. After the meeting with Hollister, steps were taken to more effectively institutionalize ICA-university relationships. A new Office of Contract Relations was established to centralize contracting; previously, a dozen divisions had been able to negotiate, enter into, and administer contracts. Contracts had been a continual sore spot between the two organizations, and, although the standard contracting did not end the disputes, it did signal an improvement in relations. In fact, it is considered the first major agency policy change brought about by university initiative.

Agency-University Harmony, 1961–1972

By the early 1960s it had become widely understood that simply transferring the new agricultural techniques developed in America to developing countries was not sufficient to sustain long-term agricultural development. Techniques developed for American conditions and constraints were usually unsuitable to the conditions of the less developed countries. The increased emphasis on institution building and the many years of technical assistance prompted a wide range of studies and reflections on previous accomplishments and on prospects for the future of AID-university collaboration.

The Hamilton Era

The agency underwent its fourth major reorganization to become the Agency for International Development in early 1961 (see Figure 13.1). Newly elected President John F. Kennedy appointed Fowler Hamilton to administer the new agency. Hamilton, like Hollister, was primarily interested in capital transfers. His interest in AID-university relations was minimal.[17]

Under the new Foreign Assistance Act of 1961, the Development Loan Fund and the International Cooperation Administration were consolidated as AID. The Latin America bureau of the ICA was given greater visibility and labeled the Alliance for Progress (Chap. 5). The broader goals of the act were to initiate "greater emphasis on overall long-term development of recipient countries, establishment of standards of self-help, and comprehensive long-term planning." The change created in AID an administration that was more decentralized and less technically oriented. "The new doctrine held that underdevelopment was caused almost entirely by interactions among poor LDC economic planning, poor macro-economic policy, and shortage of hard currency foreign exchange to pay for capital imports."[18] As opposed to organizing bureaus according to technical function, each bureau was given a certain geographic region in which to guide all aspects of foreign aid work. Each bureau was equipped with a small technical staff in addition to administrators. The change greatly reduced the role of technical services within AID. Many technical personnel left the agency.

Although reorganization increased the agency's need for university technical experts to replace in-house agency technicians, it also impeded the agency-university relationship. The agency technical personnel who lost their jobs in the reorganization had been the primary contact people for the universities. John Gardner, president of the Carnegie Corporation of New York, in his book *A.I.D. and the Universities,* noted that if technical assistance was to be effective the agency needed to have personnel who could interact with university personnel on an equal professional level.[19] But with the new organizational structure, this capacity was further reduced.

The Bell Era

The administration of David Bell (1962–66) was characterized by a more respectful and fruitful relationship between the agency and the universities. As he began his tenure, the agency was in disarray and public confidence in it was very low. Shortly after his appointment President Kennedy wrote Bell to say, with a bit of irony, "I'm sure that my troubles with AID are over, and I hope that yours never begin."[20]

Bell was the first AID administrator with overseas experience. He had served as a member of a Harvard University advisory group in Pakistan.[21] Just before coming to AID, he had been Kennedy's director of the Bureau of the Budget. In contrast to Stassen, with his impetuous demands, Bell was much more analytical in his decision making. And unlike Hollister he strongly supported technical assistance. Policies were carefully planned, and agency staff were made aware of the reasoning behind each decision. This fostered a sense of teamwork in which the agency staff and their partners in the universities were working together for a common goal. The agency nearly doubled its university contracts during Bell's three-year administration.[22]

The stability of Bell's administration enabled the agency and the universities to evaluate more formally the accomplishments and difficulties of their efforts. A number of conferences were convened and studies initiated on agency-university collaboration. The most influential of these was the report on *A.I.D. and the Universities,* directed by John W. Gardner, president of the Carnegie Corporation of New York. The report provided the agency with some needed direction and was a significant step in improving relations between AID and the universities. Gardner insisted that the proper role of the universities was to continue institution-building programs overseas. He believed that the universities should be given a "maximum degree of autonomy" to perform their duties and to determine long-term policy and program needs. Richardson attributed its influence to the fact that it was widely read, that Gardner had put much of his own effort into it, and that Bell had strongly endorsed it.[23]

Soon after the Gardner report was published, AID contacted the International Rural Development Subcommittee of the National Association of Land-Grant Colleges to collaborate in conducting "An Analytical Study of AID University Contract Projects in Agricultural Education and Research." The study was a massive, three-year project that summoned the input of nine universities and the agency to help shape the future of the agency-university effort. Because of the breadth of university involvement in the study, the insights uncovered, and their continuing relevance, the 10 recommendations that emerged from the study are listed in Exhibit 9.1.[24]

Exhibit 9.1
Principles for AID-University Cooperation

- There should be a stronger commitment on the part of all participating agencies to an expanded and long-term program of building institutions to serve agriculture.
- More flexible project agreements and improved liaison between AID and the university community would effect needed improvements in AID-university relations.
- Research on the institution-building process should be significantly increased, and existing knowledge should be utilized more effectively.
- The basic ideas that underlie the land-grant type institution are highly relevant in technical assistance projects if properly understood and employed.
- Agreement on goals and commitment to an overall strategy by host and U.S. personnel should be strengthened by wider participation in project planning and review.
- Those aspects of technical assistance programs which have contributed to the highly negative attitudes of many university staff members and department heads should be changed.
- There should be fundamental changes in orientation programs to prepare team members adequately for both the technical and the cross-cultural requirements for successful accomplishments of their overseas assignments.
- Programs of participant training should be more carefully planned and more adequately supported so that they conform to the developmental needs of host institutions.
- The university should exert its leadership in developing a fuller public understanding of international technical assistance.
- AID and the universities should cooperate in strengthening the international capabilities of U.S. universities.

Source: Committee on Institutional Cooperation—US/AID Rural Development Research Project, *AID University Rural Development Contracts and U.S. Universities* (Urbana: University of Illinois, June 1968), 4–26.

New Directions in U.S. Foreign Assistance, 1973–1982

University involvement in foreign aid reached its peak during the Kennedy and Johnson administrations. In 1969, the newly elected Nixon administration quickly activated changes in the foreign aid program. In a message to Congress on 28 May 1969, Nixon expressed support for economic, military, and technical assistance programs that served both to aid other nations and to achieve security, market expansion, and goodwill for the United States.[25] Nixon proposed three new initiatives: (1) the establishment of a semiprivate organization called the Overseas Private Investment Corporation to expand private enterprise, (2) increased support for the international development banks and additional support for the U.N. technical assistance programs, and (3) the expansion of U.S. technical assistance.

To expand U.S. technical assistance, Nixon proposed the establishment of an AID Technical Assistance Bureau that would "devise new techniques, evaluate the effectiveness of programs, and seek out the best possible people in universities and other private groups to direct the programs." The United States also increased its support for the U.N. specialized agency programs and began to fund up to 25 percent of the core costs of the Consultative Group on International Agricultural Research (CGIAR).[26]

The early 1970s were a time of reevaluation within the development assistance community. Widespread hunger and new food shortages, particularly in South Asia, tempered the excitement of the Green Revolution and caused many people to question the means by which development was being achieved (Chap. 8). Congress too was impatient and dissatisfied with the ability of U.S. foreign aid quickly to improve the welfare of the poorest people in the poorest countries. Reformers who were critical of foreign aid claimed that U.S. aid primarily served the elite of recipient countries or funded government programs that did not affect the poorest citizens.

In 1973, Congress amended the Foreign Assistance Act of 1961 to include a new emphasis on growth with equity. This new policy was patterned after the basic human needs strategy of development recently adopted by the International Labor Organization and the World Bank. One effect of the BHN strategy was to shift the U.S. assistance effort away from institution building, in which the universities were heavily involved, and toward programs that provided services directly to the poor, such as integrated rural development (Chap. 6). The effect was to weaken university participation and strengthen private voluntary organization participation in AID programs. One response to this bias was a search for new forms of university-agency cooperation.

The Board for International Food and Agricultural Development

In 1975 Representative Paul Findley (D-Ill.) and Senator Hubert Humphrey (D-Minn.) introduced the Freedom from Hunger and Famine Prevention Act of 1975 as an amendment (Title XII) to the Foreign Assistance Act of 1961.[27] The proposed amendment consisted of three components: (1) It established a Board for International Food and Agricultural Development (BIFAD) comprising members from both universities and the general public to oversee the work of the AID-university partnership. (2) It strengthened the grants program to develop the capability of U.S. universities to carry out international development projects. (3) It established the Collaborative Research Support Program (CRSP) to support research on constraints on food production and to develop strategies to overcome these constraints in both the less developed countries and the United States. The Title XII amendment was a potential turning point in AID-university relations because of its implied promise of strong congressional support.

The heart of the Title XII legislation was the creation of the Board for International Food and Agricultural Development, a semiautonomous advisory board of seven members chosen by the president to act as a liaison between AID and the universities. It was designed to empower and focus attention on U.S. universities to better utilize their expertise in foreign assistance and to bridge the often difficult communications gap between AID and the universities. The BIFAD would be responsible for helping to develop and administer research programs, to strengthen university involvement in AID, and to evaluate AID-university projects.[28] The BIFAD's advisory role was designed to extend beyond Title XII to PL 480 and other programs related to AID's agriculture, food, and nutrition account.[29] Rather than designing BIFAD simply to represent a special interest competing for AID funding, "the agreed broader approach permitted the Board to make its recommendations on the apportionment of funds to Title XII activities in the context of other requirements of the developing countries and to seek optimum complementary relationships between Title XII and other activities."[30]

Although Daniel Parker, AID administrator, encouraged the Humphrey-Findley initiative, some senior staff members viewed it as an effort by the university community "to get the camel's nose inside the tent." When it was clear that the initiative had sufficient support to be passed, AID management worked assiduously to modify the language to limit the autonomy of BIFAD. Even after the act was passed, the source and extent of BIFAD's authority remained controversial. A legal staff opinion of AID in 1976 determined that BIFAD was officially an advisory committee. But the first BIFAD chairman, Clifton Wharton, declared that "there is agreement that the Board is not simply an advisory committee, although for AID management purposes, BIFAD is so classified." He went on to say, "The Board is not in a position to operate programs independently. Its influence on policy and programs will be largely dependent on its close ties to universities, its relationship to the Administrator and his immediate deputies, and its independent reporting authority to Congress on Title XII programs." The process of integrating BIFAD into Title XII leadership was both complicated and slow. Although BIFAD was commissioned in October 1976, its full involvement did not begin until fiscal year 1979 because of continued foot dragging by the AID.[31]

The Strengthening Grants Program

Congress initiated the Strengthening Grants Program under Title XII to build greater university capacity to work with AID in fields related to agricultural development. Funds were provided directly to universities and were spent primarily in the United States. Universities were chosen for strengthening grants based on several criteria: evidence of faculty and administrative interest, demonstrated capabilities in agricultural research, and willingness to commit the institution to the program by matching all AID funds, covering all overhead expenses or indirect costs, and using the effect of the grants to strengthen the capability for AID-related research.[32] The program provided each institution with approximately $100,000 yearly for five years. By the mid-1980s the Strengthening Grants Program had successfully enhanced and expanded the capacity for international work in a number of universities.

Title XII was controversial both within the university community and in AID. Universities that were not involved in agricultural or food-related research were not included in the program. Within the land-grant colleges there was often resentment, particularly on the part of faculty associated with area studies programs, of what they regarded as a narrow focus on food and agriculture issues. The grants programs did have the intended effect of strengthening the universities' capacity in international agricultural education and research. But AID missions did not actively seek out new contracts with universities. Rather, throughout this whole period, support for AID-university collaboration within AID, and particularly in the AID country missions, was weak. Consequently, universities were increasingly better prepared to make effective contributions to the foreign assistance effort just as AID was becoming disenchanted with their partnership with the universities.

Collaborative Research Support Programs

The Collaborative Research Support Program is, in retrospect, perhaps the most effective program initiated under Title XII. Institution building, which created the capacity for less developed countries to develop their own indigenous agricultural technology, had been the focus of much of the AID-university partnership in the 1950s and 1960s. However, the commitment of AID to institution building had declined dramatically by the early 1970s. The adoption of the basic human needs approach to development reinforced a perception in the international development community that U.S. foreign assistance should finance action rather than research.[33] Even agricultural research was regarded by some as too elitist. Furthermore, because institution-building programs lacked a strong domestic constituency, the support of Congress had always been difficult to sustain. As AID decreased its commitment to institution-building programs, it sought new institutional arrangements for the support of research.

The Collaborative Research Support Program was designed to give renewed emphasis to strengthening the linkages between U.S. universities and research institutions in less developed countries. The CRSPs also signaled a fundamental philosophical shift in U.S. foreign assistance to LDC agriculture. Rather than the U.S. seeking either to inform other nations about proper agricultural techniques or to build the capacity to engage in teaching, research, and extension patterned after the U.S. model, the program fostered collaborative work. It recognized the benefit to U.S. agriculture from advances in the knowledge of other countries. The relationship between the United States and less developed countries in the program was viewed more as a partnership than as assistance. The program also changed the relationship between AID and the universities. The work involved a collaborative rather than a direct-hire relationship.[34] In general, CRSPs have built on the lessons of past university experience and have become an effective means of developing appropriate agricultural techniques. The CRSPs have been a highly effective initiative in the AID-university relationship. Their design is much more consistent with current academic career patterns than were the old-style institution-building programs of the 1950s and 1960s.

The Bi-national Agricultural Research and Development Fund (BARD)

An alternative approach in bilateral collaborative research was begun in 1977, when the United States and Israel developed the Bi-national Agricultural Research and Development program. Like the CRSPs, this program is collaborative, although it links only the United States and Israel. The program is funded by interest earned on an endowment created by the equal contributions of monies from both nations rather than through the political process inherent in CRSP budgeting. The focus of its research is on high-value agricultural products—including nuts, fruits, fish, dairy, and poultry—in the arid regions of both countries. Of the 208 BARD projects completed by 1988, 20 had produced a commercial application in the United States, and 23 more had commercial potential.[35]

An Alternative to the University Model

In the early 1970s, AID began to support a significant parallel development in agricultural research on the problems in developing countries. It committed itself to funding 25 percent of the annual budget of the Consultative Group on International Agricultural Research, which directs the work of the International Agricultural Research Centers (IARCs). The IARCs were begun in the early 1960s as a collaboration of the Rockefeller and Ford foundations. During the 1950s the Rockefeller Foundation had put together a strong cadre of scientists during its sponsorship of educational and research-oriented programs in Mexico. After success with its wheat breeding program in Mexico, the Rockefeller Foundation initiated, in cooperation with the Ford Foundation, a study of how it might contribute to advancing food production in Asia.[36]

The first joint project of the two foundations was the establishment in 1960 of the International Rice Research Institute (IRRI) in the Philippines. The combination of the Rockefeller Foundation's research experience and cadre of scientists and the Ford Foundation's financial backing created a strong institute that contributed to significant increases in agricultural productivity, particularly in Asia, popularly termed the *Green Revolution.* Between 1960 and 1966 the two foundations also established the International Maize and Wheat Improvement Center (CIMMYT) in Mexico, the International Institute of Tropical Agriculture (IITA) in Nigeria, and the International Center for Tropical Agriculture (CIAT) in Colombia. In 1967, each foundation agreed to limit contributions to the four centers to $3 million annually. The funding cap encouraged the research centers to seek funding from other public sources.[37] One of these sources was AID.

AID became committed to funding the International Agricultural Research Centers in 1969 at a conference held at the Rockefeller Foundation Conference Center in Bellagio, Italy, to consider how to expand support for international agricultural research. AID had earlier provided grants of $350,000 (in 1965) and $400,000 (in 1968) to IRRI to develop machinery and to assist in responding to the disastrous harvests in India and Pakistan. The Bellagio meeting included representatives of the World Bank, the United Nations Development Programme (UNDP), the United Nations Food and Agriculture Organization, the Rockefeller and Ford foundations, and the bilateral aid organizations of the United States, Canada, Sweden, and Great Britain. Forrest F. Hill of the Ford Foundation expressed the need for international cooperation to sustain research for development of agricultural technology for the tropics. In response, the president of the World Bank, Robert S. McNamara, suggested the concept of a Consultative Group on International Agricultural Research to coordinate fund-raising efforts and to provide oversight. The AID administrator, John Hannah, committed the United States to contribute 25 percent of the CGIAR's operating budget.[38]

Since the Bellagio Conference, the United States through AID has been the largest supporter of the IARCs. From the early 1970s through the mid-1980s, AID continued to contribute nearly 25 percent of CGIAR's budget. The IARCs have grown to include institutes or programs that conduct research on plant genetics, livestock production, plant and animal diseases, food policies, farming systems research, and national agriculture research systems in addition to the original research on a variety of specific commodities. By the early 1990s the work of the IARCs was expanding to include research on inputs and on resource and environmental aspects of technical change in agriculture.

The success of the IARCs can be attributed to three areas in which they differ from bilateral technical assistance agencies. The IARCs are not subject to direct political intervention. Each institute is an independent corporate entity that can determine its research goals on the basis of need and opportunity rather than political priorities. They have been able to draw from a broad international scientific community in building their staffs. And, finally, they have developed an effective management system to guide their programs.[39]

The effectiveness of the IARCs has led some observers to question the need for the AID-university programs to strengthen national agricultural educational, research, and extension centers in developing countries. These national agriculture research systems (NARSs) are needed for a variety of reasons. Two are especially pertinent. First, a majority of the research of IARCs is strategic or generic in nature. To be useful to a farmer, the research must be adapted to the local agroclimatic region by scientists working in the region. Second, the IARCs possess only limited technology transfer capacity. The centers must rely on the NARSs to adapt and transmit the new technologies to farmers. The skill to transmit technology requires a sophisticated system and technically trained faculty. "It has been widely accepted that the ability to screen, borrow, and adapt scientific knowledge and technology requires essentially the same capacity as is required to invent new technology."[40]

An effective international agricultural research system requires the services of both international and national research systems. The IARCs are able to capitalize upon intercountry economies of scale to perform broad commodity-based research and to assist in the coordination of technology transfer and adoption. An important role of university collaboration with AID is to carry out research, teaching, and extension that strengthens the capacity of the NARS. As a result of this complementary interaction, there exists a synergistic relationship between the IARCs and the NARSs. In an effort to improve the application of strategic research findings at the IARCs, CGIAR established the International Service for National Agricultural Research (ISNAR) in 1979 to identify problems in and encourage the development of national agricultural systems.

The Decline of University Participation in U.S. Foreign Assistance, 1983–1991

Under the Reagan administration foreign assistance was intended less to support long-term growth than to secure short-term political and strategic goals (Chap. 7).[41] The Reagan administration's economic policy emphasized the privatization of public services and encouragement of private enterprise. The foreign assistance programs reflected this ideology by increasing the use of private consulting firms for research and private voluntary organizations for technical and relief services. This new policy direction, coupled with an increasing dissatisfaction of AID personnel with the Title XII program, led to continued decline of university involvement in foreign assistance. The number of Title XII institution-building projects declined from 42 in 1982 to just 8 in 1988.[42] During the same period, the percentage of agency resources allocated to agriculture and rural development declined.

From 1981 to 1987 the agency had an administrator, M. Peter McPherson, who actively supported the goals of Title XII. McPherson had previously served as a member of the BIFAD. A few months after taking office, McPherson and BIFAD Chairman Clifton Wharton signed a joint resolution between AID and the BIFAD regarding Title XII. It expressed mutual support at the highest levels for the AID-university collaboration. However, this resolution was insufficient to bolster support for Title XII throughout the agency, particularly among AID country missions.

In 1986 McPherson conducted a survey of AID officials and university representatives regarding the Title XII program. The AID missions criticized the universities for showing little commitment to the program, for supplying long-term personnel to AID projects who were of poor quality, and for ineffective contract management. The universities expressed concern that their capabilities in agriculture were not fully appreciated by AID, that AID relied too heavily on procedures for project implementation which interfered with addressing substantive issues, that bidding procedures were skewed toward private firms, and that universities should be more involved in planning processes.[43]

According to a 1989 GAO review of Title XII programs, the reasons for the decline in the program include a decrease in the overall funding for the Agriculture, Rural Development and Nutrition account that finances Title XII; congressional earmarks to PVOs that compete with Title XII; and the trend toward developing private sector initiatives.[44] E. T. York, Jr., chancellor emeritus of the state university system of Florida, in a paper prepared for the Office of Technology Assessment, described the circumstances limiting the achievements of the Title XII program: (1) decline in support for Title XII assistance, (2) decentralization of AID decision making, (3) lack of continuity of AID and university personnel, (4) shortage of technical personnel in AID, (5) lack of support for Title XII by AID professionals, (6) competition with private sector firms, (7) procurement and contracting procedures, and (8) failure of universities to involve their best personnel.[45]

In December 1990, the agency published a series of position papers outlining a plan to reorganize AID. The final paper discussed AID's new strategic management system by which the agency plans to improve quality and efficiency as it streamlines operations: "AID is working on its ship of state in two ways: one will repair and remove the barnacles from the hull and tighten the rigging, revitalize the crew and polish the brass, while the other will adjust the navigational instruments and set the course for the right place on the horizon." The report implied that the university programs were among those "barnacles" that would be removed from AID. "No longer can AID afford exclusive, entitlement-style relations with U.S. universities. We need to create processes that are inclusive and competitive, able to adapt to changing times and requirements, and to grow with the dynamic change occurring in the developing countries."[46] The concerns of the university community about their future relationship with the agency were heightened by the failure of Acting Administrator Mark Edelman (July 1989 to February 1990) to find time on his calendar to meet with BIFAD Executive Director Lynn Pesson.

In March 1990, Dr. Ronald Roskens, president of the University of Nebraska, was appointed AID administrator. Roskens spent much of his first year reorganizing the agency. A new Agency Center for University Cooperation in Development (the University Center) was established on 20 September 1990. It combined BIFAD's support staff and AID's Office of Research and University Relations under the authority of the Bureau for Research and Development (formerly the Bureau for Science and Technology). The center, headed by Ralph H. Smuckler, formerly dean of International Programs at Michigan State University, was authorized to administer all Title XII programs, which increasingly will be limited to linking U.S. universities with LDC institutions. It also served as secretariat for the newly named Board for International Food and Agricultural Development and Economic Cooperation (BIFADEC). The new BIFADEC, chaired by Wales H. Madden, Jr., was designed to broaden the pool of university resources available to AID beyond those of the land-grant colleges. Particular emphasis was placed on making the capacities of the nation's business and management schools available to the agency. The purview of BIFADEC was extended to include all aspects of development and to an expanded program in partnership with the broader university community. The report of the BIFADEC Task Force on the University Center Programs emphasized that "programs and projects should not be

FIGURE 9.1
University Projects: 1950–1990

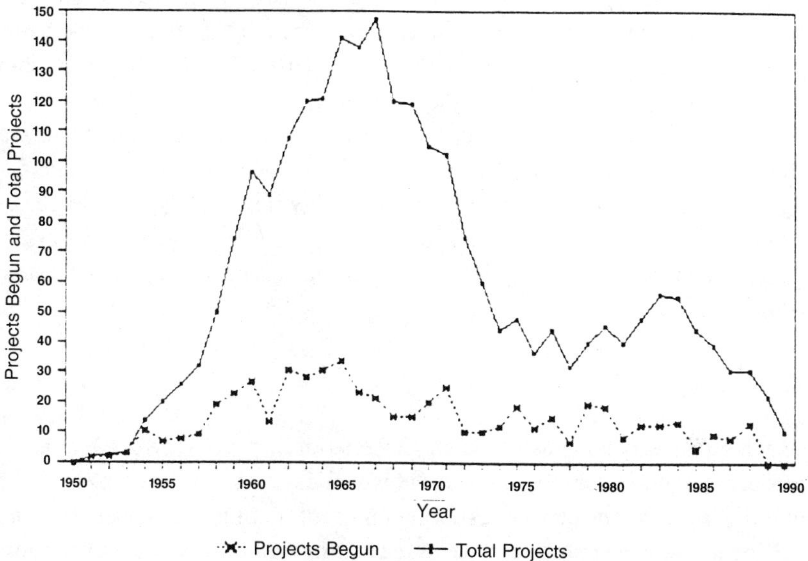

U.S. university projects in AID bilateral technical assistance programs (all development sectors).

Source: Erven J. Long and Frank Campbell, *Reflections on the Role of AID and the U.S. Universities in International Agricultural Development* (Rockville, Md.: Statistica, 1989), app. B.

expected in every instance to conform to current AID development strategies in a particular country and or program area."[47]

In spite of the positive interpretation advanced by AID, the creation of the University Center and the renaming of BIFAD to BIFADEC have been interpreted by some within the university community as a signal that AID intended to reduce its traditional reliance on universities. There has been a rapid decline in the number of university projects since 1982 (Figure 9.1).

In February 1992 a Task Force on Development Assistance and Economic Growth commissioned by BIFAD and headed by G. Edward Schuh, dean of the Hubert H. Humphrey Institute of Public Affairs at the University of Minnesota, called for a renewed emphasis by AID on agricultural development and the establishment of a Center (or Institute) for Scientific and Technical Cooperation, either as an autonomous institution such as the National Institutes of Health or as a substantially strengthened and redirected University Center within AID.[48] A combination of budget stringency and the report's completion during the last year of the Bush administration meant that the report was dead on arrival. While the focus of university programs was changing, the resources to support programs carried out in cooperation with universities declined. Fewer dollars were being spent with more universities to meet a broader program agenda. During the 1991 legislative session, considerable tension was evident between Congress and the agency about the future of Title XII and the University Center. Title XII was dropped in both the administration's version of the foreign assistance act and the version advanced by the House Foreign Affairs Committee. It was replaced in the House committee's version of the bill by the University Center. AID Administrator Roskins assured the university community that Title XII would be re-established by executive order. The university community regarded this assurance with considerable skepticism, since it would not be binding on any future administration.

Perspective

The long history of frustration in the relationship between AID (and its predecessor organizations) and the universities is due in large part to the differing perceptions of administration and staff, both in the universities and the agency, on the appropriate role of the two institutions. AID administrators and staff have typically approached the university relationship in terms of how the universities could be used to accomplish agency objectives.[49] The universities, in contrast, have typically viewed their role as extending beyond the AID program objectives to the building of viable institutions capable of generating the human capital and the knowledge to sustain recipient country development. University credibility has often been compromised, however, by willingness to be used by AID to conduct program activities that have been inconsistent with university objectives and capacities.

It is unlikely that this frustration can be resolved without the establishment of a fully autonomous institution to manage and fund university cooperation. Any successful funding policy must recognize the need for relatively unrestricted core budget support as well as support for specific institution-building and technical assistance projects. Several opportunities for the emergence of institutional arrangements to tap university scientific and technical resources more effectively were advanced in the 1970s but failed to achieve the political support needed to achieve effective institutionalization. It is unlikely that an opportunity for a thoroughgoing reform of the agency-university relationship will emerge in the constrained political and economic environment of the middle and late 1990s.

Private Voluntary Organizations

Concern for the less fortunate—the widow, the orphan, the homeless, and the stranger in need—has represented a fundamental tenant in many religious traditions. In the West, organized charitable activities were largely the province of religious organizations.[50] By the seventeenth century charitable work by religious organizations had begun to be supplemented by that of secular organizations. Exemption from taxes was often extended to secular charities by governments. They were seen as engaged in performing valuable social functions for which governments were unable or unwilling to assume responsibility.

There is also a long history in Western society, extending back almost to the voyages of discovery and conquest in the early fifteenth century, of international assistance activities by charitable organizations. The earliest were by church-related organizations that extended their missionary activities to include humanitarian assistance in areas such as health, social services, and education. These efforts often received partial subsidies by metropolitan governments. The Spanish government, for example, subsidized the operation of hospitals and schools by religious orders. In the nineteenth century, secular institutions also began to extend their charitable activities abroad, usually with the approval or support of metropolitan governments. The Red Cross societies, founded to assist with the care of those wounded in war, received substantial subsidies from their home governments.

The relationships between governments and private voluntary organizations and other nongovernmental organizations engaged in international assistance have become increasingly complex.[51] Governments in both donor and recipient countries have traditionally viewed most PVO and NGO activities as consistent with their own foreign and domestic policy objectives. They met important needs in which they had a comparative advantage relative to governments. As the resources that the PVOs have been able to allocate to relief and development assistance from their own resources have risen relative to resources available from official development assistance agencies, they have been able to bring greater pressure to bear on the formulation of donor government development assistance policy.[52] And some PVOs have emerged as the most vocal critics of development assistance policy and programs.

The purpose of this section is to review (1) the evolution of U.S. government policy toward the U.S. PVO community engaged in international humanitarian and development assistance activities and (2) the efforts of that community to influence official development assistance policies and programs.[53]

Relief and Welfare

Before World War II, official U.S. government support for the international activities of PVOs, other than the American Red Cross, occurred primarily in response to emergency situations. During World War I, relief efforts organized by private citizens to assist victims in Belgium and France were partially funded by the U.S. government.[54] After the war, U.S. private relief agencies, such as the American Friends Service Committee, the American Jewish Joint Distribution Committee, and various other religious groups and trade unions, joined with the American Relief Administration, organized by Herbert Hoover, to alleviate famine in the Soviet Union.

A base for continuing collaboration was established during World War II. In 1942, a War Relief Control Board was established to coordinate the activities of U.S. PVO relief activities. In 1943, a federation of U.S. PVOs, the American Council of Voluntary Agencies for Foreign Service, was formed at the urging of the War Relief Control Board. When the War Relief Control Board was dissolved in 1946, a new coordinating organization, the Advisory Committee on Voluntary Foreign Aid, was established. It was located in the State Department and consisted of representatives from both the PVOs and the government.[55] The U.S. withdrawal from the United Nations Relief and Rehabilitation Agency in 1946 because of alleged inefficiency and its relief effort in Communist-dominated countries strengthened the interest of the Advisory Committee in the relief work of the PVOs and led to increased financial support for their operations by the government.[56]

Among the most effective private relief efforts were those of a group of older "peace church"–based relief organizations, such as the American Friends Service Committee, the Brethren Service Commission, the Mennonite Central Committee, and the Unitarian Service Committee. But the secular and church-related organizations that have come to occupy dominant positions since World War II were largely established during the war or early postwar period. The new church-related relief agencies included the Church World Service (CWS, 1946), Catholic Relief Services (1943), and Lutheran World Relief (LWR, 1945). The new church-related organizations were not directly controlled by church boards. They were established to meet basic material needs rather than to engage in religious proselytizing. The secular organizations included Save the Children Federation (1932), OXFAM (1942), Cooperative for American Remittances in Europe (CARE, 1945), and Direct Relief International (1948). Because of the dominant roles that Catholic Relief Services, CWS, and CARE have continued to play, at least in terms of resource flows, it is useful, to illustrate the interplay between the U.S. government and the PVO community, to briefly review their establishment and evolution.[57]

Catholic Relief Services

Catholic Relief Services emerged out of an effort in the early 1940s to bring a measure of order and cooperation to the provision of post–World War II humanitarian assistance by numerous ethnic-based and other Catholic relief and service organizations.[58] Initiatives by the Bishops' War Emergency Relief Committee and the National Catholic Welfare Conference led to the formation of a new agency, War Relief Services, in 1943, later renamed Catholic Relief Services. Catholic Relief Services was governed by the Board of Trustees of the National Catholic Welfare Conference.

The initial objective of Catholic Relief Services was to provide relief and rehabilitation services in areas that could be reached while the war was still under way. This was expected to provide Catholic Relief Services with the experience and capacity that it would need to deliver services to other liberated areas as hostilities ceased. From the very beginning Catholic Relief Services established a policy that assistance would be provided to needy people without reference to sectarian affiliation. This official position did not, however, enable it to avoid occasional criticism that its support by the U.S. government had opened a breach in church-state relations.

By the mid-1950s Catholic Relief Services began phasing down its activities in Europe and expanding in Asia and Latin America. It was particularly active in Vietnam in the late 1950s and 1960s. By the late 1950s it had active programs in several Latin American countries. Relationships between Catholic Relief Services and local church hierarchies were not always smooth. In Brazil, for example, it took a visit by Bishop Sandstrom, Catholic Relief Services executive director, to impress on the Brazilian hierarchy the seriousness of the requirement by the U.S. government that food and supplies would have to be distributed to the poor regardless of color or creed.

Catholic Relief Services was not unmindful, however, that distribution of relief "improved the prestige of the Catholic Church." The new programs tended to follow a self-help formula. In Brazil, "teams that included an engineer, a nutritionist, an economist and an agriculturalist . . . would go into a village, discover the needs of the people, whether it be a new water well or an economic problem, and then lend whatever assistance was needed in terms of expertise."[59]

Church World Service

The motives for establishing the Church World Service were, in many respects, similar to those for establishing Catholic Relief Services. Attempts had been made in the 1920s and 1930s to bring Protestant relief organizations working in China under one umbrella.[60] In 1946 several umbrella groups, including the Commission for Church World Service, the Church Committee for Overseas Relief and Reconstruction, and the Committee for Relief in Asia merged to form CWS. This new agency was designed to carry out relief and reconstruction for the founding agencies and their member denominations. A number of churches continued to carry out their own fund-raising activities.

The official position of the CWS, like Catholic Relief Services, was to avoid using its relief and rehabilitation activities as an instrument for proselytizing. But the program did include funds for "religious rehabilitation" as well as food, clothing, and relief services. Relationships between the CWS and the Advisory Committee on Voluntary Foreign Aid were not always easy. CWS officials displayed a good deal of sensitivity about what they viewed as efforts by the Advisory Committee to exercise state control "over relief, rehabilitation and technical assistance programs carried on as voluntary service."[61]

The Cooperative for American Relief Everywhere

CARE was organized for the purpose of combatting hunger in Europe after the ending of hostilities in the spring of 1945.[62] Its initial function consisted of sending surplus food packages, originally assembled for use by the U.S. military, to designated individuals and families in Europe. By making a small payment, initially $10.00, an American donor could have a food package delivered to a specific recipient in Europe. As the military surplus packages were used up, more complete food packages were designed. By early 1947 CARE was offering donors an expanded assortment of packages that included blankets, clothing, and tools.

The proposal for a food package program had been vigorously advanced by Arthur Ringland, a consultant to the War Relief Control Board. When he failed to obtain a sympathetic response in Washington, he approached Wallace J. Campbell, director of the New York office of the Cooperative League of the U.S.A. (now the National Cooperative Business Association), the major cooperative trade association. The league was in the process of initiating a program to assist in the rebuilding of European cooperatives and was reluctant to take on any additional responsibilities. Ringland and a colleague, Dr. Lincoln Clark of the United Nations Relief and Rehabilitation Agency, continued to press the importance of an American initiative.[63] Campbell agreed to bring the idea to the attention of the American Council of Voluntary Agencies for Foreign Service (ACVAFS). "If the Cooperative League sets up a food parcel service, the Methodists will need one, too. And the Catholics will create a separate service. And the American Federation of Labor will have to have one."[64] After a series of conferences and personal meetings designed to overcome the considerable caution on the part of other members of the council, an agreement was reached to establish an organization, Cooperative for American Remittances to Europe (CARE), as a cooperative organization with a membership of 22 voluntary agencies. A District of Columbia charter was obtained in November 1945. The War Relief Control Board at first delayed registration of CARE because of skepticism about its capacity to carry out the proposed program. After an intensive personal effort to "walk through" the documents, the necessary agency approvals to begin shipments were obtained. The first shipment of food packages arrived in Havre, France, on 11 May 1946.

In 1948, a proposal to abandon the policy of sending packages only to individuals specified by donors and to provide food to anyone in need in a specific country or region resulted in a major policy crisis. A reconsideration of the initial policy was precipitated by pressure from the Advisory Committee on Voluntary Foreign Aid and by receipt of donations that had not designated specific recipients. Several member organizations that had their own general relief programs viewed a broader CARE mandate as potentially competitive. The secular member organizations—particularly the cooperatives, the unions, and the national farm organizations—viewed CARE as an agency that should assist in reconstruction as well as relief. After a series of emotionally charged board meetings, the broader mandate was approved by a narrow margin. Over the next several months, some of the member organizations that had voted against the broader mandate, including Catholic Relief Services, the Church World Service, the American Jewish Joint Distribution Committee, and the Friends Service Committee, withdrew from membership in CARE.

The new policy placed CARE (now renamed Cooperative for American Relief Everywhere) in a stronger position to explore new opportunities beyond its traditional areas of service in Europe. As prosperity returned to Western Europe, country programs there were gradually phased out. New programs were initiated in Asia, Latin America, and Africa. This shift in emphasis created a second major crisis. In 1953, CARE Executive Director Paul French recommended that the organization declare its mission completed. He argued that CARE should complete the closing of its European offices, close down its offices in other countries, and conclude the organization's history by going out in a "blaze of glory." The proposal was not greeted with enthusiasm by the CARE staff. After a series of meetings with regional staff, CARE President Murray Lincoln scheduled an Executive Committee meeting to consider both the French and staff recommendations. The Executive Committee supported the staff rather than the French position. Paul French had earlier tendered his resignation to emphasize his commitment to phase out the CARE operation. Before he was able to reconsider, the Executive Committee had offered the position to Richard Reuter, then serving as deputy to French.[65]

The change in leadership reinforced the transition of CARE to a general purpose relief agency. The shift was accompanied by a reduction in the food package approach in favor of the transfer and distribution of bulk commodities. New activities, including rural development, school meals, and refugee programs, were implemented. These changes were facilitated by Section 416 of the Agricultural Act of 1949 and by passage of the Agricultural Trade and Development Act of 1954 (Public Law 480). Section 416 authorized the secretary of agriculture to donate surplus agricultural commodities in danger of spoilage to voluntary agencies registered with the Advisory Committee. Public Law 480 provided that surplus commodities held by the Commodity Credit Corporation could be made available for distribution by PVOs in developing countries (Chap. 8). By the mid-1950s, CARE was operating in several countries in Latin America and Asia. Its program and the resources available to it were very different from those in its initial years.[66]

By the late 1950s, the activities that have characterized CARE operations since that time were in place. They included general relief, the promotion of self-help development, and the use of government food surpluses to combat hunger and malnutrition. There have been other new ventures, such as the assumption of operational responsibility for the MEDICO primary health care program in 1962. But these have had difficulty achieving sustained support and have remained peripheral to the overall program. Since at least the mid-1960s, CARE has positioned itself as a development agency rather than a relief agency. A new umbrella organization, CARE International, initiated by CARE U.S.A., includes national organizations in 10 other countries.

By the early 1990s, CARE U.S.A. had become the largest private nongovernmental organization in the field of relief and development. Several of the CARE organizations are among the largest NGOs in their respective countries. In spite of efforts to widen its bases of support in 1992, less than 10 percent of CARE U.S.A. support came from donors. Fifty-four percent was in the form of agricultural commodities from the U.S. government, and 27 percent was in the form of other support from government and nongovernment agencies.[67]

The dependence of CARE, Catholic Relief Services, and several other large U.S. PVOs on PL 480 food surpluses and other government support has meant that the size and geographic focus of their programs continue to be determined largely by the focus of U.S. strategic interests and the rise and decline of U.S. domestic food surpluses. Their heavy involvement in Somalia, beginning in the early 1980s and continuing through the peacekeeping operation of the early 1990s, is only one of the recent reminders of this dependency. The issue of how to turn the surplus food into an effective instrument for development, rather than simply relief, has not yet been adequately resolved.[68]

A New Focus

During the middle and late 1950s, the Advisory Committee on Voluntary Foreign Aid began to encourage members of the PVO community to shift the focus of their programs from Western Europe to developing countries. Prompted in part by President Truman's Point Four speech and the growth of U.S. economic assistance to the less developed countries, the PVO community began to examine the relevance of its own technical assistance efforts in fields such as education, health, and agriculture (Chap. 3). Students of economic development began to give considerable attention to the influence of the technical assistance efforts of voluntary agencies. By 1960 almost 70 percent of all PVO overseas assistance was going to developing countries in Asia, Latin America, and Africa. Government support for PVO activities in developing countries expanded. At the same time several of the church-related PVOs became concerned that the close association between the nonprofit organizations and government was part of the Cold War containment strategy. Smith notes that in 1960 the American Friends Service Committee (AFSC) "terminated its contractual arrangements with ICA to provide technical assistance to community development projects in India when the U.S. government insisted that AFSC personnel be subject to a security check before being hired."[69]

A New Partnership

Beginning in the early 1960s, a closer working relationship between U.S. official development assistance efforts and the activities of the PVO community was beginning to emerge.[70] In 1961 William Reuter, CARE executive director, was appointed Food for Peace director by President Kennedy (Chap. 7). Senator Hubert Humphrey (D-Minn.) successfully inserted an amendment into the Foreign Assistance Act of 1961 declaring that it was the purpose of U.S. policy "to encourage the development and use of cooperatives, credit unions and savings and loan associations" in its development assistance efforts (Chap. 5). Over the next two decades, this mandate was strengthened by a series of amendments to the Foreign Assistance Act. The most important was the New Directions mandate of 1973, in which Congress declared that private and voluntary organizations and cooperatives should be encouraged, through financial support by AID, to expand their overseas development efforts without compromising their private character (Chap. 6).[71]

In 1981 Congress further strengthened its commitment to the PVOs by requiring that at least 13.5 percent of all government expenditures for a variety of assistance activities be programmed through PVOs.[72] In recent years AID has consistently exceeded this goal, devoting over 20 percent of its total budget to the support of private institutions. Congress also provided that no PVO should qualify for aid under any of these provisions unless it obtained at least 20 percent of its total annual support for its international activities from sources other than the U.S. government.

AID Support for PVOs

In testimony given before the House Select Committee on Hunger in 1989, Richard Bissell, the AID assistant administrator for program and policy coordination, listed the major factors behind AID's partnership with PVOs: (1) PVOs are able to leverage additional resources from the private sector, (2) the maturation of PVOs increases the quality and influence of their contributions to human and institutional development, (3) PVOs take advantage of specialization and the ability to recruit and place experts in the field, (4) PVOs are apolitical and thus can provide assistance in areas where U.S. governmental aid might be controversial, and (5) PVOs are better able to coordinate development activities with other nongovernmental agencies abroad.[73]

Each AID mission and region has independent authority to award grants to PVOs to carry out development activities within its geographic area. Roughly 75 percent of all government assistance received by PVOs is channeled through AID's local mission offices.[74] However, the degree to which these local offices rely on the private sector to carry out their activities differs according to philosophy and staff size. In a recent paper David Korten attempted to characterize the practice of the various missions: "Practice varies widely from mission to mission, and from one mission director to another. There are surely examples of A.I.D. funding relatively activist organizations. But on balance, there is a strong bias in A.I.D. PVO funding favoring organizations engaged in routine service delivery activities over more activist organizations concerned with enhancing the ability of the poor to exercise their rights."[75]

The Office of Private and Voluntary Assistance also operates centrally managed grant programs.[76] During the 1980s these included the following.

Matching grants are awarded to PVOs that propose clearly defined, evaluative, field-oriented programs that support AID's developmental activities. These grants allow PVOs to expand their current activities to new projects. Recipients must demonstrate developmental expertise and a private fund-raising capacity. Proposals may be funded for terms of three to five years. The grants are matching in that AID contributes up to 50 percent of the cost of implementation with the PVO contributing the remainder in the form of cash or services.

Child survival grants are awarded to PVOs for primary health care activities, especially those targeted to mothers and children. Among the activities receiving the most emphasis are oral rehydration therapy to combat diarrhea and immunizations against a variety of diseases. AID will fund up to 75 percent of the cost of programs in these areas.[77]

Cooperative development grants foster the expansion of cooperative development organizations (CDOs) such as farm organizations and credit unions. Efforts under this program are focused on expanding the ability of CDOs to conduct overseas operations, funding new programs to expand trade and economic development, and managing PL 480–related Farmer-to-Farmer and Dairy Links programs, which foster communication between U.S. and LDC farmers.

The Development Education (Biden-Pell) Program awards small grants for educational efforts that increase the American public's awareness of the social, political, technical, and economic factors pertaining to world hunger and other development issues. Among other goals, the program seeks to generate a widespread public discussion of the root causes of world hunger and poverty to help Americans understand the U.S. stake in Third World development and, incidentally, the importance of U.S. aid to developing countries.

Commodity freight grants reimburse PVOs for the costs of transporting equipment, supplies, and other donated resources to LDCs. Under the Denton amendment, the Department of Defense also provides free shipment for donated medical supplies on military flights where space permits. PVOs must provide AID with documentation showing that the supplies will be given duty-free entry and will be transported to appropriate project sites.

Food development grants provide support for food distribution efforts. The program has three basic components: (1) strengthening the institutional capability of food distribution agencies, (2) funding innovative uses of PL 480 food programs in development efforts, and (3) increasing the planning capacity of PVOs with respect to the uses of food aid.

Between the mid-1960s and the early 1980s, AID funding of PVO activities doubled—from approximately $250 million to $500 million. Private outlays and commitments to PVOs registered with the Advisory Committee on Voluntary Foreign Aid had risen even more rapidly during this same period—from under $50 million to over $1.1 billion. AID support was drawn from a wide range of program accounts, including each of the AID functional accounts, the International Disaster Assistance Account, the Sahel Development Program, American Schools and Hospitals Abroad, the Economic Support Fund, excess property, Food for Peace, and the State Department Refugee and Migration Account.[78]

Using PVOs for Development

In the early 1980s AID initiated a series of reviews and evaluations of PVO effectiveness and of AID's relationships with the PVOs. The Reagan administration entered office with a strong ideological orientation toward strengthening the role of the private sector in developing countries and privatizing the delivery of development assistance (Chap. 7).[79]

There was a general presumption that the PVOs were able to provide more accountable, effective, and equitable services in many areas than were public sector agencies. But the criteria against which to evaluate performance were far from clear.[80] One response by AID to the interest of the administration in greater use of PVO capacities was to undertake a series of studies designed to evaluate the effectiveness of PVOs as development assistance organizations.

One of the most influential reports was an AID-commissioned study by Judith Tendler, *Turning Voluntary Organizations into Development Agencies.* The Tendler report began by analyzing some of the articles of faith that the PVOs believe characterize their work and distinguish it from that of government assistance agencies.[81] These "articles" are that (*a*) PVOs have a comparative advantage in their ability to reach the poor directly within target countries; (*b*) PVOs are better at ensuring the direct participation of target populations in the planning and implementation of development projects; (*c*) one of the important benefits of PVO work is the creation of a process of empowerment through the involvement of poor populations; (*d*) PVO work stresses people-to-people rather than institution-to-institution or government-to-government contact; (*e*) the smaller size and independence of PVOs gives them scope for greater flexibility and experimentation in project design; (*f*) PVOs contribute to the development of local institutions, fostering a sense of pluralism in the target country; and (*g*) PVOs' access to voluntary help and their freedom from bureaucratic inefficiency make them more cost-effective than other aid providers.

The Tendler study concluded that, not only did these articles of faith fail to characterize many PVO projects, but also they were not necessarily good indicators of the characteristics that make a particular development project successful. Under some circumstances these characteristics were not conducive of project success. In some situations, project effectiveness could be enhanced by reduced public participation and more effective management. Tendler argued that PVOs with limited budgets often achieve better performance when they limit their activities to well-defined tasks rather than comprehensive community development.

The Tendler report also highlighted the ambiguity inherent in PVO-government relations. PVOs often make a point of criticizing government programs as being too bureaucratized and inefficient. This rhetoric strengthens the perceived differences between private and government activities. In reality, however, PVOs and governments are often heavily dependent upon each other for the success of their respective activities. Close cooperation between the private and public sectors is a crucial requirement for the creation and duplication of successful projects. Ideological perspectives that create artificial separations between the combined efforts of the government and private sectors tend to be counterproductive. Each sector has its own strengths and weaknesses. Tendler argued that each party should focus on these differences and assign the responsibility for parastatal development activities accordingly.

The early and mid-1980s were also a period of internal stress within PVOs and within the PVO community.[82] The attempts to become broad-based development assistance organizations, in addition to maintaining traditional disaster relief functions, placed new strains on management systems that had often experienced little change since the early 1960s. Increased reliance on public resources had, in some cases, been accompanied by a weakening of the sense of responsibility by private donors. In the late 1970s, for example, CARE experienced a sharp decline in private funding from individuals, foundations, and corporations. One response was to reorganize and professionalize its management structure. Management salaries were made more competitive, the solicitation and processing of donations was strengthened, and efforts were made to improve the monitoring and evaluation of development project activities.[83]

The 1980s was also a period of increasing tension within the PVO community regarding the appropriate relationship with governments—both the U.S. government and the governments of recipient countries. Many PVOs were concerned that excessive dependence on AID funding, and the organizational changes necessary to meet AID standards of accountability, posed a threat to both the ideology and the autonomy of PVOs.[84] This concern led several secular PVOs to join OXFAM America and the PVOs affiliated with the "peace churches" to refuse all direct government assistance. Many of the larger PVOs, particularly those that were most successful in responding to the opportunities for expanded government support for development activities, were regarded by those who were concerned with the effects of closer ties to the government as having crossed the line between voluntary agency status and the not-for-profit firm providing contract services for and at the pleasure of government—operating more in the style of parastatal than private charitable organizations.

By the late 1980s it was possible to employ a three-level topology of PVO organizations.[85] The *first* group includes the older and larger organizations originally established to assist war refugees and disaster victims—CWS, Catholic Relief Services, and CARE. Changes in these programs have lagged behind changes in rhetoric. The possibilities for change are limited by continued reliance on government resources, particularly the PL 480 food aid program, for 60–80 percent of their resources. Their capacity to shift toward a stronger development orientation is also limited by the commitment of both their donors and their boards to relief and rehabilitation. The *second* group includes smaller, more technically oriented organizations that focus on training and infrastructure in areas such as health, education, and rural development. These include organizations such as the Planned Parenthood Federation of America, Heifer Project International, International Executive Service Corps, and International Voluntary Service. A *third* category includes a group of organizations that stress long-term structural solutions to poverty. They tend to emphasize institution building, working in cooperation with Third World PVOs and strengthening local community organizations. Their programs emphasize consciousness raising, political awareness, and in some cases policy and political reform.

Development Thought and the PVOs

Since the late 1960s there has been a substantial shift in U.S. PVO thinking about their role in poverty alleviation. They were increasingly influenced by emphasis in the social sciences, in the media, and within AID on "the need to attack the structural sources of underdevelopment rather than to alleviate symptoms."[86] Many began to reduce their staff presence in the field in favor of collaboration designed to strengthen the capacities of indigenous PVOs.

The 1980s was a period of very considerable intellectual ferment within the PVO community. By the end of the decade, a group of intellectuals closely associated with the PVO community were beginning to have a significant influence on development thought and development policy. As noted earlier, the PVO community became increasingly sensitive to the implications of mainstream development thought for their program activities in the 1960s. But they were slow in acquiring the professional capacity either to translate development thought into program design or to confront the development policies of the official donor agencies or recipient governments. Many were deliberately self-conscious about not confronting the policies of either donor or recipient governments.

Several factors were responsible for the emergence of greater capacity and willingness to engage mainstream development thought and official development policy on the part of the PVO community. One was the pressure by the official bilateral and multilateral assistance agencies for their clients to assume the role of more broadly based development assistance organizations. A second factor was the emergence, in some developing countries, of a strong indigenous NGO community that began to question their client relationship to developed country PVOs.[87] A third factor was the shift by multilateral and bilateral donors toward policy-based structural adjustment lending in response to the LDC debt crisis in the early 1980s. The PVO community had been very supportive of the shift toward a basic human needs orientation of official development assistance in the 1970s. PVOs tended to interpret the shift away from a project and basic needs orientation and toward policy-based structural adjustment lending as subversive of their poverty-oriented, community-based development activities.

The publication, in 1984, of *A Framework for Development Education in the United States* represents an initial effort by the PVO community to engage both their own membership and the donor community in a dialogue about development.[88] The report, based on consultations among the leading voluntary organizations, emphasized the responsibility of the PVO community to build an informed and committed constituency for development both at home and abroad. The *Framework* report also insisted on the importance of motivating citizens to contribute to the formulation and implementation of policies designed to eliminate the root causes of world poverty.

PVO development thought begins with a view of the developing world that is very different from mainstream development perspectives: "As the Third World plummets further into debt and its poor become increasingly marginalized within their respective economic systems, the players in the post-war process of development assistance are at the crossroads. The development paradigm designed by the major donor and lending agencies has failed badly, but with too much at stake—financially, commercially, economically, politically, and strategically—they continue to prescribe unwaveringly the same strategy of export-led modernization and open economies."[89]

The central concept in new PVO development thought is the ideology of "empowerment" and "people centered development." This perspective, which has been most fully articulated in the writings of David Korten, was brought to bear with considerable effectiveness in the late 1980s and early 1990s. An important vehicle was a campaign to reform the envriomental policies of the multilateral development banks (Chap. 11). But the MDB campaign was not just about the redesign of projects or policies. The MDBs were targeted with the objective of modifying development theory and practice.[90]

The PVO's Influence on Assistance Policy

The increased interdependencies between the PVOs and AID have not been a one-way street. As government policies have shaped PVO organization and programs, the PVOs have also contributed to the shaping of assistance policy and programs. Since the mid-1980s there have been efforts to bring the political resources of the PVOs and the religious communities to bear effectively on development assistance policy. In 1983 the American Council of Voluntary Agencies for Foreign Service and an association of smaller PVOs (Private Agencies in International Development—PAID) presented joint testimony to the Carlucci commission (see Chaps. 7 and 13) opposing closer linkage between economic and security assistance.[91] In 1984 ACVAFS and PAID merged to form the American Council for Voluntary International Action (InterAction).

Initially, InterAction avoided establishing close institutional linkages with the political advocacy groups concerned with human rights, gender equity, and environmental policy—issues that might weaken their claims on public support in the United States or incur the displeasure of host governments. In this nonconfrontational posture the NGOs were reflecting the viewpoints of their domestic constituencies. Survey data suggest that in the mid-1980s nearly three-fourths of the U.S. public supported disaster relief, nearly two-thirds supported technical assistance in areas such as food production, health services, and family planning, and less than 10 percent supported the use of economic assistance for the promotion of democracy or social justice.[92]

By the early 1990s the PVO community was attempting to move toward a more active role in the reform of both bilateral and multilateral assistance policy. It was prompted in part by Interfaith Impact (formerly Interfaith Action and before that Interfaith Action for Economic Justice), an organization of 35 national religious organizations (Protestant, Catholic, and Jewish) that took a more explicitly activist stance on issues of poverty, peace, and justice both in the United States and abroad.

InterAction represented the interests of the PVOs that were engaged in the delivery of services abroad, while Interfaith Impact represented the social and political concerns in development of the religious community. Some organizations, such as Lutheran World Service, were members of both. But at the time this book was completed it was not yet clear, in spite of a much more vigorous dialogue with bilateral and multilateral donors, whether the two communities would be able to translate their large memberships into either stronger support for their programs or the reform of foreign assistance.

The dilemma that has continued to face the U.S. PVO community since it made the transition from relief and reconstruction in Western Europe to a focus on the relief of poverty and economic development in the Third World remains unresolved.[93] Their source of legitimacy with their members and the general public in the United States stems largely from their role as relief agencies. Their source of legitimacy with the activists in the field of basic human needs and human rights is their role in stimulating community development and empowerment. Their source of legitimacy with AID and the State Department derives from their willingness and capacity to provide relief and development services on demand in strategically impotent corners of the world—in Vietnam in the 1960s, in Central America and the Caribbean in the 1980s, and in Somalia in the 1980s and early 1990s.[94] Unfortunately, the PVOs have not been able to convince either the development professionals in the assistance agencies or the journalists who report on their activities in the field either that they have been very effective in providing relief in a manner that does not generate dependency or of their capacity to implement and manage development projects that achieve sustainability.

The Public Foundations

The emergence in the 1970s of two publicly funded "foundation-like" organizations—the Inter-American Foundation and the African Development Foundation, reflected congressional concern that neither AID nor the multilateral assistance agencies were effective in working with poor people or assisting in the development of poor communities.[95] The popular support for such institutions reflected the emergence of diverse domestic social movements with a strong anti-establishment orientation during the late 1960s. Disillusionment about the Vietnam War and the rise of environmental concerns were associated with the emergence of an anti-technology movement and the "small-is-beautiful" ideology.

These new institutions were not the first attempts to bypass the official development agencies and work more directly with indigenous people and organizations in the Third World. In the 1950s and 1960s, the Central Intelligence Agency (CIA) had encouraged a group of private U.S. citizens to form the Asia Foundation to advance American interests in Asia. The East-West Center was established with State Department support on the campus of the University of Hawaii to facilitate cultural interchange and technology transfer between the United States and Asia. The impulse to work directly with poor people and poor communities was an important motive for the organization of the Peace Corps in 1961.[96]

The Asia Foundation

The Asia Foundation was established in 1954 as a nonprofit tax-exempt organization governed by a board of trustees.[97] However, its origins trace back to the establishment of "an ostensibly private body, 'The Committee for Free Asia' in 1951, sanctioned by the National Security Council, and . . . supported by covert indirect funding." The committee was founded with the objective of finding ways to maintain and expand unofficial contact and communication with the peoples of Asia after the establishment of Communist regimes in China and North Korea. "The emphasis was on a private instrumentality that would be privately governed and would have the freedom and flexibility to do things the Government would like to see done but which it chose not to do directly."[98]

In 1954 the Committee for Free Asia was renamed the Asia Foundation and was incorporated in California as a nonprofit corporation governed by an independent board of trustees. The foundation was funded from the beginning by and through several trusts and foundations, some of which were organized to transfer Central Intelligence Agency funds to private American organizations. Offices and programs were established in Asian countries from Korea to Afghanistan. The foundation itself did not, however, engage in covert intelligence operations.

From the very beginning, the board took the position that the foundation was created for one purpose only; namely to serve American interests in Asia as a complement and supplement to official U.S. government programs and initiatives. The membership of the foundation board reflected both its commitment to U.S. official objectives in Asia and a traditional style of foundation governance. Its membership was drawn primarily from the foreign policy establishment and elite academic institutions. Its program activity was heavily directed toward strengthening the commitment of national elites—in government, in the universities, and in the media—to democratic forms of government and to a liberal economic system.

A foundation program that was highly valued was its Books for Asia Program. The foundation annually selected and shipped to Asian libraries over half a million books—mostly donated by the American publishing industry, university bookstores, and private individuals. In its grant-making activities the Asia Foundation tended to focus on the social sciences and humanities. It employed a low-key, small-grant approach rather than an institution-building approach. When I was working in Asia in the early 1960s, the Asia Foundation was almost the only donor to which an assistant professor at a provincial university in Thailand or the Philippines might apply for funds to purchase such small equipment as a typewriter.[99]

In 1967, during the Vietnam War, it became public knowledge that the Asia Foundation had been receiving a major part of its funding through trusts and foundations that received funds for that purpose from the CIA. This led to protests, by American and Asian scholars and publicists, about the CIA connection. The government of India insisted that the foundation withdraw its program and representation from India. The furor over the CIA connection can best be understood in terms of the broader protest in the middle and late 1960s over the U.S. role in Vietnam. My own impression at the time was that the CIA connection had been an open secret that the beneficiaries of the Asia Foundation had generally conspired with the donor to ignore.[100]

After the disclosure of the CIA relationship, President Lyndon B. Johnson directed that the covert funding be terminated. Since the termination of covert funding in 1967, the Asia Foundation has not received any covert funding from any source nor has it had any connections with any U.S. government intelligence agency. A high-level commission chaired by Secretary of State Dean Rusk recommended that it would be in the national interest to continue the work of the Asia Foundation. This was accomplished by making yearly general support grants through AID and the State Department. Neither agency turned out to be a very enthusiastic supporter of the Asia Foundation. Furthermore, the congressionally mandated New Directions program, which attempted to reorient AID programs toward aiding the "poor majority," was viewed as increasingly incompatible with the Asia Foundation's more elitist approach to "building democratic institutions and encouraging the development of democratic leadership."[101]

In 1975 the Asia Foundation board requested that the U.S. government try to seek an arrangement that would provide more secure long-term funding for the foundation. A distinguished study panel chaired by Edwin Canham, editor emeritus of the *Christian Science Monitor*, was commissioned. Other panel members included James Clark of the Chase Manhattan Bank and Ambassadors Samuel Berger and Leland Burrows. The Canham panel concluded that

> the Asia Foundation is an effective instrument for the furthering of U.S. interests in Asia. It is well managed, has a body of competent and experienced personnel, is widely established and well-regarded in Asia, and has demonstrated the ability to use a limited amount of money to reach a wide range of individuals and institutions beyond the reach of official U.S. representatives and programs. The Foundation has shown itself to be sensitive and responsive to local needs and priorities, and is innovative and expeditious in the administration of the small projects . . . it supports, it is an effective proponent of pluralism and democratic social and political values. It makes efficient use of the USG funds which provide most of its financing. In brief, the Panel has concluded that the policy of providing government funds to this privately managed foundation is wise and sound, fully justified by law, and should be continued.[102]

During the Carter administration the programs of the Asia Foundation were regarded as complementary to the administration's human rights initiative, yet funding continued to remain uncertain. Operations within AID guidelines became increasingly restrictive. In 1979 the Office of Management and Budget directed the State Department to take over from AID the responsibility for providing the foundation with core budget support. This recommendation initiated a bureaucratic game that lasted until mid-1982. OMB insisted that the State Department make offsetting cuts in the other budget categories in order to fund the foundation. The State Department emphasized its high regard for the Asia Foundation program but insisted that it could not reasonably be expected to eliminate existing funding to implement the transfer. As a result no funding for the Asia Foundation was included in the president's budget request for fiscal 1981 (submitted in early 1980). The partisans of the Asia Foundation in Congress added funds for the foundation in the State Department appropriation for fiscal year 1981. The president vetoed the appropriations bill, leaving the funding for the State Department, including the Asia Foundation, to a continuing resolution.

The Reagan administration initially took an even more negative approach than the Carter administration toward continued funding for the Asia Foundation. The Senate Foreign Relations Committee, chaired by Senator Charles Percy (R-Ill.), continued to support the foundation. In both FY1982 and FY1983, the committee authorized $4.5 million for the foundation and included a stipulation that the Department of State, in cooperation with the trustees of the Asia Foundation, should develop proposals for a more permanent funding structure for the foundation. The report, prepared by the State Department in consultation with the trustees, contained an exceedingly favorable evaluation of the foundation program. Yet the version that emerged from the administration's budget review process in the spring of 1982 indicated that "the Budget Review Board decided on March 29 [1982] that there would be no request for funds for fiscal 1983 because of budget stringencies and the relatively lower priority of the Asian Foundation for a claim on the resources within the Department's budget."[103] Apparently, the Budget Review Board, composed of presidential advisors Edwin Meese, James Baker, and Michael Deaver, overruled the State Department when the department continued to insist that the funding for the Asia Foundation be additional to that needed for regular State Department operations.

During the summer of 1982, the administration reversed its earlier position on the value of the Asia Foundation. In a speech to the British Parliament on June 8, President Reagan committed the United States to "fostering the infrastructure of democracy, a free press, unions, political parties, universities, which allows a people to choose their own way to develop their own culture . . . It is time that we committed ourselves as a nation—in both the public and the private sector—to assisting in democratic development."[104] In August 1982 the Asia Foundation was asked to develop, in response to the Reagan initiative, a program that would be funded at the $5.0 million level, over and above the continuing $4.5 million State Department level. On 30 June 1982 Chairman Percy of the Committee on Foreign Relations requested the Congressional Research Service to conduct a complete review of the "past, present and future" of the Asia Foundation.

The Congressional Research Service report, submitted in January 1983, notes that the Asia Foundation "program emphases are currently changing as it adjusts its focus from AID-related activities back to its original objectives of strengthening democratic institutions, especially those pertaining to law and the judiciary, the protection of individual rights, and the training for public service in Asia." Throughout the period of uncertainty regarding future funding, the foundation trustees had continued to emphasize the significance of its programs for U.S. "vital security interests" in Asia, including its "work with Asian intellectuals, writers, lawyers, economists, political scientists, and journalists in an effort to encourage private discussion and action on national needs and goals and on regional and international problems of importance to the United States." The organizational and funding arrangement preferred by the foundation was to continue as a private, publicly supported organization with "separate earmarked annual appropriations to be channeled to the Foundation through the Department of State."[105] In 1983 the U.S. Congress enacted the Asia Foundation Act as part of the Department of State Foreign Relations Authorization Act for fiscal years 1984 and 1985. Appropriations of $5 million for fiscal 1983, $10 million for 1984, and $10 million for 1985 were authorized.

The discovery by the Reagan administration that the traditional focus of the Asia Foundation—strengthening the institution of representative government and market economy—was consistent with its own foreign policy objectives on Asia has been followed by a period of renewal and growth. The foundation was able to drop its awkward attempts to come to terms with the New Directions mandate of the 1970s. It established a subregional program thrust by organizing a Center for Asian-Pacific Affairs designed to promote dialogue and cooperation between the United States and countries of the Asia Pacific region in such areas as security and economic affairs. The foundation continued to receive strong bipartisan political support in Congress, particularly from the Senate Foreign Relations and Appropriations Committees. By 1989, when William P. Fuller succeeded Hayden Williams as president of the foundation, support by the U.S. government (from the State Department and AID) had risen to $22.6 million. Private support, mainly donations to the books program, amounted to $19.1 million.

By the early 1990s the program of the Asia Foundation differed substantially from that of a decade earlier. Its staff had become more professional. Its grant making was more focused and less diffuse. Its program was consistent with the first of the four strategic initiatives for the 1990s outlined by AID Administrator Roskens—"to help promote and consolidate democracy."[106] The Asia Foundation attempts to support indigenous political development through a range of projects aimed at improving the formal administration of justice and law, strengthening the capacity of public sector financial and economic policy institutions, supporting government mechanisms to develop and implement environmental and natural resource management policies, improving the staffing of national and local legislative bodies, and encouraging the devolution of power and authority from the center to regional and local administration. In the early 1990s the foundation was beginning to explore how to add an economics dimension to its program, particularly the issues of the interrelationship between political and economic factors in democratization, structural reform, and transition from centrally planned to market economies.

The Inter-American Foundation

By the mid-1960s there was substantial disillusionment with the results being achieved by AID in Latin America. The Alliance for Progress, initiated with great enthusiasm and much publicity by the Kennedy administration in 1961, was viewed by Congress as bogged down in disputes between donors and recipients over excessive U.S. covert and overt policy intervention. The 1966 Foreign Assistance Act included language urging more participatory approaches to both economic and political development (Chap. 6).

The search for an alternative approach began in late 1968 during a trip to Guatemala by several members of the House Foreign Affairs Committee—Dante Fascell (D-Fla.), Bradford Morse (R-Mass.), and Donald Fraser (D-Minn.)—who had gone there to see how AID programs were working. After the trip Marion Czarnecki, staff director of the House Foreign Affairs Committee, took the leadership on drawing up a proposal for a new agency that would focus its efforts on social and civic development.[107]

After several months of hearings in early 1969, the House Foreign Affairs Committee issued a report urging a recommitment to the goals of the Alliance for Progress—transformation of Latin American society, economic growth, elimination of illiteracy and disease, achievement of better income distribution, extension of social benefits, and development of democratic institutions. But the report was also highly critical of the lack of progress toward these objectives. It found that U.S. assistance had produced little positive effect on the daily lives of the masses of the Latin American people. Social development goals were not being achieved in any substantially meaningful sense, and programs operating at a government-to-government level had not been effective in responding to the requirements of social and civic change.

After the hearings Representatives Dante Fascell (D-Fla.) and Bradford Morse (R-Mass.) succeeded in incorporating into the Foreign Assistance Act of 1969 an amendment (Title IV) authorizing the establishment of an Inter-American Social Development Institution. The proposal was greeted by considerable lack of enthusiasm within the Nixon administration. The State Department regarded the act as premature, since the Peterson commission, appointed by President Nixon to consider the priorities and organization of the U.S. assistance effort, had not issued its report. AID received approval from State to testify favorably on the proposal because of concern that, if the Fascell-Morse initiative were defeated, it would not be possible to get any AID legislation through the House in 1969. In retrospect, it seems likely that, if the House had waited until the Peterson commission completed its work, something quite different might have emerged. The Peterson commission recommended the creation of an International Development Institute to provide development-related research and technical assistance.[108]

The 1969 Foreign Assistance Act authorized the transfer of $50 million from the AID appropriation, to be available until spent, to enable the new institution to operate much like a private foundation. It was expected to support innovative programs in agriculture, education, and institution building with the objective of achieving more equitable participation in the development process and in the benefits of economic development without being dependent on annual congressional appropriations.

Action to implement the 1969 legislation proceeded slowly. It was not until May 1970 that President Nixon recommended the establishment of the institute—now to be named the Inter-American Foundation. Initially, the foundation was governed by a seven-person board of directors, of whom four were to come from the private sector and three from government. The board was later expanded to include six persons from the private sector, of whom a majority would be from the party represented in the White House. The board was to serve staggered six-year terms to avoid politicization. An attempt by the White House personnel office to name board members on the basis of political patronage was effectively opposed by Viron Vaky and Arnold Nachmanoff, advisors for Latin America on the staff of Henry Kissinger, who then headed the National Security Council. In the summer of 1970, the president nominated a board of seven prominent Republicans, chaired by Augustine S. Hunt, Jr. (then Vice Chairman, Quaker Oats), who were strongly committed to the objectives for the Foundation established by Congress. In addition to its governing board, the enabling legislation called for the establishment of an advisory council of persons knowledgeable about development. The council was not established, however, until after Peter Jones succeeded Augustine Hart as chairman of the board in 1978. Hart was selected as chairman of the Advisory Council. The board of directors met for the first time on 2 October 1970.

OMB interpreted the legislative intent rather narrowly—placing an annual $10 million spending limit on foundation activity. The State Department and AID, which visualized the IAF as a Latin American version of the Asia Foundation, were anxious to have it assume responsibility for the Title IX program (of the Foreign Assistance Act of 1966), which sought maximum participation in economic development, support for indigenous democratic institutions, and support for education and training, to be funded by annual transfers from AID to IAF. The board of the foundation insisted, however, that congressional intent implied almost complete autonomy from the State Department and AID, including exemption from normal administration and civil service appointment regulations. At its first meeting the board initiated an organization study and appointed a management consultant firm to conduct a search for a president. William M. Dyal, Jr., whose background included the Peace Corps, the Christian Life Commission, and the Baptist Foreign Missions, was selected in February 1971 and appointed the next month. A career foreign service officer, Irving Tragen, was appointed as deputy director. By the spring of 1971, the foundation was ready to assure a restive House Foreign Affairs Committee that it was ready to initiate program activities.

When the foundation began operations in 1971, it was characterized by a mandate and a degree of operational autonomy that were highly unusual, if not unique, among U.S. government entities in four fundamental aspects. It was to

1. enter into direct relationships with private, grassroots organizations in Latin America and the Caribbean and not operate through government-to-government channels;
2. seek social and institutional development as much as economic advancement;
3. respond to the concerns and initiatives of indigenous groups and not impose its own priorities upon them;
4. operate outside the network of official U.S. policy making, priority setting, and interagency coordination.[109]

The IAF staff has been limited, by statute, to one hundred. In practice, it has been held, by OMB-imposed personnel ceilings, to well below that level. Program development is highly decentralized. Field representatives have been drawn largely from academic, Peace Corps, church, or private voluntary organization sources. The field representatives report to four regional directors, who report, in turn, through a vice president for programs to the president of the foundation. The field representatives are located in Washington. They make four or five trips per year to field locations.

The foundation budget ran in the $12 million to $15 million per year range during the 1970s and upwards of $25 million in the 1980s. Roughly half of the funding is from congressional appropriations, and the other half is from repayments in national currencies from the Social Progress Trust Fund of the Inter-American Development Bank.[110] About two-thirds of IAF annual disbursements have typically gone to NGO intermediary support organizations that work with the poor, while about one-fourth go directly to grassroots organizations. Very little attempt is made to impose priorities or structure on the type of projects funded or even the geographic distribution of funds. In general, about two-fifths of the funding has been for agricultural and rural development projects, with 10–20 percent falling in areas identified as education and training, community services, urban enterprises, and research and learning. Administrative costs have been low—typically less than 14 percent of the total budget.

The IAF has been the object of critical attention almost from its inception. In 1972 and 1973 the House Sub-Committee on Inter-American Affairs asked IAF to respond to criticism that it was "doing the same thing" as AID under Title IX and the Peace Corps.[111] An initial assessment by the General Accounting Office in 1973 raised questions about the reluctance of the foundation to use U.S. PVOs as intermediaries and the high proportion of projects that did not meet stated objectives.[112] In 1978 the Office of the Inspector-General for Foreign Assistance (IGA) criticized the foundation for poor project selection and design, inadequate specification of objectives, poor monitoring, and insufficient coordination with other development entities.[113]

In 1978 the Heritage Foundation initiated a study of the IAF designed to provide policy guidance in the transition to a new administration should a conservative president be elected in 1980.[114] The report grudgingly acknowledged the unique role of the foundation—"it has been able to conduct activities which AID would have difficulty conducting because of its traditional bureaucracy . . . The United States is fortunate to have a mechanism like the IAF." The report concluded, however, that, although the IAF "is not all black" and should not be eliminated, it should acquire a new economic and political philosophy. The report approved the involvement of poor people in development projects, but it opposed putting them in charge. And it admonished that "the IAF should not use U.S. tax dollars to promote, wittingly or unwittingly, groups which favor communism and whose basic ideology is inimical to the traditional interests of the United States."[115] This gratuitous advice was offered even in the absence of evidence that the IAF had "wittingly or unwittingly" promoted such groups. The foundation's response to criticism from the Republican Right was to commission studies of IAF programs by leading students of Latin American development. The general tenor of these reports was highly favorable to the work of the IAF. Their criticisms of program effectiveness and priorities tended to be somewhat muted by the reviewers' sympathy for the program's grassroots approach and the strong staff commitment.[116]

The staggered terms of the executive board were less than a fully effective protection against politicization when confronted by an administration that was intent on changing the "philosophical orientation" of the program. Politicization of the IAF began during the Carter administration. In 1978 the Carter White House named as board chairman Peter T. Jones, senior vice president and general counsel of Levi Strauss—a prominent Democrat who had formerly been active in the aid field. Jones in turn brought Peter D. Bell, a Ford Foundation staff member—also a "clearly identifiable Democrat"—into the foundation as president in 1980. There was initially some resentment of Bell's appointment on the part of the IAF staff. His concerns about project quality, reflected in an effort to introduce more systematic project development and monitoring, were viewed as an attempt to impose Ford Foundation culture on the more informal IAF style of operation. It is generally conceded that Bell was an effective executive. He did nothing to politicize the staffing of the foundation. Yet his appointment angered the critics and enemies of IAF and set a precedent that led to his forced resignation three years later (in 1983), which plunged the foundation into crisis.

When the Reagan administration assumed office in 1981, there was an opportunity to immediately fill the two public sector vacancies on the IAF board. Two of the private sector vacancies became open in the fall of 1982 and a third in 1984. The new board appointed its own study group, consisting of Dr. Sidney Weintraub (of the Lyndon B. Johnson School of Public Affairs), former Ambassador William P. Stedman, Jr., and Peter L. Szanton to review of the foundation's purposes, policies, procedures, and management. The report noted that the foundation continued to draw "strong bi-partisan support in both houses of Congress and from members of differing ideologies. OMB, which had opposed its creation, now regards the Foundation with what might be termed reluctant admiration . . . Attitudes toward the Foundation in State and AID vary and have shifted over time but now can be summarized as, at worst, bemused tolerance in Washington and growing respect in the field . . . Among academics familiar with Latin American affairs, and with development issues more generally, the Foundation appears to enjoy high regard."[117]

The Weintraub report was, however, critical of several aspects of the IAF program. It noted that it could "find no fully satisfying rationale for the observed allocation of IAF resources" but qualified this criticism by noting that the problem has been difficult to resolve in an organization in which responsiveness to client priorities is given high priority. The report noted that, during its early years, the IAF was "activist almost to the point of being anti-intellectual in spirit. [It] has over the past few years intensified efforts in evaluation and self-analysis, and has expanded its dissemination of the most important findings." And it emphasized that the IAF had not resolved the issue of how to achieve effective articulation between responsiveness to client priorities and the provision of the technical assistance necessary to assure a higher project success ratio.[118]

The Reagan administration, using the Heritage Foundation report as a guideline, moved to gain control of the IAF board. In November 1981, Victor Blanco, an immigrant from Cuba and then president of Multi-Media Management (Monrovia, California), was appointed as chairman of the board of directors. Both Blanco and Vice Chairman Harold K. Phillips, a California businessman with interests in Central America, were strongly committed to the Reagan agenda in Central America. They were particularly concerned by what they saw as the lack of consistency between the IAF program and the Reagan administration's political and strategic objectives in the Americas (see Chaps. 7 and 10). After Bell's departure, Robert W. Mashek, an IAF staff member, served as interim president until he was replaced by Deborah Szekley, a Republican activist and businesswoman from southern California, in 1984. Within less than a year, some members of the board became concerned that Szekley had been co-opted by the IAF staff and were pressing for her removal. The effort failed because, in Szekely's words, "They tried to get rid of me too soon. I still had strong support in the White House."[119] Before the end of her term, Szekely had established a reasonably effective working relationship with Blanco.

> The Reagan appointees on the Board . . . spent the ensuing years in an unsuccessful effort to tie the Foundation's funding into the administration's foreign policy agenda. There are several reasons for its failure to do so. First, and foremost, the Foundation staff, particularly its project personnel, have maintained a high level of professionalism and commitment under the most trying circumstances and have held the IAF to its mandate. Second, supporters on the outside . . . have, through Congress and the press, brought public scrutiny to bear on the board's efforts. Finally, . . . the very structure of the Foundation has made it difficult for even the board to divert it from its mandate.[120]

William Dyal, Jr., also credits the efforts of the Development Group for Alternative Policies (Development GAP), "an activist policy organization," whose leadership had been associated with IAF in the early 1970s, with helping to mobilize congressional and PVO efforts to maintain the integrity of the IAF program: "Without the Development GAP's extensive efforts, the autonomy of the Inter-American Foundation, and possibly the Foundation itself, would have been a thing of the past, and the African Development Foundation certainly would not have been created."[121] It is possible that the Reagan administration might have been more successful in redirecting the IAF program if participation by the government members of the board had been more effective. There was a tendency for the government members to become only marginally involved in IAF policy. When they attended board meetings, they often "arrived late and left early."

The IAF has continued to receive a sympathetic response to its program from the Senate and House Foreign Relations and Foreign Affairs committees and appropriations subcommittees. Committee members have expressed concern about efforts of the board of directors to redirect programs and about efforts by some board members, particularly Harold Phillips, to influence staff on grant activities. When pressed by Congressman Obey about this problem in the 1989 Appropriations Subcommittee hearings, IAF President Szekely responded that "it is very difficult for me to instruct board members who have the power of hiring and firing me."[122]

One of Szekely's initiatives was to strengthen in-country program support capacity. Initially, motivated by the slogan "They Know How," the IAF established direct working relationships with grassroots membership organizations. By the end of the 1970s, the IAF had begun to rely more heavily on contracts with grassroots support organizations, employing host country development professionals and paying host country salary levels, for assistance in in-country project identification and monitoring. In 1984 Szekely moved to formalize such arrangements in each country along the lines of a successful model that had been developed in Costa Rica by foundation representatives. The arrangement made it possible to expand project activity and provide a broader range of support functions. It relieved the foundation representatives of a good deal of logistical and administrative burden and enabled the representatives to focus more attention on matters of program substance. By transferring funds to in-country service (ICS) organizations, the foundation also was able to avoid some of the congressional and OMB strictures on funding and to respond in a more flexible manner to each country's program needs.[123]

In 1988, Weintraub, Stedman, and Szanton completed a second evaluation of IAF. The report found that IAF remained a "distinctive and valuable" institution in working directly with the poor; that it was emerging from an "extremely difficult" period of conflict between elements of the board, staff, and management; and that significant management improvements had been made. Despite these accomplishments the report found that IAF lacked a general strategy and operational plan to focus and carry out its program and learning activities. IAF responded favorably to the report, saying that it agreed with the majority of its recommendations and that many of them were already being implemented.[124]

The African Development Foundation

Legislation authorizing the establishment of an African Development Foundation (ADF) was enacted by Congress in December 1980 as part of the International Security and Development Cooperation Act of 1980 (PL 96-533, Title V). The ADF legislation was modeled on the Inter-American Foundation. But the history of ADF has been very different from that of its sister institution.

The proposal for an ADF began with a series of conversations in the mid-1970s among staff members of the IAF, the AID Africa Bureau, the Senate Subcommittee on Foreign Assistance, and the Development Group for Alternative Policies. Legislation based on a Development GAP concept paper was introduced in the House in 1977 by Representatives Don Bonker (D-Wash.) and Candiss Collins (D-Ill.) and in the Senate by Senators Edward Kennedy (D-Mass.) and George McGovern (D-S.Dak.).[125] The draft legislation addressed several perceived weaknesses in the IAF by requiring that the ADF provide support only to African organizations and limiting public sector membership on the seven-person board to two. The proposal had difficulty generating a significant political constituency. It received little support from either the U.S. PVO community or public or private sector aid contractors. Neither the OMB nor AID was enthusiastic. By 1979 the proposal had picked up sponsorship from Congressman William H. Grey (D-Pa.) and several other members of the black caucus. It was reintroduced by Grey and passed in 1981.

It took almost as long after the legislation was passed for the ADF to begin operations as it had to move the proposal through Congress. The administration delayed the nomination of a board until 1983. Neither the board chairman, William F. Pickard, a Detroit businessman, nor any of the other four private sector board members had any relevant African or development assistance experience. The board conducted its own search for a president and vice president. They selected as president Constance Hillard, a foreign policy specialist who had worked for Senator John G. Tower (R-Tex.). Reginald E. Petty, a development specialist who had been Peace Corps director in Swaziland and Kenya, was employed as vice president for programs.

There were strong pressures from congressional supporters to get a program under way as fast as possible to provide some justification for the funds that had been appropriated, and unused, since 1981.[126] Hillard and Petty had been in office only a few months when differences over program development broke out. The General Accounting Office later reported that "attempts were made by the vice president and some members of the Board to usurp the authority of the president, resulting finally in the resignation of the vice president. That was subsequently followed by the Board requesting and the president offering his resignation." When he resigned in late April 1984, Petty attributed his departure to disagreements about the effort involved in project development.[127]

Intervention from congressional sponsors forced a change in the ADF leadership. In June 1984, Leonard Robinson, Jr., the deputy assistant secretary of state for African affairs, who had served as one of the government board members, assumed the position of acting president. He was confirmed as president on 1 October 1984. By the end of 1984, key staff positions had been filled. During the summer of 1984, Robinson hired six contractors with prior development experience in Africa to serve as field representatives to explore project possibilities and develop project proposals. Emphasis was placed on "low risk–high potential" projects. By the end of the year a planning process designed to provide guidelines for program development over the 1986–90 period had been initiated.

The evaluation conducted by the Office of Technology Assessment (OTA) in 1987 generally gave the ADF administration good grades for rescuing the foundation from its nearly disastrous beginning. But its endorsement of the program can best be described as cautious. Most of the projects were still in the early stages of implementation. One-half of the 12 projects visited by the OTA evaluation teams were judged to have a high degree of participation; 11 were judged to have high to moderate potential for sustainability; 10 were viewed as having moderate to high replicability. There was relatively heavy reliance on intermediary as opposed to grassroots organizations. OTA also found that (*a*) ADF's prefunding analysis and monitoring of project implementation was weak, with African field staff being underutilized in these efforts; (*b*) communication with other private and official African development groups was not sufficient; and (*c*) country-specific planning strategies were absent. ADF responded to the OTA assessment by conducting training for its program staff in project analysis and by delegating more responsibility to African field staff in proposal review and project analysis. It chose to avoid country planning strategies to maintain its responsive grassroots posture.[128]

A brief analysis of ADF's project portfolio reveals a total of approximately $14 million obligated to 152 projects from 1984 to 1988. This included projects in agriculture (33 percent), integrated rural development (11 percent), water (12 percent), credit (13 percent), education and training (17 percent), and small business (10 percent).[129] ADF also supports newer programs for African researchers and evaluators. A total of $682,000 was obligated during FY1986–88. Successful projects that ADF has presented to Congress include pond and well development in northern Niger, entrepreneurial skills training in Lesotho, assistance to cottage industries in Zimbabwe, supply of drinking water to schools in Tanzania, and small-scale hydroelectric generation in Sierra Leone.[130] These presentations have generally received a sympathetic hearing.

ADF has a small group of supporters and no real opponents.[131] The House Subcommittee on Africa is the main supporter of ADF. William Gray remains a key supporter but less so than in the past because of shifting congressional duties. ADF cultivated a similar relationship with Congressman Burton (R-Ind.), the ranking Republican on the subcommittee. For budget requests ADF works through the staffs of Obey (D-Wis.), Gray (D-Pa.), Porter (R-Ill.), and Lewis (R-Calif.) and the House Foreign Affairs committee staff. In the 1989 House Appropriations Committee hearings, Congressman Gray noted that, "after a stormy birth, the Foundation has gotten into the groove of doing the things that many of us originally wanted to see the Foundation do, which is to provide help at the grassroots level." He also expressed concern that there had been a lack of bipartisanship on the board. The response from foundation President Robinson was that he had "raised this issue in the past with the previous administration . . . the various attempts we made to try and recommend Board members as candidates basically fell on deaf ears."[132] Gray also expressed considerable concern about a possible conflict of interest that might emerge with the possible appointment of the president's daughter, Maureen Reagan, to the ADF Advisory Council.

There is typically little time or interest on the Senate Foreign Relations Committee for small initiatives like ADF.[133] On the Foreign Operations Committee ADF finds its main supporter in Senator Leahy (D-Vt.). The Foreign Operations Committee, while supportive, exercises its oversight function and takes a "very active" interest in ADF.

The administration exerts a continuing influence on ADF policy because it largely determines ADF's budget. It has allowed only moderate increases compared to ADF requests. By 1989 ADF's budget had risen from the $2.0 million level of the early 1980s to $8.8 million. In 1990 ADF received a budget increase to $11.5 million. Both ADF and OMB saw this as a major accomplishment. The administration also exercises influence over ADF when it nominates board members.[134]

Nongovernmental supporters of ADF include the Development GAP, which supplies an Advisory Council member; the Inter-American Foundation, which supplies an organizational model; and Bread for the World, which supplies limited advocacy.[135] Each group has a stake in the grassroots development model represented by ADF. To some extent the private voluntary organizations view ADF as competition. To the extent that ADF builds a track record for indigenous groups, it undermines the PVO case for American advice and assistance. The biggest threat foreseen by the ADF during the 1990s is funding. Unlike IAF, ADF depends solely on Congress for funding. At the same time ADF wants to expand its program portfolio—to become active in more countries and to become more active in countries of current operations. ADF has pressed Congress to waive the $250,000 ceiling on projects and to consider a permanent versus a five-year authorization. ADF sees opportunities in the African economies becoming more liberalized and hopes that Congress will use this mechanism to channel resources directly to African entrepreneurs.[136]

During the 1990s ADF plans to pursue three main objectives: to continue to support grassroots development in Africa, to enhance its own grants management program, and to launch a learning and dissemination program. For the latter objective ADF looks to IAF as being a highly successful model.[137]

The Political Viability of Public Foundations

Two rather clear-cut generalizations concerning the political—and economic—viability of the "official" foundations emerge from this review. The first is that the administration—including the Office of Management and Budget, the Department of State, and the Agency for International Development—will generally oppose their development. Exceptions have included occasional support from the White House security apparatus, as in the case of the CIA in the establishment of the Committee for Free Asia and of the National Security Council in protecting the integrity of the Inter-American Foundation. This reflects traditional bureaucratic tension between the White House staff agencies and the State Department.

The second is that the emergence and continued viability of the public foundations (and other foundation-like activities) is dependent on a congressional champion or champions. The Senate Foreign Relations Committee, particularly during the chairmanship of Senator Percy (R-Ill.), was able to protect the Asia Foundation until the administration perspective turned favorable. Support by the New Directions block in the House Foreign Affairs Committee, particularly by Congressman Dante B. Fascell (D-N.J.), has been essential to the continued viability of the Inter-American Foundation. Support by Congressman William H. Gray (D-Pa.) was decisive in moving the proposal for the African Development Foundation through the legislative process and assuring its financial support.

The attractiveness of the direct access and patronage of a congressional committee and a line item in the foreign assistance or State Department budget enjoyed by the public foundation has not gone unnoticed by other client groups. There have, for example, been suggestions that a foundation-like structure be established to further institutionalize support for PVOs engaged in humanitarian and development work overseas.[138]

Patrons and Clients

Policy toward the universities, the private voluntary organizations, and the public foundations has changed over time in response to trends and cycles in the political and ideological environment. During periods when technical assistance, human capital development, and the strengthening of institutional capacity represented major themes in development assistance, the university community was viewed by the U.S. assistance agency as an important resource. When university support for development assistance was mobilized by strong leadership within the university community, the universities played an influential role in shaping U.S. development assistance policy.

Since the mid-1970s, after passage of the Famine and Freedom from Hunger (Title XII) amendment to the Foreign Assistance Act under the leadership of Senator Hubert H. Humphrey (D-Minn.) and Congressman Paul Findley (R-Ill.), the role of the universities both as instruments of assistance programs and as major factors in influencing assistance policy has declined sharply. AID administrators have come to view the resources channeled through the universities as "entitlements" rather than as a productive use of assistance resources. At the same time leadership within the university community has given lower priority to the university-AID relationship. As responsibility for aid relationships has shifted downward within the university bureaucracy, universities have become less effective in mobilizing support for programs in the areas of technology transfer and development and institution building. Within the university community there is a tendency to view as symbolic of this changing relationship the merger in 1990 of the BIFAD (subsequently BIFADEC) with the AID Office of Research and University Relations to form an Agency Center for University Cooperation in Development administered by the AID Bureau for Research and Development.

While relationships between AID and the universities have weakened over the last several years, the role of private voluntary organizations has expanded. During the 1950s and 1960s, the PVOs were viewed as useful instruments in the delivery of food and emergency assistance. But their capacity to influence assistance policy was limited—more symbolic than substantial. Since the early 1970s, however, the PVO community has both increased its capacity to influence assistance programs and its role in program delivery. The Reagan administration's emphasis on strengthening the role of the private sector provided an ideological umbrella that legitimized a larger role for the PVO sector. Support for a larger PVO role was also a product of disenchantment among some development practitioners with the effectiveness of both the state and the market in meeting the needs of the poor. Greater PVO capacity for political mobilization was also a factor. The PVO environmental community played an important role in pushing AID into taking a leading role among bilateral donors in shifting program emphases toward environmental concerns. PVO lobbying was effective in maintaining and even enlarging the AID budget for population programs against strong administration opposition.

The role of the public foundations, either as instruments of development assistance or in terms of their capacity to influence assistance policy, is more difficult to characterize. The Asia Foundation, the oldest of the public foundations, emerged with new vigor in the mid-1980s as the administration discovered that its program emphasis was highly consistent with the administration's "privatization and democratization" theme. The other public foundations—the Inter-American Foundation and the African Development Foundation—were, however, born out of the "basic human needs" and "small is beautiful" orientation of the congressionally mandated assistance reforms of the 1970s. Their programs elicited little sympathy within either the Reagan or the Bush administrations. They have remained political and economically viable largely as a result of support by a few congressional champions and a limited constituency that remains committed to the assistance reforms of the 1970s.

The future role of these three sets of institutions that have in the past occupied a dual role as both clients and patrons is less clear. The easing of tensions between the United States and the USSR and increased budget stringency have led, since the mid-1980s, to a decline in aid budgets. This leaves all three groups in a position of having to use their influence to maintain their share of a declining pool of assistance resources. It is my impression, at present, that the PVO community is more effectively mobilized than either the universities or the public foundations to maintain or even expand their role. They are also the beneficiaries of a shift in public ideology that has reinforced their capacity to bring their own influence to bear on assistance policy.

Chapter 10

Economic Assistance for Strategic Objectives

Economic assistance for strategic purposes occupies an ambiguous place among U.S. foreign assistance programs.[1] Some analysts have viewed it as integral to assistance for economic development, others as a complement to military assistance. This chapter traces the shifts in the domestic political environment and in the international environment which have induced changes in the level and direction of economic assistance resources to strategically important countries.

Every administration since the beginning of the Cold War in the late 1940s has regarded such economic assistance as vital to the conduct of foreign policy.[2] Since 1978 the support for strategic purposes has been programmed primarily under the Economic Support Fund. Earlier the assistance for strategic purposes had been programmed under rubrics such as Economic Support for Defense, Security Supporting Assistance, and Supporting Assistance. In this chapter, except where explicitly noted, I use the term *Economic Support Fund (ESF)* to refer to programs carried out under the earlier titles.

In discussing economic assistance to strategically important countries, however, reference to the flow of resources budgeted under other programs is unavoidable. Such assistance is, to a substantial degree, fungible. In its internal evaluations AID does not typically distinguish whether a project is funded under the Development Assistance Program or ESF. ESF resources have been used, at times, to provide assistance that might otherwise have been funded under the Military Assistance Program (MAP). Resources programmed under the Food for Peace (PL 480) Program have been made available to circumvent congressional constraints on the availability of ESF resources. In the last Bush administration budget (fiscal 1993), assistance programmed under the ESF amounted to $3.1 billion, roughly 21 percent of the total foreign assistance budget of $14.5 billion. In comparison, bilateral development assistance ran in the neighborhood of $2.3 billion, Food for Peace in the neighborhood of $1.3 billion, and MAP in the range of $3.6 billion.

The State Department, the Department of Defense, and the Department of Agriculture, as well as the Agency for International Development, are all involved in the planning and administration of the several assistance programs. Country allocations of development assistance funds are proposed by AID with State Department concurrence. In contrast, allocations of economic support funds are proposed by the State Department in consultation with AID. Both the Department of Agriculture and AID are involved in the allocation of food aid. Military assistance is jointly managed by the Department of Defense and the State Department, with the latter serving as lead agency on policy matters. Agency proposals are often modified by congressional earmarks and budget reductions.

A large share of the resources programmed under the ESF and its predecessor programs has been channeled to relatively few countries (Figure 10.1). In the 1950s South Korea, Taiwan, and South Vietnam were major recipients. From the early 1960s until the mid-1970s, aid to South Vietnam rose to close to 90 percent of total ESF resources. From 1977 until the early 1990s, roughly two-thirds of ESF resources have been concentrated in Egypt and Israel. Substantial ESF resources were also channeled to Central America during the 1980s. Pakistan has traditionally been a major recipient of ESF support. Countries in which U.S. military bases were located (base countries) have been continuing claimants. In addition, during the 1980s smaller amounts of ESF resources were channeled to other countries, such as Somalia and Zaire, to circumvent what the administration viewed as the excessive constraints of congressional programmatic restrictions. Substantial ESF resources were allocated to the formerly centrally planned states of Eastern Europe and the republics of the former Soviet Union.[3]

When I began this book I was reluctant, because of the controversies that have been associated with assistance to strategically important countries such as Vietnam and Israel, to write this chapter. Interpretation of U.S. experience in Vietnam continues to be controversial. It is difficult to write about the efforts of Jewish interest groups to influence U.S. assistance to Israel without being confronted with the issue of anti-Semitism. The issue of U.S. economic and military assistance in Central America remains highly sensitive. I had intended at first to focus only on those parts of the U.S. assistance program that had economic development as a primary objective.[4] But the distinctions among security, political, and economic objectives typically have been blurred. Furthermore, mechanisms other than economic and military assistance, Commodity Credit Corporate and Export-Import Bank credit guarantees, trade incentives or sanctions, and others have also been employed. It is not possible

Resources, 1951–1993

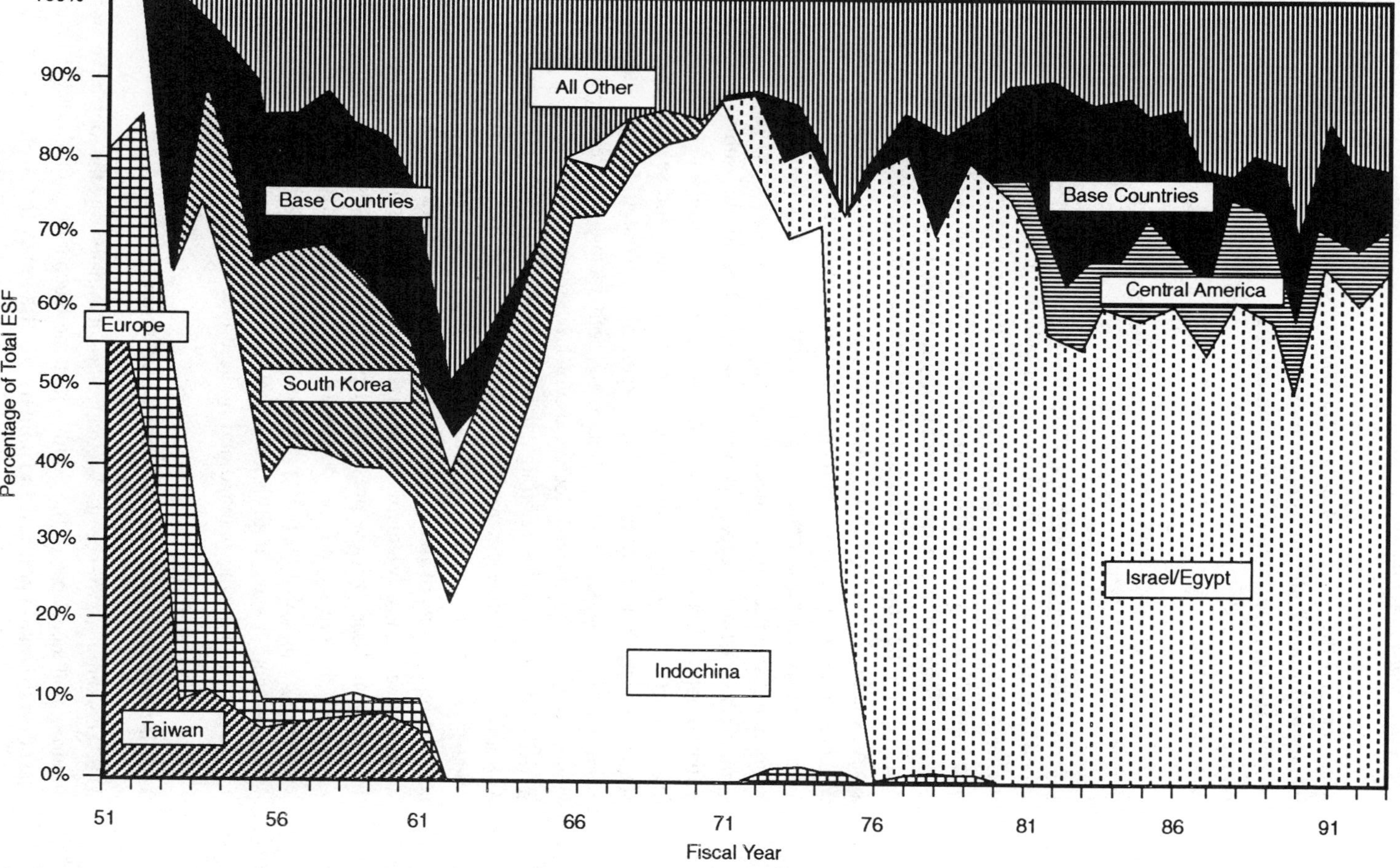

Source: U.S. Agency for International Development, *Congressional Presentation* (Washington: US/AID, various years); *U.S. Loans, Grants, and Assistance from International Organizations and Authorizations* (Washington: US/AID, various years).

to understand the sources of economic assistance policies toward countries where the United States has important strategic interests without taking into account the broader economic and political factors bearing on U.S. foreign policy.

Assistance to South Vietnam

Between the mid-1950s and the early 1960s, Vietnam became the testing ground for the often mutually inconsistent lessons that had been drawn from earlier American assistance to Latin America, Western Europe, Greece, China, and Korea (Chap. 3). The lesson drawn from experience in Latin America in the 1940s was that a modest program of education and technical assistance can become the source of substantial economic growth. The lesson drawn from experience in China was that military and economic assistance, in the absence of a viable economy and an effective government, is ineffective. The lesson drawn from assistance to Greece and Korea was that military and economic assistance can be effective in enabling even weak governments with limited administrative capacity to resist the threat of internal subversion and external oppression if the United States is prepared to involve itself deeply in the support and management of a country's economic and security system. The lesson drawn from Marshall Plan experience in Western Europe was that effective planning and administration by both recipient governments and donors is a prerequisite to effective use of large resource transfers.

All of these lessons were brought to bear at some stage during the period of U.S. involvement in Vietnam. By the time the United States withdrew from Vietnam in 1976, the credibility of each doctrine had been substantially eroded and the reputations of many advocates severely compromised.

In this section on Vietnam, I first discuss the succession of stages in U.S. intervention. I then review presidential policy. Finally, I discuss the role of Congress, the press, and the public as sources of change in policy.[5] My emphasis on presidential policy reflects the fact that, until the early 1970s, U.S. intervention was "at all times conceived by an extremely small group of top policy makers who planned and orchestrated it."[6]

U.S. Intervention in South Vietnam: Five Stages

U.S. economic assistance to Vietnam was dominated by the objective of assuring that a collapse of the South Vietnamese economy would not weaken the effort to contain political and military penetration by the North. Failure of economic growth and rampant inflation were viewed by U.S. policy makers as potential sources of civil unrest. U.S. policy was not, however, monolithic. There were advisors who insisted that a stable government and a secure countryside were prerequisite for economic development and those who argued that, lacking economic growth, a viable government and a viable defense against the North would not be possible.[7]

It is possible to distinguish five successive stages in U.S. intervention in Vietnam (Table A.1).[8] In the first period, 1954–59, primacy in assistance was placed on economic development. In the second period, 1960–64, the emphasis shifted toward pacification. In Stage 3, 1965–68, military assistance in the pursuit of the war intensified and large economic resources were used for commodity imports to try to dampen inflation. In the fourth period, 1968–73, the focus of military assistance was disengagement from ground combat, while, on the economic side, assistance focused on economic and political reform, including the strengthening of governance processes and the completion of land reform. This was followed by defeat and withdrawal during 1974 and 1975. In the rest of this section I elaborate the stages of U.S. intervention and trace the flow of assistance resources.

Each of the five stages was characterized by a shift in the relative importance of the several program categories through which aid was channeled to Vietnam and through the government of Vietnam (GVN) to military and civilian beneficiaries (Figure 10.2, Table A.1). These programs included (1) the Commercial Import Program (CIP), (2) the Food for Peace Program (PL 480), (3) Project Aid, and (4) Piaster Subsidy Aid (PSA). For purposes of this section, the CIP can be thought of as a predecessor to ESF and Project Aid as a predecessor of development assistance.

The involvement of the United States in the shaping of post–World War II Vietnam began even before the war was over. President Franklin D. Roosevelt took the position that "the French had been in control in Vietnam for a hundred years, that the natives were worse off than before, that the French had milked Indochina dry, and that the Vietnamese people were entitled to something better."[9] As the war was ending, he refused to permit U.S. forces in southern China to support French resistance to the Japanese. The allied governments decided that Chinese forces should occupy the North and British forces the South of Vietnam.

Revolution, 1950–1954

Within less than a month after V-J Day, on 2 September 1946, while Vietnam was occupied by Chinese, British, and French military forces, Ho Chi Minh organized a Vietminh (Revolutionary League for the Independence of Vietnam)–led government—the Democratic Republic of Vietnam. At the official

FIGURE 10.2
The Sources and Uses of Aid in Vietnam

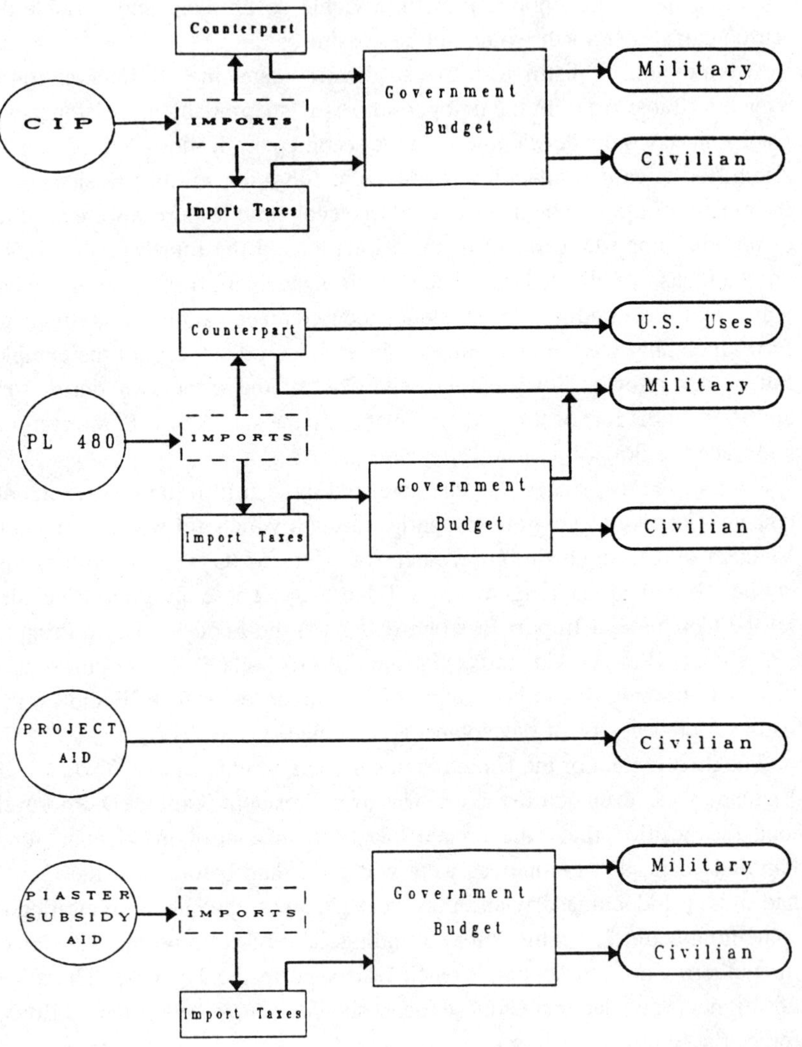

Source: Douglas C. Cacy, *Foreign Aid, War and Economic Development: South Vietnam, 1955–1975* (Cambridge: Cambridge University Press, 1986), 195.

surrender of the Japanese forces in Tonkin on September 27, the French were not invited to participate in the ceremony. The French interpreted correctly the lack of support during the last years of the war and their exclusion from the peace negotiations as deliberate American policy to exclude them from a postwar role in Indochina.

The French attempt to recapture and hold Vietnam was, in retrospect, finished with their loss of a series of northern garrisons in September and October of 1950, although the war dragged on until the final defeat at Dien Bien Phu in 1954. Meanwhile, the United States, engaged in its own war in Korea, reversed its earlier position and sought to pressure China by reinforcing the French effort in Vietnam. The war in Vietnam was transformed from a war to free the Vietnamese from French colonialism to a vital link in the effort to control Communist expansion! Initially, the United States channeled military and economic assistance through France. A United States Special Technical and Economic Mission (STEM) and a Military Assistance Advisory Group (MAAG) were sent to Vietnam in 1950. In September 1951 an agreement for direct economic assistance between the United States and the French-supported "State of Vietnam," headed by Bao Dai, was signed.

On 8 May 1954 the Vietminh succeeded in overrunning the base at Dien Bien Phu where the French had concentrated 15,000 troops. The war, which ended on 21 July 1954, had cost the French 172,000 casualties and the Vietminh three times that many. Civilian casualties were in the neighborhood of 250,000. The military and economic assistance provided by the U.S., primarily through the Marshall Plan, to support the French effort to reestablish authority in Vietnam amounted to approximately $2 billion.[10]

Reconstruction and Nation Building, 1955–1959

The Geneva Accords of 1954 provided for a provisional demarcation line between North and South Vietnam roughly along the 17th parallel. Bao Dai appointed Ngo Dinh Diem, back from exile in the United States, to the position of premier and asked him to form a government. Diem moved rapidly to establish control over the government and the military. In October 1955 he replaced Bao Dai as head of state.

When the United States moved to expand economic assistance to the Diem government in late 1955, two immediate challenges faced the U.S. Operations Mission (USOM). The first was to assist in the resettlement of refugees from the North. This population, characterized as "doubly alien"—northern and predominantly Catholic—was initially settled in temporary refugee camps near Saigon. Resettlement was largely accomplished by mid-1957.[11]

The second challenge was to replace French assistance. The budgetary support required to establish and maintain a Vietnamese military force of approximately 250,000 was largely assumed by the United States. High priority was given to economic assistance for reconstruction and development of the transportation, communication, and related physical infrastructure. Assistance was also provided for land reform, enhancement of agricultural production, health services, industrial and mineral development, and the strengthening of higher education, including the establishment of a National Institute of Administration and a College of Agriculture. During 1955–59, economic assistance amounted to close to a quarter of South Vietnam's GNP.

Several development indicators such as rice yields, employment, and school enrollment suggested that U.S. assistance and Vietnamese policy were moving the country toward economic viability. Political development, however, was less encouraging. A land reform effort, intended to strengthen the peasants' political support for the government, became bogged down. Its failure reflected the perception by many peasants that they were being forced to pay for land that they had already confiscated from landowners.[12] Peasant resistance to the Diem government was particularly strong in the rubber-producing areas, where Vietnamese landowners proved as repressive as the departed French. Industrial development was hindered by conflict between the emphasis of U.S. advisors on development through the private sector and Diem's preference for government ownership and his aversion to foreign investment.

Neither the Diem government nor its American advisors were adequately sensitive to the growing strength of the Vietminh or to the kind of policies needed to defeat an indigenous guerrilla force. The effort to develop an effective village-based Civil Guard that would both improve village infrastructure and provide security to village populations foundered on President Diem's concern that an effective Civil Guard could emerge as a threat to his own security. Beginning in 1955 the USOM funded a police advisory team (from Michigan State University) to develop a Civil Guard Program. The team was frustrated by Diem's rejection of almost every recommendation and by weak support from the U.S. ambassador. The Michigan State team withdrew in 1959.[13] Military training focused on developing a capacity to withstand a Korea-type North Vietnamese invasion, and the Vietnamese police were trained to handle normal criminal behavior. The development of a paramilitary force capable of protecting the safety of village chiefs and local officials continued to be neglected even as they were being murdered in increasing numbers.

Insurgency, 1960–1964

By 1960 the economic development objectives of U.S. assistance had been displaced, or subverted, by efforts to prevent the collapse of the Diem regime.

The level of insurgency in the countryside generated increasing concern in both Saigon and Washington. At the project level, assistance shifted from longer-term development to shorter-term political and security objectives. The Diem government sought to counter Communist-level terrorist activity first by moving large numbers of the rural population into fortified "agrovilles" and then by a "strategic hamlet" program.[14] The latter, like its predecessor, succeeded in alienating the intended beneficiaries. It proved to be ineffective as a pacification measure and was in turn abandoned after a few years.

The land reform program, promulgated in 1957, was a second casualty of heightened insurgency. The complexity of the program—which involved land surveys, legal transfer of title, and compensation of landowners—made it impossible to administer. The programs instituted by the Vietcong in areas under their control encompassed three elements that were more favorable to the tenants: land redistribution, rent reduction, and higher wages for rural workers. The effect of the heightened insurgency shifted the flow of U.S. aid resources toward pacification and away from development. It is not clear that the Diem regime had ever been committed to the success of efforts to achieve rural development. What does seem clear is that neither the Diem regime nor the Americans had the political resources or the knowledge of the country's problems that would have been needed to gain the loyalty of the peasants.[15]

War, 1965–1968

The third stage in American intervention in Vietnam lasted from the time the U.S. Marines arrived in Vietnam in March 1965 to the collapse of the Communist Tet offensive in mid-1968. The assassination of President Ngo Dinh Diem in November 1963 was followed by a period of extreme political instability, with five changes in government, until a faction of younger officers named General Nguyen Van Thieu as president and Air Vice Marshall Nguyen Cao Key as vice president after an election in September 1967.

During this period the size of the Vietnamese armed forces doubled, to about one million. U.S. troop strength rose to over half a million, and other external forces, mainly South Korean, were brought in. There was also a rapid escalation in technical assistance. Thousands of Americans took up posts throughout the country as agricultural advisors, supporters of medical services, refugee coordinators, and logistical experts. The effect again was to dramatically change the focus of the U.S. assistance effort, this time to finance almost the entire war. The Vietnam domestic economy became even more dependent on the CIP and PSA. The performance of the economy in the late 1960s was better than might have been expected. Inflation, though high, did not run completely out of control. Agricultural production, stimulated by the introduction of improved rice varieties, improvements in irrigation, and strong growth in demand, began to recover from the low production levels of the early and mid-1960s.

The Tet offensive of 31 January 1968 began with major attacks by Communist forces against all major cities and towns of South Vietnam. "The fighting over the next several months resulted in a major psychological victory for the Communist side and changed the course of history in Southeast Asia." An immediate effect of the Tet offensive was to deplete the ranks of the Vietcong. The longer-term effect was increased political pressure in the United States for withdrawal from Vietnam. The Nixon administration, convinced that the war could not be won, announced a program (the Nixon Doctrine) of "peace through negotiations, disengagement of U.S. troops from ground combat, and Vietnamization of the war effort."[16]

Vietnamization and Defeat, 1969–1975

The United States pledged to continue its military and economic assistance while the Vietnamese assumed greater responsibility for both military and civil affairs.[17] The number of AID personnel in Vietnam declined from approximately 2300 in 1968 to 700 in 1973 while the number of U.S. troops and expenditures in Vietnam on troop support were also reduced.

The period 1969–71 was the high point in the effectiveness of U.S. economic assistance. A sweeping economic reform program involving extensive revision of the interest rate, exchange rate, and tariff structures was carried out with American technical advice during 1970–71. The inflation rate was brought down, and the investment climate improved. The introduction of new rice varieties contributed to an increase in rice production, and a new and more effective "land to the tiller" land reform program, backstopped by AID, was pursued vigorously.[18]

But the initial legitimacy that Vietnamization had given to the Thieu-Ky government rapidly eroded. While U.S. officials in Vietnam were telling the press that Vietnamization was working well, land reform failed, urban unrest was rife, police and security forces were virtually out of control, and the regular forces tended to avoid or perform poorly in battle.[19]

The end of U.S. involvement in Vietnam and the occupation of South Vietnam by the North began in March 1972. By the end of the year, the civilian economy had begun to crumble. There were dramatic increases in the price of imported oil and fertilizer. The withdrawal of economic and military assistance weakened the economy. Refugees became burdensome. Agricultural production could not be sustained. The GVN lost the capacity to maintain a viable military posture. The primary U.S. objective—the prevention of the demoralization of the civil economy—was no longer viable.[20] The army of North Vietnam entered Saigon on 30 April 1975.

The interpretation offered here has not been accepted by all observers. There is still a view that with sufficient U.S. resolve a viable independent South Vietnam would have been possible. "Perhaps the United States could not have prevailed in Vietnam, but we cannot know because . . . it did not stick around long enough to find out."[21]

Perspective

Except for a relatively brief period from the middle to late 1950s, assistance for economic and political development in Vietnam clearly was little more than a sideshow to the achievement of security objectives. This is not to question the motives or competence of the large number of Americans who were involved in the management of economic and technical assistance for political and economic development. Many brought high levels of professional capacity to their work. Most were seriously committed to their missions. Why were their efforts were so ineffective? The answer requires an examination of the domestic sources of U.S. policy toward Vietnam.

Presidential Policy toward Vietnam

The most consistent element in the American involvement in Vietnam was an almost limitless capacity for self-delusion, what George F. Kennan referred to as "that curious trait of the American political personality which causes it to appear reprehensible to voice anything less than unlimited optimism about the fortunes of another government one has adopted as a friend and protégé."[22]

The capacity for self-delusion affected each administration involved in security assistance to Vietnam, from Eisenhower to Nixon.[23] It pervaded the military and civilian bureaucracies responsible for managing security assistance. It blinded the technicians managing the assistance and the media personnel who observed, analyzed, and reported. And it was pervasive among the general public until the evidence of failure became so unavoidable that public revolt finally forced U.S. withdrawal from Vietnam. Few participants, from the highest level of government to the most mundane field operators, departed from encounter with Vietnam with enhanced reputations.

Eisenhower, 1953–1960

The Eisenhower administration inherited from the Truman administration a policy legacy that included a wide gap between what the government told the

American people and what the administration actually knew about the situation in Vietnam. Policy toward Vietnam continued to be both confused and duplicitous; President Eisenhower "could conceive of no greater tragedy than for the United States to become involved in an all-out war in Indochina." While the president was assuring the country that military intervention in Vietnam was unlikely, Secretary of State John Foster Dulles was pressuring the French to stay and fight for as long as possible and the Pentagon was busy developing plans for a larger military presence in Vietnam. On 7 April 1954, Eisenhower declared, "The loss of Indochina will cause the fall of Southeast Asia like a set of dominoes." Aid administrator Harold Stassen thereupon announced an economic assistance budget that included an allocation of $1.13 billion to Indochina.[24]

Throughout the rest of the Eisenhower presidency, the official administration line was that the U.S. military and economic assistance was successful in generating viable political and economic development in South Vietnam. Internal reports from the field during the middle 1950s, however, suggested that the Saigon government was rapidly losing control in the countryside. By the late 1950s local government cadres were being decimated by assassination, and terrorism against American economic and military assistance personnel was escalating. American officials in Vietnam and Washington found themselves caught in a trap of their own making; they could not continue to maintain that everything was going well in Vietnam and, at the same time, request larger appropriations and more personnel for security and economic assistance.

By the end of the Eisenhower administration, Americans had replaced the French as the major source of support for the government of South Vietnam. Eisenhower "kept America out of the war, and he kept America in Vietnam." Yet Bernard Fall insists that "the Eisenhower Administration left office apparently without ever having understood the extent to which America was committed to Vietnam's survival."[25]

Kennedy, 1961–1963

In 1954 John F. Kennedy had warned, in a Senate speech, that no amount of military aid could conquer an enemy "which has the support and covert appeal of the people." But in 1956, in an address to the American Friends of Vietnam, Kennedy described South Vietnam as the cornerstone of the Free World in Southeast Asia—"It is our offspring and we cannot abandon it, we cannot ignore its needs."[26] Shortly after taking office Kennedy was faced with abandoning "our offspring" or increasing the U.S. commitment in Vietnam.

Beginning in 1961 the Kennedy administration embarked on a vigorous reexamination of assistance policy toward Vietnam. The result was a renewal of the crisis cycle in which the government of Vietnam promised reforms and America promised more aid. Yet Kennedy's ambivalence toward U.S. involvement in Vietnam continued. He inherited from Eisenhower an increasingly dangerous if still limited commitment and did not, as some critics have alleged, eagerly take up the burden in Vietnam. He delayed making a firm commitment for nearly a year and then he acted only because the shaky Diem government seemed on the verge of collapse.

In the short run, such a course offered numerous advantages, but over the long run it was delusive and dangerous. "It encouraged Diem to continue his self-destructive path, while leading Americans to believe they could secure a favorable outcome without paying a heavy price."[27] To Kennedy, Vietnam was a test of his administration's capacity to successfully support wars of liberation. He and most of his advisers accepted without critical analysis the assumption that a non-Communist Vietnam was vital to America's global interests.[28]

By the beginning of the Kennedy administration, there were serious doubts in both Hanoi and Washington that the Diem regime could survive. Diem was pressured for reforms. He reacted angrily and publicly by informing Ambassador Frederick Nolting that South Vietnam did not want to be a protectorate. The administration responded by slowing resource transfers. But when it could not identify a potential replacement for Diem it backed down.[29]

During 1962 and 1963 the press corps in Vietnam, as well as the lower echelons of the American bureaucracy in both Washington and Vietnam, became increasingly convinced that the war was going badly and Diem could not survive. This view was vigorously contested by the embassy and the military command in Vietnam. Sensing that his U.S. support was eroding, Diem initiated contact with Hanoi. His objective was to explore a possible settlement that would result in an American withdrawal from Vietnam.[30] A group of South Vietnamese generals opened secret contact with the United States to determine how the United States would react if they attempted a coup.

On 16 June 1963 an elderly Buddhist monk seated himself at a busy intersection in downtown Saigon and set fire to his gasoline-soaked robes. In an effort to defuse the Buddhists, Diem's army attacked the Central Pagodas in Saigon, Hue, and other central cities. In October he ordered thousands of student demonstrators, many the sons and daughters of his officials and officers, arrested. Many were tortured. The American mission in Saigon "watched Diem tear apart the fabric of Vietnamese society more effectively than the Communists had ever been able to do."[31] Kennedy authorized Ambassador Lodge to assure the generals that the United States would not assist in a coup but would support a new government if it had a good chance of success. The plans for the coup fell apart, however, when the generals were unable to mobilize sufficient support.

The administration continued to pressure the Diem government by reducing support for the Special Forces Program and for commodity imports. The generals were encouraged to continue their plotting. Kennedy continued to vacillate, leaving the final judgment up to Ambassador Lodge. On 1 November 1963, the generals mounted a well-organized coup. Diem and Ngo Dinh Nhu, Diem's brother and chief advisor, were captured and, despite promises of safe conduct, were murdered in the back of an armored personnel carrier. When Kennedy himself was assassinated three weeks later (22 November 1963), he left to his successor a Vietnam problem that was even more dangerous than the one he had inherited from Eisenhower.[32]

Johnson, 1963–1968

The new American president, Lyndon Baines Johnson, inherited from Kennedy a rapidly deteriorating situation in Vietnam. His foreign policy advisors—McNamara, Rusk, and McGeorge Bundy, held over from the Kennedy administration—still insisted that South Vietnam represented a key component of U.S. security concerns in East Asia. Johnson himself viewed the American commitment in Vietnam as part of the Kennedy program he was sworn to uphold.[33] Both military and economic assistance were expanded. As the 1964 election approached, President Johnson felt increasing pressure from Senator Goldwater and the Republican Right for not taking a sufficiently aggressive position on Vietnam.

In August 1964 the Gulf of Tonkin incident provided Johnson with an opportunity to refute the criticism of the hawks and the authority to pursue the war in Vietnam more vigorously. The destroyer *Maddox* was attacked by North Vietnamese patrol boats on August 1 while engaged in electronic monitoring off the coast of North Vietnam. On August 4, during operations in heavy seas about 60 miles off the North Vietnamese coast, the *Maddox* and the *Turner Joy* reported, based on sonar and radar contacts, that they were under attack. Retaliation was ordered against North Vietnam torpedo boat bases and oil storage facilities.

The president asked for a congressional resolution authorizing him to take "all necessary measures to repel any armed attacks against the United States and to prevent further aggression."[34] Although new evidence suggested that no attack had actually taken place, the Senate voted 88 to 2 to support the resolution. Senator J. William Fulbright, apparently more concerned with countering the Goldwater challenges to Johnson's handling of Vietnam affairs than with giving Johnson a blank check to continue the war in Vietnam, effectively shepherded the resolution through the Senate. Johnson's popularity, as measured by the Harris poll, rose from 42 to 72 percent. He had effectively neutralized Goldwater and went on to an overwhelming electoral victory in November 1964.

Johnson, like Eisenhower and Kennedy before him, continued trying to straddle the issue of American responsibility in Vietnam. He emphasized his commitment to limit American involvement by stating, in numerous speeches, that "we seek no wider war."[35] By the spring of 1965, however, confronted by continued political deterioration of the South Vietnamese government and a series of attacks on U.S. bases, Johnson ordered massive air attacks in the North and introduced U.S. ground forces into combat. Johnson sought to deflect emerging domestic concern by placing greater emphasis, in public pronouncements, on U.S. development assistance in Southeast Asia. On 7 April 1965, in a speech at Johns Hopkins University, he pledged support for a Tennessee Valley authority–type regional development scheme for the Mekong River Valley region and for an Asian Development Bank (see Chap. 11).

The first American combat troops, two marine battalions, arrived in Vietnam on 8 March 1965. Their initial assignment was to protect American facilities. By April, two more battalions were sent in. By the end of July, the South Vietnam army was in disarray and Johnson agreed to General Westmoreland's request for 180,000 additional troops. The commitment of American troops to the ground war in Vietnam in 1965 was accompanied by an illusion that the application of its technically sophisticated military power would quickly end the war. By 1967, the United States had nearly half a million combat troops in Vietnam and had dropped more bombs than in all theaters in World War II. Lyndon Johnson, unable to end the war by military means and unwilling to make the concessions necessary to secure a negotiated settlement, discovered belatedly what George Ball had warned in 1964: "Once on a tiger's back we cannot be sure of picking the place to dismount."[36]

By early 1966 both the Saigon government and American involvement were the foci of continuing civil protest in major U.S. urban centers. Johnson again sought to deflect criticism by making a renewed commitment to expand assistance for rural development. "Under intense prodding from Washington, the Americans and South Vietnamese devised an ambitious Revolutionary Development Program (RD), consciously imitative of Vietcong techniques in which fifty-nine-men teams trained in propaganda and social services, would go to the villages, live with the people, and carry out hundreds of tasks to build popular support for the government and undermine the Vietcong." The program, like earlier rural development efforts, faltered because of the inability to provide security to RD teams and their clients and the apathy and corruption of the Vietnamese civil and military bureaucracies. "Ky had initially no power to implement any of the reforms the Americans pressed on him. He could not fire bad officials because they had bought their jobs; he could not promote the good officials because they had not."[37]

The decision to send combat troops to Vietnam in the spring of 1965 turned out to be one of the most critical of the war. "Yet it had hardly stirred a ripple either in Congress or in the American press—largely because Johnson had skillfully presented it as a short term expedient." There was, however, serious debate within the administration and among a few leading members of Congress with direct access to Johnson on the wisdom of sending U.S. ground combat troops to Vietnam.[38] Vice President Hubert H. Humphrey advanced strong reservations about the wisdom of escalation during the winter and spring of 1965; he was rewarded by being put in limbo and excluded from National Security Council meetings. George Ball was most forceful in advancing his reservations. On October 5 he forwarded a long (67-page) memorandum to Rusk, McNamara, and McGeorge Bundy in which he outlined what, in retrospect, was a compelling argument against military escalation. Ball recalled that at a meeting on 7 November 1964, which was convened to consider his arguments, "Bob McNamara in particular seemed shocked that anyone would challenge the verities in such an abrupt and unvarnished manner and implied that I had been imprudent in putting such doubts on paper."[39]

Reservations were also advanced by several senators who had been particularly close to Johnson during his Senate years and who continued to have personal access to him in the White House. William Fulbright, chairman of the Senate Foreign Relations Committee; Richard Russell, chairman of the Senate Armed Services Committee; and the Senate Majority leader, Mike Mansfield, each stressed the dangers of escalation in both personal conversation and written communications. Clark Clifford, one of the "Wise Men" whom Johnson consulted informally, also expressed serious reservations.

Disintegration of the consensus on Vietnam within the administration had begun shortly after Johnson had assumed office. In 1964 Roger Hillsman, assistant secretary of state for the Far East was told to find other employment because of his dissenting views. In 1966 Bill Moyers and Michael Forrestal of the White House staff and Under-Secretary of State George Ball resigned; they had become totally alienated from the policy but felt helpless to change it. By the summer of 1967, Secretary of Defense McNamara, who had led the charge for escalation in 1965, had become disillusioned about the possibility of successfully concluding the Vietnam War. As McNamara's doubts had grown, his relationship with Johnson "had so soured by late 1967 that the Secretary gladly accepted an appointment to head the World Bank."[40]

In an effort to provide the Vietnam government with some legitimacy, the United States pressed the Ky regime to hold elections in September 1967.

Observers have argued that despite considerable fraud the elections "were neither as corrupt as critics charged nor as pure as Johnson claimed . . . The large turnout and the fact that the elections had been held in the midst of war were cited by Americans as evidence of growing political maturity. The Thieu-Ky ticket won 35 percent of the vote, but Truong Dinh Dzu, a virtually unknown lawyer who had run on a platform of negotiations with the Vietcong, won 17 percent.[41] Tensions between Americans and South Vietnamese increased as the American presence grew. The United States found, to its chagrin, that as its commitment increased its leverage diminished.

In the early morning darkness of 31 January 1968, the second day of the Tet holiday, a team of Vietcong snipers blasted a hole in the wall surrounding the U.S. embassy in Saigon and dashed into the courtyard of the compound. That same day "the Vietcong launched a series of attacks that extended from the demilitarized zone in the north to the southern tip of Vietnam. In all, they struck sixty-four district capitals and forty hamlets . . . assaulted Saigon's Ton San Nhut Airport, the presidential palace and the headquarters of South Vietnam's general staff. In Hue, 7,500 Vietcong and North Vietnamese troops stormed and eventually took control of the ancient Citadel, the interior town which had been the seat of the Emperors of the Kingdom of Annam."[42] In retrospect, the offensive was a military disaster but a political success for North Vietnam. The South Vietnamese people did not rise up to welcome the Vietcong and North Vietnamese as "liberators," the regular units of the Vietcong were decimated, and its political infrastructure was crippled. In the United States the Tet offensive destroyed the remaining credibility of the claims by President Johnson and General Westmoreland of success in Vietnam.

Clark Clifford, who had replaced McNamara as secretary of defense, initiated an intensive review of Vietnam policy. "He was encouraged . . . by the senior civilians in the Pentagon, men such as Paul Warnke, Townsend Hoopes, and Paul Nitze, who had been partially responsible for McNamara's conversion. Thus, Clifford immediately began raising at the highest levels questions that had been avoided for years."[43] The review recommended that General Westmoreland's request for more troops be denied, that Thieu be forced to shoulder greater responsibility for the conduct of the war, and that the GVN be informed that continued American assistance would depend on South Vietnam's assuming a greater burden of the fighting. Even Secretary of State Dean Rusk had forced himself to conclude that only marginal gains could be had from continued bombings. Among Johnson's closest advisors, only National Security Advisor Walter W. Rostow still urged continued escalation.

By March 1968 Clifford had infuriated Johnson by urging a policy of deescalation in Vietnam. The Council of Wise Men abandoned their 1967 position; they advised that American objectives in Vietnam could not be achieved and that moves should be made toward eventual withdrawal.[44] In Johnson's words, "the establishment bastards have bailed out." Halberstam commented that "Clifford forced Johnson to turn and look honestly at the war: it was an act of friendship for which Johnson could never forgive him."[45]

On March 31, in a television address to the nation, Johnson announced that the bombing of North Vietnam would be limited to the area just north of the demilitarized zone. He named Averell Harriman as his personal representative should peace talks materialize. And he announced, "I shall not seek and I will not accept, the nomination of my party for another term as your President."[46] Despite this dramatic turn of events, Johnson, reinforced by Rusk and Rostow, still believed that an independent, non-Communist South Vietnam was possible. A peace conference opened in Yves (France) on May 13, but it became clear that neither the North Vietnamese nor the Americans were willing to make the concessions necessary to advance the process. The Thieu government continued to resist effective Vietnamization of the fighting. To bolster the presidential campaign of Senator Hubert H. Humphrey, Johnson unilaterally stopped the bombing and gave Harriman somewhat more latitude to negotiate an "understanding" about mutual de-escalation a few weeks before the election.

Nixon and Ford, 1969–1975

When Nixon assumed office in 1969, both his secretary of defense, Melvin Laird, and his national security adviser, Henry Kissinger, recognized the necessity of ending the war.[47] The Nixon Doctrine was first enunciated at an informal briefing to newsmen on Guam on 25 July 1969 and elaborated at a Washington press conference on 3 November 1969. In its initial formulation President Nixon declared that the United States would keep its treaty commitments but that problems of internal security would increasingly be handled by Asian nations themselves. In Vietnam this meant building up Saigon's forces and the withdrawal of U.S. forces; in other words Vietnamization. "It was a policy that Laird pushed, Nixon accepted and Kissinger disparaged."[48]

But Nixon and Kissinger remained committed to maintaining a viable non-Communist government in South Vietnam. And both were initially committed to a "peace with honor" that would leave the South Vietnam government in power and avoid the appearance of U.S. defeat.[49] On 15 July 1969, Nixon secretly sent what he regarded as a conciliatory letter to President Ho Chi Minh in which he called for serious negotiation and an early end to the war. On August 25, a week before his death, Ho Chi Minh responded to Nixon, reiterating his determination to settle for nothing less than complete U.S. withdrawal from Vietnam. When the North Vietnamese remained intransigent, Nixon again escalated the war. Nixon and Kissinger were convinced that, faced with the superiority of American military might, North Vietnam could be pushed to a breaking point.[50]

During the next four years, Nixon alternated the intensification of the bombing of North Vietnam and expansion of ground warfare, including excursions into Cambodia and Laos, with renewed attempts to advance negotiations that could lead to U.S. withdrawal. The North Vietnamese continued to insist, however, on Thieu's removal as a precondition to any peace agreement. On several occasions they hinted that it might simplify the peace process if the United States arranged for his assassination.[51] While insisting on peace with honor, Nixon was trying to placate domestic criticisms by gradually withdrawing U.S. troops from South Vietnam.

The establishment of diplomatic relations with China after Kissinger's visits in July and October of 1971 and Nixon's visit in February 1972 made continuation of the war in Vietnam seem ever more anachronistic.[52] The inconclusive Paris talks were followed, in March 1972, by a massive invasion from the North. The U.S. mined Haiphong Harbor and intensified the bombing of Hanoi. By May the invasion was contained. Efforts to bring negotiations to a close were intensified. But Thieu refused to be sold out. During the fall of 1972, the United States delivered over a billion dollars worth of military hardware to reinforce the Thieu regime. It also unleashed the most intensive bombing effort of the entire war during the 1972 Christmas season, with a promise to halt the bombing if peace talks were resumed.

After Nixon's reelection in 1972, "Nixon and Kissinger . . . washed their hands of Vietnam. It could go down any drain for all they cared."[53] Talks were resumed on January 8. The peace agreement that was finally worked out left the North Vietnamese on the ground in the South and the political future of South Vietnam unresolved. This time the United States imposed the agreement on Thieu. If Thieu accepted the treaty, Nixon indicated in a secret agreement, he would provide South Vietnam with continued support and would respond with full force if North Vietnam violated the agreement. If Thieu continued to resist Nixon, he would cut off further assistance and was prepared, if necessary, to sign the treaty alone. "Peace with honor" had come at a very high price. The fighting between 1969 and 1973 accounted for over 100,000 Vietnamese and 20,000 American additional battle deaths.[54]

By the time the peace agreement was signed in January 1973, the Nixon administration had lost its capacity to govern. And the Saigon government was incapable of surviving without assistance. Because of the Watergate scandals and American war-weariness, Nixon was not able to live up to his commitments to Thieu. After his forced resignation on August 1974, Congress drastically cut back aid to South Vietnam, thus further eroding the Saigon government's will and capacity to resist. "When North Vietnam mounted a major offensive in the spring of 1975, South Vietnam collapsed with stunning rapidity, dramatically ending the thirty-year war and leaving the United States, on the eve of its third century, frustrated and bewildered."[55] On 23 April 1975, President Gerald R. Ford declared the war ended.

The failure of each administration from Truman to Nixon was a failure of analysis. Challenges to policy within the administrations were frequent, and sometimes they were substantial. But "no comprehensive and systematic examination of Vietnam's importance in the United States was ever undertaken within the executive branch. Debates revolved around how to do things better and whether they could be done, not whether they were worth doing."[56]

Congress, the Press, and the Public

From the initial U.S. involvement in Vietnam during and immediately after World War II until the mid-1960s, U.S. military and security assistance policy toward Vietnam was directed and often managed by the White House—the president and a small group of executive branch advisers.[57] By the late 1960s presidential autonomy had begun to erode. Public pressure and congressional initiative were largely responsible for forcing President Johnson to begin and President Nixon to complete the process of withdrawal.

Congress

To the general public the U.S. interest in Vietnam in the 1950s was hardly differentiated from other economic and security interests in Southeast Asia. Perceptions about Vietnam were probably influenced more by the simplistic attack on foreign aid in the 1958 novel, *The Ugly American* by William Leaderer and Eugene Burdick,[58] than by the limited media attention given to the region. The foreign aid budget was under continuous assault by a small but influential group of southern Democrats and Midwestern Republicans. This group did not advocate abandoning Vietnam to the Communists, but they did not think that aid would be effective. They objected to squandering American military and economic resources to fight the Communists at a time and place where the United States was at a disadvantage (see Chaps. 4 and 5).[59] By and large, however, the leadership in Congress supported the concept of linking economic assistance to U.S. security assistance and aiding Vietnam in particular.

Before the massive buildup of military assistance in the summer of 1965, the dominant congressional supporters of the involvement in Vietnam were a group of liberal Democrats and internationalist Republicans. "For years [they] had carried the burden of justifying the military and economic assistance programs as a way of promoting economic development and stable democracies as a substitute for direct American military involvement. They also argued that if these programs were threatened by Communist aggression or Communist inspired insurgency, there was virtue in fighting a limited war to avoid fighting a wider war later."[60] After 1965 liberals and conservatives began switching sides. The conservatives felt that, once commitments had been made, they had to support the flag. At the same time the former Cold War liberals began to oppose the war.

The erosion of congressional support can perhaps best be illustrated by tracing the evolution of thought on the Vietnam conflict by Senators Mike Mansfield and William Fulbright. Mansfield was first attracted to Ngo Dinh Diem in the late 1940s while he was residing in the United States and lecturing widely on South Vietnamese national aspirations and the importance of maintaining a non-Communist Vietnam.[61]

When Diem ascended to the premiership in 1954, American support initially was somewhat ambiguous. The U.S. embassy helped him to survive several coup attempts in the fall of 1954 and a crisis with the militant Buddhist sects in 1955. In the spring of 1955, however, General J. Lawton Collins, the U.S. ambassador to Vietnam, succeeded in convincing President Eisenhower, over the objections of Secretary of State Dulles, that Diem would have to be either completely removed or shunted to a largely symbolic role as head of state if there was to be any hope for American success in Vietnam. Diem's success against the efforts of the sects to topple his government, however, convinced the CIA and the military that he had the loyalty of the army and could emerge as a successful leader. Senator Mansfield, along with several other Senate leaders, lobbied the State Department urging support for Diem. Diem was persuaded to ignore a cable from Vietnamese Emperor Bao Dai calling for his resignation. By the mid-1950s Mansfield was recommending that American assistance efforts to Vietnam give greater attention to long-term development efforts with the objective of eventually eliminating aid to Vietnam.[62]

By the early 1960s reports from the American press corps in Vietnam were beginning to cast serious doubt about the success of American efforts to support the South Vietnamese war effort. In December 1962 President Kennedy, concerned with the growing criticism, asked Senator Mansfield to make a personal visit to Vietnam to assess the situation. Mansfield returned with a highly pessimistic report; he noted that he could find little progress since he had last visited Vietnam in 1955. In a private report to the president, Mansfield warned that the United States was being sucked into a futile conflict reminiscent of the French conflict a decade earlier. Kennedy was exceedingly disturbed by the tone of Mansfield's report. He dispatched Roger Hillsman, director of the State Department Bureau of Intelligence, and Michael Forrestal of the National Security Council staff on a second fact-finding mission. Their report contained a pessimistic appraisal of the current situation balanced by a cautiously optimistic projection of the possibilities of achieving U.S. objectives.

By the winter of 1965, Mansfield found himself one of the very few of President Lyndon Johnson's advisors to argue against an escalation of bombing. As the emphasis shifted from an air war against North Vietnam to the war in the south, Mansfield joined with other senators, such as Frank Church and George McGovern, in calling for a search for a negotiated settlement.[63] Students at campuses throughout the United States conducted "teach-ins" to protest the bombing, and in April they organized a march on Washington. The protests were sufficiently disturbing so that Johnson assured Senator Mansfield in July that he would increase efforts to seek a diplomatic settlement while at the same time increasing the deployment of military forces in Vietnam.

On 27 July 1965, Mansfield advised Johnson that his support was based on his office and not on his policy in Vietnam and that, beneath the surface, there was confusion and uncertainty that would, in time, explode into outright opposition. Mansfield correctly perceived the flimsiness of Johnson's backing. "As long as the U.S. objectives could be obtained at minimal cost, Americans were willing to stay in Vietnam. When the war turned out to last much longer and cost much more than had been anticipated, however, the President's support began to wither and the advocates of escalation and withdrawal whom he had parried so skillfully in July 1965 became less manageable."[64] Johnson ignored Mansfield's advice and committed the United States to a war that destroyed both him and his successor.

Fulbright, chairman of the Senate Foreign Relations Committee, also made the transition from support of U.S. policy toward Vietnam to active opposition in the mid-1960s. In 1964 he shepherded President Johnson's Tonkin Bay resolution through the Senate, with an overwhelming 88 to 2 margin. His active opposition began when it became clear to him that Johnson had used an attack that had not actually occurred to obtain a grant of authority to carry out an expanded war. By early 1966 Fulbright had concluded that the United States was committing men and resources to a part of the world that had only marginal security interest for the United States. Johnson angrily attributed Fulbright's defection to disappointment in not being appointed secretary of state. Fulbright continued his opposition into the early years of the Nixon administration; he was increasingly offended by Nixon's and Kissinger's lack of candor with Congress and the American people.

The Press

During the 1950s press interest in Vietnam was largely confined to periodic exposés of aid ineffectiveness or excesses. An example is the series of articles by Albert M. Colegrove that appeared in the newspapers of the Scripps-Howard syndicate under the title, "Our Hidden Scandal in Vietnam." Colegrove charged waste, corruption, bad judgment, and incompetence by both Americans and Vietnamese. The charges led to hearings in the House and Senate and a joint House-Senate hearing in Saigon. The anecdotal cases reported by Colegrove were largely disproved. Both the House report and the more critical Senate report were generally supportive of the Vietnam program. However, they found serious flaws in program management and coordination. John Montgomery concluded that when the hearings were completed no opinions had been changed.[65]

By the early 1960s some members of the American press corps in Saigon, particularly David Halberstam of the *New York Times,* Neil Sheehen of United Press International, Charles Mohr of *Time,* and Stanley Karnow of the *Saturday Evening Post*, were questioning the official U.S. optimism about the progress in Vietnam. They were not yet questioning the rationale for containing communism in Vietnam. But they were arguing that the war was being lost and that it could not be won as long as the United States persisted in its policy of "sink or swim with Ngo Dinh Diem."[66]

This critical reporting was not received well in Saigon or in Washington. In Saigon a top U.S. military official demanded that the press "Get on the team!"[67] President Kennedy tried (unsuccessfully) to get the *New York Times* to recall Halberstam. *Time* magazine editors regularly rewrote dispatches to reflect editorial preconceptions.[68] I recall being told by a reporter for a major U.S. news magazine during a visit I made to Vietnam in 1963 that his editor had cabled that Secretary of Defense McNamara had told him during a lunch that the war was going well in Vietnam, "so why don't you get out in the field and find out what is going on?"[69]

Much of the early journalistic criticisms focused on the failure of the Diem regime to reform its civil and military administration and its repressive approach to rural development.[70] The escalation of American forces in Vietnam was accompanied by growing American media presence. At the beginning of 1966, some five hundred American journalists, including television crews and administrators, were accredited to the U.S. Military Assistance Command in Vietnam (MACV). Although most went along with the government's policy, they had little enthusiasm for it and questioned how long it would take to win. The more recent arrivals, however, were often less skeptical than the old Vietnam hands. The new reporters tended to view themselves as "war correspondents" rather than political analysts.[71]

Development and Defense Intellectuals

Before the mid-1960s the strong support provided by the elite-directed establishment press for U.S. intervention in Vietnam was reinforced by a group of development and defense intellectuals both within and outside the government. Scholars and analysts in universities and independent research institutes were called upon for program design and management. Michigan State University, which provided technical assistance in the area of police and public administration, was only one of a large number of research centers that became actively involved as contractors to support the U.S. development assistance effort in Vietnam.

Kattenburg noted that "parts of the academic and general intelligentsia, many of whom were themselves dependent in some personal or institutional way on government interests or on government financial largess, contributed strong support to the war effort and Johnson's policies. At the same time it was from within this group more than from any other that opposition to the war rose after 1965–66 and that the anti-war lobby was eventually constituted and led."[72]

The Shattering of AID

"In September of 1967, four staff members of the International Voluntary Services (IVS) in Vietnam resigned from their posts and with forty-nine of their colleagues wrote a letter to President Johnson condemning the American war." The IVS, a private voluntary organization with a record of success in rural development in Thailand and other southeast Asian countries, was one of a large number of PVOs that, in addition to the direct hire AID personnel, attempted to carry out the economic assistance and development missions in Vietnam. Don Luce, John Sumner, and their colleagues resigned reluctantly, "not just because they had decided that the AID program was a failure but because they had come to realize that the main efforts of the United States in Vietnam were destructive rather than constructive."[73]

Luce and Sumner were not neophytes in Vietnam. Each had worked with rural people there long before the arrival of the first U.S. troops. They understood that both U.S. direct hire and contract personnel were caught in contradictions that were grinding out their integrity and their careers. They were forced by their bureaucratic situations to believe that their efforts could succeed, while experience, at least for those who had contacts in the field, was confirming that there was no prospect for success.[74]

Between my first visit to Vietnam in 1963 and my last visit in 1965, I saw AID staff who had arrived in Vietnam with energy and enthusiasm leave with careers ground down as if by a meat grinder. The situation worsened as the war continued. Contradictions were inherent in an environment where no rewards were given for discovering that the American effort was failing. The rewards were for success. This contradiction extended to the highest levels.

> In 1966, for example, Vice-President Hubert Humphrey went to Vietnam on Johnson's bidding to congratulate the Saigon government on the progress it had made in the area of Revolutionary Development. In the course of a ritual visit to the Rural Development training camp in Vung Tao, he heard the chief instructor of the program, Major Nguyen Be, assert that the program was not working because the entire Saigon government was corrupt. The Vice-President, who had made his political fortunes in Minneapolis as a muck-raking reformer, found himself in the position of defending a government that he must have known was corrupt against a Vietnamese reformer.[75]

In 1954, when American assistance to Vietnam began, the prospect for an agriculture-led development program had been highly promising. With a modest amount of aid, primarily technical assistance, it is possible that the relatively skilled people of Vietnam could have succeeded in breaking out of the cycle of poverty and underdevelopment. But the United States had little direct interest in the economy of Vietnam. The American aid programs were designed for a hypothetical country that did not exist.

Among the most difficult problems faced by US/AID in Vietnam, as well as other countries with authoritarian governments, was the distinction between aid to the people and aid to the government. The objective of development assistance has been to aid people, whereas that of strategic assistance, in contrast, is to aid governments. Leaders of recipient country governments, such as Diem, typically have considered U.S. assistance as assistance to their regimes rather than to their people.[76]

Summing Up

In the end it was not only the opposition in Congress or the increasingly critical reporting by the press that ended the Vietnam conflict. Every administration involved failed to effectively relate the values being served by the war to the costs in lives and materials being expended. The discrepancy between means and ends widened dramatically after 1968, when the objective shifted from preserving an independent South Vietnam to withdrawal—"peace with honor." The indiscriminate bombing, the escalation of military and civilian casualties, the extension of the war to Cambodia and Laos, and attempts to deceive the American people about the extent of the intensification bore little relation to the limited objective being sought.[77]

American failure in Vietnam began with two fundamental mistakes in the late 1940s. The first was abandoning Roosevelt's anti-colonial impulse and attempting to preserve a French presence in Vietnam. The second was according Vietnam a strategic importance that it did not possess. A continuing derivative mistake was the refusal to learn from failure. These, and other errors, were direct consequences of (*a*) a commitment to anti-communism as the central dogma through which the United States interpreted events in the rest of the world, (*b*) a narrow interpretation of the containment doctrine as the primary strategic approach to dealing with communist expansion, and (*c*) the domino theory as a basis of policy. The dogma, the doctrine, and the policy all led to elevating Indochina (and South Vietnam) to a strategic importance it did not have.

In retrospect, it would be easy to conclude that the United States should not, in the mid-1950s, have committed itself to the preservation of an economically and politically viable non-Communist state in South Vietnam. But this would be too easy. During the early 1950s, which were dominated by a strident McCarthyism (1949–54), any suggestion of withdrawal from Vietnam would have been labeled "soft on communism." Even during the late 1950s, it would have been difficult to find convincing reasons for a weaker commitment to the economic and political development of South Vietnam than to other countries in East and Southeast Asia. Beginning about 1960, however, the mistakes in judgment should have become more obvious. U.S. commitments to the short-run viability of the Diem regime and its successors placed us at odds with the longer-run interests and aspirations of the Vietnamese people.

It is not so easy, however, to excuse the U.S. presidents—from Truman to Nixon—and their senior advisers for their lack of realism in their understanding of U.S. interests in Vietnam and, more broadly, in the Indochinese region.[78] The only defensible U.S. economic and political interest in Southeast Asia was support for the emergence of postcolonial successor states that would be governed in the interests of their own citizens. This insight, which informed U.S. policy during World War II, was abandoned with the emergence of Cold War containment policy.

Are there lessons from the Vietnam experience? My own response is that, although the Vietnam experience has had important consequences for the United States, there are few lessons! The lessons that we brought to the conflict in Indochina—from previous experience in Latin America, Western Europe, Greece, China, and Korea—were not useful in Vietnam. We should not let our perspectives on the experience in Vietnam harden into dogma or doctrine.

Assistance to Israel and Egypt

U.S. economic and military assistance to the countries of Southeast Asia was driven by the strategic concerns of six successive administrations. These concerns were initially shared by Congress and reinforced by public opinion. As strategic assistance escalated into military involvement, support by Congress and the public turned into active resistance.

American economic and military assistance to Israel and other countries in the Middle East drew on very different social and political forces.[79] Assistance to Israel drew on the large emotional capital among the American public generated by the inhumane treatment of the Jewish people in Europe and the exodus to Palestine. This emotional capital was mobilized by Jewish interest groups to build support for assistance to Israel even when such assistance was viewed by incumbent administrations as inconsistent with U.S. strategic interests in the Middle East. Assistance to Egypt, as well as to Jordan, Lebanon, and Syria, has largely been derivative of assistance to Israel.

When the United States withdrew from Southeast Asia, the flow of ESF resources shifted more strongly toward resolving Arab-Israeli tensions in the Middle East (see Figure 10.1; Tables A.2 and A.3). Before 1970 U.S. economic assistance to Israel had never exceeded $100 million. Assistance escalated rapidly after the 1973 October (Yom Kippur) War between Israel and Egypt and Syria. It exceeded $500 million by the beginning of the Carter administration and rose to close to $2.0 billion by the end of the first Reagan administration. Military assistance rose by a similar order of magnitude (Table A.2). During this same period both economic and military assistance to Egypt also escalated rapidly to a level in the range of one-half to two-thirds of that received by Israel (Table A.3).

The form in which assistance was granted to Israel became increasingly favorable. In 1971 economic assistance shifted from support for specific programs, such as agricultural development, to the Commodity Import Program for purchase of U.S. goods. When CIP ended in 1979, it was replaced by largely unconditional direct budgetary transfers. The 1974 emergency aid for Israel, following the 1973 war, included the first military grant aid. Economic aid became all grant cash transfers in 1981, and military aid became all grants in 1985 (Table A.2).[80] Assistance to the region—Israel, Egypt, Jordan, and Syria—which was less than 10 percent of the ESF budget in fiscal 1970, rose to almost 90 percent by 1976 and has remained at near that level. Israel and Egypt have been the largest recipients of total U.S. bilateral economic assistance since the mid-1970s (Table A.3).[81]

Why has such a large share of U.S. economic assistance been concentrated in these two countries? The level of per capita income in Israel ranks it above any of the developing countries of Latin America, Asia, and Africa. Egypt has experienced a reasonably adequate rate of growth of gross domestic product, approximately 5 percent per year since 1952–53, rising to almost 9 percent per year from the mid-1970s to the mid-1980s.[82] However, the event that triggered rapid escalation of economic and military assistance to both Israel and Egypt was not economic need but, rather, the October War of 1973.

Three Constituencies

One of the more careful students of the politics of U.S. policy toward Israel, Steven L. Spiegel, has argued that American policy toward the Middle East, and Arab-Israeli tensions, have involved three constituencies. The first is made up of key executive officials—the president, the national security assistant, the secretaries of state and defense, the ambassador to the United Nations, and the White House foreign policy staff—who tend to interpret Middle East events in terms of broader global concerns.[83] Although some presidents (Lyndon Johnson and Ronald Reagan, for example) publicly expressed deep sympathy for the Israeli cause, all presidents tended to view the Israeli-Arab conflict primarily within the context of Cold War tensions. Presidents were drawn into the peace process in the Middle East largely as a result of domestic political pressure. But they were compelled to rationalize their efforts by interpreting the Israeli-Arab conflicts in terms of preventing Soviet penetration into the oil-rich region of the Persian Gulf.

The second constituency reflects a regional approach to the Middle East; it includes the Near East and South Asian Affairs Bureau of the State Department. A regional approach has also been pervasive within the policy analysis community outside the government and within the oil and the arms supply industries. The oil industry wanted stable, moderate, pro-American regimes in the Arab world. They feared or opposed nationalization or the independence of oil producers. "Oil men and diplomats have not always addressed precisely identical concerns but their policy preferences . . . tended to coincide on the Arab-Israel issues."[84] The arms supply industries, while profiting from the tensions within the region, have benefited from the flow of oil revenues to the region.

Spiegel also argues that, despite appearances, the oil and other business interests have been less influential in the formation of policy toward the Middle East than many critics have suspected. Their influence was strongest after the 1973 October War and during the period of high oil prices that lasted into the early 1980s. Their interests were shared by construction companies, banks, real estate developers, and even universities, which wanted to capitalize on petro dollars flowing into the oil-producing states. The oil industry made very large contributions to Nixon's 1972 campaign, but they had little direct influence on policy. A Mobil representative complained that, during the Nixon administration, "We could always get a hearing, but we felt we might as well be talking to the wall."[85]

A third constituency for policy toward the Middle East included those people for whom the Israeli-Arab conflict was a central concern. The government of Israel and the pro-Israeli lobby in the United States sought to advance the concept that Israel represented a strategic asset for the United States. But Spiegel argues that few American Jewish leaders regarded Israel's strategic role as the primary reason for backing the Israeli government. Their support has been based on religious, cultural, and historical roots reinforced by concern for Jewish survival.

Other constituencies for whom the Israeli-Arab conflict was central included the American labor movement, liberal and fundamentalist churches, and the Arab-American community. American labor has been supportive of Israel because of labor's important role in Israeli society and government. The mainline liberal Protestant denominations were strong supporters of Israel for several decades after the formation of the state but more recently have become critical of what they regard as Israel's repression of legitimate Palestinian aspirations. Many fundamentalists are convinced that the emergence of Israel as a state represents the fulfillment of Biblical prophecy about the "last days." Until very recently the Arab-American community has not been organized as an effective lobbying force. Arab governments have worked individually or through paid lobbyists, as well as through joint lobbying and pressure in cooperation with oil interests and construction companies in Washington. Their lobbying has had little effect.

The major focus of the following sections is the ethnic and presidential politics of assistance to Israel and Egypt. This is not because there have not been other domestic constituencies for U.S. policy toward the Middle East, but it is because the constituencies identified above—the Office of the President, the State Department bureaucracy, the arms supply industry, the major oil companies, the Arab-American community, and the liberal movement—were forced to define and advance their interests amidst the continuing tension between Israel and the Arab states and the strong domestic popular and political support for the Israeli state.

The Ethnic Politics of Assistance to Israel

To understand the growth of U.S. economic assistance to Israel and Egypt, one must understand the increasing role of the U.S. Jewish community, particularly after the 1967 June War (see Exhibit 10.1 for a listing of the major Jewish lobbying organizations).[86] The effectiveness of the Jewish community can best be appreciated by tracing the ability of the Jewish lobby to influence the policies of presidents and secretaries of state.

Reluctant Support

During World War II the Roosevelt administration maintained an open dialogue with Zionist leaders. Roosevelt, however, shared the opinion of his foreign policy and defense advisors that a Jewish state in Palestine was inconsistent with U.S. interests in the Middle East. Caught between his cautious instincts and the pressures from Congress and the public, "he authorized two prominent Zionist leaders, Rabbis Wise and Abba Hillel Silver, to issue a statement suggesting future American support for a Jewish national home. But he congratulated speaker Sam Rayburn for keeping the House in line against a resolution favoring a Jewish commonwealth in Palestine. A few days later he assured six Arab leaders that no decision would be made on the future of Palestine without full consultation with both sides."[87]

Before World War II, Jewish organizations had exerted relatively little influence on U.S. foreign policy. Their first major triumph was Truman's decision to recognize the new state of Israel against his own earlier judgment and the continuing opposition of his most trusted foreign policy advisors. Truman's special counsel, Clark Clifford, was a strong supporter of early recognition. Secretary of State General George Marshall, Under-Secretary Robert Lovett, and other key State Department officials vigorously opposed recognition. But Truman held firm despite concern that Marshall had threatened resignation. On 14 May 1948, the State of Israel was proclaimed in Tel Aviv at 6:00 P.M. Washington time. At 6:11 P.M., the president's press secretary announced recognition of Israel.[88]

The Eisenhower administration was less sympathetic to Jewish ambitions. It regarded the Middle East as an important arena for the containment of the USSR. The new policy, according to Secretary of State John Foster Dulles, was "friendly impartiality" to Arabs and Israelis. Impartiality did not mean equality; to Eisenhower the Arabs offered assets, whereas Israel was a liability to American interests.[89] Jewish leaders interpreted this attitude as hostility toward Israel. Relations worsened when Israel disregarded a U.N. plan (supported by the United States) to develop the Jordan River to benefit both Israel and the surrounding nations. The ill feeling was exacerbated further by an Israeli military raid on an Arab village near the project site, in which the Israelis blew up at least 30 houses after "systematically killing" their inhabitants.[90]

In 1956 Israel cooperated with the British and the French in an invasion of

EXHIBIT 10.1
Major Jewish Lobby Organizations

B'nai B'rith. A Jewish fraternal organization founded in 1843 by German-American Jews. It became strongly pro-Zionist during World War II.

Zionist Organization of America (ZOA). Founded in 1897 as the American Branch of the World Zionist Organization. It began to expand rapidly and draw membership from the AJC after Louis Brandeis, a well-known Boston lawyer and later Supreme Court justice, joined in 1912.

American Jewish Committee (AJC). Founded in 1906 by assimilated leaders of Reform Judaism to deal with the political and social problems faced by the Jewish immigrant community. The AJC was initially opposed to Zionism.

American Jewish Congress. Founded in 1943 as an association of 64 national and regional Jewish organizations. The American Jewish Congress rapidly became the leading advocate in the United States of a Jewish state in Palestine.

Council of Presidents of Major American Jewish Organizations. Founded in 1954 as an informed forum to discuss how American Jewish organizations could help Israel. Its organization was stimulated by the perceived hostility of the Eisenhower administration toward Israel. It was viewed by its founders as an alternative to the declining influence of the American Jewish Conference.

American Israel Public Affairs Committee (AIPAC). Founded in 1954 as the American Zionist Council of Public Affairs by the American Zionist Council. Its objective was to engage in lobbying on behalf of Israel. It is the only registered lobby for Israel. By the 1980s it had become the dominant voice of the American Jewish community on policy toward Israel.

Egypt to reverse Egypt's seizure the Suez Canal. Israel occupied the Sinai, the Gaza Strip, and the Straits of Tiran, which had been closed to Israeli shipping. The United States pressured Britain and France to withdraw from Suez, and the Israelis withdrew from the Sinai.[91] Many leaders of the American Jewish community were embarrassed by Jewish terrorism in Kibya and Gaza, the Israeli cooperation with the British and French in the Suez invasion, and the failure of the Israeli government to deal honestly with them in such matters. But they were not embarrassed enough to criticize Israel publicly.

By the end of the Eisenhower administration, the Jewish community looked for a 1960 presidential candidate who would be more sympathetic to the Israeli cause. Jewish leaders were favorably impressed with John F. Kennedy and financially supported his campaign. Kennedy was forced to learn, however, that Jewish electoral support did not translate into support for a Middle East peace plan perceived by the Israeli government as opposing its self-interest. In 1962 he announced a plan (the Johnson plan) that called for Arab refugees to be given a chance to return to their homes in what is now Israel or to be resettled in other parts of Israel or in other Arab countries. Prime Minister Ben Gurion regarded the demographic implications of the plan as infeasible and informed his ambassador in Washington, in a letter distributed to American Jewish leaders, that Israel regarded the plan as a threat to her existence. Kennedy had hoped to win Israel's cooperation with a $23 million loan to buy the HAWK guided missile system. The peace plan was "a classic example of a president miscalculating how hard an Israeli government and the American Jewish community will fight any measure that it perceived to be against Israel's interests—regardless of how much the White House insists it is in American interests."[92]

Lyndon Johnson viewed himself as the strongest supporter that the Jewish state had ever had in the White House.[93] His biblically based religious background, he said, reinforced his sympathy toward Israel. The Jewish community strongly supported his 1965 election campaign. Jews were well represented in his administration: Abe Fortas (nominated to the Supreme Court), Arthur Goldberg (ambassador to the United Nations), Walt Rostow (national security advisor), Eugene Rostow (under-secretary of state), and Myer Feldman (domestic policy advisor). Johnson became the first U.S. president officially to receive the prime minister of Israel at the White House. But Johnson was no more successful than Kennedy had been in converting this close working relationship into support for de-escalation of a Middle East arms race. Tensions between Israel and Egypt remained high.

From the Six-Day War to the October War

On 14 May 1967, Egypt's President Nasser put Egyptian forces on a state of "maximum alert" and requested withdrawal of U.N. observers from the Sinai. On May 22, he announced the closure of the Straits of Tiran to Israeli shipping. On June 5, Israeli planes bombarded Egyptian airfields. Impelled by fear of a new Holocaust, the U.S. Jewish community mobilized more than $100 million to support the Israeli war effort. By July 11 the Arab armies of Egypt, Syria, and Jordan were defeated. In the opinion of U.S. intelligence agencies, the closing of the Straits of Tiran was a diplomatic ploy. Egypt had not intended to attack Israel, and there was no threat to the existence of Israel in 1967. "The only question in intelligence circles at the time was whether the war—the 'turkey shoot' as Walt Rostow called it—would be over in six days or seven."[94]

The peace process remained elusive. Israel offered to withdraw to the international border with Egypt in exchange for freedom on the Strait of Tiran and the Suez Canal, provided the Sinai was demilitarized. The Arab response was "no peace, no recognition, no negotiation." In November 1967 the United Nations, drawing heavily on views spelled out by President Johnson, passed Resolution 242 to encourage negotiations. The key section of the resolution called for "withdrawal of Israeli armed forces from territories occupied in the recent conflict, . . . termination of all states of belligerency and . . . acknowledgement of the sovereignty . . . of every state in the area and their right to live in peace with secure and recognized boundaries."[95]

The resolution received very different interpretations by the several parties. To Israel, Resolution 242 required each of its neighbors to recognize Israel's right to exist and to negotiate bilaterally a secure border. To the Arab states—Egypt, Jordan, and Syria—the resolution required Israel to give back all of the territory captured during the war. To the United States, the resolution established the principle of trading land for peace. And to Palestinians the resolution was a betrayal. Its only reference to the establishment of a Palestinian state was a mandate for a "just settlement of the refugee problem." The Arab states indicated a willingness to go along with 242. The PLO rejected it. The United States adopted it as a basic policy guide adhered to with remarkable consistency by every president since Johnson.[96] Israel seemed content with the status quo—assuming that, with support from the U.S. Jewish community and the U.S. government, they could maintain military superiority. This view was seemingly confirmed when, in December 1968, after a massive lobbying effort by the American Jewish community, President Johnson acceded, over State Department opposition and his own better judgment, to a request by Israel to purchase 40 F-4 Phantom jet fighters.

When Nixon entered the White House in 1969, he prided himself on "not being beholden to the pro-Israeli lobby, since relatively few Jews had voted for him." Nixon and Henry Kissinger, his national security advisor, saw Israel's relations with the Arab states primarily in terms of U.S. relations with the USSR. Nixon believed that the Middle East situation was potentially explosive, and he quickly set in motion efforts to design a new peace initiative. In November and December, Secretary of State Rogers began discussing a plan that included Israel's withdrawal from most of the occupied territories, the right of Arab refugees to choose between repatriation and resettlement, and Jordanian and Israeli participation, with interested parties, in the civic and religious life of the Old City of Jerusalem. The plan was immediately rejected by Israel. American Jewish leaders raised an almost unified protest against the Rogers plan. To deflect Nixon's irritation Meir emphasized Israeli support for the Vietnam War. Arthur Hertzberg, a member of the World

Zionist Organization's executive board, was one of the few American Jewish leaders to question Meir.[97] The death of the Rogers plan was due, in retrospect, to the guerrilla warfare within the Israeli and U.S. governments: between Secretary of State William Rogers and National Security Advisor Henry Kissinger in the United States and between Israel's Foreign Minister Abba Eban and Ambassador to Washington Yitzhak Rabin.

The Nixon administration's second conflict with the American Jewish community centered on the issue of Jewish emigration from the USSR. In September 1972 Senator Henry Jackson, in a speech before the National Conference on Soviet Jewry, supported the linking of U.S. trade benefits for the USSR to Jewish emigration rights from the USSR. Jackson was joined by Congressman Charles Vanik (D-Ohio). The proposed legislation received the enthusiastic support of AIPAC. Nixon and Kissinger warned Meir and Rabin against pressuring Congress to support the Jackson-Vanik proposal, but neither the Israeli government nor AIPAC was willing to withdraw its support from the Jackson initiative because, in the view of many Jewish leaders, Jackson had a "shot at being President."[98]

The death of Egypt's President Nasser on 28 September 1970 opened the possibility of fruitful negotiations between Israel and Egypt. His successor, Anwar Sadat, frustrated in his dealings with the USSR, attempted to enlist U.S. assistance in negotiating an Israeli withdrawal from the Sinai. When his efforts were rebuffed in Washington, Sadat concluded that the only way to break the deadlock in Washington and Jerusalem was to cross the Suez Canal into the Sinai. The attack on 6 October 1973 (Yom Kippur, the holiest day in the Jewish calendar) caught both Israel and the United States by surprise. During the first three days Israel lost 50 aircraft and hundreds of tanks; only U.S. intervention to resupply Israel's logistical needs prevented even greater losses.[99]

This war dampened incipient criticism of Israeli policy among Jewish leaders in the United States and induced a new outpouring of emotional and financial support for Israel.[100] I. L. Kenan was succeeded as executive director of AIPAC by Morris Amitay. The two major tasks set by Amitay were to expand U.S. aid to Israel and to establish strong direction over the lobbying and campaign resources of the Jewish community. When the Campaign Financing Act of 1974 sharply limited individual contributions to a candidate for Congress, Jewish fund raisers quickly established legal political action committees (PACs).[101]

Shuttle Diplomacy

After replacing Rogers as secretary of state in the fall of 1973, Kissinger initiated a series of three-way conversations with Moshe Dayan and Anwar

Sadat to disengage troops from the Suez Canal area. The result was a step-by-step approach to peace rather than a return to the comprehensive peace plan envisioned by U.N. Resolution 242 and the Rogers plan.[102] At each step American Jewish leaders, suspicious that Kissinger was plotting to abandon Israel, became more critical. After Nixon's resignation Kissinger returned to his shuttle diplomacy with the full support of President Gerald Ford. Israeli leaders worried about the willingness of Ford and Kissinger to stand up to Arab threats to use the "oil weapon." Kissinger expressed increasing frustration with what he regarded as Israeli intransigence.

Both Kissinger and Ford became convinced that the Egyptians had bent over backward to advance the peace process while the Israeli government was unwilling to yield anything to get anything in return. "At Kissinger's urging, Ford decided to lean on Israel in an effort to break what they perceived as its intransigence. In a speech on the Middle East in March 1975, Gerald Ford called for a reassessment of U.S. policy."[103] He also delayed the delivery of weapons, including the F-15 fighter plane, and suspended negotiations for pending financial and military aid to Israel. He then began discussions on the possibility of a major speech in which he would spell out America's basic interest in the Middle East, which included Israeli withdrawal from Sinai.

According to Edward Tivnan, "Henry Kissinger had just tossed a bomb into the American Jewish community, and it quickly, and expertly, heaved it back."[104] By 21 May 1975, AIPAC had succeeded in mobilizing significant support and put a letter on the president's desk, signed by 76 senators, indicating their support for Israel and threatening to hold the 1976 foreign aid request hostage: "Within the next several weeks, the Congress expects to receive your foreign aid request for fiscal year 1976. We trust that your recommendations will be responsive to Israeli's urgent military and economic needs."[105] President Ford abandoned his plan for a Middle East policy speech, and the step-by-step process toward peace was reactivated.

Writing six years later, Senator Charles Mathias, Jr. (D-Md.), was extremely critical of how AIPAC had been able to stampede him and his colleagues into signing "the letter of seventy-six." "Seventy six of us promptly affixed our signatures although no hearing had been held, no debate conducted, nor had the administration been invited to present its views." A new round of shuttle diplomacy finally brought a semidisengagement agreement. "The Israelis showed new flexibility after the Ford-Rabin summit in June because they had resolved to accept American diplomatic, military, and economic assistance instead of Egyptian concessions."[106]

To Camp David

The Jewish community responded to Jimmy Carter's presidential campaign with considerable skepticism. Jewish interest groups had strong ties to Henry Jackson. Many were bothered by Carter's southern Baptist background. But Carter left no doubt, in a series of campaign speeches and policy statements, of his commitment to Israel's survival and to a peace process that would end the Arab boycott of Israel, establish diplomatic relations between Arab states and Israel, open frontiers, and result in a peace treaty. The Jewish community was even more skeptical of Zbigniew Brzezinski, Carter's national security advisor. In a 1975 *Foreign Policy* article, Brzezinski had criticized Israel for excessive rigidity in its unwillingness to engage in negotiations that could lead to the establishment of a Palestinian state on the West Bank in exchange for a peace agreement with the Arab states.[107]

After his election Carter was anxious to move rapidly to secure a Middle East peace accord. He saw the importance of initiating steps toward a Middle East settlement while he still had the political resources to "take the lead" from the American Jewish community. If he was successful domestic opposition would turn into support. In a speech in Clinton, Massachusetts, on 16 March 1977, Carter insisted that a solution to the Palestinian problem was a requirement for peace in the Middle East.[108] Although he did not explicitly advocate a Palestinian state, the American Jewish community reacted vigorously. Their concern had already been aroused by an unpleasant meeting on March 7 between Carter and Israeli Prime Minister Yitzhak Rabin. Carter came away from the meeting impressed with Rabin's inflexibility, whereas Rabin left with an impression that Carter was dangerously naive about Middle East politics. However, the Carter people were insensitive to Rabin's remarks on his return to Israel, in which he suggested some flexibility on the Palestine issues. Rabin indicated that Israel would not object to including Palestinians in a Jordanian delegation to peace talks and that Israel might be willing to share West Bank administration with Jordan.

Any hope that Carter might have had for advancing the Middle East peace process seemed to vanish in May 1977 when Menachem Begin was elected prime minister of Israel. Begin's position since his youth as a terrorist leader had been that the West Bank and Gaza—Judea and Samaria—were integral parts of Israel. With Begin the American Jewish community was again forced to swallow its principles in order to preserve a unified front. Rabbi Alexander Schindler, chairman of the Conference of Presidents of American Jewish Organizations and head of the Union of American Hebrew Congregations (an association of Reform congregations), persuaded himself that Begin would become more liberal in his policies once he assumed the responsibilities of office—like Nixon had. Besides, "It's impossible to say, 'Begin's terrible, but we want you [the American government] to support the state of Israel anyway.'" Schindler's shift had the effect of undercutting advocates of the peace process both in Israel and within the American Jewish community. It so angered Nahum Goldman (former head of the World Jewish Congress and a founder of the Conference of Presidents of Major Jewish Organizations) that he told Carter the only way to advance the peace process would be to "break the Jewish lobby in the United States."[109] Neither Carter nor his advisors had any stomach for such a task.

By November 1977 the Carter administration had become a bystander in the peace process. President Anwar Sadat, in an address to the Egyptian parliament in early November, said that he was prepared to go to Jerusalem to meet with Begin.[110] Begin could hardly refuse. On November 20 Sadat addressed the Knesset in Jerusalem and outlined his plan. Both Begin and Sadat agreed on one point: the Sinai was not part of the Biblical Land of Israel and should be returned to Egypt. But they did not agree on the governance of the West Bank and Gaza.

Begin continued to acquire land and establish settlements in the two territories and even proposed new settlements in Sinai. His position on settlement was deeply disturbing to many American Jews as well as to the peace movement in Israel. When the Carter administration succeeded, after furiously twisting arms in the Senate, in completing the sale of 15 F-15 jet fighters to Saudi Arabia, the Jewish lobby again turned up the heat. Morris Amitay was so upset by George McGovern's vote in favor of the F-15 sale that he branded McGovern (a consistent supporter of Israel) an "enemy of Israel." "Worried more about the effects of Jimmy Carter's policy . . . on the U.S.-Israel relationship than . . . on Begin's policies, more concerned about preserving the U.S.-Israeli relationship than the moral and democratic ties that assure that friendship, American Jewish leaders . . . questioned the motives of anyone who dared criticize Israel—Jew, gentile, or President of the United States."[111]

Despite domestic opposition by the Jewish community, Carter persisted in his efforts to find a solution to peace in the Middle East.[112] In September 1977 he succeeded in bringing Menachem Begin and Anwar Sadat together at Camp David. At the core of the Camp David agreements were arrangements for a transition to self-rule by the Palestinians of the West Bank and Gaza and for negotiations among Israel, Egypt, Jordan, and "representatives of the Palestinian People" about the final status of those territories. The solution, according to Camp David, "must also recognize the legitimate rights of the Palestinian people and their just requirements"—precisely the phrase that Israeli and Jewish leaders had created a furor over when it had appeared in

Carter's joint communique with the Russians in October 1977. There were also provisions governing the negotiation of a peace treaty between Egypt and Israel, the key being Israel's withdrawal from the Sinai to the 1967 border.

Another six months of tense and often discouraging negotiations and a personal trip by President Carter to Egypt and Israel in early March 1979 were needed to move from the Camp David agreements to the signing of a formal peace treaty. The treaty was achieved by an exercise in presidential personal diplomacy unequaled since the time of President Woodrow Wilson. The Camp David accords of September 1978 and the 29 March 1979 peace treaty between Israel and Egypt are the Carter administration's greatest achievement. Without Carter's personal commitment there would have been no treaty. Although the accords were broadly supported in Israel, some members of the Knesset denounced Carter's efforts as "a crime against our people" and "selling out Israel." The Jewish lobby, and many American Jewish voters, continued to view Carter as an enemy of Israel. Columnist William Safire insisted that Carter had deliberately betrayed the Israelis. In the 1980 election Carter received only 45 percent of the Jewish vote—down from 68 percent in 1976.[113]

A Strategic Asset

The Reagan administration came into office with a set of concerns about the Middle East much different from those of the Ford and Carter administrations.[114] Reagan personally saw Israel in terms of Biblical prophecy—as a vibrant democracy that had arisen out of the ashes of the Holocaust. His policy was guided by the belief that the Soviet Union was the source of American problems around the world. Reagan and his advisors saw the Middle East as an arena of confrontation between the United States and the USSR. Israel represented a potentially important strategic asset. Aid to Israel would be based on a view that the United States needed Israel at least as much as Israel needed aid from the United States. But Israel's value as a strategic asset could be fully realized only if tensions between Israel and the Arab states in the region were reduced and attention was focused on the threat from the USSR.

The policy of the Reagan administration was not only to strengthen Israel but also to strengthen the defense capacity of Saudi Arabia and the other moderate Arab states. A first step in this strategy was to respond to the request made by the Saudis to the Carter administration the previous June for approval to purchase the missiles, bomb racks, and fuel pods for the F-15s they had ordered previously; for KC-135 tankers to refuel the F-15s in midair; and for five airborne warning and command system (AWACS) aircraft.[115]

As rumors about the proposal began to surface in Washington, the Reagan administration was immediately confronted by opposition from AIPAC and its allies. Thomas A. Dine, who had succeeded Morris Amitay as director of AIPAC in 1980, had served as legislative assistant to Frank Church, as advisor to Senator Edmund Muskie, and as a foreign policy advisor to Senator Edward Kennedy. He came to AIPAC with a much more sophisticated appreciation of the congressional potential to formulate foreign policy. When he learned of the proposed arms sale, Dine visited Edwin Meese, White House counsel and a close friend of the president. He informed Meese that "the American Jewish community was prepared to 'fight all the way.' He outlined the intense opposition of American Jews and their 'friends' in Congress. The results, Dine noted, 'would not be in the best interests of anybody.'"[116] The Reagan administration was slow to recognize the seriousness of Dine's challenge and inept in its handling of relations with Congress. After all, no administration had been defeated in an arms sales deal.

The difficulty of the administration's position was brought home to Secretary of State Alexander Haig on a trip to the Middle East in early April 1981. Prime Minister Begin informed him that the proposed sale would threaten the overall strategic situation in the region and jeopardize Israel's security. In Riyadh Prince Saud insisted to Haig that Israel rather than the Soviet Union was the main cause of instability in the region.[117] As the seriousness of the challenge became clearer, the administration's responsibility for pulling its chestnuts out of the fire fell on Senate majority leader Howard Baker and the president's chief of staff, James Baker. The president could not afford defeat on a foreign policy issue this early in his presidency. Presidential lobbying shifted the choice from "Reagan or Begin?" to "Reagan or else!" Under pressure from the White House and Senator Baker, key senators moved to support the president. The Senate approved the AWACS sale by a vote of 52 to 48. The victory cost the president very large political resources. The victory also cost Senator Charles Percy (D-Ill.), chairman of the Senate Foreign Relations Committee, his Senate seat, and it placed Thomas Dine and AIPAC in a position to dominate the American Jewish community on issues involving Israel for more than a decade.

Prime Minister Begin welcomed and took full advantage of the Reagan administration's view of Israel as a strategic asset. But his subsequent actions had the effect of devaluing what little strategic value Israel, in fact, had to the United States. (1) Begin pursued his Greater Israel policy through an aggressive settlement program in the occupied territories; (2) bombing raids were conducted against the Iraqi's nuclear reactor site in June and against PLO sites in Beirut in July 1981; (3) on 14 December 1981 Israel formally annexed the Golan Heights; (4) in 1982 Israel invaded Lebanon in an attempt to wipe out the PLO infrastructure; (5) this was followed by the massacre, by Christian Phalange soldiers, of women and children in two Palestinian refugee camps (Sabra and Shatila), which Israeli soldiers observed but did not choose to stop. The public outcry in Israel against Begin's policies in Lebanon, particularly the Sabra and Shatila massacres, resulted in a demonstration involving some 400,000 people in Tel Aviv and a threat by some of Begin's coalition partners to resign.[118]

In July 1982 George Shultz replaced Alexander Haig as secretary of state. The time seemed ripe for a fresh start on Middle East policy. U.N. Resolution 242 and the Camp David accords were dusted off, and a few new wrinkles were added. The Reagan plan proposed a freeze on Jewish settlements and a self-governing entity in association with Jordan on the West Bank. The plan received initial support from Thomas Dine and AIPAC. Begin denounced it immediately and categorically. The plan also failed to get support from King Hussein of Jordan. The Reagan plan suffered the same fate as had that of each of his predecessors since John Kennedy.

Yet, no matter how hard Begin's actions undercut the value of Israel as a U.S. strategic asset, military and economic assistance to Israel continued to grow. Since 1981 all ESF transfers to Israel have been on a grant basis. Unlike other countries, ESF aid to Israel is not tied to specific development projects. In 1985 and 1986, a special ESF "emergency" transfer, above and beyond the regular ESF program, was initiated in Congress as a "bail out" for the costs incurred by Israel in the Lebanese invasions (see Table A.2).[119] When official aid levels are adjusted to reflect the host of other concessions and special privileges granted to Israel, aid totals are substantially above the amounts shown in Table A.2. In 1989, for example, when ESF cash transfers amounted to $1.2 billion, adjustment to include related support—interest earned on advance lump sum transfers, refugee assistance, and several other transfers—brought the total to $1.4 billion. George and Douglas Ball estimate that the reported $1.8 billion in military sales would rise to $2.3 billion if adjusted to include other related support.[120]

By the early 1980s there had emerged, in both Israel and the United States, a substantial body of economic analysis suggesting that the rapid growth in economic and security assistance after the October War had become a burden rather than a source of strength to the Israeli economy.[121] During the first two decades after 1948, Israel experienced one of the highest economic growth rates in the world. The growth rate began to fall after the 1973 Yom Kippur War. By the early 1980s, economic growth had come to a virtual halt. Foreign aid, along with massive foreign borrowing, enabled Israel to avoid fiscal discipline and maintain an overvalued currency. The effects were felt in inflation rates reaching the 1000 percent per year range in 1984 and the 500 percent range in 1985, in the inability of Israeli industry to compete in international markets, and in massive importation of consumer goods. Several Israeli and U.S. economists and journalists urged the United States to use its aid program to induce Israel to undertake the reforms that it was unwilling to impose on itself.[122] In the mid-1980s, the new national unity government that replaced Begin launched a comprehensive stabilization program. Inflation fell to below 20 percent per year. Economic growth resumed but, in part because of accelerated immigration from the USSR, unemployment remained high.[123]

By the end of the 1980s, the emotional capital sustaining U.S. assistance to Israel was eroding.[124] The erosion of public support began in the early 1970s when Israel tightened its control on Jerusalem. It intensified after the invasion of Lebanon in 1982, the failure of the Israeli army to prevent the massacre of refugees in Sabra and Shatila in 1983, and the severity with which the mass uprising—the *intifada*—that began in the Gaza Strip in December 1987 was repressed. Public concern with the congruence between U.S. and Israeli interests in the Middle East was heightened by the discovery in 1985 that a Navy counterintelligence analyst, Jonathan Pollard, had been transferring classified documents to Israeli agents. These events generated substantial distrust of Israel and sympathy for the plight of the Palestinian people in the United States, particularly among memberships of the mainline Protestant churches associated with the National Council of Churches. At the same time, the fundamentalist and evangelical churches, who saw the events unfolding in the Near East as confirmation of Biblical prophesy, were pressing for even stronger U.S. government support for the policies being pursued by the Begin and Shamir governments.[125]

This erosion of political capital gave the Bush administration sufficient flexibility to delay action on a September 1991 request by Israel for loan guarantees to support housing construction. Bush asked Congress to postpone consideration for 120 days to allow Secretary of State Baker to complete arrangements for an Arab-Israeli peace conference in October 1991. In January 1992, Secretary Baker indicated that the administration would place conditions on the loan guarantees to assure that the loan would not be used to fund Jewish settlement construction in the occupied territories. The Likud government and its supporters among Jewish interest groups and in Congress opposed attaching any conditions to U.S. aid. The last time an administration had successfully imposed conditions was in 1953, when the Eisenhower administration had withheld aid until Israel stopped a water diversion project along the Israel-Syria boundary. By the early 1990s the political cost of supporting the president had become much lower than during the fight over the F-15s during the Carter administration or over the AWACS during the Reagan administration.[126]

In 1992 Yitzhak Rabin replaced Shamir as prime minister. Rabin had campaigned on a platform that included support for the peace process and the curbing of settlement construction in the occupied territories. He is reported to have informed Thomas Dine, AIPAC executive director, and other AIPAC leaders that he regarded their pressuring of Congress to override the Bush administration's efforts to delay the housing loan guarantees as counterproductive. Rabin's position was that American Jewish organizations should not play a central role in the diplomacy between the United States and Israel.[127] In September 1992, after a year of negotiations with Israel, President Bush requested Congress to approve up to $10 billion in loan guarantees: $2 billion for each year from 1993 through 1997. Although the president and Congress imposed conditions on the loan guarantees that were intended to limit their use, the limitations are largely meaningless because the money from the loan is largely fungible.

Assistance to Egypt

United States assistance to Egypt has been largely a product of Cold War tensions between the United States and the USSR and of relations between Israel and its Arab neighbors. In response to these political concerns, Egypt received more economic aid, Israel excepted, than the rest of Asia and the Near East combined.[128]

U.S. economic assistance to Egypt began in 1951 with the signing of a technical cooperation agreement between the United States and the Royal Government of Egypt. The United States agreed to provide Egypt with technical advisors, equipment, and materials and to train Egyptian personnel in the United States. In July 1952, the overthrow of King Farouk's weak government by the "Free Officers" led by Colonel Gamal Abdel Nasser installed General Mohammed Nagib as the head of the Egyptian government. (Nassar removed Nagib and replaced him as premier in February 1954.) The coup was welcomed in the State Department and the CIA. A stronger Egyptian government was viewed as dampening the possibilities of expanding Soviet influence in the region. Closer relations with Egypt might reverse the erosion of U.S. influence caused by American involvement in the creation of Israel. In 1953 the United States signed a new assistance agreement with the revolutionary government for a project, the Egyptian-American Rural Improvement Service (EARIS), aimed at community development and rural rehabilitation in two provinces. The political motivation was emphasized by an agreement to fund the project with a $10 million lump sum, up front, cash payment.[129]

Before the Six-Day War

In the mid-1950s U.S. assistance to Egypt foundered on the negotiations over military assistance, the financing of the Aswan High Dam, and the British-French-Israeli invasion of the Suez Canal and Sinai.[130] Negotiations between Egypt and the World Bank over funding for the Aswan High Dam began in 1953. In 1955 the bank initiated conversations with U.S. and British representatives about participation in the financing. Both Britain and the United States began to lose enthusiasm for the project because of arrangements for the exchange of cotton for military supplies from the USSR and the purchase of military equipment from Czechoslovakia. Concern was growing in London and Washington about Premier Nasser's support for nationalist movements in other areas of North Africa and the Middle East.

In the United States support for the Aswan High Dam project came under attack during the hearings on the foreign aid bill in March 1956. In May, the Egyptian government extended diplomatic recognition to the People's Republic of China. By June, Dulles had backed away from his earlier commitment to World Bank President Eugene Black that financing the dam was "one of the most important things facing the U.S. government." He assured the Senate Appropriations Committee that there "was no commitment of any kind" to the Aswan scheme.[131] In July 1956, the United States informed the Egyptian government that it was withdrawing support for the financing of the Aswan High Dam. This was followed by withdrawal of support by Great Britain and the World Bank.

The following week Nasser nationalized the Suez Canal. In the chain of events that followed, Britain, France, and Israel invaded the Suez Canal and the Sinai. Egypt expropriated other British and French property and turned to the USSR for assistance in financing the Aswan High Dam. Between 1957 and 1971 Egypt signed six separate aid loan agreements, carrying highly attractive terms, with the USSR. More than one-third of all the economic assistance from the USSR was devoted to construction of the dam.

The Eisenhower administration did not try to translate Egypt's brief glow of appreciation for U.S. opposition to the British-French-Israeli attack into longer-term political advantage. Eisenhower and Dulles were more concerned with countering Nasser's influence in the Arab world. At the outbreak of hostilities, in October 1956, American technical advisors working on Egyptian development projects were withdrawn and shipments of food aid were curtailed. Egypt received no U.S. economic assistance during 1957. Dulles and Eisenhower took the position that containing Soviet influence was more important than accommodating revolutionary Arab nationalism.

Nasser and his ambassador to Washington, Mustapha Kamel, proposed a way out of the corner into which the Eisenhower administration had painted itself. In meetings with Dulles and Eisenhower in November 1958, Kamel outlined what he termed the *icebox approach.* "The United States and Egypt would agree to 'freeze' their differences, and—with sources of friction safely stowed in the 'icebox'—they could expand their areas of common interest."[132] What Egypt actually wanted, and badly needed, was food aid. Confronted with burdensome food surpluses at home, Eisenhower and Dulles found it easy, despite sniping from the Israel lobby, to use food aid to ease U.S.-Egyptian tensions. During 1959–60 the United States provided $153 million in food aid, renewed U.S. participation in EARIS, and appointed an aid director for Egypt.

Relations improved even more dramatically during the Kennedy administration. Kennedy came to power convinced that a more prosperous world would also be a safer world (Chap. 5). His administration adopted a more positive view toward Third World nationalists—viewing them as an obstacle to Soviet expansionism. An experienced Middle East scholar-administrator, John S. Badeau, was appointed as U.S. ambassador to Egypt. Between January 1961 and February 1962, the Kennedy administration signed three Title I Food for Peace agreements with the Egyptian government. "In 1961, PL 480 shipments accounted for 77 percent of Egyptian wheat imports, and 38 percent of Egypt's net supply of wheat and wheat flour." On 8 October 1962 a new agreement calling for $432 million in food aid for fiscal years 1963–65 was signed.[133]

By 1963, however, relations between the Kennedy administration and Nasser were beginning to cool under the strain of Nasser's support for the overthrow of Imam Bader, the ruler of Yemen, by a group of Yemeni "Free Officers." In January 1965, under pressure from Congress, Johnson reacted to Nasser's inflammatory anti-American rhetoric with a temporary halt to food aid shipments to Egypt. However, Johnson successfully resisted legislative efforts to cut off the remaining shipments under the 1962 PL 480 agreement. He then used congressional opposition as an excuse to impose a "short lease" on aid shipments to try to leverage Egyptian foreign policy. Sensing some relaxation in Nasser's attitude, Johnson authorized the remaining $37 million in food shipments. Yet, even as negotiations were proceeding for a new agreement in the spring of 1966, Nasser continued his attacks on U.S. policy.

By 1966, however, U.S. food surpluses had begun to decline. Disastrous harvests in South Asia in 1965 and 1966 placed increased demands on food aid reserves (Chap. 8). When Nasser declared, in his 1967 May Day speech, that he could get along without food aid that was used as a political lever, further food aid was discontinued. After the Six-Day War with Israel (June 5–11), Lyndon Johnson was in no hurry to resume aid to Egypt.

Nasser, who died in the fall of 1970, was succeeded by Anwar Sadat, his vice president. Sadat inherited a polity and an economy that were on the edge of disaster.[134] During negotiations with the Soviets over military assistance in 1970 and 1971, he found the USSR to be an increasingly unreliable source of assistance. By the summer of 1972, Sadat had ordered the withdrawal of Soviet personnel and equipment from Egypt.

After the October War

On 6 October 1973, Sadat, against Soviet advice, launched an invasion across the Suez Canal into the Sinai. It was a war he did not expect to win. He did expect, however, sufficient success to force the United States to engage actively in resolving Arab-Israeli tensions. This effort was successful. After the cease fire on October 22, Secretary of State Kissinger initiated a period of shuttle diplomacy that gradually led to disengagement. Kissinger also recognized that Egypt needed U.S. economic support to enable Sadat to improve domestic economic conditions in compensation for the loss of support from Saudi Arabia and other Arab oil states, to allow him to take domestic political risks in the disengagement of Egyptian and Israeli forces, and to justify his participation in a comprehensive regional peace process. Economic assistance to Egypt resumed in 1974 and military assistance resumed in 1979.

In January 1974, after the separation-of-forces accord between Egypt and Israel, the United States announced a commitment of $8.5 million for an initial program to help clear the Suez Canal of war debris and to begin reconstruction of the canal cities. In March, the Nixon administration asked Congress for a total of $250 million for FY1975 and programmed an additional $50 million to Egypt in the 1976 budget. By mid-May 1974, however, U.S. ambassador in Cairo Hermann Eilts reported to Washington that higher levels of aid were needed, including immediate shipments of commodities and spare parts to help Egypt conserve its meager foreign exchange. Ambassador Eilts was concerned, however, that the level of aid not be viewed by the Egyptians as the principal basis on which improved relations would rest.

In fact, however, this is essentially what President Sadat had in mind: economic aid that, even if packaged differently, should be given to Egypt in rough parity with Israel. Sadat pressed his case directly in March 1975 during the shuttle diplomacy that led to the second Sinai disengagement agreement. Kissinger had already approved raising assistance to Egypt to $500 million, of which $300 million was to be for commodities. But during the March talks the figure of $750 million emerged—an amount close to the economic support that Israel was receiving from the United States. An additional $200 million was set aside for PL 480 Title I food aid.[135] During the Camp David negotiations of 1977 and 1978, the Carter administration found it necessary to promise that Egypt would receive the same amount of aid as Israel in order to obtain Sadat's commitment to a peace treaty. Congress, however, succeeded in holding U.S. assistance to Egypt closer to 70 percent of the level of aid to Israel. U.S. economic assistance never reached a level sufficient to compensate Egypt for the cessation of Arab aid, trade, and capital flows. Furthermore, although military aid was placed on a grant basis in 1985, interest on obligations under earlier U.S. military assistance has absorbed 75–90 percent of the amount of the economic grand aid. In effect, the United States was granting Egypt aid to enable it to pay back interest on earlier U.S. military assistance loans.[136]

The level of aid has never reflected a careful assessment of Egypt's needs or even the amount it could absorb successfully.[137] The level was viewed by Kissinger and Eilts as a signal of evenhandedness in negotiations with Egypt and Israel and as an incentive to Egypt to move away from the statist economic policies of the Nasser period. The policies being advanced under the rubric of *Infitah*—literally "opening"—and supported by the United States implied that greater reliance would be placed on the private sector and market forces in making investment and production decisions.

Since the mid-1970s Egypt has continued to be the second largest, after Israel, recipient of U.S. economic assistance—almost entirely through the Economic Support Fund and PL 480 programs (Table A.3). From the mid-1970s until the early 1980s, Egypt experienced high annual rates of economic growth, in the 8–9 percent per year range. The rapid growth reflected the effects of substantial increases in foreign exchange earnings from oil exports, worker remittances, tourism, and Suez Canal traffic, as well as the growth in foreign aid. Since the mid-1980s, however, foreign exchange earnings have fallen off and growth rates have declined.[138]

Massive U.S. aid was not effective in inducing the policy reforms to sustain growth. The U.S. aid program was confronted by an Egyptian bureaucracy that was largely committed to the statist approach of the Nasser period. The bureaucracy resented external pressure—whether from the United States, the World Bank, or the IMF—for policy reform. In addition, the US/AID mission lacked the ability to bring adequate knowledge and technical capacity to bear on problems of Egyptian development. It was easier to allocate assistance funds for commodity imports and large-scale, capital-intensive infrastructure projects, such as water and sewer systems and power plants, than for rural development. Congressional advocates of aid for basic needs and agricultural and rural development had relatively little leverage. And the AID professionals themselves had limited leverage to influence Egyptian policy when their Egyptian counterparts understood very well that the level of AID funding was determined by political rather than economic considerations.[139]

A constant objective of U.S., IMF, and World Bank efforts to achieve policy reform in Egypt since the mid-1970s has been the limiting of consumer subsidies for food and fuel and producer subsidies for commodity inputs. The aim has been to eliminate fixed prices and subsidies and to move domestic prices toward international prices. "But the remarkable international transfer of capital and commodities to Egypt since 1974 can take much of the credit for the survival of pricing and subsidy policies . . . U.S. PL 480 grain sales and the Commodity Import Program have, in particular, propped up the country's urban biased pricing system and allowed Egypt's economic planners to avoid facing the worsening problems in the food and agricultural sectors."[140]

In the late 1980s US/AID officers were still fighting many of the battles of the 1970s. There were, however, indications that significant progress was finally being made toward reforming the agricultural commodity price structure. A reform program, the Agricultural Production and Credit Project (APCP), was negotiated in 1986. It called for elimination of controls on production, pricing, and marketing and the phasing out of input subsidies. It was to be implemented in three steps with the aid transfers (tranches) for each step contingent on the successful implementation of the previous step. By 1990 all of the benchmarks had been met, at least to the satisfaction of AID.[141]

The success of agricultural policy reform was not matched, however, by the reform of consumer subsidies or of the industrial structure or by liberalization of the capital markets and the foreign exchange regime. Robert F. Zimmerman, a former AID staff member, has argued, in an otherwise favorable assessment of U.S. assistance to Egypt, that the Egyptian government apparatus, including its administrative apparatus, is less able to cope with effective management and maintenance of its infrastructure today than in the mid-1970s. One interpretation of the failure to achieve broader economic reform is that the government of Egypt has not been able to acquire the political legitimacy necessary to carry out the reforms needed to stimulate economic growth.[142]

In 1991, U.S. political interests in the Middle East were again responsible for relieving Egypt of some of its external burden. Egypt's international debt of almost $50 billion was the fourth highest among developing nations—following Brazil, Mexico, and Argentina. As a reward for Egypt's support for the war with Iraq, the United States forgave some $6.7 billion of outstanding debt and Egypt's Gulf Arab allies canceled an additional $6.5 billion. The Paris Club of donors forgave an additional $10 billion and, partly in response to U.S. pressure, Egypt was able to negotiate a new loan in 1991 with the most lenient terms ever granted by the IMF. As a condition for debt forgiveness, Egypt agreed to liberalize its capital and foreign exchange markets.[143]

Robert Zimmerman, in his assessment of U.S. assistance to Egypt, insists that aid has been effective in achieving U.S. short-term political objectives. But, despite massive assistance, Egypt's economy is stagnant and its debt burden is unsustainable. The use of aid to advance U.S. strategic interests has impeded the use of those resources and of Egypt's own resources to stimulate self-sustaining development. "In the end the United States weakened its capacity to maintain its political objectives without continued massive infusions of aid."[144] One indicator of this loss in ability to pursue U.S. political objectives was the revision from the "warm peace" of the late Sadat period to a "cold peace" between Israel and Egypt when Hosani Mubarak succeeded to the Egyptian presidency after the assassination of Sadat in 1981.

Summing Up

The interests of the United States in the Middle East and the interests of Israel and the Arab states in the region have never been fully coincident. U.S. interest in the Middle East has been primarily derivative of Cold War tensions. It has also been sustained by domestic political pressure for support of the state of Israel. The Soviet Union was viewed as the principle threat to political stability and to Western access to the region's petroleum resources. For Israel and the Arab states, the Cold War was never a principal concern. Israel regarded the Arab policy of three no's—"no peace, no recognition, no negotiation"—as a major obstacle to stability in the region. Initially the very existence of Israel was viewed by the Arab states as the dominant major obstacle to stability. As the more moderate Arab states came to accept Israel implicitly, Israeli's aggressive settlement policy and its commitment, particularly by the Likud leadership—Menachem Begin, Yitzhak Shamir, and Ariel Sharon—to the concept of Greater Israel represented an insurmountable obstacle.

What drove each U.S. president to invest substantial time and political resources in the peace process in the Middle East was a perspective that the achievement of U.S. objectives in the region depended on the reduction of Israeli-Arab tensions. This does not imply that sympathy for Israel and the Jewish people has not, at times, carried considerable weight in U.S. policy. Rather, it is to argue that the perceived U.S. national interests in the region led each administration to try to bring substantial political and economic resources to bear on efforts to resolve the Israeli-Arab crises.

The United States, in its uncritical support for Israel, clearly allowed its own legitimate interests in the region to be subverted by the flouting of international law regarding the acquisition of territory by force, the circumvention of U.S. law on arms trafficking, and the violation of the human rights of Palestinians in areas occupied by Israel.[145] It is also clear that it has often been in Israel's own interest to view U.S. peace initiatives with considerable skepticism. No small nation can afford to allow itself to become dependent on the United States, or any other great power, for its national security. A valid criticism of the Begin government is that it became, during the 1980s, too dependent on the United States.

What has the United States accomplished during two decades of very substantial economic and military assistance to Egypt? One can argue that the assistance was the necessary price for peace between Egypt and Israel and for continuity in an Egyptian policy of supporting U.S. initiatives in the Arab world. What has Egypt gotten out of U.S. economic assistance? Some improvement in physical infrastructure (the Cairo sewer system, for example), modest agricultural policy reform, and a contribution to the growth of human capital. But it is hard to argue that Egypt has achieved more rapid economic growth or that the average citizen, rural or urban, is better off today than if U.S. assistance had been much more modest. And one can make the argument that a more modest level of U.S. assistance would have induced policy reforms that would have enabled Egypt to acquire the political and economic institutions needed to realize much more rapid economic growth.

Policy toward Central America

The United States has been concerned since the initial days of the republic with security in the Americas. During the twentieth century it has been increasingly concerned when internal problems, particularly in the countries of Central America and the Caribbean, seemed to create opportunities for foreign rivals to gain political advantage. Robert Pastor used the metaphor of the whirlpool to characterize U.S. involvement in the economic and political life of the nations of the Caribbean. Caught up by the centripetal force of the whirlpool, U.S. attention becomes intensively focused on countries previously regarded as unimportant. Intense involvement is then followed by disengagement, the names of the countries that occupied center stage—Nicaragua and El Salvador, for example—disappear from the media, and the lessons from the involvement are forgotten.[146]

In the first decade after World War II, the U.S. policy community largely shared a belief that instability in Latin America was caused by Communist adventurism which, if left unchecked, would threaten U.S. security. By the late 1950s or early 1960s, a growing consensus emerged that, while Communist adventurism was not unimportant, poverty was the fundamental source of instability in the region. By the late 1970s a growing number of participants in the policy process no longer viewed instability as a threat to U.S. security but, instead, as the price Latin America was forced to pay for political and economic development.[147]

During the 1980s policy toward Central America became dominated by President Reagan's obsession that "the Caribbean is rapidly becoming a communist lake in what should be an American pond."[148] As the Reagan administration's commitment to weakening the Sandinista government in Nicaragua intensified, economic assistance, primarily through the ESF, and military assistance to other countries of the region (El Salvador, Honduras, Guatemala, and Costa Rica) rose dramatically. After the election of the Chamorro government in 1990, economic assistance to Nicaragua was resumed while assistance to other countries in the region was cut back (Tables A.4 to A.8).

In this section I give attention primarily to policy toward Nicaragua and secondarily toward El Salvador.[149] Policy toward other countries in the region during the 1980s has been derivative of policy toward Nicaragua and El Salvador.

U.S. Policy in Nicaragua

U.S. Marines were stationed in Nicaragua almost continuously from 1912 to 1933.[150] When Henry Stimson became Herbert Hoover's secretary of state, he was determined that, after supervising Nicaragua's elections in 1930 and 1932, the marines would be withdrawn and the United States should adopt a policy of strict neutrality with respect to Nicaraguan domestic affairs. When the marines departed they left behind a modernized military, the National Guard, and a government that had become accustomed to looking to Washington for support and direction.

Fears in both Washington and Managua that the National Guard would become the private army of the party in power were quickly realized. In 1932, just before leaving office, President Moncada promoted Anastasio Somoza Garcia, the husband of the niece of the incoming President Juan Sacasa, to the rank of general and appointed him director general of the National Guard. Somoza Garcia used his position gradually to solidify control over the Liberal party and, in June 1936, he pushed Sacasa out of the presidency and out of the country. He was elected president on 8 December 1936 and remained in power as president and commander of the National Guard until he was assassinated in 1956.[151]

The Somozas and U.S. Policy

After World War II the United States assumed a more activist role in relations with Nicaragua. In 1945, Nelson Rockefeller, assistant secretary of state for inter-American affairs, informed the Nicaraguan ambassador that if Somoza should run for reelection there might be "difficulties for him which would seriously affect relations between the two countries."[152] Somoza stepped down, nominated 70-year-old Leonardo Arguello as the Liberal candidate, assured his election, but then deposed Arguello when he tried to remove Somoza as head of the National Guard.

When Anastasio Somoza was assassinated in 1956, his two sons moved rapidly to consolidate their power. Luis, a graduate of Louisiana State University, was chosen to complete his father's term. Anastasio Somoza, Jr. (Tachito), a West Point graduate, was promoted to the position of director of the National Guard. His first act was to arrest the leadership of the opposition party and to purge the guard of officers whose loyalty to the Somozas was regarded as questionable.[153]

In the early 1960s Luis Somoza began to relax restrictions on political activity. The economy, fueled by rapid growth of cotton exports and credit liberalization, was growing rapidly. Land reform, partially funded by AID, was initiated. Luis stepped down from the presidency in 1963 and was succeeded by his father's private secretary René Schick. In 1966 Anastasio Somoza, Jr., received the Liberal party nomination for president and, after a campaign marked by violent suppression of the opposition, he was elected in February 1967 with 70 percent of the vote.

During 1961 Luis Somoza cooperated with the United States by making facilities on Nicaragua's Caribbean coast available as a training area for the Bay of Pigs expedition. During the Alliance for Progress period, after 1962, Nicaragua received modest amounts of economic assistance for land reform, rural development, and institutional development.[154] By the early 1970s the Somoza regime was beginning to come under increasing internal pressure. Archbishop Miguel Obando y Bravo attempted to disassociate the church from Somoza's embrace. Political opposition became more militant, and Somoza's excessive profiteering from the 1972 Managua earthquake relief effort turned the business community against him.[155]

The Nixon administration shared much of the same concerns as Anastasio Somoza about the Communist threat to authoritarian regimes in Latin America. Nixon's ambassador, Turner Shelton, became a close confidante of Anastasio Somoza, Jr. He supported Somoza's decision to seek another presidential term in 1974. However, U.S. policy changed again with Nixon's departure from office in 1974. Kissinger appointed William D. Rogers, former deputy coordinator for the Alliance for Progress in the Kennedy administration, as assistant secretary of state for inter-American affairs. Rogers accepted Kissinger's offer subject to two conditions: "First, the CIA would not do anything serious in Latin America . . . without his knowledge; and second, he wanted to make basic changes in policy and personnel, particularly with regard to several ambassadors."[156] Turner Shelton was one of the ambassadors he had in mind.

Rogers conveyed the new U.S. policy directly to Somoza, in the presence of the new U.S. ambassador, James Theberg. He underscored two points. First, "the U.S. was [henceforth] absolutely neutral both publicly and privately in all its actions with regard to Somoza and the opposition, and the United States would begin a dialogue with the opposition. Second, the United States was going to be watching the accounts of the Agency for International Development much more closely to ensure that the money was not misspent."[157] Rogers replaced the collaborationist policy of the Nixon years with the Roosevelt-Truman policy of noninterference.

Anastasio Somoza, Jr., was forced to resign on 17 July 1979 as a result of broad-based pressure from virtually all elements of Nicaraguan society—the Catholic Church, the business community, students, and the Sandinista movement.

The Sandinista Movement and U.S. Policy

The Somozas were a target of sporadic guerrilla activity almost from the assumption of power by Anastasio Somoza Garcia in the 1930s. But it was the success of Fidel Castro in skillfully mixing Marxism, nationalism, and anti-Americanism to create a new recipe for revolution that inspired leftists throughout Latin America to action. In Nicaragua Carlos Fonseca Amador and Tomás Borge quit the pro-Moscow Nicaraguan Socialist party because of its reluctance to pursue an armed struggle. They organized El Frente Sandinista de Liberación Nacional (FSLN) and then joined with several other groups, including the Frente Revolucionario led by Edén Pastora.[158]

During the 1960s the Sandinista movement was an irritant but posed no real threat to the Somozas. The somewhat more liberal regime of Luis Somoza combined with a period of relative prosperity to dampen political discontent. In the early 1970s, however, the combination of Somoza repression and avarice and the more effective Sandinista organization widened support for the Sandinistas. The 1972 earthquake was the defining event for popular opposition to the Somoza regime. The Somoza family diverted substantial amounts of earthquake aid to extend their control over the economy.

In December 1974 a successful raid on the farewell party for Ambassador Shelton gave new visibility to the Sandinista movement.[159] In exchange for the prisoners captured at the party, Somoza agreed to pay a cash ransom. He released a large number of imprisoned Sandinistas, including Daniel Ortega, and allowed the members of the raiding party to fly to Cuba. The raid attracted many young people to the Sandinista movement. But determined efforts by the National Guard over the next two years decimated the Sandinista leadership. Carlos Fonseca Amoder was killed, and Tomás Borge was arrested. Decapitation of the Sandinista leadership was followed by a good deal of ideological debate in which the less ideological and more activist wing, lead by Daniel and Humberto Ortega, assumed leadership.

The Carter administration initially devoted little time to the problems of Nicaragua. But Carter's emphasis on the advancement of human rights and democracy as a central theme in foreign policy could not help but pose problems for the Somoza regime's use of repression to maintain itself in power. The State Department's paper on human rights in Nicaragua, issued in April 1977, cited reports of many disappearances and torture. The Carter administration moved to call off military assistance to Nicaragua. Somoza hired lobbyists and public relations firms in Washington to try to reverse the policy. He was aided by two influential congressmen, John Murphy (D-N.Y.) and Charles Wilson (D-Tex.). After being defeated in the House Appropriations Committee, Murphy and Wilson succeeded in restoring the deleted funds on the House floor. Carter, however, assured the House Appropriations Committee that he would not sign a military aid agreement unless there was "an improvement in the human rights situation."[160]

Somoza realized that he could not influence the United States to resume military aid unless the human rights situation in Nicaragua improved. In the spring of 1977, he instructed the National Guard to curb its abuses. A heart attack on 28 July 1977 brought Somoza to the Miami Heart Institute for treatment. When he returned to Nicaragua in September, he was urged by many associates, including his cousin Luis Pallais, president of the Nicaraguan Congress, to step down in order to undermine the opposition and to preserve his own interests. But as Somoza's health improved, his urge to remain in power strengthened. After considerable internal debate, the United States announced that it would continue the suspension of military and economic aid.

The Sandinistas correctly perceived the U.S. effort to end martial law and democratize Nicaragua as a threat to their own plan. To generate support they stepped up their efforts to weaken the National Guard by launching simultaneous attacks in the main urban centers. A democratic front was established to form a provisional government. Meanwhile a group led by church and private sector leaders, encouraged by the United States, tried to arrange for a peaceful transition. But Somoza insisted that he planned to finish out his term in 1981. On 10 January 1978, Pedro Joaquin Chamorro, publisher of the leading opposition newspaper, *La Prensa,* was assassinated. The act became the catalyst that galvanized the private sector into action against Somoza.[161]

Alfonso Robelo, president of the major business association in Nicaragua, organized a successful general strike that lasted from January 23 until the second week in February. In March, Robelo organized an umbrella opposition organization, the Broad Opposition Front (FAO). In April he met with the Ortegas in San Jose, Costa Rica, and came away convinced that they were pragmatic, though leftist, social democrats.

Meanwhile the Carter administration was sending out conflicting signals on its policy toward Somoza. In May 1978, after a year of delays, it approved the basic human needs loans to Nicaragua: $3 million for education and $7.5 million for nutrition. At the same time it reiterated both its policy of nonintervention and its concern for a nonviolent transition to democratic rule. Under pressure from both Washington and the Inter-American Human Rights Commission, Somoza indicated that he would consider signing the American Convention on Human Rights and declaring an amnesty for political prisoners.

Carter interpreted Somoza's statements as a sign that he was becoming more responsive to American concerns. He instructed Zbigniew Brzezinski, his national security advisor, to draft a letter congratulating Somoza for his positive response and urging him to move forward with implementation of the reforms. Despite considerable concern at the staff level within the National Security Council and the State Department about the wisdom of sending the proposed letter, it was finally transmitted to the U.S. ambassador in Nicaragua on July 11 and delivered to Somoza on July 21.[162] Somoza initially interpreted it as a sign of success in his campaign to obtain Carter's support. However, after a more careful reading of the letter his reaction was that the letter was designed more to undermine than support his position.

The most significant effect of the letter episode was to force Carter and Brzezinski to focus greater attention on the situation in Nicaragua. The focus intensified after 22 August 1978, when Edén Pastora and a group of 25 Sandinistas captured the National Palace and 1500 people in it. Somoza resisted pressure by the National Guard to storm the palace. He negotiated withdrawal by the Sandinistas by agreeing to most of their demands. He released 59 political prisoners, including Tomás Borge, paid $500,000 in cash, permitted the Sandinistas to air their grievances in the newspapers and over the radio, and guaranteed the Sandinistas a safe exit. The crowds that massed along the road to the airport turned the exit into a victory parade. The events of August 1978 resulted in a shifting of U.S. policy toward Nicaragua from concern with human rights to a political security issue. From then on the State Department's Human Rights Bureau played a much less visible role in policy discussions, and the policy of noninterference that had been reinstated by Secretary of State Rogers was once again nonoperational.

In September 1978 fighting broke out in five major cities. The Sandinistas struggled to stay ahead of the mass movement. But as Humberto Ortega would later admit: "The mass movement went beyond the vanguard's capacity to take the lead . . . It was a spontaneous reaction on the part of the masses."[163]

The issue now facing the United States was to determine what role it should play in a Nicaragua engulfed in a civil war. The State Department reiterated a U.S. policy of "non-intervention in the domestic politics of other countries." The Sandinistas accused the United States of planning to defend Somoza. Somoza accused the Carter administration of being dominated by leftists and Communists. In the United States, liberals criticized Carter for being too soft on Somoza while conservatives accused him of abandoning old friends.[164] Carter's own preference was to encourage democracy and dialogue among competing groups within Nicaragua but not to arbitrate that dialogue.[165] But his preferred position was impaired by Somoza's decision to eliminate the reformist option. In August and September of 1978, Somoza revoked the charter of the largest business association and arrested about 50 leaders of the moderate opposition, including Adolfo Calero, a leader of the Conservative party.

During early fall of 1978, the Carter administration was forced by events in Nicaragua and the concerns of Venezuela and Panama to take a more active role in Nicaragua.[166] Efforts to organize an initiative through the Organization of American States (OAS) proved impractical because too many other Latin American governments were also military dictatorships. Assistant Secretary of State Viron P. Vaky pressed for a more forceful U.S. posture: Somoza should be informed that the only way to prevent Nicaragua from going Communist was for him to resign before the moderate opposition was pushed all the way into the Sandinista camp. Brzezinski resisted such a direct U.S. role and pressed for organizing a mediation team from countries in the region. Conservatives in Congress criticized the administration for planning to abandon Somoza, while liberals pressed for suspension of all aid to Nicaragua. The division of opinion in Congress left the administration free to pursue the Brzezinski option.

On October 6 a mediation team consisting of representatives from the Dominican Republic, Guatemala, and the United States arrived in Managua. The mediation effort—from 6 October 1978 to 8 February 1979—failed. Somoza first refused to consider stepping down before the end of his term in 1981, then proposed a plebiscite on his retention of power, and finally backed off from his support of a plebiscite when the negotiation team rejected his plans to manage the plebiscite.

With the breakdown in negotiations, the United States decided that (1) the U.S. military group would be withdrawn and the military assistance program, which had been suspended, would be terminated; (2) no new aid programs would be considered and the two continuing project loan programs would be held up, but the programs that were well advanced and aimed at the "basic human needs of the poor" would continue; (3) all Peace Corps volunteers would be withdrawn; and (4) the size of the embassy would be reduced by more than half (from 82 to 37).[167]

From the time sanctions were imposed in February 1978 until the "final offensive" by the Sandinistas in July 1979, the United States was withdrawn from the crisis. Meanwhile, Congressman Charles Wilson (D-Tex.) continued to insist that he would hold up foreign aid appropriations if the administration did not remove its pressure on Somoza.

With the collapse of negotiations, the Nicaraguan moderates had most of their options closed. The Broad Opposition Front merged with the FSLN to form the new Patriotic Front. Meanwhile, Somoza received new shipments of arms from Israel, Argentina, and Guatemala. Support for Edén Pastora's wing of the Sandinistas from Costa Rica, Panama, Venezuela, and Cuba was expanded.

In June 1979, 10 months after the administration had rejected a mediation appeal by the moderate opposition, the United States was pulled back into the mediation process. Intelligence estimates suggested that Somoza would be forced out momentarily. The administration assumed that without a negotiated settlement Somoza's departure would leave the Sandinistas in a position to assume power. It also assumed that a Sandinista military victory would increase the probability that a pro-Cuba anti-American regime would emerge. At a National Security Council meeting on June 19, Brzezinski defined the objective of U.S. policy: "to move Somoza out and create in his place a viable government of national reconciliation." There were, however, different priorities within the administration. In the State Department "it was to insure Somoza's departure," while for Brzezinski it was to ensure that the resulting government would be stable and capable of negotiating with the Sandinistas.[168] Meanwhile, the junta leadership tried to assure the international community of its democratic orientation and to obscure the continued flow of arms from Cuba and Venezuela.

U.S. conservatives became increasingly concerned about the direction of U.S. policy. On June 18, one hundred members of Congress and five Senators sent a letter to the president and placed it as a full-page advertisement in the *New York Times*. It urged Carter to support Somoza and warned of a Communist takeover if the Sandinistas should oust Somoza. These protests from the Right were immediately quieted when the execution by the National Guard of Bill Stewart, an ABC news correspondent, was displayed on American television. A massive outpouring of calls and telegrams to the president demanded that Somoza be punished.

These events occurred just before an OAS meeting on June 21. At his speech to the OAS, Secretary of State Vance called for a replacement of the Somoza government, a transition to a government of national reconciliation, and intervention by an OAS peacekeeping force. Mexican Foreign Minister Jorge Castañeda took the leadership in opposing any intervention that might lead to *Somocismo sin Somoza*. Mexico and the Andean countries began working on an arrangement to clear the way for the Sandinistas to take power.

During the summer of 1979, U.S. policy was driven more by events in Nicaragua than by deliberations in Washington. The United States explored the possibility of a third force to serve as a buffer between a reconstituted National Guard and the Sandinistas. The few moderates who might have found it in their interest to risk supporting the U.S. position would do so only with assurance of support. Carter was unwilling to give that assurance without support from at least some countries in the region. The new ambassador to Nicaragua, Lawrence Pezzullo, found himself pursuing options urged by Washington that had already been precluded by events in Nicaragua.

At 1:00 A.M. on 17 July 1979, the Nicaraguan Congress accepted Somoza's resignation. He was escorted to the airport and left Nicaragua for Miami at about 4:00 A.M. Pezzullo, the U.S. ambassador, had spent a frantic week before the departure trying to put together an arrangement for the orderly transfer of power. The next several days were spent in futile efforts to influence the transfer. By July 19 the National Guard had ceased to exist as an organized force. Pastor summarized the history of U.S. policy during the Somoza era: "From the U.S. government's perspective the Somoza dynasty ended in much the same way it had begun . . . Anastasio Somoza Garcia took power in 1936 and his son fell in 1979. On both occasions, the United States was a passive witness to events it did not like."[169]

From the Sandinista triumph in 1979 until the early 1980s, U.S. policy toward Nicaragua shifted from support for the revolution to indirect war against Nicaragua. The lesson drawn by the Carter administration from the history of relations with Cuba was that hostile U.S. reaction to Castro's successful revolution had contributed to the radicalization of his regime. The administration quickly decided to pursue a policy that would take the stated promises of the Sandinista revolution—political pluralism, prompt elections, and a vigorous private sector—at face value. The underlying political premise of this strategy was that the majority of the national coalition in Nicaragua was more interested in economic development than in imposing a centrally planned economy. These views were reinforced by positive assessments of the Sandinista government by U.S. companies operating in Nicaragua.[170]

Implementation of the policy would not be easy. The Sandinistas continued to harbor and articulate deep-seated suspicions of U.S. intentions. They decided to press for economic assistance but to reject military assistance. They also moved more rapidly than had been anticipated to exclude the influence of moderate elements, such as Edén Pastora, within the Sandinista movement. By late April 1980 both Violeta Chamorro and Alfonso Robelo had resigned from the Council of State.

Within the United States the need to obtain congressional approval for new aid to Nicaragua precipitated a national debate. In November 1979 President Carter sent a supplemental request to Congress for $80 million in ESF resources for Central America and the Caribbean, of which $70 million would be a loan and $5 million would be grant funds for Nicaragua. In spite of opposition from conservatives and even moderates in Congress, the administration was able to push the authorization bill through the Senate and the House by the end of May. It was delayed further in the Appropriations Committee and finally passed on July 2. The bill contained a series of restrictive provisions, including a requirement that the president certify that the Nicaraguan government was not supporting guerrilla activity in El Salvador.[171]

During the last days of the Carter administration, new events triggered the cutoff of economic assistance to Nicaragua. The FSLN increased its harassment of the moderate opposition, Robelo was arrested on November 9, the government began to restrict access to the radio, and Archbishop Obando y Bravo was harassed. The Nicaraguan government also responded to pressure by the revolutionary leadership of El Salvador for support of a "final offensive" against the government of El Salvador. Evidence that Nicaragua was supporting the transfer of arms from Cuba to El Salvador became conclusive. In mid-January 1981, the Sandinistas were informed that aid was suspended. President Carter also approved $5.9 million in arms and ammunition for El Salvador.

> The decision by the directorate to aid the Salvadoran insurgents was a major miscalculation, which, in effect, ended the era of support by the United States. It also occurred at a moment when a new administration was coming into office with a very different perception of the revolution. Under the best of circumstances, it would have been difficult to persuade the Reagan administration to be patient and forge a long-term relationship with Nicaragua. Unfortunately, it was not the best of circumstances and the Sandinista support for the Salvadorans was a major contributing factor.[172]

The Reagan Administration's Policy toward Nicaragua

The Reagan administration interpreted both the Nicaraguan and the Salvadoran revolutions as evidence of Soviet expansionism in Central America—a Soviet-Cuban effort to destabilize Central America. Secretary of State Alexander Haig indicated in his memoirs that he had wanted to send two signals to the Soviet Union: that their adventuring in the Third World would not only be resisted but "rolled back" and that U.S. relations would be conditioned not by a government's respect for human rights but by its friendship with the U.S. government.[173] In the Americas, Haig chose to draw the line against the Soviets in Nicaragua and El Salvador.

In February 1981, shortly after assuming office, Haig instructed Lawrence Pezzullo, the U.S. ambassador to Nicaragua, to return to Washington for a policy review. The acting assistant secretary of state, John Bushnell, proposed three options for U.S. policy toward Nicaragua, all of which would end aid to the Sandinista government. Pezzulo argued that aid served as essential leverage in the negotiation of an end to the transshipment of arms to El Salvadoran opposition [Frente Farabunda Marti Tara la Liberación Nacional (FMLN)]. Haig asked Pezzullo to return to Managua and inform the Sandinistas that the new administration would no longer tolerate their overt support for the FMLN. Pezzullo was assured by Ortega that Nicaragua would not "risk our revolution for an uncertain victory in El Salvador."[174] As a result of the talks, Pezzullo felt that the Sandinistas had responded to U.S. concerns and that aid should not be terminated. The decision by the president to terminate aid on 1 April 1981, giving up what he considered the only leverage available to the United States, caught Pezzullo by surprise. But before resigning he encouraged Thomas Enders, the new assistant secretary of state for Latin America, to meet with the Sandinista leadership to explore whether a bargain was possible.[175]

> During his visit to Nicaragua in August 1981, Enders "developed a proposal composed of five points: (1) Nicaragua would end its support for foreign insurgencies; (2) Nicaragua would cease its military build up and reduce its armed forces to a level of about 15,000 (down from an existing level of 23,000); (3) the United States would pledge not to intervene in Nicaragua's internal affairs and to enforce U.S. neutrality laws; (4) the United States would renew economic aid; and (5) the United States and Nicaragua would expand cultural relations. Enders also communicated U.S. concerns about political pluralism, a mixed economy, and Nicaraguan relations with the Soviet Union and Cuba, though the proposal did not explicitly cover these points.[176]

Enders had trouble selling his proposal in both Managua and Washington. As the Sandinistas considered the proposal, which they thought amounted to "the terms of surrender," the United States took actions that cast doubt on the credibility of the proposals. It began a large naval exercise off the Caribbean coast of Honduras. It canceled $7 million of the ESF that it had said it would hold in suspension. The Sandinistas were particularly perturbed about the failure of the United States to enforce its own neutrality laws, which was demonstrated by its support of the training of Nicaraguan and Cuban exiles in Florida and California.

Pastor regarded the failure of the negotiations as a significant missed opportunity that both sides, and especially the Sandinistas, would regret. The administration took the position that it had "tried" negotiations and found the Sandinistas uninterested. On 17 November 1981 President Reagan signed National Security Document No. 17. Among other provisions it authorized $19 million for the CIA to field and direct a 500-man Nicaraguan secret anti-Sandinista guerrilla force—the Contras—aimed at the Cuban infrastructure in Nicaragua. Haig opposed the decision on three grounds. "First, that 'covert action' was a contradiction in terms. There were no secrets. Second, the problem of Cuban-Soviet intervention was larger than Nicaragua and needed a broader response. Third, the Contras were a 'cop-out,' providing the illusion of solving the problem while escalating the level of violence."[177]

On 14 March 1982 a group of former National Guardsmen and dissident Sandinistas, the Contras—who had been trained in demolition by CIA agents—destroyed two bridges in northern Nicaragua. "The attack—the first major assault in Nicaragua—represented a watershed both for the administration and for the Sandinistas . . . Henceforth, abandoning the Contras would be perceived as a sign of weakness by the Sandinistas and Moscow, and in the Reagan administration, no charge was more fatal."[178] The response of the Sandinista government was to declare a state of national emergency. The Sandinistas imposed censorship, increased surveillance, and arrested moderate leaders. Others fled the country. These policies resulted in internal polarization and forced many moderate leaders to make a common, though uneasy, cause with the Contras.

Congress was even more skeptical about Reagan's plans to support the Contras than about Carter's plans to provide aid to Nicaragua.[179] When briefed about the administration's plans, both Democratic and Republican members of the House Select Intelligence Committee expressed concern about the objectives of the Contras. The committee approved covert actions with the understanding that they would be taken only to interdict arms transfers. Statements by the Contra leaders that their objective was to overthrow the Sandinista government raised even greater concern in Congress. On 8 November 1982, the Boland amendment, sponsored by Representative Edward Boland (D-Mass.), chairman of the House Intelligence Committee, which specifically prohibited the use of U.S. funds for that purpose, was adopted by a vote of 411 to 0 by the House of Representatives.[180]

In September 1983 the Reagan administration submitted a Presidential Finding authorizing material support and guidance to the Nicaraguan resistance groups in order to press the Nicaraguan government "to enter into negotiations with its neighbors, and putting pressure on the Sandinistas and their allies to cease provisioning of arms, training, command, and control facilities and sanctuary to leftist guerrillas in El Salvador."[181] A major objective of the finding was to circumvent the Boland amendment. The United States also held naval exercises off each coast of Nicaragua and constructed several airfields in the south of Honduras to support the Contras. The invasion of Grenada in October 1983 enhanced the credibility of U.S. threats. The Sandinistas interpreted that invasion as a possible training exercise for the invasion of Nicaragua. To reduce the excuse for such an event, they closed down the Salvadoran guerrilla command and control center in Nicaragua. The Reagan administration was so obsessed with rolling back the Sandinista revolution that it failed to turn the Nicaraguan concerns to diplomatic advantage. However, a group of Central American and Caribbean countries, the Contadora Group (Mexico, Venezuela, Colombia, and Panama), began to negotiate a treaty along the line that had earlier been suggested by Thomas Enders.

The administration tried to use its success in Grenada to gain congressional approval for additional aid to the Contras. However, among the general public and in Congress there was considerable resistance to the Reagan administration agenda. Memories of Vietnam were still vivid. In the spring of 1984, a series of disclosures that the CIA had supervised the mining of Nicaragua's harbors, the destruction of oil storage facilities, and other operations inside Nicaragua resulted in the collapse of whatever limited enthusiasm had existed in Congress for continuing aid to the Contras. The inability, or unwillingness, of the administration to provide credible evidence of Cuban arms shipments through Nicaragua to El Salvador raised further doubts about the rationale for support to the Contras. "As an acknowledgement of the unpopularity of the program President Reagan stopped campaigning for the Contras and began campaigning for re-election on a peace platform."[182]

While the American public and Congress were becoming more skeptical of U.S. intervention in Nicaragua and El Salvador, the print and television media were increasingly allowing events in Central America to be framed in Washington rather than in the field. When the press reported from the field, it adopted a "war correspondent" mentality—often questioning the tactics of the U.S. intervention but seldom questioning the objectives. It reported the murder of American land reform experts and of members of religious orders but continued to report at face value the assurances of progress in military and political reform.[183]

On 19 July 1983, President Ronald Reagan appointed a 12-member National Bipartisan Commission on Central America, chaired by Henry A.

Kissinger. The commission was charged to study the nature of U.S. interests in the Central American region and to advise the president on the elements of a long-term policy "that will best respond to the challenges of social, economic, and democratic development in the region, and to internal and external threats to the region."[184] The commission's findings, which challenged many of the assumptions of the Reagan administration, were reported to the president on 10 January 1984. It recommended that an immediate and substantial increase in economic assistance to the region—an additional $400 million over and above the $477 million programmed for fiscal year 1984—be directed to the strengthening of urban and rural infrastructure and to housing and also an economic assistance package over the five-year period beginning in 1985 that would total $8 billion, directed to education, health, and agricultural and rural development. The report concluded that present levels of military assistance to El Salvador were inadequate—"There is . . . no logical argument for giving some aid but not enough." It recommended "significantly increased levels of aid as quickly as possible." The commission also concluded that a political solution in Nicaragua and El Salvador was still possible and should be pursued—"Nicaragua's willingness to enter into a general agreement should be thoroughly tested through negotiations and actions"—while continuing support for the Contras. In February 1984 President Reagan sent a request to Congress for an $8.4 billion five-year aid program for all of Central America, excluding Nicaragua. Congress preferred annual appropriations and funded the first year of the program at 80 percent of the level requested. During the next several years, the United States contributed in the neighborhood of $1 billion per year in economic and military assistance to the region.[185]

Reagan was reelected in 1984 with an overwhelming majority. Two days earlier Daniel Ortega had also been reelected. He received 63 percent of the votes in an election in which the opposition was prevented by Sandinista intimidation from running an effective campaign. In his 1985 State of the Union address, President Reagan transformed his Contra program into a policy on national liberation movements—"We must not break faith with those . . . risking their lives on every continent from Afghanistan to Nicaragua to defy Soviet-supported aggression and secure rights which have been ours from birth."[186] The members of Somoza's National Guard, the core of the Contra forces, had by Reagan's rhetoric been transformed into freedom fighters—"the moral equivalent of the founding fathers" who fought against the British in the American revolution.[187]

Meanwhile, the Contadora Group (with support from Argentina, Brazil, Uruguay, and Peru) met with Secretary of State George Shultz in January 1986 to urge the United States to stop funding the Contras. Their efforts were ignored. By June, however, the Contadora Group had moved the Central

American states toward a treaty that would end support for the Contras and other guerrilla groups; place a freeze on new arms purchases; gradually reduce armaments, foreign military advisors, and foreign military bases; and take steps toward national reconciliation. The proposed treaty generated considerable tension both within and between the State and Defense departments. Philip Habib, the president's special envoy for Central America, took the position that the U.S. should cease its support for the Contras if Nicaragua signed the treaty. The Defense Department objected that, if the Contadora Pact were signed, it would simply delay the date when the United States would have to dispose of the Sandinistas. Assistant Secretary of State Elliott Abrams objected to withdrawing support for the Contras until the treaty was implemented. Nicaragua refused to sign, criticizing the proposed treaty as a U.S. plot to subvert the revolution. On June 7 the Contadora Group withdrew its deadline for signing the treaty, and on June 20, five days before the U.S. House of Representatives was to vote on aid to the Contras, the Nicaraguan government announced that it would sign the treaty.[188]

As the Contadora process was getting under way, a controversy over the illegal funding of the Contra operation erupted. On 2 November 1986, an Arabic language magazine in Beirut reported that the United States had transferred military equipment to Iran in an effort to obtain the release of American hostages held by Islamic extremists in Lebanon. On November 26 Attorney General Meese, in a damage control effort, held a press conference in which he admitted that the United States had diverted to the Nicaraguan Contras funds from the sale of weapons to Iran. The operation had been directed by William Casey, director of the Central Intelligence Agency, and Admiral Poindexter, the national security advisor. Both the secretary of state and the secretary of defense, who had earlier lost intraadministration battles to limit the Contra operation, had largely been cut out of the information loop, partly by their own volition, as the Contra operation escalated.[189]

Senate Intelligence Committee hearings that began in May 1987 confirmed that Lieutenant Colonel Oliver North of the National Security staff "had organized and directed a vast covert operation outside the government that involved retired military officers, former intelligence agents, and arms smugglers . . . to assist the Contras during the period when Congress prohibited it . . . Congress established that North solicited funds, and President Reagan helped by meeting with several potential donors . . . Although President Reagan denied he knew that the profits from the arms sales were diverted to the Contras, after less than three weeks of hearings, only 24 percent of the American people believed him."[190] Later evidence confirmed that President Reagan had played the central role in the arms for hostage deal with Iran and in directing the funds realized from the transaction to the Contras.[191]

Reconciliation

While the Iran-Contra affair was unfolding, Costa Rican President Osear Arias succeeded, at a meeting of Central American presidents held in August 1987 at Esquipulas, Guatemala, in developing a formula for a peace process. "Arias persuaded Daniel Ortega and the other Central American presidents to accept his proposal to end conflicts in the region by supporting democracy, national reconciliation, and an end to support for insurgencies. By making each country responsible for securing democracy in all five, the plan cut the cord that had tied internal conflict to external interventions."[192]

Reagan insisted that the plan was "fatally flawed." He insisted that the Sandinistas would never agree to free elections except under more effective pressure by the Contras. Congress refused, however, to go beyond providing additional humanitarian aid. "With the political space permitted by suspension of aid to the Contras, President Ortega called for elections on February 25, 1990. He firmly believed that a free election would not only return him to power but would also unlock aid from Europe, lift the U.S. embargo, and end the contra war."[193] The Nicaraguan opposition united behind the candidacy of Violeta Barrios de Chamorro. Pastor argues that the election was made possible by the fact that both the Sandinistas (FSLN) and the Chamorro-led National Opposition Union (UNO) were convinced that they could win.

The successful election, on 25 February 1990, and the transition to democratic rule after the election were facilitated by prudent restraint by the Bush administration, reluctant intervention by the United Nations and the OAS, and the good offices of former U.S. president Jimmy Carter.[194] The Bush administration, anticipating an FSLN victory, avoided actions that might have undermined the elections. The United Nations and the OAS, under pressure from the five presidents, broke precedent and sent missions to observe the elections. President Carter, who had organized a Council of Freely-Elected Heads of Governments to act as observers of earlier elections in Panama, arranged to have the council invited by Ortega to observe the electoral process. When early returns confirmed that Chamorro was winning by a large margin, it was Carter who played a critical role in helping both Ortega and Chamorro to accept the results with more grace than the partisans of either the FSLN or the UNO might have hoped. The FSLN transition team was led by Daniel Ortega's brother Humberto, and the UNO team was led by Antonio Lacayo, Chamorro's son in law. Chamorro agreed to respect the integrity of the army and appointed Humberto as army chief.[195]

During its first two years, the Chamorro government made exceptional progress. The war was ended, the Contras were demobilized, and the military was reduced by over 50 percent. By the second year, inflation had been reduced and economic growth was beginning to revive. Support from the United States, however, was more reluctant and niggardly than had been anticipated. The right wing of the Republican party mounted a vigorous criticism to the effect that Chamorro had sold out to the Sandinistas. As of late 1993, economic recovery was less vigorous than had been anticipated. The Bush administration withheld $104 million in aid that had been committed to Nicaragua.[196] Nicaragua, which had occupied a central role in U.S. foreign assistance and national security policy for a decade and a half, was again becoming an object of benign neglect by the United States.

U.S. Policy toward El Salvador

The realization by the Carter administration in 1978 that the Somoza regime in Nicaragua was no longer viable forced the issue of growing instability in El Salvador onto the U.S. policy agenda. Except for a brief period during the Alliance for Progress in the early 1960s, El Salvador had received little economic or military assistance. In 1977 the U.S. ambassador to El Salvador had testified in Congress that "the United States has no vital interests in the country."[197] In 1978 total economic assistance amounted to only about $11 million. How, within a matter of five years, did the U.S. perception of its vital interest in El Salvador so change that it became the fourth largest recipient of U.S. economic and military assistance—after Israel, Egypt, and Turkey?

Repression and Reform

During its final two years, the Carter administration vigorously denounced the brutal human rights abuses of the Salvadoran government. General Carlos Humberte Romero assumed the presidency of El Salvador after fraudulent elections of 1977. Faced with the prospect of losing a second Central American nation to the Communists, however, the administration felt compelled to adopt a more activist policy.

The tradition of governance by a right-wing repressive dictatorship supported by a conservative oligarchy extends back at least into the 1930s in El Salvador. An opportunity to bring about progressive change presented itself to the Carter administration in October 1979 when, four months after the fall of Somoza, General Romero was replaced in a bloodless coup led by a group of reform-minded junior officers. They established a military-civilian government that incorporated progressive elements from the civilian sector. But the Carter administration was not prepared to grasp this opportunity. The U.S. ambassador, Frank J. Divine, distanced himself from the leader of the revolution. The reformers were outmaneuvered by more conservative senior military officers. The Carter administration requested Congress to approve $5.7 million in "nonlethal" military aid. This was taken by conservative military and civilian elements in El Salvador as evidence of U.S. approval. Within two and a half months, the reformist officers had been forced out of the junta. In early January the liberal civilian members of the government resigned when it became clear that the army was unwilling to submit to civilian control.[198]

The U.S. ambassador then pressured the military to incorporate representation of the Christian Democrat party into the government in order to preserve a semblance of civilian participation. The Christian Democrats, a center-right political party, agreed to participate in the government with an understanding that the armed forces would be brought back under civilian control. When it became clear that the military had no intention of honoring this commitment, most of the Christian Democrats who had come into the government resigned. Jose Napoleon Duarte, who had lost a bid for the presidency in 1972 because of fraudulent vote counting, had remained outside the government; he expected to gain more by running for president in what he had hoped might be an honest election. Nevertheless, he agreed to join the junta shortly after his colleagues had resigned.

Meanwhile, the Carter administration rapidly increased its economic aid to El Salvador. Much of the aid was directed toward support of a major reform effort that had initially been proposed by the reform junta and that was strongly supported by the embassy and the aid mission. The reform program consisted of three components: (1) comprehensive land reform, (2) nationalization of commercial banks, and (3) nationalization of agricultural exports.[199] The major purpose of the land reform was to break the power of the landed oligarchy and secure the loyalty of the peasantry. It was to proceed in three phases: (1) nationalization and reorganization of all land holdings above 500 hectares into cooperatives, (2) division and redistribution of holdings between 100 and 500 hectares, and (3) a "land to the tiller" program that would transfer to tenant farmers title to the land they were already working. The first phase of the land reform was largely implemented before the Carter administration left office. However, issuance of titles was delayed. In some cases the military carried out mass executions of the peasants to whom the land had been transferred.

On March 11 Ambassador Devine was replaced by Robert E. White, who was much more sympathetic to the reform effort. On March 24, Archbishop Oscar Arnulfo Romero, who had opposed both the counter coup by the military and military aid by the United States, was assassinated while conducting Mass.[200] Lack of sensitivity in Washington to the significance of Romero's murder was reflected in the fact that two days later John Bushnell, the deputy assistant secretary of state for Inter-American affairs, went before the House Appropriations Subcommittee on Foreign Affairs to argue for immediate approval of the military aid request. During 1980 assassinations of local officials, school leaders, and peasants by the military became more frequent. It was not until late 1980 and early 1981—when several Americans (four churchwomen and two land reform specialists), along with the head of the agrarian reform program, were murdered—that the escalating repression in El Salvador began to attract much attention in the United States.[201]

The Repression of Reform

In early February 1981, Ambassador White was recalled. He was replaced on June 1 by Deane Hinton, who saw his mission more as limiting the negative publicity generated by the Salvadoran government's repressive policies than as changing the policies themselves. The Reagan administration, recognizing that the adverse reports from El Salvador would limit its ability to secure congressional support for its efforts to suppress insurgency in El Salvador, pressed for an early election. In the "demonstration election," held on 28 March 1982, the Christian Democrats emerged with 35 percent of the ballots cast and 24 of 60 deputies in the Constituent Assembly. Finishing second with 26 percent and 19 deputies was the ultraconservative National Republican Alliance (ARENA) led by Roberto D'Aubuisson. A third conservative party, the National Conciliation Party (PCN), which represented the traditional military leadership, received 17 percent and 14 deputies. Pressure by the Reagan administration prevented D'Aubuisson from being named provisional president, although he was elected president of the National Assembly. In April 1983 President Reagan, in an address to a joint session of Congress, made the incredible assertion that the Salvadoran government was "making every effort to guarantee democracy, free labor unions, freedom of religion and a free press."[202]

One of the first acts of the assembly was to suspend land reform. The final blow to land reform was a constitutional provision, passed in December 1983, that raised the limit on the size of farms that could be privately owned, thus effectively nullifying the second phase. Landlords began immediately to evict tenants who had been beneficiaries of the law but had not yet been granted title. Meanwhile, the military continued to attack cooperative farms and to torture and murder cooperative members.

Toward Democratization

The Reagan administration continued to place major emphasis on elections as a means to provide the Salvadoran government with democratic legitimacy in the eyes of Congress and the U.S. public. By 1989 five more elections would have been held for legislative, municipal, and presidential officers.[203] In the first, held in the spring of 1984, Jose Napoleon Duarte was elected president of El Salvador. His inauguration was attended by Secretary of State George Shultz and a congressional delegation that included Senators Strom Thurmond (R-S.C.) and Jesse Helms (R-N.C.), both strong supporters of U.S. intervention in El Salvador and Nicaragua.

The election of Duarte had the required effect in the United States. Congressional opposition to the Reagan policy in El Salvador was effectively dissipated. In El Salvador, however, the repression continued as President Duarte, constricted by a military that remained unresponsive to civilian direction, found himself with little power to influence the course of events.

Duarte's presidency, from 1984 to 1989, was characterized by limited political liberalization. "By the end of his term in office, he was widely associated with corruption, bitter division within his party, and, most important, the failure to achieve peace . . . Duarte led the government when the military killed tens of thousands of Salvadorans and implemented a failed strategy of marginalizing the FMLN; his tenure served to prolong the war and postpone democratization. If democracy was what Duarte desired, his drift to the right and close ties to the United States probably doomed his effort from the start."[204]

In the legislative elections of 1988, the right-wing ARENA replaced Duarte's Christian Democratic Party (PPC) as the dominant party. And in the presidential elections of 1989 the ARENA candidate, Alfredo Cristiani, was elected president. Cristiani, who represented the somewhat more liberal, probusiness branch of ARENA, had come up through the ranks of the military as a D'Aubuisson protege. He was able to use D'Aubuisson's support to obtain the commitment of ARENA to the peace process.

A Transition to Democracy?

A more serious approach to the peace process was facilitated by external events. Among the most important were the decline of the Cold War, the electoral defeat of the Sandinistas in Nicaragua, and the election of George Bush in November 1988. In mid-1989 the Bush administration indicated to Salvadoran officials that the decline in the Cold War made it unlikely that Congress would continue indefinitely to provide aid at the level of the 1980s. Over the objections of the administration, Congress appended a provision to the 1991 aid bill, passed on 27 October 1990, to withhold half of the $85 million scheduled for military assistance pending progress in the peace process. The action by Congress left the government of El Salvador with the choice of negotiating with the rebels or losing U.S. aid.[205]

The efforts by President Cristiani to advance the peace process were initially undermined by the murder of four American Jesuit priests, their housekeeper, and her daughter and by an attack on the headquarters of the National Trade Union Federation of Salvadoran Workers. The FMLN initiated a major offensive in November to increase their bargaining power by strengthening their hold on several eastern provinces. In late 1989 President Cristiani, supported by the presidents of other Central American countries, approached the secretary general of the United Nations, Perez de Cuellar, to use his good offices to bring together the parties involved in the Salvadoran conflict. This was followed in January 1990 by Cristiani's visit to New York to request the secretary general's help. Despite the United Nations' traditional avoidance of involvement in internal conflicts, the secretary general responded favorably. Negotiations began in May 1990 and, punctuated by a series of disruptions, concluded on 16 January 1992 with the signing of a peace accord between the Salvadoran government and the FMLN.[206]

The peace plan signed on January 16 is a remarkable document. It envisioned a cease-fire by 1 February 1992 and the complete demobilization of the FMLN as a fighting force by 31 October 1992. In exchange for demobilization, the FMLN negotiated a basic restructuring of the Salvadoran armed forces and a redefinition of their role in society. The redefinition involved the withdrawal of the military from all internal security functions. The rapid-retaliation infantry battalions, associated with some of the most horrendous massacres of the war, would be disbanded. The Treasury Police, the National Guard, and the National Police were to be disbanded, and a new National Civil Police would be created under close international supervision.[207]

The euphoria associated with the signing of the peace pledge, both in El Salvador and among observers of Salvadoran political events, can only be described as remarkable. At the signing ceremony, former adversaries embraced each other and wept. Even long-term critics of U.S. policy in El Salvador credited the Reagan administration policy of reform through election: "U.S. policy was more farsighted than those of us who at that time were considered to be activists could envision." Furthermore, "outside of Costa Rica, El Salvador's chances for democracy may be the strongest in Central America."[208]

It is still too early at this writing to make a firm judgment on the success of the transition to democracy in El Salvador. But it is not too early to count the humanitarian and economic costs to Salvadorans of a U.S. policy that for almost a decade preferred military victory to negotiation. Political development is an uncertain process. While hoping for the best, it is worth remembering that human rights abuses in El Salvador have only partially been related to the rhythm of war. They predate the outbreak of civil conflict and helped give rise to it.[209]

Summing Up

Any attempt to interpret the confusion that surrounded U.S. policy toward Central America during the Carter and Reagan administrations must take into account both (1) the lack of consensus, referred to at the beginning of this section, about the sources of instability and the significance of that instability for U.S. security and (2) the active participation of organized constituencies, both supporters and opponents of intervention, in the policy process. It was the loss of consensus that prevented the Carter administration from developing a coherent interpretation and response to the Sandinista-led revolution. And the active role of organized constituencies with widely different interpretations of the events in Central America made it impossible for the Reagan administration to achieve the congressional support needed to aggressively pursue a policy of rolling back presumed Communist adventurism in the region. As in the latter years of the Vietnam War, the administration and the foreign policy establishment lost control of the agenda.

What should we have learned from the very substantial expenditure of resources—economic and political—in Central America? In Nicaragua the United States was unable and often unwilling to use economic assistance as an instrument to induce political and economic reform by the Somoza regime. After the success of the Sandinista revolution, we were unwilling, because of ideological blinders, to work toward a political accommodation. We imposed sufficiently heavy economic security costs on the inept Sandinista government to contribute to its collapse. But we have been unwilling or unable to provide either the economic or the technical assistance to enable the Chamorro government to make the economic growth needed to sustain the social gains in education and health that were achieved during the initial years of the Sandinista government. In El Salvador massive economic assistance forced an exhausted government and an exhausted guerrilla movement to negotiate a settlement. The human and economic cost to the people of El Salvador has been exceedingly high.

The lessons that can be drawn from the experience of U.S. efforts to influence economic and political development in Central America through economic assistance and both covert and military assistance remain the subject of substantial debate. My conclusion is that the countries in which we have most actively intervened would be better off today if our policy had been one of benign neglect. But benign neglect does not have to be the only answer. With the end of the Cold War, the economic and political problems of the Caribbean region and Central America no longer need to be viewed through the distorted glasses of ideological conflict. It is time, therefore, to make a more constructive effort to reduce the poverty and strengthen the institutions of democracy in those nations that lie at our doorstep.

By the early 1990s the prospects for democracy in Central America were more promising than even the most optimistic observer could have predicted a decade earlier, when only Costa Rica could be counted as a stable democracy. "In Nicaragua . . . for the first time since the formation of the republic more than 150 years before, a peaceful transition of power through democratic elections had occurred . . . The 1989 transfer of power in El Salvador was the first between government and opposition as the result of an election since 1931. In Guatemala, after several decades of power transfers via military coup, a government gained power through free and fair elections . . . Competitive and open elections leading to a peaceful change of power also took place in Honduras for the first time in thirty years."[210]

It would be a mistake, nevertheless, to regard democracy in the region as firmly entrenched. The countries in the region remain the poorest in the hemisphere. There seems to be little prospect that the decline in U.S. economic assistance, which began with election of the Chamorro government and the negotiation of the cease-fire in El Salvador in 1990, will not continue. If the favorable trends in political development are to be reinforced by similar trends in economic development, it seems that we may be able, in another decade, to look back and conclude that the United States has accomplished through neglect what it was not able to achieve through massive security assistance.[211]

The cost to the integrity of U.S. political institutions of intervention in Central America has been high. In retrospect, it is clear that the war waged against the Sandinista government by the Reagan administration was at least as subversive of U.S. constitutional processes as it was of Sandinista power in Nicaragua. The United States violated its own laws in allowing the training of Contra forces in the United States. It violated international law in mining Nicaraguan harbors and in attacking facilities in Nicaragua. But its most blatant violation was the criminal action, later to become known as the Iran-Contra affair, involving the diversion of profits from arms sales to Iran to provide arms to the Contras against the expressed will of the U.S. Congress.

United States Bases Abroad

As part of its strategy to contain the Soviet Union, the United States has maintained military bases abroad. Base arrangement with allies and clients has evolved through a series of stages from perceived congruence of interest to the view of U.S. assistance as rent for base rights. This section is not exhaustive. I give primary attention to the evolution of these stages in Greece, Turkey, and the Philippines but do not discuss other obvious cases such as

Pakistan, South Korea, or the numerous other "base access" countries that have received ESF funds.[212]

From Mutual Interest to Rent

During the early postwar period, the United States retained bases in countries that had been World War II allies. Some bases were also established in defeated axis countries. Before the breakup of the colonial empires, the United States also provided substantial support to Britain and France to maintain some of their bases and to facilitate their joint use by the United States. These arrangements provided the United States "with an elaborate basing structure usable for a whole range of conventional and strategic nuclear purposes. During this period, which preceded the break up of *Pax Americana* beginning in the 1960s, there was an assumed convergence of security interests between the United States and most of its allies and clients."[213]

Since the mid-1960s this perception of mutual interest has been less apparent. When the USSR leapfrogged the containment ring on the borders of its empire, the United States was induced to seek access to facilities in a large number of Third World countries. The United States had often found it difficult to persuade former colonial countries that their security interests converged. Base strategy became a game in which developing countries sought to increase the economic benefits that might be obtained by making facilities available to either the U.S or the USSR.[214] Resources transferred to countries such as Portugal, Spain, Greece, Turkey, and the Philippines under the supporting assistance and ESF budgets were, in effect, rent payments for U.S. use of facilities on their territory.

By the end of the 1980s, it had become clear that a transition to a third stage was under way. "Basing diplomacy had, to a degree, become depoliticized (in an ideological sense) and placed increasingly on an almost crass commercial basis."[215] There were several reasons for this transition. One was the changing nature of U.S. base requirements. Robert Harkavy argues that the need for large-scale facilities investments has declined and been replaced by the need for numerous new "technical" basing facilities, which are crucial to a modern global military establishment.[216] A second reason is the reduction of U.S.-USSR tensions and the demise of the Cold War. A number of countries no longer view a U.S. presence as a guarantee of security. In some countries the U.S. presence has become a significant domestic political liability. This opposition frequently has been used in negotiations as a rationale for raising the economic rent to offset the political costs.

Base Rights in the Philippines

One effect of these changes has been the discovery by U.S. security agencies that formerly indispensable facilities are no longer necessary. This transition is illustrated in a particularly dramatic manner by the withdrawal of the United States from the Clark Air Force Base and the Subic Naval Base in the Philippines. George Kennan has argued that, in post–World War II containment policy, "the strategic boundaries of United States were no longer along the western shore of North and South America. They lay along the Eastern coast of the Asiatic continent."[217] During the 1950s the Communist victories in China, the Korean War, and the French defeats in Indochina led to the perception of the Philippines bases as having great value for American security.[218]

From his election in 1965 until his deposition in February 1986, U.S. support for the administration of President Ferdinand Marcos was based in part on his ability to hold the lid on political objections to the continuation of U.S. bases in the Philippines. This policy became more explicit in the late 1970s when the Marcos government openly demanded "rent" as part of a larger aid package.[219] The Carter administration overcame its distaste for Marcos sufficiently to send Vice President Mondale to the Philippines in 1978 to facilitate base negotiations. As part of the agreement signed on 7 January 1979, ESF resources were made available to the Philippines for the first time. By the late 1970s there was increasing concern in Congress about human rights violations by the Marcos government. As an expression of this concern, Congressman Tony P. Hall (D-Ohio) of the House Foreign Affairs Subcommittee on Asia and Pacific Affairs introduced an amendment to reduce the funds available to the Philippines under the Military Assistance Program. Both President Carter and Assistant Secretary of State Richard Holbrook stressed the continued importance of the Philippines bases and took the position that, in a choice between national security and human rights concerns, the first would have to take precedence.[220]

During the Reagan administration's first year, there was little of the internal tension over policy toward the Philippines that had characterized the Carter administration. On a visit to the Philippines in June 1981 to attend President Marcos's inauguration, Vice President George Bush praised Marcos for his "adherence to democratic principles and democratic processes."[221] Security and economic assistance to the Philippines rose dramatically during the early years of the Reagan administration.

By the mid-1980s Philippine domestic opposition to the Marcos regime had strengthened. U.S. aid began to be viewed by opposition political leaders primarily as a device to keep the Marcos administration in power and assure U.S. access to the Philippine bases. The assassination of Philippine opposition leader Bengino Aquino in August 1983 generated increased domestic opposition to the Marcos regime. In the United States public concern about human rights violations became more vocal and strengthened congressional opposition to administration policy. In November 1984 the State Department published a report that was highly critical of the Marcos government. It identified specific reforms that were necessary to prevent political and economic decline in the Philippines and assure continued U.S. support for the Marcos government. To try to convey these messages directly to Marcos, the administration dispatched Assistant Secretary of Defense Richard Armitage, Assistant Secretary of State Paul Wolfowitz, Under-Secretary of State and former ambassador Michael Armacost, and Admiral William Crowe, at that time the commander of U.S. military forces in the Pacific, to the Philippines. Their message was that, "if Marcos did not initiate the necessary reforms, the U.S. Congress was not likely to appropriate the funds for the security assistance programs." Marcos was not, however, receptive to the reform suggestions. "He did not believe the Reagan administration would jeopardize the retention of the bases by abandoning him because he refused to conduct himself as the U.S. demanded."[222]

To reduce national and international pressure on his regime, Marcos decided, in late 1985, to conduct a "snap" presidential election in February 1986. After one of the most fraudulent elections in Philippine history, Marcos had himself declared a winner. The opposition, which had united behind Corazon Aquino (wife of the assassinated Bengino Aquino), was joined by important elements of the military. Marcos was forced out of the country, and Aquino was installed as president in late February 1986.

Within the Philippines the issue of the storage of nuclear weapons on Philippine territory and the use of U.S. military facilities for vessels carrying nuclear armaments became a source of contention. The Aquino secretary of foreign affairs, Raul Manglapus, long an opponent of U.S. base arrangements, took the position that the United States should remove the bases because they perpetuate the colonial legacy between the two countries and because their presence prevents the Philippines from becoming a truly sovereign and independent country. In addition, Manglapus did not believe that the Philippines confronted a significant external threat that justified the retention of the bases. Manglapus was not, however, above using the "bases as rent" card to try to escalate U.S. assistance. He insisted that the United States provide larger economic and security assistance to the Philippines as long as the bases remained.[223]

The 1991 eruption of Mount Pinatubo, which buried Clark Air Base in ash and mud and severely incapacitated operations at Subic Bay, induced what diplomacy had not been able to accomplish. As late as the spring of 1991, the United States had still insisted that Clark Air Base and Subic Naval Base were both essential to the defense of U.S. interests in East Asia and the Indian Ocean. When faced with an estimated cost of over $500 million to rehabilitate Clark, however, the Bush administration discovered that it was no longer essential. An effort was still made, however, to retain access to the Subic Bay Naval Base. Faced with an intransigent Philippine Senate president, Corazon Aquino formally notified the United States that its departure from Subic Bay had to be completed by the end of 1992.

In retrospect, it is clear, as Zimmerman has insisted, that "sacrifice of historical, long-term political and development objectives to preserve the short-term strategic political objectives, which required access to the military bases, actually created much of the later resentment and political instability."[224] Once the fact that the United States would no longer have access to Clark Field and Subic Bay was accepted, it became apparent that neither installation was essential for the protection of legitimate security interests in a post–Cold War era. Even before negotiations with the Philippines were completed, the United States had made arrangements for U.S. naval vessels and fighter aircraft to have access to facilities in Singapore. With the issue of base rights resolved, the possibility was open for the United States and the Philippines to reestablish a more constructive relationship. In the future, U.S. efforts to assist Philippines economic and political development will be less likely to be subverted by presumed security interests.

Base Rights in Greece and Turkey

Assistance to Greece and Turkey was one of the earliest U.S. post–World War II economic and military assistance programs (Chap. 3). It was born and sustained out of efforts to contain Soviet expansionism. However, continuing hostility between Greece and Turkey, particularly over the postcolonial government of Cyprus, caused severe complications for U.S. containment efforts along the southern borders of the Soviet empire.[225] The allocation of resources between the two countries has, particularly since the return to democracy in Greece in the mid-1970s, also reflected the growing political strength of the Greek ethnic constituency in the United States.

Reacting to a perceived threat from the Soviet Union in the spring of 1947, President Truman requested and Congress approved a Greek-Turkish Aid Program. It included $250 million for Greece to restore the economy and to regain control of the country and $150 million for Turkey to modernize its economy and its military. Truman also was authorized to send American civilian and military personnel to the two countries to supervise the use of the assistance and to train Greek and Turkish personnel. (See Chap. 3.)

The program involved the United States much more directly in the support and management of economic and military affairs than had been initially intended. But by the mid-1950s it was possible to view the assistance to Greece as a success story. The Communist-led guerrilla movement had been suppressed. Agricultural production had recovered. As noted in Chapter 3 and earlier in this chapter, the significance of this involvement is the lesson drawn from assistance to Greece (and from experience in Korea during the early 1950s): security assistance can be effective in enabling governments with limited administrative capacity to resist the threat of external aggression and internal subversion if the United States is prepared to involve itself deeply in the management and support of the country's economic and security system.

Continued assistance to Greece reflects the role of Greece as a "base country" and the ability of the Greek ethnic community in the United States to mobilize support for assistance to Greece. Economic assistance to Greece continued until 1976, when both economic and military assistance was cut off to protest military rule. Military assistance to Greece was restored in 1976, after the invasion of Cyprus by Turkey and the partitioning of Cyprus between Greek and Turkish zones.

Since 1974 Congress has linked military assistance to Greece to the level of military aid to Turkey in order to achieve a balance of military strength for its two allies in the eastern Mediterranean. An understanding was reached that Greece would receive $7 of military assistance for each $10 received by Turkey (the 7:10 ratio). In 1992 Turkey received $780 million in military and economic assistance while Greece received $50 million in military assistance.[226]

It has been somewhat more difficult, at least until very recently, to call U.S. assistance to Turkey a success story, particularly when it is evaluated against economic criteria. Writing in the mid-1980s Anne O. Krueger and Vernon W. Ruttan noted that "Turkey's postwar economic development shows three strikingly similar but characteristically different cycles of growth. Each cycle started with a period during which growth was fairly rapid . . . Each cycle was also beset with difficulties: inflationary pressures, increasingly unrealistic exchange rates, various *ad hoc* measures by the government to patch up the situation, and finally, severe distortions in the economy."[227]

By the late 1980s Turkey seemed to be completing a fourth reform cycle. This fourth cycle began in 1980. It differed from the earlier reform packages in that the government announced that it planned a broad liberalization of the economy, including a move away from its traditional statist industrial policy. The 1980 reforms were clearly more successful than the earlier reform cycles. Trade liberalization has been associated with rapid growth in exports—from 7.1 percent of GNP in 1980 to 21.0 percent in 1987. The Turkish debt crisis, which was as severe as that faced by Mexico, Brazil, Argentina, and Egypt, was largely resolved and credit worthiness was reestablished by the mid-1980s. By the late 1980s, however, the inflation level was running in the 65–70 percent per year range—above the highest levels in the previous cycles, and inflation had become a potential source of economic and political instability.

By the fourth cycle the United States had become a small player in economic assistance to Turkey. It had lost much of what was left of its limited capacity to influence Turkish economic policy. Modest ESF assistance was continued during the 1980s, but the levels were so low that they played more of a symbolic than a substantial role in Turkish economic development. Support by the Turkish government for the U.S. role in the Gulf War (1991–92) and for U.S. policy toward Iraq after the war resulted in a sharp escalation in both military and economic assistance to Turkey.

It seems clear, as of late 1994, that continued assistance to Greece and Turkey must largely be justified on strategic rather than economic considerations. Per capita income was $7500 in Greece and in the $3000 range in Turkey in the early 1990s. The strategic value of Greece, both in the containment of the USSR and as a source of stability in the eastern Mediterranean, has been sharply devalued. Turkey continues to retain strategic value in terms of U.S. policy toward Iran and Iraq. Its role as a secular Muslim state also gives it substantial importance in U.S. policy toward the Turkish republics of the former Soviet Union. Given the joint interest of both Turkey and the United States in political stability in the region, there is little basis for more than symbolic economic and military assistance to Turkey at present.

Summing Up

The American network of base rights around the periphery of the Soviet Empire and in East and Southeast Asia was initially an investment in the containment of Soviet and Chinese expansion. The collapse of the Soviet empire and the advance of technology have reduced the value of large-scale base facilities. The long-term presence of concentrations of U.S. military facilities and personnel has increasingly become a political embarrassment to friendly governments in the countries in which the bases are located. This military and economic assistance has assumed the characteristics of rent for bases rather than those of an arrangement for mutual defense.

It now seems appropriate, as suggested in the report of the Defense Burden Sharing Panel, to move toward decoupling the relation between basing rights and foreign aid.[228] Where U.S. troops are stationed abroad primarily for defense of the host countries, cost-sharing arrangements should obviate the need for economic assistance in exchange for basing privileges. In countries where the United States finds it useful, for its own security purposes, to obtain access to facilities, full commercial relationships should be negotiated. U.S. expenditures for labor and technical services should represent a sufficient advantage to the country in which such services are acquired to assure their availability. An articulation of such a policy should enable the United States and the host country to consider its levels of assistance for economic and political development on their own merits.

Lessons from Economic Assistance for Strategic Objectives

Activities programmed under the ESF budget declined steadily after the mid-1980s (Chap. 7). The growth of the ESF during the late 1970s and early 1980s reflected, in large part, the more activist approach of the late Carter and Reagan administrations to contain actual and presumed Soviet political penetration of Southwest Asia, Central America, and Africa. It also reflected an effort to circumvent what the administration viewed as excessive congressional earmarking of resources allocated under development assistance in the foreign aid budget. One effect of the dramatic increase in the number of countries that received ESF aid was to erode the separate rationale of the development assistance and ESF programs. The collapse of the Soviet empire further weakened the rationale of economic assistance for strategic purposes. In draft legislation submitted to Congress late in 1993, the Clinton administration proposed eliminating ESF as a separate item in the AID budget. But elimination of ESF as a budget item will not eliminate the use of economic assistance for strategic purposes.

What lessons should be drawn from the history of economic assistance for strategic purposes? The lessons from earlier experience in Latin America, Western Europe, Greece, China, and Korea did not provide useful guides to our experience in Vietnam. Nor have the lessons that were drawn from Vietnam protected the United States from devoting excessive resources to the defense of presumed national interests in other areas of little strategic significance, such as Nicaragua and El Salvador. The lesson from assistance to Egypt—that economic assistance to strategically important countries typically produces little in the way of economic development—had been learned earlier in Turkey. The lesson that we have learned from assistance to Israel is that domestic political pressure can be mobilized to force an allocation of assistance resources that are clearly inconsistent with an incumbent administration's definitions of broader U.S. strategic interests.

One of the most difficult lessons to accept from the history of economic assistance for strategic purposes is that, in the area of foreign policy, American presidents and their senior advisers cannot be expected to be honest with the American people or their representatives in Congress.[229] Each president from Eisenhower to Nixon tried to plant both feet firmly on both sides of the Vietnamese issue, promising to minimize American commitment to Vietnam while exaggerating the significance of Vietnam to American security. And each president since Eisenhower shamelessly lied to Congress and the American people about the commitments being made in Vietnam. Peace proposals were advanced with the objective of sustaining domestic support for the war rather than with any realistic expectation that they could be accepted by North Vietnam. The art of dissembling to the public and to Congress was practiced with particular skill and deliberation by Henry Kissinger during his term as national security adviser and as secretary of state. It was practiced with at least as much deliberation, but with somewhat less skill, by President Reagan and his national security staff in defending U.S. policy toward Nicaragua and El Salvador and during the Iran-Contra controversy.

The acceptance of this practice by the establishment press has been particularly disturbing. Joseph Kraft of the *New York Times* commented about Kissinger, "While he almost certainly lied, the untruths are matters of little consequence when weighted against his service to the state." I cannot be so generous as Kraft. Lack of honesty in dealing with the American people destroys the credibility of the policies that are being advanced and of the institutions the policies are designed to protect. I am not able to go as far as the iconoclastic journalist I. F. Stone, "Every government is run by liars, and nothing they say should be believed."[230] But I do insist that we have been taught to look behind every policy pronouncement—to ask not what was said but why it was said.

The failure to deal openly with the American people and with Congress on issues of national security has been costly. In his introduction to the Tower commission report, R. W. Apple argued that "Lyndon B. Johnson was shouldered into retirement by massive disenchantment with the war in Vietnam. Richard M. Nixon was sunk by Watergate and resigned in the face of probable impeachment. Gerald R. Ford was doomed by the pardoning of his predecessor. Jimmy Carter ran aground on the shoals of Iran."[231] From the perspective of the mid-1990s, one might add that Ronald Reagan's incapacity for governance was revealed by the Iran-Contra affair and that the legacy of George Bush's presidency was severely tarnished by his failure to dislodge Saddam Hussain from power in concluding the 1990–91 war with Iraq and by his effort to deflect attention from his role in the Iran-Contra affair.

I see little hope, however, that the lessons from the past will provide substantial guidelines in considering the use of economic assistance in a post–Cold War environment. The power of the American government to act in the national interest is so influenced by parochial interests and by cycles in popular sentiment that the capacity to pursue longer-term national interests lies effectively outside the competence of those charged with the shaping and execution of foreign policy.

I argued earlier that the tendency to vacillate between the two offspring of American exceptionalism—between idealist and realist doctrine—has been a persistent aspect of U.S. political culture (Chap. 2). The tension between these two poles has been a continuing theme in the political dialogue on economic assistance for strategic purposes. Liberal politicians and their constituents have found it difficult to support economic assistance that could not be rationalized in terms of the well-being of aid recipients. Conservatives have typically insisted that economic assistance be justified in terms of U.S. economic or strategic self-interest.

From the end of World War II to the mid-1960s, liberals found it easy to support foreign economic assistance because of a presumed convergence between moral purpose and strategic interest; a more prosperous world would also be a safer world. In contrast, conservatives typically opposed foreign assistance. They could find little political or ethical justification for taxing Americans to do good for foreigners (Chap. 2).

By the late 1960s positions had reversed. Liberals found the moral costs of the Vietnamese war—the human and material costs to both Vietnam and the United States—too large to continue to rationalize when measured against the limited strategic value of South Vietnam to the United States. In contrast, conservatives came to view success, or at least "peace with honor," in Vietnam as a test of America's credibility in its effort to contain communism. By the 1980s, this same test was being applied in Nicaragua and El Salvador.

By the early 1980s liberal and conservative roles again began to reverse positions.[232] In the 1992 presidential campaign, there were calls by conservatives, in both the Republican and the Democratic parties, for a disengagement from international responsibilities. But the breakup of the Soviet empire, followed by an eruption of genocide in the former Yugoslavia, and the breakdown of civil order in Somalia provided a moral rationale, acceptable to liberals and even some conservatives, for humanitarian assistance to parts of the world of little economic or strategic value to the United States.

It is now time for the United States to undertake a thoroughgoing reassessment of its strategic interests in a post–Cold War world and of the use of economic assistance for strategic purposes. I argued earlier (Chap. 2) that ethical considerations require, at a minimum, that foreign assistance do no harm to recipients. The history of our use of economic assistance for strategic purposes suggests that this minimum criterion has seldom been met when U.S. assistance has been given for strategic purposes.

Part IV

Multilateral Assistance

Chapter 11

Policy toward the Multilateral Lending Institutions

The mid-1940s were a remarkably creative period in the evolution of multilateral development assistance institutions (Chap. 3).[1] The delegates to the 1945 United Nations organizing conference in San Francisco created an Economic and Social Council (ECOSOC) as a vehicle by which preexisting specialized agencies involved in international cooperation (such as the Food and Agriculture Organization) could be attached to the U.N. system. By the late 1940s a framework for multilateral development assistance consisting of the U.N. Economic and Social Council and the specialized agencies plus the two Bretton Woods institutions—the International Bank for Reconstruction and Development (IBRD) and the International Monetary Fund—had been effectively institutionalized. "The IBRD was there to guarantee European borrowing in international markets; the IMF was there to smooth the flow of repayments; and the ECOSOC (and the specialized agencies) was there to promote peace through shared knowledge."[2]

There has, however, been a continuous evolution and growth of the multilateral assistance machinery—in ways that would have been difficult for the original architects to anticipate. The World Bank has emerged both as the main source of direct lending and as a major source of knowledge about the development process. It has been joined by three regional development banks: (1) the Inter-American Development Bank (IADB) in 1959, (2) the African Development Bank (AfDB) in 1964, and (3) the Asian Development Bank (ADB) in 1966. The program of the World Bank was expanded by the creation of two affiliates, the International Finance Corporation (IFC), in 1956, to make loans to the private sector in less developed countries and the International Development Association (IDA), in 1960, to make "soft loans" to middle- and low-income countries. Similar soft-loan and private sector lending affiliates have since been developed at the regional banks.

The Reagan administration came into office in 1981 armed with a highly critical view of both the international development banks and the U.N. specialized agencies (Chap. 7). Its perspective was, however, only an extreme variant of a pattern that had characterized almost every U.S. administration since 1950. William B. Dale, formerly U.S. executive director of the International Monetary Fund, was only slightly exaggerating when he insisted that each new administration in Washington starts out with a passive or negative attitude toward multilateralism until, propelled by experience, a more favorable attitude toward cooperation emerges and lasts until the next team takes office.[3]

In this chapter I trace the evolution of U.S. policy toward the multilateral financial institutions. In pursuing this objective I have found it necessary to give considerable attention to the evolution of U.S. bilateral lending institutions and to the domestic economic and political forces that have led to the decline of bilateral lending relative to multilateral lending for development purposes.

This analysis is, of necessity, only partial. An analysis that focuses primarily on U.S. policy toward the international financial institutions is not an adequate perspective from which to understand the policies pursued by these institutions. The multilateral development bank management and staff can be conceptualized as embedded in a two-tiered hierarchy of principals or patrons and agents or clients.[4] At one level the banks are the agents of the donor country principals that contribute financial resources to the banks. At a second level the banks themselves occupy the position of principals with respect to the countries to which they make loans.

This two-tiered arrangement with multiple donors and recipients has traditionally given the bank bureaucracies a very wide range of discretion about which political objectives and professional commitments of bank management and staff will become major sources of bank policies and programs. This discretion, because of substantial autonomy within the two-tiered system, has been reinforced by an inherent information asymmetry, carefully cultivated by the bank bureaucracies, that limits the capacity of either the developed country principals or the developing country agents to engage in policy dialogue with the bank's bureaucracies on equal terms. One developing country minister commented to me, "Even when I know they are wrong I don't have the data or the analysis to argue my case effectively."

A partial excuse for focusing primarily on U.S. policy toward the multilateral banks is that traditionally the United States has been the largest single source of finance for the banks. This financial weight has been reflected, to a varying degree, in the weighted voting systems used in the governance of the banks. Furthermore, the autonomy of the multilateral banks has been an important consideration in arguments over the priority that the United States should place on multilateral as compared to bilateral assistance.

The Coordination of Development Lending

When the Bretton Woods agreements were drafted during World War II, it was expected that U.S. lending for reconstruction and development would be channeled primarily through international organizations. The major instrument used by the U.S. government to formulate and coordinate policy of the U.S. bilateral lending institutions and policy toward the multilateral lending institutions has been the National Advisory Council on International Monetary and Financial Problems (NAC).[5] The NAC was established under the Bretton Woods agreement of 1945 to coordinate the policies and operations of the representative of the United States on the IMF and the World Bank and of all agencies of the government that make or participate in making foreign loans or that engage in foreign finance, exchange, or military transactions. The NAC was to be chaired by the secretary of the treasury. Membership included several agencies mandated by the enabling legislation plus other agencies that have an active role in international lending. Nearly all decisions were made at lower levels—by a committee of alternates and by the NAC Staff Committee, the basic working unit within the NAC. Only issues that involve major policy decisions were brought to the council itself for resolution.[6] The primary focus of NAC activity was the coordination of the policies of the Export-Import Bank and the US/AID and its predecessor agencies with those of the U.S. executive directors of the multilateral institutions.

The role of Treasury became even more dominant after a reorganization in the mid-1960s. Treasury dominance of NAC decision making had been the subject of considerable criticism by the Agency for International Development and the State Department. The Bureau of the Budget and the Council of Economic Advisors recommended transferring responsibility toward the multilateral banks to AID and that State and Treasury retain responsibility for the IMF. In 1965 President Johnson issued a reorganization plan (No. 4) transferring NAC responsibilities to the president. This was followed, in early 1966, by an executive order (No. 11269) reestablishing the NAC and giving the secretary of the treasury full authority to instruct the U.S. representatives to the multilateral development banks. AID and State were given informal assurance that the NAC would no longer regularly review AID bilateral loans. Treasury had emerged from the interagency contest with its authority enhanced. NAC became an advisory body with its coordination function reduced.[7]

The 1966 executive order did not, however, resolve the coordination issue.

As the size of the multilateral program increased relative to the bilateral program, Congress became concerned about consistency between the two efforts. In the early 1970s Congress, led by the House Foreign Affairs Committee, acted to place a stronger focus on human rights and poverty reduction objectives in the bilateral program (Chap. 6). The 1973 Foreign Assistance Act, which incorporated the New Directions principles, also included a provision creating a Development Coordinating Committee (DCC). The congressional supporters of the DCC had hoped to give AID a platform from which it could counter Treasury's role in development policy. The DCC would be chaired by the AID administrator and empowered to advise the president "with respect to the coordination of United States policies and programs affecting the development of developing countries, including programs of bilateral and multilateral development assistance."[8]

The congressional effort to establish an alternative assistance policy coordination agency that gave a larger role to State and AID was in part a reflection of internal tension within the several assistance bureaucracies. Each of the agencies—Treasury, State, and AID—had viewed the other two as having the wrong approach to development assistance and toward the multilateral development banks in particular. Treasury viewed itself as the defender of sound development. It viewed State as too willing to trade off long-term development for short-term political gain. State, in turn, had been critical of Treasury for its narrow economic approach to project evaluation and recipient country economic policy. In the view of State, international economic policy is too important to be left to bankers and economists. The AID bureaucracy shared much of State's impatience with Treasury's narrow financial orientation but at the same time often found common ground with Treasury in opposing what AID staff regarded as State's more blatant political agenda.

The DCC failed, however, to meet congressional expectations. It was unrealistic to assume that a committee chaired by the AID administrator, who held subcabinet rank, could provide policy leadership and coordinate policy among cabinet-level officials. When the cabinet-level members reduced their participation in favor of subcabinet level staff, the DCC failed to function.

The issue of coordination emerged again in 1978 when Senator Hubert Humphrey (D-Minn.) introduced a bill (S. 2420) to create an International Development Cooperation Agency (Chap. 13). Partially in response to congressional concern, President Carter issued an executive order directing that the DCC should be expanded and become the primary instrument for foreign aid coordination. A subcommittee of the DCC on Multilateral Assistance was formed to coordinate U.S. policy toward the banks. A staff working group of the subcommittee, the Working Group on Multilateral Assistance (WGMA), was established to handle day-to-day loan policy review. When the 1979 reorganization plan was implemented, the IDCA director replaced the AID administrator as chair of the DCC. The reorganization became, in effect, a dead letter during the Reagan administration, when the AID administrator served simultaneously as director of IDCA.

As of the middle 1990s, however, the distinction between the NAC and the DCC continues to be more of a convenient fiction than a reality. The same people tend to show up in the subcommittees of both organizations. When issues come up that result in tension over agency prerogatives or lead roles, initial discussions are often held outside the formal committee, subcommittee, and working group structures. The Office of Management and Budget is drawn into the coordination process when there are significant fiscal implications, such as policy concerning IDA replenishments. When important foreign policy and national security issues are involved, the National Security Council staff assumes a dominant coordinating role. While the Treasury continues to exercise the right to instruct the U.S. representatives on the governing boards of the multilateral development banks, its authority is often more apparent than real on important policy issues.[9]

The history of aid policy coordination illustrates the limits of the congressional capacity to exercise leadership in executive branch program management. An effective reorganization requires exceptionally strong presidential commitment. When that commitment is lacking, agency power relationships remain unchanged. The congressional role in development assistance policy, with respect to the bilateral assistance programs, stems from its authorization, oversight, and appropriations functions—including earmarking by functional accounts and recipient countries. In the case of the multilateral banks, its influence through the authorization and oversight functions has been more effective than through appropriations. The hearings influence Treasury policy toward the banks and the policies of the banks more by focusing congressional and popular opinion on concerns about the lending policies of the banks than on specific lending activity. Before turning to U.S. policy toward the multilateral banks, it will be useful to review the evolution of the several U.S. bilateral lending institutions.

U.S. Bilateral Lending Institutions

In this section I discuss three institutions: the Export-Import Bank, the Development Loan Fund, and the Overseas Private Investment Corporation. I do not review the other instruments the U.S. government has used to encourage or discourage U.S. investment abroad. These have included tax incentives and disincentives, investment guarantees, antitrust policies, and intellectual property rights policies.[10]

The Export-Import Bank

The first U.S. government agency established to make foreign loans, the Export-Import Bank (Eximbank), was established in 1934 under the authority of the National Industrial Recovery Act to facilitate trade between the United States and the USSR. Its first loan was to Cuba to finance the purchase of silver for minting into silver pesos.[11] Its first development loan was made to Haiti in 1938 to finance purchases in the United States of equipment, materials, and services to be used in public works construction. During World War II its lending capacity was expanded several times. By the end of World War II, it had become a major source of lending for reconstruction and development.

The Export-Import Bank Act of 1945 established the bank as an independent agency governed by a five-person board of directors, one of whom was the secretary of state. During the 1950s its powers were widened through a series of amendments to the 1945 act. Its powers included (1) the making of loans and guarantees for the expansion of capacity and the production of essential materials in foreign countries, (2) the administration of the Foreign Investment Guarantee Program of the International Cooperation Administration, (3) the administration of the program of local currency loans to private firms abroad with funds derived from the sale of surplus agricultural commodities, and (4) the ability to act as an agent for the International Cooperation Administration and other U.S. government agencies in other foreign loan operations.[12]

In spite of the fact that the Eximbank had been established to finance export of U.S. products, it did not become an important source of U.S. export financing.[13] The expansion of the bank's lending activities during the 1950s was governed more by the "legislative history" established in congressional hearings and by the foreign policy concerns of the Eisenhower administration than by specific legislative authorization. Raymond Mikesell commented in the early 1960s that "it is not possible to find in the text of the Bank's enabling authority specific authorizations for many of the loans made by the Bank, such as general purpose loans or stabilization loans not specifically tied to imports from the United States, for the fact [is] that the bulk of its loans appear to be made more for the purposes of promoting economic development in poor countries and serving other foreign policy interests of the United States rather than specifically for promoting our foreign trade."[14]

As late as 1960 the credits authorized for reconstruction and development by the Eximbank were roughly double those that had been authorized by the World Bank.[15] The role of Eximbank as a source of balance of payments support and for reconstruction and development was questioned by members of Congress, who frequently reminded the Eximbank management that its primary objective was to enhance U.S. exports. By the late 1970s, in response to congressional pressure, the Eximbank portfolio more closely reflected its initial mandate. It tended to view itself primarily as an instrument to achieve a level playing field for U.S. exporters competing with exporters from other nations in developing countries. Its programs included (*a*) direct loans for exports, usually on a subsidized basis;[16] (*b*) guarantees to cover loans to finance exports; and (*c*) insurance for short-term receivables arising out of export transactions.

The Eximbank program was viewed by the incoming Reagan administration, particularly by Office of Budget and Management Director David Stockman, as an unneeded subsidy to American business.[17] The Reagan administration made several attempts, beginning in 1981, to eliminate the direct loan program. Congress responded by expanding the direct loan authority and mandating loans to small and medium-sized business as a priority. Resources available to the Eximbank did, however, decline substantially—its lending authority declined from $5.4 billion in 1981 to $695 million in 1989. Although the Reagan budget for 1990 again proposed terminating the Eximbank Direct Loans Program, the Bush administration took a more relaxed, though ambiguous, attitude.[18]

Is the Eximbank a development assistance agency? The bank itself is somewhat ambiguous on this question. Its export loans and guarantees largely support exports to developing countries. But an important objective of its efforts has been to neutralize the effects of competitor governments. Or, as Acting Chairman William F. Ryan testified in 1989: "Do we provide subsidies? Yes, we do. That is what the Eximbank is all about . . . The French, the Japanese, the Germans, the English and more recently the Australians, the Spanish and the Scandinavians . . . support their exports very aggressively. (They) give away gobs of their taxpayers money in the process. In the case of mixed credits they give away 35 units on the dollar."[19] The Congressional Budget Office (CBO) estimated that the subsidy cost of new 1990 Eximbank obligations amounts to 9.2 percent of loan principle. The CBO recommended that Congress directly appropriate to the Eximbank the subsidy costs of new loans, loan guarantees, and insurance.[20]

The Development Loan Fund

Most of the economic assistance to developing countries programmed under the International Cooperation Administration and its predecessor agencies (see Figure 13.1) had been provided in the form of grants and soft loans. As the Korean War came to an end, there was a determination on the part of the Eisenhower administration to return to a policy of leaving economic development to private investors and the World Bank. In 1953 Eisenhower informed Congress that he planned to terminate bilateral economic assistance in 1953. Secretary of the Treasury George Humphrey sought, at the same time, to terminate development lending by the Eximbank. When these efforts failed, because of opposition in both Congress and the administration, a decision was made to place greater emphasis on loans relative to grants. Consistent with this objective a Development Loan Fund (DLF) was established within the ICA in 1957. In 1959 the DLF became an independent agency.[21]

Most of the loans made by the DLF were project loans. The projects funded by the DLF were similar to those financed by the Eximbank—highways, electric power, railroads, hydroelectric dams, port and harbor development, factories, irrigation, telecommunications, mining, and other "directly productive" investments, with only a small amount devoted to financing "social overhead capital" such as sanitary water supplies, sewage disposal, low-cost urban housing, and rural development. A major difference was that Eximbank loans were repayable in dollars, whereas about 75 percent of DLF loans were repayable in local currencies. Thus, by the late 1950s, the United States had established substantial institutional capacity for making both hard and soft loans in support of economic development.[22] In 1961 the International Cooperation Agency and the Development Loan Fund were combined under the new Agency for International Development. The merger was not achieved without considerable internal tension. Staff who had entered the agency in the early 1950s as members of the Technical Cooperation Agency were particularly bitter about what they saw as the loss of President Truman's vision—"to make the benefits of our scientific advances and industrial progress available for the improvement and growth of underdeveloped areas." They were concerned about what they saw as a shift in orientation in the new agency from "technology transfer" to "financial transfer" (Chap. 4).

By the mid-1960s the new agency had made a substantial transition in its method of financing economic development. A policy of increasing the percentage of AID assistance in the form of loans was adopted. "In fiscal years 1959–61 an estimated 36 percent of ICA-DLF economic assistance took the form of loans, whereas in fiscal 1965 . . . about two-thirds of AID's economic assistance took the form of loans." Congressional pressure also resulted in a slight hardening of loan terms.[23] The character of the loans also changed. Congress had become concerned about the excessive buildup of foreign currency reserves in U.S. accounts in developing countries.[24] After 1961 most of the new loans became payable in dollars. (See Chap. 8 for a discussion of the accumulation of foreign currency under the food aid programs.)

The Overseas Private Investment Corporation

In 1969 Congress created a new agency, the Overseas Private Investment Corporation, to "mobilize and facilitate the participation of United States private capital and skills in the economic and social programs of less developed countries and areas, thereby complementing the development assistance objectives of the United States."[25] The legislation transferred to OPIC most of the functions previously administered by AID (and before AID by DLF and ICA) designed to protect the American investor against political risk—including inconvertibility, expropriation, and war.[26] The establishment of OPIC was, to a significant degree, the result of a persistent effort by Senator Jacob K. Javits (D-N.Y.) in support of the concept of a federally chartered corporation to promote private investment in less developed countries. The concept was first developed by Benjamin A. Javits, the senator's brother, in a 1950 book, *Peace by Investment*.[27]

AID and its predecessor agencies had been issuing investment guarantees since 1948.[28] Initially, the guarantees were issued primarily to countries in Europe. During the 1950s, the investment guarantee program expanded primarily in Latin America, South Asia, and Korea. The program was expanded rapidly, particularly in Latin America, in the early 1960s as a result of concern about the expropriation of American investment after the ascension to power of President Castro in Cuba and the initiation of the Alliance for Progress program in the first year of the Kennedy administration (Chap. 5). Throughout its administration under AID and predecessor agencies, the program was viewed by its managers primarily as an instrument to further U.S. development assistance and foreign policy objectives. Most guarantees were for investment in basic industries or public utilities, such as bauxite in Jamaica, copper and telephone communications in Chile, and fertilizer and chemicals in Korea. The program operated under a series of bilateral agreements with host countries. It was typically assumed that there was little conflict between furthering U.S. foreign policy and furthering the economic development of the host country.

A 1968 AID reorganization by President Lyndon B. Johnson placed the program within a new Office of Private Resources (OPR). In the same year Senator Javits succeeded in attaching an amendment to the Foreign Assistance Act requesting the president to make a comprehensive review of the foreign aid program, including consideration of proposals for a federally chartered private corporation to stimulate the flow of private U.S. capital to developing countries. Earlier, in 1966, Javits had sponsored an amendment to the Foreign Assistance Act of 1966 to create an International Private Investment Advisory Council on Foreign Aid (IPIAC). In 1968 IPIAC and the president's Advisory Committee on Foreign Assistance Programs (the Perkins committee) both urged the formation of a government corporation to handle the guarantee programs. In 1969 the presidential Task Force on International Trade and Investment Policy (the Peterson committee) urged the formation of an autonomous public loan guarantee agency that would be less subject to political influences than was the program administered by AID.

Legislation establishing the Overseas Private Investment Corporation was passed on 30 December 1969, as part of the Foreign Assistance Act of 1969. The new agency was to be governed by an 11-member board of directors, a majority of whom would not be government officials. The administrator of the Agency for International Development would serve as chairman. OPIC's capital stock, amounting initially to $40 million, would be held by the secretary of the treasury, and it would operate under the policy guidance of the secretary of state. President Nixon did not issue an executive order transferring the private investment programs being administered by AID to OPIC until 19 January 1971. The delay was due, at least in part, to disagreements between members of Congress and the administration over the appointment of the president and vice president of OPIC.

The transfer of responsibility from AID to the new OPIC for insuring investors from political risk occurred just in time for AID to avoid assuming responsibility for dealing with the consequences of a major series of expropriations in Chile.[29] After the election of Salvador Allende, the Socialist candidate, as president of Chile in November 1970, steps were taken by the Chilean government to nationalize economic activities, including the mineral resources and related facilities of the large foreign-owned copper mining companies, most of the foreign and private banks, and major communications facilities. The situation became increasingly complicated as a result of revelations that the International Telephone and Telegraph (ITT) Company's Chilean affiliate had actively intervened in the 1970 presidential elections.

Congressional concern led to (1) the establishment in 1972 by the Senate Foreign Relations Committee of a special Subcommittee on Multinational Corporations chaired by Senator Frank Church (D-Idaho), (2) hearings on the operations of OPIC by the Subcommittee on Economic Policy of the House Committee on Foreign Relations in 1973, and (3) a Congressional Research Service analysis of OPIC operations. The supporters of OPIC in Congress generally took the position that it was a useful instrument in preventing disputes over political intervention or expropriation from rising to the level of government confrontation. The critics, led by Senator Church, were concerned that many of the private sector activities insured by OPIC did not promote, and sometimes subverted, LDC economic development. There was also concern by organized labor that OPIC guarantees encouraged runaway industries and job exportation. Negative attitudes were also reinforced by the political environment engendered by the Watergate disclosures and the disclosures of political influence and bribery by ITT and other American firms, including several insured by OPIC.

A second controversy centered on the issue of whether political risk insurance could be privatized. "The most important provision of the Overseas Private Investment Corporation Amendment Act of 1974 authorized and encouraged OPIC to involve the private insurance industry in its programs with the objective that by 1981 OPIC would function solely as a reinsurer . . . No later than March 1, 1974, it would submit an analysis of the possibilities of transferring its program to the private sector."[30]

OPIC had already had some experience with reinsurance. It had been successful in attracting Lloyd's of London after being rebuffed by U.S. insurance and reinsurance companies on the grounds that they had no experience with political risk insurance. In 1975 OPIC organized an Overseas Investment Insurance Association (the Group) consisting of 12 U.S. private insurers and Lloyd's. It soon became apparent, however, that most members of the Group were unwilling to take on significant risk exposure—they had joined more to project a good public relations image than with any expectation that reinsurance would become a profitable activity.

A third controversy, which continued throughout the 1970s, was whether OPIC's main purpose should be to support U.S. interests in the development of the LDCs or whether its purpose should be primarily to protect the U.S. investment in LDCs. The critics viewed these two objectives as inconsistent. They argued that the more successful the privatization effort became, the less effective OPIC would be in supporting the interest of the United States in LDC economic development. Private sector representatives argued that the U.S. government had some responsibility to provide subsidized political risk insurance because political risk in LDCs was often a consequence of U.S. policy.

Action on the Overseas Private Investment Corporation Act of 1978 was conducted in a much less emotionally charged atmosphere than in the 1974 reauthorization. The 1974 mandate to transfer OPIC's insurance underwriting activities to the private sector by 31 December 1979 was dropped. Opposition to continuation of OPIC came primarily from organized labor and the basic human needs constituencies. Labor again objected that OPIC was part of the package of tax incentives and subsidies that favored runaway industries. The chairman of the Interreligious Task Force on U.S. Food Policy argued that the OPIC policies were not consistent with the New Directions focus in U.S. assistance policy, which emphasized small business and rural development. Senator Frank Church and Clifford P. Case (R-N.J.) argued that OPIC should give a higher priority to development objectives.[31] The Overseas Private Investment Corporation Act of 1978 incorporated only modest revisions. OPIC was instructed to give preferential treatment to projects in the lowest-income countries. Greater emphasis on small business in both the loan guarantee and the direct lending program was mandated. The mandatory privatization program was terminated, but OPIC was encouraged to seek reinsurance by the private insurance industry. OPIC was enjoined from supporting investment in projects producing competitive products for export to the United States—palm oil, sugar, or citrus, for example.

The 1978 act gave OPIC operating authority through 30 September 1981. In 1980, Senator Paul S. Sarbanes (D-Md.) presided over hearings on a bill proposed by Senator Jacob K. Javits to extend OPIC's authority for four more years.[32] Labor and the human needs constituencies again reiterated their concerns. But there was little opposition within either the Senate or the House of Representatives. The extension was passed in the House and Senate in late September and was signed by the president on 16 October 1981. The major changes from earlier legislation were an indication of congressional intent, inserted in the purposes clause, that the OPIC should give preferential treatment in its direct investment program to investment in LDCs with per capita incomes of $690 or less and restrict activities in countries with per capita income of $2950 or more in U.S. dollars. OPIC was instructed to consider the "positive trade benefits for the United States" in its activities, but the restrictions on projects involving copper, palm oil, sugar, or citrus crops for export were removed.

During the middle and late 1980s, OPIC programs and policies were again subject to an upsurge of critical attention both from within the administration and from external interest groups. As the 1985 reauthorization hearings approached, the corporation acceded to pressure by the Reagan administration to initiate a study that would produce a plan for the privatization of some or all of its programs by the end of fiscal year 1988. Application of the Gramm-Rudman-Hollings budget ceilings resulted in the curtailment or termination of some activities, such as investment feasibility studies. A delay in reauthorization until March 1986 forced OPIC to suspend its political risk insurance coverage during the first three months of 1986. As the 1988 reauthorization approached, pressures on OPIC from the administration receded while external pressures accelerated. Beginning in the mid-1980s corporation lending policies came under increasingly critical scrutiny from environmental interest groups, particularly the Natural Resources Defense Council (NRDC). The issue of the influence of OPIC investment guarantees on domestic employment continued to emerge at annual hearings. A 1987 GAO report criticized OPIC for the use of a method that led to underestimation of employment displacement effects. In self-defense OPIC employed a consultant, Arthur Young International, to review the GAO study. The Arthur Young report argued, correctly in my view, that the GAO had erred in focusing its criticism on only the direct employment effects.[33]

When the dust settled the 1988 OPIC reauthorization act widened the OPIC mandate. It authorized participation in equity investments in small business projects in the Caribbean and in sub-Saharan Africa, raised the ceiling on the size of the projects that could be covered under the investment guarantee program, and broadened OPIC's authority to cooperate in pools or consortia involving the private political risk insurance industry. The OPIC mandate was extended until 1 October 1992.

In concluding his analysis of OPIC, Alan Brenglass argues that "there has always existed in OPIC legislation and its implementation . . . an inherent conflict between the foreign development mandate and the directives pertaining to business management principles." My own perspective is slightly different. The conflict is more appropriately viewed as among foreign policy interests, foreign development objectives, the protection of American investment abroad, and the expansion of markets for American exports.[34] OPIC's record of performance suggests that it is time to put aside some of the traditional concerns, such as the issue of additionality—would a particular investment not be made in the absence of the political risk insurance provided by OPIC? It should be enough that purchaser premiums on the risk insurance are sufficient to cover program costs. It is also time to put aside the issue of whether OPIC is a development agency. The evidence suggests that OPIC has responded to the 1978 congressional mandate by increasing its activity in the poorer developing countries and by giving greater preference to the stimulation of investment by smaller U.S. businesses. The evidence also suggests a concentration of lending in the more "friendly" developing countries.[35] OPIC has been able to operate without replenishment of its resources. It should be enough that OPIC's political risk insurance portfolio is financially viable and reasonably consistent with U.S. foreign policy and development assistance priorities.

By the early 1990s it was clear that the three bilateral institutions, whose programs have been reviewed in this section, had become minor actors in the field of development finance. The Agency for International Development, which had absorbed the Development Loan Fund in the early 1960s, had largely withdrawn from development lending during the 1980s. Its development assistance activities were mostly funded through grants rather than loans. The Export-Import Bank and the Overseas Private Investment Corporation both continued to employ the rhetoric of development assistance when it was politically convenient. But both were engaged mainly in advancing

U.S. commercial interests in developing countries and in the former centrally planned economies.

The Multilateral Lending Institutions

The International Monetary Fund and the International Bank for Reconstruction and Development were the central institutional innovations designed to assure a liberal economic order in the post–World War II era (Chap. 3).[36] The two institutions owed their origins, as Lord Keynes remarked, "primarily to the initiative and ability of the United States Treasury."[37] The World Bank articles of agreement contain explicit provisions, based on the Treasury's preliminary draft, that the bank should avoid interference in the domestic political affairs of member countries: "The Bank and its officers shall not interfere in the political affairs of any member; nor should they be influenced in their decisions by the political character of the member or members concerned. Only economic considerations shall be relevant to their decisions, and these considerations shall be weighted impartially."[38] Similar provisions were included in the charters of the three regional banks. Politics would be left to the politicians. Economics would be handled by technocrats.

If the United States had maintained its commitment, there would be little need to write this chapter. It was hardly reasonable, however, to expect that the political interests of the United States, the bank's most powerful member throughout most of its history, would not impinge on bank lending activity. During the first several postwar decades, U.S. policy toward the World Bank and the new regional banks emerged out of internal bureaucratic politics in which the Treasury Department played a dominant role. By the early 1970s, however, as multilateral lending came to play a much larger role relative to the U.S. bilateral assistance program, congressional and popular concerns widened the political agenda and forced debate about the lending policies of the MDBs into the public arena.

The first quarter century after the Bretton Woods agreement was a period of rapid institutional innovation. The lending activities of the World Bank were broadened by the establishment of two bank affiliates. The International Finance Corporation was created in 1956 to make loans to the private sector in less developed countries without requiring an investment guarantee by the government of the recipient country. The International Development Association was established in 1960 to make *soft loans,* loans at concessional rates, for development projects in the poorest countries. By the mid-1960s the World Bank had been joined by three regional development banks: (1) the Inter-American Development bank (1959), (2) the African Development Bank (1964), and (3) the Asian Development Bank (1966). This period of rapid institutional change was coincident with the presidencies of Eugene Meyer (1946), John J. McCloy (1947–49), Eugene Black (1949–63), and George Woods (1963–68) (see Appendix B).

I do not, in this section, attempt an exhaustive history of these institutional innovations. The record of the first two decades of the World Bank and the other multilateral financial institutions has been documented by the massive scholarship of Edward S. Mason and Robert E. Asher in *The World Bank since Bretton Woods*.[39] Rather, I attempt to trace the evolution of U.S. policy toward the multilateral lending institutions. Although this history is rather complex, it can be stated rather briefly: The United States initially opposed each of the new initiatives. When confronted by strong support by the other donors and Third World beneficiaries, however, opposition turned to grudging acceptance.

Competition with the Eximbank

During the late 1940s and early 1950s, the World Bank and the U.S. Eximbank became engaged in a competitive struggle over their relative roles in development finance. The ink from President Truman's signature on the Bretton Woods Agreements Act of 31 July 1945 was hardly dry before the issue of the appropriate relationship between the lending activities of the Eximbank and the World Bank emerged as a major policy issue. Legislation signed the same day raised the lending authority of the Eximbank to $3.5 billion.

U.S. policy at the time of the establishment of the World Bank was that it would become the principal agency through which to make loans for reconstruction and development that could not be furnished by private capital. The large needs for capital transfers to Western Europe in 1945 and 1946 were, however, beyond the capacity of the newly established World Bank. More by default than by policy, the more experienced Eximbank was able to respond to these needs. By the end of 1947, however, its lending role in Western Europe was largely superseded by grant support for reconstruction under the Economic Cooperation Administration, which administered the Marshall Plan.

Disagreements about the appropriate relationship between the World Bank and Eximbank lending intensified in April 1948, when President Truman asked Congress for an increase of $500 million in Eximbank lending authority to be used to assist economic development in Latin America. Although public relations considerations dictated that the World Bank maintain a public posture of cooperation, Bank President John J. McCloy and U.S. Executive Director Eugene Black expressed strong reservations about the proposed increases in lending authority to John W. Snyder, U.S. secretary of the treasury and chairman of the NAC. The World Bank was particularly concerned about the effect of interest rate differentials charged by the two institutions—the bank's interest on long-term loans was then 4.5 percent as compared to 3.5 percent on Eximbank loans and 2.5 percent on loans administered by the ECA. In the opinion of the World Bank, Eximbank lending should be limited to purposes that concerned either the political and security interests of the United States, such as the financing of the procurement of strategic materials, or to the financing of U.S. foreign trade. Long-term development lending should be the prerogative of the IBRD. Mason and Asher note that "each institution suspected the other of 'stealing' its clients, concealing information on pending negotiations, and engaging in other forms of unfair competition. To some extent both were right. And borrowers were not above playing the two agencies off against each other."[40]

By the early 1950s there were significant differences in the lending activities of the two institutions. The bank's portfolio was largely concentrated in large infrastructure projects—particularly electric power and communication—while the Eximbank's loans were more heavily focused on manufacturing, mining, forestry, and water resource development. Furthermore, Eximbank credits were generally available only to finance the purchase of material, equipment, and technical services from firms based in the United States.

An initial showdown between the two institutions came in 1952, when the World Bank successfully insisted that it, rather than the Eximbank, should finance a $40 million loan to Japan for the construction of two steam power plants.[41] The bank's position became U.S. policy during the initial years of the Eisenhower administration. Eugene Black, then World Bank president, found it relatively easy to convince Eisenhower's economy-minded secretary of the treasury, George Humphrey, that a smaller role for the Eximbank represented a promising opportunity to save money. On 30 April 1953 President Eisenhower sent to Congress a reorganization plan designed to reduce Eximbank's autonomy and make it more subservient to Treasury. The reorganization was described by one observer as leaving the Eximbank with little more than a bookkeeping rather than a policy function and making the executive director a $17,500 per year errand boy for Treasury.[42] This change was, however, acceptable to neither American industry nor Congress. The American economy was beginning to feel the effects of the post–Korean War *rolling readjustment*—the then-current euphemism for recession. Senator Homer Capehart (R-Ind.), "one of the highest-powered, highest-pressure salesmen this country has ever produced," succeeded, after a tour of Latin America and Senate hearings, in pushing through Congress legislation that not only reestablished the Eximbank as an independent agency, but also increased its lending authority by $500 million—to $5.0 billion.[43]

The World Bank had fewer misgivings about the bilateral capital transfer activities of US/AID and predecessor agencies (the Foreign Operation Administration, the International Cooperation Administration, and the Development Loan Fund). It saw the direct grants and foreign currency lending activities of the U.S. bilateral program as useful in meeting the capital requirements for social infrastructure projects that contributed to economic development but that could not expect to earn a direct financial return.[44]

By the late 1950s, the tension between the World Bank and the Eximbank had also moderated. The credit demands by the less developed countries were larger than had been anticipated in the early 1950s. The World Bank reluctantly accepted the Eximbank's position that clients should be free to patronize both institutions. By the 1970s the functions of the two institutions had become further differentiated with, as noted earlier, the Eximbank turning to advancement of the commercial interests of U.S. exporters.

Reluctant Support for Bank Affiliates

Pressure had been building among the less developed nations, almost from the World Bank's establishment, for international support for a new facility to finance non–self liquidating, "low-yielding and slow-yielding" projects.[45] The United States agreed to them only when it became convinced that the United Nations might create an alternative financial institution that would be competitive with the World Bank and the U.S. Eximbank—"the IFC and the IDA were the price the United States had to pay to protect the World Bank's central role as a bulwark for sound, conservative standards of development in the poorer nations."[46]

In 1949 V.K.R.V. Rao, then chairman of the Subcommission on Economic Development of the U.N. Economic and Social Council, had suggested a United Nations Development Administration (UNEDA) to be financed by contributions from member governments to support development projects in the form of loans offered on liberal terms and at nominal interest rates. The U.S. representative on the subcommission, Emilio G. Collado, previously U.S. executive director at the World Bank, was "unable to concur."

Further impetus for establishment of the IFC and IDA came in 1951 from a recommendation by the U.S. International Development Advisory Board, chaired by Nelson Rockefeller, for the establishment of two new international financial institutions, one to finance concessional loans to the poorest countries and another to encourage private investment in developing countries. The Rockefeller report was not welcomed by the new Eisenhower administration—then engaged in a costly war in Korea and in escalation of the Cold War armaments race. The Treasury, Eximbank, and Federal Reserve opposed further proliferation of international bureaucracy and objected to intergovernmental institution participation in equity financing.

Pressure from the less developed countries continued to build. In 1953 the U.N. Department of Economic Affairs urged the formation of a Special United Nations Fund for Economic Development (SUNFED). The proposal was taken up at the 1954 meeting of the ECOSOC development council, where it received enthusiastic support from the poorer nations. The U.S. delegation to the United Nations advised Washington that it would be unproductive to continue the negative posture and urged some expression of sympathy toward the developing countries. They urged the IFC as the least costly available initiative. World Bank President Black also urged U.S. support for the IFC and had the plan redrafted to meet the objections to IFC participation in equity financing of developing country private firms. Treasury Secretary Humphrey responded by announcing support for the plan at a November 1954 meeting of the inter-American finance ministers. The plan was considered by the House and Senate finance committees in the spring of 1955 and passed unanimously by the Senate on June 21 and by an overwhelming majority in the House on September 1.

Establishment of the IFC did not, however, satisfy the demands of the less developed countries for a soft-loan facility. The World Bank was initially less favorably disposed to soft loans than to grants. But the pressure for the formation of SUNFED led the bank gradually to modify its position. Pressure for the United States to modify its opposition originated in the U.S. Senate. In 1956 Senator A. S. (Mike) Monroney (D-Okla.) proposed a soft-loan program that would administer, in a nonpolitical manner, the embarrassing accumulation of local currencies being generated by U.S. development and food aid loans. The proposal was endorsed by the Senate in July 1958. The administration, which had originally opposed the Monroney proposal, reversed itself shortly before the Senate vote. It wanted to avoid an approach that would finance "needy lands with rich countries' monies" by a U.N. institution governed on a one-country, one-vote basis.

The final version of the IDA articles of agreement that was submitted to member governments in January 1960 was quite different from the original Monroney proposal. In spite of strong support for a program that would include both grants and loans, the United States prevailed, in deference to domestic political pressure, in its insistence on a loan program—no matter how soft the terms. There was little enthusiasm at the World Bank for the Monroney proposal that the IDA assume responsibility for the use of the local currencies owned by the United States. Initial lending authority was set at $1.0 billion, considerably below the level desired by the less developed countries. It was agreed that the president of the World Bank would also serve as president of IDA and that the program would be administered by bank personnel rather than as, in the case of the IFC, a semiautonomous institution.

What was it that had been created as a result of more than a decade of pressure to transform an institution that started out viewing itself as a bank into something that more nearly resembled a development institution? Mason and Asher, writing in 1973, referred to the IDA as "an elaborate 'fiction.' Called an 'association' and possessed of Articles of Agreement, officers, governmental members, and all the trappings of other international agencies, it is . . . simply a fund administered by the World Bank. Its aim is to finance the same types of projects as does the Bank, selected according to the same standards, but on terms that place a lighter burden on the balance of payments of the borrowing country. The result was to broaden substantially the range of nations with which the Bank Group deals and to increase the amount of financing it provides."[47] It also made the bank dependent on member governments for the replenishment of IDA resources.

Responding to Regional Interests: The Regional Development Banks

The emergence of the three regional development banks—the Inter-American Development Bank (1959), the African Development Bank (1964), and the Asian Development Bank (1966)—was due in large part to continuing dissatisfaction on the part of developing countries with what they regarded as overly rigorous lending and project evaluation procedures of the World Bank and the dominant role of the developed market economies in the world economy. The U.S. government was generally unsympathetic to proposals for the establishment of regional banks, preferring the World Bank and its affiliates as its primary instrument for multilateral lending and assistance.[48]

The timing of U.S. acquiescence in support for the establishment of the regional institutions was attributable less to concern about development than to the emergence of U.S. policy interests in the particular part of the world. U.S. support for an Inter-American Development Bank reflected a concern to reverse the decline in relations with Latin America after Vice President Nixon's disastrous trip to Latin America in 1958 (see Chap. 5). Support for the establishment of an Asian Development Bank coincided with escalation of the war in Vietnam. U.S. participation in the African Development Bank followed a period of rising tension and increased Soviet interest in southern Africa that began with the Portuguese revolution and withdrawal from their African colonies.

The Inter-American Development Bank

Impetus for the creation of an Inter-American Development Bank can be traced to the First International Conference of American States, 1889–90. The fact that the IADB was not established until 1960 is a reflection of continuing U.S. opposition. The United States was unenthusiastic about the establishment of an institution that might compete with U.S. private banking interests. Franklin Roosevelt's Good Neighbor policy represented an attempt to establish better relationships with the countries of Latin America, but it did not involve substantive new initiatives nor increased aid. With the Eximbank and the World Bank, the U.S. government saw little reason for the establishment of a regional lending institution. Eugene Black, president of the World Bank (1949–63), expressed strong hostility toward the establishment of an IADB. Latin American countries resented the World Bank for its use of leverage and the United States for the relatively minor share of U.S. bilateral assistance to the region.[49] In the 1950s a series of conferences were held in Latin America calling for the establishment of a development bank that would be more responsive to the needs of the region.

Postwar relations between the United States and Latin America were strengthened with the signing of the charter of the Organization of American States in 1948, but it was not until the late 1950s that a Latin American entity became an issue for U.S. policy makers. The fall of commodity prices and decline of Latin economies transformed a longstanding political suspicion of the United States into specifically focused economic resentment against the United States and the existing international institutions. This was manifest in a demand for a more imaginative, political, and social approach to development. The United States, however, appeared insensitive to the Latin position. The State Department continued to convey a positive impression that U.S.-Latin relations were progressing fine. This position became untenable during Vice President Richard M. Nixon's catastrophic visit to Latin America in the winter of 1958.[50]

A few months before the Nixon visit, the Latin American nations had initiated preparatory steps toward setting up an inter-American bank. The impetus for a Latin American development bank was reinforced by U.S. interest in the formation of a Middle East regional development bank. An announcement of the willingness of the United States to participate in an inter-American financial institution was made in August 1958 at the OAS in Washington by Douglas Dillon, then under-secretary of state, immediately before a speech by President Eisenhower calling for the establishment of a Middle East regional bank.

The new climate of accommodation was reflected in the unusual speed with which negotiations to organize an Inter-American Development Bank proceeded. Negotiations started in January 1959 and were completed in April. An important innovation was the establishment of a soft-loan window, the Fund for Special Operations (FSO), which became a model for the World Bank's soft-loan window, the International Development Association. The IADB was supplemented in October 1960 by the creation, within the framework of the Alliance for Progress, of a Social Progress Trust Fund (SPTF) to respond to the need for so-called social lending. There was considerable concern within the IADB that the SPTF might become an instrument of excessive U.S. leverage on IADB policy. This issue was resolved by an agreement that the monies would be utilized within four sectoral program areas: (1) agrarian reform, (2) low-income housing, (3) water supplies and sewage, and (4) higher education.

The Asian Development Bank

A proposal for an Asian regional development fund was made by Japanese Prime Minister Kishi in 1957. Another proposal for a regional commercial bank was made by the Japanese government in 1962. Formal proposals for the organization of an Asian Development Bank (ADB) were initiated by the U.N. Economic Commission for Asia and the Far East (ECAFE) in August 1963. The initiative was prompted, in part, by the 1963 Khartoum agreement among African ministers of finance to establish an African Development Bank.[51] By December 1965 an agreement on the establishment of the bank and on its charter had been achieved.

The process moved through two stages. From August 1963 to April 1965, the leadership came almost entirely from working groups established under ECAFE auspices. Technical assistance was supplied by the IADB. Neither the United States nor other potential developed country members, except Japan, indicated significant enthusiasm for the venture. Even Japan, mindful of the lack of response to its 1962 initiative and fearing that it might find itself the only major donor, maintained a cautious posture—insisting that the cooperation and participation of developed countries outside the region would be essential to Japan's participation. The implication of this position was that only if substantial American support was assured would Japan accept what it clearly felt was its natural role.

The momentum for the establishment of the bank changed sharply in April 1965. In a speech at Johns Hopkins University on April 5, President Johnson announced that the United States was prepared to join in "a greatly expanded cooperative effort for development" in Southeast Asia and that its own contributions, if Congress gave its approval, would include "a billion dollars in

American investment in this effort when it is underway."[52] The impetus for the Johnson pledge was the rapidly expanding American commitment to the war in Vietnam and the need to seek broader sharing of the U.S. commitment to economic development in the region.

With American support Japan was ready to enter into a firm commitment. The United States and Japan both offered to subscribe $200 million each, which would amount to 40 percent of the proposed initially authorized capital. The United States also offered to contribute $100 million to a soft-loan fund for Southeast Asia. President Johnson further emphasized his support by appointing Eugene Black, former World Bank president, as his special advisor on Southeast Asia. During the final negotiations in Manila, the issue of the bank's location became a major source of tension. Both Japan and Iran were intent on having the bank in their capitals. The Southeast Asian countries preferred either Manila or Bangkok. The United States was reluctant to support the Tokyo location. The final choice of Manila led to the withdrawal of Iran from membership and to considerable resentment on the part of Japan.[53]

Japan's concerns were subsequently assuaged by the appointment of Takeshi Watanabe, who had served on both the ECAFE working group and the Ministerial Conference consultative committee, as ADB president. The ADB got off to what White described as a "brilliant beginning." The backing of Eugene Black, coupled with the selection of Watanabe, assured the confidence of the member governments and of the private financial community.[54]

The African Development Bank

The establishment of the African Development Bank drew on political and economic motivations much different from those for either the Inter-American Development Bank or the Asian Development Bank. In the case of the IADB and the ADB, developed country donors played an active entrepreneurial role and became major contributors of equity capital when the banks were established. The African Development Bank, in contrast, was established over the active opposition of the metropolitan countries to which the African countries continued to be closely linked, both economically and politically, even after independence. "The African Bank was shaped almost exclusively by the way in which Africans themselves perceived their needs and their place in the broader global environment."[55]

The impetus for the establishment of the AfDB was strengthened by the failure of the effort in the 1950s to expand the role of the United Nations in development financing through a Special United Nations Fund for Economic Development. The African countries responded by resolving, at the All-African

People's Conference in Tunisia in January 1960, to explore the possibility of setting up an African investment bank to promote development projects. This proposal was adopted at the third session of the Economic Commission for Africa in February 1961. Robert Gardiner, executive secretary of the Economic Commission for Africa, was interested to "undertake a thorough study of the possibilities of establishing an African Development Bank and to report to the Commission at its next session."[56]

The Gardiner commission—the Committee of Nine—found it necessary to contend with political tensions both within and outside the region. There was an initial concern that, if the bank were controlled by the Economic Commission for Africa, it would give the commission greater power than many African countries were prepared to accept. A decision was made, therefore, to establish the bank as an autonomous institution outside of the commission's direct influence. There was also division between the more radical group of African states—the Casablanca group, consisting of Ghana, Guinea, Mali, Morocco, and the United Arab Republic (UAR)—and the more moderate group—referred to as the Monrovia group. The most serious external difficulty, however, stemmed from the opposition of the French government and the campaign by the French government against the proposal among the more pliant francophone countries. When the French government reluctantly moderated its opposition, it was made clear to the organizing commission that France had strong reservations against American participation. The American government expressed some enthusiasm for the bank to the Gardiner committee representatives who visited Washington but found the French objections an adequate reason for muting its support.

As a result of consultations between the Gardiner commission and the developed countries, it became "firmly and finally convinced that the African nations would have to set up the institution, and make it work, on their own." The Committee of Nine prepared a series of reports on its missions and, at its third session, in January 1963, it adopted a draft agreement that was distributed to African governments for comment. The agreement was discussed in a preparatory meeting and then at a conference of finance ministers at Khartoum in July 1963. A number of technical issues had to be resolved at the Khartoum conference: "How to devise an institutional base for African cooperation, how to allay the smaller countries' fears that cooperation would lead to domination by those African countries which were already relatively advanced; and how to devise . . . a style appropriate to the peculiar conditions of African dependence and African balkanization." The representatives of the developed countries who participated as observers in the organizing conference had apparently arrived without formulated instructions. George Woods, then-president of the World Bank, sent a message through the director of the

Africa Department to exercise caution in the allocation of scarce resources and to avoid duplicating the work of other institutions. The only strongly positive external response was from Felipe Herrera, president of the IADB, who stressed the political significance of the creation of what he regarded as a sister institution.[57] Advice was sought from the World Bank, the Inter-American Bank, the U.N. Secretariat, and the Economic Commission for Africa. The draft was closely modeled on the precedents of the World Bank group combined with some features of the IADB Social Progress Trust Fund. After a series of heated debates, it was decided that the anglophone-francophone tensions could best be released by locating the bank in Abidjan (Ivory Coast) and by appointing as president Mamoun Beheiry, the distinguished governor of the Sudan Central Bank.

The African Development Bank finally came into existence on 10 September 1964 with ratification by the 12 governments whose subscriptions summed to the required 65 percent of authorized capital. The total capital subscription of $217.8 million was, however, paid in rather slowly. Egypt (UAR) deliberately cut its subscription when it failed to receive what it regarded as an acceptable number of positions on the AfDB staff. The bank opened its doors for business on 1 July 1966 and made its first loan—for highway construction on the Kenya-Uganda and Kenya-Tanzania borders—in August 1967.

Once the AfDB became operational, it was possible to reduce tensions with the French government and open the way for modest U.S. participation. In 1966 the AfDB proposed to the United States and other potential donors the formation of a new soft-loan facility. The fund was finally established in 1973. Beginning in the mid-1970s the United States, in response to major changes in the African political landscape and the growing political power of the domestic Afro-American community, sought membership in the African Development Fund (AfDF).

By the late 1970s the AfDB was ready to reverse its own longstanding opposition to non-African membership. This reflected, in part, the fact that the AfDF was becoming too large relative to the limited capitalization of the bank. In May 1978 the bank issued a membership invitation to non-African countries. The donors to the AfDF had urged that, if the African countries wanted broader access to their resources, they ought to be willing to accord them a larger role in the bank. The regional countries would have preferred to maintain the exclusive pan-African character of their institution. However, by 1978 it was clear they were having trouble financing each other's development through the AfDB. They needed the broader access to outside capital markets and sources of financing which would only come with active participation by the developed nations. The Carter administration would have been willing to support a larger role in AfDB funding and governance in spite of the lack of a strong domestic and congressional constituency. But it became evident during the talks that the AfDB was unwilling to increase the share of capital held by nonregional countries beyond 33 percent. The final arrangement provided for only the same modest level of U.S. participation in the bank as had previously been the case.[58]

The European Bank for Reconstruction and Development

The European Bank for Reconstruction and Development (EBRD) is the newest regional development bank. An EBRD was proposed by President Mitterand of France in the fall of 1989. It was endorsed by the Council of the European Economic Community on 9 December 1989. After a series of technical and planning meetings in the winter and spring of 1990, an agreement establishing the EBRD was signed by 40 countries, the European Investment Bank (EIB), and the EEC on 29 May 1990.

The impetus for the establishment of the EBRD was to support the transition of the formerly centrally planned economies of Eastern Europe. The EBRD charter was quite explicit that its mandate is to support recipient countries that are committed to both economic and political liberalization. This is in contrast to the charters of the World Bank and the other regional development banks, which specifically prohibit them or their officers from being influenced by political considerations. The United States is expected to play a modest role in the EBRD.[59] Its initial contribution of $10 million amounts to 10 percent of paid-in capital.

Responding to Domestic Politics

Support by the U.S. government for the multilateral lending institutions that it had helped create remained strong throughout the 1960s. Negotiations over replenishment and borrowing authority, particularly the second IDA replenishment, often involved tortuous negotiations to resolve differences within the administration, between the administration and Congress, and with bank management and other donors.[60] Nevertheless, the U.S. government continued to play a generally strong, positive role in strengthening the capacity of the multilateral institutions.

It became clear, by the completion of negotiations for the third IDA replenishment in 1970, that establishment of the soft-loan windows that required periodic replenishment had changed the relationship between the bank management and member governments. In the case of the World Bank, this change has been characterized by Mason and Asher.

> Until the advent of IDA, the president of the World Bank could exercise great freedom in allocating available resources because he had raised the resources in private capital markets and could raise even more when "good" projects were presented for financing. By and large, allocation was not a problem. When IDA entered the picture, allocation became a problem because every IDA project that was approved reduced the balance available for commitments to other projects. The resources were contributed by governments, and governments (through their executive directors) gradually became more interested in eligibility criteria, economic performance, development strategy, and the means proposed for stimulating previously neglected sectors of the economy. The full impact of the board of directors' growing interest in development policy became most apparent only toward the end of the 1960s.[61]

Initially, the policy concerns of developed country member governments were typically formulated and expressed through treasurics, ministries of finance, and central banks and their representatives. They tended to be more interested in financial policy than development policy. With the emergence of IDA, other ministries and agencies began to pursue policy agendas toward the banks that reflected their particular concerns. In the case of the United States, the State Department became increasingly concerned with the consistency between lending by the banks and U.S. foreign policy. The U.S. Agency for International Development was concerned about consistency with U.S. development assistance priorities. Congress began to attempt to have a more direct influence on the priorities of the banks. And the domestic U.S. development assistance constituency, as well as special interests (agriculture, environmentalists, and others), began to attempt to exert pressure on bank policy through their access to the administration and Congress. By the early 1980s, after the Reagan administration assumed office, the Treasury itself became a more consistent critic of bank policy.

In this section we explore the effects of these several domestic constituencies—administration, congressional, societal, and intellectual—on U.S. policy toward the World Bank. We also explore how external sources—changes in the international economic environment—have influenced U.S. policy toward the multilateral development banks.

Administration Policy

Since the late 1960s administration support for the programs of the multilateral development banks has varied from active support to outright hostility.

The Nixon and Ford Administrations

The Nixon administration was the first in which presidential attention focused on specific multilateral bank operations. Coming into office in 1969, the Nixon administration was committed to a more modest—or more realistic—role for the United States in international economic affairs. This perspective, which came to be termed the *Nixon Doctrine,* was enunciated in a speech in Guam in July 1969 and in an elaborated speech to Congress on 18 February 1970 (Chap. 6).

The Nixon Doctrine translated into more restrained support for the multilateral development banks, particularly the regional banks. The administration supported the third IDA replenishment in the 1969–70 negotiations but had to be "cajoled and embarrassed" into agreeing to contribute $100 million to an expansion of IADB concessional lending capacity in 1970.[62] It finally agreed to contribute $1.0 billion to a $1.5 billion IADB Fund for Social Operations after extracting concessions, including a requirement that loans would be repaid in the currency lent and the selection of the candidate favored by the United States for IADB president. In spite of the concessions achieved during the negotiations, the administration was not able—or was not willing—to prevent the Senate from defeating the FSO replenishment proposed in December 1970.

Administration support for development assistance, and the multilateral banks in particular, turned even more negative after the 1971 devaluation of the dollar. The implications of the Nixon Doctrine and the devaluation were spelled out by Deputy Treasury Secretary Charles E. Walker at the annual meeting of the Asian Development Bank in Vienna in the spring of 1972. "There is a . . . sharply heightened feeling in the United States today that the economic interests of our country have not been given sufficient weight in international policy making. What follows from this is that financial and other burdens traditionally accepted without question by the United States can no longer be automatically accepted on that basis."[63]

Attempts to exert direct pressure on MDB lending, however, produced mixed results. In 1971, when India moved its troops into East Pakistan (now Bangladesh) to support the independence movement, the Nixon administration condemned the Indian move in the United Nations, cut off bilateral assistance to India, and urged the World Bank to defer IDA credits to India. The Nixon-Kissinger position was regarded as ill-advised at the staff level within AID and the departments of State and Treasury. It was opposed by the management of the World Bank and IDA and failed to gain support from other countries represented on the IDA board. The experience was hardly consistent with the view of some critics from the Left that World Bank and IDA action was dominated by the largest donor.[64]

The United States appeared, at least superficially, to be more successful in pressuring the MDBs to limit lending to Chile during the presidency of Salvadore Allende. The World Bank made no new loans to Chile between

Allende's election in 1970 and January 1974, a few months after the fall of Allende's government. In retrospect, it seems that Allende's antagonism toward the international financial institutions was at least as important as U.S. pressure. After Allende's death, when the United States wanted the banks to speed up lending to Chile, disbursements actually declined for a few years because of a lack of new projects in the pipeline. The official position of the two banks (the World Bank and the IADB) during the Allende presidency was that the lack of new loans was a response to their lack of confidence in the management of Chile's domestic economy.[65]

During the fourth IDA replenishment negotiations in 1973, Treasury extracted concessions, including a reduction in the U.S. IDA quota to one-third and a spreading out of its contributions over four years instead of three, as the price for agreeing to the replenishment. The administration waited two years to submit to Congress the proposal to increase ADB capital funds it had agreed to in 1971, and in 1973 actively resisted the establishment of a proposed soft-loan window, the Asian Development Fund. In the talks that began on IADB/FSO replenishment in 1974, the United States extracted further concessions, including a shift from FSO borrower to donor status on the part of the more wealthy Latin American countries and increased emphasis on ordinary capital lending relative to soft-loan funding.

The energy and food crisis that began in 1973 had the effect of inducing a more positive attitude toward the multilateral banks on the part of the administration. In a speech to the United Nations General Assembly in September 1975, Secretary of State Henry Kissinger proposed "the establishment of two new special lending institutions, an International Fund for Agricultural Development (IFAD) and an International Resources Bank (IRB) and announced U.S. support for the World Bank and IFC."[66] The IRB proposal was dropped when it failed to elicit support from either other donors or the proposed recipients. IFAD, which had been proposed with the hope of using it to mobilize for development some of the new resources enjoyed by the oil-producing countries, was brought into existence in 1977. The expansion of IFC capital was accomplished with relatively little stress.

Secretary Kissinger did, however, experience considerable difficulty in bringing Treasury along on his commitment to expand World Bank resources. The disagreement was exacerbated by bank president Robert McNamara's campaign to double World Bank lending capacity. Treasury Secretary Simon objected to any increase in the level of World Bank operations, partly on the grounds of its potential inflationary effect, and insisted that the IBRD loan rates be set slightly above the World Bank borrowing rate. Treasury also delayed action on the 1975–76 IDA replenishment talks until after the 1976 elections.

The Carter Administration

The Carter administration came into office with a commitment to put greater emphasis on multilateral relative to bilateral aid. It was determined to make the multilateral banks "a keystone for U.S. foreign economic development policy."[67] In the summer of 1977, the administration was successful in persuading Congress to appropriate in a single package the funds for a World Bank capital replenishment, the funds to make up the arrearages that remained unpaid under the fourth IDA replenishment, the first year funding for a fifth (IDA-V) replenishment, and an increase in its supplemental contribution to the AfDF. In exchange, it was able to negotiate a reduction in the U.S. share of the World Bank capital replenishment from 25 percent to 19 percent. (The initial U.S. share of World Bank capitalization had been 41 percent.) It also was successful in late 1977 in pushing through replenishment of the AfDF and the ADF. In the process it was able to get agreement on guidelines that would direct a large share of the new resources to the poorest countries and, it hoped, to the poorest people.

By 1978, however, the Carter administration had begun to run into increasing opposition to its agenda for the MDBs. Its attempt to earmark 50 percent of capital replenishment of Inter-American Development Bank resources to the poor majority in the poorest countries and to increase the contributions of the more prosperous countries in the region while simultaneously reducing concessional resources proved difficult to negotiate. In 1978, when the AfDB finally concluded that its viability depended on opening up its membership to non-African countries, the initiative was supported by the Carter administration. But it had difficulty mobilizing sufficient congressional support to enlarge its earlier modest role in the AfDF.

The Carter administration gave strong rhetorical support to World Bank President McNamara's revived plan to double the size of the bank's capital stock. But, sensitive to congressional budget concerns, it tried to find ways to do it on the cheap. It supported a proposal to expand the bank's near-market lending capacity by increasing the bank's capital at a rate of roughly 12 percent per year over the next decade. But it sought to reduce the cost by arguing that the increased lending capacity should be based primarily on callable capital rather than paid-in capital. Although there were objections by some other developed member countries to what they perceived as a major change in policy, the United States did succeed in reaching an agreement to lower the paid-in portion to 7.5 percent. The Carter administration supported the proposal to increase IDA real lending capacity by 5–8 percent per year. But it also pressed for a substantial reduction in the U.S. share of the IDA replenishment. The other countries made it clear that there would be no IDA replenishment without substantial U.S. participation. The United States finally agreed to provide $3.24 billion, or 27 percent, of a new $12 billion three-year funding package—well below the 31 percent that the United States had contributed to the previous replenishment. The net effect of the bank and IDA replenishment negotiation was a substantial broadening of burden sharing and a reduction in the U.S. role. Lack of enthusiasm in Congress for the new package and what some regarded as inept handling of the congressional submission forced postponement of action on both the IDA and World Bank authorizations until the first year of the Reagan administration.

The Reagan Administration

When the Reagan administration came into office in January 1981, it carried in its train a large burden of anti–multilateral assistance intellectual and ideological baggage.[68] The 1980 Republican platform had stressed bilateral rather than multilateral assistance. "Bilateral programs provide the best assurance that aid programs will be fully accountable to the American taxpayer and wholly consistent with our foreign policy interests."[69] The Reagan administration transition team for foreign aid, headed by Edwin J. Feulner, Jr., president of the Heritage Foundation, was severely critical of the leadership of the World Bank during Robert McNamara's term as president and, more generally, of the lending programs of the multilateral development banks.[70] David Stockman, Reagan's first director of the Office of Management and Budget, regarded the banks as purveyors of socialist doctrine in the Third World. This view was shared by Secretary of the Treasury Donald Regan and Assistant Secretary Beryl Sprinkle (Chap. 6). In addition, Treasury Secretary Regan resented the role played by former Treasury Secretary George Shultz in negotiating an agreement between the Carter administration and the Reagan campaign advisors, arranging for the appointment of Bank of America President Alden W. (Tom) Clausen as president of the World Bank just a few days before the election.[71]

The State Department, led by Secretary of State Alexander Haig, Jr., insisted that the banks were sound institutions and that U.S. credibility in international fora would be undermined by failure to honor the previous administration's international commitments. Haig's well-honed skills in bureaucratic infighting, combined with a lag in filling top policy positions at Treasury, enabled State to force an administration commitment to request from Congress the full authorization of the package negotiated by the Carter administration—including support for the IADB, ADF, and AfDF, as well as the World Bank. In his presentation to Congress, Treasury Deputy Secretary Tim McNamara insisted, however, that this should not be interpreted as a commitment to the multilateral institutions. He also indicated that Treasury was initiating an in-depth inquiry into the performance of the banks. This was followed by a letter from President Reagan to key congressional leaders requesting support for the legislation. The package was passed, with very few changes, by Congress in the final days of the 1981 session.[72]

While the new administration was pressing Congress to move the Carter administration's proposals through Congress, it was also moving rapidly in an attempt to advance the policy perspective of the Republican Right. Treasury persuaded the Inter-American Development Bank to replace its executive vice president with a friend of Deputy Secretary McNamara. It reversed the Carter administration position and opposed the creation of a World Bank energy affiliate. And the Treasury took a much more active role in voting against loans, based on both economic and ideological considerations, when they came to the boards of the World Bank and the regional MDBs.[73]

In the spring of 1981, Treasury initiated the promised "comprehensive and dispassionate examination" of the MDBs. The study was designed to establish a policy and budgetary framework for U.S. participation in the banks during the 1980s. Although the study listed 19 criticisms of the MDBs, ranging from excessive staff salaries to their systems of project selection and evaluation, its overall tone was generally positive regarding support of the MDB institutions.[74] The report was particularly critical of the overemphasis on loan quantity rather than loan quality during the rapid growth of lending by the MDBs during the 1970s. The major conclusions of the study, which were not always consistent with the body, were that the United States should (1) participate in the MDB capital increases negotiated during the Carter administration but seek agreement that no new paid-in capital would be required; (2) reduce, in real terms, participation in the soft-loan windows, especially in the IDA; and (3) work to implement a more consistent "graduation" policy from the soft-loan to the hard-loan windows.[75]

The global debt crisis, signaled by Mexico's currency devaluation announcement in 1982, set in motion a process that led to the Reagan administration's taking a more positive position toward the MDBs. This transition was initiated in early 1985, when James A. Baker III succeeded Donald T. Regan as secretary of the treasury, and was completed in 1989, the first year of the Bush administration, when Treasury Secretary Nicholas F. Brady announced a more comprehensive debt reduction program.[76]

The Baker plan, outlined in an address to the World Bank's board of governors in Seoul (Korea), proposed that the multilateral banks and the private banks should substantially increase their short- and medium-term lending sufficient to enable the severely indebted countries to grow out of their difficulties. The Baker plan floundered, however, as the private banks sought to reduce rather than increase their exposure in the heavily indebted developing countries.

As the failure of the Baker plan became increasingly acknowledged, Secretary of the Treasury Nicholas Brady (who had succeeded Baker) proposed on 10 March 1989 a program of debt renegotiation. "The Baker Plan had emphasized domestic reforms to encourage growth, such as privatization and market liberalization. The Brady Plan shifted emphasis to new investment flows, the return of flight capital, and strengthened domestic savings."[77] The Brady initiative envisioned that as much as 20 percent of commercial lendings to Third World debt might be written off. The plan was adopted by the World Bank on 1 June 1989. The bank set aside $100 million from its earnings to fund a debt reduction facility designed to help low-income countries reduce their commercial debt burden and $91 million from IDA reflows to help some of the poorest IDA borrowers to convert old World Bank market rate loans to lower IDA terms, thus reducing their debt service requirements. Although the Brady plan was initially badly underfunded, Brady and his Treasury colleagues successfully pressured the major private U.S. banks to take a more active role in relieving the debt burden in a number of countries, variously estimated at between 15 and 35, where debt overhang remained a serious obstacle to the resumption of economic growth.[78]

The transition to a more positive view of the role of MDBs on the part of the second Reagan administration coincided with the emergence of a more critical stance on the part of the U.S. Congress. Congress became increasingly concerned that the greater emphasis on debt reduction and economic reform was being achieved at the expense of MDB lending and country programs to alleviate the condition of the poor. Congress also became concerned about whether economic policy reforms, designed to increase foreign exchange earnings and reduce this debt overhang, were not resulting in major environmental damage.

Congressional Pressure

The U.S. Congress has become an increasingly important actor toward the multilateral development banks.[79] This larger role, as noted earlier, is due to the continuing need to replenish the funds loaned on highly concessional terms through the MDB's soft-loan windows (IDA, FSO, ADF, and AfDF). It is an understatement to note that congressional activism on U.S. policy toward the MDBs has not been welcomed by either Treasury or the banks. Since the early 1960s Treasury has been engaged in a continuing rear-guard action to protect from Congress its freedom of action on MDB policy.

The World Bank was created, in the view of its founders, to serve strictly economic purposes. "Only economic considerations shall be relevant to their decisions, and these considerations shall be weighed impartially."[80] The separation of politics from economics has been a useful fiction in bank relationships with both donor and recipient members and has frequently been used by Treasury as an argument that the unique role of Congress in determining U.S. policy toward the multilateral banks is a source of frequent emotional stress and occasional embarrassment to both Treasury and the MDBs. "In most countries with parliamentary or executive dominated systems, the initiative for international policy lies with the cabinet or executive. The role of the legislature is basically one of ratifying or confirming decisions already reached by government leaders . . . In the U.S. system, by contrast, the President has limited authority to make binding international commitments without the consent of Congress, and there is often considerable uncertainty about whether Congress will pass the laws needed to implement the administration's initiatives."[81]

Other countries hammer out their internal differences about multilateral bank policies in privacy while the bank replenishment talks are under way. The U.S. government arrives at its final decisions in public fora after international negotiations are complete. Neither the banks, the U.S. representative in replenishment talks, nor other governments can be sure that what they have agreed on in replenishment talks will not have to be renegotiated. Treasury has, however, often been more ready to fault Congress than credit it for the advantage that it gives the United States in the negotiation process. U.S. negotiators are in a position to leverage their bargaining power, beyond their voting strength, by simultaneously asserting agreement in principle with a proposed increase in capital or concessional funds while pleading that "it is doubtful that we could get it by Congress."

The U.S. Congress has attempted to exercise its authority primarily in two ways. One is by directing the secretary of the treasury to "instruct" the representatives to act in accordance with policies promulgated by Congress. Congress has also used the authorization and appropriation process to influence MDB policy.

In attempting to understand the role of Congress, it should be kept in mind that Congress speaks with multiple and often competing voices. Five committees consider MDB legislation. The House Banking, Finance and Urban Development Committee and the Senate Foreign Relations Committee have jurisdiction over authorizing legislation. The House Foreign Affairs Committee, which has responsibility for bilateral aid authorization legislation, also takes an active interest in possible competition or consistency between bilateral and multilateral assistance programs. Budget requests are handled by the House and Senate Appropriations committees. And within each of these committees, the chairs of the several subcommittees, particularly the Foreign

Operations subcommittees of the two appropriations committees, have a great deal of autonomy and power. Congressional committees also influence policy and the conduct of operations by the executive agencies through channels other than authorization and appropriations. Hearings and committee reports are used to focus attention on issues that are important to individual members. Personal contact between executive agency personnel and an expanding congressional staff is an important channel of influence.

Even before the era of concessional lending, Congress occasionally played an important role in the evolution of U.S. policy toward the international financial institutions. Jonathan Sanford has commented on the important role played by Senate Foreign Relations Committee Chairman J. William Fulbright and Senator Mike Monroney: "In 1955 . . . (Fulbright) took the lead in developing congressional support for the new International Finance Corporation. Later, intrigued by Mike Monroney's ideas on new approaches to international development assistance, Fulbright put him in charge of the new Banking Committee subcommittee on international finance and encouraged him to use it for building congressional support for his ideas. The Banking panel later got Senate support for Monroney's 1958 resolution which called for the establishment of a new International Development Association."[82]

The committees have also at times attempted to use leverage over multilateral bank legislation and budget to advance other policy agendas. In 1967, for example, the Senate Foreign Relations Committee held the administration's request for funds for the Asian Development Bank hostage to its attempts to influence the Johnson administration's pursuit of the Vietnam War. That same year Congress amended the IADB legislation to require independent audits of IADB operations (the Selden amendment).

Nevertheless, it is probably safe to generalize, at least through the 1970s, that congressional support for the MDBs has been more consistent than executive branch support. Sanford, writing in 1982, concludes that

> subscriptions to MDB ordinary capital have generally passed by substantial majorities. There has been more suspense about congressional action on MDB concessional aid contributions. Yet even though legislation for each bank has suffered defeat at least once at some point in the process, the basic level of congressional support for the MDB concessional loan program also seems substantial. The question usually has not been whether the bill would ultimately pass but whether the so-called "crippling" amendments or possible cuts in the increased U.S. contributions would be adopted.[83]

Since the mid-1970s Congress has taken the lead in redirecting the U.S. bilateral assistance program to place greater emphasis on human rights, growth with equity, and sensitivity to environmental concerns (Chap. 7). Concern with these issues resulted in legislation mandating that the secretary of the treasury instruct the U.S. MDB board members to use their "voice and vote" to advance these same policies at the banks.

> The International Financial Institutions Act (1982) states that it is U.S. policy to encourage MDB lending to countries that pursue development strategies to meet basic human needs and growth-with-equity. Additional provisions mandate that the United States promote sound environmental policies, encourage the economic integration of women, and urge more MDB lending for projects aimed to meet domestic food needs instead of supporting the export of politically sensitive agricultural products. Congress has also used MDB legislation as a media through which to announce its concerns about issues such as Taiwan's status in the ADB and the need for more aid to Africa.[84]

It is difficult to assess how much weight to give these attempts to influence MDB bank policy through generalized policy guidance. In the early 1970s, World Bank President Robert McNamara was himself attempting to redirect bank policy to place greater emphasis on rural development and other poverty-related programs. Expression of concern for these issues in Congress strengthened his authority within the bank. He actively resisted attempts by U.S. commodity interest groups to limit agricultural lending to develop commodity exports from LDCs.[85] McNamara's successors, however, moved slowly and, most observers would agree, primarily at the rhetorical level to respond to the efforts of the environmental interest groups to incorporate "sustainability" criteria into project design until well into the 1980s.

The results of efforts by Congress to use the appropriations process—the "power of the purse"—to influence MDB bank policy have also been mixed. The most dramatic example concerned an attempt by Congress in the late 1970s to stop World Bank lending to the Socialist Republic of Vietnam. "In 1977, responding to concerns that the new Carter administration might use the multilateral agencies as vehicles for paying reparations to Vietnam, the House adopted several amendments to the fiscal 1978 foreign aid appropriations bill prohibiting the use of U.S.-appropriated funds to finance 'directly or indirectly' any loans to Vietnam and five other countries (Cambodia, Laos, Uganda, Angola, and Mozambique). World Bank President McNamara responded that his agency could never accept an earmarked contribution."[86]

To resolve the dispute, President Carter indicated to Congress that he would instruct the U.S. representative to the World Bank to oppose all lending for these nations. The problem was compounded the following year when the World Bank approved a $60 million IDA loan to Vietnam for agricultural development. After the loan was approved, the House adopted an amendment to the fiscal 1978 authorization that provided that no U.S. funds could be used for IDA loans to Vietnam. The same amendment was attached to the 1980 appropriation legislation. In both years the Senate insisted that the restriction must be dropped from the measure, and after vigorous discussion it was excluded from the final act. In 1979, McNamara assured Congress, in a letter drafted by Treasury, that his agency would not make any loans to Vietnam during the coming year. Although McNamara justified his decision on the grounds that the economic policies being pursued by the government of Vietnam provided an unfavorable environment for successful lending activity, his direct communication with the U.S. Congress was severely criticized by his board. The significance of the event was that "Congress demonstrated its ability to politicize the Bank without actually incorporating politically oriented directives or restrictions on the statute books . . . The threat of such legislation was more than adequate to permit Congress to impose its will upon the Bank."[87]

In 1983 Congress made an unsuccessful attempt to counter the efforts of the Reagan administration to cut support for concessional funding at the Inter-American Development Bank. In 1984 it pushed a reluctant administration to contribute $225 million to the IDA for the Special Facility for Sub-Saharan Africa. In the 1980s the support of the Afro-American community, and of the Black Caucus in Congress, resulted in greater success in securing congressional support for new funding by the AfDB and the AfDF than by the two other regional development banks.

Three Interest Groups

Since the mid-1970s, congressional efforts to influence MDB policies directly have been, by and large, a response to the interests of domestic political constituencies. This has been particularly true of attempts to influence policies and programs in areas such as agricultural commodity production, poverty reduction, and preservation of the environment. A common charge against the multilateral institutions, particularly the IMF and the World Bank during the mid-1980s, was that the conditionality imposed in structural adjustment loans forced countries with heavy debt burdens to reduce social infrastructure investment and focus their development investment on the generation of commodity exports—thus contributing both to the depression of world agricultural commodity prices, to the impoverishment of rural people, and to the degradation of domestic resources and environments.[88]

Agriculture

The interest of organized agricultural producers in foreign assistance policy is not new (Chaps. 4 to 7). Attempts to limit bilateral assistance in support of development that would stimulate competitive commodity production have ebbed and flowed with the strength of international commodity markets. The collapse of agricultural commodity prices in domestic and international markets in the early 1980s focused the attention of agricultural commodity organizations on the MDB programs. The American Soybean Growers Association was particularly concerned about the expansion of soybean production in Brazil and of oil palm production in Malaysia. The decline in commodity prices was mistakenly attributed by commodity organizations to rapid growth in commodity exports from less developed countries, stimulated by development assistance, rather than to the decline in demand associated with the global recession of the early 1980s.

In 1979 commodity groups were successful in incorporating language into the Foreign Assistance Act instructing the president to initiate international consultations with other members of the Organization for Economic Cooperation and Development to develop standards for the allocation of development assistance for the production of commodities in oversupply in world markets. In 1986 legislation was passed instructing the NAC to include in its annual report a list of World Bank project proposals that would enhance a country's capacity to produce commodities for export that are likely to be in surplus on world markets or to cause injury to U.S. producers. The International Financial Institution Act of 1988 contained language requiring the secretary of the treasury to use the "voice and vote" of the U.S. representatives to the MDBs to oppose lending in support of the production of commodities likely to be in surplus on world markets.[89] The producer groups also attempted to bring less formal pressures on the MDBs, particularly the World Bank, through consultations with bank officers and the generation of anti-MDB publicity. In these efforts they were often joined by elements of the "basic human needs" interest groups, who viewed commodity exports from LDCs as diverting food from the poor.

It is doubtful, however, that the commodity groups had very significant influence on MDB bank policy. The complaints by the agricultural commodity producers often suffered from lack of credibility—they had not done the homework necessary to show that MDB bank loans in support of competitive commodity production were significant enough to damage U.S. producers. A series of academic papers, written in opposition to the commodity group pressures, purported to show that LDC economic growth, stimulated by commodity exports, generates growth in consumer demand for animal proteins and stimulates the growth of imports of U.S. feed grains.[90]

Basic Human Needs

A second important U.S. interest group that has been increasingly concerned about U.S. policy toward the multilateral banks has been the "basic human needs" constituency. In 1973, in his address to the board of governors in Nairobi, World Bank President Robert S. McNamara had pledged the bank to direct its resources toward improving the productivity and the welfare of the rural poor in the poorest countries.[91] The themes of integrated rural development and growth with equity that were being used to redirect bank policy were similar in spirit to the New Directions or basic human needs orientation in the U.S. bilateral assistance program mandated in the Mutual Development and Cooperation Act of 1973 (see Chap. 6).

Although the bank's emphasis on growth with equity received strong support in Congress and in the basic human needs constituency, it was viewed with considerable skepticism by Treasury Secretary Simon who, McNamara complained, wanted him "to run the World Bank as if it were a financial institution."[92] In the 1980s, during the Clausen presidency, the bank turned away from distributional considerations to emphasize policy-based "structural adjustment" lending. The basic needs constituency became bitter opponents of the World Bank programs, which they saw as attempts to rescue developed country financial institutions on the backs of the world's poor. But it is doubtful whether their opposition had a significant influence on structural adjustment lending.

Environmental Interest Groups

A third U.S. group that has focused substantial attention on multilateral bank policy is the environmental interests.[93] The success of the environmental advocates in influencing MDB policy, particularly World Bank policy, is of interest because this was the first time that U.S. nongovernmental organizations had achieved significant success in challenging World Bank policy. The success of the environmental NGOs involved four major elements: (1) political pressure exerted through the U.S. Congress and the Department of the Treasury, (2) direct pressure on the banks involving criticism by environmental interest groups of particular policies and projects, (3) indirect pressure exerted through alliances with environmental interest groups in recipient countries, and (4) liaison with elements of the World Bank bureaucracy sympathetic to the environmental interest groups' policy agenda.

By the early 1970s the World Bank was beginning to take notice of rising concern about the relationships between development and the environment. In an address to the United Nations Economic and Social Council in 1970,

World Bank President McNamara questioned "whether and how we can help the developing countries to avoid or mitigate some of the damage economic development can do to the environment without at the same time slowing down the pace of economic progress."[94] McNamara's response to his own question was to establish a small unit that would review the environmental consequences of development projects.[95]

The response of the World Bank staff was first to view environmental concerns as a distraction from the objective of fostering economic growth and then, as environmental concerns intensified, to argue that in developing countries poverty has been the primary source of environmental degradation. Economic growth was seen as reducing the pressure on natural resources and fragile environments, and environmental degradation was seen as a threat to sustainable development.

During the late 1970s pressure by environmental interest groups was successful in forcing AID to give specific attention to watershed protection, reforestation, soil conservation, protection of wildlife habitat, water pollution, resource surveys, and training efforts designated to establish the capacity to conduct environmental impact studies as part of project design and implementation. The Natural Resources Defense Fund and the Environmental Defense Fund brought a suit against AID asking that it institute environmental policies and regulations consistent with the provisions of the U.S. Environmental Protection Act of 1975. Sensing defeat, AID agreed to a court-approved settlement. As a result AID established, in spite of its own inclinations, a leadership position within the international donor community in the environmental area. Since 1987, when environmental interests were successful in getting language inserted in appropriations legislation requiring AID to establish an "early warning" system to monitor and report on MDB projects that might have adverse environmental effects, bilateral foreign assistance legislation has repeatedly emphasized environmental priorities, particularly improved environmental and natural resource management to achieve sustainable patterns of development.

After these successes with AID, the several environmental interest groups began in the early 1980s to turn their attention to the MDBs. Starting in 1983 a loose coalition that included the Environmental Defense Fund, the Natural Resources Defense Council, the Sierra Club, the National Wildlife Federation, and the Environmental Policy Institute initiated a "MDB-Campaign" that included a variety of tactics, particularly a series of well-publicized case studies of World Bank–financed "ecological disasters" in Brazil, India, Indonesia, and elsewhere. Congressional and parliamentary hearings in the United States and several European countries in the mid-1980s had the effect of drawing media attention to bank-supported projects that had displaced native populations or contributed to tropical deforestation.[96] Senator Robert Kasten (R-Wis.), chairman of the Subcommittee on Foreign Operations of the Senate Appropriations Committee, and Representative David Obey (D-Wis.), chairman of the Foreign Operations Subcommittee of the House Appropriations Committee, were persuaded to write letters of inquiry to the Treasury Department on specific bank projects and to draft legislation directing U.S. executive directors at the multilateral banks to press for reform.

These efforts to influence MDB policy were initially frustrated by the strong anti-MDB stance of the Reagan administration. However, James Baker, who succeeded Donald Regan as secretary of the treasury in 1985, saw an opportunity to use the somewhat shrill complaints of the environmental interests to reinforce the administration's own MDB agenda. Treasury then took steps to assure the U.S. environmental community greater access to MDB internal information and decision processes. The political resources that U.S. environmental interest groups were able to bring to bear on MDB policy were reinforced during the late 1980s by the ability of U.S. environmental NGOs to establish liaison and provide technical assistance to emerging environmental interest groups in developing countries. Indigenous protests against MDB projects could then be used to strengthen domestic pressure on MDB policy and projects.[97]

The environmental community has been even more critical of the regional development banks than of the World Bank.[98] It was not until 1990 that the IADB established an Environmental Protection Division. The ADB and AfDB are also regarded by the environmental community as lacking in sensitivity to environmental concerns. In 1990 the U.S. Treasury Department criticized both the ADB and the AfDB for what it regarded as inadequate staffing of their environmental units and for failure to incorporate environmental impact assessments into lending procedures. However, the location of the Asian Development Bank and African Development Bank headquarters outside the United States has led to less attention and less access to their projects and policies on the part of U.S. environmental interests.

In May 1987 World Bank President Barber Conable publicly acknowledged that the bank had been "part of the problem." He announced that the bank would substantially strengthen the staff of its Office of Environmental and Scientific Affairs (OESA).[99] He emphasized in his speech that the centerpiece of the bank's new environmental lending would be a global program in support of tropical forest conversion—the Tropical Forestry Action Plan. The plan had been developed jointly by the bank, the U.N. Food and Agriculture Organization, and the United Nations Development Programme, with substantial intellectual input from the World Resources Institute. Senator Robert W. Kasten of the Senate Appropriations Committee and several members of the House Banking Committee found it politically advantageous to attempt to advance the agenda of the environmental interest groups.

By the early 1990s there was substantial concern within the environmental community that the commitment by both the bilateral and the multilateral development assistance agencies was more symbolic than substantive.[100] The environmentalists belatedly discovered what knowledgeable observers of the World Bank already knew—that the bank's operating divisions—not its central research and policy units, such as the Office of Environmental and Scientific Affairs—are where project planning, implementation, and monitoring actually occurs and that the relationship between bank policy and project development is often rather tenuous.

Much of the discontent in the late 1980s focused on the Tropical Forestry Action Plan (TFAP).[101] Reports prepared by both Third World and developed country environmental interest groups insisted that projects financed under the TFAP were engaged in forest exploitation rather than conservation and renewal—that the TFAP was contributing to the acceleration of deforestation through increased logging. By the fall of 1990, the World Resources Institute, the Natural Resources Defense Fund, the Sierra Club, and other environmental groups were engaged in a campaign to "stop the Tropical Forestry Action Plan." In response, the bank developed and circulated for comment a forestry policy paper. During the early 1990s, the environmental NGOs continued to be very critical of bank policy and lending in the forestry area. Exceedingly critical reviews were that by the Morse commission, appointed by Conable to investigate charges of economic, technical, and environmental deficiencies (including negligence and deception) on the part of the bank staff and the Indian government in the planning and development of the Narmada scheme, and the Wapenhans report, which found that the quality of the bank's loan portfolio had been declining for more than a decade. These added additional fuel to the criticisms of bank policy by the environmental community.[102] In 1994 a coalition of environmental organizations, organized under the rubric of Fifty Years Is Enough, were calling for a sharp reduction in World Bank funding and the separation of the IDA and the newly established Global Environment Facility (GEF) from World Bank management.

Right and Left Populists

There has been remarkable unity in popular opinion, from both the Left and the Right, that the multilateral development banks—the World Bank, in particular—have had a pernicious influence on the development of the poor countries. The MDBs have been viewed by the Right as responsible for the politicization of economic activity and the excessive growth of the public sector in client countries. The Left has held the banks responsible for weakening the capacity of the governments in developing countries to resist capitalist penetration and for the emergence of neocolonialism.[103]

In the United States the criticism by the Right has largely come through journalists associated with the American Enterprise Institute, the Cato Institute, and the Heritage Foundation. Edwin Feulner, Jr., president of the Heritage Foundation, headed the Reagan administration's US/AID transition team. The populist critics from the Right have also drawn substantial inspiration from the polemical scholarship of Lord Bauer of the London School of Economics and the Hoover Institute.[104] The tone of the indictment brought by the Right against the World Bank is reflected in the following quotations. The bank has pursued policies that "debase standards for international commercial lending: (1) substitution of welfare for development; (2) preference for state enterprises over private companies; (3) focus on projects in disregard of borrowers' economic policies; and (4) uncritical acceptance of statist development themes." The bank's policy-based lending program has been counterproductive. Its Structural Adjustment Loans (SALs) "have allowed the Bank to claim credit whenever a recipient government makes any economic reform that is not patently idiotic."[105]

Criticisms from the Left stem both from the traditional Marxist view of the IMF and the World Bank as agents of imperialism and from a more recent populist or grassroots criticism that views World Bank "policy-based lending" as an assault on social infrastructure and bank-supported development projects as destructive of natural environments and indigenous communities. The tone of criticism from the left side of the political spectrum is illustrated by the following: "The World Bank is perhaps the most important instrument of the developed capitalist countries for prying state control of its Third World member countries out of the hands of nationalists and socialists who would regulate international capital's inroads and turning that power to the service of international capital. The United States government, as the largest shareholder in the Bank and contributor to IDA, has always been able to control the direction of its lending."[106]

A review of the evolution of World Bank lending policy lends little support to the exaggerated rhetoric or the scholarly pretensions of the critics from either the Right or the Left.[107] But the convergence of criticism from the Left and the Right, including that of the environmental community, serves as a reminder that the political spectrum should be diagrammed as a full rather than a half circle.

Professional Influence

In his opening remarks at the July 1944 Bretton Woods conference, Lord Keynes noted that the draft document being considered by the conference was due "primarily to the initiative and ability of the United States Treasury."[108] Harry Dexter White, advisor to Secretary of the Treasury Henry Morgenthau, was the central figure in drafting the initial proposals. Emelio Collado and members of his staff at the State Department Division of Financial and Monetary Affairs contributed to a revised proposal. The predominant role of the Treasury bureaucracy in U.S. policy toward the multilateral banks has continued. It is doubtful, however, that any American professional, outside of the Treasury bureaucracy, has made an identifiable contribution to U.S. policy toward the MDBs.

This is not to argue that research and policy analysis by American professionals, primarily economists, have not had an important role in framing the concepts that have informed both bilateral and multilateral assistance policy. Hollis Chenery and a series of collaborators developed and operationalized the "two-gap" model that has been used by both AID and the World Bank to estimate the magnitude of "required" aid flows. Professor Theodore W. Schultz and his students have been influential in persuading the development assistance agencies of the high rates of return to be realized from investments in agricultural research and in human capital development. Research by Bella Balassa, Anne O. Krueger, Jagdish Bhagwati, and their collaborators provided much of the intellectual and empirical support for the liberal policy reforms urged on the developing countries during the debt crisis of the 1980s. Hollis Chenery, Anne O. Krueger, Stanley Fischer, and Lawrence Summers have occupied the positions of vice president and chief economist of the World Bank. But enumeration of these direct contributions to MDB policy and analysis is quite different from identification of the intellectual or professional sources of U.S. policy toward the MDBs.[109]

Has U.S. Policy Influenced the Multilateral Development Banks?

In this concluding section, I return to the question of how much influence the United States really has over MDB policy or operations. The U.S. Treasury's practice of carefully monitoring the MDB loan review process, studying prospective loans in detail, and pursuing issues of concern during the early part of the review does at least create a presumption that the United States attempts to influence MDB lending activity. Furthermore, the MDBs have in the past followed agendas quite similar to the agendas of the U.S. bilateral assistance agencies. When the United States emphasized basic human needs, the MDBs followed; when the United States emphasized policy-based lending, the MDBs followed; when the United States became concerned about environmental issues, the MDBs followed.

This conclusion is not shared, however, by the critics of MDBs. As noted above, critics from the Right believe that the policies pursued by the MDBs have been subversive of U.S. interests, whereas critics from the Left assert that the United States has always been able to bend MDB lending policies to its own economic and political interests. The author of a Heritage Foundation "scorecard" on World Bank lending during the 1980s found that, during 1983–87, the bank regularly ignored U.S. interests: "74 loans of the World Bank which the U.S. has opposed through either abstention or voting 'no,' nonetheless were approved by the bank."[110] In contrast, Robert L. Ayres has argued, based on the 20 largest recipients of World Bank loans, that the bank and IDA have loaned the bulk of their resources to countries highly important to America's geopolitical and geostrategic interests. The list of these World Bank (IDA) borrowers reads like a "who's who of development countries" in terms of their historical and contemporary importance to American foreign policy interests. Writing in 1986 and referring specifically to the World Bank, Richard E. Feinberg noted that U.S. influence "is built on much more than U.S. voting power and its ability to nominate the President. Many factors guarantee that American options will be heard: the Bank's location in Washington, in shouting distance of the U.S. Treasury Department; the strength and attentiveness of the U.S. Executive Director's Office; the use of English as the Bank's official language; and the fact that Americans account for one-quarter of the higher level professional staff, as well as senior management."[111]

The official Treasury position on U.S. influence reflects a structural view. In testimony before the Senate Committee on Appropriations in 1988, James W. Conrow, deputy assistant secretary for developing nations, pointed out that there is a real difference in the ability of the U.S. government to influence IADB and ADB policy. In the ADB, a combination of nonregional donors and the regional nonborrowing countries have majority ownership of the institution. In the case of the AfDB, two-thirds of the shares are owned by the African member countries. Conrow noted that there was a great deal of concern, when membership was opened to non-African countries in 1983, that "we would come in and try to turn the institution immediately into a World Bank or an IMF."[112]

The only two reasonably careful quantitative analyses of which I am aware suggest a cautious assessment of the influence of U.S. interests on World Bank policy. In a 1981 University of Pennsylvania Ph.D. thesis, Michael E. Akins attempted to determine for 1972–73 whether there was a statistical relationship between U.S. economic and strategic interests and the geographic distribution of IBRD and IDA lending. Four indicators of U.S. interests were used: (1) dependency on U.S. aid, (2) dependency on U.S. trade, (3) U.S. military arms sales, and (4) U.S. military assistance. IDA lending was weakly associated with U.S. aid flows, and IBRD loans were weakly associated with U.S. trade. But there was no association with arms sales or military assistance. Akins interpreted his results as unable to support a conclusion that the United States exercised any meaningful control over the geographic distribution of either IDA or IBRD lending during the period studied.[113]

A second study by Stephen D. Krasner, also published in 1981, focused on the relationship between U.S. interests, measured in terms of bilateral financial resource transfers and trade, and the lending activities of the IADB and the ADB during 1971–76. Krasner found a weak relationship between IADB lending and U.S. resource transfers, no relationship between U.S. trading interests and IADB transfers, and a negative association between ADB country allocations and U.S. assistance flows. Krasner argued that "in their dogged fixation on communism American policy makers tended to ignore specific interests."[114]

The policies pursued by the MDBs have, however, generally been consistent with the broader objectives of U.S. policy in advancing a more liberal international economic order. Much of U.S. support for policy-based lending during the 1980s was motivated by a desire to prevent the global debt crisis from inducing a reversal of the trend toward liberalization. There is little basis, however, for criticisms that the United States has been successful, or has even attempted in a very serious manner, to bend MDB policies to favor U.S. economic interests. Congress, as Asher and Mason suggested, has used the replenishment process to attempt to exert more direct influence on MDB policies and projects. It has been successful in pressing the administration to negotiate reductions in the U.S. share of IDA replenishments. It has also occasionally been successful in reducing or stretching out the term of MDB soft-loan replenishments.

There can be little question that the emergence of the soft-loan windows, and the periodic need to replenish the funds that support the soft loans, has contributed to widening of the political debates within the administration about MDB policy, has expanded the opportunity for Congress to attempt to influence U.S. policy toward the MDBs, and has contributed to a more active effort on the part of domestic interest groups and constituencies to influence policy toward the MDBs through their access to the administration and Congress. The Treasury monopoly on administration policy toward the MDBs has been weakened. AID has at times exerted pressure to achieve greater consistency between MDB lending and U.S. development assistance priorities. During the first Reagan administration, Treasury itself, under pressure from the conservative wing of the Republican party to assume a more critical role in policy toward the MDBs, found its efforts countered by Secretary of State Alexander Haig, Jr.

Among the several domestic interest groups, environmental groups have been particularly successful, since the mid-1980s, in their efforts to exert pressure on MDB policies and projects through their access to the administration and Congress. The extent of their influence must, however, be evaluated against the background of emerging environmental problems that were becoming increasingly apparent to the engineers, agronomists, and economists who inhabit the MDB bureaucracies.

Nevertheless, their successes carry important implications for the future. Mason and Asher identified the establishment of IDA as providing the lever for increased politicization of the World Bank by member governments. In my judgment the success of U.S. environmental interests in complementing their own MDB policy agendas by mobilizing both developed and developing country interest groups against MDB projects will, in the future, be viewed as a second major event in the politicization of MDB policy or, depending on one's perspective, making MDB policy and project lending more responsible to public interests. The success of the environmental interest groups is important because it is the first time that public interest groups or constituencies outside of member government executive agencies or legislative bodies have successfully mounted a substantial challenge to MDB policies and projects.

Chapter 12

Policy toward the Specialized Agencies and Voluntary Programs of the United Nations

The U.N. system of international organization[1] that emerged after 1945 was "the product of American idealism, imagination, and political creativity."[2] The United States acted as host to the July 1945 U.N. organizing conference in San Francisco. For the half century since 1945, it has been official policy of the United States to support the United Nations and its specialized agencies and voluntary programs. The United Nations has also received broad support from the general public and from the mass media.

But U.S. policy toward the United Nations has often been held hostage to the exaggerated expectations of both its advocates and its opponents. Many liberals have been disappointed that the United Nations has not been able to play a more decisive role in the resolution of conflicts among states and the alleviation of poverty in poor countries. Many conservatives have viewed the United Nations as an unacceptable infringement on U.S. national sovereignty and as "antagonistic to the U.S., the West and the free enterprise system."[3]

There have also been continuing differences within the U.S. government on U.S. policy toward the U.N. system. Prior to the 1945 organizing conference, the State and Treasury departments held quite different views on how postwar economic and social issues should be addressed. The State Department wanted to see a comprehensive approach to relief and reconstruction issues. The Treasury preferred to address individual technical issues, such as exchange rate stabilization and reconstruction, separately from broader political arrangements.

Among proponents of development assistance, particularly within the academic community and among aid activists, there is often a view that multilateral assistance is a more desirable form of aid than bilateral assistance. It is often argued that bilateral assistance suffers from domination by political, security, and other nondevelopment interests. In contrast, it is often argued that multilateral assistance is more responsive to recipient needs and is governed by more objective criteria. On the other hand, supporters of U.S. bilateral assistance have argued that the technical competence of the U.S. bilateral agencies has been higher than that of the U.N. agencies.[4]

The purpose of this chapter is to review the evolution of U.S. policy toward the U.N. agencies and programs most directly involved in development assistance. These include four specialized agencies—the Food and Agriculture Organization (FAO); the International Labor Organization (ILO); the Educational, Scientific and Cultural Organization (UNESCO); and the World Health Organization (WHO). They also include three voluntary programs—the United Nations Development Programme (UNDP), the United Nations Children's Fund (UNICEF), and the United Nations Environmental Program (UNEP). The primary focus of my interest is in the domestic sources of U.S. policy toward the development activities of the U.N. programs and agencies. U.S. policy has, however, often reflected concerns about the effectiveness of the agencies for the promotion of U.S. economic and political interests.

I have not been able, in this chapter, to give specific attention to several other agencies and programs whose activities are, at least in part, supportive of economic development.[5] These include the High Commissioner for Refugees (UNHCR), the Industrial Development Organization (UNIDO), and several others. The work of the World Food Program and the International Fund for Agricultural Development is referred to in Chapter 8. I do not, in this chapter, give specific attention to the more generalized development policy debates, such as those within the United Nations Conference on Trade and Development (UNCTAD) beginning in the mid-1960s about a new international economic order—designed to stabilize primary raw material and commodity prices, promote the transfer of technology on more favorable terms, expand the flow of financial resources on concessional terms, regulate the activities of transnational corporations, and reform the international system. Nor do I give explicit attention to the work of the Department of Economic and Social Affairs (ESA) or to agencies such as the regional economic commissions (for Europe, Asia and the Pacific, Latin America, Africa, and Western Asia). Although these organizations are concerned primarily with regional economic cooperation, statistical reporting, and analysis, they have had, at times, important effects on development policy.[6]

In attempting to understand U.S. policy toward the U.N. system, I have been somewhat surprised at how little assistance I have found in the literature on international organizations.[7] Political scientists have tended to view the nation-states as the dominant actors and the international organizations as agents with little independent power or initiative. Organization sociology has viewed international organizations as actors capable of pursuing their own independent objectives. I find both views useful in attempting to understand the tensions that have arisen between the United States and the several U.N. specialized agencies and programs. But neither view is fully consistent with the policy formation process. Policy toward each of the agencies and programs is often made by special interests within the bureaucracy in association with nongovernmental interest groups that have only a tenuous relationship with each other or with the foreign policy process. The process of policy formation toward the International Labor Organization, for example, typically includes officials of the AFL-CIO, the U.S. Chamber of Commerce, and other employer organizations. The process of policy formation toward the Food and Agriculture Organization involves officials in the departments of Agriculture and State, as well as the officers of major farm and commodity organizations and the agriculture business community.

I also find that both functionalist and realist perspectives are useful in attempting to understand the process of policy formation toward the agencies and programs. The emergence of the U.N. specialized agencies reflected, at least implicitly, a functional theory of international organization. The functionalist view starts with the position that certain tasks for which governments have responsibility cannot be effectively provided within the territorial boundaries of the individual nations. Functionalists go on to argue that it is possible to decouple cooperation among nations around mutual technical, humanitarian, and economic concerns from the more overtly political disputes among nations. Realists, in contrast, would argue, to paraphrase Mark Imber, "that an expectation that politicization in even a highly technical agency could be avoided is excessively naive—the discovery of politicization in the United Nations or one of its specialized agencies is rather like discovering gambling in a casino."[8] Commitment to an idealized functionalist perspective has, however, provided a rationale for frequent U.S. charges of politicization in the specialized agencies and programs. Imber has argued that these charges, and U.S. withdrawal from the ILO and UNESCO, represent a challenge to functionalist theory. It is clear, however, that those agencies whose functions have been primarily scientific or technical, such as WHO, have been freer of criticism on the grounds of politicization, while those whose activities have impinged more directly on areas of domestic political debate have received the greatest criticism.

The Specialized Agencies and Voluntary Programs

The U.N. agencies created or brought into the U.N. network in the immediate post–World War II era each addressed a specific interwar or war-related problem. Some were expected to disband after a short period, as in the case of the United Nations Relief and Rehabilitation Agency and the United Nations Children's Fund. Others were given broader mandates and the status of a permanent agency, as in the case of the Food and Agriculture Organization, the United Nations Educational, Scientific and Cultural Organization, the International Labor Organization, and the World Health Organization. In the initial debates about the form and functions of the U.N. system, development assistance received little attention. Nevertheless, the organization and support of the specialized agencies and programs reflected recognition of a need to address economic and social as well as political issues through intergovernmental collaboration.[9]

The U.N. system currently includes 16 specialized agencies and 23 voluntary programs and funds. Each specialized agency is headed by a director-general elected by its own governing body, whereas each voluntary program or fund is headed by an under-secretary-general elected by the U.N. General Assembly upon the recommendation of the secretary-general. (In the case of UNICEF, an executive-general is appointed by the secretary-general, with the advice of the UNICEF Executive Board.) The specialized agencies were established as autonomous bodies. They are responsible to their own governing bodies rather than to the U.N. Economic and Social Council. The agencies do report to and consult with the United Nations in the preparation of budgets and transmit the budgets for review by the General Assembly. There were major disagreements at the meetings of the Preparatory Commission of the United Nations between those who favored greater control by the United Nations of international economic and social activities and those who supported decentralization and almost complete independence on the part of the specialized agencies. Those favoring decentralization prevailed. This has been a central issue in the periodic efforts to reform the U.N. development system.

Although the U.N. multilateral lending institutions—the International Bank for Reconstruction and Development, the International Monetary Fund, the International Development Association, and the International Finance Corporation—are technically specialized agencies, they are governed quite differently than the other specialized agencies and are not commonly referred to as *specialized agencies* (Chap. 11). The International Fund for Agricultural Development is a specialized agency, although its contributions are voluntary rather than assessed.

The voluntary programs clearly have less autonomy within the U.N. system. An even more important difference is in the way they are financed. The specialized agencies receive contributions based on U.N. assessments which, once established, obligate the member nation to a fixed percentage contribution of the budget as approved by the organization. In addition to their regular or assessed budgets, the specialized agencies may also raise supplementary voluntary funds for special purposes and development assistance. Some voluntary programs or funds (UNDP, WFP, UNICEF, UNHCR) hold periodic pledging conferences at which states declare their level of contribution for the specified time period; others, such as UNEP, work directly with individual donor agencies.

In fiscal year 1991 the United States contributed $291 million to the budgets of the specialized agencies and programs discussed in this chapter.[10]

The Issue of Arrears

Criticism of the United Nations by the U.S. government during the Reagan administration was particularly vigorous. The United States withdrew from UNESCO in 1984. During the 1980s the United States also delayed or withheld its assessed contributions to the ILO and several other U.N. agencies. Because arrears have been used to attempt to influence policy in a number of agencies, the issue is discussed here before the discussion of U.S. policy toward specific agencies or programs.

There are several ways to withhold assessed contributions from U.N. agencies. *Withholdings* are sums deliberately withheld from a member's assessed contributions as a matter of announced policy and are technically illegal. *Delayed payments* are payments that are staggered or phased within the permitted guidelines.[11] Once the payments are outside the required time period, they are referred to as *arrears.* Arrears are usually followed by a loss of voting rights after some finite period (usually two years).

During the 1980s both Congress and the administration adopted a strategy of general withholdings to induce budgetary reforms in the U.N. General Assembly and the specialized agencies.[12] In 1985 Congress enacted the Kassebaum-Solomon amendment, which limited U.S. contributions to the assessed budgets of the United Nations and its specialized agencies to 20 percent of the agencies' budgets after October 1986. This condition was to be lifted only after the particular U.N. agency had adopted procedures so that voting rights on budgetary matters would be proportional to contributions. The United Nations attempted to respond to U.S. concerns through a General Assembly resolution of 18 December 1986.[13] The resolution was a compromise whereby the United States and major donors were to be consulted in the year when a budget was not presented for adoption about both the programs and the budget for the upcoming biennium, and decisions about budget would be taken on the basis of a consensus in the Committee for Programme and Coordination (CPC) before being considered in the plenary session of the General Assembly.

Secretary of State Shultz pointed out that the administration opposed the withholding provisions but that Congress passed the measure because the United Nations and its specialized agencies had not "paid sufficient attention in the development of their budgets to the views of member governments who are major financial contributors to those budgets."[14] The Kassebaum-Solomon amendment was revised in 1987 to reflect the movement toward consensus-based budgeting. However, Assistant Secretary for International Organizations Richard Williamson suggested to the House Foreign Affairs Committee that underpayment had become official U.S. policy toward the U.N. agencies.[15] The United States adopted guidelines as of 23 February 1988 that were more reflective of budgetary concern than policy reform. The guidelines listed four categories of institutions: (1) a group that would receive full funding at all times (NATO and ITO); (2) institutions that had changed their budget procedures and would normally be fully funded [OECD, GATT, International Atomic Energy Agency (IAEA), WHO, and International Civil Aviation Organization (ICAO)]; (3) a less deserving group that would be funded at 85 percent of their assessment (OAS, the Pan American Health Organization [PAHO], ILO, UNIDO); and (4) "less responsive" organizations that would receive only 75 percent of the assessed amount (FAO). FAO was singled out because it continued to be the only agency not to adopt consensus-based budgeting.

The Balanced Budget and Emergency Deficit Control Act of 1985 (Gramm-Rudman-Hollings act) also had important implications for the funding of the United Nations and its specialized agencies. If the president's budget did not meet the legislation's deficit ceilings and zero budget growth targets, automatic spending reductions would be triggered. The legislation required most U.S. nondefense agencies to sustain a 4.3 percent "sequestration." In 1986 the 4.3 percent sequestration resulted in $18 million being withheld from the U.N. agencies.[16] Negotiations on the legislation, known as the budget summit compromise of 1987, limited the growth of the 1989 Department of State budget to 2 percent. This also led to an appropriations shortfall for U.N. agencies in 1989.

Two other legislative restrictions resulted in the withholding of $7.8 million from the United Nations in fiscal years 1985 and 1987.[17] From 1987 to 1989 the administration withheld $38 million in tax equalization adjustments.

These adjustments reflect the difference between what the United States believes that the United Nations should reimburse American employees for U.S. taxes and the amount that the United Nations budgets and assesses the United States for this purpose. Other methods have recently been instituted to promote budget austerity, including legislatively mandated withholdings to fund the war on drugs. The United States has also withheld funds for specific activities to which it has objected. From 1980 to 1989, the United States withheld $15 million as its proportionate share of costs related to specific U.N. activities, such as those that provided support for the Palestine Liberation Organization or the South West Africa People's Organization.[18]

U.S. withholdings grew from $9 million in 1985 to over $590 million by 1991. Of the total arrearages accumulated to international organizations and peacekeeping forces by November 1989, over 75 percent was owed to seven U.N. agencies—the United Nations, FAO, ILO, WHO, ICAO, UNIDO, and WHO. The Reagan administration had proposed to Congress a plan that would achieve full payment of assessments in five annual installments. The first payment was made in 1991, and payments should be completed in 1995.[19]

The United Nations Development Programme

Before proceeding to a discussion of the several specialized agencies and voluntary programs, it will be useful to review the developments that led to the establishment of the United Nations Development Programme. UNDP is a voluntary fund created in 1966 by a merger of the United Nations' Expanded Program of Technical Assistance (EPTA) and the Special Fund. It was established to become the central financing and coordinating authority of the United Nations for technical assistance activities.[20]

UNDP's New York–based Secretariat is headed by an administrator who has traditionally been an American national. A governing council of 48 states—21 members from developed countries and 27 from developing countries—meets once a year to act as a policy-making body on operating policies, programs, and budgets. The Governing Council is elected by the Economic and Social Council. The organization is mandated to provide systematic and sustained assistance in fields essential to the technical, economic, and social development of countries.

UNDP Predecessor Programs

At the end of World War II, there was no doubt that a massive reconstruction effort had to be undertaken. Much of the post–World War II relief and reconstruction responsibilities were assumed by the United Nations Relief and Rehabilitation Agency. The agency's responsibilities were redistributed after 1946 to various U.N. agencies with particular expertise. The agencies that took over specialized functions were expected to carry on what were seen as nonpolitical activities of technical assistance and relief.

An Expanded Program of Technical Assistance was created in 1949 to provide funds not available through the regular U.N. budget to carry out short-term, small-scale, and low-capital-input projects under its chairman, David Owen. There was a desire, particularly on the part of less developed countries, to expand EPTA so that it could supply capital investment as well as technical assistance. This led to a proposal for a capital development fund, the Special United Nations Fund for Economic Development. The United States and other developed countries resisted the proposal, but the debate continued until a compromise was reached through the creation of the Special Fund in 1958. The Special Fund carried out preinvestment activities and, like the EPTA, provided experts and fellowships. Its projects generally were larger in scale, were longer in term, and included more capital inputs.[21] An American, Paul Hoffman, was chosen by the secretary-general to be the managing director (Table B.1).

During the 1950s and early 1960s, resources and activities expanded rapidly. More and more countries requested EPTA and Special Fund assistance. There was a generally recognized view that U.N. development activities needed to be better coordinated. The specialized agencies were becoming increasingly involved in development assistance. A merger of EPTA and the Special Fund in 1966 into the United Nations Development Programme was expected to improve coordination and financing.

The Jackson and Pearson Reports

The merger of the EPTA and the Special Fund to form the UNDP did not, however, achieve instant improvement in performance. The program was characterized by extended delays at almost every phase of the project cycle—from project formulation and implementation to evaluation and follow-up. There was concern that the preinvestment and technical assistance activities consisted of a series of unrelated projects that reflected the narrow interests of the sectoral ministries rather then a comprehensive assessment of national priorities.

In 1968, the United Nations commissioned a study on the capacity of the United Nations' development system.[22] The report was to examine how effectively and efficiently the system used its funds and to determine how it might be able to handle a doubling of funds. During virtually the same period, a second study (the Pearson report) was financed by the World Bank in an attempt to determine the effectiveness of all multilateral development assistance and to suggest improvements.[23]

The Jackson report characterized the U.N. development system as lacking in central direction—"For many years I have looked for the 'brain' which guides the policies and operations of the U.N. development system. The search has been in vain."[24] One of the main recommendations of the report was that the U.N. central administration should be strengthened to improve effectiveness. The position of administrator of UNDP should be given increased authority, and the administrator's appointment should be made by the General Assembly, thus raising his or her authority relative to that of the specialized agency directors-general. More effective support for development assistance could be achieved by centralizing the budgets of all of the specialized agencies (excluding IBRD and the IMF) and by vesting coordination control in ECOSOC. The report suggested that the proposed reforms could be achieved without any amendments to the U.N. charter or the constitutions of any agencies. The Jackson report urged improvement in accountability through centralized financing through UNDP but at the same time sought to improve planning through maximum decentralization to the field level. Indicative planning should be arrived at in conjunction with government ministries at the country level.

As a result of the report, country-wide indicative planning guides were established to bring more continuity to the system. A position of director-general of development was established. UNDP resident representatives were assigned to work with recipient governments to prepare longer-term development plans, which were submitted to the Governing Council for approval. U.N. specialized agencies were to be represented in the host country through the UNDP representative. Critics have contended that one effect of indicative planning was to introduce intense competition within UNDP over long-term budget allocations. Some donors, particularly the United States, were concerned that indicative planning also weakened donor control over budget allocation and growth.

The reforms were viewed by the specialized agencies as a threat to their independence. The specialized agencies regard themselves as responsible to their governing bodies rather than to the United Nations. Their elected heads outrank the appointed head of UNDP. In the United States, the U.S. Department of Agriculture favored direct funding and the State Department favored centralized funding through UNDP for technical assistance activities. In the 1970s the FAO, under Director-General Saouma, reintroduced FAO resident representatives, thus reversing the decision of former Director-General Sen to put FAO representation under the direction of the UNDP representative.

Donors sometimes viewed contributions made through UNDP as characterized by excessive overhead in contrast to contributions directly to the specialized agencies. The specialized agencies maintained their ability to raise funds and establish extrabudgetary sources of funding for their projects. The United States lent verbal support, but little financial support, to the proposals for strengthening the UNDP advanced in the Jackson report. U.S. contributions to UNDP have declined in real terms from the 1970s to the early 1980s.

The Commission on International Development (the Pearson commission) was established in 1968 by the World Bank to evaluate the performance of the multilateral development assistance institutions and to make recommendations on how the system could become effective. The commission was headed by former Canadian Prime Minister Lester Pearson. The preface to its report noted that the "climate surrounding foreign aid programs is heavy with disillusion and distrust."[25] The report argued that development assistance needed a clearer purpose and greater coherence. The volume of aid should be increased. Its administration should be made more effective, and aid should not be tied to purchases in the home country. Technical assistance needed to be redirected because it had not been adequately integrated with capital assistance. Debt and population growth were also identified as areas of concern. The report called for the revitalization of aid to education and research and for an increasing share of aid to be channeled through multilateral sources. It also stressed the creation of a framework for free and equitable trade and the promotion of "mutually beneficial" flows of foreign private investment.

The report of the Pearson committee was interpreted as forming a basis for increased funding for assistance channeled through the multinational banks relative to the UNDP. The World Bank, IMF, IDA, and IFC system had the capacity for concessional aid, through the International Development Association, lacked by the United Nations–administered system. The United States seemed to have a clear preference for the recommendations of the Pearson commission rather than those of the Jackson commission. This preference reflected U.S. concern that increasing U.N. and specialized agency membership affected U.S. influence in the agencies. As early as 1971 Congress was calling for voting reform to strengthen the hand of the United States, a strengthening of ECOSOC, and a weakening of the specialized agencies.[26]

A 1978 restructuring resolution adopted by the General Assembly attempted to wrest control from the specialized agencies through the appointment of a director-general for development and international cooperation by the secretary-general of the United Nations. The measure also included the appointment of resident coordinator at the country level. However, once again the executing agencies remained "too strong" because they maintained their ability to govern their budgets.[27]

UNDP, 1966–1992

The publication of the Jackson and Pearson reports coincided with President Nixon's emphasis on multilateral relative to bilateral assistance. An implication of the Nixon Doctrine was that multilateral lending institutions would become the primary channel for development assistance. In this way, the United States could promote the defense and development of allies and friends without being responsible for the complete design and execution of all such programs (Chaps. 6 and 11). In essence, the Pearson report of 1967 paved the way for the World Bank to play an expanded role in multilateral assistance. Already in 1967, 60 percent of gross disbursements of the multilateral agencies were accounted for by the World Bank and its affiliates.[28]

It will become even more clear in subsequent sections that one effect of declining U.S. support for UNDP was a successful search by the specialized agencies for new funding sources for technical assistance. Despite declining resources available through the UNDP, the specialized agencies were able to expand their activities through supplementary funding for special projects and programs provided by individual donor countries. The effect of U.S. policy was to increase the independence of the specialized agencies rather than to enhance coordination.

During the 1980s U.S. contributions to UNDP continued to decline in real terms as nominal increases in contributions were more than offset by inflation. Other countries' contributions continued to grow more rapidly than U.S. contributions, and the U.S. share of the UNDP budget fell to only about 15 percent by 1981.[29] By 1990 the United States was contributing barely 10 percent of the voluntary funds available to UNDP. During this same period the U.S. assessed contributions to several of the specialized agencies and voluntary programs experienced significant growth in real terms. Those increases have usually been resisted by the United States. But, since the specialized agencies do not have weighted voting systems like the multilateral lending banks, the United States had little leverage until it adopted a policy of withholding assessed contributions to resist budget growth.

The decline in U.S. support for U.N. programs during the 1980s was not sufficient to quiet conservative critics. One focus of criticism has been the performance of the UNDP, and the U.N. system more generally, in the area of development assistance. In a study for the Heritage Foundation, Erikson and Sumner argue that U.N. development assistance is so small and ineffective relative to total assistance flows that its demise would not be noticed. A second focus is that UNDP has been part of a socialist conspiracy. Because the UNDP projects "seek to be ecologically sound, self-sustaining and equitable in their distribution of resources and opportunities, they are socialist by design." Christopher Whalen warned that debt forgiveness is secretly in the works for developing countries and that Maggie Thatcher would make a wonderful candidate to replace Perez de Cuellar as U.N. secretary-general.[30]

Whelan's criticisms were echoed in a November 1991 article by Amity Shales in the *Wall Street Journal*. Shales was particularly critical of the State Department for not putting forward a candidate for U.N. secretary-general. In her view the United Nations has an agenda that runs counter to U.S. interests. The unsuccessful Polish candidate for secretary-general, Kryzsztov Skubiszewski, would have better served U.S. interests. "His current task, cleaning his foreign service of communists, has given him experience that could prove useful in undertaking reform at the U.N."[31]

Summary

The UNDP has not become the major coordinating and financing agency visualized when it was established in 1966. The resources available to the UNDP have declined in real terms since the 1970s. Specialized agency regular budgets and extrabudgetary resources combined have exceeded the UNDP's resources since 1982.[32] Several factors help to explain why UNDP has failed to become an effective financing and coordinating authority. One is the rise of the multilateral development banks. A second is unwillingness on the part of the United States to concentrate multilateral funding in UNDP. A third is resistance on the part of the specialized agencies to giving up their budget authority. A fourth was the inability of the UNDP to articulate an intellectually compelling doctrine for its assistance efforts. The initiation of an annual *Human Development Report* in 1991 is viewed by some observers as a successful attempt to stake out an intellectual foundation for a more coherent UNDP program focus.[33]

As the specialized agencies and voluntary programs have become less dependent on the UNDP, there has been an increasing tendency for the UNDP to utilize its own Office for Project Services (OPS) to implement projects in developing countries.[34] This has been viewed with a good deal of concern by the specialized agencies because, in their interpretation, the UNDP does not have a mandate to provide technical assistance—only to coordinate technical assistance among the agencies. In the early 1990s there was considerable pressure to remove the OPS from UNDP.

The Food and Agriculture Organization

The FAO is the largest and among the most highly regarded of the U.N. specialized agencies and voluntary programs.[35] FAO's activities can be grouped into three broad categories: (1) international consultation and dialogue on issues of agricultural development and food policy; (2) the collection, analysis, and dissemination of information and data on food, agriculture, and rural affairs; and (3) technical assistance and training for developing countries on a wide range of food and agricultural development activities.

The FAO plenary body, the Conference, elects the director-general, as well as the 49-member Governing Council. The Conference meets biennially while the council acts on policy and the program between conferences. For the 1992–93 biennium the approved Programme of Work, on an annual basis, was $338.5 million, of which $317.3 million was assessed contributions. The United States contributed 33.3 percent of the assessed contributions prior to 1 January 1974, when U.S. legislation (PL 92-544) placed a 25 percent limitation on the U.S. contribution.[36]

Establishing the FAO

Efforts to establish an international organization concerned with food and agriculture extend back well before World War II. In the mid-1930s Stanley Bruce, the prime minister of Australia, had urged the League of Nations to consider the linkages between nutrition, agriculture, and public health. Similar ideas were advanced during the war, particularly by the British nutritionist John Boyd Orr and by Frank McDougall, economic advisor to the Australian mission to the League of Nations.[37]

President Roosevelt offered to convene a conference in Hot Springs, Virginia (18 May to 3 June 1943) to explore the proposal. John Boyd Orr was not asked to attend the conference as a British delegate because his views on world food policy differed too strongly from those of the British government. Two groups emerged at the conference, one that wanted to create a strong organization to increase world production with stabilized prices and another that sought to limit the organization to fact finding and advisory work. Boyd Orr was greatly disappointed when the conference recommended an organization that would limit its activities to the collection of statistics, promotion of research, and technical assistance.[38]

The conference recognized the need for international cooperation to increase world agricultural production, provide technical assistance to member governments, assure sufficient food supplies, and enhance food consumption. But it did not act on these concerns! The United States was among those who sought a restricted scope of work and budget. A budget of $5 million per year was a compromise between two extremes ranging from $1–1.5 million to $10 million. The conference chose an interim commission, chaired by L. B. Pearson of Canada, to draw up a constitution for the U.N. Food and Agriculture Organization.[39]

A second conference was held in Quebec, at the same time as the U.N. organization meeting in San Francisco, in late 1945. John Boyd Orr attended the conference as an advisor to the British delegation. His disdain for research is evident in his comments on the conference: "No research was needed to find out that half the people in the world lacked sufficient food for health, or that with modern engineering and agricultural science the world food supply could be easily increased to meet human needs."[40]

Despite his reservations about the FAO mission, the Quebec Conference resulted in the appointment of John Boyd Orr as the first director-general of the FAO (Table B.2). His lifelong dream was to alleviate hunger through the establishment of a World Food Board with the authority and funds to stabilize world food markets. Boyd Orr, knowing the resistance that awaited his program, reluctantly accepted the appointment. He assumed the office with a commitment to work to expand FAO's activities and authority.[41]

Advice and Technical Assistance, 1945–1970

During his term (1945–47), John Boyd Orr tried, without success, to advance his proposal to establish a World Food Board with the capacity to (1) stabilize world agricultural prices, (2) manage an international food grains reserve, (3) fund agricultural surpluses to be sold on concessionary terms to underprivileged countries, and (4) cooperate with other organizations responsible for assigning agricultural and industrial development loans and formulating international trade policy.[42]

Boyd Orr moved rapidly to set up a strong Economics Division to work on commodity policy issues. Plans for the World Food Board were delayed as FAO got caught up in efforts to relieve postwar food shortages. The United States took the position that it would not offer financial support for a World Food Board. Both Britain and the United States indicated that they believed that the International Trade Organization being discussed at the time would be the more competent body to address these matters. The American position was influenced by an assumption that it would be called on to bear most of the cost of any world food policy. The British government feared that guaranteeing producer incomes would threaten their economy, which was based on the importation of food on very favorable terms. Despite support on the part of France, Austria, Poland, Greece, and a number of food deficit countries, the world food reserve and price stabilization proposals failed primarily because the American delegate insisted that the United States and the other powers would not provide the organization with the funds or authority to establish a World Food Board.[43]

Boyd Orr was succeeded by directors-general with much less ambitious agendas. Norris Dodd (1948–54) had been U.S. under-secretary of agriculture. He set about repairing what he, and others, regarded as Boyd Orr's rather casual approach to management. Dodd was followed by Philip Cardon (1954–56), who had served as head of the USDA Agricultural Research Administration. Cardon found himself unable to cope with the complex administrative and political problems he faced within the FAO organization and with member governments. He resigned after two years.[44]

By the early 1950s the FAO had initiated an active program of (*a*) survey missions in support of agricultural project development; (*b*) the collection and publication of statistical, technical, and economic information; (*c*) the organization of commodity advisory groups, such as the International Rice Commission and the International Wheat Commission under a committee on commodity problems; and (*d*) liaison with member country agricultural leaders. Technical assistance funded through the regular budget had been provided to Greece, Nicaragua, Poland, and Thailand, and assistance funded through UNRRA had been given to nine other countries.[45] During the mid-1950s, field activities expanded rapidly. Funds roughly equivalent to FAO's regular budget were made available through the Expanded Program of Technical Assistance, a forerunner to UNDP. FAO technical assistance activities were characterized by a strong technology transfer or extension bias. Little attention was given to strengthening agricultural research capacity in recipient countries. A major accomplishment during the mid-1950s was the development of guidelines for the disposal of agricultural surpluses (Chap. 8). The fact that the surplus disposal guidelines were adopted, whereas the earlier proposals for a World Food Board and an International Commodity Clearing House had been rejected, suggests the outer limits of agricultural commodity coordination that the major food-exporting countries, particularly the United States, were willing to accept.

The appointment of FAO's fourth director-general, Binay Ranjan Sen (1957–66), was characterized by a rapid expansion of membership of newly independent states and by a substantial broadening of the FAO program. Sen came to the FAO with wide diplomatic experience after a distinguished career in food administration in India. Under Sen the FAO continued its constitutionally mandated duties through the regular budget while simultaneously attempting to expand its development project activities through extrabudgetary sources. The U.N. Special Fund, created in 1959, permitted the rapid growth of FAO field activities.[46] Sen put the FAO country representatives under the direction of the U.N. resident representatives and used the savings, along with funds from the U.N. Special Fund, to expand FAO's field staff. World Bank/FAO cooperation on preinvestment studies started in 1964.

Sen also embarked on an aggressive campaign to alert the world to the problem of hunger. A principle vehicle was the Freedom from Hunger Campaign, initiated in 1959.[47] The campaign began with a World Food Survey to document the extent of hunger. The study, completed in 1962, estimated the number of undernourished at some 200 million to 300 million people. It documented geographically where consumption exceeded FAO standards and where supply fell short of the standards. The World Food Congress, held in Washington, D.C., in June 1963, was the highlight of the three-year-long public education campaign. Thirteen hundred people, including many representatives from nongovernmental organizations, participated in the congress. The realities of hunger and malnutrition were recognized worldwide.

The Declaration of the World Food Congress urged international cooperation in the broadest terms to alleviate hunger. Many proposals were put forward to address the issues of hunger, but no plan of action was adopted. Despite the vague nature of the declaration's pledge to do everything possible to relieve hunger and malnutrition, the Congress chairman, U.S. Secretary of Agriculture Orville Freeman, informed Sen that the terms of the declaration were far too radical and that he would refuse to preside over the session if Sen pressed it.[48] Freeman refused to preside on the final day, when the declaration was adopted by acclamation.

Although the World Food Congress accomplished less than Director-General Sen had hoped, it did contribute to advancing progress on two items that were high on his agenda. One was the establishment of a multilateral World Food Program under the joint oversight of the United Nations and the FAO (see Chap. 8). The second was the preparation of an Indicative World Plan for Agricultural Development that outlined the issues that would confront the global food and agricultural system into the mid-1980s. Sen had put into place at least part of the agenda that John Boyd Orr had advanced in the late 1940s.[49]

It is difficult to characterize U.S. policy toward the FAO before the late 1960s. Although the United States was generally supportive of FAO technical assistance activities, it was critical of attempts to achieve greater coordination of commodity policy activities and opposed the rapid budget increases proposed by Sen. The United States sponsored a 1961 constitutional amendment limiting the term of the director-general to four years plus a possible two-year extension. But it had not formalized a coherent policy toward FAO. A working party chaired by the assistant secretary of agriculture for international affairs was appointed in 1965 to prepare a policy statement of objectives, reflecting the views of U.S. government agencies directly concerned with FAO. The GAO reported in 1969 that a policy statement had not yet been completed and that the available drafts had not ranked FAO programs by priority.[50]

The World Food Crisis

FAO's fourth director-general, Addeke Boerma (1967–75), who had previously served as the Netherlands' commissioner for foreign agricultural relations and as FAO's regional representative for Europe, had the misfortune to preside over the organization during a period of great stress on world food supplies. The indicative World Plan for Agricultural Development, completed in 1969, concluded that agricultural output in the developing countries would have to increase by 4 percent per year during the 1970s if world food needs were to be met. At the time that the report was issued, new high-yielding wheat and rice varieties were beginning to have some success in expanding food production in developing countries. There was considerable optimism that this "green revolution" technology would redress the disequilibrium between food supplies and developing country needs. The FAO did not emphasize research in its own programs because of lack of scientific capacity. But Director-General Boerma strongly supported the FAO role as a co-sponsor (with the World Bank and the UNDP) of the new network of international agricultural research centers being organized under the auspices of the Consultative Group on International Agricultural Research (CGIAR).[51]

During the early 1970s, however, the FAO was forced to confront the challenge of a world food crisis. Adverse weather conditions led to poor harvests, particularly in South Asia, in 1972 and 1973. The drought coincided with U.S. attempts to decrease North American grain surpluses. The United States withheld 40 million acres from production in 1972 and 15 million in 1973. The FAO came under severe criticism on the grounds that it had not anticipated the crisis. A World Food Conference, held under the auspices of the United Nations rather than the FAO, was convened in Rome in December 1974 (Chap. 8).

The World Food Conference witnessed an increasingly acrimonious debate on North-South issues. "The World Food Conference introduced, within the FAO policy bodies, the North-South ideological conflict that was to supersede the agro-technical approach that had pervaded the organization until the late 1960s."[52] The developing countries' share in international trade had declined from 40 percent to 30 percent between 1961–63 and 1970–72. The issue became not just the food crisis, but a discussion of a new international economic order (NIEO) that was designed to correct the unequal terms of trade between the developed and developing countries. The major results of the conference included a commitment to an annual food aid target of 10 million tons, the establishment of a Committee of Food Aid Policies and Programs as the policy guidance body for the World Food Program, the organization of a U.N. World Food Council to provide a forum on world food issues, and the establishment of an independent International Fund for Agricultural Development. The establishment of the council and the fund were, in effect, a vote of no confidence on the FAO and its director-general (Chap. 8).

Revitalization and Controversy, 1976–1992

Boerma was succeeded as director-general in 1976 by Edouard Saouma, a French-trained Lebanese agronomist, who had spent most of his professional career within the FAO—most recently as director of the Land and Water Division. He was elected with strong support by the countries of the Organization for African Unity and the members of the Islamic Conference and the League of Arab States, defeating the Canadian, W. David Hopper, whose candidacy had been advanced by the United States, Great Britain, and Canada.

Saouma set about immediately to attempt to repair FAO's damaged image. He embraced the agenda advanced by the World Food Conference. He instituted a series of internal reforms that sought to (1) reduce headquarters staff, (2) direct the savings to the Technical Cooperation Programme (TCP), and (3) reorient programs toward action rather than research. He also reversed former Director-General Sen's decision to make FAO field staff responsible to the UNDP. This was an agenda with which the U.S. government, particularly the State Department Bureau for International Organizations, was exceedingly uncomfortable.

In the mid-1960s the GAO began to press the administration to develop a statement of policy toward the FAO and the other specialized agencies. A preliminary statement had been developed by 1970. It was not formalized, however, until 1976. The activities that the United States regarded as appropriate for FAO were "(a) stimulating global economic development; (b) increasing national agricultural output through the effective international exchange of scientific and technological information; (c) improving the quality of and availability of global agricultural commodity information, as a basis for planning production and facilitating international trade in agricultural products; and (d) facilitating U.S. participation in international agricultural markets."[53]

The Government Accounting Office commented that U.S. objectives reflected a "traditional" view of FAO that was not really "consistent with the nature of most FAO programs (i.e., development programs) today or the primary thrust of current U.S. foreign aid policy, which seeks to maximize aid to the 'poorest of the poor'." The GAO also noted that emphasis in FAO was shifting from information gathering toward action. "We believe the United States should give recognition to the changing nature of FAO and the statement of objectives should be revised so that the United States will be in a more favorable position to provide appropriate influence, direction and guidance in FAO."[54]

In the same report, the comptroller-general expressed concern about the creation of the Technical Cooperation Programme because it financed its activities through the assessed budget, which departed from U.S. and traditional U.N. policy that such activities be funded through voluntary contributions to UNDP. The report estimated the TCP budget at $18.5 million and noted that the TCP planned to decentralize operations and move more of its staff and decision making to the country level.[55] The United States had grudgingly accepted the creation of the TCP during the July 1967 meeting of the FAO council. Funding the TCP would increasingly become a target for criticism as U.S. anti–United Nations sentiment grew and the United States pushed strongly for a no-growth FAO budget. It called for financing of technical assistance exclusively through voluntary funds and called on the FAO to return to its "original purpose."

Among Saouma's other major initiatives during the late 1970s and early 1980s were a World Conference on Agrarian Reform and Rural Development in 1979, which attempted to give renewed impetus to agrarian reform; the adoption, in 1983, of an International Undertaking on Plant Genetics Resources, which advanced a perspective that plant genetic resources represented "a common heritage of mankind"; the adoption in 1985 of an international code to govern pesticide trade, distribution, and utilization; a 1991 conference on agriculture and the environment, which led to the incorporation of stronger sustainability considerations in the FAO agricultural, forestry, and fisheries programs; and a 1992 international conference on nutrition, which sought to obtain stronger commitments to a cooperative plan of action to assist governments and nongovernmental organizations in nutrition improvement programs.

During the Reagan and Bush administrations, these initiations were often viewed as driven more by the ideological rhetoric of the NIEO than by objective agricultural development considerations. Critics of the FAO and other U.N. agencies received a receptive hearing. The most vocal criticism came from the conservative Washington think tank, the Heritage Foundation. In 1984, the Heritage Foundation published a report criticizing U.S. participation in FAO.[56] Its primary complaints centered on a perceived lack of commitment to the private sector, support for the agenda of the NIEO, and its refusal to criticize inappropriate government policies. Saouma was also criticized for politicization of the personnel system to assure his reelection and for an overly acute sense of his own importance in dealing with member governments. Some governments were particularly upset at his insistence on being granted the courtesies of a head of state when he traveled to their countries.[57]

In early 1988 the ambassador at the U.S. mission to FAO, Fred J. Eckert, forwarded an exceedingly critical "letter of inquiry" to Director-General Saouma raising questions about "pork-barrel allocation of FAO funds and projects designed to assure his 1977 reelection."[58] In the fall of 1989, the FAO incurred additional U.S. displeasure when the council voted support for a program to assist Palestinians in the Israeli-occupied territories with agricultural production. The United States and Israel cast the only dissenting votes.[59] The council also adopted a budget for 1990 and 1991 that called for a 1 percent increase. The United States showed its disapproval with the two actions by paying only $18 million of its $61.4 million assessment for 1989—the minimum necessary to maintain voting rights in the FAO. The United States also warned that continued disregard of its concerns could lead to withdrawal from the FAO.

As recently as October 1990, the House of Representatives held a hearing on U.S. policy toward the Food and Agriculture Organization that focused on the TCP. Representatives Bereuter (R-Nebr.) and Miller (R-Ohio) implied that TCP funds were "confidential/top secret" funds and asked whether they had been used for campaign purposes in the last election for director-general. John Bolton, assistant secretary of state for the Bureau of International Organizations, replied that the allegation was certainly made. Dawson Ahalt, agricultural attache at the U.S. Mission to FAO, followed up with a letter insisting that the fund is not a slush fund. Bolton also implied that the FAO had not been as forthcoming as other U.N. organizations in responding to pressure from the United States and other major donors for improvements in program and budget processes. The FAO was slow to accept zero real (corrected for inflation) budget growth as the path to efficiency and "stands alone" as the only U.N. agency that has not adopted a consensus-based decision-making process on budgetary matters. Bolton was vague, however, about the specific reforms sought by the United States. "I wish I could be more concrete regarding the much needed process of reform in the FAO. But quite frankly it is too early to tell." The ambiguity of Bolton's testimony was reflected in his comments that an external review of the FAO had concluded that "the performance of FAO . . . has been impressive both in terms of the quantity of outputs and their quality." Testimony by Duane Acker, administrator of the USDA Office of International Cooperation and Development, emphasized the importance of FAO programs for U.S. agriculture and its unique capacity to address such international issues as the maintenance of global databases, the monitoring of environmental change, and the coordination of pest control programs.[60]

The 1983 Kassebaum amendment, which required that 20 percent of U.S. assessed contributions should be withheld unless consensus-based budgetary procedures had been adopted, has also affected the U.S. position in the FAO. As of 1990, the United States had reduced its contributions well below the requirement of the Kassebaum amendment, keeping them just high enough to maintain voting rights while hoping that eventually the FAO would agree to its demands—which had never been clearly articulated to the FAO or the other member nations. As of January 1990, the United States owed $192 million to FAO, $70 million of which was the U.N. calendar year 1990 assessed contribution. To maintain voting rights the United States needed to pay $56 million before the end of the year because the FAO charter imposes loss of voting rights for countries more than two years in arrears. Based on the results of the 1990 council meeting, the United States paid the 1990 assessment and participated freely in the budget formulation process for the upcoming biennium. The Programme of Work and the budget for 1992–93 were adopted by the 1991 conference by consensus, and the United States was then (in the 1990s) paying its full assessed contribution and was in the process of paying its arrears.

In spite of initial opposition by the United States and most other Anglophile countries, Saouma was easily reelected director-general for six-year terms in 1981 and 1987. As his third term drew toward a close, there was considerable speculation that Saouma might stand for a fourth term. In early 1993, however, Saouma indicated that he intended to step down at the end of his third term. In November 1993, after intense competition among eight candidates (including four from Europe), Jacques Douf, an agricultural economist who was Senegal's ambassador to the United Nations, was elected to succeed Saouma.

UNESCO and the Triumph of Ideology

The creation of the United Nations Educational, Scientific, and Cultural Organization evolved from a European interest in planning for post–World War II educational and cultural reconstruction. The United States was one of the principal architects of UNESCO, yet almost from the beginning it has been a reluctant supporter. It has repeatedly complained about mismanagement and excessive budgetary expansion. The events leading to U.S. withdrawal in

1984 suggest that the U.S. action was largely a response to ideologically motivated domestic political pressure.[61]

Cooperation in Education, Science, and Culture, 1942–1945

Planning for a transnational organization dedicated to collaboration in the areas of education, science, and culture began in Europe before the end of World War II. Transnational intellectual cooperation organizations already existed in the Paris-based Institut International de Cooperation Intellectuelle (IICI) and the Geneva-based International Bureau of Education (IBE). In 1942 the chairman of the British Council invited the ministers of education from the United Kingdom and eight exile governments of the German occupied countries to meet in London to establish the Conference of Allied Ministers of Education (CAME).[62]

CAME's early focus was on postwar reconstruction in the area of education. However, by the end of 1943, representatives in CAME were expressing the need for a permanent international organization for education. The push for permanency convinced U.S. observers that an intergovernmental organization would be established with or without U.S. participation. The U.S. observers to the conference urged the State Department to seek a more active role. By the time a constitution-drafting conference was organized in London for November 1945, both the U.S. and the French governments had advanced draft constitutions. The mandate that emerged from the conference was for an organization that would "contribute to peace and security by promoting collaboration among nations through education, science and culture."[63] At American insistence the mandate also encompassed collaboration in the area of mass communications.

The UNESCO constitution established three main organs: the Secretariat, headed by the director-general, the General Conference, and the Executive Board. An early debate centered on the strength of the director-general. The U.S. preference for a strong executive head won out.[64] The director-general prepares the draft program and budget, assumes primary responsibility for program execution, and appoints the members of the Secretariat. The Secretariat provides all staff support for the two main UNESCO governing bodies, the General Conference and the Executive Board. The director-general has almost complete control over the organization, since he directs the Secretariat and the Secretariat provides information that serves as a basis for the policy action of the Executive Board and the General Conference. The constitution also provides for a unique feature, the establishment in each member state of a national commission to represent the nongovernmental communities concerned with the fields of competence of the organization.

The UNESCO mandate, to promote "collaboration among nations through education, service and culture," has resulted in a very different style of organization and program than in the other specialized agencies. UNESCO has operated "more in the style of a university than an aid agency."[65] The effects of its many activities have been difficult to identify with great precision. And the controversial nature of many of the issues that fall within its mandate has meant that it could hardly be effective without becoming subject to charges of politicization. In this section I review the evolution of UNESCO and discuss the events that led to U.S. withdrawal on 31 December 1984.

The Formative Years

When the first General Conference met in Paris in 1946, its most important action was the choice of director-general. It was agreed that the director-general would be British and that Paris would be the site of the UNESCO headquarters. The United States presumed that the director-general would be American, but when Truman's suggested appointee, Francis Biddle, received little support the position went to Julian Huxley, an Englishman (Table B.3).[66] U.S. delegates perceived Huxley as a weak administrator, a socialist, and an atheist. They worked to impose two conditions on his selection—his term would be limited to two years, and he would appoint a U.S. citizen as deputy director-general.[67] The United States was determined to make an impact and began a longstanding policy of instructing the U.S. representative to the Executive Board in violation of UNESCO's charter, which anticipated that country delegates would participate in their personal capacity rather than as instructed delegates from their countries.

As noted earlier, the United States pushed hard to include a communications role in the UNESCO mandate. The United States saw mass communications as an opportunity to combat communism. In 1946 the United States tried but failed to promote interest in the creation of a worldwide radio network. William Benton, as the U.S. representative to UNESCO, argued that mass communication was the organization's most important area of work. However, the U.S. radio network proposal made little headway and was dropped within a year. The United States supported the election of Mexican Foreign Minister Jaime Torres-Bodet as director-general in 1948. President Truman emphasized the vital importance of UNESCO at a meeting of the U.S. National Commission in April 1950. But William Benton remained critical of the failure of UNESCO to take a firm position on East-West conflict. During the Korean War the United States requested UNESCO assistance in the American propaganda campaign against North Korea. The Executive Board convened, at U.S. request, in a special session in August 1950. The

United States and UNESCO's director-general both put forward proposals. The U.S. plan was regarded as too politicized, and the director-general's proposal was accepted. The director-general's plan provided for the production and distribution of educational materials about the Korean action. The United States was disgruntled with UNESCO's avoidance of the communism issue and threatened to withhold its assessment. These threats led to Director-General Torres-Bodet's resignation in December 1952. He was succeeded by an American, Luther Evans.[68]

Despite the squabbling, important work was done during this period. UNESCO carried out studies and adopted several standard-setting instruments. The standard-setting conventions include the 1948 Agreement for Facilitating the International Circulation of Visual and Auditory Materials of an Educational, Scientific and Cultural Character; the 1950 Agreement on the Importation of Educational, Scientific and Cultural Materials; the Universal Copyright Convention; and the 1958 Convention Concerning the International Exchange of Publications.

The USSR, although a member of the United Nations, did not join UNESCO until 1954. The U.S. response to Soviet membership was to emphasize the more technical functions of UNESCO. The United States also supported a British proposal to transform the Executive Board into a body of member state representatives by amending the UNESCO constitution. Eisenhower commented that "there has been . . . a lot of suspicion about UNESCO . . . in many quarters of the United States."[69]

Under René Maheu, who became director-general in November 1962, UNESCO expanded its budget rapidly and added several new scientific and technical responsibilities.[70] In 1960, the Intergovernmental Oceanographic Commission was initiated to promote cooperative scientific investigation of the ocean space. This period also saw the launching of the International Hydrological Decade to promote the transfer of technical advice on water resource management to the developing world. UNESCO was also able to provide teachers and technical help to the Congo during the 1960 crisis. The new initiatives were funded by both regular and extrabudgetary resources. Among UNESCO's most popular activities have been efforts to preserve endangered cultural monuments such as Machu Picchu in Peru, Borobudur in Indonesia, and Abu Simbel in the Nile Valley.[71]

The emergence of the newly independent nations was rapidly changing the composition of membership in both the United Nations and UNESCO. For the United States the changes in UNESCO's membership meant a perceived loss of influence. In the 1960s UNESCO began a transition toward furnishing more advisory services on development planning and handling the administration of development assistance projects. This trend was led by a very active deputy director-general, Malcolm Adiseshiah. By the late 1960s the United States had become increasingly uncomfortable with UNESCO's budget growth; it saw the creation of the United Nations Development Programme in 1966 as a way to achieve greater influence over the UNESCO budget.[72]

Controversy and Withdrawal

During the 1970s the United States became increasingly concerned about what it characterized as the excessive politicization of UNESCO. Controversy was particularly intense around the proposals for a new world information and communications order and policy toward Israel. Although these issues were largely resolved in a manner satisfactory to the United States, they helped to create an environment that led to U.S. withdrawal from UNESCO at the end of 1984.

A New World Information and Communication Order

In the 1974 Sixth Special Session of the U.N. General Assembly, the developing countries organized in a voting coalition known as the Group of 77 and called for a new international economic order to redress the perceived general imbalance in the world economy.[73] In UNESCO the perception of imbalance translated into a charge that Western domination of information channels was resulting in both excessive bias and neglect in the coverage of news from Third World countries. At the UNESCO General Conference in Nairobi in 1976, those countries introduced a demand for a new international information order. Later, as part of a compromise package that was adopted by consensus, this became known as the "new world information and communications order" (NWICO).

American press coverage generally interpreted the call for a NWICO as a direct attack on the free flow of information.[74] Although the perception in the United States was that UNESCO was dominated by the advocates of a new order, none of the originally proposed limitations on the free flow of information had been adopted by UNESCO. The United States has been generally successful, contrary to popular opinion, in defending free press concepts. Leonard Sussman, executive director of Freedom House and a frequent critic of UNESCO activities in the communications field, testified in 1984 that "throughout the decade of bitter communications controversies there has never been a single resolution or program approved at UNESCO that supports press censorship, the licensing of journalists, or other programs to harm press freedom."[75]

In 1974, 1976, and 1978, Soviet-initiated draft declarations on the media that would sanction the supremacy of the state over the press were brought up and defeated. But the Soviet proposals tended to become confused in the minds of many U.S. government officials and in press coverage with Third World calls for a NWICO. The USSR was not, however, particularly interested in NWICO issues. It took the position that a new order was not needed and that the current order based on state sovereignty was sufficient.[76] The net effect of the debates in the late 1970s and the early 1980s was a series of declarations and actions that supported the position of the United States and other free press advocates.

UNESCO and Israel

In 1974 and 1975 three resolutions critical of Israel were successfully passed at UNESCO. One concerned an allegation that Israel's excavation techniques were resulting in violation of Islamic artifacts in East Jerusalem. A second concerned the restriction of educational opportunities in the occupied territories. A third dealt with Israel's right to participate in regional groupings. Israel's application to join the European group was rejected, and it was not invited to join the Asian group. Congress reacted to the UNESCO resolutions by eliminating funding for UNESCO for 1975 and 1976 in the Foreign Assistance Act of 1974 (PL 93-559).[77] When UNESCO reversed the resolution that excluded Israel from joining the European regional organization in 1976, the president authorized the resumption of contributions to the organization. By June 1977, the United States had paid all of its contributions that had been withheld since 1974.

Withdrawal

The election of President Reagan in 1980 created a more favorable environment for influence by critics of UNESCO. Steps toward withdrawal were initiated on 28 December 1983, when Secretary of State George Schultz wrote a letter of intention to withdraw to UNESCO's Director-General Amadou Mahtar M'Bow. The letter indicated that, because the trends in management, policy, and budget of UNESCO were detracting from the organization's effectiveness and leading UNESCO away from its original constitutional principles, the U.S. government would formally terminate its membership on 31 December 1984.[78] The State Department elaborated on the charges in various documents. Its complaints can be put into four categories: (1) excessive politicization, (2) excessive statism, (3) unrestrained budgetary expansion and poor management, and (4) an endemic hostility toward the basic institutions of a free society, especially the free market and a free press.[79]

Several Western member countries shared the U.S. concern about need for reform in UNESCO management. There were legitimate concerns about management and personnel policy. But they were caught by surprise by the U.S. decision to withdraw. The State Department report on participation in the United Nations for 1982 had stated that U.S. participation that year was successful. The report gave no indication that U.S.-UNESCO relations were nearing a breaking point. The report noted that, at the General Conference meetings of November 23 to December 3, the United States had (1) eliminated numerous "potentially dangerous" NWICO proposals, (2) succeeded in incorporating key free press concepts, and (3) excluded from the MacBride Commission Report references that might potentially endanger press freedoms and journalistic activities.[80] In 1983 an interagency working group headed by the National Science Foundation indicated that the scientific benefits from continued participation warranted continued U.S. participation.[81] In 1984 a congressional staff study noted that "the substance of U.S./UNESCO assessment and credibility of the U.S. decision would have been enhanced had the Department examined its own management of U.S. relations with UNESCO."[82]

What happened between 1982 and 1983? One factor was the series of attacks on UNESCO launched by the conservative Washington think tank, the Heritage Foundation. During the early 1980s the Heritage Foundation published a series of books, pamphlets, background papers, and memorandums attacking the United Nations and its specialized agencies. UNESCO was attacked for conducting a "war against the western press"; for advocating "a global welfare state"; for the teaching of "international human rights," "disarmament education," and "amoral education"; and for trying to move world opinion in the direction of a planned socialist economy. The Heritage Foundation urged that Congress investigate UNESCO and that U.S. tax dollars supporting education and social science programs be cut off. Finally, "the United States should withhold its financial support of these programs until all vestiges of the anti-Western, NIEO policy and its social welfare state schemes are eliminated."[83] A second Heritage Foundation document published on 13 December 1982 portrayed the 1982 UNESCO Mexico City Conference, which the State Department had described as successful, as serving mainly as an arena for communist and Third World propaganda. The report urged that the United States either fight back or get out of UNESCO.[84]

David Stockman, director of the Office of Management and Budget, had proposed withdrawal from UNESCO soon after Reagan took office in 1981. Although his objective was retrenchment in foreign aid rather than discontent with UNESCO, he found it useful to exploit anti-U.N. feelings within the administration and among groups influenced by the Heritage Foundation briefings. Stockman's recommendation was blocked by vigorous objections from the U.S. National Commission on UNESCO and, in effect, was placed on hold until the appointment in 1982 of Gregory Newell, a Reagan campaign aid, as assistant secretary to head the State Department's International Organizations Bureau. Newell made withdrawal his issue.[85] Beginning in 1982 he was particularly effective in his efforts to manipulate the press and other media to secure a favorable climate of opinion for withdrawal. Internal reports critical of U.S. management of policy toward UNESCO were suppressed. Expressions of support by federal agencies and scientific associations whose activities would be negatively affected by withdrawal were disregarded.

Despite calls for reform, U.S. officials were not willing to enumerate the specific reforms that would be needed to avoid U.S. withdrawal. The Western countries interested in reform took on the task through members of the Western Information Group (WIG). The WIG caucus, made up of 21 Western delegates, was set up in 1984 as a working group on reform. It was headed by Ambassador Marten Mourik of the Netherlands and included U.S. Ambassador Jean Gerard, who headed the subgroup on budget. The Reagan administration sent observers to UNESCO to monitor the organization, yet neither the U.S. mission nor the State Department's Bureau of International Organization would state clearly what reforms, if any, might lead to a reversal of the withdrawal decision.[86] The U.S. mission did provide an unattributed list of 13 proposed reforms, but it was understood that this was not necessarily a list that would satisfy the U.S. government. Despite the frustration, on 12 March 1984 the WIG group offered a draft working paper on reform that identified three categories of problems: (1) structural/institutional, (2) political, and (3) program/administrative.[87] At a meeting of the Executive Board in Paris on 9–23 May 1984, the members of WIG were prepared to offer concrete reforms based on their deliberations. The United States participated in the debates but, when the board created a 13-member Temporary Committee on Reform, the U.S. ambassador declined to be a member, saying later that "our strategy was not to seek a place on the committee, itself, but influence it through active work within the Western Information Group."[88]

In July 1984 Assistant Secretary of State Gregory Newell sent a second letter to UNESCO indicating that more sweeping reforms were needed.[89] The July letter called for constitutional reforms that would (1) create mechanisms to ensure that UNESCO budgets would be approved by members who contribute the majority of the organization's funds, (2) return UNESCO to the organization's original purpose, and (3) permit the assumption by member states of their rightful authority in the General Conference and Executive Board. The U.S. position can best be interpreted as a method of justifying U.S. withdrawal rather than as an effort to advance UNESCO reform. "The context, tone and inconsistencies in the public record demonstrate that the withdrawal from UNESCO was prompted overwhelmingly by the pressure of domestic concerns. UNESCO's failings represented the clearest target for an ideologically motivated campaign to achieve the public humiliation of a major U.N. agency."[90] For the Reagan administration, withdrawal from UNESCO represented a relatively inexpensive payoff to its right-wing constituency. A somewhat more generous conclusion might be that the Reagan administration was frustrated by the lack of success of U.S. efforts to use UNESCO as an effective instrument of U.S. foreign policy.

The position of the Bush administration on UNESCO membership remained essentially unchanged from the U.S. position at the time of withdrawal at the end of 1984. A 1990 report to Congress reiterated the complaints outlined in the 1984 *Perspectives on U.S. Withdrawal from UNESCO* and, in addition, insisted that there had been further deterioration in the management and administration of UNESCO since the election of Frederico Mayor to the position of director-general in 1987.[91] The report also noted that the United States, in spite of withdrawal from membership, had continued to participate in several technical programs in which it is interested, such as the Intergovernmental Oceanographic Commission, the World Heritage Commission, and the Man and Biosphere Program.

The Bush administration did, however, assume a more favorable attitude toward the United Nations. It committed itself to payment of U.S. arrearages. The disintegration of the Soviet empire and the U.N. role in the Gulf War had also created a more favorable attitude toward the United Nations and its agencies on the part of the general public in the United States. However, the United States had not, at the end of the Bush administration, taken steps to rejoin UNESCO. In May 1993 the American Panel on UNESCO of the United Nations Association of the United States released a report that argued that the three areas on which the Reagan administration had conditioned its reentry—politicization, budgetary expansion, and management reform—had been successfully addressed by UNESCO.[92] The Clinton administration has publicly recognized the constructive role that UNESCO could play in addressing the new problems of the post–Cold War era. When this book was being completed, the administration was considering a recommendation that the United States reenter the organization in October 1995 but had not yet made a final decision.

The International Labor Organization

The International Labor Organization was founded in 1919 "with an explicitly political purpose—to diffuse the appeal of Bolshevism."[93] When the ILO was founded, Europe had just gone through the ravages of World War I. The Russian revolution signaled that instability could come from within a country as well as from outside. It was believed that international cooperation to improve working conditions, minimum wages, and social security would permit improvement of the living conditions of workers without threatening comparative advantage.

This section reviews the history of the U.S.-ILO relationship from 1919. After outlining the foundation of the ILO and its evolution, I examine the recurring conflicts between the United States and the ILO and discuss the events leading to the two-year U.S. withdrawal (6 November 1977 to 18 February 1980).

The Early History of the ILO, 1918–1944

When the ILO was established in 1919, it was structured to assure that it would not become an international workers' union. The ILO created tripartite delegations, unique among international organizations, in which a workers' representative, an employers' representative, and a government representative from each country came together to establish international labor guidelines. Albert Thomas, a leading figure in the history of the French socialist movement, became the first director-general (Table B.4). Neither the United States nor the Soviet Union joined in 1919. Thomas died suddenly in 1932. Harold Butler from the United Kingdom was appointed by the Governing Body to replace him. Butler engaged in an aggressive effort to broaden the ILO membership. Franklin Delano Roosevelt's election in 1932 created a more favorable political environment for U.S. participation.[94]

Butler resigned in 1938 in protest against U.S. pressure to appoint a deputy in whom he had no confidence. John Winant, former Republican governor of New Hampshire and New Deal advocate, took his place.[95] Winant, the first American director-general, had been the first chairman of the U.S. Social Security Board and an assistant director of the ILO. As World War II approached, he negotiated a move of the ILO to Montreal from Geneva for the duration of the war. In 1941 Winant resigned to become U.S. ambassador to London. He was succeeded by former deputy director Edward Phelan of Ireland. Phelan managed to schedule a regular conference in April-May of 1944, which brought together government, employer, and worker delegates from 41 countries.

The 1944 conference promulgated the Declaration of Philadelphia, which set out the basic principles of the ILO for the post–World War II world. The declaration marked a transition from the confinement of communism to the promotion of economic development as a primary concern of the ILO.

The declaration committed the ILO to support full employment, the expansion of consumption, the provision of industrial training, and the advancement of the less developed regions of the world. The fundamental principles of the declaration are that (1) labor is not a commodity, (2) freedom of expression and association are essential, (3) poverty anywhere is a danger to prosperity everywhere, and (4) work through ILO promotes the common welfare.[96] This shift in emphasis was to become an important factor in the U.S. charges of politicization of the ILO in the mid-1970s.

The Postwar ILO, 1945–1970

Director-General Phelan had hoped that the ILO might be given more authority over postwar economic policy. However, the establishment of the U.N. Economic and Social Council precluded a larger role for the ILO. In 1948, Phelan was replaced by David Morse, who had served as assistant undersecretary in the U.S. Department of Labor. Morse brought a New Deal perspective, supportive of the principles of the Declaration of Philadelphia, to the ILO.

During the long period, from 1948 to 1970, that David Morse served as director-general of the ILO, the organization's most important efforts were in the areas of international labor standards and technical cooperation. The greatest areas of controversy were, however, around efforts by the USSR and the Arab states to use the ILO General Conference to advance political agendas that were viewed by the U.S. government and by labor and employer representatives as outside the competence of the ILO. The ILO constitution provides that the annual General Conference may adopt, by a two-thirds majority, international conventions or recommendations with respect to working conditions and the protection of human rights. When conventions are adopted each member state is supposed to submit them to competent authorities for legislative action.

As of the late 1970s, the United States had ratified only seven, the least of any major power, of the 151 conventions that had been adopted by the ILO conference. The U.S. government has taken the position that, in areas such as minimum standards for social security, unemployment and old age benefits, compensation for work injuries, family allowances, and medical care and hospitalization, the U.S. federal-state structure is an impediment to ratification. Walter Galenson has argued, however, that the real reasons have been employer opposition and the historical reluctance of the Senate to ratify international conventions. The American labor movement, on the other hand, has generally been favorably disposed toward ILO standard setting through conventions. But it has rarely either had the political resources or been willing to place sufficient priority on the ILO conventions to secure passage in the U.S. Senate.[97]

Director-General Morse also sought a more activist role for the ILO than that provided by the labor standards effort. President Harry S. Truman's commitment in his January 1949 inaugural address to a "bold new program" of technical assistance (Chap. 4) was the lever Morse had been looking for to advance his agenda. Although the ILO governing body was cautious about assuming an operational role, they responded favorably when it became apparent that most of the money would come from the United Nations (initially the EPTA and later the UNDP) rather than from the ILO regular budget.[98]

Technical assistance by the ILO began in the early 1950s. The largest individual program consisted of vocational training and management development in newly emerging states. Other activities included assistance in the areas of labor legislation, collective bargaining, employment service administration, the establishment of social security systems, and related areas. In 1969, just before his departure, Morse succeeded in initiating a new World Employment Program that focused on employment planning, income distribution, population and manpower policies, technology choice, and other programs designed to address more directly the emerging employment crisis in most developing countries.[99] Short-term missions were sent to different countries to evaluate how employment could be increased. The missions produced volumes of material on each country—on issues such as agricultural policy, land reform, industrial development, foreign trade, and fiscal and monetary policy. Several of the reports have become important reference works for academic research.[100] But they had little influence other than to provide an opportunity, on their completion, for well-publicized visits by the ILO director-general to the recipient countries.

The first crisis in U.S. relations with the ILO emerged in the mid-1950s after the readmission of the USSR to membership in the ILO. The adoption by the ILO of a convention on disability insurance led the U.S. employer representative to declare that the ILO was "communist dominated." The U.S. Chamber of Commerce adopted a resolution in 1957 calling for Congress to investigate continued American participation. In April 1957, a bill was passed by the Senate limiting U.S. financial contributions. The Eisenhower administration, which favored continued U.S. participation, finessed the opposition by appointing a special committee, headed by Joseph E. Johnson, president of the Carnegie Endowment, to investigate the U.S. role in the ILO. The Johnson report, although highly critical of the role of the State, Labor, and Commerce departments in formulating U.S. policy toward the ILO, was strongly supportive of continued U.S. participation in ILO. The U.S. labor movement was also strongly supportive.[101]

In spite of considerable dissatisfaction with the ILO on the part of the U.S. delegates and the U.S. government, the government failed to develop a coherent policy toward the ILO. Commenting on the period between readmission of the USSR and U.S. withdrawal, Galenson, writing in 1981, echoed the findings of the 1957 Johnson report: "The U.S. government has rarely played an active role in ILO affairs. Moreover, the division of responsibility between the State, Labor, and Commerce departments in the determination of the U.S. government policy led inevitably to bureaucratic struggles."[102]

U.S. Withdrawal, 1970–1979

The difficulties that led to withdrawal began when David Morse retired in 1970 and Wilfred Jenks was designated director-general. Jenks was a respected ILO civil servant. He had narrowly won the position over Francis Blanchard, also an ILO careerist, who was supported by many delegates from developing countries.[103] Jenks, who had the support of the United States, won by two votes.

Four weeks after his appointment, Jenks announced the appointment of Pavel Astapenko of the USSR as assistant director-general. The Soviet Union, as one of the major industrial countries, had been pushing for an assistant director-general position since rejoining in 1954. George Meany, U.S. worker representative and president of the AFL-CIO, was furious about the appointment. Meany used his standing and influence with the House Appropriations Committee, which cut $3.7 million from a requested $7.5 million for 1970 and eliminated the projected funding for 1971. By the end of 1971, the United States was $11.6 million in arrears. Congress authorized partial payment. At the end of 1974, the U.S. arrears was still $2.2 million.[104]

A second flash point occurred in June 1974, when the General Conference adopted a resolution condemning the Israeli occupation of Arab territories. This was followed by admission of the Palestine Liberation Organization to observer status in June 1975. Henry Kissinger forwarded a notice of withdrawal on 5 November 1975. His letter said that the United States did not want to withdraw and would continue to promote reform of the ILO. He then outlined several U.S. grievances. He indicated that the United States could not accept the erosion of tripartism. He also accused the ILO of selective concern for human rights, disregard for due process, increasing politicization, and excessive attention to extraneous issues. The concern about politicization was a reference to the accusations against Israel. Extraneous issues referred to ILO participation in the NIEO debates.

Meany's role in pressing for U.S. withdrawal was well publicized in the *Washington Post* and the *New York Times*. The *New York Times* commented that "Mr. Meany is using his muscle against an old whipping boy, the International Labor Organization; and official Washington is meekly bowing to his will." In the 1970s, unlike the 1950s, it was not just the employers that favored withdrawal. This time the Department of Labor, the Department of Commerce, the AFL-CIO, and the U.S. Chamber of Commerce favored withdrawal. The State Department and the National Security Council preferred to hold off withdrawal. When the end of the two-year notice period came up, a new president, Jimmy Carter, had to make the final decision. On 1 November 1977 he paid his debts to Mr. Meany by deciding to withdraw even though Soviet activity in the ILO in the late 1970s was "very low-key."[105] The State Department, committed to the value of multilateralism, pushed for postponement of withdrawal to the very end.

U.S. Participation—Again

The United States watched conference results closely and was pleased that the 1978 session failed, for want of a quorum, to pass a resolution critical of Israel. In 1979 the United States was satisfied at the absence of any abuse of due process or new initiatives against Israel. In addition, the conference voted to adopt secret ballot procedures for some votes in the plenary sessions. The United States rejoined the ILO in February 1980. How should one evaluate the withdrawal episode? Imber argues, "Viewed as a discrete exercise, the toughening response had worked. Criteria for both withdrawal and reentry had been publicly stated, a warning issued and the threat carried through. During the period of withdrawal, reforms had been observed and, true to previously stated intentions." But Imber also insists, in my view correctly, that, although the concern about politicization was appropriate, the issue of extraneous issues was flawed. "To deny the ILO the right to debate relations between the North and the South, the global impact of Western recession and protectionism, would be to deny much of the Philadelphia Declaration on which our postwar U.S. enthusiasm for the organization was largely based."[106]

Rejoining the ILO did not, however, resolve all outstanding issues. Lane Kirkland, president of the AFL-CIO, testified before the Senate in 1985 that the United States needed to ratify more conventions than the 6 of 160 it had ratified to date. He argued: "The federal structure is not the real reason for our nonratification record. Rather, it stems from the resistance in the past by employer organizations because ratification would involve a supervisory scrutiny of our democratic laws and practices and involve some of our domestic labor standards."[107]

There continues to be a lack of careful analysis of the effectiveness of the technical assistance provided through the ILO. U.S. policy has continued to be guided by the same principles, or lack thereof, that guided policy before withdrawal. The ILO budget continues to be affected by U.S. withholdings. As of 1990 the shortfall in appropriated funds had led to a shortfall in U.S. payment of its assessed contribution of $2.7 million. The United States continues to object to much of the standard-setting work of the organization and its use of the ILO enforcement mechanisms to criticize regimes that the United States regards as friendly.

With the decline of East-West tensions, the U.S. government seems again to be in the process of redefining U.S. policy toward the ILO. Congress has recently addressed the subject of U.S. ratification of ILO conventions. There has been some support for increasing the number of conventions ratified by the United States. There has been criticism that the conventions are meaningless exercises signed by many member governments with no intention of implementation. If the United States intends to retain membership, it should take a much stronger and more well-informed role in ILO program and policy reform.

The World Health Organization

The World Health Organization has, until recently, received much less critical media attention than has the FAO, UNESCO, or ILO. It has rarely been subject to official criticism from the United States. The United States has often contributed more to WHO's assessed regular budget than to any other specialized agency. In this section I identify the historic reasons that explain the strength of U.S. support for WHO. WHO has some structural advantages relative to other specialized agencies in the area of development assistance. WHO was created as a service agency. From the beginning, WHO's mandate was to address the issues of disease and its prevention rather than the broader issue of health service delivery.[108]

Establishing an International Health Organization

The process of establishing the World Health Organization began at the United Nations Conference on International Organizations held in San Francisco in April 1945. The United Kingdom and the United States had agreed not to put questions regarding health issues on the conference agenda, but other delegations insisted. The Chinese and Brazilian delegations eventually drafted a joint declaration calling for a General Conference to establish an international health organization.

In March 1946, the Technical Preparatory Committee, comprising 16 health experts nominated by governments designated by ECOSOC, met in Paris. Dr. Thomas Parran, surgeon-general of the United States Public Health Service (USPHS) from 1936 to 1948, represented the United States. A draft constitution prepared by Dr. Parran and his USPHS colleagues was accepted virtually in whole by the committee. A second meeting, the International Health Conference, took place in New York on 19 June to 22 July 1946. It adopted a constitution for the World Health Organization and established an Interim Commission to act for the future WHO, pending the constitution's ratification. The constitution provided that the WHO would assume the relevant functions of the League of Nations Health Organization, the Office International d'Hygiene Publique (OIHP), and the UNRRA Health Division. U.S. influence assured that the WHO mandate was to address medical questions in terms of disease and its prevention and not how medical services were delivered. The American Medical Association in particular wanted to ensure that the WHO would not take any action that might promote socialized medicine.[109]

U.S. influence was also evident in discussions on defining the relationship between the previously established Pan American Sanitary Board (PASB) and WHO.[110] The PASB was the strongest of the existing regional health organizations and its director, former U.S. surgeon-general Dr. Hugh S. Cummings, strongly advocated the continued separate existence of the PASB. Even today, the Pan American Health Organization, which now serves as WHO's regional office for the Americas, is the only regional body to maintain an independent budget. It is regarded by some as the best example of how effectively a regional health organization can operate. Other observers have been critical of what they regard as needless friction between the PAHO and the WHO headquarters.

Brock Chisholm of Canada was elected executive secretary and later as first WHO director-general (Table B.5). New York was named as the official headquarters, but by the time the first World Health Assembly met the headquarters had been shifted to Geneva.[111] The Interim Commission mentioned above continued its organizational work until April 1948, when the necessary 26 ratifications had been obtained to permit WHO to enter into existence.

The Early Years

Although the United States was active in WHO's creation, several U.S. concerns contributed to the delay between the completion of preparatory work in 1946 and the ratification of the WHO constitution by the requisite 26 member states in 1948. The United States was concerned that WHO might move into social and policy aspects of the provision of health services, which would create potential budgetary implications.[112] Intensification of the Cold War affected the

U.S. position on several WHO policy decisions. In 1949, the World Health Assembly, acting on a recommendation of the Executive Board, decided that the WHO should not normally provide medical supplies to recipients. The United States feared that supplies would be provided to Communist states. U.S. influence was also exerted in a 1952 decision not to authorize a population program.

Mass Campaigns To Eradicate Disease

The campaigns undertaken before 1955 included mass treatment programs, conducted in cooperation with UNICEF, against diseases such as syphilis and yaws.[113] These programs provided immediate and dramatic results. The longer-term effects were more problematic. Elimination of the disease from an entire area required repeated visits. When and if any cases of the disease remained after the campaign ended, the disease resumed its spread.

Beginning in the mid-1950s the WHO initiated a series of disease eradication campaigns. The Pan American Sanitary Bureau had undertaken a malaria eradication program in the early 1950s. Although many scientists were not convinced that eradication was possible, the World Health Assembly agreed to embark upon a malaria eradication program. The malaria campaign required considerable financial and personnel resources. It was highly effective in reducing the incidence of malaria in many countries. Beginning in the mid-1950s, however, reports started to trickle in of mosquito resistance to DDT, the insecticide widely used to kill the malaria-bearing anopheline mosquito. Africa south of the Sahara was excluded from the program for physical, economic, and developmental reasons complicated by high endemicity and complex transmission factors. The weakness of the program was that it relied almost totally on the use of DDT within a rigid program framework.

The apparent success of the malaria program affected the decision to adopt a second eradication program—the battle against smallpox. The smallpox eradication program began in 1959. It was difficult to muster support, and the program did not really take off until an intensified program was put into place in 1966. During the 1960s, the basic concept of eradication was beginning to be questioned. The industrialized countries began to resist budget increases. Despite the controversy, the second eradication campaign was initiated.

The second program came about in large part because of U.S. activities in Africa. In 1965, the United States committed itself to providing assistance to a regional smallpox eradication program in western and central Africa, as well as to the global effort. The USSR had long been interested in a global effort because the country shared a long border with endemic Asian areas. In 1966, the assembly approved the Intensified Smallpox Eradication Program, allocated $2.4 million from the WHO regular budget, and declared a goal of eradication within 10 years. In 1966 the WHO assembly also reversed its 1952 decision and initiated a program to support family planning activities.[114]

A Broader Agenda

Since the mid-1970s the World Health Assembly, the governing body of the WHO, under the strong leadership of Director-General Halvdan Mahler, has moved to broaden the agenda of the WHO from the earlier emphasis on technical approaches to improving human health to a broader focus on health care and its role in development. This new agenda reflected a growing recognition of the importance of preventive as compared to corrective strategies. It emphasized the role of a better food supply, safe drinking water and sanitation, maternal and child care, appropriate treatment of common diseases, and the provision of essential drugs.

The defining event in advancing the broader agenda was the International Conference on Primary Health Care, organized by WHO and UNICEF, held in Alma-Ata (Khazakistan) in 1978. The location of the conference in the Soviet Union was a matter of considerable pride to the USSR and helped stimulate their strong support for WHO. The conference declared an objective of "health care for all by the year 2000." The conference went beyond the traditional WHO commitment to the training of health workers and advocated a program of essential health services to be provided through a team of doctors, nurses, and local medical workers. The proposed system would require increased health resources at the community level and less emphasis on hospital-based services.[115] The Alma-Ata conference also stressed the need to ensure the provision of essential drugs so that they could be purchased in bulk. This thrust was strongly supported by the U.S. Public Health Service, the Agency for International Development, and the Department of State.

By the early 1980s the United States found itself embroiled in several controversies with the WHO over its broader agenda.[116] One issue was the promotion of breast-milk substitutes by multinational corporations in the Third World. It was alleged by some consumer organizations in the United States and Western Europe that breast-milk substitutes were a cause of infant malnutrition among the poor in developing countries. In May 1981 the World Health Assembly adopted an international code on the marketing of breast-milk substitutes. Infant formulas were seen as a cause of malnutrition in infants, especially in developing countries, because formula marketing diverted mothers from breast-feeding, which provides a superior form of infant nutrition, and because the infant formula was often improperly prepared. The United States was the only nation to vote against the code. Three other countries—South Korea, Japan, and Argentina—abstained.

A second issue was that of quality control of internationally marketed pharmaceuticals. Concern about quality control had been on the WHO agenda since the mid-1960s. The United States successfully opposed an international regulatory approach in favor of upgrading the technical qualifications of national regulatory agencies. Another related issue was the distribution and use of pharmaceuticals in the Third World. The developing countries were concerned about *drug colonialism*—the promotion of luxury drugs, the failure to provide lower-cost generic products, and the continued marketing of drugs identified as dangerous in developed countries. In 1978 the WHO passed a resolution establishing an Action Program on Essential Drugs designed to advance the use of generic drugs.

In each of these cases, the United States, although initially opposed, responded by working for policy modifications that were, if somewhat reluctantly, responsive to the objections of U.S. constituencies. It did not respond either by making punitive budget reductions or by withdrawal, as in the cases of the FAO, ILO, and UNESCO. What accounts for this differential response? Mingst argues that the difference was due, at least in part, to the close relationship between the American medical/scientific community and the WHO and the medical leadership in many developing countries. She also notes that, during much of its life, at least until the appointment of Dr. Hiroshi Nakajima, WHO directors-general exercised considerable political skill in dealing with the United States. Most important, however, was the fact that the United States continued to view the WHO as primarily a scientific/technical organization performing functions that were inherently valuable to the United States as well as its developing country members.

During the early 1990s, the United States did express considerable concern about what it regarded as unsatisfactory leadership by Director-General Hiroshi Nakajima.[117] Complaints were expressed about the lack of forward-looking leadership, the authoritarian management style, and declining staff morale. In 1993, the United States took a leadership role in opposing Nakajima's reelection. Supported by strong backing from the Japanese government, Nakajima was reelected by a divided World Health Assembly. In spite of its opposition to Nakajima's reelection, the United States has continued its tradition of strong support for the WHO.

The United Nations Children's Fund

The United Nations Children's Fund was created as a temporary agency to supply emergency assistance to children in Europe after World War II. It supplied material assistance and some training, without political prejudice, beginning in 1947. It quickly expanded its mandate and has become a permanent voluntary fund to address the long-term development needs of children and their mothers.[118] All contributions to UNICEF are voluntary. U.S. contributions have been consistent and relatively high compared to voluntary contributions to the specialized agencies. UNICEF is unique in that it receives as much as 25 percent of its funds from the public. The fund's involvement in fund raising through greeting card sales dates to its earliest years under Maurice Pate. The funds for UNICEF's general resources budget are contributed by governments, nongovernmental organizations (such as the 34 national UNICEF committees), and private individuals. Its supplemental fund is financed by governments, nongovernmental organizations, and other U.N. agencies for specific projects selected by the donor.

This chapter reviews UNICEF's evolution from an emergency fund to a development fund and explores U.S. government criticism of the expansion of UNICEF's activities. Strong public support has helped maintain the level of U.S. contributions.

UNICEF in Europe, 1946–1950

UNICEF emerged as a result of intense lobbying on the part of several key players concerned about the welfare of children in Europe and a successful public campaign to raise awareness and funds. The key advocates were interested in seeing certain aspects of the work of UNRRA continue as it became apparent that UNRRA would be shorter lived than originally thought. From its earliest days UNRRA had received constant criticism in the United States for mismanagement—both by UNRRA's own officials and by the officials of governments who received UNRRA support. Criticisms often were more a reflection of budgetary than substantive policy concern.[119]

Among those who were particularly active in seeking to establish a successor organization to the UNRRA were Ludwik Rajchman of Poland and Fiorello LaGuardia of the United States. Rajchman, who had headed the League of Nations health secretariat and who represented Poland at all UNRRA council meetings, was the most vigorous advocate of the creation of a special fund targeted specifically toward the needs of children. Rajchman was a leader in the field of social medicine and believed in the incorporation of child nutrition and maternal care into regular medical practice. He was probably not chosen to lead the World Health Organization because the United States found his views too radical. Rajchman fully understood the sources of U.S. political opposition and sought to make sure that the first executive director was an American with established Republican sympathies (Table B.6).[120]

UNRRA successfully gathered sympathy through publicity about the plight of European children. At the end of World War II, the UNRRA commissioned eight American Army Signal Corps cameramen to stay on in Europe to document the effects of war on children.[121] Their pictures of homeless, begging children and overflowing orphanages would move people to contribute some $200 million dollars for child welfare. The film "Seeds of Destiny" began its tour at a White House screening in the spring of 1946 with Fiorello LaGuardia, the new director of UNRRA and ex-mayor of New York, in attendance. He became a strong advocate for the children's fund. The film helped to generate widespread support for aid to children among the public.

In 1946 the UNRRA council decided to use UNRRA's unspent funds to create a United Nations International Children's Emergency Fund to address the needs of children in postwar Europe. In 1950 the U.N. General Assembly extended UNICEF to 1953 to address long-term children's issues in developing countries. In 1953 the United Nations changed the name of the organization to the United Nations Children's Fund, maintaining the acronym, and extended the program indefinitely.[122]

Early fund raising in the United States met with difficulties. Aake Ording, the Norwegian delegate to UNRRA who had tried to ward off the collapse of UNRRA at the Geneva council meeting of August 1946, was a strong proponent of aid to children and had proposed the United Nations Appeal for Children (UNAC). UNAC called on voluntary organizations all over the world to raise money for child relief. In the United States, the effort was not successful because of a lack of official enthusiasm and the resentment of American voluntary agencies about the invasion of their territory.[123]

In 1947, the U.S. National Committee for UNICEF was successfully brought into existence by Katherine Lenroot, director of the U.S. Children's Bureau and U.S. delegate to UNICEF's Executive Board. The slate of distinguished committee members held its first meeting in the White House at the invitation of Mrs. Harry Truman. Although the committee received extensive favorable publicity for the UNAC, they stood aloof from its fund-raising activity for fear of antagonizing supporters of congressional appropriations for UNICEF.[124] The United Nations Appeal for Children established an important precedent as the U.N. agency that appealed to private citizens for contributions.

Expanding to Developing Countries, 1950–1960

UNICEF was originally conceived as a short-term fund. On 6 October 1950 the General Assembly addressed the question of the dissolution of UNICEF. Eleanor Roosevelt represented the United States during these discussions and presented the U.S. view supporting UNICEF's dissolution and the distribution of its duties to other specialized agencies. Other countries rallied to prolong the life of UNICEF and expand its work into other countries. On 1 December 1950 the General Assembly extended UNICEF for three additional years. The new objective shifted from emergency relief to long-term benefit to children in less developed countries.[125]

The Truman administration had objected to UNICEF's efforts to prolong its mandate past 1950. UNICEF also became a target of McCarthyism. Ludwik Rajchman, who had done so much work to establish UNICEF, served as the Polish delegate and chairman of the UNICEF Executive Board. When he walked out of a UNICEF board meeting to protest its refusal to seat the People's Republic of China because of the presence of Taiwan, the *New York Times* reported the incident as "Reds Walk Out at U.N. Group's Child Aid Talks."[126] Toward the end of 1950, Rajchman was subpoenaed by Congress, despite his diplomatic status. After refusing to answer the subpoena, he was never granted another U.S. entry visa.

In the 1950s UNICEF adopted a campaign against mass disease. It brought to developing countries some of the new products developed during World War II to fight disease, such as antibiotics, sulfa drugs, and DDT. It supported campaigns for vaccination against tuberculosis and the control of yaws, malaria, trachoma, and leprosy. It also supported the training of nurses, midwives, and birth attendants.[127] UNICEF, as a supplier of material assistance, worked closely with the World Health Organization, which provided technical guidance to UNICEF. In addition to its work in health, UNICEF also provided support for child feeding and other nutrition programs. In the 1960s it began, in collaboration with UNESCO, a program for support of education in Africa.

The campaigns made headlines, were popular, and raised funds, but were one-time undertakings that were not part of the basic health services of a country. By the end of the decade, there was much discussion of how to incorporate disease control into basic health services so that children could always be treated against the ailments treated in the campaigns of the 1950s. By the end of the 1950s, UNICEF was moving toward a larger definition of children's needs. In 1959 the General Assembly adopted a Declaration of the Rights of the Child. In response, UNICEF carried out a survey of the needs of children and developed the concept of the "whole child."

A Partner in Development, 1960–1980

The idea of the whole child places the child within the family and the community and asserts that a child's needs cannot be treated in isolation from the larger problems in the family or community. This concept encouraged a new trend within UNICEF which permitted increased flexibility in UNICEF's approach to children's problems. Country programming became an integral part of the organization's work. UNICEF strengthened its collaboration with other agencies, particularly WHO and FAO. By 1963 the United States was expressing concern that some UNICEF projects only indirectly served the needs of children. U.S. policy favored a more restricted scope of work for UNICEF.[128]

UNICEF had some advantages that other members of the "development club," such as the specialized agencies and multilateral banks, did not recognize in the early 1960s. From the beginning, UNICEF had worked primarily in the field, whereas the specialized agencies had concentrated much of their expertise in their international or regional offices. Experience in the field convinced UNICEF that governments must incorporate greater concern for women and children in their national economic development plans. Beginning in 1962, UNICEF's Executive Board called for governments to take children's and young people's needs into account when designing national development plans.[129] The rhetoric of "human capital" and "economic development" worried some of the board members, who found it far removed from helping children in distress.

During the 1950s UNICEF had assiduously avoided becoming embroiled in the issue of population control in spite of pressure from the Scandinavian countries. The appointment of Henry Labouisse as executive director in January 1965, combined with pressure from India, Pakistan, and Nigeria for assistance for family planning, created an environment that was conducive to a more positive policy on the part of UNICEF toward the support of family planning efforts. The policy was strongly opposed by Belgium and some Latin American countries. At the May 1966 meeting of the UNICEF Executive Board in Addis Ababa, a proposal by Labouisse to initiate a modest program that would provide poor mothers with access to family planning information to facilitate birth spacing opened up the most explosive debate in UNICEF history. In 1967 the UNICEF board approved support for maternal and child health services. Although family planning was not mentioned in the resolution, it was understood that birth control would be included as one instrument of a more comprehensive maternal health program. The issue became less controversial in the international community with the establishment of a U.N. Fund for Population Activities in 1967. At the 1974 World Population Conference, the United States took a strong positive position in support of an active role on the part of both bilateral and multilateral donors for family planning. Twenty years later, at the World Population Conference in Mexico City, the United States reversed its position and assumed the role of a major opponent of the U.N. population program.

The 1970s were the second U.N. Development Decade. Its commitment to human development was consistent with UNICEF's own priorities and capacities. Country planning efforts promoted a package of basic services including food and nutrition, clean water, health, family planning, basic education, and supporting services to women in national plans. UNICEF also sought community involvement through the training of local health workers.

The formal adoption of the basic services concept took place in 1975, while U.S. involvement in Vietnam was in full swing. The call for a new international economic order had been announced in the U.N. General Assembly in April 1974. At the 1975 special session of the General Assembly, Henry Kissinger declared that the industrialized world was ready to enter into serious negotiations with the developing nations on a restructuring of global institutions. The United States had been trying to limit its financial obligations to the various U.N. organizations for years, but congressional committees were beginning to recognize that the U.S. position in the United Nations was changing and that the U.S. share of total contributions to voluntary programs was on the decline.[130]

At 1978 Senate authorization hearings, Charles William Maynes, assistant secretary for the Bureau of International Affairs in the State Department, emphasized the decline in assistance to the largest voluntary programs—UNDP, UNICEF, and the U.N. University. In particular he noted that in 1970 the United States had provided 35 percent and 34 percent of UNDP's and UNICEF's regular budgets, whereas in 1978 that percentage had dropped to 20 percent and 19.5 percent, respectively. He added that, although the United States continued to hold the top spot as the largest contributor, others had noticed that U.S. voluntary contributions had declined despite an understanding that U.S. voluntary contributions were to remain steady when the U.S. assessment to the United Nations and its specialized agencies had been lowered from 31 percent to 25 percent.[131]

The relative decline in U.S. contributions in the 1970s created a serious political problem for succession in UNICEF leadership. During the 1970s, the Scandinavian countries substantially increased their contributions. In view of their large contributions, Sweden, in particular, resented the U.S. presumption that the UNICEF chief executiveship was an American preserve. U.N. Secretary-General Kurt Waldheim, who was not known for political courage, tried to finesse the issue by twice extending the term of Labouisse. Finally, under increasing pressure from the U.S. State Department and the Swedish Ministry of Foreign Affairs, Waldheim canvassed the UNICEF Executive Board and, in May 1979, announced the appointment of the U.S. nominee, James P. Grant.

The appointment of Grant initiated a period of dynamic growth in the

UNICEF budget and program. Grant came to UNICEF from a distinguished career with the U.S. Agency for International Development and as the founding president of the Overseas Development Council. He had pioneered the development of a Physical Quality of Life Index designed as an alternative to the use of the gross national product (GNP) to measure a country's success in meeting the basic needs of its people.[132]

Under Grant's direction the activities of UNICEF were broadened even further. A "Child Survival and Development" revolution was launched in 1983 to reduce childhood death from immunizable disease and dehydration from diarrheal disease. The program included work in the areas of family spacing, the promotion of breast feeding, food production and supplementation, the promotion of child growth, and female literacy as part of the child survival strategy.[133]

U.S. contributions to UNICEF lagged during the early and mid-1980s. In 1989, the GAO reported that Sweden and Italy had surpassed the United States in donations to UNICEF. U.S. influence was perceived to be declining as a result. When UNICEF procurement offices shifted from the United States to Denmark, the U.S. share of procurement declined. The United States almost lost its seat on the executive board in 1988 when it came in fifth in voting to fill five seats. The United States continued to criticize the expansion of UNICEF activities, and in 1988 the U.S. representative to UNICEF voiced concern that UNICEF was losing its concentration on child survival by expanding into mothers' education and children's rights, which the United States saw as the domain of the ILO. However, a GAO report on U.S. participation in UNICEF recognized that most U.S. officials generally believe that UNICEF is well managed. Action had been taken to respond to a U.N. auditor's criticism in 1985 and 1986 that UNICEF had exceeded its budget authority. The GAO called for increased oversight of projects and added that increased collaboration with other U.N. agencies would be beneficial, as would an increased effort to create sustainable projects.[134]

Although support for UNICEF has varied during different administrations, congressional support has been more consistent. During the 1980s and the early 1990s, Congress has, each year, appropriated more than the administration requested for UNICEF. This has reflected both strong public support for programs to improve the status of children and a congressional perspective that UNICEF has been effective in advancing the children's agenda.

Since the late 1980s, UNICEF has been effective in substantially expanding its funding. Its total budget rose from $571 million in 1987 to $866 million ($509 million in general resources and $357 million in supplemental funds) in 1993. A 1990 World Summit for Children adopted a World Declaration on the Survival, Protection and Development of Children and an exceedingly ambitious action plan.[135] The goals of the action plan included specific targets for the reduction of infant and maternal mortality, access to safe drinking water, sanitary disposal of excreta, access to basic education, and reduction of illiteracy, with special emphasis on female literacy. As of early 1994, 158 governments, not including the United States, had signed the Declaration Plan of Action. UNICEF was given a prominent role in the achievement of these objectives.

The United Nations Environmental Program

In June 1972, the United Nations sponsored a Conference on the Human Environment in Stockholm, Sweden. The conference assembled high-level environmental officials and advocates from around the world for the first time. It brought together industrialized and developing nations to delineate the "rights" of the human family to a healthy and productive environment through meetings on the rights of people to adequate food, sound housing, safe water, and access to the means of choosing the size of their families.[136]

The conference focused on a wide range of national and international environmental issues and stressed the need to incorporate environmental concerns into national development strategies. After much heated debate and political maneuvering, the conference agreed on a declaration, which consisted of a proclamation and 26 principles, and an Action Plan for the Human Environment, which contained 109 recommendations.[137] The Stockholm Conference also adopted a Resolution on Institutional and Financial Arrangements, which determined how the United Nations Environmental Program would function. Since the 1972 meeting, sensitivity about the potential effects of environmental change—including desertification, loss of biological diversity, ozone depletion, and global climate change—has placed environmental issues higher on the international policy agenda.

What Is UNEP?

UNEP was created by the U.N. General Assembly in December 1972 on the recommendation of the June 1972 Stockholm Conference on the Human Environment. It is not an executing agency for U.N. programs. Its mandate is to coordinate the environmental activities of the U.N. agencies and other international organizations and to stimulate the incorporation of human environmental concerns in governmental and nongovernmental strategies and programs for economic development. UNEP's headquarters is in Nairobi, Kenya. It was the first U.N. body to locate its headquarters in a developing country. It is headed by an executive director who oversees a small secretariat of about 230 professional staff (about 250 worldwide). The secretariat stimulates work on the environment, coordinates environmental programs within the U.N. system, provides advisory services, administers the Environment Fund, prepares the organization's long-term plan, and submits it to the Governing Council. The 58-member Governing Council decides on program activities, provides policy directives for the U.N. system and UNEP's secretariat, and convenes drafting conferences for international environmental agreements. Each council member is elected by the General Assembly for a four-year term.[138]

UNEP's secretariat and program are funded through the regular budget of the United Nations (on the order of 10 percent), voluntary contributions to the Environment Fund (approximately 70 percent), trust funds (some 15 percent), and counterpart contributions (about 5 percent). UNEP's activities depend largely on voluntary contributions. This fact effectively limits its role to one of catalyst, coordinator, and educator. UNEP's total budget, of which the United States contributed about one-third, was approximately $70 million in 1993.[139]

Although UNEP is the first international agency devoted exclusively to environmental issues, it is not the first effort in international cooperation on environmental issues. International environmental cooperation had previously taken place through the efforts of several U.N. specialized agencies. The International Maritime Organization (IMO) began addressing the control of marine pollution in 1952. The FAO had a constitutional mandate, dating from 1945, for the "conservation of natural resources." Since 1920 the ILO had established international agreements to protect workers against environmental hazards. The World Meteorological Organization has coordinated the sharing of atmospheric data since the nineteenth century. Other agreements had been established to protect migratory birds and to manage water resources even before World War I.[140]

The Nixon administration was relatively unsympathetic to environmental concerns. The White House Council on Environmental Quality (CEQ) had been established in 1969 by Congress over the objections of the White House. Nixon was prompted, however, by public opinion to appear responsive to environmental concerns. His first official act on 1 January 1970 was to sign the National Environmental Policy Act, which established the CEQ and mandated environmental assessments of public investment.[141] Resistance by the Nixon administration to the domestic environmental agenda was not reflected in U.S. participation in the 1972 Stockholm Conference on the Human Environment.[142]

The 1972 Stockholm Conference

The conference emphasis on the relationship between development and environment came largely from concerns expressed by developing countries that emphasis on environment would detract from their developmental efforts. This issue was addressed at the conference by a panel report of Third World scientists. Their 1971 report (the Founex report) was tabled to the conference as a working paper. The report emphasized that it is important to recognize not only the potential environmental hazards of industrialization, but also that poverty itself is both a cause and an effect of environmental degradation. The U.S. delegation also made a major contribution in shaping the Declaration on the Human Environment. At Stockholm, the phrase "poverty is the worst form of pollution" was coined.[143] The institutional arrangements agreed upon, however, were much more modest than the ambitious objectives outlined by the conference.

Nongovernmental organizations played an important though unofficial role at the 1972 Stockholm Conference. An unofficial NGO conference, the Environment Forum, which was partially funded by the Swedish government, took place simultaneously with the official conference. Its influence on the conference was more limited than expected because of the tendency of some delegates to attempt to advance other agendas, such as opposition to the Vietnam War and anticolonialism.[144]

The UNEP was established in spite of U.S. objections. The U.S. delegation had arrived at the conference with instructions to "get a headline a day" but was forced to make the best of what amounted to a series of defeats in battle over the statement of principles.[145] UNEP was designated as a voluntary program rather than a specialized agency. Maurice Strong, a Canadian businessman and development agency official, was appointed its first executive director. He was succeeded in 1976 by Mostapha Tolba, an Egyptian microbiologist and government official (Table B.7). Both Strong and Tolba were characterized by strong entrepreneurial and weak administrative capacities.[146]

UNEP Activities, 1973–1992

Since the 1972 Stockholm Conference, the UNEP has used its position to encourage governmental, international organizational, and nongovernmental action on environmental issues. As a catalyst to governmental action, UNEP has worked to facilitate international cooperation on the monitoring of the earth's environment, the disposal of hazardous wastes, the management of freshwater resources, the fight against desertification, and other critical issues. UNEP works with the specialized agencies to identify and coordinate environmental projects and with nongovernmental industry and community organizations to raise consciousness of the importance of environmental issues. It has made significant efforts to induce developing countries to take part in world environmental programs.

During its first two decades, the UNEP played a leading role in facilitating and sponsoring several important international programs and agreements, including the Global Environmental Monitoring System (GEMS), the 1985 Vienna Convention on ozone-depleting substances and the subsequent 1987 Montreal Protocol on the phasing out of chlorofluorocarbons and other ozone-deleting chemicals, the international agreement on the Basil Convention of 1989 limiting transboundary movement of hazardous waste, and the negotiations leading to agreements to reduce pollution in 10 regional seas, including the Mediterranean and the Caribbean. It played a lead role, along with the World Meteorological Organization, in preparations for the Climate Change Convention and in the negotiation of the Convention on Biological Diversity signed at the 1992 Earth Summit Conference in Rio de Janeiro.[147]

UNEP cooperates with nongovernmental organizations as well as other U.N. and national agencies. It has established strong working relationships with international NGOs, including the International Council of Scientific Unions (ICSU), the International Union for the Conservation of Nature and Natural Resources (IUCN), the World Wildlife Foundation (WWF), and the International Institute for Environment and Development (IIED). The importance that UNEP attaches to nongovernmental organizations is illustrated by the Outreach Network begun in 1982. Through this network UNEP helps to disseminate information on environmental and health issues to schools and the media.[148]

To commemorate the 10th anniversary of UNEP's creation, a special meeting of the Governing Council of Governments met in Nairobi in 1982. The environmental concerns that the United States had expressed at Stockholm had become pervasive by the time of the 1982 Nairobi meeting. But in Nairobi the Reagan administration took the position that nations should rely primarily on market forces—"free market environmentalism"—in preference to regulations to cope with environmental problems. The U.S. delegation insisted that international agreements were not an appropriate means to effect environmental protection. The Conference Declaration reaffirmed the principles of the Stockholm Declaration and called on all nations to implement the action plan more fully. The declaration also reiterated the concerns of developing countries, insisting that "threats to the environment are aggravated by poverty as well as by wasteful consumption patterns; both can lead people to overexploit their environment."[149]

An important step toward a broader consensus on the issue of environment and development was achieved in the 1987 report of the United Nations World Commission on Environment and Development, *Our Common Future.* The report became known as the Brundtland report after the prime minister of Norway, Gro Harlen Brundtland, who chaired the World Commission on Environment and Development. The commission advanced the concept of "sustainable" development as a comprehensive response to an interlocking set of global crises in the areas of environment, development, population, and energy. "Sustainable development is development that meets the needs of the present without compromising the ability of future generations to meet their own needs."[150] The report asserted that the needs of both the present and future generations must be considered in making resource and environmental policy.

The Brundtland commission report saw its most urgent task as persuading nations of the need for a multilateral approach. It identified the United Nations as the preferred locus for a new institutional initiative because it is the only international organization with universal membership. It also recognized that the independent character of the specialized agencies and weakness in coordination have made the U.N. system less effective than desired, but asserted that these shortcomings were correctable.[151]

The commission discussed at length a reorientation of UNEP in view of the leveling off of funding despite a substantial increase in range of activities. "UNEP should be the principal source on environmental data, assessment, reporting, and related support for environmental management as well as the principal advocate and agent for change and cooperation on critical environment and natural resource protection issues."[152] It urged that UNEP's catalytic and coordinating role in the U.N. system be reinforced and extended.

The Bush administration continued the Reagan emphasis on market forces and minimal government involvement. However, its "no regrets" policy doctrine led it to adopt a somewhat more positive posture on global environmental issues. The president supported the moratorium on mining in Antarctica and recommended spending $50 million to clean up past pollution from U.S. research bases there. In 1990 Presidents Bush and Gorbachev announced their decision to create an international park across the Bering Straits. The United States participates actively in the UNEP/World Meteorological Organization (WMO) Intergovernmental Panel on Climate Change. In February 1990, the president signed the U.N. Economic Commission for Europe's Treaty on Trans-boundary Environmental Impact Assessment and sent it to the Senate for ratification. The president supported the establishment of a center in Budapest to assist in the development of environment protection programs. He made a commitment to the elimination of chlorofluorocarbons and authorized a $220,875 contribution to the U.N. Trust Fund in support of the Vienna Convention and the Montreal Protocol.[153]

On the negative side, the Reagan and Bush administrations provided limited financial support for the UNEP. Funding ran in the $7–10 million range in the early and mid-1980s. Congress has, however, consistently voted more funding than requested by the administration. By fiscal 1992, U.S. funding for UNEP had risen to $22 million. In general, the Bush administration preferred that multilateral environmental funds be channeled through a World Bank/UNDP/UNEP Global Environment Facility (GEF) established in 1990, where the United States is perceived as having greater influence on programming.[154] The United States has participated little in the new UNEP regional seas organization, insisting that customary international law is sufficient. During the first two years of the Bush administration, there was often considerable conflict between White House Chief of Staff John Sununu and EPA Administrator William Reilly. Sununu's own calculations, on his personal computer, led him to conclude, for example, that concerns about climate change had been blown out of proportion.

The United Nations Conference on Environment and Development

In June 1992, the United Nations sponsored a major international Conference on Environment and Development (the Earth Summit) in Rio de Janeiro. UNEP, although not the sponsor, played an important facilitating role in the conference. UNEP organized the negotiations for the Convention on Biological Diversity and placed observers on all of the conference's preparatory committees. UNEP was also given a substantial role in the implementation of conference outputs. There was reference to strengthening UNEP, discussion of combining UNEP with UNDP, and, finally, the creation of a Commission on Sustainable Development as an institution to help implement the conference agenda.

The United States anticipated limited results from the Earth Summit. Curtis Bohlen, as the assistant secretary of state for oceans and international environmental and scientific affairs, testified that the United States would commit itself to ensuring that ongoing and future bilateral and multilateral assistance projects are sustainable. But he foresaw little prospect of new funding. Any new funding would, according to Bohlen, be channeled through the new Global Environment Facility.[155]

At the three preparatory conferences, the United States made constructive contributions in key areas such as oceans, freshwater resources, toxic waste substances, waste management, and institutional arrangements. The United States was also a strong proponent of opening the process to nongovernmental organizations.[156] On some more contentious issues, however, the U.S.

position was dominated by "three no's." It expressed strong opposition to any "new and additional" funding for environmental programs, to proposals for new programs of international cooperation, and to new commitments on fossil fuels and forests that would require changes in U.S. policy.

After considerable indecision, President Bush attended the Rio Conference, more for symbolic than for substantive purposes. His appearance was marred by embarrassing disagreement with the head of the U.S. delegation, EPA Administrator William Reilly, over signing the proposed Convention on Biological Diversity. A letter from Reilly to the White House requesting approval to seek agreement on relatively minor adjustments that would meet U.S. objections and the reply refusing such approval were leaked to the press by a White House source, causing considerable embarrassment to the U.S. delegation to the conference.[157]

The U.S. delegation to the Rio Conference included representatives from both the Senate and the House. The Senate delegation was headed by Senator Albert Gore, Jr. (D-Tenn.), and the House delegation was headed by Representative George Miller (D-Calif.). The acrimony between the congressional delegation and the administration was reminiscent of the dissension at the 1973 World Food Conference (Chap. 8). Several members of the congressional delegation made speeches in which they expressed substantial criticism of U.S. lack of leadership.

The achievements of the Rio Earth Summit included the adoption of binding conventions on climate change and biodiversity. The provisions of the climate change convention were substantially weakened to assure signature by the United States. The United States was the only participant that failed to sign the biodiversity convention at Rio. An agreement on tropical forestry was adopted only in the form of a nonbinding statement of principles. A wide-ranging 800-page action program, *Agenda 21,* was adopted. It included a recommendation for the establishment of an institutional arrangement, the Commission on Sustainable Development (CSD), as a functional commission of the U.N. Economic and Social Council.[158]

In December 1992, the United Nations General Assembly authorized the establishment of the Commission on Sustainable Development. The commission was established at the February 1993 meeting of the Economic and Social Council.[159] U.N. Secretary-General Boutros-Ghali has appointed an Under-Secretary-General, Nitin Desai, to oversee the work of the CSD. Its establishment required that the United States, the United Kingdom, and other developed countries relax the "no new institutions" stance that they had adopted in the late 1980s. Its establishment also raises serious questions about the future role of the UNEP. A key to the future is the implementation of *Agenda 21*. However, no new or additional funding was provided to implement the work of the United Nations Conference on Environment and Development (UNCED). An increase in the UNEP budget from the $70 million level of the early 1980s to an estimated $250–300 million, which would be needed to implement the program, is difficult to imagine in the constipated fiscal environment of the mid-1990s.

Perspective

The primary objective of this chapter has been to understand U.S. policy toward the formation and development of the several U.N. specialized agencies and voluntary programs. Particular attention has been devoted to four specialized agencies—FAO, ILO, UNESCO, and WHO—and three voluntary programs—UNDP, UNICEF, and UNEP.

The United States played an important leadership role in the establishment of the U.N. system. From its founding in the mid-1940s until the mid-1970s, the United States was largely supportive of the specialized agencies and voluntary programs. U.S. criticism was more likely to emphasize the failure of the system to live up to the expectations of its founders or constitutional mandates than the failure of its specific activities or programs. During the mid-1970s the criticisms began to change. The United Nations began to be viewed by some segments of U.S. society and polity as a dangerous place—as a threat to U.S. sovereignty and to U.S. economic and political institutions. The United States has consistently attempted to limit the programs and budgets of the specialized agencies and voluntary programs. Coate has argued, however, that a coherent explanation of the shift in policy toward the U.N. specialized agencies and voluntary programs since the late 1960s is not available. He rejects the view that a decline in U.S. power provides an adequate explanation and points to the particular issues involved, their relation to American liberal and conservative ideologies, the organizational characteristics of the particular agencies, the roles and personalities of particular directors-general, the attitudes of U.S. administrators and officials, biases in reporting by the U.S. media, and the agendas of U.S. interest groups. He argues that an adequate bases for weighing the importance of these factors is not available.[160]

The basis for U.S. policy toward U.N. agencies concerned with nonsecurity issues has been poorly defined. The GAO has repeatedly pointed out that evaluation of the work of the specialized agencies is rendered difficult because of the lack of established U.S. policy guidelines toward the U.N. specialized agencies and affiliated organizations. One of the reasons that U.S. policy is not well defined is that there are often differences of opinion and little coordination among the various U.S. departments concerned and the State Department.[161] Another is that, historically, the United States has been less interested in the nonsecurity aspects of multilateral relations than in those directly related to U.S.-USSR relations. The United States has also been averse to being party to international agreements that might seem to infringe on U.S. sovereignty or violate the principle of federalism.

The sources of U.S. policy toward the United Nations and its specialized agencies have also changed. The general public has been, at least until the United Nations expanded its peace-keeping activities in the mid-1990s, broadly supportive of the United Nations.[162] But its knowledge of the activities of the specialized agencies and programs, with the possible exception of UNICEF, has been slight. Constituency groups such as the United Nations Association and the National Commission for UNESCO have been moderately effective in using the media to make information about U.N. activities available to the public and in lobbying Congress on behalf of the United Nations and its agencies and programs. The agencies themselves have also utilized publicity campaigns such as the FAO-sponsored annual World Food Day in an attempt to create a favorable impression.

Since the mid-1970s critics of the United Nations have become more effective in arousing public opinion against specific programs. In the early and mid-1980s, the Heritage Foundation conducted an active program of criticism against the FAO, UNESCO, and other specialized agencies. The American Jewish community brought pressure on Congress to eliminate funding for UNESCO after the adoption by UNESCO of the resolutions concerning Israeli rights of participation in the European regional grouping and violations of Islamic cultural artifacts and of education policy in the occupied territories. Since the mid-1970s Congress has played a more active role in policy toward the U.N. specialized agencies and programs. This more active congressional role has been in part a reflection of constituency interests. During the 1980s, however, congressional policy was driven more by budgetary constraints than by concern about substantive issues. The Kassebaum amendment in the Foreign Relations Authorizations Bill of 1985, which called for a reduction in the U.S. assessed contribution to the U.N system from 25 percent to 20 percent, and the Gramm-Rudman-Hollings sponsored Balanced Budget and Emergency Deficit Central Act of the same year both had severe consequences on the budget and programs of the specialized agencies and voluntary programs. However, when, in 1987, the administration adopted a policy of paying the arrears that had been accumulated during the Reagan administration, Congress responded by appropriating amounts that exceeded the administration's requests for fiscal year 1988.

Before 1980, presidential policy had been largely favorable to the U.N. specialized agencies and programs. They were viewed, consistent with the functionalist perspective, as valuable if somewhat flawed instruments of U.S. policy. President Carter reluctantly acceded to AFL-CIO President George Meany's pressure for withdrawal from ILO and resumed participation two years later in response to ILO reforms. The Reagan administration adopted, at least at the rhetorical level, a strong anti–United Nations stance. The administration's position was strongly influenced by the right wing of the Republican party and the personal antagonism of Gregory Newell, the assistant secretary of state for international affairs (1982–85), toward the U.N. system and UNESCO in particular.

A continuing puzzle has been the failure of a series of administrations to develop a more coherent policy toward the specialized agencies and voluntary programs. There was broad agreement by the early 1970s—even among sympathetic observers—that in many of the agencies and programs personal and political considerations rather than professional qualifications often dominated the selection of candidates for senior positions, that secretariats had become increasingly unresponsive to the concerns of member states, that the translation of general conference resolutions into policy was often distorted, that headquarters staffs had been excessively expanded, and that the general conferences were often used as a forum for the articulation of political issues that were extraneous to the functions of the particular agency or program.

Genuine reforms were and are needed. When adequately qualified U.S. delegations have participated with patience and perseverance, reforms proposed by the United States have often been realized. But the quality of U.S. participation, reflected in the selection of representatives and the staff work by the Bureau for International Organization Affairs, particularly since the early 1980s, has often been inadequate. The U.S. comptroller-general's office has issued a series of reports that have been highly critical of the failure of the State Department and the sectoral departments to develop coherent policy toward the specialized agencies and programs. It is somewhat ironic that the staffing of leadership positions in the Bureau for International Organization Affairs has been criticized on essentially the same grounds as the bureau has directed toward the U.N. agencies (Table A.16).

With the end of the Cold War and the decline in the intensity of ideological debate in international fora, it is time to rethink U.S. interests in international cooperation and the rationale for U.S. participation in multilateral organizations. Critics of the U.N. system within recent administrations have, at least at the staff level, been more concerned with the effectiveness of program delivery by the agencies and with the North-South divisiveness that has hindered the performance and credibility of the agencies. Criticisms have more frequently focused on specific activities than on overall agency performance. These concerns, if effectively anticipated in U.N. fora, should contribute to a more effective program. The critics on the Right, however, have been motivated by a deeper agenda. They are concerned with the implications of formal structures of international interdependence on the erosion of sovereignty—and they hope to reverse, stall, or at least slow down the erosion. The defenders share the critics' perception—but they welcome the erosion of sovereignty as a step in taming the exercise of excessive economic and political nationalism. They hope, in effect, that the Lilliputians can effectively tame the American Gulliver. These issues will not easily be resolved.

Part V

Reform and Redirection

Chapter 13

Reforming U.S. Foreign Economic Assistance

When the Clinton administration assumed office in 1993, the U.S. development assistance program was in disarray. The bilateral development assistance budget had declined continuously in real terms since the mid-1980s. The Economic Support Fund, which had experienced rapid growth during the first Reagan administration, had declined even more rapidly than development assistance during the second Reagan administration. Contributions to multilateral assistance programs had risen modestly in nominal terms but were lower in real terms than a decade earlier (see Figures 7.1 and 7.2)[1]

During the second Reagan administration, the easing of political tensions between the United States and the Soviet Union had contributed to a decline in the willingness of Congress to continue to sustain foreign assistance at the level achieved in the mid-1980s. The demise of the Soviet empire and the end of the Cold War during the first two years of the Bush administration placed additional demands on a beleaguered assistance agency. Inept AID administration and a proclivity on the part of Secretary of State James Baker to improvise rather than draw on staff capacity contributed to further weakening of the role of the AID. During 1991–93, the outgoing Bush administration and the incoming Clinton administration were confronted with an outpouring of commission and task force reports from official sources and from the assistance community urging either the reform or the dismemberment of the agency.

These were not the first efforts to reform or reorganize the U.S. economic assistance effort. Between 1950 and 1959 there were eight major official program and policy reviews of the U.S. assistance programs.[2] U.S. technical and economic assistance activities had gone through a series of reorganizations (Figure 13.1). It was not until 1961, however, that the several U.S. bilateral assistance programs were merged into a single organization—the Agency

FIGURE 13.1
Changes in U.S. Foreign Aid Administration and Aid Programs

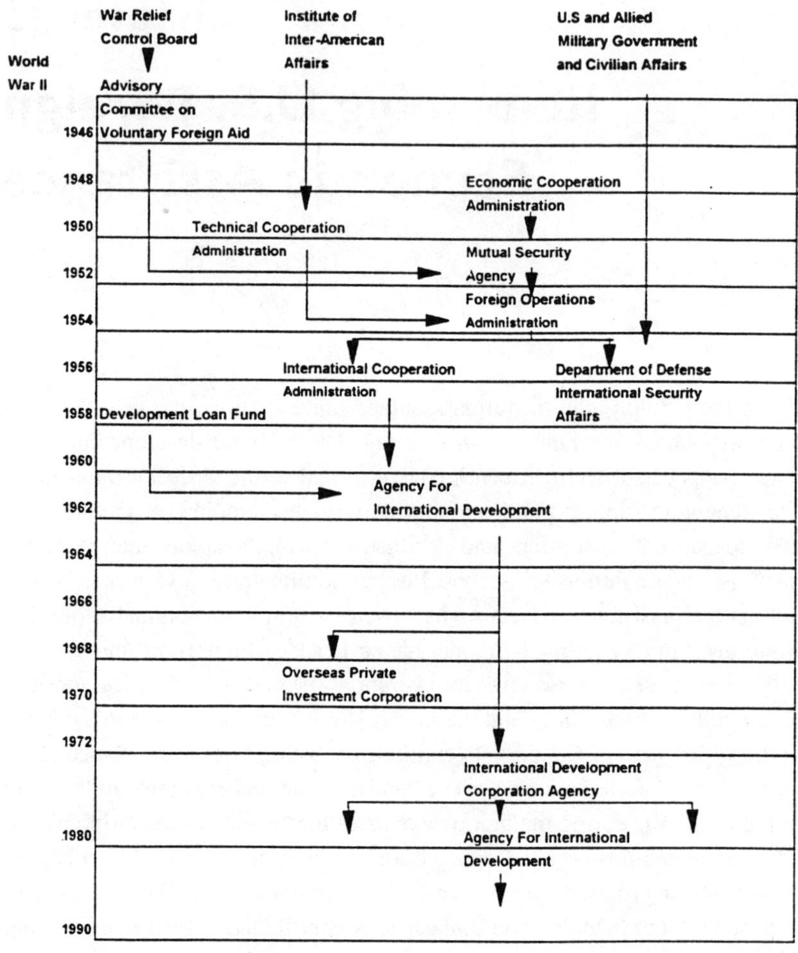

for International Development. During the 1960s and 1970s, reports of study commissions continued to proliferate. In the late 1970s an effort was made to create a coordinating body, the International Development Cooperation Agency, that would provide policy guidance and coordination for the entire U.S. economic assistance effort.

In this chapter I review efforts, including the proposals made in the late 1980s and early 1990s, to reform or reorganize the U.S. foreign economic assistance effort. A remarkable feature of the reforms proposed for the 1990s is the continuing relevance of tension between idealist (or liberal) doctrine and realist (or conservative) doctrine. This tension has been described by Charles William Maynes: "The post-war foreign policy consensus that shattered in Vietnam was after all, the result of a coalition between the iron-willed and the big-hearted. The former urged huge defense budgets and committed anti-communism. They raised the clenched fist. The later embraced developmental assistance and the policies of interdependence. They extended the helping hand. Each tolerated the other. Each made compromises it might have preferred to avoid. But the result was an uneasy concord about the direction and content of American foreign policy. As long as the American economy was strong, the casualties were low, and the consensus endured."[3]

From Mutual Security to AID

During the early 1950s, the U.S. assistance effort was dominated by Cold War tensions and the containment doctrine. The major aid recipients were countries on the periphery of the Soviet Union and China. By the mid-1950s, the nature of the competition between the United States and the Soviet Union was beginning to change. In 1953 the Soviet Union became a contributor to the U.N. Expanded Program of Technical Assistance. In 1956 it replaced the United States and the World Bank as a source of assistance to Egypt for construction of the Aswan High Dam (Chap. 10). The competition moved to areas further from the periphery of the Soviet Empire—to Latin America, Africa, and Southeast Asia.

In his study, *The Politics of Foreign Aid,* John White notes that the transition from harmony to competition in aid giving was accompanied by a transition to greater emphasis on the developmental uses of aid. The attachment of explicit political conditions on aid was increasingly seen "as likely to drive the recipients into the arms of the Russians as to win new allies for the United States."[4] The emergence of a series of newly independent states in Africa, beginning with Ghana in 1957, widened the opportunities for competition. Vice President Nixon's disastrous trip to Latin America in 1958 propelled the issues of "neglect of Latin America" into the debate of the 1960 election campaign (Chap. 5). During the 1960 presidential election campaign, Kennedy, sensing Nixon's vulnerability, attacked the Eisenhower administration for its failure to assist the people of Latin America to realize their economic and political aspirations.

After his election President Kennedy moved rapidly to strengthen the U.S. commitment to Latin American economic development. In November 1960 he asked Adolf Berle, professor of international law at Columbia University and an assistant secretary of state for Latin America, to head a task force to formulate the outline for U.S. policy toward Latin America. On 13 March 1961, in a speech at a White House reception for members of Congress and for the diplomatic corps of the Latin American republics, Kennedy called on all people of the hemisphere to join in a new Alliance for Progress—an *Alianza para Progresso*—to satisfy the basic needs of the American people for homes, work and land, health, and schools (Chap. 5).[5]

President Kennedy also moved rapidly to reorganize the U.S. assistance effort. In his inaugural address, President Kennedy pledged increased assistance to the poor countries of the world, "not because the Communists are doing it, but because it is right." Under-Secretary of State George W. Ball headed an informal internal study group to establish the framework for a reorganized aid program. This was followed by a presidential message to Congress in March. A week later President Kennedy formally appointed a Task Force on Foreign Economic Assistance, directed by International Cooperation Administration Director Henry R. Labouisse. In June the task force proposed the creation of a new foreign economic assistance agency to be named the *Agency for International Development.*[6] The task force recommended that

> the Agency for International Development will combine under the direction of a single administration the present Washington and field operations of the International Cooperation Administration, the Development Loan Fund, the Food-for-Peace Program in its relation with other countries, the local currency lending activities of the Export-Import Bank, the donation of nonagricultural surpluses from stockpiles of excess commodities and equipment, and the related staff and program services now provided by the Department of State and the International Cooperative administration.[7]

During the summer the Senate Foreign Relations Committee and the House Foreign Affairs Committee held hearings. Much of the controversy centered around the president's request for long-term financing of development loans for industrial and infrastructure development. After a good deal of rather acrimonious debate in Congress, the Kennedy proposals were incorporated into the Foreign Assistance Act of 1961 (S. 1983, PL 87-195). The bill was passed with faint praise but by very large margins and signed into law by President Kennedy on September 4. (See Chap. 5 for further discussion of the House and Senate debates.)

Kennedy was able to obtain from Congress much of what he had requested in his reorganization proposals. The 1961 act combined the responsibilities of the International Cooperation Administration and the Development Loan Fund under a single agency. Other major departures from previous policy included (*a*) an emphasis on long-range economic planning by the recipient country as a basis for the allocation of assistance resources, (*b*) a clear emphasis on the priority of economic development objectives relative to strategic and military objectives, (*c*) organization of the field activities of the new agency along regional rather than technical lines, and (*d*) the authority to make long-term assistance (five-year) commitments—although without the long-term borrowing authority for aid lending that Kennedy had requested. Congress also expressed strong support for multilateral assistance and for closer collaboration with other bilateral donors and indicated a preference that assistance for the poorest countries should emphasize human development rather than the financing of capital facilities. The 1961 act placed greater emphasis than had earlier legislation on grants in support of technical assistance and authorized the new agency to undertake a program of research and development in support of the U.S. assistance effort. Kennedy was not successful, however, in bringing the Peace Corps or the development lending activities of the Export-Import Bank under the new agency. The Department of Agriculture retained major responsibility for the Food for Peace Program, and the military assistance component of the foreign assistance effort remained larger than either Kennedy or the task force had hoped.

Implementation of the new policies enunciated in the 1961 act was delayed by difficulties in establishing effective leadership of the new agency. The position of administrator was first offered to George Wood, a New York investment banker and later president of the World Bank. When the Wood nomination ran into trouble in Congress because of his firm's involvement in an effort of the Eisenhower administration to privatize the Tennessee Valley Authority, Kennedy turned to Fowler Hamilton, a New York lawyer with government experience during World War II.[8] But the momentum of the reforms was dampened by what Walt Rostow referred to as "administrative problems."[9] Within the agency there was strong resistance to moving from organization along technical lines—agriculture, public health, housing, and others—to a regional pattern of organization. Hamilton was replaced by David E. Bell, then-director of the Bureau of the Budget, in January 1963. By that time there was increasing resistance in Congress to growth in AID funding. One consequence was a rapid shift in project funding from grants to loans.[10]

The initial momentum for improved relations with Latin America generated by President Kennedy's Alliance for Progress proposal was rapidly dissipated. The invasion of Cuba on April 17 by Cuban exiles—organized, financed, armed, and transported by the Central Intelligence Agency—became a divisive element in the August Punta del Este conference convened to write a charter for the alliance.[11] U.S. support for economic and social development in Latin America was seen as motivated primarily by the U.S. concern to contain and weaken the Castro regime. Within a year of the Punta del Este meeting, there had been a major turn away from constitutional government in Brazil, Argentina, and Peru. In retrospect, however, it was the U.S. preoccupation with security that subverted our efforts to contribute to economic and social reform in Latin America and to the alliance.[12]

Focus on the Poor

The Foreign Assistance Act of 1973 represented the first major reform in the U.S. foreign economic assistance program since passage of the 1961 act. This time the initiative originated in Congress rather than the administration (Chap. 6). The stage was set for the reform, however, by the enunciation of the Nixon Doctrine in July 1969. The Nixon Doctrine reversed the Kennedy "bear every burden" commitment. In a 1970 amplification Nixon insisted that "the United States . . . cannot—and will not—conceive all plans, design all programs, execute all decisions, and undertake all the defense of the free nations of the world."[13] Support for AID in Congress was eroded by growing tension with the administration over continued involvement in the Vietnam conflict. On October 9 the Senate, for the first time, voted down a foreign aid bill. The AID budget declined in both 1972 and 1973. The deadlock was broken, as detailed in Chapter 6, by a congressional initiative that dramatically shifted the direction of the foreign aid program. The new policy was described somewhat overenthusiastically by Robert A. Pastor:

> The thrust of the bilateral development program changed from an economic strategy of maximizing gross national product and industrialization and a political strategy of providing the largest amounts of aid and food commodities to military allies to a more socially-oriented strategy of helping the poorest countries and the poorest sectors of the population in these countries. A complete reorganization of AID from an agency defined by geographical categories to one based on the three principal functions of a development process aimed at the "poorest 40 percent," food and nutrition; population, planning and health; and education and human resources.[14]

Much of the initiative for change came from Congress. Congressmen Dante Fascell (D-Fla.) and Donald Fraser (D-Minn.) of the House Foreign Affairs Committee were key players. A group of Washington-based scholars grouped around the Overseas Development Council also played important roles in feeding ideas into the legislative process. Both efforts were reinforced by the subtle hand of AID Administrator John Hannah, who encouraged the proposed changes in spite of opposition from the State Department and the White House.

It is clear, in retrospect, that the shift in AID programming lagged behind the shift in policy and rhetoric. By the late 1970s, however, the new personnel streams and the merging of loan and grant systems were resulting in greater consistency between assistance programming and the objectives of the New Directions policy.

The Coordination of U.S. Assistance Programs

At the time of the 1961 reorganization, the United States accounted for over two-thirds of bilateral economic assistance and close to three-fourths of all assistance flows. The World Bank was just completing a transition from regarding itself primarily as a finance agency to assuming a broader role as a development institution (Chap. 11). Within the U.S. government the new Agency for International Development appeared to have both the mandate and the resources to assume the role of lead agency for foreign economic assistance.

By the mid-1970s, it was clear that the capacity of AID to function as a lead agency in assistance policy and coordination had weakened. Several factors were involved. One of the most important was the effect on the agency of the major responsibility that it had been assigned for the Vietnam program beginning in the early 1960s (Chap. 10). Responsibility for program implementation remained with AID even after Defense and State had asserted control over all decision making with respect to Vietnam. One former AID officer has commented, "AID was a failure in Vietnam not only because the U.S. was a failure, but because AID did not hold onto its responsibilities within the total U.S. effort."[15] The very large growth of agency staff during the Vietnam war, followed by an equally major contraction after the war, had a major negative influence on agency personnel capacity and morale. Suspension of AID to India during the Bangladesh War in 1971 tended to confirm the perspective that the agency's development objectives were secondary to its role in support of security objectives.

A second factor was a shift in relative emphasis toward greater multilateral assistance (Chap. 12). In 1979 U.S. support for the programs of the multilateral development banks was larger than the bilateral assistance program administered by AID. Responsibility for policy toward and liaison with a series of U.N. programs—the U.N. Development Programme, UNICEF, the U.N. Disaster Relief Organization, and several other programs—rested with the International Organizations Bureau of the State Department rather than with AID. This shift gave the Treasury, which is the major policy and financial link with the multilateral banks, and the State Department, which had major responsibility for relations with the U.N. organizations, a larger role relative to AID. A further change was a relative shift in bilateral aid from program assistance to project assistance. This change was largely a response to the New Directions and basic human needs approaches to development assistance (Chap. 6). It was accompanied by a reduction in the capacity of AID to undertake macroeconomic analyses of national development plans and programs and to interact effectively at a professional level with the multilateral banks. Another important factor was the growth, particularly during the 1970s, of nonaid resource transfers. As the earnings of the oil-exporting countries rose dramatically during the 1970s, the funds were rapidly recycled through the international banking system into loans to a rapidly growing group of newly industrializing developing countries.

The traditional mechanisms for coordination of the aid effort among U.S. government agencies were the National Advisory Council on International Monetary and Financial Policies (NAC) and the Development Coordinating Committee (DCC). The NAC was a longstanding interagency body, chaired by Treasury, that reviewed all international loans of the United States—including AID loans. The DCC is an interdepartmental body, created in 1973, to coordinate U.S. bilateral and multilateral assistance programs. It was chaired by the AID administrator and staffed by the agency. The effectiveness of the DCC was limited, almost from the beginning, by what one observer described as "a fatal design flaw." It was unrealistic to expect that a committee chaired by the AID administrator, who held subcabinet rank, could provide policy leadership and coordination to cabinet-level officials. Lack of enthusiasm for the concept of aid coordination by Secretary of State Kissinger further undermined the potential effectiveness of DCC during the Ford administration. When the cabinet-level members reduced their participation in favor of sub–cabinet level staff, the DCC lost any hope of performing its lead agency function. At the beginning of the Carter administration, DCC staff effort was first directed to a review of the AID program and only later to the development of proposals for AID reorganization.

Increased concern with the organization and effectiveness of the U.S. foreign economic development assistance effort became evident to both the administration and Congress. In the spring of 1978, the Department of State contracted with the Brookings Institution to conduct an assessment, directed by Lincoln Gordon, of U.S. development assistance strategies and organization. The work was carried out under the guidance of Henry Owen, director of the Brookings Institution Foreign Policy Studies Program, and by an advisory committee chaired by David E. Bell, then a Ford Foundation vice president. The study recommended that "new legislation should be sought authorizing the establishment of a Development Cooperation Agency which would be AID's successor; and an International Development Foundation, which would be concerned with research and development and with training."[16]

The mission of the Development Cooperation Agency would be to continue AID's operational programs and technical assistance. This report recommended a renewed commitment to the poverty reduction objectives of the 1973 New Directions legislation (Chap. 6). The Development Cooperation Agency was envisaged as an independent agency reporting to the president. The issue of aid coordination was discussed, and several alternative approaches, with their advantages and limitations, were outlined.

The new International Development Foundation (IDF) would be organized as an autonomous, permanent agency somewhat comparable to the National Science Foundation. It would serve as the central source of knowledge concerning research priorities in the field of development. It would strengthen the contribution of U.S. universities and guide and support U.S. government research on development problems. And it would help build research and training capacity in the developing countries. A major impetus for the IDF was the recent demonstration of the potential power of agricultural research to remove technical constraints on food production through the establishment of research capacity in the tropics. Although there was no specific reference in the Brookings report, the proposed IDF would function in a manner remarkably similar in design to the highly regarded Canadian International Development Research Center (IDRC).

Congress was, during this same period, becoming increasingly critical of what it perceived as the disorganization of the aid effort. Just before his death in the winter of 1978, Senator Hubert H. Humphrey (D-Minn.) had completed work on a bill proposing the establishment of an International Development Cooperation Agency to replace AID. Shortly after Senator Humphrey's death, Senator Sparkman (D-Ala.) (with 20 co-sponsors) introduced the bill formulated by Senator Humphrey. In the Humphrey bill, "the Director of IDCA was to report directly to the President rather than to the Secretary of State and was to have major responsibility for policy relating to . . . bilateral assistance, multilateral development banks, aid programs of international organizations, the Overseas Private Investment Corporation, certain Public Law 480 functions, policy toward activities of the International Fund for Agricultural Development, and the Peace Corps."[17] The Humphrey bill, like the Brookings report, also proposed the establishment of an autonomous foundation-like organization to manage scientific and technical cooperation—an Institute for Technological Cooperation (ITC). Similar legislation was introduced in the House by the chairman of the House Foreign Affairs Committee, Congressman Clement Zablocki (D-Wis.).

President Carter assigned to Henry Owen, who had been brought into the White House as special representative for economic summits, responsibility for liaison with Congress and for initiating the additional staff work needed to support the proposed reorganization. On April 10 President Carter submitted a reorganization plan to Congress and on May 17 he issued a presidential directive reorganizing the DCC to meet some of the concerns expressed about the proposed legislation.[18] Although Congress took no action on the Humphrey-Zablocki bill, it did direct the president to institute a strengthened system of coordination of U.S. development assistance policies and urged the creation of a new agency with primary responsibility for coordination of international development-related activities. The reorganization plan proposing the establishment of the IDCA and an ITC was submitted to Congress in April 1979.

The reorganization proposals precipitated a period of intense debate both within and outside of the administration. Treasury, as might be expected, vigorously resisted transfer of responsibility for the multilateral development banks to the proposed IDCA. The Peace Corps, although initially compliant, began a campaign of resistance once it became apparent that other agencies were resisting the transfer of activities. The AID administrator, former governor of Ohio John J. Gilligan, acting in his role as chairman of the DCC, appointed an internal study group to propose options for the organization and responsibilities of the IDCA and an advisory committee headed by David Bell and a planning office headed by Ralph Smuckler of Michigan State University to work out a blueprint for an Institute for Scientific and Technical Cooperation (ISTC).

The reorganization plan that President Carter forwarded to Congress attempted to balance the conflicting interests of Congress to exert stronger coordination of the U.S. assistance effort and those of the administration, particularly Treasury, to preserve agency prerogatives. The plan provided for an IDCA with far weaker coordination responsibilities than had been proposed in the original Humphrey bill. The GAO evaluation, referred to above, characterized this plan as weaker than any of the three that had been included in Administrator Gilligan's options—including the weakest option that had been favored by Gilligan.

Ambassador Owen was apparently more strongly committed to the establishment of ISTC than to an IDCA with strong policy coordination authority. At the House and Senate hearings held in May 1979, supporters of the proposed reorganization repeatedly sought assurances from him that the plan would give the IDCA director sufficient authority to coordinate U.S. policy toward the multilateral development banks and to resist pressures from the State Department to direct assistance resources to short-term political purposes.[19] Neither congressional supporters nor critics found the reassurances offered by the administration to be very compelling. It is clear, in retrospect, that the reorganization plan that was put into place was an exceedingly weak response to the concerns that had led Senator Humphrey to propose the establishment of an IDCA.

The establishment of an autonomous Institute for Scientific and Technological Cooperation (ISTC) proved at least as controversial as the establishment of the IDCA. Impetus for the establishment of ISTC stemmed largely from concern by the federal science agencies, the university community, and the private sector that, in spite of the commitment in the original Point Four Program and in the 1961 reorganization plan, the U.S. development assistance program had failed to adequately bring U.S. research and development capacity to bear on the solution of the technical and economic problems faced by the developing countries. In the late 1960s and early 1970s, there was concern among the academic community that the AID research program had been distorted to serve political and strategic concerns rather than development objectives. These were reinforced in the late 1970s by a concern that support for scientific research and technology for development had faltered as a result of the program changes associated with the New Directions and basic human needs initiatives.[20]

The strongest support for ISTC came from the House, where it was vigorously supported by Congressmen Dante B. Fascell (D-Fla.) of the Foreign Affairs Committee and George E. Brown (D-Calif.) of the Science, Space, and Technology Committee. Support in the Senate was less enthusiastic. Senator Adlai Stevenson (D-Ill.) favored a completely autonomous ISTC, but Senator Dennis DeConcini (D-Ariz.) vigorously opposed ISTC. DeConcini was reportedly disturbed by what he regarded as inappropriate lobbying for ISTC by some universities and by Ralph Smuckler and Princeton Lyman of the ISTC Planning Office. There was also some resentment on the part of White House congressional liaison staff over the congressional perception that Smuckler and Lyman were the authoritative spokesmen, on behalf of the administration, on matters pertaining to ISTC.

After being passed by an overwhelming vote in the House, the bill failed to win approval in the Senate. DeConcini persuaded the Senate Appropriations Committee to strike out any funds for the ISTC, which he described as "a new bureaucracy created just to satisfy the universities that get millions of dollars for research projects."[21] On the Senate floor he successfully inserted an amendment prohibiting the use of any money for ISTC planning in fiscal year 1980. David Bell's advisory committee (of which I was a member) was discharged, and the Planning Office was closed down. Dr. Nyle Brady, the director-general of the International Rice Research Institute, who had been scheduled to head the ISTC, withdrew from consideration. The 1981 Carter budget did recommend an appropriation of $95 million as start-up costs for ISTC. When Brady was appointed as senior assistant administrator for the

AID Bureau for Science and Technology a year later, he found that Congress had appropriated only an additional $5 million for a competitive grants program to support scientific research on issues related to development.

The reorganization plan creating IDCA was approved by Congress in the fall of 1979. Dr. Thomas Erlich, president of the Legal Defense Fund and formerly dean of the Law School at Stanford University, was brought into the administration as IDCA director. But IDCA failed to find an effective role within the Carter administration. The failure to institutionalize IDCA successfully reflected, to a substantial degree, lack of commitment to the IDCA concept within the Carter administration. The death of Senator Humphrey had created a favorable political environment to resolve congressional concern about aid coordination. AID Administrator Gilligan, who had failed to establish credibility with Congress, with the White House staff, and within his own agency, was regarded as less than fully committed to aid coordination.[22]

The White House congressional liaison staff were slow to get their act together, and President Carter was, himself, ambivalent about how much coordination he wanted. Treasury, in addition to its lack of enthusiasm for coordination, was concerned with the budget implications of a major World Bank IDA replenishment. Treasury Secretary Blumenthal, in a personal meeting with Secretary of State Cyrus Vance, forced an agreement that the role of the NAC in coordinating bilateral and multilateral lending activity would not be weakened. IDCA Director Erlich failed to establish an effective interagency working relationship. His aggressive stance toward AID brought him into continuing conflict with AID Administrator Douglas Bennet. Although IDCA had budget review authority, only AID had the staff to engage in program development. Director Erlich had, in effect, no one to coordinate. The Reagan administration left IDCA on the books but finessed its role by appointing Peter McPherson, the AID administrator, concurrently as director of IDCA.

Reforms for the 1990s?

During the closing years of the second Reagan administration, it became increasingly clear to both critics and defenders of development assistance that reform of the U.S. development assistance effort was overdue. This consensus reflected both changes in the circumstances and perspectives of domestic constituencies for assistance and changes in the international economic environment, particularly the reduction in tensions between the United States and the USSR.

Since the initial passage of the Mutual Security Act of 1957, a substantial component of the economic assistance program has been budgeted under rubrics such as Defense Support, Supporting Assistance, Security Supporting Assistance, and, more recently, the Economic Support Fund. Regardless of the terminology used, three general objectives have been emphasized: "To protect nations threatened by communist or communist-inspired aggression; to encourage (friends) to grant military base and facility access rights to American forces; and to support countries with which the United States maintains a special political and security relationship" (Chap. 10).[23]

The Reagan administration found the New Directions legislation governing the use of funds programmed under Development Assistance too restrictive in its attempt to achieve a closer linkage between development and security assistance in advancing its foreign policy goals. Resources allocated to the Economic Support Fund could, on the other hand, be transferred in the form of program grants to relieve balance-of-payment difficulties, to assist in debt restructuring, and to support commodity imports.

The rapid growth in the ESF during the first Reagan administration also led to a proliferation in the number of ESF recipients. Traditionally, the number of countries receiving ESF-type assistance ranged between 10 and 20, with fewer than 5 countries receiving 70–80 percent of the total. By 1986 ESF funds were being distributed to over 60 countries. Critics began to point out that the relationship between the use of ESF funds and priority foreign policy goals was more difficult to discern. Reductions in the ESF budget during the second Reagan administration forced very large cuts in assistance to countries such as Sudan, Jordan, Thailand, Tunisia, and Peru.

In May 1986 Secretary of State George Shultz characterized the reductions in the 1987 AID appropriations proposed in the congressional budget recommendations as "a tragedy for United States foreign policy" and a "reversal of 40 years of constructive American leadership for peace and freedom."[24] Exaggerated rhetoric is not unexpected from a secretary of state who is attempting to defend his budget. But there can be no doubt that, by the end of the second Reagan administration, the U.S. economic assistance program was plagued by the same disparity between limited means and inflated objectives with which it had begun in 1951.

One solution to the deficiency of resources to meet the expanded approach to economic security would have been to revise the basic foreign assistance legislation, as recommended by the Carlucci commission, to merge the two major bilateral economic assistance programs—development assistance and security assistance (ESF)—into one program that would be used primarily as an instrument of U.S. foreign policy.[25] A second option would have been to relax the restrictions on the use of development assistance resources associated with the New Directions mandate. There also have been suggestions that the costs of supporting American access to overseas military bases and facilities be shifted from the foreign aid to the defense budget.

Advancing the Reform Agenda

During the last two years of the Reagan administration, studies and proposals put forward assistance policy reforms in the spirit of the liberal reforms of the mid-1970s. In an article in the summer 1988 issue of *Foreign Policy,* Representative David R. Obey (D-Wis.) and Carol Lancaster insisted that the problems faced by most of the approximately 70 countries that receive U.S. aid were primarily economic. They were skeptical that assistance to Egypt, Israel, and Jordan has been effective in reducing regional tensions and resented the priority given to the countries hosting U.S. military bases—Greece, Portugal, Spain, Turkey, and the Philippines—in the allocation of assistance resources. They argued that, for most of the countries receiving U.S. aid, the transfers were too small to have any significant effect on either development or security.[26]

Obey and Lancaster insisted that the first priority of U.S. policy toward the developing world should be resolution of the debt problem. In the middle and late 1980s, "developing countries as a group exported more capital to repay their debts than they imported through foreign aid and commercial borrowing."[27] They insisted that the United States could not resolve the debt problem on its own. It could only do so in concert with other bilateral donors and the multilateral lending institutions. Obey and Lancaster also argued that, if the macroeconomic issues of debt, trade, and growth were resolved, it should be possible for the United States again to refocus its assistance efforts on generating productive employment for the poor, investing in health and education, and addressing concerns about the environment.

An even stronger plea for the redirection of resources from security to development was made by John W. Sewell and Christine E. Contee of the Overseas Development Council in an article in the 1987 issue of *Foreign Affairs.*[28] The Overseas Development Council had been a leading source of ideas for the basic human needs strategy of the 1970s (see Chap. 6). In their 1987 article, Sewell and Contee called for reforms that would direct aid resources in support of (1) policy reforms leading to more liberal economic and political regimes in recipient countries, (2) projects directed toward the alleviation of poverty in the poorest countries, and (3) increased U.S. exports to Third World countries.

Sewell and Contee also insisted that "the security interests of the United States are best protected by fostering capable developing country governments, willing and able to meet the economic and political aspirations of their people." They faulted the idea that the large resources transferred to politically sensitive countries could be effectively used to purchase political reform or economic growth. "The irony of a politically determined aid program is that, where the aid program is large enough to make a difference to the country in question, funds are not likely to be withheld for any reason, as such action might threaten perceived political or strategic interests."[29] They argued that, in those countries where the United States did have clear security interests, assistance should be provided in the form of program rather than project aid.[30]

Sewell and Contee also suggested several changes in the organization of the U.S. assistance program. They noted that, when the U.S. Agency for International Development had been established in 1961, it had been designated as the lead agency for U.S. development policy. It no longer was able to fulfill that task (see Chap. 7). "United States policy toward the World Bank and other multilateral development banks is determined instead by the Treasury (although AID contributes to the decisions), and country allocations of bilateral security aid are largely determined by the Departments of State and Defense. AID does not have the clout to deal with decisions on trade and debt . . . and is often too encumbered to work easily at the grass-roots level."[31] AID should be incorporated into a new agency that would address its efforts primarily to problems of poverty in low-income countries and in selected middle-income countries. The United States should leave to the World Bank the financing of infrastructure, the building of institutions, and the conduct of policy dialogue. The new agency should be empowered to act more like a foundation in dealing with local agencies in developing countries. The Peace Corps should be expanded into a more effective institution for technical assistance.

Both the Obey-Lancaster and Sewell-Contee papers assumed that U.S. resources for development assistance would be more severely constrained in the 1990s than during the 1980s. But what would the U.S. assistance program look like if assistance efforts were guided more by the needs of the developing world than by budget constipation? In a series of conferences beginning in the spring of 1986, which had been organized by Ralph H. Smuckler of Michigan State University and Robert J. Berg of the International Development Conference, an effort was made to mobilize the best thinking of a wide range of individuals and organizations, primarily outside of the official assistance community, about the future direction of U.S. assistance policy and the structure of the U.S. assistance agency. The results were summarized in a report issued by the Center for Advanced Study of International Development at Michigan State University.[32]

The Michigan State University report argued that in the 1990s the U.S.

development assistance effort should be "broadly-based growth, an effective attack on poverty, and an end to the destruction of the environment." It urged that it was now time to forge a more mature relationship with the Third World that would involve a shift away from the old idea of aid to a new focus on mutual gain through cooperation. Development assistance should give priority to four areas: (1) the enhancement of physical well-being through health systems and population planning, (2) the development of sustainable agricultural systems for production of food, (3) the development of environmental programs and policies to protect natural resources and assure energy security, and (4) the implementation of sound urban development policies. The report urged greater reliance than in the past on (1) human resource investment, (2) the application of science and technology, and (3) policy reform and institutional development to achieve the priority objectives.

The study also urged reorganization of the U.S. assistance effort. It reaffirmed (1) the need for stronger coordination of the aid effort at the White House level, (2) the desirability of a semiautonomous foundation to strengthen research and the use of science and technology for development, and (3) greater use of binational councils and boards and other intermediaries, such as universities and private voluntary organizations, in program implementation. The study urged the separation of responsibility for development assistance from security-oriented strategic and military assistance. The agency envisaged in the report would, however, have a much broader mandate for economic cooperation than the present AID.

Opportunities Lost

By the last year of the Reagan administration, there was general agreement, both in the administration and in Congress, that substantial restructuring of the AID effort would be required. There was little agreement, however, on the policy framework for reform. AID constituency organizations—private voluntary organizations and agricultural, health and population, and environmental interest groups—that tended to reflect their interests through Congress remained strongly committed to the human rights, basic needs, and poverty reduction orientation of the 1970s. The agency's administration and the State Department, and the constituencies that tended to reflect their views through the administration, regarded these views as incongruent with the changes in the domestic and international economic environment of the 1980s. Issues of debt restructuring and growth-oriented policy reform, particularly the liberalization of domestic and trade policies, were at the top of the administration's agenda.

These perspectives were reflected in two important policy documents issued in the winter of 1989. In February, the Agency for International Development released an internal study under the imprimatur of AID Administrator Alan Woods, *Development and the National Interest: U.S. Economic Assistance into the 21st Century* (the Woods report).[33] The report was an exceedingly critical assessment, at least for an official document, of the limitations and accomplishments of the U.S. assistance effort. The report downplayed the importance of economic assistance as a source of development

> Where development has worked, and is working, the key has been economic growth. And this is largely the result of individual nations making the right policy choices and making the most of internal human and material resources. A strong expanding American economy, a healthy trade climate, and the development assistance provided by profit-based and nonprofit private organizations are critical elements. Direct U.S. development assistance, overall, has played a secondary role and has not always succeeded in fostering growth-oriented policies among recipient states.

Furthermore, "much of what has haphazardly evolved as development assistance over the past four decades has not worked, has sometimes not even been aimed at the correct objectives, and, above all, has been overtaken by events."[34]

The report did not, however, realize its promise. It did not draw on AID's own documentary evidence of AID's effectiveness. And it did not provide the promised strategy for economic assistance into the twenty-first century or even a road map for the 1990s. It is possible that the failure of the Bush administration to lay out its own agenda for reform was due to the illness of AID Administrator Alan Woods in the latter months of 1988 and into the spring of 1989. But it is also clear that Secretary of State James Baker did not put the same priority on the AID program that Secretary Haig had placed on AID at the beginning of the Reagan administration. As of January 1990, AID had been without a functioning administrator for almost one year. The Woods study was not followed up by an administration agenda for assistance policy reform.[35]

In January 1988 the chairman of the House Committee on Foreign Affairs, Dante B. Fascell (D-Fla.), appointed a bipartisan Task Force on Foreign Assistance under the direction of Lee Hamilton (D-Ind.) and Ben Gilman (R-N.Y.). This task force "grew out of frustration"—that the assistance program was unfocused, that it is ineffective, and that it did not reflect the changing nature of the international economy and America's declining role as a source of economic assistance.[36] It would not be entirely cynical to suggest that another motivation for the task force effort grew out of frustration on the part of the leadership of the House Committee on Foreign Affairs about its inability to exercise leadership in the area of foreign assistance policy during the

Reagan administration. In the 1970s the committee had been a source of the New Directions mandate (Chap. 6). During the 1980s Congress had only twice, in 1981 and 1985, succeeded in passing an AID authorization bill. Foreign assistance policy in Congress, to the extent that it existed, had passed from the authorizing to the appropriation committee, particularly to the Foreign Operations Subcommittee of the House Appropriations Committee, chaired by David Obey (D-Wis.).

The task force issued its report in February 1989.[37] The report was critical of the large resources devoted to the Economic Support Fund. It argued that the AID program was burdened by too many objectives and was spread too thin over too many countries. And it agreed with the longstanding AID staff complaint that the program was hampered by excessive reporting requirements, earmarks, and restrictions. The task force recommended that, in the area of economic assistance, the committee should consider the following:

—the enactment of a new international economic cooperation act to replace the Foreign Assistance Act;
—the creation of a restructured foreign aid–implementing agency to replace AID;
—the identification of economic growth, environmental sustainability, poverty alleviation, and democratic and economic pluralism as the principal objectives;
—the provision of greater flexibility in the implementation of assistance programs;
—the provision of more effective accountability focused on results rather than on allocations; and
—the improvement of coordination with other U.S. international economic policies, with other donors, and within country programs.

In the area of security assistance, the task force recommended that the committee should consider the following:

—the separation of grant assistance and concessional military assistance from cash sales authorities;
—the creation of a new defense trade and export contract act to replace the Arms Export Contract Act;
—the establishment of one military assistance account;
—the provision of more effective accountability, again focused on results;
—the phasing out over a five-year period of military assistance as a *quid pro quo* for base access rights.[38]

The task force was particularly critical of what it regarded as program rigidity due to the functional accounts (agriculture, health, education), country earmarking, and excessive reporting requirements imposed by Congress.[39]

The House committee, under the leadership of Chairman Fascell, acted rapidly to move the proposed legislation through the committee and to the House floor. However, the International Economic Cooperation Act (H.R. 655), which was overwhelmingly passed (314 to 101) by the House on June 9, included few of the reforms proposed by the task force. The opening paragraphs (Sec. 110) elaborated on the four objectives identified in the task force report—broad-based economic growth, environmentally and economically sustainable development, alleviation of the worst manifestations of poverty through human resource development, and promotion of political, social, and economic pluralism. The bill transferred $1.0 billion from the Economic Support Fund to development assistance. It eliminated a large number of obsolete and redundant reporting requirements. But it was almost completely unsuccessful in reducing the earmarking of country and program allocations in the functional accounts. The committee defeated Hamilton's proposal to phase out the giving of aid in exchange for base rights.

The House bill shared with earlier assistance legislation an almost cynical disregard for the disparity between the idealistic goals enunciated in the legislation and the limited means dedicated to the achievement of those goals. An example of this tendency was the incorporation of proposals that had previously surfaced as the Global Poverty Reduction Act. Section 101-e of the House bill directed the president to submit to Congress a plan that would eradicate the worst aspects of poverty by the year 2000.[40] The objectives enunciated in Section 101-e are exceedingly important. But Section 101-e was only one section in a $6.6 billion bilateral aid authorization, which would allocate only slightly more than $2.0 billion to the development assistance account! (In contrast, the authorization for the Economic Support Fund was to be $2.4 billion in 1990.)

Other initiatives in the House bill included (*a*) a proposal to strengthen the Overseas Private Investment Corporation to mobilize greater participation of private capital and skills for development and (*b*) a proposal to create, within the new IDCA, a Trade and Development Agency to promote U.S. private sector participation in development projects. Funds would be provided for project planning and support. The bill also provided for closer cooperation between AID and the universities through the establishment of a Center for University Cooperation in Development and with the PVO community through a Center for Voluntary Cooperation in Development (see Chap. 9).

The Senate Foreign Relations Committee, unlike the House committee, made little effort to rewrite the 1961 legislation. An International Security and

Development Cooperation Act was approved by an 18 to 0 vote by a generally apathetic Senate Foreign Relations Committee on July 1.[41] The Senate authorization bill was, however, never brought to the floor for debate and a vote. A frequently expressed view in Congress was that Senate Majority Leader George Mitchell (D-Maine) was reluctant to bring the bill to the Senate floor because he was not confident that Senator Claiborne Pell (D-R.I.) could effectively contain efforts that would be made by Senator Jesse Helms (R-N.C.) to amend the bill on the floor.[42] It has also been reported that Senator Paul Sarbanes (D-Md.), chairman of the International Economic Policy, Trade, Oceans and Environment Subcommittee of the Senate Foreign Relations Committee, resented what he considered to be insufficient consultation by the Hamilton task force with his subcommittee. The result was that prospects for reform of the AID program in the first session of the 101st Congress were effectively dead by midsummer. It also meant that serious consideration of foreign assistance policy issues would again be left to the House and Senate appropriations committees rather than being dealt with by the authorizing committees.[43]

The failure on the part of the authorizing committee to move the aid reform legislation forward brought the administration once more into direct and increasingly intensive conflict with Congressman David R. Obey (D-Wis.), chairman of the House Appropriations Subcommittee on Foreign Operations. As noted in Chapter 5, Obey had, since the mid-1980s, expressed his disapproval of the Gramm-Rudman-Hollings deficit reduction bill by insisting that foreign aid should share, to the same degree as domestic programs, in the G-R-H budget constraints.[44] In June Obey announced that he was planning for a $14.3 billion foreign aid bill for fiscal 1990—$300 million below the administration request. But his spending priorities would cut $800 million from administration-supported programs. The administration proposed an increase in funding to the Export-Import Bank for subsidies for U.S. industrial exports and to the International Finance Corporation (the World Bank arm that lends to the private sector). Obey placed greater priority on programs that were more in line with the 1970s emphasis on basic needs and the poor majority. He favored the International Development Association replenishment and the payment of arrears to the U.N. specialized agencies. He would cut the Economic Support Fund and military aid.

On 1 July 1989 the House passed a $14.3 billion fiscal 1990 aid appropriations bill (H.R. 939). Senator Patrick J. Leahy (D-Vt.), chairman of the Senate Appropriations Subcommittee on Foreign Operations, finally succeeded in getting his subcommittee to approve a $14.4 billion foreign aid measure on September 14. Congressman Obey, in deference to his colleagues on the House Foreign Affairs Committee, held up conference committee action to resolve differences between the House and Senate versions of the appropriations bill, hoping to force the Senate to act on an authorization bill. On November 9, after a series of bitter disputes between Obey and Senator Daniel K. Inouye (D-Hawaii) over earmarking and security provisions, a House-Senate conference committee completed work on draft legislation.

The draft contained provisions that the Bush administration identified as unacceptable, including new money for the U.N. population program and a provision prohibiting the administration from using foreign aid to induce other countries into taking action, such as supporting guerrilla operations, that the U.S. government cannot legally take on its own.[45] President Bush vetoed the appropriations bills on November 19. On November 20 Congress passed a revised $14.6 billion aid package. It dropped the features President Bush had found unacceptable and included $40 million in funds for aid to Poland and $60 million for aid to Hungary. The president signed the bill on December 1.

It is not possible to understand what happened to the aid authorization and appropriations legislation through the fall of 1989 without referring to the remarkable political events in Eastern Europe. By late summer the lack of enthusiasm for aid reform was being replaced by what the *Congressional Quarterly* referred to as a "boomlet" of support for foreign aid. Members of Congress began to compete to take credit for boosting aid to Poland. The mood was reinforced by the remarkable outpouring of sympathy for Poland during the November 13–19 visit to the United States by Polish Solidarity leader Lech Walesa. His addresses to a joint session of the House and Senate and to an assembly of the AFL-CIO were received with great public enthusiasm. Congress, which had been unable to pass general aid authorization legislation in midsummer and which was unable to act on State Department authorization and appropriations legislation, had no trouble in November in passing an authorization measure (H.R. 340) for Poland and Hungary for fiscal 1990–91. Funds for the two countries for fiscal 1990–91 were included in the foreign aid appropriations bill. By the end of the 1989 legislative session, the value of Polish ancestry had come close, at least for a few months, to replacing that of Irish ancestry in the political marketplace.

More Studies, Task Forces, and Commissions

From early 1989 until the end of the Bush administration, AID was plagued by ineffective and, at times, incompetent leadership. Even as the Woods report was being completed, Alan Woods was progressively incapacitated. In July 1989 Woods was succeeded by Deputy Administrator Mark Edelman, who served as interim administrator until the appointment of Ronald Roskens as administrator in March 1990 (Appendix A).[46]

Disintegration

Roskens was never able to establish either the autonomy from the State Department or the effective command over the agency that would have been required to establish policy or manage programming at AID. At his swearing in ceremony in March 1990, Secretary of State James Baker outlined five major foreign policy challenges—referred to in the agency as *Baker's Charge*—for his new administrator:

—Consolidate the world wide trend toward democracy;
—Build strong, free-market economies;
—Help the peacemakers . . . strengthen the hand of regional actors committed to peace;
—Address transnational threats—environmental degradation, drug trafficking and terrorism; and
—Strengthen international ties . . . to ensure that the positive world trends we see will continue . . . [We] must respond to the needs of the developing world.

A committee of top AID staff was asked to draft an agency mission statement based on Baker's Charge. The priorities that emerged—the family, democracy, environment, and business partnership—reflected the priorities of an ideologically motivated staff who were critical of the continuing commitment to building scientific and technical capacity in developing countries and of commitments to assist in meeting the basic human needs of the poor in the poorest countries. Agriculture and family planning were deemphasized. The early drafts omitted any mention of human resource investment or even of economic development. Concerned staff were successful, after substantial internal debate, in expanding the statement of objectives to include "concern for individuals and the development of their economic and social well-being."[47]

The Bush administration submitted a redraft of the Foreign Assistance Act to Congress in April 1991. One effect of the proposal would have been to reduce congressional earmarking to give the administration greater control over the allocation of assistance resources. In the proposal, building human capacity was listed as a form of humanitarian assistance rather than either a productive investment or an ultimate development goal. The reduction of poverty was also treated as humanitarian assistance need rather than as a central purpose of development.[48] The administration did not, however, expend much effort in an attempt to secure passage.

At the policy level—in the State Department and AID—the basic human needs orientation that had been strengthened by the reforms of the mid-1970s was officially dead! Critics both within and outside the agency saw in Baker's Charge the emergence of a new rationale—serving U.S. commercial interests abroad—replacing the older Cold War rationale for foreign economic assistance.[49] Comments from senior AID staff indicated concern as to why AID should be attempting to embrace responsibilities in areas where AID had little capacity and which more appropriately fell under the mandates of the Trade Representative, the Export-Import Bank, or the Overseas Private Investment Corporation.

Roskens himself seemed more interested in AID reorganization than in AID program and policy. Reorganizations were implemented in October 1991 and again in the summer of 1992. A major effect of the later reorganization was to insulate Administrator Roskens from the policy and management decisions facing the agency. The congressional concern with AID administration was reinforced by charges of corruption against several AID officers by the AID inspector-general and by concerns about AID mismanagement.[50]

It was widely rumored during late 1991 and early 1992 that Administrator Roskens would not survive through the November 1992 elections. It seemed apparent to informed observers, however, that Secretary of State Baker had little interest in economic development and was not anxious to replace Roskens with a strong administrator.[51] On program matters, particularly the newer programs in the formerly centrally planned economies, Baker and his staff at times simply bypassed Roskens' office and conveyed instructions on AID programming directly to AID bureau chiefs.

By the early 1990s the declining total resources available for bilateral programs, combined with congressional earmarks of ESF funds to specific countries, of development assistance funds to functional accounts, and of new programs in the former centrally planned economies, left many country missions with almost no program flexibility. Within the agency the regional bureaus were pressing for reallocation of resources away from the central bureaus, such as Private Enterprise and Research and Development. Outside the agency, individual constituencies, such as population and environmental activists, were pressing Congress to expand programs in their areas of concern from a declining budget.[52]

Concern on the part of AID constituencies and Congress with what seemed to be a disintegration of AID capacity and direction led, during the last two years of the Bush administration, to a series of task force and commission reports that attempted to chart a course for U.S. development assistance in the 1990s. There was broad consensus that the agency was in deep trouble. The end of the Cold War had shifted administration and congressional priorities away from the least developed countries and toward the formerly centrally planned economies. There was lack of consensus among assistance constituencies about AID priorities. The several studies and task force and commission reports can be viewed, in part, as efforts to redirect a declining pool of assistance resources in the direction of the constituencies responsible for promoting the particular studies or reports.

Reorganization

Proposals for reform ranged from a narrowing and focusing of the AID program to the transfer of responsibility for security and development assistance to the State Department. In this section I characterize several of the more substantial task force and commission reports that appeared during the last two years of the Bush administration.[53]

The Overseas Development Council seized on President Bush's 1 October 1990 address to the United Nations General Assembly calling for a "New World Order" to present an alternative international affairs budget. The ODC insisted that the US/AID had "lost its effectiveness and should no longer monopolize the distribution of US bilateral assistance." Instead, Congress should establish a Sustainable Development Fund (SDF). "The SDF would not be an operating agency, but would provide funding on a competitive basis for programs to be carried out by international organizations, private voluntary organizations and profit making firms. The SDF would be launched at $2 billion in FY 1992 rising to $5 billion in FY 1996. When it reached full operations, most US bilateral aid would flow through it."[54] The ODC proposals, in deference to the strength of political constituencies, would add a Middle East Peace Account that would continue to be budgeted at existing levels of support for Israel and Egypt. Savings would be achieved by discontinuing support assistance to the "base rights" countries and by moving military aid assistance to the defense budget. An expanded program of debt relief for the most severely indebted countries and expanded funding for the Export-Import Bank were also proposed.

The theme of sustainable development was also emphasized in a report of an Environmental and Energy Study Institute Task Force chaired by Gustav Spaeth, president of the World Resources Institute.[55] The report noted that the easing of East-West tensions was shifting attention to North-South issues. The report urges support for building the scientific, technical, and institutional capacity needed to enable low- and middle-income developing countries to shift to environmentally and economically sustainable development. The stabilization of population, elevation of the social and economic states of women, and improved access to U.S. markets under a more environmentally sensitive international trade regime were urged as essential elements of an assistance program directed to support sustainable development.

A dramatic but very different change in organization was proposed by the President's Commission on the Management of AID programs (the Ferris commission).[56] The commission was established by Congress in the 1991 Foreign Assistance Appropriation Act (PL 101-513). Its establishment was based on concern by Senator Patrick J. Leahy (D-Vt.) about what he perceived as disintegration of managerial capacity both in Washington and in the field.[57]

The Ferris commission went beyond its mandate to consider policy as well as management problems. "AID's basic management problems can never be resolved without a reappraisal of the objectives of foreign economic assistance."[58] In addition to recommendations in the areas of program and personnel management and in managerial control, it urged more effective coordination among the U.S. government agencies with the largest assistance programs.[59] The commission pointed out that the Development Coordinating Committee (discussed earlier in this chapter) had not met since 1978 and that the Reagan administration's National Security Council policy-coordinating committee, Resources for International Affairs Programs, headed by the undersecretary of state for management, had never met.[60]

The commission made two major policy proposals. It urged that the most important priorities for the U.S. foreign assistance program should be "economic policy reform programs overseas and trade and investment programs that will directly benefit the American economy."[61] The commission also recommended that AID should be fully integrated into the State Department. The Economic Support Fund should be administered by an under-secretary for international security and emergency assistance and should be used only to achieve foreign policy political objectives. Development assistance funds should be administered by an under-secretary for economic cooperation and used only for legitimate development purposes.

The perspective of the Ferris commission was echoed in two other reports released in 1992. A report from the American Foreign Policy Council found that the basic human needs mandate of the Foreign Assistance Act of 1973 had "served mainly to diminish the usefulness of development assistance in the implementation of foreign policy goals."[62] It urged, in the spirit of the Carlucci commission report of 1983, integrated management of all foreign assistance accounts and foreign policy instruments, even including the Peace Corps and International Disaster Relief, to advance foreign policy objectives.

I am highly skeptical of the recommendations that responsibility for development assistance programs can be productively located within the State Department. The Carnegie commission itself identified the primary obstacle: "The State Department's culture—its underlying tendencies and priorities—has rejected, or at least resisted, transplants of technical skill . . . A key part of the explanation is that its culture has been grounded in the 19th century tradition of gentleman diplomats: political, verbal and linguistic ability have been valued more than technical, analytical, and strategic skills."[63] The response to my concerns by a senior staff member of the Ferris commission was that the State Department had, during the last several decades, became so involved in operational responsibilities—disaster relief, refugees, and other programs—that it is being forced to reform its personnel policies to accommodate the scientific, technical, and managerial capacities consistent with its expanded responsibilities. I am also skeptical of the Ferris commission's recommendation that the U.S. development assistance or development cooperation program should be increasingly devoted to advancing U.S. economic and commercial interests abroad. The effect would be to divert AID from development and to burden the agency with an additional mandate for which it has little capacity. If such an effort is needed, it would be more appropriate to strengthen the role of the Department of Commerce, particularly with respect to policy coordination for the Export-Import Bank and the Overseas Private Investment Corporation, the two agencies that already have responsibility for advancing U.S. commercial interests abroad (Chap. 11).

Reform

A second set of reports focused more directly on program redirection than on reorganization. These included the report of the Task Force on Development Assistance and Economic Growth (the Schuh task force) and the report of the Independent Group on the Future of U.S. Development Cooperation.

The Task Force on Development Assistance and Economic Growth was commissioned by the Board for International Food and Agricultural Development. It was headed by G. Edward Schuh, dean of the Hubert H. Humphrey Institute of Public Affairs at the University of Minnesota.[64] It quickly became apparent to the task force and its advisory committee that an effective response to concerns about assistance for agricultural development would require an examination of both the broader dimensions of foreign economic assistance and the possibilities of reclaiming domestic support for foreign assistance. The task force also went beyond its original mandate to consider collaboration between AID and the university community in areas other than food and agricultural development.

The Schuh task force devoted considerably more attention to setting the stage for its recommendations by discussing in considerable detail the changed setting for development assistance and cooperation and how these changes should influence future development agendas. It also attempted to provide a more detailed assessment of the lessons from foreign aid experience. The general thrust of the report was that "the bulk of this nation's foreign economic assistance should be dedicated to investments in human capital, where the private international capital market is not likely to provide adequate resource flows."[65] It emphasized the high rates of return of these investments and of closely related activities involving collaboration in research and education.

The institutional reforms proposed by the Schuh task force to advance its more general recommendation involved strengthening the technical and scientific capacity of the agency and the establishment within AID of a new Center for Scientific and Technical Cooperation. It urged more effective collaboration with other federal agencies and the university community in carrying out the proposed program of international cooperation. The concerns of the Schuh task force were also reflected in a report by the Carnegie commission which urged the establishment of a science and technology counselor to the secretary and deputy secretary of state. It also urged, in contrast to the Schuh report, that AID be included in the responsibilities of an under-secretary for development and security cooperation.[66]

The response by the State Department and the AID administration to the Schuh report was a deafening silence. Its emphasis on the importance of public sector investment in human capital development and on support of the development of scientific and technical capacity in developing countries confronted Administrator Roskens with recommendations that were hardly consistent with administration ideology.[67]

Perhaps the most influential of the several reports was the report of an Independent Group on the Future of U.S. Development Cooperation.[68] The Independent Group urged that U.S. development assistance efforts ought to be fundamentally restructured and focused around the goal of sustainable development. By sustainable development the group meant "growth that brings with it the alleviation of poverty and preservation of the environment for successive generations in a context of government accountability and social justice consistent with the aspiration of all members of a society."[69]

To accomplish this objective the Independent Group recommended the replacement of AID by a U.S. Sustainable Development Cooperation Agency. The new agency should emphasize a series of sectoral policy and program priorities:

—*investing in people*, including employment creation, education, health promotion, and family planning;
—*protecting the earth*, including environmental management, agricultural production, energy production, forestry and fisheries programs, and biological diversity; and
—*strengthening the institutions of free societies*, including assistance in building accountability in government, strengthening of the capacities of non-

governmental and civic organizations, and protection of the rights of the disadvantaged.

Within these areas, the Independent Group urged the use of selection criteria consistent with U.S. capacities and recipient country needs and priorities. The Independent Group urged that political aid, currently Economic Support Fund activities, should be justified and administered by the State Department. Military assistance should be subsumed under the defense budget and administered by the Department of Defense. Export promotion and related efforts to enhance U.S. competitiveness should be the responsibility of the Export-Import Bank, the Overseas Private Investment Corporation, and the Office of the Trade Representatives rather than the responsibility of the Agency for International Development or whatever development assistance agency might replace AID.

The Independent Group also recognized that, given the large number of agencies involved in development assistance, neither a reorganized assistance agency nor any other cabinet department can impose coherence or coordination. It recommended the establishment in the Office of the President of a Development Coordination Group to be chaired by the vice president and staffed by the Sustainable Development Cooperation Agency and the Economic Policy Council. The Sustainable Development Cooperation Agency was visualized as being responsible for planning, overseeing, and evaluating, but not conducting, programs in the three program priority areas. It would operate through two main units—a Central Policy Unit and a Program Unit.

I find it somewhat surprising that the issues of poverty and income distribution, central themes in the reform efforts led by the House Foreign Affairs Committee in the early and mid-1970s, seemed to carry so little weight in the reform agendas being proposed in the early 1990s. Only a report by Bread for the World, an interdenominational assistance interest group, placed (1) *improving livelihoods*—creating and enhancing opportunities for poor people to increase their earning capacity and quality of life—and (2) *meeting basic human needs*—expanding investments in health, access to safe and adequate supplies of food and water, education, and shelter—at the center of its policy agenda.[70] It seemed clear that the authors of the Bread for the World report were concerned that the emphasis given to natural resource and environmental issues in some of the other reports would divert assistance resources from the most basic problems faced by poor people in poor countries.

In spite of the differences in origin and perspective, the several reports tended to agree on at least two issues. The first was that the existing AID organization is no longer viable. Both its organization and its functions should be reorganized or reformed. A second area of substantial agreement was that the four areas of assistance—development assistance, humanitarian assistance, political or strategic assistance, and military assistance—should be administered as separate programs. A reorganized agency should be responsible only for development assistance.

There were also areas of substantial disagreement. The Ferris commission and the Carnegie commission reflected in their reports a set of concerns that had been prominent in the 1980s—how to link economic assistance more closely to U.S. political interests and economic advantage in recipient countries.[71] The Carnegie, Schuh, and Independent Commission reports urged a renewed commitment to investment in people and to scientific and technical cooperation with developing countries.

The most substantial departure from earlier themes was the emphasis on environmental security and sustainable development. This theme was particularly strong in the reports of the Environment and Energy Task Force, the ODC New World Order Budget, and the Independent Commission. In part, this concern reflected the rising tide of resource and environmental concerns, particularly among natural scientists and development assistance intellectuals, about the future health of the planet. I also interpret the focus on resource and environmental issues as a search for an integrating theme that could replace the Cold War as a motivating force to sustain the U.S. commitment to development assistance.

The Response of the Clinton Administration

As this book was being completed, more than a year after Bill Clinton assumed office as president, the response of the new administration to the flurry of reports and recommendations advanced during the closing years of the Bush administration was just beginning to take shape. J. Brian Atwood was confirmed as AID administrator in May 1993. In his confirmation hearings, he identified growing populations, mass migrations, political repression, ethnic conflict, environmental degradation, and a worsening global economy as core issues with which U.S. foreign policy must be concerned. He emphasized that the overall goal of U.S. development assistance must be sustainable development.

Changes in agency programs and organization were to be delayed, however, until the completion of a major review by a task force working under the direction of Deputy Secretary of State Clifton R. Wharton. The appointment of the task force was greeted with a good deal of cynicism in Congress and the press. A *Washington Post* editorial noted that

> the 30-year-old AID agency has been examined by more blue-ribbon panels and independent study groups than any organization around . . . We suppose that a

new look . . . can find new evidence of squandered U.S. aid, employee improprieties, a cumbersome bureaucracy, and shortcomings in management accountability . . . If the new study ends up proposing the usual remedies . . . the central issue facing AID will have been missed . . . Our guess is that much, maybe most of the old structure and setup, will have to be junked and a wholly new start made. The old program is probably beyond reforming and in need of replacing.[72]

Hearings on a draft of the "phantom Wharton report" were held by the House Committee on Foreign Affairs in July. A revised report was completed in September.[73] The delay was attributed to a pending review of foreign aid being conducted by the National Security Council, which was apparently never completed. In testimony before the Senate Foreign Relations Committee on July 14, Wharton recommended that the U.S. foreign assistance program should be based on three broadly encompassing strategies: (1) promoting sustainable growth and development, (2) building democratic participation in development, and (3) addressing global issues such as population, health, and environmental protection in developing countries. The task force report emphatically rejected recommendations that AID assume responsibility for promoting U.S. commercial interests abroad. In November 1993, Deputy Secretary Wharton resigned. His resignation was preceded by a series of leaks and denials from the secretary of state's office regarding his impending departure. The reasons for his departure remain cloudy.

As this chapter was being completed, it was clear that the framework outlined in the Wharton report had established the grounding for the administration's AID reform legislation, tentatively entitled the Peace, Development and Democracy Act of 1994. A discussion draft was submitted to Congress in November 1993. The legislation was revised and introduced in the House in early February 1994 as H.R. 3765. A distinguishing feature of the proposed bill was the unprecedented flexibility that it would give to the administration in managing foreign assistance. It would authorize funds for a few broad goals, remove many of the restrictions on country eligibility for assistance, give wide authority to transfer funds from one purpose to another, and do away with the functional accounts and earmarking. The Economic Support Fund would be eliminated.

In the proposed legislation, sustainable development was adopted as the organizing principle for a new post–Cold War assistance policy. Five objectives were identified in the proposed legislation and in the agency strategy paper:[74]

1. protecting the global environment,
2. stabilizing world population growth and protecting human health,
3. building democracy,

4. encouraging broad-based economic growth, and
5. providing humanitarian assistance and aiding postcrisis transition.

The *Washington Post,* reversing its earlier skepticism, embraced the proposed legislation as "a smaller and neater measure with a less invasive set of foreign aid policies and objectives."[75]

A disturbing feature of the proposed legislation is that it would establish AID as a statutory agency under the foreign policy guidance and supervision of the secretary of state. Such a provision would strengthen the linkage between foreign economic assistance and the political and security objectives of a current administration along the lines recommended by the Carlucci commission in 1983 (Chap. 7). By mid-1984, however, it was clear that lack of new legislation was not a serious obstacle to using economic assistance resources to support political and strategic objectives. In spite of the rhetoric about commitment to sustainable development, assistance to the poorest countries and for several of the traditional functional program areas—food and agriculture, for example—was being scraped to the bone to generate the resources needed to fulfill State Department commitments in the Middle East, to the newly independent states of Eastern Europe and the former Soviet Union, and in southern Africa.

Lessons from Reform Efforts

What are the lessons that should be drawn from the reform efforts that have been reviewed in this chapter?

One fairly obvious lesson is that reform is exceedingly difficult in the absence of presidential leadership. President Kennedy's commitment was a critical element in the successful consolidation of assistance agencies into a new Agency for International Development in 1961. The appointment of an inept administrator to head the new agency contributed to the failure to realize the reform agenda that President Kennedy had outlined during the presidential campaign and in the first months after assuming office. Lack of presidential leadership was a critical missing element in the failure of the 1979 and 1980 reform efforts. President Carter was never able to resolve in his own mind how much coordination of the aid effort he wanted to achieve. This indecision was compounded by the attempt to achieve reform during the last year in office of an administration that was losing credibility within its own party. Even under the best of circumstances, the last year of a presidential term is not the most favorable environment for a reform effort. The lesson of the 1989 reform effort is that, even in the first year of a presidential term, little can be accomplished in the presence of indifferent presidential leadership. The administration's interest in reform was focused on achieving greater flexibility to pursue strategic objectives by reducing congressional earmarking. Policy leadership from the agency was allowed to drift, first under an ailing administrator and then by failure to designate a replacement until well into 1990.

A second lesson is that reform efforts have often been made obsolete by changes in the domestic or international political environment. The idealism that President Kennedy's commitment to the Alliance for Progress engendered in both Latin America and the United States was quickly subverted by the invasion of Cuba at the Bay of Pigs on 17 April 1961. The additional resources that might have been devoted to economic assistance were, by 1963, being channeled into more intensive security assistance efforts in Vietnam. The Camp David accords of the late 1970s distorted the flow of assistance resources toward the Middle East and weakened the development focus of the U.S. assistance effort. The failure of the reform efforts of 1989 provide an even more dramatic example of the impact of economic and political change in aborting policy reform. The major consideration on the economic side was the apparent weakening of the capacity of the United States to play a central role in world economic affairs. The easing of tension between the United States and the USSR in the late 1980s and the collapse of authority of the Communist party in the centrally planned economies of Eastern Europe since the late 1980s have led to reallocation of declining economic assistance resources from the lowest-income countries to the former centrally planned countries.

In retrospect, it seems that the failure to reform the U.S. assistance effort in the late 1980s was to a substantial degree due to a combination of political and economic changes that have called into question the rationale of our assistance programs. The economic role of the United States in the world economy has been weakened by self-indulgent domestic economic policy. By the late 1980s the United States had experienced two decades of lagging productivity and output growth. It had experienced a transition from a creditor to a debtor nation. It may be somewhat overdramatic to think of the United States as sharing the weakness of the other debtor nations of the Western hemisphere—Argentina, Brazil, Venezuela, and Mexico. But the capacity of the United States for leadership in resolving the global debt crises during the 1980s was severely eroded by our own vulnerability. Two former secretaries of state have insisted that "United States political leadership in the World cannot be sustained if confidence in the American leadership continues to be undermined by substantial trade and budget deficits."[76]

The second economic consideration is the widely diverse economic performance of countries in the developing world. The Third World of the 1960s no longer exists. There is a Third World of the newly industrializing countries led by the four small tigers of East Asia—Korea, Taiwan, Hong Kong, and Singapore—and closely followed by Thailand and Malaysia. There is a Fourth World composed of large countries that have achieved very substantial economic power—Brazil, Mexico, India, and China. There is a Fifth World of resource-rich countries—with rich resources but poor people—countries such as Iraq and Iran. And there is the Sixth World of truly poor countries in Africa, Latin America, and South Asia. The way in which the United States relates economically and politically to these several worlds is obscured when they are viewed through the traditional lenses of economic and security assistance.

These economic factors can be viewed as background conditions that influence the capacity of the United States to respond to the assistance needs of the poor countries. But it has been the reduction of tension between the United States and the USSR and the replacement of Communist party authority in Eastern Europe that has removed much of the security rationale for the U.S. foreign economic assistance program. Increases in the U.S. assistance budget have, in the past, been a direct response to rising tension between the United States and the USSR. Rising tension was associated with the Marshall Plan and Point Four initiatives of the late 1940s and early 1950s (see Chaps. 3 and 4), with the growth of assistance budgets in the late 1950s and early 1960s, and with the doubling of economic and military assistance during the late 1970s and early 1980s.

Unless tension between the United States and the USSR revives, it will become increasingly difficult for either the administration or the assistance constituencies to persuade Congress to maintain even the level of AID funding of the mid-1990s. The most likely prospect is for a continuation of the decline that began in the mid-1980s. It also seems likely that there will be a continuing shift in regional priorities away from Latin America and Asia. As the resources available to the US/AID have declined, the role of the international financial institutions and the United Nations and its specialized agencies and programs in setting the global development agenda has grown. For a time this trend was obscured by the presence of a strong US/AID professional capacity in this field. But as that intellectual capital has continued to erode along with the decline in U.S. financial assistance, this influence of the United States on the global development agenda has also declined.

Chapter 14

Does AID Have a Future?

During the late 1980s and early 1990s, the Agency for International Development was subject to even more than the usual criticism.[1] Several of the reform proposals outlined in the last chapter proposed extensive reorganization or even the elimination of AID. Proposals have been made for moving many of the functions of AID to the State Department or to other agencies. It seems clear that the changes under way in both the domestic and the international political environment suggest that the U.S. economic assistance program as we have known it—as it has been conceived and managed since the early 1950s—is no longer viable. Some critics view this as a cause for celebration. But I come to this conclusion reluctantly.

In this chapter I first identify the series of visions that have guided U.S. development assistance in the past and review some of the lessons that we have learned, or should have learned, from our experience with development assistance. I then suggest some options for the future that are consistent with both U.S. capacities and U.S. interests. Finally, I suggest some elements of a new vision that should guide U.S. development assistance policy in the future.

Six Visions

U.S. development assistance policy, since the post–World War II relief and recovery efforts in Western Europe and East Asia, has been guided by a series of six successive strategic visions.[2]

The *first* was a vision of a post–World War II liberal political and economic order. This vision was articulated by the architects of the new postwar institutions—the World Bank, the International Monetary Fund, the General Agreement on Tariffs and Trade, and the United Nations and its specialized agencies and voluntary programs. The vision was induced by a perception that economic autarchy and political repression during the interwar period were major sources of the Great Depression and World War II (Chap. 3).

The *second* vision was outlined as the fourth point in President Harry S. Truman's inaugural address of 20 January 1949. In that speech, Truman proposed "a bold new program for making the benefits of scientific advances and industrial progress available for the improvement and growth of underdeveloped areas." This was the technical assistance vision (Chap. 4).

The *third* was the vision articulated by John F. Kennedy in his presidential campaign and in his first years in office that "a more prosperous world would also be a more secure world." This articulation held out the promise of refocusing the security concerns of the Eisenhower administration from containment to development. The assistance policy that emerged emphasized the transfer of large financial resources by both bilateral and multilateral institutions (Chap. 5).

The *fourth* vision was articulated by members of the House Foreign Affairs Committee in the late 1960s and early 1970s—a New Direction in foreign assistance that would focus on basic human needs and human rights. Aid should be directed to achieving greater equity among peoples, both within and among countries—to achieving political empowerment and improvement of the economic well-being of the poor majority in the poorest countries (Chap. 6).

The *fifth* was the doctrine of closer linkage between economic and security assistance articulated in the report of the Commission on Security and Economic Assistance (the Carlucci report) and in speeches by Secretary of State Alexander Haig and U.N. Ambassador Jeane Kirkpatrick during the first Reagan administration. Translation of the doctrine into policy was, however, confronted by an AID administrator whose emotional commitments were closer to the New Direction themes than to the right wing of the Reagan administration (Chap. 7).

A *sixth* vision, sustainable development, emerged during the closing years of the Bush administration. Its central theme was intergenerational equity—"sustainable development is development that meets the needs of the present without compromising the ability of future generations to meet their own needs." Unlike earlier visions, the vision of sustainable development did not emerge from official levels—from either the administration or Congress. It was advanced first by the international environmental community and later by a broad coalition of NGOs. It was initially greeted with cautious skepticism at official levels. Its momentum was enhanced when environmental crisis became a central issue in the vice presidential campaign of Senator Al Gore. It was embraced as a unifying foreign assistance theme by the Clinton administration.[3]

Throughout the almost five decades since the 1940s, there have been two overarching constraints on the pursuit of the several visions or strategies outlined above.

The *first* is that U.S. development assistance policy has largely been derivative of Cold War containment strategy. The growth and decline in the magnitude of assistance flows have been dominated by the intensity of the Cold War. The decline in Economic Support Fund and development assistance resources since the mid-1980s is only the most recent manifestation of this relationship. When effectiveness in the use of aid resources for development purposes has seemed to be in conflict with short-term strategic objectives, the strategic objectives have generally dominated assistance policy.

A *second* constraint is the continuing gap between the articulated objectives of assistance policy and the limited resources that have been made available to realize these objectives. The commitments to global poverty reduction in the 1970s, to debt restructuring in the 1980s, and to sustainable development in the 1990s are among the examples of the gap between rhetoric and resources. In the last Bush administration budget and the first Clinton administration budget, authority for U.S. bilateral economic assistance, including both development and strategic or supporting (ESF) assistance, amounted to less than $8 billion. The continuing gap between America's pretensions and its willingness to support them can hardly avoid leading to greater disillusionment with the U.S. aid effort.[4]

The plethora of development assistance reform proposals advanced during the closing years of the Reagan and Bush administrations have lacked the sense of compelling purpose that would be necessary to unlock the two constraints (Chap. 13). There has been no articulation of what might become a common vision of the relationship between the U.S. assistance effort and the kind of world Americans want to live in during the first half of the twenty-first century. There are several reasons why our vision has become blurred.

One reason for the blurring of vision has been the emergence of a much broader conception of national interest. Traditionally realist doctrine has defined national interest as the capacity to bring power to bear effectively in international relations in defense of national security. A more pragmatic perspective on political behavior suggests, however, that in practice national interest has been defined more broadly to include the extension of representative government, the advancement of economic well-being both at home and abroad, a search for a more stable world order, and a concern for basic human rights and civic virtue (Chap. 1).

During the Cold War this broader vision was often constrained by the perceived need to combat Soviet imperialism both along the borders of the USSR and in the Third World. It is no longer possible, however, for a U.S. president, supported by the consensus of a relatively homogeneous foreign policy establishment, to invoke the specter of Soviet adventurism to mobilize public opinion and congressional support for a foreign aid budget that allocates a large share of assistance to strategically important countries. There has been a vigorous search, by realists, at both the bureaucratic and the policy level in Washington, for new issues that might replace the Cold War in mobilizing support for foreign economic assistance. But appeals to "a war on drugs" or "environmental security" have not been able to tap a sufficient sense of immediacy to generate the necessary level of political commitment. And appeals to America's role in building a New World Order remain an empty rhetorical capsule in search for policy content.[5]

A second reason for the blurring of vision is the very substantial disillusionment of the American public with the aid effort. This is sometimes cast in terms of "aid weariness."[6] There is also concern over the effects of intervention, either economic or military, when guided primarily by strategic objectives. There have been some dramatic successes in development assistance. Higher-yielding crop varieties have eased the burden of food scarcity in South Asia. The oral rehydration technique has reduced infant mortality due to diarrheal disease. But the view that foreign assistance could, within a generation, dramatically reduce the incidence of poverty throughout the world is now seen as an illusion. Within the largest and most committed sources of support for development assistance among the general public, there is a deep resentment that too much aid has been directed to strategically important countries where it has often done more harm than good—where it has not met the basic criterion that at least aid should do no harm (Chap. 2; Chap. 10).

A third reason for the blurring of vision is that Americans are in the midst of a substantial realignment of conservative and liberal perspectives on the appropriate role of the United States in foreign affairs. I noted earlier that "American exceptionalism"—the view that the nation is endowed with unique political virtue—had spawned two conflicting doctrines about the appropriate relation of the United States to the rest of the world (Chap. 1). An implication of the idealist (or liberal) doctrine is that it is the mission of the United States to lead the world—by example, assistance, and cooperation—into a more democratic and prosperous future. An implication of the realist (or conservative) doctrine is that the United States must be continuously on guard against excessive entanglements with countries whose interests and ideologies we do not share—that we should manage our relations with the rest of the world primarily in our own interests.

The period from the late 1940s to the late 1960s was characterized by a broad bipartisan consensus on foreign policy. Although there was a resurgence of right-wing isolationism during the late 1940s and early 1950s, "the Cold War reformulated America's world role and made it possible for former isolationists to become internationalists."[7] During this period, idealist doctrine dominated U.S. assistance policy. We viewed ourselves as involved in a mission to reconstruct the rest of the world in our image—democratic, liberal, and prosperous. The domestic political discensus associated with the Vietnam War and the growth of disorder in international relationships that has followed the end of the Cold War generated a powerful shift away from idealist and toward realist doctrine.

Associated with this shift is a reversal of perspectives on the part of the more liberal and conservative wings of both the Democratic and the Republican parties. From the late 1940s through the mid-1960s, the liberals supported and the conservatives opposed a more activist international economic and political role for the United States (Chaps. 4 and 5). As U.S. involvement in Vietnam progressed, there was a reversal of roles, with conservatives adopting a more activist and liberals a less activist stance. For a brief period during the late 1960s and early 1970s, while conservative realists continued to focus on the Communist threat and liberal idealists on withdrawal from excessive commitment in Asia, President Richard Nixon was able to break through the bounds of ideology and pursue a pragmatic foreign policy. Nixon's pragmatic approach led to an opening of relations with China, more productive arms control negotiations with the USSR, and an excruciatingly slow withdrawal from Vietnam.[8]

By the early 1990s a reversal of roles was again under way.[9] Conservatives were urging a less activist role in the Middle East, toward the former centrally planned economies, and toward the poor countries of Asia, Africa, and Latin America. Liberals were urging a more activist role in response to humanitarian concerns—in the Horn of Africa, in the Balkans, and in the Caribbean—even if it meant getting bogged down in extended conflict.

Lessons from Development Assistance

In spite of the constraints of doctrine, resources, and vision under which U.S. assistance policy has labored, there are important lessons from past experience.[10] Let me turn first to some of the lessons from assistance for sector development and then to the lessons from assistance for policy reform.

Sector Development

Assistance to Physical Infrastructure Development

During the 1950s and 1960s, large-scale investment in transport facilities (roads, railroads, ports, airports) and multipurpose resource development projects (power, flood control, irrigation) occupied a very prominent place in both bilateral and multilateral development assistance portfolios. Many of these projects made substantial contributions to the development of recipient countries. Others became a burden. During the 1970s, infrastructure projects were severely criticized on technical grounds. Cost overruns were often substantial; the technology was often incompatible with the level of country development; failure to consider exchange rate distortions often led to inappropriate investments. During the 1980s, infrastructure investments became the subject of intense scrutiny and severe criticism by the environmental community. Some of this criticism was valid. Much of it was overblown. It is, however, again possible to take a much more positive view of lending for infrastructure development. The technical, environmental, and economic aspects of project evaluation and design have become more sophisticated. And the services provided by infrastructure are essential for economic growth.

Agricultural and Rural Development

Sustained growth in agricultural production requires a close articulation of public and private sector support for research, development, and technology transfer. The private sector has generally been relatively efficient in the development and transfer of mechanical and chemical technology and in the distribution of technical inputs. The public sector has been more effective in the development of biological and information technology. Public sector agricultural research and extension have achieved rates of return that are among the highest available to either national governments or development assistance agencies. The underinvestment in agricultural research and related activities in agricultural production, processing, and distribution development reflects a continuing failure on the part of both donor agencies and national governments to understand the role of agricultural development in generating economic growth and in contributing to more equitable income distribution.

Efforts by bilateral and multilateral donors to assist in community and rural development programs have met with much less apparent success than have attempts to enhance agricultural production. One of the major sources of disillusionment has been the lack of consistency between the dynamics of rural development and the imperatives of donor assistance. Successful rural development programs tend to be small in geographic scope and slow to implement; impose intensive demands on professional and administration capacity; are difficult to assess within the framework of conventional cost-benefit analysis; and are difficult to monitor. A second source of disillusionment has been the difficulty of achieving congruence between the local self-help and resource mobilization philosophy of rural development programs and the objectives of donors to achieve measurable improvements on basic human needs indicators within the space of the project cycle.

Assistance for Investment in Human Resource Development

Both development theorists and assistance agencies were slow to recognize that investment in education and other forms of human capital represented a high pay-off source of economic growth. As evidence began to accumulate, indicating high rates of return to education, perspectives began to change. It is time for the United States to review its commitments to cooperation in the development of educational systems and to draw on the knowledge that is gained in the redesign and reform of our own systems.

Assistance in health and family planning also came to be recognized as an investment in human capital. The initial transfer of health technology from Western society to developing countries has often been inappropriate. We have transferred sickness recovery systems rather than health systems. There is an enormous challenge facing the development assistance community, as well as national health systems, to design systems that enable families to live healthy lives so they do not have to enter the sickness recovery system. There is also an enormous need for the establishment of health research capacity in the tropics. The resurgence of malaria and tuberculosis, the high cost of dealing with infectious disease, the failure to make progress in dealing with parasitic disease, the emerging AIDS epidemic, and the health effects of environmental change suggest that over the next two decades the health dimension of human resource development should command a level of attention similar to that received by agriculture in the 1960s and 1970s.

Policy Reform

The Influence of Domestic Economic Policy on the Effectiveness of Donor Economic Assistance

The effectiveness of economic assistance has been strongly conditioned by both the macroeconomic and the sectoral economic policies of the host country. The contrast between the effectiveness of assistance to Korea before and after 1961 and the effectiveness of assistance to Ghana and Ivory Coast during the 1960s and 1970s is among the more dramatic examples. In the early 1960s Korea was still regarded as an economic "basket case." The Syngman Rhee government managed economic policy to maximize foreign economic assistance rather than to enhance economic growth. It was only after more growth-oriented policies were adopted in the mid-1960s that investments in the physical and institutional infrastructure, funded by U.S. economic assistance in the 1950s, began to pay off. At independence in 1957 Ghana had a well-established export sector, a reasonably well-developed physical infrastructure, a relatively high level of literacy, and the highest per capita income in Africa. The Ivory Coast lagged behind Ghana in practically every indicator of development. By the early 1980s the economic situation in the two countries was essentially reversed. Ghana has pursued policies of import substitution and direct state intervention in almost every area of economic activity. In the Ivory Coast government policy was directed toward guiding rather than controlling the private sector. Since the late 1980s the situation in these two countries has again changed—with Ivory Coast lagging and Ghana advancing more rapidly as a result of a vigorous program of policy reform.

Policy Dialogue and Policy-based Lending

The effectiveness of economic assistance is influenced (1) by the degree of convergence in the views of the donors and recipient countries concerning the latter's economic policies and (2) by the importance of economic development objectives relative to other donor motivations in decisions concerning the volume and allocation of economic assistance.[11] The dominance of donor strategic interests relative to commitment to economic policy reform has been demonstrated repeatedly in the case of Turkey. The willingness of the United States to support Turkish policy in trading off economic reform against short-term strategic concerns contributed to the severity of the series of growth cycles experienced by the Turkish economy (1950–58, 1959–69, 1970–79). For an even more extreme example, one can turn to the history of U.S. economic assistance to Egypt (Chap. 10).

Among the many factors that have influenced the effectiveness of policy dialogue between donors and recipients, two have been particularly important. One is the degree of convergence of the views of donors and recipients concerning the need for and importance of proposed reforms. A second, and closely related factor, is the ability of recipients to bring substantial professional capacity and experience to bear on issues of institutional reform, policy analysis, and program implementation. When these factors are not present, reforms are often implemented both reluctantly and ineffectively.

The Influence of the Size of Assistance Flows on National Economic Growth

The effect of the size of development assistance flows on the rate of economic growth of recipient countries represents a continuing theoretical and empirical puzzle. The evidence to support a conclusion that differences in the level of development assistance have accounted for major intercountry growth differences is not available. There is some evidence that rates of return from economic assistance to the OECD countries have been relatively high.[12] There is evidence, though somewhat inconclusive, that in the absence of effective macroeconomic policy there is a negative relationship between the size of foreign aid transfers and the rate of economic growth. But the evidence to support a conclusion that differences in the level of development assistance have accounted for major differences in intercountry economic growth rates or other foreign development indicators is not available.

Economic Assistance and the Achievement of Noneconomic Objectives

There is a consistent pattern of jeopardizing the achievement of the principle economic objectives when projects are burdened with divergent objectives. Divergent objectives sharply reduce the chances for achieving success even of the most immediate primary goals.[13] In the Philippines, for example, linking economic assistance to the continuation of base rights failed to generate economic development, contributed to political repression, and failed to secure continued access to base facilities. It is too much to ask a multiple purpose water development project to be a catalyst for regional economic development. It is enough if it delivers power and water efficiently to users. It is too much to ask a legal training program to become a catalyst for democratic development. It is enough if the competence of the legal system can be enhanced to render justice more effectively. The linkage between the two major components of basic human needs and rights—improvement in economic well-being and the strengthening of civil society—is not always as obvious as their advocates suggest.

Political Development

The strengthening of democratic institutions has traditionally ranked relatively high, at least at a rhetorical level, among the objectives of U.S. foreign assistance policy. With the end of the Cold War, there have been renewed calls "to promote freedom and democracy around the world." Building democratic participation in development was among the four major initiatives listed in early pronouncements by Deputy Secretary of State Wharton and AID Administrator Atwood. But U.S. commitment to political development has, like commitment to economic development, often faltered when confronted with short term strategic considerations (Chap. 10).

In the case of economic development, both sector development and policy reform efforts have been able to draw on a powerful body of economic thought—primarily neoclassical economic theory—that provides the analytical tools with which to address issues of development practice and the design of economic reform. The application of these tools, even when used with skill and sensitivity, has not represented a guarantee against failure in project, program, or policy design. There is no similar body of theory that can serve as a guide in the design of a program to strengthen the institutions of governance or of a program to achieve a liberal political order.

One of the few guides available is the empirical generalization that political liberalization is more sustainable when it is preceded by a successful program of economic liberalization.[14] The generalization is sufficiently strong to support a conclusion that a poor country is fortunate if economic liberalization runs sufficiently ahead of political liberalization to generate economic growth at the same time that political reforms are being put in place. This generalization is clearly consistent with recent East Asian experience. The East Asian tigers—Korea, Taiwan, Hong Kong, and Singapore—certainly cannot be classified as liberal democracies. Nor can the second echelon of rapidly growing economies in the region—Thailand, Malaysia, and Indonesia. They have, however, developed political systems capable of sustaining policies consistent with economic growth. And that economic growth seems to be inducing effective demands for modest political liberalization.

What is the bottom line? What should we have learned from the past? At the risk of only slight overstatement, let me make two assertions. The first is that the removal of distortions in monetary, fiscal, trade, commodity, and consumer policy is a prerequisite for effective economic performance. Structural reform raises the rate of return of growth-enhancing investment, but it is not a primary source of economic growth. At best it can reduce the "X inefficiency"—the gap between the level of output that has already been achieved and the level of output that is potentially feasible.

The second is that the real sources of economic growth are investments in human and physical capital and in productivity-enhancing technical and institutional change. These more fundamental investments must draw on resources—financial, political, intellectual—that are not readily mobilized in the short run and often not mobilized by the private sector. They do not generate immediate increments in economic growth. They often require a generation or more to mature. The failure to make investments needed to expand technical and institutional capacity in the 1970s is a major reason why the response to the policy reforms of the 1980s has often been so disappointing.

One way of summing up is to insist that advising "shock treatment," as we have often done in Eastern Europe and the former USSR, for countries with weak or missing market institutions or limited technical capacity—that they go cold turkey on policy reform—must be viewed as little more than self-indulgent intellectual sloth. It reflects a lack of willingness to invest the intellectual energy necessary to understand the economies and the societies for which reform prescriptions are being made. In the pursuit of reform, motivation has often outrun knowledge and capacity.[15]

Toward Renewed Commitment?

Now let me turn to the future of U.S. development assistance. I will lay out two scenarios. The first will be a more substantial program that I view as consistent with U.S. interests and capacities in a post–Cold War world. The second will be a more limited program—the minimum that we should ask of ourselves—even in an environment of constrained budgets and a growing weariness with the burdens of world leadership. Both scenarios will be conditioned by a search for a post–Cold War rationale for U.S. development assistance. Is there anything that can, or will, replace the Cold War as a rationale for the mobilization of U.S. resources to assist in the development of poor countries? Both scenarios attempt to take into consideration the changes in the global economy over the last several decades and the changing role of the United States in the world economy and polity.

The evolution of the global economic system has dramatically altered the demands of and the opportunities for effective foreign economic assistance. Until the late 1960s the world operated under a fixed exchange rate regime. The transfer of resources from dollar surplus countries to deficit countries could be viewed as part of the cost of maintaining the institutional infrastructure of an increasingly liberal international economic order—at least until the "dollar shortage" was replaced by a "dollar glut." We now have lived with a flexible exchange rate system for more than two decades. The international capital market that has been put in place makes it possible for countries that pursue reasonably sound domestic monetary and fiscal policies to borrow the financial resources they need. The rationale for concessional resource transfers, other than to the very poorest countries, has largely disappeared. Indeed, large concessional transfers can, unless carefully managed, result in perverse distortions in the exchange rates of the recipient countries.

The position of the United States in the world economy has also changed. The United States is no longer as confident of its leadership as it was when President Truman announced the Point Four Program. It is no longer as confident of its capacity to assist in the design of educational and health systems as it was when economists first started conceptualizing the role of human capital in economic development. It is no longer as confident of its capacity to contribute to the solution of either domestic or global poverty as it was when President Johnson outlined his New Society programs. And our confidence in our ability to prescribe monetary and fiscal policy for others ought to be much weaker than it was when the United States was the world's largest creditor nation rather than the largest debtor nation.

Organizing for Effective Development Cooperation

These changes in the international and the domestic economy imply a much different mission for a U.S. economic assistance program than in the past. We need to reform our bilateral program to operate in a mode of economic cooperation rather than economic assistance. U.S. assistance efforts should focus largely on the high pay-off areas of human capital development and of technical and institutional change. My own preference would be for an Economic Cooperation Administration with much of its bilateral economic development and humanitarian assistance activity organized in two semiautonomous institutes, along with the several public foundations, under an ECA umbrella. It would also encompass a somewhat larger role for multilateral assistance. Neither the State Department nor an assistance agency that operates under direct State Department policy guidance could be relied on to give substantial weight to the perspective suggested by this model or to defend the allocation of resources needed to support long-term development objectives in those countries of the world that fall outside short-term security interests—even though this would be in our long-term national interest.

An Institute for Scientific, Technical, and Economic Cooperation

In today's world the United States has as much to learn from as to teach by strengthening technical and intellectual interchange. The mandate of an Institute for Scientific, Technical, and Economic Cooperation (ISTEC) should be to enhance the two-way exchange of knowledge and technology among all nations rather than simply to give technical assistance to poor countries.[16] The ISTEC mandate should include the OECD and the formerly centrally planned economies, as well as the less developed countries. Emphasis should be strongest in areas such as agriculture, health, population, and environment. It should also include cooperation in the areas of institutional reform, policy analysis, and program implementation. Program operations should be largely subcontracted to universities, research institutes, and the sectoral departments and agencies such as Agriculture; Health, Education and Welfare; Environmental Protection; and the National Institute of Standards and Technology—

in which the scientific and technical capacity to implement the ISTEC program resides. The funding necessary to maintain the capacity for the nation's major research universities to participate in ISTEC programs should be placed on a long-term institutional grant basis, somewhat similar to that provided by the Hatch Act for domestic agricultural research.

An Institute for Private Voluntary Cooperation

Humanitarian concerns for the poor in the poorest countries and for those displaced by international conflict and domestic repression will continue to represent a basic impulse for foreign assistance for a wide spectrum of the American public.[17] Official assistance agencies do not have a strong record of performance in this area. The Institute for Private Voluntary Cooperation (IPVC) should be organized to fund programs by PVOs, cooperatives, and private firms on a competitive basis. Too much of present funding has been treated as an entitlement. A major emphasis should be placed on strengthening indigenous PVOs. Much of food aid, except that allocated for so-called market development, should be channeled through the IPVC. The PVO community should be encouraged to become more effective in using food aid as an instrument of development than in the past.

The Public Foundations

In addition to the ISTEC and the IPVC, support should be expanded for the publicly supported development foundations. These include the Asia Foundation, the Inter-American Development Foundation, and the African Development Foundation. The historical roots of the Asia Foundation were deep in Cold War doctrine. During the last decade, however, it has emerged with substantial capacity to work on issues of democratization and privatization—items that should be high on the foreign policy and foreign assistance agenda. The Inter-American Foundation and the African Development Foundation are products of the New Directions and basic human needs foreign assistance thrust of the 1970s. They have now emerged with substantial capacity to work directly with the poor and with the informal sectors in poor countries. A cautious expansion of support for the programs of these public foundations and for the creation of several new public foundations—such as the recently established Eurasia Foundation and the proposed public foundation to work in the area of sustainable energy systems—would seem warranted. My caution stems from concern that rapid growth in support could outrun the capacity of the public foundations.[18]

Security Assistance

The component of the foreign economic assistance budget allocated to the support of strategically important countries under the Economic Support Fund has declined more rapidly than has development assistance since the mid-1980s. The overwhelming share of ESF resources is now allocated to the Middle East. As security assistance budgets have declined, there has been a frantic search in Washington to find new threats that might reverse the decline. It is now time for a complete reassessment of U.S. policy, including assistance policy, toward the Middle East.

The Nixon Doctrine, first articulated on Guam in 1969, prepared the way for U.S. military disengagement from Southeast Asia. It is now time for the United States to promulgate a new Middle East doctrine along the lines suggested by George Kennan in the mid-1970s.[19] The first element in that doctrine should be that the United States no longer has vital strategic or security interests in the Middle East.[20] A second element should be that the United States does have an interest, short of direct military intervention, in the continued reduction of tensions between Israel and the Arab states in the region. A third element should be that the United States would welcome the emergence of representative governments in the region. As progress is made in reducing the flow of ESF resources to the region, the funds should be shifted to other bilateral and multilateral assistance activities.

Multilateral Assistance

The United States should continue to look favorably on requests for modest expansion of the borrowing authority and replenishment of soft-loan lending facilities at the World Bank and the regional development banks. The relationship between the United States and several of the U.N. specialized agencies and voluntary programs remains troubled. The ascendancy of the State Department Bureau for International Organizations, relative to the sectoral departments, in the formulation of U.S. policy toward the U.N. specialized agencies, combined with personal antagonisms between bureau administrators and specialized agency directors-general and growing arrears in U.S. budget contributions, have resulted in a weakening of the U.S. role in several of the specialized agencies during the 1980s and the early 1990s (Chap. 12).

In spite of this troubled history, it is now in the U.S. interest to provide stronger U.S. support for the work of the United Nations Development Program and the specialized agencies and voluntary programs in the 1990s. The easing of U.S.-USSR tensions has removed some of the ideological tensions that have frequently spilled over into U.S. relationships with the specialized agencies—multilateral assistance should be viewed by the U.S. government as a less expensive, and often less frustrating, approach to assisting some of the economically and politically least developed countries.

Building on U.S. Capacity

I do not see anything on the horizon that will be as effective as the Cold War was in generating the political resources necessary to support a program as broad as that outlined in the previous section. The prospect is for continued decline in the resources for foreign economic assistance. In this section, I outline a minimum program to which the United States should commit itself, even in the constrained environment of the late 1990s.

Decisions being made when this chapter was being written indicate that in the mid-1990s more than half of bilateral economic assistance will continue, in the immediate future, to be allocated to advancing the peace process and related political objectives in the Middle East. A significant portion of the remaining economic assistance will be allocated to support the economic and political transition process in Eastern Europe, Russia, and the other successor states to the USSR. A much smaller but still substantial flow will probably be directed to facilitating democratic reform in Southern Africa. As these priorities are met, it seems that substantially less than $1.0 billion will be available for U.S. bilateral economic assistance to the poorest countries in Asia, Africa, and Latin America.

My vision for the U.S. bilateral assistance program in the severely constrained economic environment of the mid-1990s is much less ambitious than the United States is capable of delivering. But it is a program that would draw on U.S. capabilities to cooperate with poor countries in advancing their own development priorities. The program would be built around a reorganization and refocusing of the functional accounts in the AID development assistance budget in five important areas.

AGRICULTURE AND FOOD SECURITY

Agricultural commodities have been available on relatively favorable terms in world markets since the early 1980s. But most countries in the developing world have not yet succeeded in developing and sustaining the agricultural research, extension, and infrastructure investment that will enable them to meet the demands that will be placed on agricultural production capacity during the early decades of the next century. Even fewer have been able to design and put in place the institutions needed to assure the poor equitable entitlement to their basic subsistence needs. The food situation in much of

Africa has become increasingly precarious. The decline in support for agricultural development, and particularly the decline in support for agricultural research, should be reversed.

NATURAL RESOURCES, ENERGY USE, AND ENVIRONMENTAL PROTECTION

The closing decades of the twentieth century have seen a major transition in concern about the capacity to achieve sustainable economic growth. It is now clear that technical change is capable of releasing the most serious threats to growth arising out of resource constraints. But the environmental effects of agricultural and industrial intensification are posing new threats to the sustainability of economic growth. These threats range from groundwater and soil pollution to global climate change. Only a few developed countries and even fewer developing countries have begun to put in place the technologies and institutions needed to resolve these threats.

HEALTH AND POPULATION

The design of health systems to meet the needs of the poor majority in the least developed countries continues to evade the efforts of assistance programs. A series of health threats—the resurgence of malaria and tuberculosis, the failure to make significant progress in parasitic disease, the high cost of responding to infectious disease, the health effects of environmental change, and the debilitating effect of the AIDS epidemic on working-age populations—point toward the emergence of a global health crisis in the early decades of the twenty-first century. We need to strengthen the capacity for essential national health research. We need to design and implement health delivery and maintenance systems that give the family and the community a central role in the health system. Population stabilization before the end of the second quarter of the twenty-first century is clearly feasible. It must represent an important component of efforts to achieve food security and sustainable improvements in other dimensions of human development.

EDUCATION AND HUMAN CAPITAL

It has been clear since midcentury that broad-based economic growth can be sustained only if all people have the opportunity to acquire the basic skills and knowledge that facilitate effective participation in the economic, social, and political development of their country. Advances in science and technology have raised both public and private returns to improvements in education. Yet in too many countries there is strong bias against access to even the most basic levels of education for rural areas, girls, and the urban poor.

INSTITUTIONAL REFORM

During the 1980s political and economic reform occupied a relatively high priority in the U.S. bilateral assistance agenda. The uneven success of economic reform efforts has been due, to a substantial extent, to the lack of institutional capacity to respond to the incentives made available by the reform programs. The even more limited success of U.S. efforts to assist in political reform reflected not only the inadequate knowledge base and capacity of the U.S. bilateral assistance agency, but also the frequent conflict between U.S. strategic objectives and the imperatives of political reform. In spite of limited success in the past, it is appropriate for the U.S. assistance agency to expand its efforts to strengthen the institutions needed to sustain economic and political development.

These priorities are not inconsistent with the priorities of the Clinton administration as outlined by the 1993 Wharton task force (Chap. 13). They do imply a far less adequate assistance effort than is consistent with either U.S. capacities or responsibilities. They are, however, consistent with the limited resources that are likely to be available for economic assistance by the United States to the poorest countries in the late 1990s. They are consistent with but do not exhaust the elements usually included in the sustainability agenda. Each draws on scientific, professional, and technical capacity in which the United States has much to offer. There is no presumption that all program areas will be operative in all countries. The program initiative should draw on the capacities of universities, private voluntary organizations, and public foundations in a way that assures sustainability in the development of program capacity.

A New Vision?

The decline in the relative strength of the U.S. economy has weakened its capacity to play a hegemonic role in global economic and political affairs. I have (reluctantly) found myself in agreement with Jeane Kirkpatrick, who insisted (a bit prematurely) in a 1990 article in *Foreign Affairs* that the United States must reconcile itself to being "just a power." Henry Kissinger has insisted that in the emerging world order "the United States can neither withdraw from the world nor dominate it."[21] But the declining capacity of the U.S. economy to sustain a first class global posture in economic and security affairs cannot fully account for the constraints under which U.S. foreign economic assistance will be forced to operate in the middle and late 1990s. The effects of the irresponsible fiscal policies pursued since the early 1980s will continue to dampen policy initiatives. For at least the next decade, the U.S. government will continue to tailor both its foreign and its domestic policies to a very constipated fiscal environment.

As the Clinton administration struggles to repair the erosion in the capacity of the domestic economy and the dysfunction of social institutions that became increasingly apparent during the closing decades of the Cold War, its capacity and inclination to pursue foreign policy goals aggressively, particularly foreign economic assistance, have become increasingly tentative. Thomas L. Friedman has noted that, while continuing to project a vision and commitment to a more peaceful, democratic, and prosperous world, the Clinton administration has, in practice, defined a new policy of self-containment.[22]

Are there any forces at work which might reverse the anticipated decline in assistance resources? One could be the emergence of one or more common threats to the well-being of both developed and developing countries.[23] As noted above there was a good deal of rhetoric in the early and mid-1990s about sustainable development and environmental security. There is little doubt that the transnational nature of some environmental threats—global climate change, ozone depletion, acid rain, and others—will require the strengthening of transnational or international institutions. There is also the possibility of global health and food crises emerging as we move into the first decades of the next century.[24] Either could result in an international resource mobilization effort to resolve the crisis. But I do not visualize, at least in the short run, any of these common concerns generating the political support that will be needed to prevent the erosion of U.S. assistance resources. I am concerned that the gap between AID's articulation of its vision of sustainable development and the resources that are being allocated to the achievement of its vision will contribute to the discrediting of the concept of sustainable development.

The most likely prospect is for each assistance constituency, within the government and outside, to continue to attempt to carve out for its favored program area (population, environment, agriculture) a larger share of a declining assistance budget. The lack of a central policy focus has left the assistance budget particularly vulnerable to such efforts.

The continuing fatigue and disorientation in the U.S. bilateral effort will not be resolved by the typical Washington remedy—by reorganizing AID. Moving organizational boxes around (as in the 1979 reorganization that created IDCA), rationalizing interagency conflict and cooperation (as in the 1990 food aid reforms), or granting parts of the aid program greater autonomy from political pressures (as in the case of the public foundations or my suggestions for reorganization in this chapter) will not resolve this problem.

A New World Order?

The problem of lack of focus will not be resolved until a new post–Cold War vision of the kind of world in which we want to live during the first half of the twenty-first century captures the political and popular imagination. Such a vision can now be perceived only dimly. I have been pressed by friends in the development community to embrace the rhetoric of sustainable development in an attempt to capture a vision for the future. I have resisted, however, because the concept of sustainability has become so elastic that it can be stretched to cover almost any reform agenda. It has become an umbrella under which constituencies with widely diverse and often inconsistent agendas can march without confronting their disagreements.[25]

The international environment in which assistance efforts will be conducted in the early decades of the twenty-first century will be vastly different then the bipolar world of the Cold War era. We will be confronted with what Harlan Cleveland has termed "a new world disorder."[26] Many centralized nation-states are perceived by large numbers of their peoples as increasingly less relevant to their economic and political needs. This trend is apparent in large multinational states. But it also includes many small multinational states and states that incorporate geographically based national minorities—whether Amer-Indian nationals in the United States and Guatemala, ethnic minorities in the former Yugoslavia and the USSR, or tribal minorities in Rwanda and Burundi.

Governments will be forced to deal more creatively with their constituent nationalities than in the past. The constitutional design challenge of the next several decades will be how to simultaneously achieve political autonomy and economic viability. On the political side this means a pragmatic search for constitutional arrangements that will assure ethnic and other communities sufficient autonomy to satisfy their civic needs. Economic viability requires that political autonomy be achieved within a constitutional framework that will permit financial resources, commodities and services, and people to move freely across political borders.

What should be the role of U.S. economic assistance in an environment of pervasive economic and political disorder? U.S. national security will rarely be threatened by the small conflicts of natural liberation or ethnic cleansing. Nor will conventional military responses be particularly effective in restoring order.[27] But the idealist version of American exceptionalism will continue to represent a compelling source of American foreign policy. The liberal impulse that led to U.S. leadership in the design of the post–World War II international system—the United Nations, the World Bank and the International Monetary Fund, and the General Agreement on Tariffs and Trade—is capable, if effectively mobilized, of sustaining an activist role for the United States in responding to the new international disorder.

But the implications for U.S. development assistance policy are far from clear. The U.S. bilateral development assistance program, as we have known it throughout most of the postwar period, is already largely eroded. It is doubtful that, in the absence of a new vision and a new consensus, US/AID can survive in its present form. A new vision grounded in today's realities and tomorrow's promise, however, could lead our bilateral assistance program in a new direction—more toward development cooperation than toward assistance.

The more developed societies of today have inherited modern economies and the science, technology, and institutions that have enabled them to find a way out of the poverty trap. If we want to contribute to the building of a safer and more prosperous world, we must return to the vision articulated by President Harry S. Truman in his 1949 inaugural address, "to make the benefits of our scientific and industrial progress available for the improvement of underdeveloped areas." And we must combine that vision with that of the 1973 House Foreign Affairs Committee, linking the advances in basic human needs and human rights. The poor countries must learn to use their own material and human resources more effectively. They must transform traditional institutions and reform their economic and social policies to achieve both more rapid growth and equitable development.

The United States, with its vast capacity in science and leadership, its excellent higher education system, its committed PVOs, and its long experience with assistance in the development of modern economic and political institutions, is capable of playing a major role in this cooperative effort. It is in our own interest to live in a more prosperous world, in a sustainable environment, and in a world with a more liberal and progressive civic culture and international order.

Appendixes
Notes
Index

Appendix A

U.S. Assistance to Strategically Important Countries

TABLE A.1
U.S. Economic and Military Assistance to South Vietnam by Fiscal Year, 1955–1975 (million dollars)

Fiscal year	AID	PL 480	Piaster subsidy	Total economic aid	Military assistance	Total assistance
Reconstruction and Nation Building						
1955	320.2	2.2		322.4		322.4
1956	195.7	14.3		210.0	176.5	386.5
1957	259.4	22.8		282.2	119.8	402.0
1958	179.4	9.6		189.0	79.3	268.3
1959	200.9	6.5		207.4	52.4	259.8
Insurgency						
1960	170.6	11.3		181.8	72.7	254.5
1961	140.5	11.5		152.0	71.0	223.0
1962	124.1	31.9		156.0	237.2	393.2
1963	143.3	52.6		195.9	275.9	471.8
1964	165.7	59.1	5.8	230.6	190.9	421.5
War						
1965	225.0	49.9	15.4	290.3	318.6	608.9
1966	593.5	143.0	57.4	793.9	686.2	1,480.1
1967	494.4	73.7	98.5	666.6	662.5	1,329.1
1968	398.2	138.5	114.4	651.1	1,243.4	1,894.5
Vietnamization						
1969	314.2	99.4	146.9	560.5	1,534.0	2,094.5
1970	365.9	110.8	178.7	655.4	1,577.3	2,232.7
1971	387.7	188.0	202.3	778.0	1,945.6	2,723.6
1972	386.8	67.8	133.1	587.7	2,602.6	3,190.3
1973	313.3	188.3	29.5	531.2	3,349.4	3,880.6
Defeat						
1974	384.3	269.9	3.2	657.4	941.9	1,599.3
1975	191.3	49.6		240.9	625.1	866.0
Total	5,954.4	1,600.7	985.2	8,540.3	16,762.3	25,302.6

Source: Douglas C. Dacy, *Foreign Aid, War and Economic Development: South Vietnam, 1955–1975* (Cambridge: Cambridge University Press, 1986), 200.

Table A.2

U.S. Assistance to Israel, 1970–1994

		Economic assistance									Military assistance	
		AID and predecessor agencies			Food for Peace		Other economic assistance		Total			
Administration	Year	Loans	Grants	(ESF)	Loans	Grants	Loans	Grants	Loans	Grants	Loans	Grants
Nixon	1970	0.0	0.0	(0.0)	40.7	0.4	0.0	0.0	40.7	0.4	30.0	0.0
	1971	0.0	0.0	(0.0)	55.5	0.3	0.0	0.0	55.5	0.3	545.0	0.0
	1972	0.0	50.0	(50.0)	53.8	0.4	0.0	0.0	53.8	50.4	300.0	0.0
	1973	0.0	50.0	(50.0)	59.4	0.4	0.0	0.0	59.4	59.4	307.5	0.0
Nixon & Ford	1974	0.0	50.0	(50.0)	0.0	1.5	0.0	0.0	0.0	51.5	982.7	1,500.0
	1975	0.0	344.5	(324.5)	8.6	0.0	0.0	0.0	8.6	344.5	200.0	100.0
	1976	225.0	475.0	(700.0)	14.4	0.0	0.0	0.0	239.4	475.0	750.0	750.0
	TQ	25.0	50.0	(75.0)	3.6	0.0	0.0	0.0	28.6	50.0	100.0	100.0
	1977	245.0	490.0	(735.0)	7.0	0.0	0.0	0.0	252.0	490.0	500.0	500.0
Carter	1978	260.0	525.0	(785.0)	6.8	0.0	0.0	0.0	266.8	525.0	500.0	500.0
	1979	260.0	525.0	(785.5)	5.1	0.0	0.0	0.0	265.1	525.0	2,700.0	1,300.0
	1980	260.0	525.0	(785.0)	1.0	0.0	0.0	0.0	261.0	525.0	500.0	500.0
	1981	0.0	764.0	(764.0)	0.0	0.0	0.0	0.0	0.0	764.0	900.0	500.0
First Reagan	1982	0.0	806.0	(806.0)	0.0	0.0	0.0	0.0	0.0	806.0	850.0	550.0
	1983	0.0	785.0	(785.0)	0.0	0.0	0.0	0.0	0.0	785.0	950.0	750.0
	1984	0.0	910.0	(910.0)	0.0	0.0	0.0	0.0	0.0	910.0	850.0	850.0
	1985	0.0	1,950.1	(1,950.1)	0.0	0.0	0.0	0.0	0.0	1,950.1	0.0	1,400.0
Second Reagan	1986	0.0	1,898.4	(1,898.4)	0.0	0.0	0.0	0.0	0.0	1,898.4	0.0	1,722.6
	1987	0.0	1,200.0	(1,200.0)	0.0	0.0	0.0	0.0	0.0	1,200.0	0.0	1,800.0
	1988	0.0	1,200.0	(1,200.0)	0.0	0.0	0.0	0.0	0.0	1,200.0	0.0	1,800.0
	1989	0.0	1,200.0	(1,200.0)	0.0	0.0	0.0	0.0	0.0	1,200.0	0.0	1,800.0
Bush	1990	0.0	1,194.8	(1,194.8)	0.0	0.0	0.0	0.0	0.0	1,194.8	0.0	1,792.3
	1991	0.0	1,850.0	(1,850.0)	0.0	0.0	0.0	0.0	0.0	1,850.0	0.0	1,800.0
	1992	0.0	1,200.0	(1,200.0)	0.0	0.0	0.0	0.0	0.0	1,200.0	0.0	1,800.0
	1993	0.0	1,200.0	(1,200.0)	0.0	0.0	0.0	0.0	0.0	1,200.0	0.0	1,800.0
Clinton	1994[a]	0.0	1,450.0	(1,200.0)	0.0	0.0	0.0	0.0	0.0	1,450.0	0.0	1,800.0

Source: U.S. Agency for International Development, *Congressional Presentation* (Washington: US/AID, various years); *U.S. Loans, Grants and Assistance from International Organizations, Obligations and Loan Authorizations* (Washington: US/AID, various years).

[a] Request.

TABLE A.3

U.S. Assistance to Egypt, 1970–1994

		Economic assistance									Military assistance	
		AID and predecessor agencies			Food for Peace		Other economic assistance		Total			
Administration	Year	Loans	Grants	(ESF)	Loans	Grants	Loans	Grants	Loans	Grants	Loans	Grants
Nixon	1970	0.0	0.0	(0.0)	0.0	0.0	0.0	0.0	0.0	0.0	0.0	0.0
	1971	0.0	0.0	(0.0)	0.0	0.0	0.0	0.0	0.0	0.0	0.0	0.0
	1972	1.5	0.0	(0.0)	0.0	0.0	0.0	0.0	1.5	0.0	0.0	0.0
	1973	0.0	0.0	(0.0)	0.0	0.8	0.0	0.0	0.0	0.8	0.0	0.0
Nixon & Ford	1974	0.0	8.5	(8.5)	9.5	3.3	0.0	0.0	9.5	11.8	0.0	0.0
	1975	194.3	58.5	(252.8)	104.5	12.8	0.0	0.0	298.8	71.3	0.0	0.0
	1976	150.0	108.2	(252.8)	201.7	4.4	0.0	0.0	351.7	112.6	0.0	0.0
	TQ	429.0	107.8	(536.8)	14.6	1.1	0.0	0.0	443.6	108.0	0.0	0.0
	1977	600.0	99.2	(699.3)	196.8	11.7	0.0	0.0	796.8	110.9	0.0	0.0
Carter	1978	617.4	133.3	(750.8)	179.7	12.5	0.0	0.1	797.1	145.9	0.0	0.2
	1979	250.0	585.0	(835.0)	230.7	22.4	0.0	0.0	480.7	607.4	1,500.0	0.4
	1980	280.0	585.0	(865.0)	285.3	16.1	0.0	0.0	565.3	601.1	0.0	0.8
	1981	70.0	759.0	(829.0)	272.5	28.9	0.0	0.0	342.5	787.9	550.0	0.8
First Reagan	1982	0.0	771.0	(771.0)	262.0	31.9	0.0	0.0	262.0	802.9	700.0	202.4
	1983	0.0	750.0	(750.0)	238.3	16.8	0.0	0.0	238.3	766.8	900.0	426.9
	1984	0.0	852.9	(852.9)	237.5	13.7	0.0	0.0	237.5	866.6	900.0	466.7
	1985	0.0	1,065.1	(1,065.1)	213.8	13.2	0.0	0.0	213.8	1,078.3	0.0	1,176.7
Second Reagan	1986	0.0	1,069.2	(1,069.2)	217.5	6.6	0.0	0.0	217.5	1,075.8	0.0	1,245.8
	1987	0.0	819.7	(819.7)	191.7	3.9	0.0	0.0	191.7	823.6	0.0	1,301.8
	1988	0.0	717.8	(717.8)	153.0	2.6	0.0	0.0	153.0	720.4	0.0	1,301.5
	1989	0.0	816.5	(815.0)	150.5	1.2	0.0	[b]	150.5	817.7	0.0	1,301.5
Bush	1990	0.0	900.5	(898.4)	192.9	0.0	0.0	0.0	192.9	900.5	0.0	1,295.9
	1991	0.0	782.8	(780.8)	165.0	0.0	0.0	0.0	165.0	782.8	0.0	1,301.9
	1992	0.0	815.0	(815.0)	150.0	0.0	0.0	0.0	150.0	815.0	0.0	1,301.8
	1993	0.0	747.0	(747.0)	3.2	0.0	0.0	0.0	3.2	747.0	0.0	1,301.8
Clinton	1994[a]	0.0	818.8	(815.0)	7.6	0.0	0.0	0.0	7.6	818.8	0.0	1,300.8

Source: U.S. Agency for International Development, Congressional Presentation, (Washington: US/AID, various years); *U.S. Loans, Grants and Assistance from International Organizations, Obligations and Loan Authorizations* (Washington: US/AID, various years).

[a] Request. [b] Less than $50,000.

TABLE A.4

U.S. Assistance to El Salvador, 1978–1994

		Economic assistance									Military assistance	
		AID and predecessor agencies			Food for Peace		Other economic assistance		Total			
Administration	Year	Loans	Grants	(ESF)	Loans	Grants	Loans	Grants	Loans	Grants	Loans	Grants
Carter	1978	5.7	2.3	(0.0)	0.0	1.7	0.0	1.2	5.7	5.2	0.0	[a]
	1979	4.2	2.7	(0.0)	0.0	2.9	0.0	1.6	4.2	7.2	0.0	[a]
	1980	37.4	14.9	(9.1)	3.0	2.5	0.0	0.5	40.4	17.9	5.7	0.2
	1981	53.8	24.5	(44.9)	26.2	9.1	0.0	0.4	80.0	34.0	10.0	25.5
First Reagan	1982	43.9	110.7	(115.0)	19.9	7.7	0.0	[b]	63.8	118.4	16.5	65.5
	1983	47.6	151.2	(140.0)	39.0	7.8	0.0	[b]	86.6	159.0	46.5	34.8
	1984	32.2	129.2	(120.2)	49.0	5.5	0.0	[b]	81.2	134.7	18.5	178.1
	1985	21.0	355.1	(285.0)	49.0	8.8	[b]	0.0	70.0	363.9	10.0	126.3
Second Reagan	1986	8.0	260.2	(181.9)	44.0	10.4	0.0	0.0	52.0	270.6	0.0	121.8
	1987	0.0	414.5	(281.5)	42.0	6.4	0.0	0.0	42.0	420.9	0.0	111.5
	1988	0.0	265.7	(195.0)	35.5	12.9	0.0	0.0	35.5	278.6	0.0	81.5
	1989	0.0	253.2	(190.9)	40.0	13.8	0.0	0.0	40.0	267.0	0.0	81.4
Bush	1990	0.0	199.7	(136.4)	40.2	6.8	0.0	0.0	40.2	206.5	0.0	81.0
	1991	0.0	179.7	(124.0)	34.0	14.1	0.0	0.0	34.0	193.8	0.0	66.9
	1992	0.0	234.4	(125.5)	34.3	29.4	0.0	0.1	29.4	239.4	0.0	22.7
	1993	0.0	141.4	(95.7)							0.0	41.4
Clinton	1994[a]	0.0	91.4	(61.2)	0.0	0.0	0.0	0.0	0.0	91.4		

Source: U.S. Agency for International Development, Congressional Presentations, (Washington: US/AID, various years); *U.S. Loans, Grants and Assistance from International Organizations, Obligations and Loan Authorizations* (Washington: US/AID, various years).

[a] Request.

[b] Less than $50,000.

TABLE A.5

U.S. Assistance to Honduras, 1978–1994

		Economic assistance										Military assistance	
		AID and predecessor agencies			Food for Peace		Other economic assistance		Total				
Administration	Year	Loans	Grants	(ESF)	Loans	Grants	Loans	Grants	Loans	Grants		Loans	Grants
Carter	1978	10.0	3.0	(0.0)	0.0	2.4	0.0	1.7	10.0	7.1		2.5	0.7
	1979	16.0	6.0	(0.0)	2.0	2.8	0.0	2.3	18.0	11.1		2.0	0.3
	1980	38.6	7.2	(0.0)	2.0	3.2	0.0	2.1	40.6	12.5		3.5	0.4
	1981	20.2	5.5	(0.0)	3.6	4.6	0.0	2.5	23.8	12.6		8.4	0.5
First Reagan	1982	54.5	13.4	(36.8)	7.0	3.1	0.0	2.7	61.5	19.2		19.0	12.3
	1983	35.0	52.3	(56.0)	10.0	5.5	0.0	3.2	45.0	61.0		9.0	39.3
	1984	23.3	47.7	(40.0)	15.0	5.2	0.0	3.8	38.3	56.7		0.0	77.4
	1985	19.8	184.8	(150.2)	15.0	4.4	[b]	5.0	34.8	194.2		0.0	67.4
Second Reagan	1986	15.6	96.2	(66.5)	15.0	4.6	0.0	5.2	30.6	106.0		0.0	61.1
	1987	15.4	159.1	(131.8)	12.7	5.4	0.0	5.2	28.1	169.7		0.0	61.2
	1988	13.0	116.9	(85.0)	12.0	8.4	0.0	6.6	25.0	131.9		0.0	41.2
	1989	0.0	53.0	(15.0)	18.0	10.2	0.0	6.9	18.0	70.1		0.0	41.1
Bush	1990	0.0	166.6	(130.1)	12.0	9.6	0.0	4.4	12.0	180.6		0.0	21.3
	1991	0.0	99.0	(60.9)	0.0	6.2	0.0	4.6	0.0	109.8		0.0	33.5
	1992	0.0	65.2	(30.0)	0.0	20.9	0.0	3.2	0.0	89.3		0.0	6.4
	1993[a]	0.0	52.6	(5.9)	0.0	18.3	0.0	0.0	0.0	50.8		0.0	8.1
Clinton	1994[a]	0.0	18.4	(0.0)	0.0	16.9	0.0	0.0	0.0	35.3			

Source: U.S. Agency for International Development, *Congressional Presentations* (Washington: US/AID, various years); *U.S. Loans, Grants and Assistance from International Organizations, Obligations and Loan Authorizations* (Washington: US/AID, various years).

[a] Request.

[b] Less than $50,000.

TABLE A.6

U.S. Assistance to Guatemala, 1978–1994

		Economic assistance									Military assistance	
		AID and predecessor agencies			Food for Peace		Other economic assistance		Total			
Administration	Year	Loans	Grants	(ESF)	Loans	Grants	Loans	Grants	Loans	Grants	Loans	Grants
Carter	1978	0.0	4.5	(0.0)	0.0	4.6	0.0	1.5	0.0	10.6	0.0	0.0
	1979	14.6	2.8	(0.0)	0.0	5.3	0.0	2.0	14.6	10.1	0.0	0.0
	1980	5.0	2.8	(0.0)	0.0	3.3	0.0	1.9	5.0	8.0	0.0	0.0
	1981	5.5	3.6	(0.0)	0.0	7.5	0.1	2.3	5.6	13.4	0.0	0.0
First Reagan	1982	3.0	5.2	(0.0)	0.0	5.6	0.0	1.7	3.0	12.5	0.0	0.0
	1983	17.5	4.8	(10.0)	0.0	5.4	0.0	2.0	17.5	12.2	0.0	0.0
	1984	0.0	4.5	(0.0)	6.7	6.5	0.0	2.6	6.7	13.6	0.0	0.0
	1985	39.7	36.0	(12.5)	20.0	8.2	0.0	3.0	59.7	47.2	0.0	0.5
Second Reagan	1986	29.8	60.0	(52.8)	18.1	5.9	0.0	2.9	47.9	68.8	0.0	5.4
	1987	10.2	143.3	(115.5)	22.7	8.5	0.0	3.1	32.9	154.9	0.0	5.5
	1988	9.9	99.6	(79.4)	13.2	5.4	0.0	4.1	23.1	109.1	0.0	9.4
	1989	0.4	113.8	(80.0)	17.1	11.5	0.0	4.4	17.5	129.7	0.0	9.4
Bush	1990	0.0	86.0	(56.5)	17.1	9.0	0.0	2.6	17.1	97.6	0.0	3.3
	1991	0.0	60.0	(30.5)	17.3	12.3	0.0	2.7	17.3	75.0	0.0	0.4
	1992	0.0	33.8	(8.4)	14.9	7.7	0.0	5.4	14.9	46.9	0.0	0.2
	1993[a]	0.0	32.6	(5.9)	13.0	5.2	0.0	0.0	13.0	37.8		0.4
Clinton	1994[a]	0.0	18.4	(0.0)	11.0	5.9	0.0	0.0	11.0	29.4		

Source: U.S. Agency for International Development, *Congressional Presentations* (Washington: US/AID, various years); *U.S. Loans, Grants and Assistance from International Organizations, Obligations and Loan Authorizations* (Washington: US/AID, various years).

[a] Request.

TABLE A.7

U.S. Assistance to Costa Rica, 1978–1994

		Economic assistance									Military assistance	
		AID and predecessor agencies			Food for Peace		Other economic assistance		Total			
Administration	Year	Loans	Grants	(ESF)	Loans	Grants	Loans	Grants	Loans	Grants	Loans	Grants
Carter	1978	5.5	1.4	(0.0)	0.0	0.8	0.0	1.4	5.5	3.6	0.0	0.0
	1979	15.1	1.4	(0.0)	0.0	0.0	0.0	1.5	15.1	2.9	0.0	0.0
	1980	12.0	1.6	(0.0)	0.0	0.4	0.0	2.0	12.0	4.0	0.0	0.0
	1981	10.0	1.5	(0.0)	0.0	1.8	0.0	2.0	10.0	5.3	0.0	0.0
First Reagan	1982	24.7	6.8	(20.0)	18.0	1.1	0.0	1.1	42.7	9.0	0.0	2.1
	1983	138.2	46.0	(157.0)	28.0	0.2	0.0	1.7	166.2	47.9	0.0	4.6
	1984	47.4	98.1	(130.0)	22.5	0.0	0.0	1.9	69.9	100.0	0.0	9.1
	1985	10.7	184.8	(169.6)	21.4	0.2	0.0	2.9	32.1	187.9	0.0	11.2
Second Reagan	1986	6.3	132.9	(126.0)	20.0	0.3	0.0	3.3	26.3	136.5	0.0	2.6
	1987	14.7	146.1	(142.5)	17.2	0.1	0.0	3.2	31.9	149.4	0.0	1.7
	1988	0.0	101.3	(90.0)	15.0	0.1	0.0	4.0	15.0	105.4	0.0	0.2
	1989	0.0	114.8	(93.5)	0.0	3.4	0.0	3.8	0.0	122.0	0.0	0.2
Bush	1990	0.5	77.0	(64.9)	15.0	0.2	0.0	2.6	15.5	79.8	0.0	0.2
	1991	3.0	39.1	(27.0)	0.0	0.0	0.0	2.9	3.0	42.0	0.0	0.3
	1992	0.0	17.4	(10.0)	0.0	0.2	0.0	2.2	0.0	16.8	0.0	0.2
	1993[a]	0.0	5.9	(0.2)	0.0	0.1	0.0	0.0	0.0	6.1	0.0	1.2
Clinton	1994[a]	0.0	3.3	(0.0)	0.0	0.0	0.0	0.0	0.0	3.3		

Source: U.S. Agency for International Development, *Congressional Presentations* (Washington: US/AID, various years); *U.S. Loans, Grants and Assistance from International Organizations, Obligations and Loan Authorizations* (Washington: US/AID, various years).

[a] Request.

TABLE A.8

U.S. Assistance to Nicaragua, 1978–1994

		Economic assistance									Military assistance	
		AID and predecessor agencies			Food for Peace		Other economic assistance		Total			
Administration	Year	Loans	Grants	(ESF)	Loans	Grants	Loans	Grants	Loans	Grants	Loans	Grants
Carter	1978	10.5	2.0	(0.0)	0.0	0.1	0.0	1.4	10.5	3.5	0.0	0.4
	1979	0.0	9.7	(8.0)	2.6	4.4	0.0	1.8	2.6	15.9	0.0	[b]
	1980	15.0	4.4	(1.1)	15.0	3.0	0.0	1.3	30.0	8.7	0.0	0.0
	1981	48.0	10.4	(56.6)	0.0	1.2	0.0	0.3	48.0	11.9	0.0	0.0
First Reagan	1982	0.0	5.8	(5.1)	0.0	0.4	0.0	0.1	0.0	6.3	0.0	0.0
	1983	0.0	0.0	(0.0)	0.0	0.0	0.0	[b]	0.0	[b]	0.0	0.0
	1984	0.0	0.0	(0.0)	0.0	0.0	0.0	0.1	0.0	0.1	0.0	0.0
	1985	0.0	0.0	(0.0)	0.0	0.0	0.0	0.0	0.0	0.0	0.0	0.0
Second Reagan	1986	0.0	0.0	(0.0)	0.0	0.0	0.0	0.0	0.0	0.0	0.0	0.0
	1987	0.0	0.0	(0.0)	0.0	0.0	0.0	0.0	0.0	0.0	0.0	0.0
	1988	0.0	0.0	(0.0)	0.0	0.0	0.0	0.4	0.0	0.4	0.0	0.0
	1989	0.0	3.5	(3.5)	0.0	0.0	0.0	0.4	0.0	3.9	0.0	0.0
Bush	1990	0.0	220.1	(214.7)	0.0	2.8	0.0	0.4	0.0	223.3	0.0	0.0
	1991	0.0	215.3	(204.1)	0.0	1.9	0.0	1.5	0.0	218.7	0.0	0.0
	1992	0.0	42.3	(40.4)	0.0	4.8	0.0	2.9	0.0	55.0	0.0	0.0
	1993[a]	0.0	135.3	(97.4)	15.7	2.0	0.0	0.0	15.7	137.3	0.0	0.0
Clinton	1994[a]	0.0	78.2	(50.8)	13.0	0.0	0.0	0.0	13.0	50.8		

Source: U.S. Agency for International Development, *Congressional Presentations* (Washington: US/AID, various years); *U.S. Loans, Grants and Assistance from International Organizations, Obligations and Loan Authorizations* (Washington: US/AID, various years).

[a] Request.

[b] Less than $50,000.

Appendix B

U.N. Agency Administrators and U.S. Assistant Secretaries of State for International Affairs

TABLE B.1
UNDP Administrators

Paul G. Hoffman	United States	1967–72
Rudolph A. Peterson	United States	1973–76
F. Bradford Morse	United States	1977–86
William H. Draper III	United States	1986–93
James Gustave Speth	United States	1993–

TABLE B.2
FAO Directors-General

John Boyd Orr	United Kingdom	1945–47
Norris E. Dodd	United States	1948–54
Philip V. Cardon	United States	1954–56
Binay Ranjan Sen	India	1957–66
Addeke Hendrik Boerma	Netherlands	1967–75
Edouard Saouma	Lebanon	1976–93
Jacques Douf	Senegal	1994–

TABLE B.3
UNESCO Directors-General

Julian Huxley	United Kingdom	1945–48
Jaime Torres-Bodet	Mexico	1948–52
John W. Taylor[a]	United States	1952–53
Luther Evans	United States	1953–58
Vittorino Veronese	Italy	1958–59
René Maheu[a]	France	1959–61
René Maheu	France	1962–73
Amadou Mahtar M'Bow	Senegal	1974–87
Frederico Mayor Zarazoga	Spain	1987–

[a] Acting Director-General.

TABLE B.4
ILO Directors-General

Albert Thomas	France	1919–32
Harold Butler	United Kingdom	1933–38
John Winant	United States	1939–41
Edward Phelan	Ireland	1941–48
David Morse	United States	1949–70
Wilfred Jenks	United Kingdom	1970–74
Francis Blanchard	France	1974–89
Michel Hansenne	Belgium	1989–94

TABLE B.5
WHO Directors-General

Brock Chisholm	Canada	1948–53
M. G. Candau	Brazil	1953–73
Halvdan Mahler	Denmark	1973–87
Horoshi Nakajima	Japan	1988–

TABLE B.6
UNICEF Executive Directors

Maurice Pate	United States	1947–65
Henry Labouisse	United States	1965–80
James P. Grant	United States	1980–94

TABLE B.7
UNEP Executive Directors

Maurice Strong	Canada	1973–76
Mostapha K. Tolba	Egypt	1976–93
Elizabeth Dowdeswell	Canada	1993–

TABLE B.8
Assistant Secretaries of State for International Organization Affairs

Dean Rusk	9 February 1949–26 May 1949
John D. Hickson	8 August 1949–27 July 1953
Robert D. Murphy	28 July 1953–30 November 1953
David Mck. Key	18 December 1953–31 July 1954
Francis O. Wilcox	6 September 1954–20 January 1961
Harlan Cleveland	23 February 1961–8 September 1965
Joseph John Sicso	10 September 1965–9 February 1969
Samuel De Palma	11 February 1969–20 June 1973
David H. Papper	25 June 1973–2 January 1974
William B. Buffum	4 February 1974–18 December 1975
Samuel W. Lewis	24 December 1975–13 April 1977
Charles William Maynes	14 April 1977–9 April 1980
Richard Lee McCall, Jr.	10 June 1980–21 January 1981
Elliott Abrams	13 May 1981–1 December 1981
Gregory J. Newell	4 June 1982–12 November 1985
Alan L. Keyes	13 November 1985–17 November 1987
Richard S. Williamson	18 February 1988–19 March 1989
John R. Bolton	5 May 1989–19 January 1993
Douglas J. Bennet, Jr.	26 May 1993–

Appendix C
Agency Administrators, 1942–1991

Economic Cooperation Administration (ECA)

PAUL G. HOFFMAN (APRIL 1948 TO AUGUST 1950)

An automobile executive, Hoffman rose from a salesman to become the president of Studebaker Automobile Company in 10 years. During the war, he guided that company's production of aircraft engines and military trucks. He was hesitant to accept the post as head of the new Economic Cooperation Agency until Truman forced his hand by announcing his appointment. He called the ECA's distribution of Marshall Plan goods "the first line of defense for Western civilization" and explained that "Communists have fought us with riots, strikes, terror, and sabotage. We've used food, tools, and hope and just beat the hell out of them." He left the agency to join the Ford Foundation. He was instrumental in campaigning for Eisenhower's presidency and eventually became a member of the U.S. delegation to the United Nations.

WILLIAM C. FOSTER (OCTOBER 1950 TO AUGUST 1951)

Foster was an officer and director of the Pressed and Welded Steel Production Company, Inc., from 1922 to 1946. He began his government service in 1941 as a consultant to the War Board and continued as under-secretary of war on procurement for the Army Air Force during World War II. Foster began work with the Marshall Plan in 1948 and rose to administrator in 1950. He later became deputy secretary of defense and was director of the U.S. Arms Control and Disarmament Agency for 1961 to 1969.

Technical Cooperation Administration (TCA)

HENRY G. BENNETT (JUNE 1950 TO DECEMBER 1951)

The first of the Point Four directors, Bennett had served since 1928 as the president of Oklahoma A & M. His appointment may be attributable to his participation in the U.N. Food and Agriculture Organization's Conference on the Relief of Post-War Hunger. Bennett became acquainted with Ethiopian Emperor Haile Selassie on a trip in April 1950. He advised President Truman that Ethiopia would be the "ideal testing place" for the new program. Bennett died in a plane crash in Ethiopia in 1951. He was once called "a dreamer of no little dreams, with the magic for transposing them into reality."

STANLEY ANDREWS (MAY 1952 TO DECEMBER 1952)

An agriculturalist and newspaper editor, Andrews was chosen to head the TCA after the death of Bennett. He struggled to maintain the mission of the TCA to transfer technology to lesser developed countries as the agency merged with the Mutual Security Agency to form the new Foreign Operations Administration. Andrews lost that battle as the new FOA centered its activities around security issues. After his work with the agency, Andrews published two books, was an active consultant to Michigan State University, and eventually became executive director of the Kellogg Foundation.

Mutual Security Administration (MSA)

W. AVERILL HARRIMAN (OCTOBER 1951 TO JANUARY 1953)

Harriman began an illustrious foreign affairs career in 1941 coordinating the lend-lease aid with Great Britain and the Soviet Union. During numerous trips abroad he won the trust of Joseph Stalin, and in 1943 Harriman became the U.S. ambassador to the Soviet Union. He attended the Tehran and Yalta conferences of allied leaders to plan the postwar world. Harriman believed in a firm stance in relations with the Soviet Union and was instrumental in Truman's Soviet policy. He was ambassador to Great Britain and secretary of commerce in the Truman administration before becoming chairman of the President's Committee on Foreign Aid, which formulated the Marshall Plan program and lobbied for its passage. In 1948 he became head of the Economic Cooperation Administration's Office of the Special Representative in Europe, where he remained for two years. He became a troubleshooter for Truman in 1950 and was instrumental in the U.S. decision to enter the Korean War. Harriman was director of the Mutual Security Administration from 1951 to 1953. He was governor of New York from 1954 to 1958 and served in various posts in the State Department until his retirement in 1969.

Foreign Operations Administration (FOA)

HAROLD STASSEN (AUGUST 1953 TO JUNE 1955)

Stassen became governor of Minnesota in 1938 at the age of 31. He was twice reelected before resigning to enter active service in the U.S. Naval Reserve in 1943. After the war, he participated in the development of the United Nations. He began his first bid for the presidency in 1948. Unsuccessful, he ran again in 1952 but was forced to drop out. The shift of his delegates led to the nomination of Eisenhower. In return for this support, Eisenhower named Stassen to lead the Mutual Security Administration, which later became the Foreign Operations Administration. He revamped the agency to become much more involved in security assistance and encouraged the contributions of universities and charitable organizations to carry out U.S. development assistance work. In March 1955 Stassen was appointed by Eisenhower to a new post as special assistant to the president for disarmament. He became a perennial candidate for president but was not a contender after 1960.

International Cooperation Administration (ICA)

James B. Hollister (July 1955 to September 1957)

A lawyer from Cincinnati, Ohio, Hollister was a member of the board of education from 1921 to 1929. He won election as a U.S. congressman and served from 1931 to 1937, when he returned to his law practice. From 1953 to 1955 he was executive director of the Hoover Commission, which studied efficiency in government management. One of their findings was that "mistakes and waste" characterize the foreign assistance program. He became head of the new International Cooperation Administration from 1955 to 1957 and instituted strict control of the administration. After his work with the agency, he returned to his private practice in Cincinnati.

James H. Smith (October 1957 to January 1959)

An aviation expert, Smith held numerous military positions within government in addition to his brief term as ICA administrator. He was a decorated navy pilot during World War II and later became an advocate for maintaining a strong Naval Air Force. As a businessman, Smith was vice president in charge of the Atlantic Division for Pan American Airways. During his term as ICA administrator, the agency continued its funding for military aid and began the Development Loan Fund.

James W. Riddleberger (May 1959 to February 1961)

A career officer of the U.S. Department of State Foreign Service from 1929 to 1968, Riddleberger directed the International Cooperation Administration from 1959 to 1961. His other posts included ambassador to Greece, Yugoslavia, and Austria and chairman of both the Population Crisis Committee and the Development Assistance Committee To Organize for Economic Cooperation and Development.

Henry Labouisse (March 1961 to November 1961)

An American U.N. official, Labouisse served numerous foreign policy posts during the war before becoming director of the International Cooperation Administration. He served for only a brief period at the end of the Eisenhower administration. After his work with the ICA, Labouisse became the executive director at the United Nations Children's Fund (UNICEF).

Agency for International Development (AID)

Fowler Hamilton (September 1961 to December 1962)

A lawyer and Rhodes scholar, Hamilton was special assistant to the U.S. attorney general from 1938 to 1942. He served in a variety of government posts during the war until becoming a partner in the law firm of Cleary, Gottlieb, Steen & Hamilton in 1946. The only interruption in his work for that firm was his appointment to serve as administrator for the new Agency for International Development, where he had the challenge of a new agency that was in disarray.

David E. Bell (December 1962 to July 1966)

The first AID administrator with extensive overseas service in the Third World, Bell had served in Pakistan with a Harvard University Economic Advisory Group from 1954 to 1957. He was an assistant in the White House from 1947 to 1953. He directed the Bureau of the Budget from 1961 to 1962, when Kennedy appointed him to be AID administrator. He ably served AID until 1966, when he took a post with the Ford Foundation. He has also served as director of the Harvard Center for Population Studies.

William S. Gaud (August 1966 to 1969)

A lawyer and law school professor, Gaud became assistant administrator for AID's Bureau for the Near East and South Asia in 1961. He was deputy administrator of AID for two years before becoming AID administrator in 1966. He carried on much of the work begun by his predecessor, Bell. In 1969 he left AID to become executive vice president for the International Finance Corporation. He served two years as consultant to the World Bank. In 1976, he became national chairman for the Population Crisis Committee.

John A. Hannah (April 1969 to September 1973)

An educator and civil servant, Hannah was president of Michigan State University from 1941 to 1969. During that period he served on various national committees, including the U.S. Civil Rights Commission, of which he was chairman. As president of the National Association of State Universities and Land-Grant Colleges, he offered the expertise of the universities to serve in the U.S. foreign assistance programs. In 1969, he became administrator of AID under Nixon. During his tenure, the United States expanded its contributions to the multilateral assistance organizations. Hannah actively participated in the formation of the Consultative Group on International Agricultural Research and pledged U.S. contributions to cover 25 percent of CGIAR's operating budget.

Daniel S. Parker (October 1973 to January 1977)

Parker was an executive with the Parker Pen Company from 1950 to 1973, when he became administrator for AID. While at AID, he was also the president's special coordinator for International Disaster Assistance. He left the agency in 1977 to become chairman and chief executive officer of Omniflight, Inc. Parker was an active member of the Republican National Finance Committee from 1961 to 1973 and served on numerous other trade and investment committees.

John J. Gilligan (March 1977 to March 1979)

An ardent supporter of social programs throughout his career, Gilligan lobbied for the Great Society programs as a congressman from Ohio. During his successful bid for governor of Ohio in 1970, he emphasized the need for new taxes to finance the budget and convinced Ohio voters to approve the first state income tax. Gilligan administered the agency during a period of tight budgets and is famous for noting that AID personnel were "over-age, overpaid, and over here."

Douglas Bennet (August 1979 to January 1981)

Bennet began with the agency while finishing his graduate work at Harvard in 1963. Subsequently he served in the State Department as special assistant to Ambassador Bowles and was on staff with Senators Hubert Humphrey, Thomas Eagleton, and Abraham Ribicoff. Before coming back to AID, Bennet served as director of the Senate Budget Committee staff and was the assistant secretary of state for congressional relations. After his work with the agency, Bennet served as president of the Roosevelt Center for American Political Studies and president and CEO of National Public Radio.

M. Peter McPherson (February 1981 to August 1987)

Considered one of the finer AID administrators, McPherson gained overseas experience with the Peace Corps and was on the Board for International Food and Agricultural Development before becoming AID administrator in 1981. He had also worked for the IRS and as a private lawyer before becoming acting counsel to President Reagan in 1981. McPherson's long tenure helped build stability in the agency. Under his leadership, AID dramatically increased its support for security assistance.

Alan Woods (November 1987 to June 1989)

A businessman and public servant, Woods was appointed AID administrator after his tenure as deputy U.S. trade representative. Woods also served as assistant secretary of defense, chief of staff for the governor of Missouri, and press assistant to President Nixon before entering the private sector. He held positions as president or vice president for international services for Sears World Trade and DGA International. Woods died in office in 1989 before completing many of his programs and was succeeded by Deputy Administrator Edelman.

Mark L. Edelman (July 1989 to February 1990)

A veteran of AID, Edelman served as ambassador of Cameroon from 1987 to 1989 before returning to AID as deputy and eventually interim administrator. He had previously held positions with AID as senior advisor to the administrator and assistant administrator for Africa. Before his work with AID, Edelman served in the State Department and was a legislative assistant to Senator John C. Danforth of Missouri. Upon the appointment of Ronald Roskens as administrator, Edelman returned to his post as deputy administrator.

Ronald Roskens (March 1990 to December 1992)

An educator, Roskens was a professor and administrator in various positions at Iowa State University and Kent State University before becoming president of the University of Nebraska System in 1977. During his tenure at the University of Nebraska, he served on the American Council of Education and the National Association of State Universities and Land-Grant Colleges. In March 1990, he became the first post–Cold War administrator of AID. He attempted to focus the efforts of the agency on democratization and private enterprise and to reform AID administration.

J. Bryan Atwood (May 1993 to present)

Before being nominated as AID administrator, Atwood had been undersecretary of state. Prior to joining the Clinton administration, he had served as president of the National Democratic Institute for International Affairs (1985–83). The institute, which is affiliated with the Democratic party, promotes democracy in transitional societies. Atwood had previously served in the Foreign Service on the Ivory Coast and Spain, as deputy assistant secretary of state for congressional relations, and as dean of professional studies/academic affairs at the Foreign Service Institute.

Appendix D
Presidents of the World Bank

Eugene Meyer (June 1946 to December 1946)

A highly successful president of the Wall Street investment banking house with a record of distinguished public service dating back to World War I, Meyer was a close friend of Secretary of State Byrnes and Secretary of Treasury Vinson, was well known to President Truman, and was highly regarded on Wall Street. He was appointed at age 70 and quickly wearied of the infighting over the relative power of the executive directors and the president.

John J. McCloy (1947 to 1949)

McCloy turned down the opportunity to be general counsel to the bank under Meyer and initially refused the opportunity to succeed Meyer. McCloy agreed to return to Washington as bank president when assured that he would have adequate authority plus the full backing of the U.S. government. A quintessential member of the foreign policy establishment, he served as assistant secretary of war from 1941 to 1945 and left the bank in 1949 to become high commissioner for Germany.

Eugene Black (1949 to 1963)

While vice president of the Chase National Bank of New York, Black had been instrumental in persuading McCloy to accept the World Bank presidency. He was named U.S. executive director after the resignation of Emilio Collado in 1947. During Black's presidency, many of the internal administrative tensions were resolved and the bank made the transition from viewing its role as that of financing postwar reconstruction to that of financing major infrastructure investments in developing countries.

George D. Woods (1963 to 1968)

Woods came to the bank from the position of chairman of the board of the First Boston Corporation. He had been active, on a volunteer basis, in a number of bank missions. Wood strengthened the bank's development focus, strengthened its capacity for economic analysis, and built a strong relationship with the rest of the U.N. family.

Robert S. McNamara (1968 to 1981)

A former professor of business administration at Harvard, president of the Ford Motor Company, and secretary of defense, McNamara came to the bank with a reputation as the man who had exercised the firmest leadership ever provided at Defense. He was the first World Bank president without a banking background. McNamara attempted to refocus bank lending to give greater priority to poverty alleviation and rural development.

A. W. Clausen (1981 to 1986)

Appointed by the Carter administration in consultation with the transition team of the incoming Reagan administration, Clausen shifted from McNamara's poverty-oriented approach to a renewed emphasis on economic growth, structural reforms, and greater emphasis on the role of the private sector.

Barber Conable, Jr. (1986 to 1991)

Conable served in the U.S. House of Representatives for 20 years. He was the ranking Republican on the Ways and Means Committee when he retired from Congress in 1984. He served as a professor at the University of Rochester before accepting the presidency of the World Bank. At the bank he initiated a major reorganization, continued the emphasis on structural reform, and emphasized greater consideration of the environmental consequences of bank lending.

Lewis Preston (1991 to the present)

Retired Chairman of J. P. Morgan's Executive Committee before his appointment, Preston had previously served as chairman of the J. P. Morgan and Morgan Guarantee Trust boards.

These sketches are drawn primarily from Edward S. Mason and Robert E. Asher, *The World Bank since Bretton Woods* (Washington: Brookings Institution, 1973). See also Barend A. deVries, *Remaking the World Bank* (Washington: Seven Locks Press, 1987).

Notes

Preface

1. Harry S. Truman, "Inaugural Address of the President," *Department of State Bulletin* 33 (30 January 1949): 125.

2. Anne O. Krueger and Vernon W. Ruttan, *The Development Impact of Economic Assistance to LDC's*, 2 vols. (St. Paul/Minneapolis: University of Minnesota Economic Development Center for the Agency for International Development and the Department of State, March 1983, mimeo).

3. Raymond F. Mikesell, *The Economics of Foreign Aid and Self-sustaining Development* (Boulder: Westview Press, 1983).

4. See Anne O. Krueger, Constantine Michalopoulos, and Vernon W. Ruttan (with Keith Jay, Gayl Ness, J. Dirck Stryker, Vasant Sukhatme, and Hasan A. Tuluy), *Aid and Development* (Baltimore: Johns Hopkins University Press, 1989).

5. Vernon W. Ruttan and John Lewis, *The World Bank in Pakistan: Review of a Relationship, 1960–1984*, Operations Evaluation Department Report 6048 (Washington: World Bank, 27 January 1986).

6. The results of this review are summarized in Keith Fuglie and Vernon W. Ruttan, "Value of External Reviews at the International Agricultural Research Centers," *Agricultural Economics* 3 (1989): 365–80.

7. James P. Grant, *Disparity Reduction Rates in Social Indicators: A Proposal for Measuring and Targeting Progress on Meeting Basic Needs* (Washington: Overseas Development Council, Monograph 11, 1978): 9.

8. Vernon W. Ruttan, "Integrated Rural Development Programs: A Skeptical Perspective," *International Development Review* 17 (December 1975): 9–16.

9. William H. Sewell, Jr., "Theory of Action, Dialectic and History: Comment on Coleman," *American Journal of Sociology* 93 (July 1987): 166–71 (quote at 171).

10. Vernon W. Ruttan and Yujiro Hayami, "Toward a Theory of Induced Institutional Innovation," *Journal of Development Studies*, 20 (July 1984): 203–23.

11. Vernon W. Ruttan, "Cultural Endowments and Economic Development: What Can We Learn from Anthropology?" *Economic Development and Cultural Change* 36 (May 1988): 5247–72.

12. Stephen D. Krasner, *Defending the National Interest: Raw Materials and U.S. Foreign Policy* (Princeton: Princeton University Press, 1978): 12–36. Krasner insists that the ideological commitment to a liberal international economic and political order can be treated as an independent variable in explaining U.S. foreign policy in the post–

World War II world. This idea stands in sharp contrast to the Marxist view that ideology is a dependent variable reflecting the interest of the ruling class, in contrast to the liberal perspective that policy is the result of pluralist bargaining among interest groups.

Chapter 1 The Domestic Sources of Foreign Assistance Policy

1. The author is indebted to Charles E. Kindleberger, Raymond H. Hopkins, and John D. Montgomery for comments on an earlier draft of this chapter.

2. Hans Morgenthau argued that development aid does not differ substantially from the bribes employed in nineteenth century diplomacy in "A Political Theory of Foreign Aid," *American Political Science Review* 56, no. 2 (1962): 301–9. John White noted that "the transfer of resources between nations, for a wide variety of purposes, had long been a feature of international relations. The sheer volume of resources transferred, however, coupled with the degree of government involvement, constituted a new element in a new situation." John A. White, *The Politics of Foreign Aid* (New York: St. Martins Press, 1974), 11. For a history of earlier American assistance efforts, see Merle Curti and Kendal Birr, *Prelude to Point Four: American Technical Missions Overseas: 1838–1938* (Madison: University of Wisconsin Press, 1954), and also Emily S. Rosenberg, *Spreading the American Dream: American Economic and Cultural Expansion, 1890–1945* (New York: Hill & Wong, 1982).

3. The exodus metaphor has exerted a powerful influence on American historical scholarship and popular thought. David W. Noble pointed out that Frederick Jackson Turner and Charles A. Beard emphasized the encounter with the frontier in the formation of American culture, and Sacvan Bercovitch traced the origins of American exceptionalism to Puritan theology. The "English Puritans had defined themselves as a New Israel trapped within the bondage of the medieval establishment. They knew, however, that as a Chosen People they could engage in an exodus that would lead them to the Promised Land. . . . The Puritans defined an Old and New England on the basis of an elaborate theory of history that they brought with them across the Atlantic." David W. Noble, *The End of American History* (Minneapolis: University of Minnesota Press, 1985), 4–5. By 1776, "the key metaphors of Puritan theology had become secularized and then widely accepted throughout the English colonies. . . . The promise was a virtuous Republic. The Revolution was the exodus from the Egyptian bondage of monarchy." Noble, *The End of American History,* 6.

4. For the distinction between liberal (or idealist) and conservative (or realist) doctrine, see Louis Hartz, *The Liberal Tradition in America: An Interpretation of American Political Thought since the Revolution* (New York: Harcourt, Brace, 1955), and Robert A. Packenham, *Liberal America and the Third World: Political Development Ideas in Foreign Aid and Social Science* (Princeton: Princeton University Press, 1973). Hartz and Packenham have used the liberal doctrine as the primary lens through which to interpret American economic and political relations with the rest of the world. In Packenham's definition the liberal doctrine includes four propositions: (1) change and development are easy, (2) all good things go together, (3) radicalism and revolution are

bad, and (4) distributing power is more important than accumulating power. Packenham, *Liberal America,* 111–60. Most realists share a world view that includes four key assumptions about the forces involved in international relations: (1) human nature is seen pessimistically, (2) the state is the only important actor in international relations, (3) the struggle for power is a permanent and prominent feature of relations between states, and (4) states act as rational actors in pursuit of national interest. Michael Joseph Smith, *Realist Thought from Weber to Kissinger* (Baton Rouge: Louisiana State University Press, 1986), 1:218–26. See also Henry Kissinger, *Diplomacy* (New York: Simon & Schuster, 1994), 18. "The singularities that America has ascribed to itself throughout its history have produced two contradictory attitudes toward foreign policy. The first is that America serves its values best by perfecting democracy at home, thereby acting as a beacon for the rest of mankind; the second that America's values impose on it an obligation to crusade for them around the world."

5. Packenham, *Liberal America,* 25.

6. Walter Lippmann, *The Cold War: A Study of U.S. Foreign Policy* (Cambridge: Harvard University Press, 1947). The book is based on a series of articles that appeared in the *New York Herald Tribune* in 1947. An excerpt from the book, "The Cold War," was published in *Foreign Affairs* 65 (Spring 1987), 870–84. The spring 1981 issue of *Foreign Affairs* also included retrospective articles by Walter W. Rostow and George F. Kennan. More recent scholarship has tended to support the Lippmann view. See Charles P. Kindleberger, *Marshall Plan Days* (Winchester, Mass.: Allen & Unwin, 1987), 28. For a revisionist view that the differences between the approaches of the Truman Doctrine and the Marshall Plan were more tactical than strategic, see Richard M. Freeland, *The Truman Doctrine and the Origins of McCarthyism: Foreign Policy, Domestic Politics, and Internal Security, 1946–1948* (New York: Alfred A. Knopf, 1972).

7. The contribution of George F. Kennan to the containment doctrine has been the subject of considerable debate. Deborah Welch Larson, *Origins of Containment: A Psychological Explanation* (Princeton: Princeton University Press, 1985), noted that "Cold War historians generally agree that George Kennan's long telegram of February 22, 1946 had a galvanizing effect on U.S. officials' attitudes toward the Soviet Union, providing the intellectual justification for the emerging containment policy" (p. 28). According to Kennan, "the Soviets perceived the world as divided between socialist and capitalist centers, between which there could be no permanent peaceful coexistence" (p. 255). The reaction to Kennan's "discursive, somewhat academic discussion of Soviet policy was astonishing. It was not only brought to the attention of Secretary Byrnes, Under-Secretary Acheson, Assistant Secretaries Benton, Clayton, and Dunn and the several State Department offices, but was sent to diplomatic missions around the world. Navy Secretary James Forrestal had the text reproduced and made it required reading for hundreds of military officers" (p. 256). But it is doubtful that President Truman ever read or was even aware of Kennan's long telegram (p. 352). Its influence was probably due as much to its timing as its content. Events were inducing American leaders to abandon the assumptions of Roosevelt's grand design for a postwar order based on the collective leadership of the great regional powers—the United States, Britain, the Soviet Union, and China—in favor of a policy that

would contain further expansion. It also seems clear that the excitement generated by Kennan's long telegram and the subsequent "X" articles reflected his intellectual rationale for a policy that was in the process of emerging in response to events. Larson argued that, if anyone should be designated as the architect of containment, Acheson is a more likely candidate than Kennan.

8. George F. Kennan's paper was first published under the pseudonym of "X" in "The Sources of Soviet Conduct," *Foreign Affairs* (July 1947), 566–82. It was reprinted in *Foreign Affairs* 65 (Spring 1987), 852–68. Kennan urged that the United States initiate "a policy of firm containment, designed to confront the Russians with unalterable counterforce at every point where they show signs of encroaching upon the interests of a peaceful and stable world" (p. 867). In retrospect it seems that, although Kennan was flattered by the attention his ideas received from Forrestal and Acheson, he quickly became concerned with the broad thrust that the concept was given both in the Truman Doctrine and in the subsequent development of the containment doctrine. See George F. Kennan, *Memoirs: 1925–1950* (Boston: Little, Brown, 1967), 320; also "Containment Then and Now," *Foreign Affairs* 65 (Spring 1987), 885–90. Kennan and Assistant Secretary William L. Clayton each drafted papers that were then crafted into a draft that was the basis for Marshall's Harvard commencement address by Charles (Chip) Bohlen. Walter Isaacson and Evan Thomas, *The Wise Men: Six Friends and the World They Made—Acheson, Bohlen, Harriman, Kennan, Lovett, and McCloy* (New York: Simon & Schuster, 1986), suggested that Kennan viewed his contribution to Marshall's speech as "an opportunity to rectify the excesses of the Truman Doctrine" (p. 405). Anders Stephanson, *Kennan and the Art of Foreign Policy* (Cambridge: Harvard University Press, 1989), refers to a response, drafted by Kennan but never sent, in which he indicated that he was offended "that Lippmann had identified him with the Truman Doctrine, which he had opposed, and then compared that policy unfavorably with the Marshall Plan, of which he had been a proprietor" (p. 101). It is hard to avoid a conclusion, in spite of Kennan's protests, that the long telegram served to mobilize sentiment inside the administration while the "X" article tended to strengthen the anti-Soviet mood among the informed public and hence strengthen the forces associated with the Truman Doctrine of containment. The most complete articulation of containment doctrine is contained in a National Security Council document issued on 14 April 1950 (NSC-68) prepared under the direction of Paul Nitze, who succeeded Kennan as director of the State Department Policy Planning Staff on 1 January 1950. By this time Kennan had become an active opponent of containment doctrine and was particularly concerned by what he regarded as the exaggerated view of the threat of Soviet expansionism in NSC-68. The full text of NSC-61 was first made publicly available in 1975. It has been reproduced in Thomas H. Etvzold and John Lewis Gaddis, eds., *Containment: Documents on American Policy and Strategy* (New York: Columbia University Press, 1978), 385–442.

9. Lippmann, *The Cold War,* 54. Lippmann insisted that a policy of containment "cannot be made to work, and that the attempt to make it work will cause us to squander our substance and our prestige." Lippmann, *The Cold War,* 10.

10. Lippmann, *The Cold War,* 64. In his March 1947 speech, President Truman

proposed $400 million for aid to Greece and Turkey. During the four-year period 1947–48 to 1949–51, U.S. economic and military assistance to Greece amounted to approximately $1.2 billion. The U.S. assistance program in Greece involved direct U.S. intervention in economic, military, and political affairs. The series of agreements under which assistance was granted gave so much authority to American representatives that the Greek government was dependent on American approval for almost all major fiscal decisions. In 1950 American intervention resulted in the replacement of Sophocles Venizelos by Nicholas Plastiras as prime minister. In 1952 the United States exerted strong pressure to change the electoral system from a proportional representation to a majority system. William H. McNeill, *Greece: American Aid in Action, 1947–1956* (New York: Twentieth Century Fund, 1957), 33–84; Howard Jones, *A New Kind of War: America's Global Strategy and the Truman Doctrine in Greece* (New York: Oxford University Press, 1989).

11. Krueger, Michalopoulos, and Ruttan, *Aid and Development.*

12. Melvyn D. Leffler, "The United States and the Strategic Dimensions of the Marshall Plan," *Diplomatic History,* 12 (Summer 1988), 277–306; John D. Montgomery, *The Politics of Foreign Aid: American Experience in Southeast Asia* (New York: Praeger, 1962), 11–60; Goran Ohlin, "The Evolution of United States Aid Doctrine," in Benjamin J. Cohen, ed., *American Foreign Economic Policy* (New York: Harper & Row, 1968), 347–61.

13. Robert O. Keohane, *After Hegemony: Cooperation and Discord in the World Political Economy* (Princeton: Princeton University Press, 1984), 34.

14. These examples are drawn from the more extensive discussion in Robert L. Paarlberg, "United States Attention to the Third World, 1945–74: The Logic of Policy Agenda Formation" (Ph.D. diss., Harvard University, 1975), 201–20. For additional examples see Stephen D. Krasner, *Defending the National Interest: Raw Materials Investments and U.S. Foreign Policy* (Princeton: Princeton University Press, 1978). Krasner argues that before World War II (except during the Woodrow Wilson administration), American foreign policy can best be understood in terms of economic interest. American policy was directed to securing material benefit for American society and for particular American interests. He goes on to argue that after the second world war foreign policy was directed to the achievement of ideological objectives—"American leaders were moved by a vision of what the global order should be like—liberal, democratic, and prosperous" (p. 16).

15. This issue has been particularly troublesome to analysts following the Marxist tradition who are committed to an economic interpretation of historical development. See, for example, Harry Magdoff, *The Age of Imperialism* (New York: Modern Reader Paperbacks, 1969). Even less ideologically committed observers have mistakenly interpreted U.S. economic and political assistance in Southeast Asia as being based on the importance of "raw materials and food supplies." Paul Kennedy, *The Rise and Fall of Great Powers: Economic Change and Military Conflict from 1500 to 2000* (New York: Random House, 1987), 383.

16. Keohane, *After Hegemony,* 131.

17. Hans Morgenthau argued that it is "pointless to even raise the question of whether

the United States ought to have a policy of foreign aid—as much so as to ask whether the United States ought to have a foreign political or military policy. For the United States has interests abroad which cannot be secured by military means and for the support of which the traditional methods of diplomacy are only in part appropriate." Hans P. Morgenthau, "A Political Theory of Foreign Aid," 301.

18. Krasner, *Defending the National Interest,* 13–20, 342–46.

19. Isaacson and Thomas, *The Wise Men: Six Friends,* 342–438.

20. Dean Acheson, *Present at the Creation: My Years in the State Department* (New York: Norton, 1969), 219. Later administrations required new metaphors to characterize the cumulative effects of Soviet penetration. References to rotten apples were replaced by references to dominoes during the Eisenhower administration.

21. Krasner, *Defending the National Interest,* 31. Krasner's view of the role of the White House and the State Department derives from his perspective on the role of the state. "It is useful to conceive of a state as a set of roles and institutions having particular drives, compulsions, and aims of their own that are separate and distinct from the interests of any particular societal group. These goals are associated with either general material objectives or with ambitious ideological goals related to beliefs about how societies should be ordered. They can be labeled the national interest" (p. 10).

22. For a classification of interest groups by type of assistance, see John Wilhelm and Gerry Feinstein, *U.S. Foreign Assistance: Investment or Folly?* (New York: Praeger, 1984), 5. See also the discussion in David A. Baldwin, *Foreign Aid and American Foreign Policy: A Documentary Analysis* (New York: Praeger, 1966), 3–9. In 1959 Bernard C. Cohen warned that a major weakness of scholarly writing on interest group influence was that too much of it was based on impressionistic evidence and too little drawn on empirical research. Bernard C. Cohen, *The Influence of Non-Governmental Groups on Foreign Policy-Making* (Boston: World Peace Foundation, 1959). In spite of the significant body of research on this issue since the late 1950s, our knowledge in this area remains highly subjective.

23. David A. Stockman, *The Triumph of Politics: The Inside Story of the Reagan Revolution* (New York: Harper & Row, 1986; Avon Books, 1987), 126.

24. Edward S. Mason and Robert E. Asher, *The World Bank since Bretton Woods* (Washington: Brookings Institution, 1973), 136–57, 406–2.

25. Drawing on extensive interviews with State and AID officials, Packenham noted that "AID has a strong bias toward strict economic criteria and is therefore constantly threatened by the Department of State, whose criteria tend to be short-term political. As a result anything 'political' is anathema to many AID officials. For its part, the Department of State . . . sees AID as naive, idealistic, and apolitical." Robert A. Packenham, "Political Development Doctrines in the American Foreign Aid Programs," *World Politics* 17 (January 1966): 231.

26. For a useful discussion of the changing role of Congress in foreign affairs, see the papers in Randall B. Ripley and James M. Lindsay, eds., *Congress Resurgent: Foreign and Defense Policy on Capitol Hill* (Ann Arbor: University of Michigan Press, 1993).

27. Barbara Hinckley, *Less than Meets the Eye: Policy Making and the Myth of the Assertive Congress* (Chicago: University of Chicago Press, 1994), 101–24.

28. Charles Whalen, *The House and Foreign Policy: The Irony of Congressional Reform* (Chapel Hill: University of North Carolina Press, 1982).

29. "Passman Interview," *Congressional Quarterly,* 2 September 1961, 312. According to Packenham, "Representative Otto Passman, the chairman of the subcommittee dealing with foreign aid of the Appropriations Committee of the House of Representatives, is perhaps the best example of the 'eccentric' type of critic; he was also regarded as reactionary . . . he had a significant influence on aid policy." Robert A. Packenham, *Liberal America and the Third World: Political Development Ideas in Foreign Aid and on Social Science* (Princeton: Princeton University Press, 1973), 117.

30. Frank Ballance, "State of the Aid Mandate in the United States and Canada" (Washington: Overseas Development Council, June 1984, mimeo).

31. I. M. Destler, Leslie H. Gelb, and Anthony Lake, *Our Own Worst Enemy: The Unmaking of American Foreign Policy* (New York: Simon & Schuster, 1984), argue that during the 1960s power was passing from an old establishment, the community of eastern bankers and lawyers, to a new professional elite drawn from academic institutions and think tanks. See particularly 92–126.

32. Steven L. Spiegel, *The Other Arab-Israeli Conflict: Making America's Middle East Policy from Truman to Reagan* (Chicago: University of Chicago Press, 1985), 395–97.

33. See, however, John M. Richardson, Jr., *Partners in Development: An Analysis of AID University Relations: 1950–1966* (East Lansing: Michigan State University Press, 1969). The period during which Harold Stassen served as director of the Foreign Operations Administration (FOA) was decisive in establishing the pattern of cooperation between the U.S. assistance agency and the universities. Clearly, Stassen valued and understood the role that universities could play in technical assistance and their political value as a constituency for the agency.

34. Popular concern with international and domestic policy issues has varied over time. In a series of Gallup polls taken between 1940 and 1973, American leaders and the public almost always assigned a high ranking to foreign policy and security issues. International sentiment was clearly eroding during the 1960s and 1970s. In surveys taken between the early 1970s and early 1980s, there was a strong shift toward giving a higher priority to domestic issues, such as inflation, unemployment, and access to energy supplies. Polls conducted by the Chicago Council on Foreign Relations (CCFR) in 1974, 1978, 1982, and 1986 indicate a return to greater sensitivity to foreign affairs after the early 1980s. However, the 1986 poll showed substantial gaps between the views of the general public and those of opinion leaders on both military and economic assistance. Only 36 percent of the general public, in contrast to 78 percent of opinion leaders, favored foreign military assistance. The gap with respect to economic assistance was not so great: 60 percent of the general public to 93 percent of opinion leaders favored aid for foreign economic development and technical assistance. See John E. Rielly, "America's State of Mind," *Foreign Policy* (Spring 1987): 39–55. For a more complete report on the CCFR studies, see John E. Rielly, *American Public*

Opinion and U.S. Foreign Policy, 1987 (Chicago: Chicago Council on Foreign Relations, 1987), and the earlier reports on the 1974, 1978, and 1982 studies. For an analysis of the effect of popular and elite perspectives on foreign policy, see Barry B. Hughes, *The Domestic Context of American Foreign Policy* (San Francisco: Witt-Freeman, 1978).

35. Bernard C. Cohen, *The Influence of Non-Governmental Groups in foreign Policy-Making* (Boston: World Peace Foundation, 1959), 8; Mohammed E. Ahrari, ed., *Ethnic Groups and U.S. Foreign Policy* (Westport, Conn.: Greenwood Press, 1987).

36. Michael Clough, "Grass-Roots Policy Making: Say Good-Bye to the 'Wise Men'," *Foreign Affairs* 73 (January/February 1994): 2–7.

37. See James R. Simpson, "The Origin of United States' Academic Interest in Foreign Economic Development," *Economic Development and Cultural Change* 24 (April 1976): 633–44; Hans W. Arndt, *Economic Development: The History of an Idea* (Chicago: University of Chicago Press, 1987).

38. See Anne O. Krueger and Vernon W. Ruttan, "Development Thought and Development Assistance," in Krueger, Michalopoulos, and Ruttan, *Aid and Development*, 13–31.

Chapter 2 Why Foreign Economic Assistance?

1. For an earlier draft of this chapter, see Vernon W. Ruttan, "Why Foreign Economic Assistance," *Economic Development and Cultural Change* 37, no. 2 (1989): 411–24.

2. Anne O. Krueger, "Aid in the Development Process," *World Bank Research Observer* 1 (January 1986): 57–78, esp. 64, 65.

3. For an exception see David H. Lumsdaine, *Moral Vision in International Politics: The Foreign Aid Regime, 1949–1989* (Princeton: Princeton University Press, 1993). Lumsdaine insists that the primary reason for foreign economic assistance lies in "the humanitarian and equalitarian principles of the donor countries."

4. Commission on Security and Economic Assistance, *A Report to the Secretary of State* (Washington: CSEA, 1983), 31; George Shultz, "Foreign Aid and U.S. National Interests," in *Realism, Strength, Negotiation: Key Foreign Policy Statements of the Reagan Administration* (Washington: Department of State, Bureau of Public Affairs, 1984), 142–45.

5. Teresa Hayter, *Aid as Imperialism* (London: Penguin, 1971); Francis M. Lappe, *Aid as an Obstacle: Twenty Questions about Our Foreign Aid and the Hungry* (San Francisco: Institute for Food and Development Policy, 1980).

6. Alfred Maizels and Machiko Missanke, "Motivations for Aid to Developing Countries," *World Development* 12, no. 9 (1984): 879–900; Lumsdaine, *Moral Vision in International Politics,* 73–103.

7. Steven J. Rosen, "The Open Door Imperative of U.S. Foreign Policy," in *Testing Theories of Economic Imperialism,* ed. Stephen Rosen and James R. Kurth (Lexington, Mass.: D. C. Heath, 1974), 117–42.

8. John W. Mellor and Bruce F. Johnston, "The World Food Equation: Interrela-

tions among Development, Employment, and Food," *Journal of Economic Literature* 22 (June 1984): 531–74, esp. 541.

9. G. Edward Schuh, *The United States and the Developing Countries: An Economic Perspective* (Washington: National Planning Association, 1986), 31–42.

10. John A. Pincus, "The Cost of Foreign Aid," *Review of Economics and Statistics* 45 (November 1963): 360–367; Jagdish Bhagwati, *Amount and Sharing of Aid* (Washington: Overseas Development Council, 1970).

11. Theodore W. Schultz, "Value of U.S. Farm Surpluses to Underdeveloped Countries," *Journal of Farm Economics* 62 (December): 1019–30; Paul Isenman and Hans Singer, "Food Aid: Disincentive Effects and Their Policy Implications," *Economic Development and Cultural Change* 25 (January 1977): 205–38.

12. Krueger, "Aid in the Development Process," 66.

13. Paul Mosley, "The Political Economy of Foreign Aid: A Model of the Market for a Public Good," *Economic Development and Cultural Change* 33 (January 1985): 373–93, esp. 375.

14. Hans Morgenthau, "A Political Theory of Foreign Aid," *American Political Science Review* 56, no. 2 (1962): 301–9; John W. Sewell and John A. Mathieson, *The Third World: Exploring U.S. Interests,* Foreign Policy Association Headline Series no. 259 (Washington: Foreign Policy Association, 1982).

15. Samuel P. Huntington, "Foreign Aid for What and for Whom, Part 2," *Foreign Policy* 2, no. 2 (1971): 114–34.

16. R. D. McKinlay and A. Mughan, *Aid and Arms to the Third World: An Analysis of the Distribution and Impact of U.S. Official Transfers* (New York: St. Martin's, 1984), 31–34.

17. W. W. Rostow, *Eisenhower, Kennedy, and Foreign Aid* (Austin: University of Texas Press, 1985).

18. Commission on Security and Economic Assistance, *Report to the Secretary,* 46.

19. Harry Eckstein, "The Idea of Political Development," *World Politics* 34 (July 1982): 451–86.

20. McKinlay and Mughan, *Aid and Arms.*

21. Francis I. West, "The Effectiveness of Military Assistance as an Instrument of U.S. Foreign Policy," paper prepared for the Commission on Security and Economic Assistance (Washington, 1983).

22. Samuel P. Huntington, "Foreign Aid for What and for Whom, Part 1," *Foreign Policy* 2, no. 1 (1970–71): 161–89, esp. 170.

23. Edward C. Banfield, "American Foreign Aid Doctrine," in *Why Foreign Aid?* ed. Robert A. Goldwin (Chicago: Rand McNally, 1963), 10–31; P. T. Bauer, *Equality, the Third World, and Economic Delusion* (Cambridge: Harvard University Press, 1981), 86–134.

24. Roger C. Riddell, "The Ethics of Foreign Aid?" *Development Policy Review* 4 (March 1986): 24–43; Roger C. Riddell, *Development Assistance Reconsidered* (London: James Currey, 1987).

25. Peter Singer, "Reconsidering the Famine Relief Argument," in *Food Policy,* ed. Peter Brown and Henry Shue (New York: Free Press, 1977), 36–53; Robert Tucker, *The Inequality of Nations* (New York: Basic Books, 1977), 117–26.

26. Charles Beitz, *Political Theory and International Relations* (Princeton: Princeton University Press, 1979), 134–43; Robert L. Simon, "Troubled Waters: Global Justice and Ocean Resources," in *Earthbound,* ed. Tom Regan (New York: Random House, 1984), 179–212.

27. Mark Blaug, "Economic Imperialism Revisited," *Yale Review* 50 (Spring 1961): 335–49.

28. Kenneth E. Boulding and Tapan Mukerjee, "Unprofitable Empire: Britain in India, 1800–1967: A Critique of the Hobson-Lenin Thesis on Imperialism," *Peace Research Society Papers* 14, Rome Conference (1970): 1–21; Stephen D. Krasner, "Trade in Raw Materials: The Benefits of Capitalist Alliances," in *Testing Theories of Economic Imperialism,* ed. Stephen Rosen and James R. Kurth (Lexington, Mass.: D. C. Heath, 1974), 138–98.

29. Jane Jacobs, *Cities and the Wealth of Nations: Principles of Economic Life* (New York: Random House, 1984), 59–71.

30. Richard N. Cooper, "The Oceans as a Source of Revenue," in *The New International Economic Order: The North South Debate,* ed. Jagdigh N. Bhagwati (Cambridge: MIT Press, 1977), 104–20.

31. F. A. Hayek, "The Atavism of Social Justice," in *New Studies in Philosophy, Politics, Economics, and the History of Ideas* (London: Routledge & Kegan Paul, 1978), 57–70 (quote at 58).

32. Banfield, "American Foreign Aid Doctrine," 24.

33. Bauer, *Equality and Economic Delusion,* 86–133; P. T. Bauer, *Reality and Rhetoric: Studies in the Economics of Development* (Cambridge: Harvard University Press, 1984), 38–62.

34. C. B. MacPherson, *The Rise and Fall of Economic Justice, and Other Papers* (Oxford: Oxford University Press, 1985), 1–20.

35. John Rawls, *A Theory of Justice* (Cambridge: Harvard University Press, 1971), 54–192.

36. Beitz, *Political Theory and International Relations,* 141, 142; C. Ford Runge, "American Agricultural Assistance and the New International Economic Order," *World Development* 5, no. 8 (1977): 225–46.

37. Frederick Crews, "In the Big House of Theory," *New York Review of Books* 33 (29 May 1986): 36–42, esp. 36.

38. Richard N. Cooper, panel discussion of "The New International Economic Order," in Bhagwati, *The New International Economic Order,* 354–85.

39. Ibid., 355.

40. Keohane, *After Hegemony,* 120–24; Richard N. Cooper, *Economic Policy in an Interdependent World: Essays in World Economics* (Cambridge: MIT Press, 1986), 1–22.

41. Kenneth J. Arrow, *Social Choice and Justice* (Cambridge: Harvard University Press, 1983), 175–89 (quote at 188).

42. Beitz, *Political Theory and International Relations,* 143–61.

43. Singer, "Reconsidering the Famine Relief Argument."

44. Ibid., 37.

45. Huntington, "Foreign Aid for What and for Whom," 175.

46. Willis Peterson, "Rates of Return on Development Assistance Capital: An International Comparison," *Kyklos* 42, fasc. 2 (1989): 203–17.

47. Jere R. Behrman and Raj Kumar Sah, "What Role Does Equity Play in the International Distribution of Development Aid?" in *Economic Structure and Performance,* ed. L. Taylor, M. Syrquin, and L. E. Westphal (New York: Academic Press, 1984), 295–315; William N. Trumbull and Howard J. Wall, "Estimating Aid-Allocation Criteria with Panel Data," *Economic Journal* 104 (July 1994): 876–82.

48. Bauer, *Equality and Economic Delusion,* 86–137.

49. Henry Shue, *Basic Rights: Substance, Affluence, and U.S. Foreign Policy* (Princeton: Princeton University Press, 1980).

50. Thomas W. Pogge, "Liberalism and Global Justice: Hoffman and Norden on Morality in International Affairs," *Philosophy and Public Affairs* 15 (Winter 1986): 67–81.

51. Joseph S. Nye, Jr., "Ethical Dimensions in International Involvement in Land Reform," in *International Dimensions of Land Reform,* ed. John D. Montgomery (Boulder: Westview Press, 1984), 7–29.

Chapter 3 Before Point Four

1. I am indebted to Harlan Cleveland for comment on an earlier draft of this chapter.

2. Harry S. Truman, "Inaugural Address of the President," *Department of State Bulletin* 33 (30 January 1949): 125.

3. Merle Curti and Kendall Birr, *Prelude to Point Four: American Technical Missions Overseas, 1838–1938* (Madison: University of Wisconsin Press, 1954).

4. I am indebted to Harlan Cleveland, who served as director of the China Aid Program and the China Area Aid Program under the Economic Cooperation Administration during 1948–50, and to Haldore Hanson, who served as director of the Interdepartmental Committee on Cultural Cooperation with Latin America, for personal insights into the issues discussed in this chapter. Three books from which I have drawn, beyond my capacity to acknowledge, are William Adams Brown, Jr., and Redvers Opie, *American Foreign Assistance* (Washington: Brookings Institution, 1953); Philip M. Glick, *The Administration of Technical Assistance: Growth in Latin America* (Chicago: University of Chicago Press, 1957); and Charles Wolf, Jr., *Foreign Aid: Theory and Practice in Southern Asia* (Princeton: Princeton University Press, 1960).

5. John A. White, *The Politics of Foreign Aid* (New York: St. Martin's, 1974), 34–67.

6. This section draws very heavily on Brown and Opie, *American Foreign Assistance,* 1–11, 22–24.

7. Calvin Coolidge, quoted in Daniel J. Boorstin, *The Americans: The Democratic Experience* (New York: Random House, 1973), 573.

8. For a review and assessment of the events leading to the depression of the 1930s, see Charles P. Kindleberger, *The World in Depression, 1929–39* (Berkeley: University of California Press, rev. ed. 1986). It is argued by Michael J. Hagen that liberal business leadership in a series of Republican administrations attempted to forge a

more liberal international economic order in the first decade and a half after World War I. This effort failed, in part, because "public policy throughout the Republican Ascendancy was pulled in opposite directions by promoters of organized capitalism and defenders of an older more conservative order." Michael J. Hagen, *The Marshall Plan: America, Britain and the Reconstruction of Western Europe, 1947–1952* (Cambridge: Cambridge University Press, 1987), 10.

9. This section draws very heavily on Brown and Opie, *American Foreign Assistance,* 16–22, and Glick, *The Administration of Technical Assistance,* 6–30.

10. Glick, *The Administration of Technical Assistance,* 17.

11. Brown and Opie, *American Foreign Assistance,* 19; see also 414–417. The Export-Import Bank was established in 1934 as a temporary instrument to finance and facilitate U.S. exports during the depression. By the late 1930s it had gone beyond its initial objective and was lending money to foreign governments to support U.S. foreign policy objectives. After the United States entered World War II, Lend-Lease credits replaced Export-Import Bank loans to Europe and most bank lending was directed to Latin America. After World War II bank lending declined until lending in support of U.S. assistance policy was renewed by the Act for International Development (1950) and U.S. entry into the Korean War. See Philip P. Boucher, "United States Foreign Aid to Latin America: Hypotheses and Patterns in Historical Statistics, 1934–1974" (Ph.D. diss., University of California, 1979). For more detail on the development of the Export-Import Bank, see Chapter 11.

12. Brown and Opie, *American Foreign Assistance,* 124–31.

13. For a popular but detailed account, see William H. McNeill, *Greece: American Aid in Action, 1947–1956* (New York: Twentieth Century Fund, 1957). Also Howard Jones, *A New Kind of War: America's Global Strategy and the Truman Doctrine in Greece* (New York: Oxford University Press, 1989).

14. Melvyn P. Leffler, "The United States and the Strategic Dimensions of the Marshall Plan," *Diplomatic History* 12 (Summer 1988): 277–306. Also Brown and Opie, *American Foreign Assistance,* 384.

15. For a detailed discussion of the negotiation in Washington and in Europe between the time of Marshall's speech and the passage of the Economic Cooperation Act of 1947, see Michael J. Hagan, *The Marshall Plan: America, Britain and the Reconstruction of Western Europe, 1947–1952* (Cambridge: Cambridge University Press, 1987), 45–87. See also 101–9 for more detailed discussion of the debates in the United States about administrative strategy for the ERP. The issue of USSR participation in the Marshall Plan has been a matter of continuing debate. There has been considerable speculation that the American terms of participation were deliberately designed to exclude the USSR. Seven junior State Department officers (Thomas C. Blaisdall, Jr., Harold Van B. Cleveland, Ben T. Moore, Paul R. Porter, Theodore Geiger, Charles P. Kindleberger, and Walt W. Rostow) who were working on the economic aspects of the Marshall Plan were convinced that a division of Europe, by preventing the restoration of trade, would preclude a successful recovery effort. Charles P. Kindleberger insists that Marshall was fully committed to the participation of the USSR. Clearly, however, opinions were shifting rapidly in the early summer of 1947, and a number of senior

State Department officials, including Under-Secretary Dean G. Acheson and George F. Kennan, were pleased that the USSR decided not to join the Organization for Economic Cooperation and Development (OEEC). In addition to Hagan, *The Marshall Plan,* 251–53, see Charles P. Kindleberger, *Marshall Plan Days* (Winchester, Mass.: Allen & Unwin, 1987), particularly 100 and 109.

16. Frank Kofsky, *Harry S. Truman and the War Scare of 1948: A Successful Campaign To Deceive the Nation* (New York: St. Martin's, 1993).

17. Immanuel Wexler, *The Marshall Plan Revisited: The European Recovery Program in Economic Perspective* (Westport, Conn.: Greenwood Press, 1983), 5.

18. Wolf, *Foreign Aid,* 41.

19. Ibid., 40–43.

20. The Foreign Economic Assistance Act of 1950 included separate sections covering aid to Europe under the Economic Cooperation Act (ERP), aid to the "general area of China" under the China Area Act, and global technical assistance under the Act for International Development. The authorization for use of ERP and China Aid funds in the "general area of China" was preceded by the dispatch in March 1950 of a mission to survey the assistance needed by Burma, Indochina, Indonesia, Thailand, and Malaya. The mission was headed by R. Allan Griffin, the former deputy chief of the U.S. aid program in China. See Wolf, *Foreign Aid,* 81–84, 114.

21. For U.S. assistance to Korea after the Korean War, see Anne O. Krueger and Vernon W. Ruttan, "Assistance to Korea," in Anne O. Krueger, Constantine Michalopoulos, and Vernon W. Ruttan, *Aid and Development* (Baltimore: Johns Hopkins University Press, 1989), 226–49.

22. The architects of the World Bank and the IMF, particularly Henry Dexter White (United States) and John Maynard Keynes (United Kingdom), anticipated that the organizations needed for international cooperation in the postwar world would involve an International Trade Organization (ITO). Preparatory meetings were held in 1946 and 1947, and an ITO charter was agreed upon at the Havana Conference on Trade and Employment in November 1947. Pending ratification of the charter, a General Agreement on Tariffs and Trade was put into operation. The charter of the ITO was not ratified, thus leaving the GATT as the sole outcome of the effort.

23. Both the World Bank and the IMF technically are specialized agencies of the United Nations. However, their early relations with the United Nations and several of its specialized agencies were troubled. Mason and Asher, *World Bank since Bretton Woods,* refer to the bank as "a rather 'special' specialized agency" (p. 8).

24. For the origins and early history of the International Monetary Fund, see J. Keith Horsefield, *The International Monetary Fund, 1945–1965* (Washington: IMF, 1969). For the origins and early history of the International Bank for Reconstruction and Development, see Mason and Asher, *World Bank since Bretton Woods.*

25. In this section I draw heavily on Lvon Luard, *A History of the United Nations,* vol. 1, *The Years of Western Domination, 1945–1955* (New York: St. Martin's, 1982).

26. Brown and Opie, *American Foreign Assistance,* 9.

27. Ibid., 76–80, 109–13.

28. Gove Hambridge, *The Story of the FAO* (New York: Von Nostrand, 1955), 73–76.

Chapter 4 Technical Assistance for Economic Development

1. For an earlier draft of this chapter, see Joseph V. Kennedy and Vernon W. Ruttan, "A Reexamination of Professional Popular Thought on Assistance for Economic Development: 1949–1952," *Journal of Developing Areas* 20 (April 1986): 297–326. The author is indebted to Harlan Cleveland, David E. Bell, John R. Lewis, Arthur Schlesinger, Jr., Theodore W. Schultz, and Willard L. Thorp for comments on an earlier draft.

2. Harry S. Truman, "Inaugural Address of the President," *Department of State Bulletin* 33 (30 January 1949): 125.

3. See Harry G. Johnson, *Economic Policies toward Less Developed Countries* (Washington: Brookings Institution, 1968), 35; Mahbub ul Haq, *The Poverty Curtain: Choices for the Third World* (New York: Columbia University Press, 1976), 12–26; Christopher D. Gerrard, *Promoting Third World Agriculture: Lessons of Recent Experience* (Ottawa, Ont.: North-South Institute, 1983), 2–3; Elliot R. and Victoria A. Morss, *U.S. Foreign Aid: An Assessment of New and Traditional Development Strategies* (Boulder: Westview Press, 1982), 21–24; and Albert O. Hirschman, "The Rise and Decline of Development Economics," in *The Theory and Experience of Economic Development,* ed. Mark Gersovitz, Carlos F. Diaz-Alejandro, Gustzav Ranis, and Mark Rosenzweig (London: Allen & Unwin, 1985), 380.

4. For a personal account, see Clark Clifford (with Richard Holbrooke), *Counsel to the President: A Memoir* (New York: Random House, 1991), 248–53. See also Harry S. Truman, *Memoirs: Years of Trial and Hope* (Garden City, N.Y.: Doubleday, 1956), 2:223–39; Harlan Cleveland, *The Future Executive* (New York: Harper & Row, 1972), 87–88; Arthur Schlesinger, Jr., personal interview, 28 February 1985; Harlan Cleveland, personal interview, 14 February 1985; David Bell, personal letter, 22 October 1985.

5. H.R. 5615, reprinted in U.S. Congress, House Committee on Foreign Affairs, *Hearings on an Act for International Development,* 81st Cong., 1st sess., 1949, 1–3.

6. H.R. 6026, reprinted in U.S. Congress, House Committee on Foreign Affairs, *Hearings on an Act for International Development,* 81st Cong., 1st sess., 1949, 174–80.

7. The Act for International Development, 64 *U.S. Statutes at Large,* no. 204, chap. 220, tit. 4, sec. 401–18.

8. Gordon Gray, *Report to the President on Foreign Economic Policies* (Washington: USGPO, March 1951); *Partners in Progress: A Report to the President by the International Development Advisory Board* (Washington: USGPO, March 1951); *Measures for the Economic Development of Under-Developed Countries: A Report by a Group of Experts Appointed by the Secretary-General of the United Nations* (New York: United Nations, May 1951).

9. David H. Blelloch, "Technical Assistance: Programmes and Policies," *International Affairs* 28 (January 1952): 49–58; Nelson Rockefeller, "Widening Boundaries of National Interest," *Foreign Affairs* 29 (July 1951): 533.

10. Ragnar Nurkse, "Some International Aspects of the Problem of Economic Development," *American Economic Review* 42 (May 1952, supplement): 571–73; John

H. Adler, "The Fiscal and Monetary Implementation of Development Programs," ibid., 584; Hans W. Singer, "Comments," ibid., 607–8; Blelloch, "Technical Assistance," 56; Gray, *Report on Foreign Economic Policies,* 59; Theodore W. Schultz, "The Declining Economic Importance of Agricultural Land," *Economic Journal* 61 (December 1951): 725–40; Oscar Zaglits, "Comments," *American Economic Review* 42 (May 1952, supplement): 609.

11. Blelloch, "Technical Assistance," 54–58; Gray, *Report on Foreign Economic Policies,* 9, 12, 15–17, 57, 70, 75–87; George Hakim, "Point Four and the Middle East: A Middle East View," *Middle East Journal* 4 (April 1950): 186–87; Rockefeller, "Widening Boundaries," 529.

12. Blelloch, "Technical Assistance," 54–56.

13. Peter T. Bauer and B. S. Yamey, "Economic Progress and Occupational Distribution," *Economic Journal* 61 (December 1951): 744; Nurkse, "Some International Aspects," 577–80, 583; Blelloch, "Technical Assistance," 49; Hakim, "Point Four," 187–89; Singer, "Comments," 607; Gray, *Report on Foreign Economic Policies,* 5, 8–9, 57; Rockefeller, "Widening Boundaries," 523, 533.

14. Nurkse, "Some International Aspects," 574–75; Hakim, "Point Four," 189–91; William A. Brown, Jr., "Treaty, Guaranty, and Tax Inducements for Foreign Investments," *American Economic Review* 40 (May 1950, supplement): 491; Bruno Foa, "Comments," ibid., 519; Gray, *Report on Foreign Economic Policies,* 61–63.

15. Adler, "Fiscal and Monetary Implementation," 588, 590, 593; Horst Mendershausen, "Comments," *American Economic Review* 42 (May 1952, supplement): 603; Hans P. Neisser, "Comments," ibid., 604; Rockefeller, "Widening Boundaries," 533; Gray, *Report on Foreign Economic Policies,* 63.

16. Mendershausen, "Comments," 603; Rockefeller, "Widening Boundaries," 535–36; Hakim, "Point Four," 185–86; Foa, "Comments," 519; Gray, *Report on Foreign Economic Policies,* 13–14, 29, 66–67.

17. Arthur Z. Gardiner, "Point Four and the Arab World: An American View," *Middle East Journal* 4 (July 1950): 297.

18. U.S. Congress, House Committee on Foreign Affairs, *Hearings on an Act for International Development,* 81st Cong., 1st and 2d sess., 1949–50 (hereafter cited as *1950 House Authorization Hearings*); U.S. Congress, Senate Committee on Foreign Relations, *Hearings on an Act for International Development,* 81st Cong., 2d sess., 1950 (hereafter cited as *1950 Senate Authorization Hearings*); U.S. Congress, House Committee on Appropriations, Special Subcommittee on Foreign Aid Appropriations, *Hearings on Foreign Aid Appropriations for 1951,* 81st Cong., 2d sess., 1950, (hereafter cited as *1950 House Appropriation Hearings*); U.S. Congress, Senate Committee on Appropriations, *Hearings on Foreign Aid Appropriations for 1951,* 81st Cong., 2d sess., 1950 (hereafter cited as *1950 Senate Appropriation Hearings*); U.S. Congress, House Committee on Banking and Currency, *Hearings on Export-Import Bank Loan Guarantee Authority,* 81st Cong., 1st sess., 1949 (hereafter cited as *1949 House Investment Guarantee Hearings*); U.S. Congress, Senate Committee on Banking and Currency, *Hearings on Foreign Investment Guaranties,* 81st Cong., 1st sess., 1949 (hereafter cited as *1949 Senate Investment Guarantee Hearings*); U.S. Congress, House Committee on

Foreign Affairs, *Mutual Security Act Extension: Hearings on H.R. 7005,* 82d Cong., 2d sess., 1952 (hereafter cited as *1953 House Authorization Hearings*); U.S. Congress, Senate Committee on Foreign Relations, *Hearings on Mutual Security Act of 1952,* 82d Cong., 2d sess., 1952 (hereafter cited as *1952 Senate Authorization Hearings*). See also Walter M. Daniels, ed., *The Point Four Program* (New York: H. W. Wilson, 1951); Ellen Ziskind Berg, "The 1973 Legislative Reorientation of the United States Foreign Assistance Policy: The Content and Context of a Change" (M.A. thesis, George Washington University, 1976, 206–15).

19. Testimony of James E. Webb, Acting Secretary of State, reprinted in *1950 House Authorization Hearings*, 21; testimony of Willard L. Thorp, Assistant Secretary of State for Economic Affairs, reprinted in ibid., 29.

20. Webb testimony, *1950 House Authorization Hearings,* 5–6; testimony of Julius A. Krug, Secretary of Interior, ibid., 299–300; testimony of Winthrop Aldrich, Chairman, President's Advisory Committee on Foreign Financial Problems, *1949 Senate Investment Guarantee Hearings,* 28–29; testimony of Herbert E. Gaston, Chairman of the Export-Import Bank, *1949 House Investment Guarantee Hearings,* 68; Webb testimony, ibid., 30; Webb testimony, *1950 House Authorization Hearings,* 5; Thorp testimony, *1950 Senate Appropriations Hearings,* 363, 588–92.

21. In addition to coverage of Truman's speech, the *New York Times* also reported on a major retreat by the Nationalist forces in China. *New York Times,* 21 January 1949, 1.

22. Testimony of Dean Rusk, Assistant Secretary of State, *1950 Senate Appropriations Hearings,* 494–95.

23. Thorp testimony, *1950 Senate Appropriations Hearings,* 14, 392; testimony of Capus W. Waynick, Acting Administrator, Point Four Program, ibid., 574; testimony of Paul G. Hoffman, Administrator, Economic Cooperation Administration, *1950 House Authorization Hearings,* 432; testimony of Raymond T. Moyer, Chief ECA Representative in China, ibid., 356; testimony of Philip M. Kaiser, Assistant Secretary of Labor, ibid., 278; testimony of Oscar R. Ewing, Federal Security Administrator, ibid., 65–68; Webb testimony, ibid., 5; Thorp testimony, ibid., 13; Webb testimony, *1949 House Investment Guarantee Hearings,* 30.

24. Testimony of Dean Acheson, Secretary of State, *1952 Senate Authorization Hearings,* 119; testimony of Jonathan B. Bingham, Acting Administrator, TCA, ibid., 629; Acheson testimony, *1950 Senate Authorization Hearings,* 13; Webb testimony, *1950 House Authorization Hearings,* 6; testimony of Maurice J. Tobin, Secretary of Labor, ibid., 174–75.

25. Webb testimony, *1949 House Investment Guarantee Hearings,* 31; Acheson testimony, *1950 Senate Authorization Hearings,* 13; Thorp testimony, *1950 Senate Appropriations Hearings,* 362, 386, 443, 444, 509; Hare testimony, ibid., 573.

26. Thorp testimony, *1950 Senate Appropriations Hearings,* 517; Webb testimony, *1950 House Authorization Hearings,* 6; testimony of Charles Sawyer, Secretary of Commerce, ibid., 130–31; Krug testimony, *1950 House Authorization Hearings,* 297.

27. Acheson testimony, *1950 Senate Authorization Hearings,* 10, 23; testimony of Philip C. Jessup, Ambassador at Large, ibid., 25–26; Thorp testimony, *1950 Senate Appropriations Hearings,* 362, 383, 393, 445, 585.

28. Krug testimony, *1950 House Authorization Hearings,* 302; Moyer testimony, ibid., 357; Thorp testimony, ibid., 16, 482, 485; Thorp testimony, *1950 Senate Appropriations Hearings,* 390, 442.

29. Thorp testimony, *1950 Senate Appropriations Hearings,* 430, 451; Thorp testimony, *1950 House Appropriations Hearings,* 19; Webb testimony, ibid., 7; Hoffman testimony, *1950 House Authorization Hearings,* 416; Hoffman testimony, *1950 Senate Appropriations Hearings,* 236–37; testimony of Austin T. Foster, Chairman, Treaty Committee, National Foreign Trade Council, Inc., *1950 House Appropriations Hearings,* 438.

30. Thorp testimony, *1950 House Authorization Hearings,* 13–15; testimony of Charles F. Brannan, Secretary of Agriculture, ibid., 45, 52; Hare testimony, *1950 Senate Appropriations Hearings,* 570–73; Miller testimony, ibid., 424–25; Acheson testimony, *1950 Senate Authorization Hearings,* 4; Hoffman testimony, *1950 House Authorization Hearings,* 430; Moyer testimony, ibid., 353–54; Webb testimony, ibid., 21; Ewing testimony, ibid., 71; Moyer testimony, ibid., 356–57; Thorp testimony, ibid., 22; Webb testimony, ibid., 32; Ewing testimony, ibid., 65; Moyer testimony, ibid., 358.

31. Testimony of John W. Snyder, Secretary of the Treasury, *1949 House Investment Guarantee Hearings,* 2; Thorp testimony, *1950 Senate Appropriations Hearings,* 362; Thorp testimony, *1950 House Authorization Hearings,* 458; Sawyer testimony, ibid., 122; Snyder testimony, *1949 Senate Investment Guarantee Hearings,* 113; testimony of S. R. Carpenter, Secretary, Board of Governors, Federal Reserve System, ibid., 112; testimony of Ernest A. Gross, State Department, ibid., 114; Webb testimony, ibid., 17.

32. Acheson testimony, *1950 Senate Authorization Hearings,* 6; testimony of Herbert E. Gaston, Chairman, Export-Import Bank, *1949 Senate Investment Guarantee Hearings,* 113; Gross testimony, ibid., 114; Snyder testimony, ibid., 3; Webb testimony, ibid., 17; Aldrich testimony, ibid., 30; Snyder testimony, *1949 House Investment Guarantee Hearings,* 4.

33. Acheson testimony, *1950 Senate Authorization Hearings,* 6–7; Sawyer testimony, *1950 House Authorization Hearings,* 122–23; Webb testimony, *1949 House Investment Guarantee Hearings,* 31.

34. Gaston testimony, *1949 Senate Investment Guarantee Hearings,* 41, 49, 113; Gross testimony, ibid., 115–16; Sawyer testimony, *1950 House Authorization Hearings,* 123–24; Webb testimony, ibid., 19, 37; Snyder testimony, *1949 House Investment Guarantee Hearings,* 9.

35. Gaston testimony, *1949 Senate Investment Guarantee Hearings,* 37–39, 41, 43–45, 47, 52–53, 71, 113–14; Snyder testimony, ibid., 2, 5, 10, 13, 16; Webb testimony, ibid., 18; Gaston testimony, *1949 House Investment Guarantee Hearings,* 73; Carpenter testimony, *1949 Senate Investment Guarantee Hearings,* 112; Gaston testimony, ibid., 35, 114, 37; Gross testimony, ibid., 116; Webb testimony, ibid., 23; Snyder testimony, *1949 House Investment Guarantee Hearings,* 5.

36. Webb testimony, *1949 House Investment Guarantee Hearings,* 30; Snyder testimony, ibid., 22–23; Webb testimony, *1949 Senate Investment Guarantee Hearings,* 25–26; Carpenter testimony, ibid., 112; Acheson testimony, *1950 Senate Authorization Hearings,* 20, 5; Snyder testimony, *1949 Senate Investment Guarantee Hearings,* 2;

Krug testimony, *1950 House Authorization Hearings,* 305; Thorp testimony, *1950 Senate Authorization Hearings,* 362.

37. Thorp testimony, *1950 House Authorization Hearings,* 459–67, 471, 483; Webb testimony, ibid., 6–7; Acheson testimony, *1950 Senate Authorization Hearings,* 10.

38. Kaiser testimony, *1950 House Authorization Hearings,* 278–79, 283, 285–86, 288; Tobin testimony, ibid., 273, 174, 275.

39. Report of the Special Committee on Point IV Program, "Chamber of Commerce of the United States" (hereafter cited as "Chamber of Commerce Report"), *1952 House Authorization Hearings,* 155–56; testimony of Norman M. Littell, Chairman, Foreign Economic Cooperation Committee, American Bar Association, ibid., 75.

40. Littell testimony, ibid., 75, 83–84; Roy W. Gifford, Chairman, Foreign Commerce Committee, Detroit Board of Commerce, *1949 Senate Investment Guarantee Hearings,* 57, 63; Gifford testimony, *1950 House Authorization Hearings,* 313, 318–19; Richard B. Frost, Secretary World Affairs Committee, Detroit Board of Commerce, *1949 House Investment Guarantee Hearings,* 147–48.

41. Gifford testimony, *1949 Senate Investment Guarantee Hearings,* 58, 59; Frost testimony, *1949 House Investment Guarantee Hearings,* 148, 149–50; Littell testimony, *1950 House Authorization Hearings,* 75, 79–82.

42. Foster testimony, *1950 House Authorization Hearings,* 101–2; Frost testimony, ibid., 102; testimony of Robert F. Lorce, chairman, National Foreign Trade Council, Inc., *1950 House Authorization Hearings,* 504; "Chamber of Commerce Report," ibid., 158; Littell testimony, *1949 Senate Investment Guarantee Hearings,* 80–81.

43. "Chamber of Commerce Report," *1950 House Authorization Hearings,* 159–60; Foster testimony, ibid., 102; testimony of J. D. A. Morrow, President, Joy Manufacturing Co., *1949 Senate Investment Guarantee Hearings,* 115; testimony of Harry S. Barger, National Economic Council, Inc., *1949 House Investment Guarantee Hearings,* 159–60; Frost testimony, ibid., 145–46, 148; Littell testimony, ibid., 86; Littell hearings, *1949 Senate Investment Guarantee Hearings,* 78, 80; Gifford testimony, ibid., 58.

44. Foster testimony, ibid., 102, 114, 117–18; Gifford testimony, ibid., 196, 313; "Chamber of Commerce Report," ibid., 155, 156; Frost testimony, *1949 House Investment Guarantee Hearings,* 152; testimony of E. P. Thomas, President, National Foreign Trade Council, *1950 Senate Authorization Hearings,* 117–18; Littell testimony, *1950 House Authorization Hearings,* 79–82; testimony of Spruille Braden, former Assistant Secretary of State for American Public Affairs, *1950 House Authorization Hearings,* 221, 230; testimony of Clarence R. Miles, Chamber of Commerce of the United States, *1952 Senate Authorization Hearings,* 538.

45. Thomas testimony, *1950 House Authorization Hearings,* 118; Gifford testimony, ibid., 314; "Chamber of Commerce Report," ibid., 155–56; Foster testimony, ibid., 104–5.

46. Testimony of Donald Montgomery, United Auto Workers, Congress of Industrial Organizations, *1950 House Authorization Hearings,* 439–41.

47. Montgomery testimony, ibid., 438; statement of the United Textile Workers of America, American Federation of Labor, *1952 Senate Authorization Hearings,* 113; testimony of George P. Delaney, American Federation of Labor, *1950 Senate Authorization Hearings,* 72; Montgomery testimony, *1950 House Authorization Hearings,* 440, 443.

48. Montgomery testimony, *1950 House Authorization Hearings,* 437–40; United Textile Workers statement, *1950 Senate Authorization Hearings,* 113.

49. Testimony of John C. Lynn, Legislative Director, American Farm Bureau, *1950 House Authorization Hearings,* 486; testimony of J. T. Sanders, Legislative Council, National Grange, ibid., 392; Lynn testimony, *1950 Senate Authorization Hearings,* 114; Lynn testimony, *1950 House Authorization Hearings,* 486–87; testimony of Allan B. Kline, President, American Farm Bureau Federation, ibid., 345; Lynn testimony, *1950 Senate Authorization Hearings,* 114; testimony of Wallace J. Campbell, Cooperative League of the USA, ibid., 54; Lynn testimony, *1950 House Authorization Hearings,* 487; Kline testimony, ibid., 346.

50. Lynn testimony, *1950 House Authorization Hearings,* 487; Kline testimony, ibid., 345, 346; Sanders testimony, ibid., 394; Campbell testimony, *1950 Senate Authorization Hearings,* 55.

51. Testimony of Michael Straight, Chairman, American Veterans Committee, *1950 House Authorization Hearings,* 512.

52. Statement of the Council for Social Action, Council of Christian Churches (hereafter cited as Council for Social Action Statement], ibid., 515; testimony of Wynn C. Fairfield, Secretary for General Administration, Foreign Missions Conference, ibid., 133, 141–42; testimony of Walter V. VanKirk, Federal Council of Churches of Christ in America, *1950 Senate Authorization Hearings,* 42; testimony of Clarence E. Pickett, Honorary Secretary of the American Friends Service Committee, ibid., 45–46; testimony of Rowland M. Cross, Foreign Missions Conference of North America, ibid., 96.

53. Testimony of Maxine Y. Wollston, American Association of University Women, *1950 Senate Authorization Hearings,* 119; VanKirk testimony, ibid., 42; Straight testimony, ibid., 56; testimony of Theodore Waller, United World Federalists, Inc., ibid., 60; Fairfield testimony, *1950 House Authorization Hearings,* 151; Council for Social Action Statement, ibid., 517.

54. Fairfield testimony, *1950 House Authorization Hearings,* 133; Waller testimony, ibid., 514; testimony of Clark M. Eichelberger, Director, American Association for the United Nations, ibid., 510.

55. Testimony of Mrs. Clifford A. Bender, Women's Division of the Methodist Church, ibid., 51–58; testimony of Reverend Monsignor John J. McClafferty, National Conference of Catholic Charities, ibid., 267; statement of the Executive Committee of the Federal Council of the Churches of Christ in America, ibid., 448; Straight testimony, *1950 Senate Authorization Hearings,* 56; testimony of Norman Thomas, Socialist Party, ibid., 115; Waller testimony, ibid., 58, 60–61.

56. Eichelberger testimony, *1950 House Authorization Hearings,* 510; Waller testimony, ibid., 514; testimony of Benjamin Marsh, Executive Secretary, People's Lobby, ibid., 523; testimony of Reverend Herman Reissig, Council for Social Action, Congressional Christian Churches, *1950 Senate Authorization Hearings,* 65; Eichelberger testimony, *1950 House Authorization Hearings,* 510; Bender testimony, ibid., 517.

57. Straight testimony, *1950 Senate Authorization Hearings,* 56–57; Straight testimony, *1950 House Authorization Hearings,* 512–13; Cross testimony, *1950 Senate Au-*

thorization Hearings, 92; Marsh testimony, ibid., 107; testimony of Rayford Logan, National Association for the Advancement of Colored People, *1950 House Authorization Hearings,* 210.

58. Marsh testimony, *1950 Senate Authorization Hearings,* 107, 112; testimony of Constance W. Anderson, Young Women's Christian Association, ibid., 120; Council for Social Action Statement, *1950 House Authorization Hearings,* 517; Bender testimony, ibid., 517; H. A. Howard, National Director, Phi Beta Sigma, ibid., 331.

59. Straight testimony, *1950 Senate Authorization Hearings,* 56; Pickett testimony, ibid., 48; VanKirk testimony, ibid., 42; testimony of Philip Schiff, American Association of Social Workers, ibid., 49; testimony of Reverend R. A. McGowan, National Catholic Welfare Conference, ibid., 123; Fairfield testimony, *1950 House Authorization Hearings,* 133–34, 141; testimony of Hyde G. Buller, Agricultural Development, Inc., ibid., 213; Laubach testimony, ibid., 382.

60. Testimony of Harry E. Ewing, *1950 Senate Authorization Hearings,* 66–70; testimony of Burlin B. Hamer, *1950 House Authorization Hearings,* 347; testimony of Dr. Gerald F. Winfield, ibid., 170–74; testimony of L. G. Shreve, President, Council Services, Inc., ibid., 163–70.

61. Woolston testimony, *1950 Senate Authorization Hearings,* 119.

62. Pickett statement, ibid., 47; Thomas statement, ibid., 115; Reissig statement, ibid., 65–66; Council for Social Action Statement, Congressional Christian Churches, *1950 House Authorization Hearings,* 517.

63. Statement of Congressman Jacob K. Javits, *1950 House Authorization Hearings,* 34, 58; statement of Congressman John Kee, ibid., 76; statement of Congressman Abraham A. Ribicoff, ibid., 57–58.

64. Javits statement, ibid., 190, 203–4, 432; Kee statement, ibid., 264, 308–9; statement of Congresswoman Helen G. Douglas, ibid., 288–90, 293; Douglas statement, ibid., 287; Kee statement, ibid., 293; Congressman Joseph P. O'Hara, *1949 House Investment Guarantee Hearings,* 56.

65. Statement of Congressman Christian A. Herter, *1950 House Authorization Hearings,* 181, 473; statement of Congressman Henry O. Talle, *1950 House Investment Guarantee Hearings,* 9, 40; Herter statement, ibid., 129.

66. Herter statement, *1950 House Authorization Hearings,* 184–86; statement of Congressman Robert B. Chipperfield, ibid., 236; statement of Congressman James G. Fulton, ibid., 145–46; Herter statement, ibid., 193–94.

67. Chipperfield statement, ibid., 236; Herter statement, ibid., 189; statement of Congressman Charles A. Eaton, ibid., 191; Javits statement, ibid., 202; statement of Congressman John M. Vorys, ibid., 196; statement of Congressman Donald L. Jackson, ibid., 428; Herter statement, *1949 House Investment Guarantee Hearings,* 130; statement of Senator J. William Fulbright, *1950 Senate Authorization Hearings,* 14; statement of Senator A. Willis Robertson, *1950 Senate Appropriations Hearings.*

68. Vorys statement, *1950 House Authorization Hearings,* 24–25, 84–85; statement of Congressman John Davis Lodge, ibid., 250; Fulbright statement, *1950 Senate Authorization Hearings,* 13–14, 28–29; statement of Senator H. Alexander Smith, ibid., 27–30, 39; Vorys statement, *1950 House Authorization Hearings,* 74, 77, 91–92.

69. Statement of Congressman Albert M. Cole, *1949 House Investment Guarantee Hearings,* 15; Herter statement, ibid., 127; statement of Senator Tom Connally, *1950 Senate Authorization Hearings,* 23, 26–27; statement of Senator Kenneth S. Wherry, *1950 Senate Appropriations Hearings,* 382–83, 439.

70. Javits statement, *1950 House Authorization Hearings,* 203–4, 432; statement of Congressman Walter H. Judd, ibid., 446; Wherry statement, *1950 Senate Appropriations Hearings,* 444–48; statement of Senator Sheridan Knowland, ibid., 453–54.

71. Douglas statement, *1950 House Authorization Hearings,* 302; statement of Congressman Francis P. Bolton, ibid., 303; Fulton statement, ibid., 202; Judd statement, ibid., 54. But see Connally statement, ibid., 34–35; Judd statement, ibid., 197, 397–400, 412; statement of Thomas E. Morgan, ibid., 22–23.

72. Statement of Senator Guy Cordon, *1950 Senate Appropriations Hearings,* 386; Wherry statement, ibid., 431–34, 441; Knowland statement, ibid., 440.

73. Testimony of C. Tyler Wood, Associate Deputy Director, Mutual Security Agency, *1952 Senate Authorization Hearings,* 270–71.

74. Acheson testimony, *1952 House Authorization Hearings,* 162; testimony of W. Averell Harriman, Director for Mutual Security, ibid., 2.

75. Harriman testimony, *1952 Senate Authorization Hearings,* 65; testimony of Jonathan B. Bingham, Acting Administrator, TCA, ibid., 628; Wood testimony, *1952 House Authorization Hearings,* 858–59, 1120; Harriman testimony, ibid., 7; testimony of Harlan Cleveland, Assistant Director for Europe, MSA, ibid., 954.

76. The Mutual Security Act of 1951, 65 *U.S. Statutes at Large,* no. 373, tit. 5, sec. 511(b).

77. Ibid.; Bingham testimony, *1952 House Authorization Hearings,* 1011–12; Wood testimony, ibid., 858–61, 1119; testimony of Johnston Avery, Assistant Administrator, TCA, ibid., 1134; "The Mutual Security Program," reprinted in ibid., 1047.

78. Harriman testimony, *1952 House Authorization Hearings,* 6.

79. Acheson testimony, ibid., 137; Harriman testimony, ibid., 7; Wood testimony, *1952 Senate Authorization Hearings,* 592–93; Acheson testimony, ibid., 105–6, 117; Bingham testimony, ibid., 628–29; Acheson testimony, ibid., 105–6, 117; Cleveland testimony, ibid., 792–93; Acheson testimony, *1952 House Authorization Hearings,* 13, 137, 149; Bingham testimony, ibid., 958, 996.

80. Bingham testimony, *1952 House Authorization Hearings,* 989–90; Cleveland testimony, ibid., 931–38, 949; Wood testimony, ibid., 804, 1125; Wood testimony, *1952 Senate Authorization Hearings,* 590–91; Acheson testimony, ibid., 804.

81. Wood testimony, *1952 Senate Authorization Hearings,* 355; testimony of Robert A. Lovett, Secretary of Defense, ibid., 167.

82. Acheson testimony, ibid., 105; testimony of Clarence R. Miles, Chamber of Commerce of the United States, ibid., 530; Acheson testimony, ibid., 119; testimony of Andrew N. Overby, U.S. Executive Director, International Bank for Reconstruction and Development, *1952 House Authorization Hearings,* 591.

83. Overby testimony, *1952 House Authorization Hearings,* 582–85, 587–88.

84. Harriman testimony, ibid., 122; Overby testimony, ibid., 600–601, 588–89, 608.

85. Testimony of Frank Southard, Jr., U.S. Executive Director, International Monetary Fund, ibid., 470–74; Overby testimony, ibid., 602–3.

86. Wood testimony, *1952 Senate Authorization Hearings,* 590, 595, 596–97; Bingham testimony, ibid., 629, 640–41; Acheson testimony, ibid., 116; Bingham testimony, *1952 House Authorization Hearings,* 959, 961, 967, 971, 1025; testimony of Stanley Andrews, Administrator, TCA, ibid., 986; Acheson testimony, ibid., 162.

87. Wood testimony, *1952 Senate Authorization Hearings,* 649; Harriman testimony, *1952 House Authorization Hearings,* 8; Cleveland testimony, *1952 Senate Authorization Hearings,* 597; testimony of John W. Snyder, Chairman, National Advisory Council on International Monetary and Financial Problems, *1952 House Authorization Hearings,* 597; Bingham testimony, *1952 Senate Authorization Hearings,* 648.

88. Wood testimony, *1952 House Authorization Hearings,* 1125; Cleveland testimony, ibid., 952–53; Snyder testimony, ibid., 597; see Mutual Security Act of 1951, 65 *U.S. Statutes at Large,* no. 373, tit. 5, sec. 522.

89. Bingham testimony, *1952 House Authorization Hearings,* 959; Bingham testimony, *1952 Senate Authorization Hearings,* 646; Wood testimony, ibid., 650; Bingham testimony, *1952 House Authorization Hearings,* 959; Harriman testimony, ibid., 7; Bingham testimony, *1952 Senate Authorization Hearings,* 631, 714, 723, 726.

90. Bingham testimony, *1952 House Authorization Hearings,* 959–60, 972–73; Bingham testimony, *1952 Senate Authorization Hearings,* 629–30, 696; Andrews testimony, ibid., 637.

91. "Policy Guidance Regarding Labor and Manpower Aspects of Technical Cooperation Program," *1952 Senate Authorization Hearings,* 742; "Mutual Security Program," *1952 House Authorization Hearings,* 1042.

92. Bingham testimony, *1952 Senate Authorization Hearings,* 634–37; Andrews testimony, ibid., 637; "Policy Guidance Regarding Labor and Manpower Aspects of Technical Cooperative Program," ibid., 742–44; Wood testimony, ibid., 599; Cleveland testimony, ibid., 597–98; Harriman testimony, ibid., 100.

93. Cleveland testimony, ibid., 792–93; "U.S. Technical and Economic Assistance in the Far East—A Part of the Mutual Security Program for 1952–1953" (hereafter cited as "Asia Report"), *1952 House Authorization Hearings,* 818–21.

94. Testimony of Clem D. Johnston, Director, U.S. Chamber of Commerce, *1952 House Authorization Hearings,* 652–53, 671; Miles testimony, *1952 Senate Authorization Hearings,* 530; testimony of L. M. Brile, President, Fairmong Aluminum Co., ibid., 550; Miles testimony, ibid., 531–32; Brile testimony, ibid., 549–50; statement of the Illinois Manufacturers Association, *1952 House Authorization Hearings,* 1095–96.

95. Brile testimony, *1952 Senate Authorization Hearings,* 549; Miles testimony, ibid., 536; Johnston testimony, *1952 House Authorization Hearings,* 663; Miles testimony, *1952 Senate Authorization Hearings,* 538; Brile testimony, ibid., 550; testimony of Sam G. Baggett, Vice President, United Fruit Co., *1952 House Authorization Hearings,* 873.

96. Johnston testimony, *1952 House Authorization Hearings,* 653, 666; statement of the National Foreign Trade Council, ibid., 1089; Rockefeller testimony, ibid., 881; statement of Detroit Board of Commerce, ibid., 1094; testimony of James S. Martin,

General Counsel, Association for International Development, *1952 Senate Authorization Hearings,* 498.

97. Johnston testimony, *1952 House Authorization Hearings,* 664–65; Brile testimony, *1952 Senate Authorization Hearings,* 550; Miles testimony, ibid., 536–37.

98. Testimony of Boris Shiskin, Economist, American Federation of Labor, *1952 House Authorization Hearings,* 903–4, 908, 900–901, 907; testimony of James B. Carey, Secretary-Treasurer, Congress of Industrial Organizations, ibid., 1086; Carey testimony, *1952 Senate Authorization Hearings,* 481; Shiskin testimony, ibid., 478; Shiskin testimony, *1952 House Authorization Hearings,* 900, 905–7; Carey testimony, ibid., 1088; Carey testimony, *1952 Senate Authorization Hearings,* 484.

99. Carey testimony, *1952 House Authorization Hearings,* 1086–87; Carey testimony, *1952 Senate Authorization Hearings,* 484, 488; Shiskin testimony, *1952 House Authorization Hearings,* 905; Carey testimony, ibid., 1088; Carey testimony, *1952 Senate Authorization Hearings,* 484–85, 488, 491.

100. Testimony of John C. Lynn, Legislative Director, American Farm Bureau Federation, *1952 House Authorization Hearings,* 632; "Long-Term Purposes and 1952–1953 Action Program of the National Farmers Union," statement of the National Farmers Union, ibid., 693; Kline testimony, *1952 Senate Authorization Hearings,* 439.

101. Lynn testimony, *1952 House Authorization Hearings,* 633; testimony of J. T. Sanders, Legislative Council, National Grange, ibid., 696–97; Kline testimony, *1952 Senate Authorization Hearings,* 439, 448; Sanders testimony, ibid., 471–73; statement of the National Farmers Union, *1952 House Authorization Hearings,* 694; testimony of James G. Patton, President, National Farmers Union, ibid., 691; Patton testimony, *1952 Senate Authorization Hearings,* 463; Sanders testimony, ibid., 469–70.

102. Patton testimony, *1952 Senate Authorization Hearings,* 463; Sanders testimony, ibid., 472; Patton testimony, *1952 House Authorization Hearings,* 691; Lynn testimony, ibid., 632; Kline testimony, *1952 Senate Authorization Hearings,* 439, 443.

103. Statement of the American Labor Party, *1952 Senate Authorization Hearings,* 545; testimony of Henry Pratt Fairchild, National Secretary, National Council of the Arts, Sciences, and Professions, Inc., ibid., 547.

104. Testimony of Bernard Weitzer, Jewish War Veterans of the United States of America, ibid., 497; testimony of Dr. John Coleman Bennett, Council for Social Action, Congressional Christian Churches, ibid., 403–4; testimony of Arthur Schlesinger, Jr., Americans for Democratic Action, ibid., 543; statement of the General Federation of Women's Clubs, *1952 House Authorization Hearings,* 1097; testimony of Dorothy Norman, Chairman, American Committee for Economic Aid Abroad, ibid., 1098; testimony of Eileen Blackey, American Association of Social Workers, ibid., 1104; testimony of Ray Gibbons, Director, Council for Social Action, Congressional Christian Churches, ibid., 1103.

105. Eichelberger testimony, *1952 Senate Authorization Hearings,* 411; Fairchild testimony, ibid., 547; Weitzer testimony, ibid., 497; statement of the League of Women Voters, *1952 House Authorization Hearings,* 1098; statement of the General Federation of Women's Clubs, ibid., 1097; Norman testimony, ibid., 1099–1100; Blackey testimony, ibid., 1104.

106. Statement of the National Board of the Young Women's Christian Association, *1952 Senate Authorization Hearings,* 546; testimony of Robert T. Henry, Executive Secretary, National Council of Churches of Christ, ibid., 401; Eichelberger testimony, ibid., 411; Blackey testimony, *1952 House Authorization Hearings,* 1104; Norman testimony, ibid., 1098; statement of the General Federation of Women's Clubs, ibid., 1097.

107. Statement of Congressman Walter H. Judd, *1952 House Authorization Hearings,* 996–97; statement of Congressman Thurmond Chatham, ibid., 936–37; statement of Senator Alexander Wiley, *1952 Senate Authorization Hearings,* 44–46, 95–96, 187, 355; Smith statement, ibid., 64, 718–19; statement of Senator Guy M. Gillette, ibid., 311.

108. Statement of Senator Theodore Francis Green, *1952 Senate Authorization Hearings,* 353; Javits statement, *1952 House Authorization Hearings,* 123.

109. Fulton statement, *1952 House Authorization Hearings,* 197–98; Wiley statement, *1952 Senate Authorization Hearings,* 352–53; statement of Senator Ralph E. Flanders, ibid., 398.

110. Javits statement, *1952 House Authorization Hearings,* 165; Connally statement, *1952 Senate Authorization Hearings,* 228; Green statement, ibid., 37–38, 100, 388, 593–94; Javits statement, *1952 House Authorization Hearings,* 585; statement of Congressman Lawrence H. Smith, ibid., 1022.

111. Javits statement, *1952 House Authorization Hearings,* 123; Judd statement, ibid., 353; Flanders statement, *1952 Senate Authorization Hearings,* 400; statement of Senator John J. Sparkman, ibid., 654.

112. Vorys statement, *1952 House Authorization Hearings,* 473; Javits statement, ibid., 472–73; Bolton statement, ibid., 476.

113. Flanders statement, *1952 Senate Authorization Hearings,* 399; Fulbright statement, ibid., 696, 581; Sparkman statement, ibid., 654; Judd statement, *1952 House Authorization Hearings,* 72, 932, 937, 996, 998; Sparkman statement, *1952 Senate Authorization Hearings,* 654, 657, 665; Fulbright statement, ibid., 659; Smith statement, ibid., 633.

114. Judd statement, *1952 House Authorization Hearings,* 1000–1001; Bolton statement, ibid., 1003; Ribicoff statement, ibid., 152; Fulton statement, ibid., 1005; Bolton statement, ibid., 1003; Judd statement, ibid., 1002; Ribicoff statement, ibid., 1001.

Chapter 5 Development Policy from Eisenhower to Kennedy

1. For an earlier draft of this chapter, see James M. Hagen and Vernon W. Ruttan, "Development Policy under Eisenhower and Kennedy," *Journal of Developing Areas* 23 (October 1988): 1–30. I am indebted to David E. Bell, Milton J. Esman, Erven J. Long, John D. Montgomery, Arthur T. Mosher, W. W. Rostow, and Martin W. Sampson for their advice and comments on an earlier draft. I also thank Donald M. Fraser, Philip M. Raup, and Barbara J. Stuhler for their participation in interviews.

2. *New York Times,* 4 June 1961, 6E.

3. Testimony of W. Averell Harriman, MSA Director, House Foreign Affairs Com-

mittee hearing, 19 March 1952 (*Congressional Quarterly Almanac* [hereafter cited as *CQA*], 1952, 163).

4. Alfred M. Guenther testimony, Senate Foreign Relations Committee hearings, 24 March 1952 (*CQA*, 1952, 165).

5. The Randall Commission called for development assistance in the sphere of private enterprise (*CQA*, 1954, 266); John Foster Dulles testimony, Joint Committee Hearing of the Senate Foreign Relations Committee and the House Foreign Affairs Committee, 5 May 1953 (*CQA*, 1953, 219).

6. Harold Stassen testimony, Senate Appropriations Committee hearings, 9 July 1953 (*CQA*, 1953, 158); *Newsweek*, 18 May 1954, 31.

7. John Taber, House debate, 27 July 1954 (*CQA*, 1954, 168); Styles Bridges, Senate debate, 14 August 1954 (*CQA*, 1954, 169); Walter George statement [*Facts on File* (New York: Facts on File, 1954), 14:280].

8. Harold Stassen testimony, House Foreign Affairs Committee hearing, 27 April 1954 (*CQA*, 1954, 276).

9. Staff Report to Senate Appropriations Committee, 6 February 1954 (*CQA*, 1954, 168).

10. *New York Times Magazine*, 26 September 1954, 13, 65–69.

11. Alexander Wiley, Senate debate, 28 July 1954 (*CQA*, 1954, 279).

12. Nikita Krushchev, *Pravda*, 22 November 1955 (quoted in Elizabeth Kridl Valkenier, *The Soviet Union and the Third World: An Economic Bind* [New York: Praeger, 1983], 4).

13. Testimony of William J. Sebald, Deputy Assistant Secretary of State for Far Eastern Affairs, Senate Foreign Relations Committee hearing, 11 May 1955; testimony of George V. Allen, Assistant Secretary of State for Near Eastern Affairs, Senate Foreign Relations Committee hearing, 12 May 1955 (*CQA*, 1955, 304); *New York Times*, 26 February 1956, sec. 4, 3.

14. John Foster Dulles in speech to Philadelphia Bulletin Forum, 28 February 1956, quoted in *Facts on File*, 1956, 66; Dwight D. Eisenhower message to Congress, 20 April 1955 (*CQA*, 1955, 303); John Foster Dulles testimony, House Foreign Affairs Committee hearing, 25 May 1955 (*CQA*, 1955, 307); Dulles testimony, Senate Foreign Relations Committee hearing, 6 May 1955 (*CQA*, 1955, 304).

15. Harold Stassen testimony, Senate Foreign Relations Committee hearing, 6 May 1955 (*CQA*, 1955, 304); John McCloy, *New York Times*, 23 May 1956, 10.

16. Senator J. William Fulbright, Foreign Relations Committee hearing, 25 February 1956 (*Facts on File*, 1956, 65); Senator Hubert Humphrey, Senate debate, 1 June 1955 (*CQA*, 1955, 306). Senator Mike Mansfield (D-Mont.) chaired a Foreign Relations Special Subcommittee directed to study technical assistance and related programs. The subcommittee staff report released March 11 warned of problems unless a "consistent concept [of the role of technical assistance] in foreign policy" were developed (*CQA*, 1955, 303).

17. Russell Long, Senate debate, 31 May 1955 (*CQA*, 1955, 306); George Malone, Senate debate, 2 June 1955 (*CQA*, 1955, 306); D. R. Matthews, House debate, 29 June 1955 (*CQA*, 1955, 308); *CQA*, 1955, 302.

18. Dwight D. Eisenhower, State of the Union Message, 5 January 1956 (*CQA,* 1956, 419); Dulles, *New York Times,* 12 January 1956, 10; Walter George, ibid., 16 January 1956, 1.

19. *Report of the President's Citizen Advisers on the Mutual Security Program* (Washington: USGPO, 1957).

20. Senate Special Committee on Foreign Aid, *Foreign Aid,* Senate Report 300, 13 May 1957 (*CQA,* 1957, 605).

21. A number of studies were commissioned by the special committee; see Special Committee to Study the Foreign Aid Program, United States Senate, *Foreign Aid Program, Compilation of Studies and Surveys* (Washington: USGPO, 1957).

22. International Development Advisory Board, *A New Emphasis on Economic Development Abroad: A Report to the President of the United States on Ways, Means, and Reasons for U.S. Assistance to International Economic Development* (Washington: USGPO, 1957).

23. Harry S. Truman, National Conference on Foreign Aspects of U.S. National Security, Washington, 25 February 1958 (*CQA,* 1958, 184).

24. Harvey S. Perloff, *Alliance for Progress: A Social Invention in the Making* (Baltimore: Johns Hopkins University Press for Resources for the Future, 1969), 207.

25. Walt W. Rostow, *Eisenhower, Kennedy, and Foreign Aid* (Austin: University of Texas Press, 1985), 141; Mason and Asher, *World Bank since Bretton Woods,* 386–87.

26. John F. Kennedy, Senate speech, 19 February 1959, quoted by Rostow, *Eisenhower, Kennedy, and Foreign Aid,* 157; Mike Mansfield, Senate Foreign Relations Committee hearing, 15 May 1959 (*CQA,* 1959, 184).

27. Report of the President's Special Committee To Study the Military Assistance Program (aka the Draper Committee), 23 July 1959 (*CQA,* 1959, 190); Charles Brown, House debate, 16 June 1960 (*CQA,* 1960, 182); C. Douglas Dillon, Senate Foreign Relations Committee hearing, 4 May 1959 (*CQA,* 1959, 183).

28. House Foreign Affairs Committee Special Study Mission to Asia, the Western Pacific, Middle East, Southern Europe, and North Africa, House Report 1386, 14 March 1960 (*CQA,* 1960, 171).

29. Richard M. Nixon letter to 20 Republican members of the House Appropriations Committee, 22 March 1960 (*CQA,* 1960, 179).

30. In his message to Congress, 16 February 1960, President Eisenhower said that the "overwhelming support of the vast majority of our citizens leads us inexorably to mutual security as a fixed national policy" (*CQA,* 1960, 168).

31. John F. Kennedy television and radio address, 25 July 1961 (quoted in *Facts on File,* 1961, 261); Kennedy in speech at Eighth National Conference on International Economic and Social Development, 16 June 1961 (quoted in *Facts on File,* 1961, 224).

32. Adlai Stevenson in his 24 July 1961 report of his 18-day Latin American tour (quoted in *Facts on File,* 1961, 275); Dean Rusk speech before the National Press Club, 10 July 1961 (quoted in *Facts on File,* 1961, 1080); Robert S. McNamara testimony at Senate Foreign Relations Committee hearing, 14 June 1961 (*CQA,* 1961, 299).

33. Che Guevara (quoted in *Facts on File,* 1961, 1985); Nikita Khrushchev (quoted in *Facts on File,* 1961, 1985); Ayub Khan address to Congress, 12 July 1961 (quoted in *Facts on File,* 1961, 255); John F. Kennedy (quoted in *Facts on File,* 1961, 1093).

34. Argued by Representative D. S. Saund (D-Calif.), House debate, 16 August 1961 (*CQA*, 1961, 306).

35. John F. Kennedy, statement to Congress, 29 August 1961 (quoted in *CQA*, 1961, 309).

36. Otto Passman interview with *Congressional Quarterly*, 2 September 1961 (quoted in *CQA*, 1961, 312).

37. Dean Rusk testimony, 31 May 1961, *International Development and Security Hearings before the Committee on Foreign Relations, US Senate, 87th Congress, First Session on S. 1983* (Washington: USGPO, 1961) (hereafter cited as *Senate Hearings*), 79, 75–76.

38. Frank M. Coffin testimony, 9 June 1961, ibid., 476; Wayne Morse, 16 June 1961, ibid., 778; Hubert H. Humphrey, 15 June 1961, ibid., 765.

39. Senator Homer E. Capehart, 14 June 1961, ibid., 631; Lloyd Neidlinger testimony, 19 June 1961, ibid., 893; Jerry Voorhis testimony, 20 June 1961, ibid., 920.

40. Hubert H. Humphrey, 14 June 1961, ibid., 767.

41. *CQA*, 1952, 165.

42. Senate debate on S. 2475, 28 July 1953: comments of Senators Andrew Schoeppel (R-Kans.), Milton Young (R-N.Dak.), Spessard Holland (D-Fla.), and Hubert Humphrey (D-Minn.) (*CQA*, 1953, 114); House Agriculture Committee testimony, 28 April 1954, by John C. Lynn, Legislative Director of the American Farm Bureau Federation. The Senate Agriculture Committee reported (S. Rept. 642) on 24 July 1953, that "farm organizations . . . evinced considerable interest" in authorization of sale or barter of surplus farm products abroad. Testimony of Reed Dunn of the National Cotton Council, in House Agriculture Committee hearing, 4 May 1954 (*CQA*, 1954, 121–22). Representative Robert K. Harrison (D-Nebr.) declared that the bill "[might] turn out to be the most important legislation ever passed in this House to expand the agricultural industry," in House debate, 15 June 1954 (quoted in *CQA*, 1954, 123).

43. Testimony of Homer L. Brinkley, National Council of Farmer Cooperatives, at Senate Agriculture Committee Hearing, 9 March 1954 (*CQA*, 1954, 121).

44. Amendment by Representative Walter Judd (R-Minn.), House floor debate, 15 June 1954; passed by voice vote (*CQA*, 1954, 123).

45. Representatives Page Belcher (R-Okla.), Thomas Abernathy (D-Miss.), and Brooks Hays (D-Ark.) in House debate, 15 June 1954 (*CQA*, 1954, 123).

46. Burton I. Kaufman, *Trade and Aid: Eisenhower's Foreign Economic Policy, 1953–1961* (Baltimore: Johns Hopkins University Press, 1982), 189–90; *PL 480 Extension: Hearings before the Committee on Agriculture and Forestry, U.S. Senate, 85th Congress, Second Session* (Washington: USGPO, 1958), 5 February 1958, 8–34 (as cited in Kaufman, *Trade and Aid*, 150).

47. W. Raymond Ogg of the AFBF urged greater emphasis on economic aid and recommended the sale abroad of $1 billion of farm surplus products, with the receipts to be used for foreign economic development, in Senate Foreign Relations Committee hearing, 23 May 1953 (cited in *CQA*, 1953, 222). In the Senate Foreign Relations Committee hearing, 22 May 1959, the AFBF called for cuts in economic aid, while the

Farmers Union recommended an expansion of technical aid (*CQA*, 1959, 165). John C. Lynn, representing the AFBF in the House Foreign Affairs hearing on 29 February 1960, said that the Mutual Security Act request should be cut from $4.2 billion to $3 billion (*CQA*, 1960, 170). Then, in House Foreign Affairs Committee hearing, 6 July 1961, Lynn stated that the AFBF was for the aid program in general but not on a long-term appropriation (House hearings, 87th Cong., 1st sess., 1961, H.R. 7372, 1418–1441).

48. Boris Shishkin, AFL, in testimony before the House Foreign Affairs Committee, 2 June 1953 (*CQA*, 1953, 220, 218).

49. George Meany testimony (*CQA*, 1956, 427).

50. *CQA*, 1959, 185; Andrew J. Biemiller testimony (*CQA*, 1959, 180).

51. Biemiller testimony, 6 July 1961, in *The International Development and Security Act: Hearings before the Committee on Foreign Affairs, House of Representatives, 87th Congress, First Session on HR 7372* (Washington: USGPO, 1961) (hereafter cited as *House Hearings*), 1410, 1408.

52. Victor Reuther testimony, ibid., 1469; Biemiller testimony, ibid, 1408; Reuther testimony, ibid., 1465.

53. House floor debate, 30 June 1954 (*CQA*, 1954, 278, 280).

54. Robert F. Loree, National Foreign Trade Council, in testimony before Senate Foreign Relations Committee, Special Subcommittee on Technical Assistance, 2 March 1955 (*CQA*, 1955, 303); Henry Ford II and James T. Duce testimony, ibid.

55. Testimony of 11 May 1956 of George J. Burger, National Federation of Independent Business, regarding a poll conducted by his organization (*CQA*, 1956, 427); J. Peter Grace testimony at 5 April 1957 hearing of Special Senate Committee To Study Foreign Aid (*CQA*, 1957, 603).

56. Gordon Canfield and Robert Griffin, House floor debate, 2 July 1958; George W. Andrews on 1 July 1958 (*CQA*, 1958, 189).

57. William C. Foster testimony, Senate Foreign Relations Committee hearing, 13 May 1959 (*CQA*, 1959, 185); J. Warren Nystrom testimony, 27 June 1961, *House Hearings*, 1182.

58. Forrest D. Murden testimony, 20 June 1961, *Senate Hearings*, 945; Emilio G. Collado testimony, 5 June 1961, *President's 1961 Tax Recommendations: Hearings before the Committee on Ways and Means, House of Representatives*, 87th Cong., 1st sess., 2674.

59. Lloyd Neidlinger testimony, 20 June 1961, *House Hearings*, 596.

60. Testimony of T. Coleman Andrews, General Bonner Fellers, and Dr. Elgin Groseclose, 21 June 1961, ibid., 735–82.

61. Walter Harnischfeger and A. G. Heinshohn testimony, 20 June 1961, *Senate Hearings*, 898–914; Robert T. Stevens testimony, ibid., 909.

62. A. C. Nielsen, Jr., testimony, 27 June 1961, *House Hearings*, 1197; Austin S. Igleheart testimony, 27 June 1961, ibid., 1203.

63. John D. Montgomery, "U.S. Advocacy of International Land Reform," in *International Dimensions of Land Reform*, ed. John D. Montgomery (Boulder: Westview Press, 1984), 119.

64. As an example, in his message to Congress on 22 March 1961, Kennedy promoted an expanded aid program "to meet the problems which confront us." Quoted in Robert D. McKinlay and Anthony Mughan, *Aid and Arms* (New York: St. Martin's, 1984), 35.

65. Barratt O'Hara comment, *House Hearings,* 1044. Dr. James H. Sheldon, representing the United Church of Christ, Council for Christian Social Action, testified that his group absolutely endorsed the long-range aid program under consideration, 26 June 1961, *House Hearings,* 1054.

66. Ian M. D. Little and Juliet M. Clifford, *International Aid: A Discussion of the Flow of Public Resources from Rich to Poor Countries* (Chicago: Aldine Publishing, 1965), 113.

67. Clifford Earle, Director of the Office of Church and Society, Board of Christian Education, United Presbyterian Church in the USA, in Foreign Affairs Committee testimony, 27 June 1961, *House Hearings,* 1187; Dr. W. G. Mather, Professor of Sociology, Pennsylvania State College, representing the American Baptist Convention in testimony before the Foreign Affairs Committee, 26 June 1986, *House Hearings,* 1061.

68. *National Voter* 10 (May 1960).

69. Barbara Stuhler testimony before the Foreign Affairs Committee, 20 June 1961, *House Hearings,* 569–77; Roberta C. Cox, member of the Washington Committee on Legislation of the National Congress of Parents and Teachers, in testimony before the Foreign Affairs Committee, 20 June 1961, *House Hearings,* 583.

70. Representative Barratt O'Hara in Foreign Affairs Committee hearing, *House Hearings,* 1148.

71. Rostow, *Eisenhower, Kennedy, and Foreign Aid,* 42.

72. Nelson Rockefeller, "Widening Boundaries of National Interest," *Foreign Affairs* 29 (July 1951): 533–38; *Measures for the Economic Development of Underdeveloped Countries,* A Report by a Group of Experts Appointed by the Secretary General of the United Nations (New York: United Nations, May 1951); David Blelloch, "Technical Assistance: Programmes and Policies," *International Affairs* 28 (January 1952): 53–58; Kennedy and Ruttan, "Reexamination of Thought on Assistance," 297–326.

73. Rockefeller, "Widening Boundaries," 524.

74. Commission on Foreign Economic Policy, *Staff Paper* (Washington: USGPO, 1954); Gunnar Myrdal, *An International Economy: Problems and Prospects* (New York: Harper & Brothers, 1956), 130; Nurkse, "Some International Aspects," 571–73; Blelloch, "Technical Assistance," 50.

75. In reporting the Economic Cooperation Act of 1948, Senator Vandenberg said, "This legislation, Mr. President, seeks peace and stability for free men in a free world. It seeks them by economic rather than by military means." See *Hearings before a Subcommittee on Government Operations, House of Representatives, 97th Congress, First Session, 6 October 1981* (Washington: USGPO), 98.

76. Max Millikan and Walt W. Rostow, *A Proposal: Key to an Effective Foreign Policy* (New York: Harper & Brothers, 1957); Howard Ellis, "A Perspective on Foreign Aid," in *The United States and the Developing Economies,* ed. Gustav Ranis

(New York: Norton, 1964), 54–62; Edward Mason, *Foreign Aid and Foreign Policy* (New York: Council on Foreign Relations, Harper & Row, 1964); John D. Montgomery, *The Politics of Foreign Aid: American Experiences in Southeast Asia* (New York: Council on Foreign Relations, Praeger, 1962), 207.

77. Milton Friedman, "Foreign Economic Aid: Means and Objectives," in Ranis, *United States and Developing Economies,* 24–38.

78. George Liska, *The New Statecraft: Foreign Aid in American Foreign Policy* (Chicago: University of Chicago Press, 1960), 65; Charles Wolf, Jr., *Foreign Aid: Theory and Practice in Southern Asia* (Princeton: Princeton University Press, 1960); Banfield, "American Foreign Aid Doctrine," 10–13.

79. Howard Wiggins, "Foreign Assistance and Political Development," in *Development of the Emerging Countries: An Agenda for Research* (Washington: Brookings Institution, 1962), 208–9; Bert F. Hoselitz and Myron Weiner, "Economic Development and Political Stability," *Dissent* 8 (Spring 1961): 172–84.

80. Our research has led us to conclude that a security concern was the dominant force motivating the call for economic development assistance in the years leading up to and including 1961. W. W. Rostow and John D. Montgomery, who were both notable participants in the foreign aid debate at that time, disagree with this conclusion. They both have recollections that would put substantially less emphasis on this security concern.

81. Nurkse, "Some International Aspects," 583.

82. Blelloch, "Technical Assistance," 56; John Adler, "The Fiscal and Monetary Implementation of Development Programs," *American Economic Review* 42 (1952, supplement): 571–73; Hollis Chenery, "Comparative Advantage and Development Policy," in *Readings in Economic Development,* ed. T. Morgan, G. Betz, and N. Choudhry (Belmont, Calif.: Wadsworth Publishing, 1963), 178.

83. *Measures for the Economic Development of Under-developed Countries,* A Report by a Group of Experts Appointed by the Secretary General of the United Nations (New York: United Nations, May 1951); International Development Advisory Board, *Partners for Progress: A Report to the President* (Washington: USGPO, 1951).

84. Hans Singer, "Comments," *American Economic Review* 42 (1952, supplement): 608; Mason and Asher, *World Bank since Bretton Woods,* 711.

85. Theodore W. Schultz, *The Economic Test in Latin America,* Bulletin 35, New York State School of Industrial and Labor Relations (Ithaca: Cornell University, August 1956), 16; Theodore W. Schultz, *Transforming Traditional Agriculture* (New Haven: Yale University Press, 1964), 70, 5.

86. Paul Rosenstein-Rodan, "Problems of Industrialization of Eastern and South-Eastern Europe," *Economic Journal* 53 (June/September 1943): 205; Raul Prebisch, *The Economic Development of Latin America and Its Principal Problems* (Lake Success, N.Y.: UN Publications, 1950). This is an essay prepared for the United Nations Economic Commission for Latin America.

87. Raymond F. Mikesell, *The Economics of Foreign Aid* (Chicago: Aldine Publishing, 1968), 57.

88. Walt W. Rostow, *The Stages of Economic Growth* (Cambridge: Cambridge University Press, 1960).

89. Mikesell, *Economics of Foreign Aid,* 39. Also Simon Kuznets, "Notes on the Take-off," in *The Economics of the Take-off into Sustained Growth,* ed. Walt W. Rostow (London: Macmillan, 1964), 22–43.

90. Albert Hirschman, *The Strategy of Economic Development* (New Haven: Yale University Press, 1958); Walter Galenson and Harvey Leibenstein, "Investment Criteria, Productivity, and Economic Development," *Quarterly Journal of Economics* 69 (August 1955): 343–70.

91. John P. Lewis, *Quiet Crisis in India* (Washington: Brookings Institution, 1962), 56; John K. Galbraith, "A Positive Approach to Economic Aid," *Foreign Affairs* 39 (April 1961): 444–57.

92. Raul Prebisch, "Joint Responsibilities for Latin American Progress," *Foreign Affairs* 39 (July 1961): 622, 627; Paul Hoffman, "Operation Breakthrough," *Foreign Affairs* 38 (October 1959): 37, 34.

Chapter 6 The Basic Human Needs Mandate

1. For an earlier draft of this chapter, see Rolf H. Sartorius and Vernon W. Ruttan, "Human Needs Mandate," *Journal of Developing Areas,* 23 (April 1989): 332–62. The author is indebted to Michael Barnett, George Ingram, Martin M. McLaughlin, John D. Montgomery, W. W. Rostow, Martin W. Sampson, Rolf E. Sartorius, Stephen G. Walker, and Maurice J. Williams for comments on earlier drafts. I also express my appreciation to Marian Czarnecke, Donald Fraser, James Grant, John Hannah, John H. Sullivan, and Maurice J. Williams for their courtesy in granting interviews on the topics covered in this chapter.

2. Before 1973 the Foreign Assistance Act comprised the following budget categories: development loans, technical assistance, Alliance for Progress, loans and grants, and population. See "Foreign Assistance Act of 1971," *United States Statutes at Large: 1972* (Washington: USGPO, 1972), 86:20. For the original text of the act, see "Foreign Assistance Act of 1961," *United States Statutes at Large: 1961* (Washington: USGPO, 1961), 85:424.

3. For a very useful analysis, see Ellen Ziskind Berg, "The 1973 Legislative Reorientation of the United States Foreign Assistance Policy: The Content and Context of a Change" (M.A. thesis, George Washington University, 1976).

4. See John Lewis Gaddis, *Strategies of Containment: A Critical Appraisal of Postwar American National Security Policy* (New York: Oxford University Press, 1982), chap. 7. Gaddis cites W. W. Rostow's 284-page draft statement of "Basic National Security Policy" as being an important guide to the administration's strategic designs (p. 200). Gaddis also cites Paul A. Samuelson and Walter Heller as being two top economic advisers to Kennedy who advocated that the economy could sustain, or even benefit from, increases in spending for both national defense and domestic economic reform (p. 204). Ibid., 215.

5. Walt W. Rostow, "On Ending the Cold War," *Foreign Affairs* 65 (Spring 1987): 836.

6. Congressional Research Service (CRS), "The New Directions Mandate and the

Agency for International Development," in *AID's Administrative and Management Problems in Providing Foreign Economic Assistance*, Hearing before a Subcommittee of the Committee of Government Operations, House of Representatives, 97th Cong., 1st sess., 6 October 1981 (Washington: USGPO, 1981), 95. See also chapter 5.

7. Report of the President's Advisory Committee on Foreign Assistance Programs, *Development Assistance in the New Administration* (Washington: USGPO, October 1968), 81.

8. CRS, *The Reorganization of U.S. Development Aid: A Comparison and Summary of Some Official and Unofficial Proposals*, a report prepared for the House Committee on Foreign Affairs (Washington: USGPO, May 1973), 2.

9. For varying perspectives on the meaning of the Nixon foreign policy, see Robert E. Osgood, ed., *Retreat from Empire? The First Nixon Administration* (Baltimore: Johns Hopkins University Press, 1973). For Kissinger's own perspective, see *Diplomacy*, 674–761.

10. Rostow, "Ending the Cold War," 836.

11. Leslie Gelb, "What Exactly Is Kissinger's Legacy?" *New York Times Magazine,* 31 October 1976; Simon Serfaty, "Brzenzinske: Play It Again Zbig," *Foreign Policy* 32 (Fall 1978): 3–21; both cited in Charles W. Kegley and Eugene R. Wittkopf, *American Foreign Policy: Pattern and Process* (New York: St. Martin's, 1979), 65.

12. Gaddis, *Strategies of Containment,* 274–308.

13. Richard M. Nixon, "U.S. Foreign Policy for the 1970's, a New Strategy for Peace," Presidential Report to Congress, 18 February 1970, reprinted in *Public Papers of the Presidents of the United States: Richard Nixon, 1970* (Washington: USGPO, 1971), 116–90.

14. Nelson A. Rockefeller, *The Rockefeller Report on the Americas: The Official Report of a U.S. Presidential Mission for the Western Hemisphere,* New York Times edition (Chicago: Quadrangle Books, 1969).

15. CRS, *United States Foreign Policy for the 1970's: A Comparison of the President's 1970 and 1971 Foreign Policy Reports to Congress* (Washington: USGPO, 1971), 745–46.

16. Ibid.

17. See statement by Senator Javits (R-N.Y.), *A Foreign Economic Policy for the 1970s,* Hearings before the Subcommittee on Foreign Economic Policy of the Joint Economic Committee, 91st Cong., 1st sess. (Washington: USGPO, 1970), 503.

18. The Task Force on International Development, "U.S. Foreign Assistance in the 1970s: A New Approach," Report to the President from the Task Force on International Development (March 1970), reprinted in *Foreign Economic Policy for the 1970s,* 460–502.

19. Richard M. Nixon, "Special Message to Congress Proposing Reform of the Foreign Assistance Program," 15 September 1970, reprinted in *Public Papers of the Presidents of the United States: Richard Nixon, 1970* (Washington: USGPO, 1971), 745–46.

20. CRS, *1970 and 1971 Foreign Policy Reports,* 18; Robert A. Pastor, *Congress and the Politics of U.S. Foreign Economic Policy* (Berkeley: University of California Press, 1980), 278; CRS, *Reorganization of U.S. Development Aid,* 27.

21. Pastor, *Congress and the Politics,* 277–78.

22. CRS, *U.S. Foreign Policy for the 1970s: An Analysis of the President's 1972 Foreign Policy Report to Congress* (Washington: USGPO, 1972), 1; CRS, *U.S. Foreign Policy for the 1970s: An Analysis of the President's 1973 Foreign Policy Report to Congress* (Washington: USGPO, 1973), 1 and 79.

23. CRS, *President's 1973 Foreign Policy Report,* 79.

24. John A. Hannah, "Memorandum for AID Employees," dated 24 January 1972 with attachment attributed to Maurice J. Williams entitled, "Reform of the U.S. Economic Assistance Program."

25. The CRS notes that, before 1973, US/AID's Latin American Bureau had been shifting away from large infrastructure projects to ones that focused more on agriculture, education, and health. Marian Czarnecke, former Chief of Staff for the Foreign Affairs Committee, supported this view in the interview of 3 November 1987, as do the papers of Berg and James P. Grant (see notes 27 and 33). In Grant's 1973 interview with Czarnecke, Czarnecke recalled that the House had toyed with the functional budget idea as early as 1971.

26. US/AID, unpublished report commonly referred to as the Stern report, transmitted to US/AID administrator on 13 December 1971 and signed by Ernest Stern, Philip Birnbaum, and Thomas Arndt.

27. Berg, "The 1973 Legislative Reorientation of the United States Foreign Assistance Policy: The Content and Context of a Change" (M.A. thesis, George Washington University, 1976), 164, 170.

28. Congressman Donald Fraser (D-Minn.) interview, 9 June 1987; Maurice J. Williams interview, 2 November 1987; Marian Czarnecke interview, 3 November 1987.

29. Williams interview, 2 November 1987.

30. Ibid. Williams noted that he served as a deputy to Hannah to run the agency and to keep him informed and that Hannah handled the sensitive relationships among the secretary of state, the president, and Congress. See also CRS, "New Directions Mandate," 117.

31. CRS, "New Directions Mandate," 232; Maurice J. Williams, "Reform of the U.S. Economic Assistance Program," US/AID, 4 January 1972 (mimeographed).

32. Statement by Maurice J. Williams, Deputy Administrator of US/AID, *Foreign Assistance Act of 1972,* Hearings before the House Committee on Foreign Affairs (Washington: USGPO, 1972), 104.

33. James P. Grant, "An Analysis of the Congressional Foreign Aid Initiative of 1973" (B.A. thesis, Harvard University, 1975), 7; CRS, "New Directions Mandate," 232–33. The CRS cites Policy Determination #48, "Employment and Income Distribution Objectives for AID Programs and Policies," US/AID, Policy Background Paper, 2 October 1972.

34. CRS, "New Directions Mandate," 117. In December 1972, a second US/AID task force reported to Hannah. See "Proposed U.S. International Development Assistance Program for the President's Second Term," an internal report of the task force headed by Sidney Brown. Berg notes that this report strengthened the recommendation for the functional budget categories. Also see Berg, "1973 Legislative Reorientation," 165.

35. CRS, "New Directions Mandate," 117. James P. Grant maintains that the bill stepped on too many bureaucratic toes and threatened to remove strategic oversight from the State Department. Berg maintains that the bill was particularly disliked by the National Security Council (NSC) because it separated military and economic assistance.

36. James P. Grant, citing a 1973 interview with James Frey, who was chief of the International Programs Division of OMB.

37. The Overseas Development Council, founded in 1969, is a privately funded organization concerned with the promotion of foreign aid and development. James P. Grant, formerly assistant administrator of US/AID, was president of the ODC during 1969–73. Pastor, *Congress and the Politics,* 279. Although the Pastor account is consistent with the perception of several former US/AID and ODC staff members, it has been disputed by some other participants.** A former staff member of the House Foreign Affairs Committee and several former US/AID staff members have insisted, in interviews, that both the agency and the council played peripheral rather than central roles in the thinking that went into the 1973 legislation and in the effort that secured its passage.

38. CRS, "New Directions Mandate," 233.

39. Cited in Ralph Braibanti, "External Inducement of Political and Administrative Development," in *Political and Administrative Development,* ed. Ralph Braibanti (Durham: Duke University Press, 1969), 11.

40. CRS, "New Directions Mandate," 99.

41. Cited in Braibanti, "External Inducement," 10. See also U.S. Congress, House of Representatives, *Foreign Assistance Act of 1962,* 87th Cong., 2d sess., H. Rept. 1788 (Washington: USGPO, 1962).

42. CRS, "New Directions Mandate," 99.

43. Braibanti, "External Inducement," 13, notes that Fraser is generally accepted as the initiator of Title IX both in Congress and in US/AID; Braibanti, "External Inducement," 15.

44. Marian Czarnecke interview, 3 November 1987; see statements by Donald M. Fraser, *Congressional Record,* 13 July 1966, 15444–15449, and by Bradford Morse, *Congressional Record,* 15 March 1966, 5852–5856.

45. Fraser interview, 9 June 1987; Braibanti, "External Inducement," 15.

46. Braibanti, "External Inducement," 13.

47. Ibid., 15–21; CRS, "New Directions Mandate," 103, 102, which cites Section 207 of the 1967 FAA.

48. CRS, "New Directions Mandate," 104.

49. Ibid., 103, which is citing Section 207 of the 1967 FAA.

50. Review of Title X by Secretary of State Elliot Richardson, *Foreign Assistance Act of 1969,* Hearings before the House Committee on Foreign Affairs (Washington: USGPO, 1969), 113.

51. CRS, "New Directions Mandate," 104; Pastor, *Congress and the Politics,* 278; William Watts and Lloyd A. Free, *State of the Nation* (Lexington, Mass.: Lexington Books, 1973), 129–37, 215.

52. Pastor, *Congress and the Politics,* 278.

53. Watts and Free, *State of the Nation,* 216.

54. Grant, "Congressional Foreign Aid Initiative," 9; CRS, "New Directions Mandate," 117, 133–40.

55. CRS, "New Directions Mandate," 128.

56. Grant, "Congressional Foreign Aid Initiative," 10; CRS, "New Directions Mandate," 232; Berg, "1973 Legislative Reorientation," chap. 5.

57. CRS, "New Directions Mandate," 133.

58. Lars Schoultz, *Human Rights and United States Policy toward Latin America* (Princeton: Princeton University Press, 1981), 194–95.

59. Ibid., 141–42, 151, 153. James P. Grant notes that Senators George Aiken (R-Vt.) and Hubert Humphrey (D-Minn.) built a base of support for the bill in the Senate. Senators J. W. Fulbright (D-Ark.), Mike Mansfield (D-Mont.), and Frank Church (D-Idaho) opposed the mandate.

60. Martin W. Sampson, "Witness for Issue Change" (Paper delivered at the 1982 Midwest Meeting of the International Studies Association, St. Louis, 13 November 1982).

61. Charles Whalen, *The House and Foreign Policy* (Chapel Hill: University of North Carolina Press, 1982), 26.

62. Krueger, Michalopoulos, and Ruttan, *Aid and Development*, 13–31; Hollis B. Chenery and Alan M. Strout, "Foreign Assistance and Economic Development," *American Economic Review* 56 (September 1966): 679–733; Yujiro Hayami and V. W. Ruttan, *Agricultural Development: An International Perspective* (Baltimore: Johns Hopkins University Press, 1985), 22–33; Theodore W. Schultz, *Transforming Traditional Agriculture* (New Haven: Yale University Press, 1964); idem, *Investment in Human Capital* (New York: Free Press, 1971).

63. Vernon W. Ruttan, "Cultural Endowments and Economic Development: What Can We Learn from Anthropology?" *Economic Development and Cultural Change* 36 (April 1988): 5247–71; idem, "What Happened to Political Development?" *Economic Development and Cultural Change* 39 (January 1991): 265–92; idem, "The Sociology of Development and Underdevelopment: Are There Lessons for Economists?" *International Journal of Sociology of Agriculture and Food* 2 (1992): 17–38.

64. See Daniel Lerner, *The Passing of Traditional Society* (Glencoe, Ill.: Free Press, 1962); David McClelland, *The Achieving Society* (Princeton, N.J.: Von Nostrand, 1962); Berthold F. Hoselitz et al., *Theories of Economic Growth* (Glencoe, Ill.: Free Press, 1960); David Apter, *The Politics of Modernization* (Chicago: University of Chicago Press, 1965).

65. See Gabriel A. Almond and James Coleman, eds., *The Politics of Developing Areas* (Princeton: Princeton University Press, 1960); Gabriel A. Almond, *Comparative Politics: A Developmental Approach* (Boston: Little, Brown, 1966); Samuel Huntington, "Political Development and Political Decay," *World Politics* 17 (April 1965): 415; idem, *Political Order in Changing Societies* (New Haven: Yale University Press, 1968).

66. John D. Montgomery, "The Populist Front in Rural Development: Or Shall We

Eliminate the Bureaucrats and Get On with the Job?" *Public Administration Review* 39 (January/February 1979): 58–66; Vernon W. Ruttan, "What Happened to Political Development?" *Economic Development and Cultural Change* 39 (January 1991): 265–92. For a polemical attack on the Cold War liberal academics, see Noam Chomsky, *American Power and the New Mandarins* (New York: Random House, 1967): 23–158.

67. Lester B. Pearson, *Partners in Development: Report of the Commission on Economic Development* (New York: Praeger, 1969); Rostow, *Eisenhower, Kennedy, and Foreign Aid*, 180. A key reaction against the Pearson report was Barbara Ward, ed., *The Widening Gap: Development in the 1970s* (New York: Columbia University Press, 1971).

68. See Teresa Hayter, *Aid as Imperialism* (Baltimore: Penguin, 1971); Samir Amin, "Development and Structural Change: African Experience," in Ward, *The Widening Gap*, 312–33; Susanne Bodenheimer, "Dependency and Imperialism," in K. T. Fann and Donald Hodges, eds., *Readings in U.S. Imperialism* (Boston: Peter Sargent, 1971); Denis Goulet and Michael Hudson, *The Myth of Foreign Aid: The Hidden Agenda of the Development Reports* (New York: International Documentation North America, 1971).

69. See P. T. Bauer, *Dissent on Development* (Cambridge: Harvard University Press, 1971). Bauer's article, "The Case against Foreign Aid," *Wall Street Journal* 3 October 1972, was inserted in the *Congressional Record* by Senator J. W. Fulbright (D-Ark.) during Senate hearings on 2 October 1973 (S. 18392–18393).

70. Bauer, "Case Against Foreign Aid."

71. See, for example, Joseph Spengler, "The Economist and the Population Question" (1965 Presidential Address to the American Economics Association), *American Economic Review* 56 (March 1966): 1–24; idem, *Population Change, Modernization and Welfare* (Englewood Cliffs, N.J.: Prentice Hall, 1974); Jay Forrester, *World Dynamics* (Cambridge, Mass.: Wright-Allen, 1971); Donella H. Meadows and Dennis L. Meadows, with Jorgen Rovders and William W. Behrens III, *The Limits to Growth* (New York: Universe Books, 1972); Robert Heilbroner, "Growth and Survival," *Foreign Affairs* (1972): 139.

72. See William Paddock and Paul Paddock, *Hungry Nations* (Boston: Little, Brown, 1964); idem, *Famine 1975!* (Boston: Little, Brown, 1967); William Paddock and Elizabeth Paddock, *We Don't Know How* (Ames: Iowa State University Press, 1973); Anne and Paul R. Ehrlich, *Population, Resources, Environment—Issues in Human Ecology* (San Francisco: Freeman, 1970); Paul R. Ehrlich and Richard Harriman, *How To Be a Survivor* (London: Pan/Ballantine, 1971); Paul R. Ehrlich, *The Population Bomb* (London: Pan, 1971).

73. Krueger, Michalopoulos, and Ruttan, *Aid and Development;* Keith Griffin and John L. Enos, "Foreign Assistance: Objectives and Consequences," *Economic Development and Cultural Change* 18 (April 1970): 313–27; Keith Griffin, *The Political Economy of Agrarian Change* (Cambridge: Harvard University Press, 1974); Ernst F. Schumacher, *Small Is Beautiful—A Study of Economics as If People Mattered* (London: Blond & Briggs, 1973).

74. Douglas Rimmer, "'Basic Needs' and the Origins of the Development Ethos," *Journal of Developing Areas* 15 (January 1981): 215–38.

75. International Labor Office, *Poverty and Landlessness in Rural Asia* (Geneva: ILO, 1977), vi. See, for example, Employment Missions to Columbia, *Towards Full Employment* (Geneva: ILO, 1970), and International Labor Office, Kenya, *Employment, Incomes, and Equality* (Geneva: ILO, 1972).

76. David Turnham, *The Employment Problem in Less Developed Countries: A Review of the Evidence* (Paris: Development Center of the OECD, 1971).

77. See, for example, Committee for Development Planning, *Attack on Mass Poverty and Unemployment* (New York: United Nations, 1972); U.N. Secretary-General, *First Biennial Review of the International Development Strategy* (New York: United Nations, 1973).

78. Robert McNamara, "Address to the Board of Governors" (Washington: World Bank, September 1973); Pastor, *Congress and the Politics,* 278, notes that McNamara first discussed the need for a new approach in a speech in 1972.

79. CRS, *Reorganization of U.S. Development Aid.* These studies were Committee for Economic Development, *Assisting Development in Low-Income Countries: Priorities for U.S. Government Policy* (New York: CED, 1969); Robert Asher, *Development Assistance in the Seventies: Alternatives for the United States* (Washington: Brookings Institution, 1970); Samuel Huntington, "Foreign Aid: For What and for Whom," *Foreign Policy* 1 (Winter 1970–71); Lester Brown, *World without Borders* (New York: Random House, 1972); Robert E. Hunter and John E. Rielly, eds., *Development Today* (New York: Praeger, 1972); Harald B. Malmgren, "Trade and Development," in Hunter and Rielly, *Development Today*; Edgar Owens and Robert Shaw, *Development Reconsidered* (Washington: Heath, 1972); Kenneth Thompson, *Foreign Assistance: A View from the Private Sector* (Notre Dame: University of Notre Dame Press, 1972). An important work on participation not cited in the CRS summary study was Max Millikan et al., *The Role of Popular Participation in Economic Development,* MIT Report 17 (Cambridge: MIT Press, 1969).

80. CRS, *Reorganization of U.S. Development Aid,* 36–38.

81. See, for example, Irma Adelman and Cynthia Taft Morris, *Economic Growth and Social Equity in Developing Countries* (Stanford: Stanford University Press, 1973); Albert Fishlow, "Brazilian Size Distribution of Income," *American Economic Review* 62 (May 1972): 391–402; Hollis B. Chenery, M. S. Ahluwalia, C. L. G. Bell, J. H. Duloy, and Richard Jolly, *Redistribution with Growth* (London: Oxford University Press, 1974); and the various ILO studies (cited in note 75).

82. Adelman and Morris, *Economic Growth and Social Equity,* 1–2.

83. Edgar Owens and Robert Shaw, *Development Reconsidered: Bridging the Gap between Government and People* (Washington: Heath, 1972). The ideas contained in the study, however, were certainly not new. The participatory strategy and the terminology "bridging the gap between government and people" had been elaborated by Millikan in 1961. See Max Millikan, ed., *Emerging Nations: Their Growth and United States Policy* (Boston: Little, Brown, 1961), 62.

84. Owens and Shaw, *Development Reconsidered,* iv; Fraser interview, 9 June 1987.

85. James P. Grant interview, 16 October 1987. See also James P. Grant, *Growth from Below: A People Oriented Development Strategy,* Development Paper 16 (Wash-

ington: ODC, 1973); James P. Grant and Susan Sammartano, *Growth with Justice: A New Partnership?* Communique on Development Issues, No. 18 (Washington: ODC, 1973); Robert E. Hunter, *The United States and the Developing World: Agenda for Action* (Washington: ODC, 1973); Paul A. Laudicina, *World Poverty and Development: A Survey of American Opinion,* Monograph 8 (Washington: ODC, 1973); and Barbara Ward, *A "People" Strategy of Development,* Communique on Development Issues, No. 23 (Washington: ODC, 1973).

86. Grant interview, 16 October 1987. Grant noted that Owens had been talking about many of these ideas earlier but had been unable to publish. He said that Shaw was a "bright young graduate student" who was assigned to the project to get the book out.

87. In the foreword of the third printing, Congressman Fraser writes that *Development Reconsidered* formed the "intellectual backdrop" to New Directions. Fraser had commented favorably on the manuscript as early as 1966. See speech by Donald Fraser, *Congressional Record,* 13 July 1966, 15444–50.

88. George C. Herring, *America's Longest War: The United States and Vietnam* (New York: John Wiley, 1979), 123, 172; Fraser interview, 9 June 1987.

89. Fraser interview, 9 June 1987, 146, 192–95.

90. Kegley and Wittkopf, *American Foreign Policy,* 144–46. See also John Spanier, *Games Nations Play,* 2d ed. (New York: Praeger, 1975).

91. Kegley and Wittkopf, *American Foreign Policy,* 146.

92. C. Fred Bergsten, "The Threat from the Third World," *Foreign Policy* 11 (Summer 1973): 102–24. See also idem, "The Threat Is Real," *Foreign Policy* 14 (Spring 1974): 84–90. Similar views were aired in Congress. See, for example, *National Security Policy and the Changing World Power Alignment,* House Hearing before the Subcommittee on National Security Policy and Scientific Developments (Washington: USGPO, 1972).

93. Bergsten, "Threat from the Third World," 102–24.

94. See, for example, Gabriel Almond, *The American People and Foreign Policy* (New York: Praeger, 1960); Bernard C. Cohen, *The Public's Impact on Foreign Policy* (Boston: Little, Brown, 1973); and Ralph B. Levering, *The Public and American Foreign Policy* (New York: Morrow, 1978).

95. Alfred O. Hero, "American Public Reactions to Non-Military Foreign Aid," an undated paper (late 1960s) prepared for the Brookings Institution, cited in Frank Ballance, "State of the Aid Mandate in the U.S. and Canada," a paper prepared for the Overseas Development Council (June 1984), 24; John E. Reilly, *American Public Opinion and U.S. Foreign Policy* (Chicago: Chicago Council on Foreign Relations, 1979), cited in Ballance, "State of the Aid Mandate," 20; American Institute of Public Opinion, Public Opinion News Service (March 1966), cited in Michael K. O'Leary, *Politics of American Foreign Aid* (New York: Atherton Press, 1967), 60.

96. Laudicina, *World Poverty and Development.* For a summary of this study, see John W. Sewell and Charles Paolillo, "Public Opinion and Government Policy," in *The U.S. and the Developing World: Agenda for Action 1974,* ed. James W. Howe (New York: Praeger, 1974), 124–39.

97. Christine E. Contee, *What Americans Think: Views on Development and U.S.–Third World Relations* (Washington: InterAction and ODC, 1987), 24.

98. See William Watts and Lloyd A. Free, "Nationalism, Not Isolationism," *Foreign Policy* 24 (Fall 1976): 3–21. In contrast to the internationalists who favored both hard-line and accommodationist attitudes, isolationists continued to oppose American intervention overseas. Kegley and Wittkopf, *American Foreign Policy,* 275.

99. Statement by Senator William Fulbright (D-Ark.), *Foreign Economic Assistance Act, 1973,* Hearings before the Senate Committee on Foreign Relations, 93d Cong., 1st sess. (Washington: USGPO, 1973), 1.

100. See Norman J. Ornstein, "Interest Groups, Congress, and Foreign Policy," in *American Foreign Policy in an Uncertain World,* ed. David Forsythe (Lincoln: University of Nebraska Press, 1984), 49–64.

101. Grant, "Congressional Foreign Aid Initiative," 14; Berg, "1973 Legislative Reorientation," 167; CRS, "New Directions Mandate," 118; Grant interview, 16 October 1987.

102. CRS, "New Directions Mandate," 118; Grant interview, 16 October 1987. Grant noted that Paolillo worked on the initiative full-time during the entire legislative process and that the ODC wrote the testimony of seven or eight different witnesses, including that of David Rockefeller and Tony T. Dechant. In the interview of 3 November 1987, Marian Czarnecke noted that he was responsible for the testimony of Lucy Wilson Benson and other witnesses.

103. Orville Freeman, testimony, in U.S. Congress, House Committee on Foreign Affairs, *Mutual Development and Cooperation Act of 1973,* Hearings, 93d Cong., 1st sess., on H.R. 7484, H.R. 8297, 12 June 1973 (Washington: USGPO, 1973), 421 (hereafter cited as *MDCA 1973 Hearings*).

104. Edward Mason, testimony, ibid., 457. Mason also noted that the "most novel" aspect of the bill resembled certain proposals put forward by the Peterson commission in 1970.

105. These representatives included John Eckland, President, Agriculture Cooperative Development International; Wallace Campbell, International Housing Cooperative Program; D. Ali Felder, Cooperative League of the U.S.A.; James Walker, National Credit Union Association; and Leon Evans, National Rural Electric Cooperative Association.

106. Tony T. Dechant, testimony, *MDCA 1973 Hearings*, 465.

107. James P. Grant, testimony, ibid., 473; CRS, "New Directions Mandate," 113.

108. Grant testimony, *MDCA 1973 Hearings*, 484, 473.

109. Edward E. Hood, letter, ibid., 495; Leonard Woodcock, letter, ibid., 654.

110. David Rockefeller, letter, ibid., 496.

111. Edgar Owens, statement, ibid., 497; James MacCracken, testimony, ibid., 517. MacCracken was accompanied by Bishop Swanstrom, Executive Director, Catholic Relief Services; Bernard Confer, Executive Secretary, Lutheran World Relief; Gottlieb Hammer, Executive Vice Chairman, United Israel Appeal; Melvin Frarey, Program Director, Community Development Foundation; Leon Marion, Executive Director, American Council of Voluntary Agencies for Foreign Service; Teymuraz Bagration,

Executive Secretary, Tolstoy Foundation; Gaynor Jacobson, Executive Director, United HIAS; and Samuel Haber, Executive Vice President, American Jewish Joint Distribution Committee.

112. Lucy Benson Wilson, letter, ibid., 647.

113. William Paddock, testimony, ibid., 370.

114. See CRS, "New Directions Mandate," pt. 4, p. 251.

115. Schoultz, *Human Rights,* 371–72.

Chapter 7 Lost Directions: U.S. Foreign Assistance Policy since New Directions

1. For an earlier draft of this chapter, see Mark McGuire and Vernon W. Ruttan, "Lost Directions: U.S. Foreign Assistance Policy since New Directions," *Journal of Developing Areas* (January 1990): 127–80. The author is indebted to John H. Sullivan, Robert Berg, Richard Blue, Carol Lancaster, Larry Q. Nowels, Caleb Rossiter, and Keith Jay for interviews on issues covered and comments on earlier drafts of this chapter.

2. For discussions of the US/AID budget process, see George M. Guess, *The Politics of United States Foreign Aid* (New York: St. Martin's, 1987), 95–108, and Caleb Rossiter, *The Bureaucratic Struggle for Control of U.S. Foreign Aid* (Boulder: Westview Press, 1985), 120–28. See also U.S. General Accounting Office, *Political and Economic Factors Influencing ESF Programs* (Washington: GAO, 1993).

3. In the absence of an authorization bill, the budget falls under a continuing resolution or an omnibus budget package. This means, in the absence of authorization bills, that a large portion of policy-related legislation falls to the appropriations process. See Representative David R. Obey and Carol Lancaster, "Funding Foreign Aid," *Foreign Policy,* 71 (Summer 1988): 147. In one interview, a Senate staffer pointed out that the Foreign Relations Committee, owing to a weak leadership, has been steadily declining in importance. This factor contributed greatly to the difficulty in passing authorization legislation beginning in the early 1980s.

4. U.S. Congress, House Committee on Foreign Affairs, *Congress and Foreign Policy—1984,* reproduced by the Library of Congress, Congressional Research Service, 15 January 1987 (Washington: USGPO, 1985), 81.

5. William Schneider came to the State Department from OMB, where he had been associate director for national security and international affairs. Before that, he had been a staff associate for the Defense Subcommittee of the U.S. House Appropriations Committee.

6. Larry Q. Nowels, Congressional Research Service, interview, 24 March 1989. Clarence D. Long was chairman of the House Appropriations Foreign Operations Subcommittee, in which Jack Kemp was the ranking minority member, and Robert Kasten was chairman of the Senate Appropriations Foreign Operations Subcommittee, in which Daniel Inouye was the ranking minority member.

7. Ibid. Long was often criticized for his inability to write an aid bill that could get through Congress. See *Congressional Quarterly*, 19 December 1981, 2492. In an interview,

Caleb Rossiter of the Arms Control and Foreign Policy Caucus, 23 March 1989, commented that Reagan "rolled" the House leadership on the tax cut issue in 1981 and that, from then on, the House was apprehensive about questioning administrative initiatives.

8. Ted Weihe, "Congressional Strategies for Development Cooperation Initiatives" (unpublished manuscript, U.S. Overseas Cooperative Development Committee, 1987). The continuing resolution permitted unpopular foreign assistance provisions (e.g., funding of the MDBs) to be added to the bill in the Senate, where they were most likely to be supported.

9. "Foreign Aid Panel Urges Special Effort for Poor," *New York Times,* 13 October 1977, 11. See also *Congressional Quarterly*, 11 June 1977, 1177.

10. Graham Hovey, "Single Agency Planned for Managing Foreign Aid," *New York Times*, 16 February 1979, A5.

11. John H. Sullivan, interview, 7 February 1989. In retrospect, it is clear that IDCA was stillborn because no influential advocate appeared after the death of Hubert Humphrey. Ed Feulner of the Heritage Foundation, head of the Reagan transition team, believed that IDCA should be abolished, calling it a "useless bureaucratic appendage." Feulner, "Foreign Aid: Debating the Uses and Abuses," *New York Times,* E5. Carol Lancaster argued that Henry Owen never really cared for IDCA and that he saw it as a way to get ISTC through Congress.

12. Military training funds were banned for Argentina, Uruguay, and Ethiopia, and all types of assistance were banned for Angola, Cambodia, and Laos. However, although the Philippines, Iran, and Panama were cited for human rights violations, aid was not cut to them. See *Congressional Quarterly*, 14 July 1979, 1402. Daniel Patrick Moynihan (D-N.Y.) commented in 1978 that the United States was part of a "worldwide ideological struggle" with the Soviet Union and that, by concentrating on North-South rather than East-West issues, the United States had lost all of the initiatives it had gained from the detente of the early 1970s. See Richard Burt, "Criticisms Ahead for Carter on Shifts in Rights Policy," *New York Times*, 10 February 1987, 14; Clyde H. Farnsworth, "Aid to Poor Countries: Even Service Gets Softer," *New York Times*, 5 October 1980, sec. 4, p. 3.

13. Cited in American Foreign Policy Council, *Modernizing Foreign Assistance: Resource Management as an Instrument of Foreign Policy* (Westport, Conn.: Praeger, 1992), 21.

14. Jimmy Carter, "State of the Union Address" (Washington: White House, January 1980).

15. Kenneth A. Oye, "The Domain of Choice," in *Eagle Entangled,* ed. Kenneth A. Oye, Donald Rothchild, and Robert J. Lieber (New York: Longman, 1979), 25.

16. Robert Berg, President, International Development Council, interview, 30 March 1989. Berg was director of evaluation in the Bureau for Program and Policy Coordination at US/AID during the Carter years and throughout the transition.

17. "Foreign Aid: Debating the Uses and Abuses," *New York Times*, 1 March 1981, E5. The article reports an interesting discussion among Hollis Chenery, Alan Cranston, and Edward Feulner on assistance to needy nations.

18. This view was supported by many in the administration. One of the more vocal

was David Stockman, director of OMB. The OMB Budget Working Group initiated sessions entitled "Foreign Aid Retrenchment," which called for drastic reductions in the foreign assistance budget and urged that the U.S. should "not support aid programs that do not offer direct political and security benefits for the U.S." See Juan de Onis, "Haig Fights Proposal for Drastic Reduction in Foreign Assistance," *New York Times,* 29 January 1981, 9.

19. Aron Raymond, "Ideology in Search of a Policy," *Foreign Affairs: America and the World* 60, no. 3 (1981): 504; Andrew Knight, "Ronald Reagan's Watershed Year?" *Foreign Affairs* 61, no. 3 (1982): 512. The first term of the Reagan administration was distinguished by the largest peacetime military buildup in the nation's history.

20. John Sewell, Richard E. Feinberg, and Valerina Kallab, eds., *U.S. Foreign Policy and the Third World: Agenda 1985–86* (Washington: Overseas Development Council, 1985), 5. For additional discussion of the Reagan economic policies with respect to the global economy, see Henry R. Nau, "Where Reaganomics Works," *Foreign Policy* 57 (Winter 1984–85): 14–37.

21. Sewell, Feinberg, and Kallab, *Policy and the Third World,* 5.

22. *Congressional Quarterly*, 19 December 1981, 2514.

23. In October 1981, Vice President George Bush traveled to Pakistan and visited the Khyber Pass with General Zia to emphasize the U.S. commitment. Reagan proposed $3.2 billion in military and economic aid. In December 1981, a House-Senate conference authorized the president to provide the aid with the provision that Congress reserved the right to veto the president's action. *Congressional Quarterly,* 19 December 1981, 2516. The Carter administration had offered $200 million to Pakistan immediately after the Soviet invasion of Afghanistan, but General Zia rejected it, calling it "peanuts." See also "Less Reticent White House Acts on Military Aid," *New York Times*, 29 March 1981, 2E.

24. M. Peter McPherson, testimony, *Foreign Assistance Legislation for Fiscal Years 1984–85, Part 1,* Hearings before the House Committee on Foreign Affairs, 97th Cong., 1st sess., 23 February 1983 (Washington: USGPO, 1984), 246. McPherson went on to say, "It is a program which fosters the political atmosphere in host countries wherein practical solutions can be applied to social and economic problems."

25. Theodor W. Galdi, "Development Assistance and Food Aid: Historical Overview," presented in *Foreign Assistance and Related Programs Appropriations for 1988,* Hearings before the House Subcommittee on Appropriations, 100th Cong., 1st sess., pt. 3, 2 April 1987 (Washington: USGPO, 1987), 105.

26. George Schultz, "Foreign Aid and U.S. National Interests," speech given at the Southern Center for International Studies, Atlanta, 24 February 1983, reprinted for publication in *Realism, Strength, Negotiation: Key Foreign Policy Statements of the Reagan Administration* (Washington: U.S. Department of State, Bureau of Public Affairs, 1984), 143; George P. Schultz, testimony, *Foreign Assistance Legislation for FY1984–85*, 16 February 1983, 93.

27. Clifford Lewis, then Deputy Assistant Administrator for Program and Policy Coordination, interview, 22 March 1989. Lewis called the four pillars a "public relations ploy." Robert Berg referred to the four pillars as the "four nonsenses."

28. The Carlucci commission was appointed to "review the goals and activities of United States foreign assistance efforts." *Commission on Security and Economic Assistance, Report to the Secretary of State* (hereafter cited as the *Carlucci Commission*), Department of State (Washington: USGPO, 1983), 3, 4. The major recommendations of the commission were to combine development and security assistance, increase overall aid, promote the private sector, and increase flexibility in both development and security assistance. The commission advocated the use of ESF to "further U.S. political and commercial objectives." See also Stephen Hellinger, Douglas Hellinger, and Fred M. O'Regan, *Aid for Just Development* (Boulder: Lynne Rienner Publishers, 1988), 28.

29. *Carlucci Commission,* 5. For example, the commission recognized that many balance-of-payments supports were being used to pay for interest on U.S. weapons. *Economist*, 6 April 1989, 21.

30. Carol Lancaster, interview, 25 March 1989, in Subcommittee on Foreign Operations, Export Financing, and Related Programs, Committee on Appropriations, House of Representatives, *Hearings* (Washington: USGPO, 1 April 1988), 78, 82.

31. For an analysis of the unsuccessful attempt to link the allocation of foreign aid resources to recipient voting behavior in the United Nations, see Charles W. Kegley and Steven W. Hook, "U.S. Foreign Aid and U.N. Voting: Did Reagan's Linkage Strategy Buy Deference or Defiance?" *International Studies Quarterly* 35 (1991): 295–312.

32. See Mikesell, *Economics of Foreign Aid,* and Anne O. Krueger and Vernon W. Ruttan, *The Development Impact of Economic Assistance to LDCs,* vols. 1 and 2 (Minneapolis: University of Minnesota Economic Development Center, March 1983). The Krueger-Ruttan study has since been revised and published as Krueger, Michalopoulos, and Ruttan, *Aid and Development.*

33. The President's Private Sector Survey on Cost Control (the Grace commission) also identified opportunities for increased efficiency and reduced costs that could be achieved throughout the entire federal government. For US/AID, the commission found that the cycle of planning, approving, and monitoring project assistance is sluggish and inefficient because of (1) pressures by congressional mandates and oversight; (2) foreign policy and strategic considerations; (3) bureaucratic inadequacies and socioeconomic weaknesses of beneficiaries; and (4) bureaucratic inertia within US/AID itself. The commission recommended that US/AID (1) increase the use of private voluntary organizations, (2) work to repeal the deobligation/reobligation authority of Congress, (3) further decentralize US/AID, (4) reduce reporting time, and (5) move to a two-year budget submission cycle. See *President's Private Sector Survey on Cost Control: Report on the Department of State/AID/USAID, Spring–Fall 1983* (Washington: USGPO, 1983).

34. M. Peter McPherson, testimony, in House Committee on Foreign Affairs, *Foreign Assistance Legislation for Fiscal Year 82: Hearings*, 97th Cong., 1st sess. 13, 18, 19, and 23 March 1981 (Washington: USGPO, 1981), 249.

35. *Private Enterprise Development,* AID Policy Paper, Bureau for Program and Policy Coordination, March 1985 (Washington: USGPO, 1985), 10.

36. See press release for *The President's Task Force on International Private Enterprise*, Report to the President, December 1984 (Washington: USGPO, 1984).

37. *Population Assistance,* AID Policy Paper, Bureau for Program and Policy Coordination, September 1982 (Washington: USGPO, 1982); Gayl D. Ness, "The Impact of International Population Assistance," in Krueger, Michalopoulos, and Ruttan, *Aid and Development,* 7.

38. See Jason L. Finkle and Barbara B. Crane, "The Politics of Bucharest: Population, Development, and the New International Economic Order," *Population and Development Review* 1, no. 1 (September 1975): 87.

39. Ness, "Impact of International Population Assistance," 8.

40. James L. Buckley, "U.S. Commitment to International Population Planning," statement presented to the International Conference on Population, Mexico City, 8 August 1984, *Current Policy,* no. 604 (Washington: U.S. Department of State, Bureau of Public Affairs, 1984), 2. Buckley found population growth to be a threat only in centrally planned economies where the concentration of economic decision making in the hands of planners and public officials tended to inhibit individual initiative and sometimes crippled the ability of average men and women to work toward a better future. He cited Hong Kong and South Korea as countries experiencing major increases in population while undergoing rapid economic growth.

41. Julian Simon, *The Ultimate Resource* (Princeton: Princeton University Press, 1981), 196. See also Vernon W. Ruttan's review of *The Ultimate Resource* in *Economic Development and Cultural Change* 32, no. 4 (1984): 886–89.

42. Constance Holden, "A 'Prolife' Population Delegation," *Science* 224 (22 June 1984): 1321. The article was prepared by the Office of Policy Development.

43. Ness, "Impact of International Population Assistance," 8. US/AID, in accordance with legislation passed in 1974, was forbidden to "provide support for abortion services or a number of other abortion-related activities." All AID-funded projects and contracts with other agencies prohibit abortion activities. See *Population Assistance,* AID Policy Paper, 6.

44. Werner Fernos, President, Population Institute/Population Action Council, noted in a prepared statement that the United States was sending mixed signals on population assistance. See *Foreign Assistance Legislation for FY1984–85,* 581–585.

45. Tom Barry and Deb Preusch, *Soft War* (New York: Grove Press, 1988), 3, 17. It can be argued that assistance to Central America is based not on need but rather on national security interests. The reaction of the administration was a direct response to the threat of revolution. Congress has been skeptical. Richard Stone, appointed special envoy—"ambassador-at-large"—for Central America in 1983, commented that "an awful lot of congressmen [who are not members of the foreign policy committees] don't know all the facts, and what they certainly don't know is the priorities, the emphasis, the nuances of administration policy on Central America." See *Congressional Quarterly,* 30 April 1983, 820, and *Congressional Quarterly*, 31 December 1983, 2776–78.

46. Joseph Pelzman and Gregory K. Schoepfle, "The Impact of the Caribbean Basin Economic Recovery Act on Caribbean Nations' Exports and Development," *Economic Development and Cultural Change,* 361 (July 1988): 753–96; Anne O. Krueger, *Economic Policies at Cross Purposes: United States and Its Developing Countries* (Washington: Brookings Institution, 1993), 137–61.

47. *Congressional Quarterly Almanac,* 1984, 94.

48. The Reagan administration proposed the Central America Democracy, Peace, and Development Initiative (CAI), for which $8.4 billion in U.S. assistance was requested over a five-year period. Congress, however, approved assistance for only one year (1985) (see Chap. 10).

In the case of El Salvador, aid for FY1987 exceeded the country's own contribution to its budget for the first time in the history of U.S. foreign aid. See "Bankrolling Failure: U.S. Policy in El Salvador and the Urgent Need for Reform," a report to the Arms Control and Foreign Policy Caucus by Senator Mark O. Hatfield (R-Oreg.), Representative Jim Leach (R-Iowa), and Representative George Miller (D-Calif.). Also, Caleb Rossiter, interview, 23 March 1989.

49. Carol Lancaster, *U.S. Aid to Sub-Saharan Africa: Challenges, Constraints and Choices* (Washington: Center for Strategic and International Studies, 1988), 27.

50. The Africa Program was expendable because funds for the high-priority recipients (i.e., Israel, Egypt, base-right countries) continued to be earmarked at high levels. Larry Nowels, interview, 24 March 1989. Carol Lancaster also argued that many BHN, innovative rural development projects were not working and that policy reform was a necessary condition for development.

51. *Congressional Quarterly,* 1 December 1984, 3041–42.

52. Ibid., 3045.

53. *Compact for African Development,* Report of the Committee on African Development Strategies, Joint Project of the Council on Foreign Relations and the Overseas Development Council (Berkeley: University of California Press, 1986), 23. Also, *Continuing the Commitment: Agricultural Development in the Sahel,* Office of Technology Assessment (OTA) Special Report, Congress of the United States, August 1986 (Washington: USGPO, 1986).

54. *Congressional Quarterly,* 1 December 1984, 3045.

55. Ibid., 3037–42. ESF was used to support the EPI in 1984. See Nowels, "Overview of ESF," 84.

56. Lancaster, *U.S. Aid to Sub-Saharan Africa,* 29–30. Among the additional reasons she cited were that projects seldom contained technological improvements to permit African farmers to expand their agricultural production in a cost-effective manner and ignored the policy and institutional environment that often discouraged African farmers from expanding their investments and production. See also OTA, *Continuing the Commitment.* U.S. aid to Africa rarely has exceeded 10 percent of the total aid to the region and remains less than 5 percent of the GNP of any recipient country.

57. Edward Tivnon, *The Lobby: Jewish Political Power and American Foreign Policy* (New York: Simon & Schuster, 1987), 131.

58. Ibid., 138.

59. George Schultz, *Turmoil and Triumph: My Years as Secretary of State* (New York: Charles Scribner & Son's Series, 1993), 104–14.

60. David A. Stockman, *The Triumph of Politics: The Inside Story of the Reagan Revolution* (New York: Avon Books, 1987), 126; John M. Goshko, "Huge Cutback

Proposed in Foreign Aid," *Washington Post*, 29 January 1981, 1A. The foreign aid retrenchment also called for withdrawal from UNESCO because of its "pro-PLO" stance.

61. Stockman, *Triumph of Politics*, 126, 127.

62. *United States Participation in the Multilateral Development Banks in the 1980s*, Department of the Treasury, February 1982 (Washington: USGPO, 1982), 1. The recommendations for U.S. policy toward the development banks were: (1) participate in the MDB capital increases (established during the Carter administration) but seek agreement that no paid-in capital is required; (2) continue callable capital subscriptions but on the basis of program limitations rather than appropriations; (3) reduce, in real terms, participation in soft-loan windows, especially in the International Development Association; and (4) work to implement a more consistent "graduation" policy in hard-loan windows and a more systematic "maturation" program in the soft-loan windows. Ibid., 4–9.

63. Clyde H. Farnsworth, "McNamara Calls on World Bank to Intensify Fight against Poverty," *New York Times*, 1 October 1980, 1; Teresa Hayter and Catherine Watson, *Aid: Rhetoric and Reality* (London: Plato Press, 1985), 198.

64. Ibid., 199–200.

65. IDA is a World Bank agency that specializes in low-interest loans to the world's poorest countries. In 1979, the Carter administration had promised $3.24 billion to IDA over FY1981–83. In 1981, Reagan concurred with the amount but insisted on its spread over four instead of three years. See *Congressional Quarterly*, 25 December 1982, 3113–14.

66. Ann Crittenden, "Foreign Aid Has Friends Back Home: Businessmen," *New York Times*, 30 July 1978, sect. 3, 1.

67. Anthony Rowley, "Ideology before Need," *Far Eastern Economic Review* (14 February 1985): 72.

68. Gregory Newell, Assistant Secretary of State for International Organization Affairs, listed the U.S. policy priorities in regard to the United Nations as (1) reassertion of the leadership role of the United States in international organizations, (2) promotion of budget responsibility, (3) strengthening of U.S. influence in international conferences via reduction in delegations, (4) increase in number of U.S. nationals serving in international organizations, and (5) increase in the role of the private sector. William Schneider called programs of the United Nations "low-priority, foreign aid pet rocks." *Congressional Quarterly*, 26 July 1986, 1675.

69. Newell, one of UNESCO's sharpest critics, said in 1983 that "there is no conceivable way that UNESCO could change its policies, its direction, its practices, such that we would be enticed to remain." See Walter Pincus, "If UNESCO Changes, Schultz Says U.S. Will Reconsider Quitting," *Minneapolis Star and Tribune*, 30 December 1983, 10A.

70. See U.S. Department of State, *U.S. Participation in the U.N., Report of the President to the Congress for the Year 1984* (Washington: Department of State Publications, Bureau of International Organization Affairs, 1985), 232.

71. Ibid., 207.

72. John W. Sewell and Christine E. Contee, "U.S. Foreign Aid in the 1980s: Reordering Priorities," in Sewell, Feinberg, and Kallab, *Policy and the Third World,* 96. Many development experts express concern with the accountability of ESF funds and the overall lack of design in the administration's private sector initiatives.

73. Larry Q. Nowels, testimony, *Foreign Operations, Export Financing, 1989,* 114.

74. *Congressional Quarterly*, 5 October 1985, 1999–2000.

75. John W. Sewell and Christine E. Contee, "Foreign Aid and Gramm-Rudman," *Foreign Affairs* 65, no. 5 (1987): 1016.

76. Ibid., 1017–18.

77. High interest rates in the United States had caused debtor nations to cut imports and compromise their already low standards of living. Baker also argued that the budget and trade deficits were closely linked: that the deficit worsened because foreign countries were unable to maintain levels of spending on U.S. imports. For discussion see "One-Armed Policymaker: A Survey of the World Economy," *Economist*, 24–30 September 1988, 1–72.

78. See Krueger, *Economic Policies at Cross Purposes,* 94–98. For Baker's own review, see James A. Baker, testimony, *Foreign Assistance and Related Programs, Appropriations for 1987, Part 3,* Hearings before a Subcommittee of the Committee on Appropriations, House of Representatives, 99th Cong., 2d sess., 13 March 1986 (Washington: USGPO, 1986), 591. See also Baker's testimony in *Economic Summit, Latin Debt and the Baker Plan,* Hearings before the Committee on Foreign Relations, U.S. Senate, 99th Cong., 2d sess., 20 May 1986 (Washington: USGPO, 1986). Also *Congressional Quarterly*, 5 December 1987, 2984, and Baker's prepared statement in *Security and Development Assistance,* Hearing before the Committee on Foreign Relations, U.S. Senate, 100th Cong., 1st sess., March 1987, pt. 1 (Washington: USGPO, 1987), 299–315.

79. For a discussion of East-West relations and the Reagan foreign policy response, see Robert W. Tucker, "Reagan's Foreign Policy," *Foreign Affairs* 68, no. 1: 1–27.

80. See Larry Q. Nowels, testimony, *Foreign Operations, Export Financing, 1989,* 114. Nowels pointed out that the use of ESF has not shifted dramatically since 1986 and that it "continues to be primarily a tool used to advance U.S. political and security objectives." However, the use of ESF for cash transfer, economic policy reform, and even long-term development projects had been on the rise. Ibid., 86.

81. Lancaster, *U.S. Aid to Sub-Saharan Africa,* 24. In 1987 President Reagan created a special interagency coordinating committee for African aid. Executive Order 12599 charges the committee with assuring that all U.S. economic programs for and policies toward Africa be "consistent with the goal of ending hunger in the region through economic growth, policy reform, and private sector development." Library of Congress, Foreign Affairs and National Defense Division, *Foreign Assistance Policy Studies: A Review of Major Reports and Recommendations* (Washington: USGPO, 1988), 20.

82. Assistance to Eastern Europe and the former Soviet Union was authorized under new legislative authority: (*a*) the Support for East European Democracy (SEED) Act and (*b*) the Freedom Support Act. By fiscal 1994 the United States was allocating

almost $1.0 billion per year in aid to the new states of eastern Europe and the former Soviet Union. Curt Tarnoff and Larry Q. Nowles, *U.S. Foreign Assistance: The Rationale, the Record and the Challenges in the Post Cold War Era* (Washington: National Planning Association, 1994), 8. Prepared for the Committee on Foreign Affairs, U.S. House of Representatives.

83. Elaine Sciolino, "Reagan, in Switch, Says U.S. Will Pay Some Old U.N. Dues," *New York Times*, 14 September 1988, 1; "Overdue U.N. Funds Released by Reagan," *Minneapolis Star Tribune*, from *New York Times*, 14 September 1988, 1A; "Aid to Poor Nations Has Been Disrupted by U.S. Failure To Pay Over $500 Million," *Wall Street Journal*, 13 September 1988, 58. In October 1988, the U.N. Peace Keeping Forces were awarded the Nobel Peace Prize for their work throughout the world. There is some speculation that the Reagan administration's renewed support occurred not only because of declining anti-Western sentiment but also because of political pressures from the Bush campaign and Reagan's desire not to have his last speech before the now popular U.N. assembly tainted by U.S. debts. See Sciolino, "Reagan, in Switch," *New York Times*, 10A; Flora Lewis, "Revitalizing the United Nations," *Minneapolis Star Tribune*, 12 September 1988, 14A.

84. See *AID's Administrative and Management Problems*, 280–85. See also the Babb committee report, *Task Force Report for the Administrator: Organization and Structure of AID* (Washington: Agency for International Development, October 1977, mimeo).

85. *AID's Administrative and Management Problems*, 284.

86. Ibid., 296, 295.

87. Ibid., 24.

88. *AID's Administrative and Management Problems*, 285. Carol Lancaster saw an additional factor in the downfall of IDCA as the conflict between Bennett and Thomas Ehrlich, director of IDCA.

89. Krueger, Michalopoulos, and Ruttan, *Aid and Development*, 28–31, 322–23; Ann Crittenden, "The Realpolitik of Foreign Aid," *New York Times*, 26 February 1978, sec. 3, 1.

90. Robert Berg, interview, 30 March 1989. The transition was very quick and very effective; political appointees were put in place and moved rapidly to change administrative policy. Berg characterized the policies as "weak in intellectual input, but powerful in ideology." Keith Jay, former Deputy Administrator of the Bureau for Program and Policy Coordination, US/AID, interview, 26 May 1989.

91. M. Peter McPherson, Acting Deputy Secretary of the Treasury and former Administrator of US/AID, interview, 10 September 1988.

92. Juan de Onis, "Sharp Reduction Expected in Foreign Aid Request," *New York Times*, 26 January 1981, 7. The paper on foreign assistance that McPherson submitted to Reagan also called for more emphasis on technical assistance and fewer transfers of agency money to developing countries. McPherson believed that foreign policy had humanitarian and development components. He also believed that foreign aid was "political" and that ESF was a useful tool in the disbursement of assistance. See M. Peter McPherson, "Advancing U.S. Interests with Foreign Assistance," *Foreign Service Journal* (December 1986): 22.

93. For the agency's perspective on assistance policy thought, see *Blueprint for Development: The Strategic Plan of the Agency for International Development*, Agency for International Development, June 1985 (Washington: USGPO, 1985). McPherson insisted that "Foreign Assistance is an instrument of U.S. foreign policy. Foreign Assistance serves our political, military, strategic, and economic interests as well as development and humanitarian objectives. Our bilateral economic assistance is meant in part—in some cases, in a very important part—to achieve objectives that have little to do with typical development indicators. The effectiveness of aid is linked to all these interests and objectives." M. Peter McPherson, testimony, *AID Oversight,* Hearings before the Committee on Foreign Relations, U.S. Senate, 99th Cong., 2d sess., 21 April 1986 (Washington: USGPO, 1986), 181.

94. Another step in the decentralization process was giving mission directors greater autonomy and regional bureaus less authority. To that end, McPherson reduced personnel in the two central bureaus and the three regional bureaus in Washington to maintain staff members at the missions. Attempts were made to ensure that the program initiatives from the field were consistent with the four pillars. McPherson indicated that this process had worked more effectively in Asia than in Africa and Latin America. M. Peter McPherson, interview, 10 September 1988.

95. Christopher Madison, "Exporting Reaganomics—The President Wants To Do Things Differently at AID," *National Journal*, 29 May 1982, 961.

96. Ibid., 961.

97. McPherson,"Advancing U.S. Interests," 24. McPherson listed the oral rehydration approach to infant diarrheal disease and US/AID support to the vaccination against childhood disease as two of the major contributions made during his tenure. McPherson, interview, 10 September 1988.

98. *Foreign Assistance Policy Studies,* 9. McPherson considered private sector development to be the "crux" through which a country can draw the more open economic policies that enable it to develop. See McPherson, "Advancing U.S. Interests," 24. Privatization for him could be "the right step at the right time to finally liberate developing countries' economies from slow growth or stagnation." M. Peter McPherson, cited in Martin Tolchin, "U.S. Links Some Foreign Aid to Privatization," *New York Times*, 20 February 1986, 13. In 1986 US/AID, like the administration, declared that "the extent of U.S. assistance for some developing countries will depend on their efforts to transfer public assets and programs to private industry."

99. *Foreign Operations, Export Financing, 1989,* 375.

100. Ballance, "State of the Aid Mandate," 41; *Private and Voluntary Organizations,* AID Policy Paper, Bureau for Program and Policy Coordination, September 1982 (Washington: USGPO, 1982), 2 (see the section on external and societal sources).

101. Despite the BHN rhetoric that was still maintained by US/AID, the only program to receive increased funding was health. Other functional accounts—agriculture, population, and education and human resources—all declined. Assistance for agriculture actually dropped from 50 percent of development assistance in 1980 to 40 percent in 1989. *Report of the Task Force on Foreign Assistance to the Committee on Foreign Affairs, U.S House of Representatives,* February 1989 (Washington: USGPO,

1989), 14–17. "It is hardly surprising, therefore, that these funds have been used primarily to advance the economic and political interests of their relatively small elite, as well as counterpart interests in the United States." Hellinger, Hellinger, and O'Regan, *Aid for Just Development,* 164.

102. President Carter repeatedly complained that Congress was placing too many restrictions on his foreign relations programs. The FY1978 Foreign Aid Authorization Bill, for example, prohibited aid to Zambia, Tanzania, Angola, and Mozambique. Exceptions were given to Zambia and Tanzania (Carter could waive the prohibition if it were determined that furnishing assistance would "further the foreign policy interests of the United States") but not to Mozambique or Angola. Other provisions included a directive that U.S. representatives of the multilateral development banks vote against loans to the aforementioned four countries and to Uganda and four other Communist countries. Furthermore, these representatives were expected to vote against loans to nations producing palm oil, citrus fruit, and sugar when U.S. producers were being injured by their importation. *Congressional Quarterly*, 3 June 1978, 1409–12; Crittenden, "Realpolitik of Foreign Aid," 1.

103. Obey and Lancaster, "Funding Foreign Aid," 147.

104. *Congressional Quarterly*, 19 December 1981, 2498.

105. *Congressional Quarterly*, 14 April 1984, 831–33. In 1982, the House passed a resolution reaffirming the New Directions mandate and criticizing the administration's private sector initiative as "lacking in descriptive detail and policy guidance." The Senate went even further. It mandated that a minimum of 50 percent of development assistance go to "productive facilities, goods and services which will directly benefit those living in absolute and relative poverty." *Congressional Quarterly*, 12 June 1982, 1412.

106. John Felton, "Who Makes Foreign Policy?" *Congressional Quarterly*, 18 June 1983, 1233.

107. Ibid., 1234.

108. The 1985 bill (PL 99–83) was the only normal aid authorization bill passed from 1981 to 1994. Barbara Hinckley, *Less than Meets the Eye: Foreign Policy Making and the Myth of the Assertive Congress* (Chicago: University of Chicago Press, 1994), 121–23, 216.

109. Obey and Lancaster, "Funding Foreign Aid," 141.

110. Ibid., 142–43. After the harsh budget reductions of 1986 and 1987 and the stock market crash (Black Monday, 19 October 1987), the administration and Congress negotiated alternatives to the Gramm-Rudman-Hollings budget reduction plans which are triggered when the administration does not meet specific budget ceilings in which a certain percentage of the funding is withheld. When this happens, a "sequestration" program is put in place to "mitigate the impact of cuts on organizations considered most responsive to U.S. interests." The right is reserved to withhold more than the allotted percentage to those organizations "least responsive to U.S. interests." United States General Accounting Office (GAO), *United Nations: Implications of Reductions in U.S. Funding* (Washington: USGPO, June 1986), 9–10. Larry Nowels argued that the budget for foreign assistance would have been cut with or without G-R-H;

the account had been growing even more rapidly than the defense budget, and Congress just could not sustain that kind of growth.

111. *Congressional Quarterly*, 16 March 1985, 498.

112. Larry Q. Nowels, "The Foreign Affairs Funding Debate in 1987," Congressional Research Service Report for Congress (22 February 1989).

113. Obey and Lancaster, "Funding Foreign Aid," 153–55.

114. Larry Nowels, interview, 24 March 1984.

115. GAO, *United Nations: Implications,* 1. The organizations affected by this measure are FAO, ILO, UNIDO, World Health Organization (WHO), the International Civil Aviation Organization, and the World Meteorological Organization. In addition, Congress consistently voted increases in assistance over the president's requests for the United Nations Children's Fund (UNICEF) and IFAD. However, Congress insists that a careful watch be maintained on the voting practices of all U.N. agencies receiving U.S. aid.

116. Ibid., 7.

117. McPherson claimed in 1986 that earmarking funds leads to "a mosaic of rules and combinations so that every dollar has some pigeon-hole into which it must fit two or three times." US/AID officials continue to request flexibility in the distribution of assistance as well as less notification and indication, the formal process by which Congress maintains close watch over the funds disbursed by US/AID. See *AID Oversight,* 7.

118. *Task Force on Foreign Assistance,* summary.

119. During the 1970s many industrialized nations accelerated the growth rate of their money supplies. Inflation and the rapid expansion of credit resulted. Interest rates rose less than that of the average price level and, thus, led to negative real interest rates, further stimulating the demand for borrowing. James B. Burnham, "World Debt and Monetary Order: Learning from the Past," *CATO Journal* 4, no. 1 (1984): 71–79.

120. Richard E. Feinberg, "International Finance and Investment: A Surging Public Sector," in Sewell, Feinberg, and Kallab, *Policy and the Third World,* 51–71.

121. Ibid., 51.

122. See Christine E. Contee, *What Americans Think: Views on Development and US–Third World Relations,* a public opinion project of InterAction and the Overseas Development Council, 1987; John E. Reilly, ed., *American Public Opinion and US Foreign Policy 1987* (Chicago: Chicago Council on Foreign Relations, 1987) and Ballance, "State of the Aid Mandate."

123. Contee, *What Americans Think,* 6. Additional highlights of the study are as follows: (1) Americans are aware of the problems of poverty and do not believe that much progress has been made in improving Third World living conditions over the past decade. (2) Americans have strong negative perceptions of Third World governments but not of the people of these countries. (3) Policy makers perceive American public support for U.S. economic assistance to be weak and fluctuating. (4) Most Americans are poorly informed about U.S. foreign relations in general but are aware that U.S. economic relations with developing countries potentially are of mutual benefits. (5) The perceived trade-off between promoting domestic well-being and helping

nations overseas limits public support to specific U.S. trade, aid, and financial policies to promote Third World growth or alleviate poverty. (6) Most Americans recognize that the United States has political or strategic interests in the Third World, but many are concerned with overinvolvement in the affairs of developing countries. (7) The major reasons for public support for economic assistance are humanitarian concern or a sense of responsibility; economics or political self-interest are generally less compelling. (8) Americans express a strong preference for those U.S. economic aid programs that most recognizably deliver help directly to poor people. (9) Economic aid is widely perceived to be ineffective or wasted; however, this opinion does not dissuade many Americans from supporting assistance efforts. (10) The American public makes little distinction between private and official aid efforts. (11) Personal experience or personal approaches are most likely to motivate Americans to become actively involved in aid efforts to promote development or to alleviate poverty in Third World countries.

124. Ibid., 21. Ballance showed that most Americans perceive outlays only in absolute terms and do not consider percentage of GNP as an important measure (Ballance, "State of the Aid Mandate," 28). As of 1988, the United States was the largest contributor of Official Development Assistance in absolute terms; Japan has recently overtaken the United States as largest contributor, however.

125. Reilly, *American Public Opinion,* 4–7; Contee, *What Americans Think,* 15. A question asked in the studies of 1947, 1956, 1974, 1978, and 1982 was "Do you think it will be best for the future of the country if we take an active part in world affairs or if we stay out of world affairs?" In the 1986 study the question was "Do you think it will be best for the future of the United States if we take an active part in world affairs or if we stay out of world affairs?"

126. Ballance, "State of the Aid Mandate," 29. Ballance also pointed out that the "anti-Communist rationale for assistance was strong at the beginning of the aid program, although polls now show that it does not figure heavily in public thinking." Ibid., 39.

127. For additional discussion of PVOs, see Hellinger, Hellinger, and O'Regan, *Aid for Just Development,* 99–122, and Robert Hunt, *Private Voluntary Organizations and the Promotion of Small-Scale Enterprise,* AID Evaluation, Special Study No. 27, U.S. Department of State (July 1985).

128. Kathleen Teltsch, "Aid Groups in U.S. Worry over Funds," *New York Times,* 13 February 1986, 11; Ballance, "State of the Aid Mandate," 43.

129. Minear, "Forgotten Human Agenda," 85, 86.

130. Ballance, "State of the Aid Mandate," 49, 46, 47. Easterbrook pointed out that, "in vigor, freshness and appeal, market-oriented theories have surpassed government-oriented theories at nearly every turn. This feat has been accomplished in the main by circumventing the expected source of intellectual development—the universities. Conservative thinkers have taken their case directly to Congress, the media and the public—to the marketplace of ideas." Gregg Easterbrook, "Ideas Move Nations," *Atlantic* (January 1986): 66.

131. From Winrock International, Summary of Recommendations of Winrock Colloquium, "Future U.S. Development Assistance: Food, Hunger, and Agricultural Issues," 1. Presented at the National Conference on Cooperation for International Devel-

opment, 15–17 May 1988, in East Lansing, Michigan. A policy statement from the American Farm Bureau Federation asserts that the federation opposes "economic and/or technological aid through any state, federal or international program which contributes to the production or distribution of any agricultural products by our foreign competitors which adversely affect the interests of U.S. producers." Remarks by Dean Kleckner, President, American Farm Bureau Federation, before the Winrock International Workshop, Washington, 4 January 1989.

132. Winrock International, Summary of Recommendations, 1.

133. Brown, "Degradation," 10.

134. Ibid.; John W. Mellor, "The Intertwining of Environmental Problems and Poverty," *Environment* 30, no. 9 (1988): overview.

135. Roger C. Riddell, *Foreign Aid Reconsidered* (Baltimore: Johns Hopkins University Press, 1987), 157; Easterbrook, "Ideas Move Nations," 66.

136. Edward Feulner, "Foreign Aid: Debating the Uses and Abuses," *New York Times,* E5. Later, Doug Brandow of the Heritage Foundation published *U.S. Aid to the Developing World: A Free Market Agenda,* a collection of works dealing with the many aspects of the foreign aid program. It takes a more conservative approach to foreign assistance and also stresses private foreign aid through charitable organizations and private corporate investment. Doug Brandow, ed., *U.S. Aid to the Developing World: A Free Market Agenda* (Washington: Heritage Foundation, 1985).

137. Ballance, "State of the Aid Mandate," 41. For example, the Heritage Foundation is extremely critical of the United Nations. See Easterbrook, "Ideas Move Nations," 72–73.

138. The administration requested policy recommendations for all governmental bodies from the Heritage Foundation; they were published as *Mandate for Leadership: Policy Management in a Conservative Administration* (Washington: Heritage Foundation, 1981).

139. Peter T. Bauer and Basil S. Yamey, "Foreign Aid: What Is at Stake?" in *The Third World: Premises of U.S. Policy,* ed. W. Scott Thompson (San Francisco: Institute for Contemporary Studies, 1983), 115–35; cited in *Foreign Assistance Policy Studies,* 47. Bauer argued that developing countries have made considerable progress without foreign assistance and would continue to do so if they were allowed; if investment funds were required for development, they could be obtained by commercial borrowing. See Anne O. Krueger and Vernon W. Ruttan, "Toward a Theory of Development Assistance," in Krueger, Michalopoulos, and Ruttan, *Aid and Development*, 32–52.

140. Quoted in Riddell, *Foreign Aid Reconsidered,* 159.

141. Hernando de Soto, *The Other Path: The Invisible Revolution in the Third World* (New York: Harper & Row, 1989).

142. Riddell, *Foreign Aid Reconsidered,* 131.

143. Frances Moore Lappé, Rachel Schurman, and Kevin Danaher, *Betraying the National Interest,* Institute for Food and Development Policy (New York: Grove Press, 1987); Teresa Hayter, *Aid as Imperialism* (Baltimore: Penguin Books, 1971). GAP is the acronym for Group for Alternative Policies; see Hellinger, Hellinger, and O'Regan, *Aid for Just Development.*

144. Riddell, *Foreign Aid Reconsidered,* 131.

145. Ibid., 265. Riddell's position does not obviate the theories of the Right and Left; both have had positive influences on the theory of development assistance, and both provided arguments for a richer analysis. Ibid., 102–27.

146. Krueger and Ruttan, *Development Impact,* 14.

147. In 1987, for example, the Micro Enterprise Loans for the Poor Act was passed to provide credit for the poor in developing countries. Also in 1987 the African Famine Recovery and Development Act was passed. This act amended the Foreign Assistance Act of 1961 to establish a separate authorization for assistance for famine recovery and long-term development in sub-Saharan Africa and for other purposes. When this chapter was initially drafted, both houses were in the process of discussing a Global Poverty Reduction Act, which sought the eradication of the worst aspects of poverty in developing countries by the year 2000.

Chapter 8 The Politics of Food Aid Policy

1. For earlier drafts of the material in this chapter, see Vernon W. Ruttan, *Why Food Aid?* (Baltimore: Johns Hopkins University Press, 1993), 2–36, 216–28; "International Food Aid: Interest Groups and Clients," *Choices* 5 (3d quarter, 1990): 12–16; "International Food Aid: Changed but Contractions Continue," *Choices* 6 (1st quarter, 1991): 3–6.

2. In writing this chapter, I have been able to draw on several exceptionally useful studies: Trudy Huskamp Petersen, *Agricultural Exports, Farm Income, and the Eisenhower Administration* (Lincoln: University of Nebraska Press, 1979); Peter A. Toma, *The Politics of Food for Peace* (Tuscon: University of Arizona Press, 1967); Mitchell Bruce Wallerstein, "The Politics of International Food Aid: U.S. Policy Objectives in an Evolving Multilateral Context" (Ph.D. diss., Massachusetts Institute of Technology, 1978); Mitchell B. Wallerstein, *Food for War—Food for Peace: United States Food Aid in a Global Context* (Cambridge: MIT Press, 1980); Hans Singer, John Wood, and Tony Jennings, *Food Aid: The Challenge and the Opportunity* (Oxford: Oxford University Press, 1987). Useful summaries of the objectives and provisions of agricultural commodity and food aid legislation are found in Willard W. Cochrane and Mary E. Ryan, *American Farm Policy, 1948–1973* (Minneapolis: University of Minnesota Press, 1967), 131–74; Susan B. Epstein, "Food for Peace, 1954–1986: Major Changes in Legislation" (Washington: Congressional Research Service, 30 April 1987); *The United States Food for Peace Program, 1954–1984: A Compilation of International Materials on the United States Public Law 480* (Washington: International Trade and Development Foundation, Spring 1985).

3. Petersen, *Agricultural Exports,* 137–51.

4. For greater detail on the earlier programs, see Kathleen Ann Cravero, "Food and Politics: Domestic Sources of U.S. Food Aid Policies, 1949–1979" (Ph.D. diss., Fordham University, 1982), 31–39, 234–52. Also Ann-Marie Bairstow, "A History of United States Food Aid: 1812–1954" (Washington: Agency for International Development, August 1988, mimeo). United States assistance during the nineteenth century, with the exception of a relief appropriation of $50,000 for Venezuela in 1912 and

assistance in the transport of gifts to Ireland in 1880 by the Navy, was entirely voluntary. Both Congress and the president generally adhered to a view that the use of public funds for charity was unconstitutional. Even the bulk of post–World War I relief to Belgium and Russia, administered by Herbert Hoover, came primarily from private sources. Daniel J. Boorstin, *The Americans: The Democratic Experience* (New York: Random House, 1973), 570–74.

5. Quoted from Petersen, *Agricultural Exports,* 9. Secretary Benson regarded PL 480 as one of his major accomplishments. See Ezra Taft Benson, *Cross Fire: The Eight Years with Eisenhower* (New York: Doubleday, 1962).

6. Whenever the subject of food aid came up, "Dulles had a nervous tremor." Sherman Adams, *First-hand Report: The Story of the Eisenhower Administration* (New York: Harper & Brothers, 1961), 389.

7. Petersen, *Agricultural Exports,* 38–40.

8. Ibid., 40.

9. Political pressure for an expanded program of sales for foreign currencies is usually traced to a resolution adopted at the 1952 National Conference of the American Farm Bureau Federation in Seattle, Washington; the resolution urged the government to expand the use of surpluses by selling them for foreign currencies. Support was reaffirmed at the 1953 National Conference. When the Farm Bureau was unable to obtain support for its proposal from the Department of Agriculture or from the leadership of the House and Senate agriculture committees, it turned to two junior members, Representative Robert D. Harrison (R-Nebr.) and Senator Andrew F. Schaeppel (R-Kans.), to introduce the proposal. By the summer of 1954, rising surpluses had created a more favorable climate for passage of the legislation. See David S. McLellan and Donald Clare, *Public Law 480: The Metamorphosis of a Law,* Eagleton Institute Cases in Practical Politics, Case 36 (New York: McGraw-Hill, 1965), 2–4.

10. Senator Humphrey had been the chief sponsor of the India Emergency Food Act of 1951. In 1952 he made a speech before the Grain Terminal Association in St. Paul urging the use of U.S. surplus commodities as aid to impoverished countries. He presented testimony in support at hearings held on 16 July 1953 by the Senate Committee on Agriculture and Forestry to consider a bill (S. 2249) to give the president emergency authority to use surplus agricultural commodities for foreign assistance. This was followed, on 25 February 1954, by the introduction of a bill (S. 3020) to use American agricultural surplus to promote peace. The bill died in committee. These early efforts by Humphrey are important for two reasons. They represented his initial involvement in food aid policy—an area in which he would play an active and sometimes dominant role throughout his career. It was also an important early expression of his pragmatic approach to legislative action—to propose a comprehensive approach to a problem and be satisfied with whatever parts of the proposal are eventually realized. See Elmer L. Menzie and Robert G. Crouch, *Political Interests in Agricultural Export Surplus Disposal through Public Law 480,* Technical Bulletin 161 (Tucson: University of Arizona Agricultural Experiment Station, September 1964), and Albert Eisele, *Almost to the Presidency* (Blue Earth, Minn.: Piper Company, 1972), 11.

11. Quoted from Menzie and Crouch, *Political Interests in Surplus Disposal,* 17, 21.

12. Ibid., 50.

13. Title I required that (1) reasonable precautions be taken that PL 480 sales not disrupt domestic commercial sales or upset world prices, (2) private trading channels be used as much as possible, (3) special consideration be given to using the act to expand markets for American goods abroad, and (4) measures be taken to make sure that purchasing nations do not resell goods brought from the United States for profit. The law authorized the Commodity Credit Corporation to handle the transportation and transfer of funds. The funds could be used by the Agriculture Department to develop markets and by the State Department to make economic development grants, to finance educational exchange, and to accomplish other U.S. government purposes. Gilman G. Udell, *Agricultural Trade Development and Assistance Act of 1954 and Amendments* (Washington: U.S. House of Representatives Document Room, 1971), 12; Menzie and Crouch, *Political Interests in Surplus Disposal,* 42, 43. The provisions for donations abroad through nonprofit voluntary agencies in Title III were the result of a continuing campaign by private relief organizations to expand the commodities distributed under their auspices and to obtain government funding to cover inland and ocean transport of the commodities that they distributed. See Robert R. Sullivan, "The Politics of Altruism: A Study of the Partnership between the United States Government and American Voluntary Relief Agencies for the Donation Abroad of Surplus Agricultural Commodities, 1949–1967" (Ph.D. diss., Johns Hopkins University, 1968), 34–59.

14. Menzie and Crouch, *Political Interests in Surplus Disposal,* 50, 52.

15. Cravero, "Food and Politics," 239.

16. Since the sales for foreign currencies program were, in effect, an elaborate deception to obscure the true nature of the food aid transaction, it is useful to trace how they worked. The first step was for the U.S. government and the foreign government to reach an agreement that enabled that government to pay for some farm product imports with its own currency rather than with dollars. The agreement specified the quantity of the product involved, the price, and, usually, the uses that could be made of the foreign currency acquired by the United States. The farm products were usually sold to the foreign government by a private exporter who was paid in dollars by the U.S. government. The foreign government in turn usually sold the imported commodities in its domestic market to recoup the funds paid to the United States for the imported commodities. Under the PL 480 legislation, the United States was authorized to lend the funds back to the country for use in its development program. In effect, this meant that the foreign government found itself borrowing its own currency, and paying interest on it, when it could just as easily have printed additional money. The primary reason the U.S. government engaged in such "fictional" transactions is that they appeared more acceptable to policy makers and the American people than outright grants of food or of dollar aid. The primary reason the importing countries were willing to engage in the fictional transactions is that they realized that it was unlikely that they would be forced to repay the loans or that the United States would ever find a way to use for its own purposes a significant share of the countries' currency that it

controlled. For an excellent analysis of the effects of counterpart funds, see Michael Roemer, *The Macroeconomics of Counterpart Funds* (Cambridge: Harvard Institute for Economic Development, February 1988).

17. The opportunity to use food aid to Poland was an important initial motivation. Following the emergence of Wladyslaw Gomulka as first secretary of the Polish Communist Party after the outbreak of riots in Poznan in October 1956, the State Department certified the new Polish government as "independent," thus making it eligible to receive surplus food. In May 1957 Senator Kennedy, in a speech in Omaha, criticized the Eisenhower administration for its lack of progress in making food aid available to Poland. George Zacher, *A Political History of Food for Peace*, Department of Agricultural Economics Staff Paper 77–18 (Ithaca: Cornell University, May 1977), 12, 13.

18. Epstein, "Food for Peace," 10.

19. Quoted from Petersen, *Agricultural Exports,* 87, 88. Davis was apparently the first to suggest the "Food for Peace" label.

20. Ibid., 89.

21. The ICA succeeded the FOA as the U.S. aid agency in 1954. The ICA urged a shift from sales to grants with foreign policy rather than disposal in mind. It argued that it was "a most undignified spectacle for a great power like the U.S. to have to press other countries to accept 'loans' of the proceeds of these 'sales' in order to perpetuate the fiction that they were really 'sales'." Quoted from Petersen, *Agricultural Exports,* 91.

22. In the account of his years as secretary of agriculture, *Cross Fire,* Secretary Benson stresses his close personal working relationship with President Eisenhower. But he completely underplays his conflicts with Charles Randall and completely omits any reference to Senator Humphrey's role in PL 480 and Food for Peace legislation.

23. Ibid., 93; Cooley, quoted from Theodore W. Schultz, "Value of Farm Surpluses to Under-developed Countries" *Journal of Farm Economics* 42 (December 1960): 1025.

24. By the late 1950s the State Department and the ICA (and later AID) were beginning to take advantage of the administrative discretion in the law. Food aid to Egypt represented a major example. "PL480 proved in 1959–60 to be a far more reliable means of improving U.S.–Egyptian relations than the politically more problematical capital and technical aid programs of 1952–56. Despite intermittent and generally ineffectual sniping from the Israel lobby the Eisenhower administration quietly signed a series of Title I agreements with Egypt in 1959–60." William J. Burns, *Economic Aid and American Policy toward Egypt, 1955–1981* (Albany: State University of New York Press, 1985), 118.

25. David S. McLellan and Donald Clare, *Public Law 480,* 32. They also assert, somewhat more realistically, that "shipments of United States surpluses are almost automatically assumed to exert a favorable influence on foreign policy. No one has really stopped to examine whether this is true or simply a semiofficial myth. No one really knows what impact PL 480 sales and grants are having on American foreign policy. Perhaps no one really wants to know."

26. Willard W. Cochrane, "Farm Technology, Foreign Surplus Disposal, and Domestic Supply Control," *Journal of Farm Economics* 41 (December 1959): 885–99. Cochrane had contributed a Kennedy campaign position paper on agricultural policy and had been closely associated with Orville Freeman while Freeman was governor of Minnesota.

27. Wallerstein, "Politics of International Food Aid," 206–9.

28. This was acknowledged by Secretary of Agriculture Orville Freeman in 1964 hearings on extension of the PL 480 program. See Toma, *Politics of Food for Peace,* 70–73.

29. I have drawn very heavily on the excellent history and analysis of the amendment and extension of the 1964 act (PL 88-638) in Toma, *Politics of Food for Peace,* 67–110, 148–54.

30. See Trudy Huskamp Peterson, "Sales, Surpluses, and the Soviets: A Study in Political Economy," in *The Role of U.S. Agriculture in Foreign Policy*, ed. Richard M. Frankel, Don F. Hadwinger, and William P. Browne (New York: Praeger, 1979), 56–79, for the debates over grain sales to the USSR and eastern Europe during the late 1950s and early 1960s. A decision to remove the 1948 embargo on sales to the USSR was finally made in October 1963. By 1963 Egypt had become the world's largest per capita consumer of food aid.

31. It strikes me as politically naive, however, to argue that by shifting the PL 480 budget from Agriculture to State the 1964 act stripped "the last vestiges of the surplus disposal facade from PL-480." Wallerstein, "Politics of International Food Aid," 213.

32. Johnson is reported to have felt that "there was no reason to maintain within the White House a bureaucratic structure which was created primarily to elect George McGovern to the Senate." Wallerstein, "Politics of International Food Aid," 597.

33. Toma, *Politics of Food for Peace,* 133.

34. Ibid, 133–39.

35. For greater detail on the origin and history of multilateral food aid, see Wallerstein, "Politics of International Food Aid," 307–407, 532–51. For an exceedingly useful review and evaluation of the history and policies of the agencies involved in multilateral food aid, see Ross B. Talbot, *The Four World Food Agencies in Rome* (Ames: Iowa State University Press, 1990).

36. For a discussion of the assistance efforts initiated under the World Food Program in its initial three-year trial period, see A. Dawson, "Food for Development: The World Food Program," *International Labor Review* 90 (August 1964): 100–29. For a retrospective view see Hans W. Singer, "Development through Food: Twenty Years' Experience," in World Food Program (Government of the Netherlands), *Report of the World Food Program of the Government of the Netherlands Seminar on Food Aid* (Rome: World Food Program, 1983).

37. The WFP often acts more as a coordinating than an implementing agency, particularly with respect to U.S. contributions. Talbot, *The Four World Food Agencies,* 63.

38. Orville L. Freeman, "Malthus, Marx and the North American Breadbasket," *Foreign Affairs* (July 1967): 579–93.

39. In the discussion of food aid during the Kennedy and Johnson administrations,

I draw very heavily on Wallerstein, "Politics of International Food Aid," 409–77, 584–634; Cravero, "Food and Politics," 177–207, 252–315.

40. Raymond F. Hopkins and Donald J. Puchala, *Global Food Interdependence: Challenge to American Foreign Policy* (New York: Columbia University Press, 1980), 88–91. Although Israel's food imports under PL 480 ended in 1976 as a result of the congressional requirement that 75 percent of Title I food aid must go to poor countries, funding for food imports was made available to Israel under the AID Commodity Import Program, which goes to countries receiving Security Supporting Assistance.

41. For a very careful analysis and assessment of the use of "food power" toward India by the Johnson administration, see Robert L. Paarlberg, *Food Trade and Foreign Policy: India, the Soviet Union, and the United States* (Ithaca: Cornell University Press, 1985), 143–69.

42. Wallerstein, "Politics of International Food Aid," 551–74. See also Arthur A. Goldsmith, "Policy Dialogue, Conditionality and Agricultural Development: Implications of India's Green Revolution," *Journal of Developing Areas* 22 (January 1988): 179–98. The depth of Johnson's involvement is suggested by Rostow: "I helped him follow the fall of rain in India and Pakistan as closely as he did along the Pedernales. He knew the dates of shipment from American ports of grain required for timely arrival in Calcutta and the state of Indian grain stocks. He personally guided the negotiation of each tranche of food aid." Walt W. Rostow, *The Diffusion of Power* (New York: Macmillan, 1972), 423.

43. Wallerstein, "Politics of International Food Aid," 609.

44. "The P.L. 480 annual congressional appropriation is deposited with the Commodity Credit Corporation (CCC), which finances Food for Peace sales, agreements, and donations. If the amounts appropriated are greater than actual needs in any one year, the excess is used to reduce future appropriate requests. If the appropriations are less than actual needs, other CCC funds may be used temporarily to finance the balance of the costs. P.L. 480 budgetary costs and program levels for any one year may not be identical. Title I sales are made on credit, and repayments reduce P.L. 480 budget costs by partially financing the program level of subsequent years. In addition, commodities shipped under Title II may have been acquired under the domestic price support program. The P.L. 480 program pays the CCC the export market price for these commodities. The amounts of commodities shipped under P.L. 480 depend not only on actual funding levels, but also on domestic commodity prices. If P.L. 480 funding levels remain constant but domestic commodity prices rise, the quantity of commodities shipped will decline." Epstein, "Food for Peace," 47.

45. Epstein, "Food for Peace," 22. There was a growing tendency in the 1970s to use the annual foreign assistance acts as vehicles for modifying food aid programs.

46. Cravero, "Food and Politics," 305.

47. The definitive analysis of U.S. food policy in the early and mid-1970s is I. M. Destler, *Making Foreign Economic Policy* (Washington: Brookings Institution, 1980), 19–128. For a shorter treatment see I. M. Destler, "United States Food Policy, 1972–1976: Reconciling Domestic and International Objectives," in *The Global Political Economy of Food*, Raymond F. Hopkins and Donald J. Puchala, eds. (Madison:

University of Wisconsin Press, 1978), 41–77. I also draw very heavily on Wallerstein, "Politics of International Food Aid," 409–77, 584–634.

48. See G. Edward Schuh, "The Exchange Rate and U.S. Agriculture," *American Journal of Agricultural Economics* 56 (February 1974): 1–13.

49. Willard W. Cochrane and Mary E. Ryan, *American Farm Policy, 1948–1973* (Minneapolis: University of Minnesota Press, 1976), 203.

50. Destler, *Making Foreign Economic Policy,* 37. Whereas Destler, writing from a "realist perspective," interprets the events associated with the Soviet Union grain sales of 1972 and 1973 as incompetence reinforced by conservative ideology, scholars working in a more "radical" tradition have interpreted the same events as a clever conspiracy by the leadership of the U.S. Department of Agriculture to create a worldwide shortage of agricultural commodities in order to drive up commodity prices and help resolve the U.S. balance of payment problem. See John Henry Frundt, "American Agribusiness and U.S. Foreign Policy" (Ph.D. diss., Rutgers University, May 1975), 275, 276. While rejecting Frundt's "conspiracy view," I find it a bit difficult to describe Secretary Butz and his senior associates at the USDA as inept or naive, as Destler implies.

51. Wallerstein, "Politics of International Food Aid," 71.

52. In an effort to raise foreign exchange in 1974, Bangladesh sold Cuba approximately $3 million worth of jute gunny sacks. The reduction in food aid shipments was in part an effort to stop trade between Bangladesh and Cuba. After Bangladesh canceled further exports of jute, the United States did agree to increase its food aid shipments, but no wheat arrived in Bangladesh until after Christmas, when the worst effects of the famine were over. Wallerstein, "Politics of International Food Aid," 488–89. See also Donald F. McHenry and Kai Bird, "Food Bungle in Bangladesh," *Foreign Policy* 27 (Summer 1977): 72–88. During 1973–78 I visited Bangladesh several times. I mistakenly attributed the delay in shipments to bureaucratic inefficiency.

53. Destler, "United States Food Policy, 1972–1976," 58. In retrospect, the zero budget can be interpreted as part of the bureaucratic infighting to determine whether the PL 480 budget should be charged against Agriculture or State.

54. As usual in issues of food policy, the influence of Senator Hubert H. Humphrey was involved. There was considerable opposition in the Senate to Kissinger's appointment as secretary of state. It has been reported that Humphrey dropped his opposition to Kissinger's appointment on condition that Kissinger endorse the World Food Conference. See Lee Egerstrom, "74 World Food Conference Resembled a Roman Circus," *St. Paul Pioneer Press Dispatch*, 4 December 1983.

55. Wallerstein, "Politics of International Food Aid," 457–60; Edward R. F. Sheehan, *The Arabs, Israelis, and Kissinger* (New York: Readers Digest Press/Thomas Y. Cromwell, 1976).

56. Wallerstein, "Politics of International Food Aid," 75, 76. For a useful analysis of the world food situation as perceived just before the World Food Conference, see U.S. Senate Committee on Agriculture and Forestry, *The World Food Conference: Selected Materials for the Use of the U.S. Congressional Delegation to the World Food Conference* (Washington: USGPO, 30 October 1974).

57. Ibid., 627.

58. Lee Egerstrom, "War on Hunger at a Standstill," *St. Paul Pioneer Press Dispatch*, 4 December 1983.

59. Destler, *Making Foreign Economic Policy*, 125, 107.

60. Thomas G. Weiss and Robert S. Jordan, *The World Food Conference and Global Problem Solving* (New York: Praeger, 1976). The authors note that "it was generally believed that Secretary-General Marei was appointed at least in part because his Egyptian nationality facilitated negotiations with Arab nations whose oil wealth made them . . . the logical contributors to a new fund" (p. 60). For additional perspective on the World Food Conference and the establishment of the International Fund for Agricultural Development, see Talbot, *The Four World Food Agencies*, 75–129; Sergio Marchisio and Antonietta Di Blase, *The Food and Agricultural Organization* (Dordrecht: Martinus Nijhoff, 1992), 74–86.

61. Don Wallace and Helga Escobar, *The Future of International Organization* (New York: Praeger, 1977), 13.

62. Ross B. Talbot, "Implications of the World Food Conference Resolutions: U.S. Government Policy with Respect to the International Grain Reserve Issue," in *The Role of U.S. Agriculture in Foreign Policy*, ed. Richard M. Fraenkel, Don F. Hadwinger, and William P. Browne (New York: Praeger, 1979), 109–36; Talbot, *The Four Food Agencies*, 99–130.

63. This discussion of the events leading to the International Development and Food Assistance Act of 1975 draws primarily on Wallerstein, "Politics of International Food Aid," 230, 231; Epstein, "Food for Peace," 27–34; Thomas R. Saylor, "A New Legislative Mandate for American Food Aid," in *Food Policy: The Responsibility of the United States in Life and Death Choices*, ed. Peter G. Brown and Henry Shue (New York: Free Press/Macmillan, 1977), 199–211.

64. For a discussion of the difficulties encountered in getting the Food for Development Program under way, see Jose M. Garzon, "Food Aid as a Tool of Development: The Experience of PL-480, Title III," *Food Policy* 19 (August 1984): 232–44.

65. Task Force on the Operation of Public Law 480, *New Directions for U.S. Food Assistance: A Report on the Special Task Force on the Operation of Public Law 480* (Washington: USDA, May 1978); Presidential Commission on World Hunger, *Overcoming World Hunger: The Challenge Ahead* (Washington: Presidential Commission on World Hunger, March 1980).

66. G. Edward Schuh, *The United States and the Developing Countries* (Washington: National Planning Association, 1986), 11–16.

67. The growth of food aid under the mutual security rubric since the early 1970s reflects the common congressional practice of making symbolic reforms in response to pressure from the "basic needs" constituency while simultaneously responding to the administration's concern that resources be available to meet needs justified under a security rationale. A similar shift in financial transfers, from development assistance to supporting assistance, occurred in the US/AID budget after passage of the New Directions legislation in 1973 (see Chap. 5).

68. Epstein, "Food for Peace," 41–48.

69. The U.S. Congress included in the Foreign Assistance Appropriations Act of 1987 a provision that "none of the funds appropriated by this or any other act to carry out Chapter 1 of Part I of the Foreign Assistance Act of 1961 shall be available for any testing or breeding feasibility study, variety improvement or introduction, consultancy, publication, conference, or training in connection with the growth or production in a foreign country of an agricultural commodity for export which would compete with similar commodity grown or produced in the United States" (Section 550). The combined effect of the Bellman and the Bumpers amendments comes very close to insisting that food aid not be used to either discourage or encourage agricultural production in recipient countries. The Bumpers amendment was, to a substantial extent, a response to concern by the American Soybean Association that U.S. economic and technical assistance was the source of increased production of soybeans for export by Brazil. See Paul B. Thompson, *The Ethics of Aid and Trade: U.S. Foreign Policy, Foreign Competition and the Social Contract* (New York: Cambridge University Press, 1992), 43–50.

70. For discussion of the changes in the Food Security Act of 1975, see Charles E. Hanrahan and Susan B. Epstein, *Foreign Food Aid: Current Policy Issues* (Washington: Library of Congress Congressional Research Service 87–923 ENR, 14 September 1987). For the administration and programming of food aid under the 1975 act, see Donald S. Ferguson, *Improving the Effectiveness of PL-480 Food and Agricultural Assistance* (Washington: USDA, Office of International Cooperation and Development, January 1988).

71. Sales for dollars and convertible local currencies under Title I also contain a large concessional element. In addition to the large interest rate subsidy, the repayment provisions provide an additional element of concessionality. "Agreements may be signed for either dollar credit with up to a 20-year repayment period or convertible local currency credit with up to a 40-year repayment period. The grace period before interest for dollar credit agreements may go up to 2 years, and for convertible local currency agreements, it may be as long as 10 years." Foreign Agricultural Service, *Food for Peace: 1986 Annual Report on Public Law 480* (Washington: USDA, April 1988), 3.

72. Donald S. Ferguson, *Food Security and Private Sector Lending under Sections 106 and 108 of PL-480* (Washington: USDA, Office of International Cooperation and Development, March 1988).

73. The EEP, TEA, and Export Credit Guarantee Programs have been reviewed in several General Accounting Office reports. See *Implementation of Agricultural Export Enhancement Program* (Washington: GAO, March 1987) and *Commodity Credit Corporation Export Credit Guarantee Programs* (Washington: GAO, June 1988).

74. The extent to which the Export Enhancement Program has actually increased sales is debatable. Robert L. Paarlberg argues that the "EEP hasn't added much to foreign sales because nine out of ten EEP bonus baskets simply displace sales that would have been made anyway." "The Mysterious Popularity of EEP," *Choices* 5 (2d quarter, 1990): 15.

75. For somewhat greater detail see World Food Institute, *World Food Trade and U.S Agriculture, 1960–1987* (Ames: Iowa State University by World Food Institute, October 1988).

76. Testimony by Winston Wilson, President of the U.S. Wheat Associates, an export market development organization funded by wheat producers and the USDA Foreign Agricultural Service, in *U.S. Agricultural Exports: Does Administration Effort Match Potential?* Hearings before a Subcommittee on Government Operations, U.S. House of Representatives (Washington: USGPO, 1980), 112.

77. Edward Clay, "Food Aid, Development, and Food Security in the 1980s" (London: Relief and Development Institute, July 1989), 39.

78. See Martin Doornhas, Manoshi Mitra, and Pieter van Stuijvenberg, "Premises and Impacts of International Diary Aid: The Politics of Evaluation," *Development and Change* 19 (July 1988): 467–504.

79. Clay, "Food Aid, Development, and Food Security."

80. Vernon W. Ruttan, "International Food Aid: Changed, but Contradictions Continue," *Choices* 6 (1st quarter, 1991), 3–6.

81. U.N. Food and Agricultural Organization, *Uses of Agricultural Surpluses To Finance Economic Development in Underdeveloped Countries: A Pilot Study in India* 6 (Rome: FAO Commodity Policy Studies, No. 6, June 1955). The supporting data for the FAO study are reported in M. Dandekar, *Uses of Food Surpluses for Economic Development* (Gokale, India: Gokale Institute of Politics and Development, Publication 30, 1956). See also Mordecai Ezekiel, "Apparent Results in Using Surplus Food for Financing Economic Development," *Journal of Farm Economics* 40 (November 1958): 915–23. For a review of the evolution and criticism of the two gap models, see Krueger, Michalopoulos, and Ruttan, *Aid and Development.*

82. Willard W. Cochrane, "Farm Technology, Foreign Surplus Disposal, and Domestic Supply Control," *Journal of Farm Economics* 41 (December 1959): 885.

83. Theodore W. Schultz, "Value of U.S. Farm Surpluses to Underdeveloped Countries," *Journal of Farm Economics* 42 (December 1960): 1019–30, 1027.

84. Lawrence W. Witt, "Development through Food Grants and Concessional Sales," in *Agriculture in Economic Development*, Carl Eicher and Lawrence Witt, eds. (New York: McGraw-Hill, 1964), 334–59.

85. R. D. Rogers, U. K. Srivastava, and Earl O. Heady, "Modified Price, Production and Income Impacts of Food Aid under Market Differentiated Distribution," *American Journal of Farm Economics* 54 (May 1972): 201–8; Paul J. Isenman and H. W. Singer, "Food Aid: Disincentive Effects and Their Policy Implications," *Economic Development and Cultural Change* 25 (January 1977): 205–37.

86. See particularly Peter Singer, "Reconsidering the Famine Relief Argument," in *Food Policy*, Peter Braun and Henry Shue, eds. (New York: Free Press, 1977), 36–53. See chapter 7 in this volume for an evaluation of the ethical or moral responsibility arguments for foreign economic assistance.

87. See, for example, Garrett Harden, "The Tragedy of the Commons," *Science* 162 (1968): 1243–48; idem, "Living on a Lifeboat," *Bioscience* 24 (October 1974): 561–68.

88. Isenman and Singer, "Food Aid," 222, 223.

89. Glenn Fox and Vernon W. Ruttan, "A Guide to LDC Food Balance Projections," *European Review of Agricultural Economics* 10 (1983): 325–56.

90. See, for example, Susan George, *How the Other Half Dies: The Real Reasons*

for World Hunger (Montclair, N.J.: Allanheld & Osmon, 1977); Emma Rothschild, "Is It Time To End Food for Peace?" *New York Times Magazine*, 13 March 1977, 15–48; Francis Moore Lappé (and Joseph Collins), *Food First: Beyond the Myth of Scarcity* (Boston: Houghton Mifflin, 1977); Tony Jackson (with Deborah Eate), *Against the Grain: The Dilemma of Project Food Aid* (Oxford: OXFAM, 1982); James Bovard, *How American Food Aid Keeps the Third World Hungry* (Washington: Heritage Foundation, 1 August 1988).

91. The findings from these studies are summarized in Hans Singer, John Wood, and Tony Jennings, *Food Aid: The Challenge and the Opportunity* (New York: Oxford University Press, 1988). The most complete guide and assessment of the literature is Edward J. Clay and Hans W. Singer, *Food Aid and Development: Issues and Evidence* (Rome: World Food Program Occasional Paper 2, September 1985). See also Edward J. Clay and Hans W. Singer, *Food Aid and Development: The Impact and Effectiveness of Bilateral PL-480 Title I-type Assistance* (Washington: US/AID Program Evolution Discussion Paper 15, December 1982), and Brady J. Deaton (and others), *Food Aid and Economic Development* (Blacksburg: Virginia Polytechnic Institute and State University, June 1988). For a more analytical treatment of the same issues, see T. N. Srinivasan, "Food Aid: A Cause of Development Failure or an Instrument for Success?" *World Bank Economic Review* 3 (May 1988): 39–65.

92. Singer, Wood, and Jennings, *Food Aid,* 201.

93. See James P. Houck, "Link between Agricultural Assistance and International Trade," *Agricultural Economics* 2 (1988): 154–66; Earl Kellog, R. Kodl, and P. Garcia, "The Effects of Agricultural Growth on Agricultural Imports in Developing Countries," *American Journal of Agricultural Economics* 68, no. 5 (1986): 1347–52; Alan de Janvry and Edith Sadoulet, "The Conditions for Harmony between Third World Agricultural Development and U.S. Farm Exports," *American Journal of Agricultural Economics* 68, no. 5 (1986): 1340–46.

94. John W. Mellor, "Global Food Balances and Food Security," *World Development* 16 (1988): 997–1011.

95. Willis W. Peterson, "International Food Stamps," *Food Policy* (August 1988): 235–39.

96. An earlier draft of this section appears in Vernon W. Ruttan, "International Food Aid: Interest Groups and Clients," *Choices* 5 (3d quarter, 1980): 12–16.

97. Dean Kleckner, "Trade and Aid Policies: How U.S. Farmers See It," in *Aid, Trade, and Farm Policies*, ed. Wayne E. Swegle and Polly C. Ligon (Morrilton, Ark.: Winrock International, 1989), 17–22. Kieckner, President of the American Farm Bureau, notes that, while farmers are generally supportive of food aid, they increasingly oppose technical assistance for agricultural development. "Most U.S. farmers cannot understand—or don't want to understand—why we voluntarily finance, train, and equip our own competition for world markets" (p. 19). In 1986 the American Soybean Association was successful in having prohibitions on foreign assistance that would encourage exports from developing countries added to the Foreign Assistance Act of 1981 (the Bumpers amendment). See Paul B. Thompson, *The Ethics of Aid and Trade,* 41–55.

98. Dan Morgan, *Merchants of Grain* (New York: Viking Press, 1979), 102.

99. See particularly Lappé (and Collins), *Food First,* 227–356; George, *How the Other Half Dies,* 164–83.

100. *Cargo preference* refers to requirements that U.S. ships handle a specified percentage of certain cargos. The 1954 act required that 50 percent of all U.S. government-generated cargo be carried by U.S. ships. For the legislative history of cargo preference, see Charles S. Gitomer and C. Ford Runge, *Cargo Preference Legislation: Agricultural Exports and the Future of the Duluth-Superior Exchange—A Legislative History and Economic Analysis* (St. Paul: University of Minnesota Sea Grant College Program Research Report 34, April 1990).

101. In this section I draw very heavily on Robert R. Sullivan, "The Politics of Altruism: A Study of the Partnership between the United States Government and American Voluntary Relief Agencies for the Donation Abroad of Surplus Agricultural Commodities, 1949–1967" (Ph.D. diss., Johns Hopkins University, 1968). See also Cravero, "Food and Politics." The US/AID identifies five functional PVO subcategories that serve as intermediaries in the delivery of AID-funded programs: cooperative and credit unions, AFL-CIO labor institutes, family planning organizations, nonprofit consulting firms, and traditional voluntary organizations. The voluntary agencies involved in food aid are classified as traditional voluntary organizations. See U.S. Agency for International Development, *AID Partnership in International Development with Private and Voluntary Organizations* (Washington: AID Bureau for Program and Policy Coordination, September 1982).

102. See testimony by Wynn C. Fairfield in U.S. Congress, House Committee on Agriculture, *Long Range Farm Program (Hearings), Serial R, Part 22* (Washington: USGPO, 1955), 4332–33. Quoted in Sullivan, "The Politics of Altruism," 234.

103. Some PVOs have engaged in 100 percent monetization of food aid in project funding. Since the U.S. government also pays the ocean freight, this means that the U.S. government has been covering close to the full cost of some PVO project assistance.

104. Edward Clay and Elisabeth Everitt, *Food Aid and Emergencies: A Report on the Third IDS Food Aid Seminar* (Discussion paper, University of Sussex Institute of Development Studies, Brighton, July 1985), 30. For a dramatic example, see Raymond Bonner, "Famine," *New Yorker* (13 March 1989): 85–101.

105. G. Edward Schuh, *Improving the Developmental Effectiveness of Food Aid* (Paper prepared for U.S. Agency for International Development, Department of Agricultural and Applied Economics, University of Minnesota, St. Paul, September 1979).

106. The General Accounting Office has been critical of the Foreign Agricultural Service for lacking objective evaluation of the influence of market development activities. U.S. General Accounting Office, *International Trade: Review of Effectiveness of FAS Cooperator Market Development Program* (Washington: GAO INSIAD-87–89, March 1987). For a more positive evaluation, see S. Elaine Grigsby and Praveen M. Dixit, *Alternative Export Strategies and U.S. Agricultural Policies for Grains and Oilseeds, 1950–83* (Washington: USDA, Economic Research Service Staff Report AGES 860616, September 1986).

107. World Food Program/African Development Bank, *Food Aid for Development in Sub-Saharan Africa* (Rome: World Food Program, 1987), 2, 12; John W. Mellor

and Rajul Pandya-Lorch, "Food Aid and Development in the MADIA Countries," in *Aid to African Agriculture: Lessons from Two Decades of Donors Experience*, ed. Uma Lele (Baltimore: Johns Hopkins University Press, 1991), 520–73.

108. John Osgood Field and Mitchell B. Wallerstein, "Beyond Humanitarianism: A Development Perspective on American Food Aid," in *Food Policy: The Responsibility of the United States in Life and Death Choices*, ed. Peter G. Brown and Henry Shue (New York: Macmillan/Free Press, 1977). For a more balanced appraisal, see Singer, Wood, and Jennings, *Food Aid*, 37–54.

109. Beryl Levinger, *School Feeding Programs in Developing Countries: An Analysis of Actual and Potential Impact* (Evaluation Special Study 30, U.S. Agency for International Development, Washington, January 1986); Michael Marin, "Good Will and Its Limits in Somalia," *New York Times*, 27 August 1993, A29; "The Food Aid Racket," *Harpers* (August 1993): 10–12. Marin suggests that the Somali government has actively discouraged domestic food production in order to maintain the revenue generated by the sale and theft of food aid supplies.

110. Thomas R. Saylor, "A New Legislation Mandate for American Food Aid," in Brown and Shue, *Food Policy*, 206.

111. Robert L. Paarlberg, "The Mysterious Popularity of EEP," *Choices* 5 (2d quarter, 1990): 14–17; Richard Ball and Christopher Johnson, "Political, Economic and Humanitarian Motivations for PL 480 Food Aid: Evidence from Africa," *Economic Development and Cultural Change* 43 (forthcoming, 1995). Ball and Johnson find that in the 1970s economic and strategic self-interest were most influential but that in the 1980s humanitarian motivation and recipient country needs predominated in explaining the programming of food aid to Africa.

112. Grigsby and Dixit, *Alternative Export Strategies*; Shahla Shapouri and Stacey Rosen, *Effect of Fiscal Austerity on African Food Imports* (Foreign Agricultural Economic Report 230, Economic Research Service, USDA, Washington, May 1987).

113. National Research Council, Board on Science and Technology for International Development, *Food Aid Projections for the Decade of the 1990s* (Washington: National Academy Press, 1988). See also *Food Aid in Africa: An Agenda for the 1990's* (Washington: World Bank; Rome: World Food Program, August 1991) and Raymond F. Hopkins, "Reforming Food Aid for the 1990s" (Statement to the House Select Committee on Hunger, 22 June 1989). For food aid trends since 1972, see Nydia R. Suarez and Linda C. Beoler, *U.S. Agricultural Exports under Public Law 480* (Washington: USDA, Economic Research Service, Statistical Bulletin 876, February 1994).

114. See Schuh, *Developmental Effectiveness of Food Aid;* John W. Mellor, "Global Food Balances and Food Security," *World Development* 16 (1988): 997–1011; Willis W. Peterson, "International Food Stamps," *Food Policy* (August 1988): 235–39.

Chapter 9 Universities, Voluntary Organizations, and Public Foundations: Interests, Clients, and Constituencies

1. Agency for International Development, *AID Partnership in International Development with Private Voluntary Organizations* (Washington: US/AID, September 1982).

The universities and PVOs also devote substantial amounts of their own resources to economic assistance. In the late 1980s AID estimated that U.S. university subsidies to foreign students amounted to about $1.5 billion and that private voluntary agencies (including churches) contributed about $10 million in their own resources. Agency for International Development, *Development and the National Interest: U.S. Economic Assistance into the 21st Century* (Washington: USAID, February 1989), 70.

2. Ibid., 2.

3. Richard O. Niehoff, *John A. Hannah: Versatile Administrator and Distinguished Public Servant* (Lanham, Md.: University Press of America, 1989), 216.

4. This section draws very heavily on Brian D. Jordahl and Vernon W. Ruttan, *Universities and AID: A History of Their Partnership in Technical Assistance for Developing Countries* (St. Paul: University of Minnesota, Department of Agricultural and Applied Economics Staff Paper P91–32, July 1991). I have also drawn heavily on an unpublished study by Ervin J. Long and Frank Campbell, *Reflections on the Role of AID and the US Universities in International Agricultural Development* (Rockville, Md.: Statistica, 1989). See also U.S. Congress, Office of Technology Assessment, *New Opportunities for U.S. Universities in Development Assistance,* OTA-BP-F-71 (Washington: USGPO, September 1991). I am indebted to Robert J. Berg, Stuart Callison, and John Stovall for comments on an earlier draft of this section.

5. Between 1960 and 1988 over half of the expenditures on AID-university programs and projects were in the field of agriculture. Long and Campbell, *Aid and the U.S. Universities,* 1–15, 16.

6. In 1951 the Mutual Security Agency was formed to assume the responsibilities of the Economic Cooperation Administration. It also assumed responsibility for aid to Southeast Asia and the Pacific regions while the Technical Cooperation Agency coordinated aid to the Middle East, South Asia, the American republics, and Africa. *New York Times,* 12 January 1953, 10. The MSA and TCA essentially were doing the same work but in different geographic regions. The MSA differed from the TCA in that its responsibilities also included military assistance. In 1952 the two organizations were merged to form the Foreign Operations Administration (see Fig. 13.1).

7. John M. Richardson, Jr., *Partners in Development: An Analysis of AID-University Relations, 1950–1966* (East Lansing: Michigan State University Press, 1969), 37.

8. "Private Aid Stressed in Stassen Cutback," *New York Times,* 11 September 1953, 5; "U.S. Technical Aid Enlists Colleges," *New York Times,* 7 October 1953, 18.

9. Richardson, *Partners in Development,* 41.

10. Paul P. Kennedy, "Separate Point 4 Urged on Stassen," *New York Times,* 17 December 1953, 30.

11. Robert Bendiner, "Point Four—Still the Great Basic Hope," *New York Times,* 1 April 1951, sec. VI, 13; Paul P. Kennedy, " Concept and Scope of Point 4 Viewed as Undergoing Shift," *New York Times,* 24 September 1953, 1.

12. Long and Campbell, *Aid and the U.S. Universities,* I-19; Richardson, *Partners in Development,* 53.

13. Long and Campbell, *Aid and the U.S. Universities,* I-20; Richardson, *Partners in Development,* sec. I, 59.

14. Ibid., 54.

15. Richard Humphrey, ed., *Universities and Development Assistance Abroad* (Washington: American Council on Education, 1967), 40.

16. Ibid., 43.

17. *Ibid.*, 109.

18. U.S. Congress, House, *Foreign Assistance Act of 1962: Hearings before the Committee on Foreign Affairs,* pt. 1, 87th Cong., 2d sess. (Washington: USGPO, 1962), 3; Long and Campbell, *Aid and the U.S. Universities,* sec. III, 10.

19. John W. Gardner, *A.I.D. and the Universities,* Report to the Administrator of the Agency for International Development (Washington: AID, 1964), 2.

20. "The Anchor Man for Foreign Aid," *Business Week,* 11 May 1963, 50.

21. David E. Bell, interview by Brian D. Jordahl, Minneapolis, Minn., 19 June 1990.

22. Projects were begun in Jordan, Argentina (2), Bolivia, Brazil (4), Costa Rica, Dominican Republic, Guatemala, Jamaica, Paraguay, Uruguay, Nigeria (5), Malawi, Zambia, Sierre Leone, Somali Republic, Uganda, and India. Projects were terminated in Cambodia, China, Iran, Guatemala, and Paraguay. Richardson, *Partners in Development* (East Lansing: Michigan State University Press, 1969), 124–25.

23. Gardner, *A.I.D. and the Universities,* 7; Richardson, *Partners in Development,* 141.

24. Committee on Institutional Cooperation–US/AID Rural Development Research Project, *Building Institutions To Serve Agriculture* (LaFayette, Ind.: Purdue University Press, 1968), ix, 4–26. The recommendations are discussed in greater detail in Brian D. Jordahl and Vernon W. Ruttan, *Universities and AID: A History of Their Partnership in Technical Assistance for Developing Countries* (St. Paul: University of Minnesota Department of Agricultural and Applied Economics Staff Paper P91–32, July 1991).

25. Niehoff, *John A. Hannah,* 141–42.

26. Ibid., 142; Long and Campbell, *Aid and the U.S. Universities,* sec. IV, 2.

27. U.S. Congress, Senate Committee on Foreign Relations and Subcommittee on Foreign Assistance, *Foreign Assistance Authorization: Examination of U.S. Foreign Aid Programs and Policies: Hearings on S. 1816 and H.R. 9005,* 94th Cong., 1st sess., 1975, 640.

28. U.S. General Accounting Office, *Aid and the Universities Have Yet To Forge an Effective Partnership To Combat World Food Problems*, ID82–3 (Gaithersburg, Md.: GAO, 1981), 7.

29. Public Law 480 (PL 480) is the primary legislation authorizing U.S. food assistance to less developed countries (see Chap. 8).

30. Agency for International Development, "Report to the Congress on Title XII—Famine Prevention and Freedom from Hunger," 1977, 6.

31. GAO, *Aid and the Universities,* 7; Olga Starakis and Sally Nelson, eds., *Proceedings of the Conference on the University and Title XII Held in Minneapolis, Minnesota, May 5–7, 1977* (St. Paul: Institute of Agriculture, Forestry, and Home Economics, July 1977), 37–38.

32. Long and Campbell, *Aid and the U.S. Universities,* 6–8; sec. V, 6.

33. David E. Bell, interview by Brian D. Jordahl, Minneapolis, Minn., 19 June 1990.

34. Ibid.; Long and Campbell, *Aid and the U.S. Universities,* 7.

35. Richard E. Just, David Zilberman, Douglas Parker, and Mark Phillips, *The Economic Impacts of BARD Research on the U.S.* (Bet Dagan, Israel: Binational Agricultural Research and Development Fund [BARD], 1 June 1988).

36. Warren C. Baum, *Partners against Hunger: The Consultative Group on International Agricultural Research* (Washington: World Bank, 1986); Vernon W. Ruttan, *Agricultural Research Policy* (Minneapolis: University of Minnesota Press, 1982), 116–46.

37. Baum, *Partners against Hunger,* 18–22, 24.

38. Ibid., 30.

39. Vernon W. Ruttan, "Toward a Global Agricultural Research System: A Personal View," *Research Policy* 15 (December 1986): 316.

40. Ruttan, "Global Agricultural Research System," 307–27.

41. For a more detailed review of the issues discussed in this section, see Congress of the United States, Office of Technology Assessment, *New Opportunities for U.S. Universities in Development Assistance,* OTA-BP-F-71 (Washington: USGPO, September 1991).

42. U.S. General Accounting Office, *Foreign Aid: Issues Concerning U.S. University Participation*, NSID-89-38 (Gaithersburg, Md.: GAO, 1989), 2.

43. John G. Stovall, "The Role of U.S. Universities in Development Assistance: What Have We Learned from Experience?" (Paper prepared for the Office of Technology, U.S. Congress, August 1989), 21.

44. U.S. General Accounting Office, *Foreign Aid: Issues Concerning U.S. University Participation,* NSID-89-38 (Gaithersburg, Md.: GAO, 1989), 2:14–16.

45. E. T. York, Jr., "An Assessment of Title XII of the Foreign Assistance Act, 'Famine Prevention and Freedom from Hunger'" (Paper prepared for the Office of Technology Assessment, U.S. Congress, December 1988), 10ff.

46. Agency for International Development, *Toward Strategic Management* (Washington: US/AID, December 1990), 3; idem, *The Partnership for Business and Development* (Washington: US/AID, December 1990), 6.

47. BIFADEC Advisory Committee on the University Center Program, *Report of the BIFADEC Task Force on the University Center Program* (Washington: US/AID Agency Center for University Cooperation in Development, 5 December 1991).

48. Task Force on Development Assistance and Economic Growth, *International Cooperation for Sustainable Economic Growth: The U.S. Interest and Proposals for Revitalization* (Washington: Board for International Food and Agriculture Development and Economic Cooperation, February 1992).

49. Dr. Robert Rosenzweig, President of the Association of American Universities, has pointed out that AID and the State Department, while consumers of the intellectual product of universities, have seldom accepted responsibility for investment in the production of either the knowledge or trained people relevant to the department and agency missions. He contrasts AID and the State Department unfavorably with the National Science Foundation, the National Institute of Health, and the Department of Defense. Robert Rosenzweig, "Presentation to BIFADEC" (Washington, 20 June 1989, mimeo).

50. In preparing this section I have drawn on a paper prepared for me by Joseph V. Kennedy, "PVOs and U.S. Foreign Assistance" (St. Paul: University of Minnesota Department of Agricultural and Applied Economics, December 1990, mimeo). Wallace J. Campbell, Catherine Coughlin, Julie Fisher, Douglas Siglin, Brian H. Smith, Carolyn Stremlau, and Cynthia Williams have provided useful comments and criticism on early drafts.

51. The terminology used to describe private voluntary organizations and other nongovernmental organizations has become increasingly baroque. See David C. Korten, *Getting into the Twenty-first Century: Voluntary Action and Global Agenda* (West Hartford, Conn.: Kumarion Press, 1990), 2.

52. In 1993, U.S. PVOs registered with AID received $2.4 billion in private contributions. The U.S. government provided them with an additional $1.5 billion. This does not include the private contributions to PVOs working abroad that do not elect to receive support from government sources. U.S. private contributions to PVOs that work abroad rank second highest, behind Norway, in the industrial world. For detailed information on sources of support, see Agency for International Development, Office of Private and Voluntary Cooperation, *Voluntary Foreign Aid Programs, Report of American Voluntary Agencies Engaged in Overseas Relief and Development Registered with U.S. Agency for International Development* (Washington: US/AID, 1994).

53. There is a serious deficiency in scholarly historical and social science literature on the role of "third sector" (nonprofit, nongovernmental) institutions in economic development. Much of the literature tends to be personal, self-indulgent, and promotional. Among the important exceptions are Merle Curti, *American Philanthropy Abroad: A History* (New Brunswick, N.J.: Rutgers University Press, 1963; 2d ed., Transaction Books, 1988); Jorgen Lissner, *The Politics of Altruism: A Study of the Political Behavior of Voluntary Development Agencies* (Geneva: Lutheran World Federation, February 1977), 87–132; Brian H. Smith, *More than Altruism: The Politics of Private Foreign Aid* (Princeton: Princeton University Press, 1990), 27–44; Julie Fisher, *The Road from Rio: Sustainable Development and the Nongovernmental Movement in the Third World* (Westport, Conn.: Praeger, 1993). For an attempt to outline a theory of the provision of goods and services by the voluntary nonprofit sector, see Burton A. Weisbrod, *The Voluntary Non-Profit Sector: An Economic Analysis* (Lexington, Mass.: D. C. Heath-Lexington Books, 1977), 51–76.

54. Smith, *More than Altruism,* 32–48; Curti, *American Philanthropy Abroad.*

55. Arthur C. Ringland, "The Organization of Voluntary Foreign Aid: 1939–1953," *Department of State Bulletin* 30 (15 March 1954): 303–91.

56. Curti, *American Philanthropy Abroad,* 487.

57. No attempt is made in this section to review comparable developments in other Western countries. Among the useful accounts are Ben Whitaker, *A Bridge of People: A Personal View of Oxfam's First Forty Years* (London: Heinemann, 1983).

58. Curti, *American Philanthropy Abroad,* 521–23. For a highly personal account of the founding of CRS and its early postwar programs, primarily in Europe, see Eileen Egon, *Catholic Relief Services: The Beginning Years for the Life of the World* (New York: Catholic Relief Services, 1988). The first director of CRS was the Rever-

end Patrick A. O'Boyle, a child welfare specialist. Reverend Edward E. Sandstrom, whose earlier work had been in labor economics and social welfare, became executive director.

59. Alfred A. Schneider, *My Brother's Keeper* (Green Bay, Wis.: Alt Publishing, 1981), 189.

60. Curti, *American Philanthropy Abroad,* 512–17.

61. Ibid., 515.

62. This account draws very heavily on the somewhat idealized account by Wallace J. Campbell, *The History of CARE: A Personal Account* (Westport, Conn.: Praeger, 1990). See also Curti, *American Philanthropy Abroad,* 491–502.

63. "The organization might never have been born if it had not been for Ringland's single minded, driving determination to enlist backing for his great idea of overseas food package distribution." Campbell, *The History of CARE,* 8.

64. Ibid., 10.

65. Ibid., 70.

66. For a less idealistic perspective on the decision by CARE to refocus its efforts on the less developed countries, see Eugene Linden, *The Alms Race: The Impact of American Voluntary Aid Abroad* (New York: Random House, 1976), 10–19.

67. Agency for International Development, Office of Private and Voluntary Cooperation, *Report of American Voluntary Agencies Engaged in Overseas Relief and Development Registered with the U.S. Agency for International Development* (Washington: US/AID, 1994).

68. For a critical perspective on PVO involvement in Somalia, see Michael Maven, "Shortsighted Charity in Somalia," *New York Times*, 27 August 1993; "The Food-AID Racket," *Harpers* (August 1993): 10–12.

69. American Council of Voluntary Agencies of Foreign Service, *The Role of Voluntary Agencies in Technical Assistance* (New York: ACVAFS, May 1953); James G. Maddox, *Technical Assistance by Religious Agencies in Latin America* (Chicago: University of Chicago Press, 1956); Smith, *More than Altruism,* 113, 54.

70. Smith, *More than Altruism,* 56–71.

71. Foreign Assistance Act of 1973, Public Law 93–189 (87 stat 71), Part I, Chap. 1, sec. 102(b)13.

72. International Security and Development Assistance Act of 1981, Public Law 97-113 (95 stat. 1519), sec. 2151 a–d.

73. Richard E. Bissell, "Statement," in U.S. Congress, House Select Committee on Hunger, *Role of Private Voluntary Organizations in the U.S. Foreign Assistance Program: Hearings*, 101st Cong. (Washington: US/GPO, 1989), 3, 31 (hereafter cited as *Hearings on PVOs in the Foreign Assistance Program*).

74. Ibid., 9.

75. David Korten, "Statement," in *Hearings on PVOs in the Foreign Assistance Program,* 117.

76. For a brief description of grants outstanding in these programs during 1989, see *FVA/PVC Project Portfolio: Fiscal Year 1989* (Washington: US/AID Bureau for Peace and Voluntary Assistance, 1990) (prepared by Automation Research Systems).

77. For a detailed review of AID's Child Survival Program, see *Child Survival: A Fourth Report to Congress on the USAID Program* (Washington: AID, 1989). See also *Office of Private and Voluntary Cooperation (PVC),* informational brochure prepared for AID by Automation Research Systems, June 1989.

78. Agency for International Development, *AID Partnership in International Development with Private and Voluntary Organizations*, AID Policy Paper (Washington: Bureau for Program and Policy Coordination, September 1982), 1.

79. Ibid., 1, 2.

80. E. A. Brett, "Voluntary Agencies as Development Organizations: Theorizing the Problem of Efficiency and Accountability," *Development and Change* 24 (1993): 269–303; Burton A. Weisbrod, "Rewarding Performance That Is Hard To Measure: The Private Non Profit Sector," *Science* 244 (May 1989): 541–44.

81. Judith Tendler, *Turning Voluntary Organizations into Development Agencies: Questions for Evaluation* (Washington: AID Program Evaluation Discussion Paper 12, April 1982). The Tendler study is widely cited in subsequent literature on PVO effectiveness. Ibid., 2–6.

82. Thomas W. Dichter, "The Changing World of Northern NGOs: Problems, Paradigms, and Possibilities," in *Strengthening the Poor: What Have We Learned?* ed. John P. Lewis (New Brunswick, N.J.: Transaction Books, 1988), 177–88. See also the articles in the special issue by Anne Gordon Drabek, ed., "Development Alternatives: The Challenge for NGOs," *World Development* 15 (Autumn 1987, supplement).

83. Amanda Bennett, "CARE Makes a Comeback after Drive to Revamp Its Management Practices," *Wall Street Journal*, 9 February 1987, sec. 2, 21.

84. Thomas H. Fox, "NGO's from the United States," in Drabek, "Development Alternatives," 11–19.

85. Smith, *More than Altruism,* 112–24. Korten has employed an evolutionary topology: (1) Generation I, Relief and Welfare; (2) Generation II, Small-Scale and Self-Reliant Local Development; (3) Generation III, Sustainable System Development. See David C. Korten, "Third Generation NGO Strategies: A Key to People-centered Development," *World Development* 15 (1987, supplement): 145–59. Clark suggests a topology of six classes: (1) relief and welfare agencies, (2) technical innovation organizations, (3) public services contractors, (4) popular development agencies, (5) grassroots development organizations, and (6) advocacy groups and networks. John Clark, *Democratizing Development: The Role of Voluntary Organizations* (West Hartford, Conn.: Kumarian Press, 1991), 34, 35.

86. Smith, *More than Altruism,* 113.

87. See Fisher, *The Road from Rio*. One of the concerns that emerges from Fisher's study is the extent to which indigenous or grassroots organizations are, in fact, dependent on international NGOs, bilateral development assistance agencies, or their own governments.

88. Joint Working Group of Development Education, *A Framework for Development Education in the United States* (New York: Private Agencies in International Development and American Council of Voluntary Agencies of Foreign Service, 1984). See also Larry Minear, "The Other Missions of NGO's: Education and Advocacy," in Drabek, "Development Alternatives," 201–10.

89. Doug Hellinger, "NGOs and the Large Aid Donors: Changing the Terms of Engagement," in Drabek, "Development Alternatives," 135.

90. David C. Korten, "Strategic Organizations for People Centered Development," *Public Administration Review* 44 (July/August 1984): 341–52; David C. Korten, *The U.S. Voluntary Sector and Global Realities: Issues for the 1990's* (Boston: Institute for Development Research, April 1989); David C. Korten, "Third Generation NGO Strategies: A Key to People-centered Development," in Drabek, "Development Alternatives," 145–59; David C. Korten, *Getting to the Twenty-first Century: Voluntary Action and the Global Agenda* (West Hartford, Conn.: Kumarian Press, 1990); David Korten, "Statement," in *Hearing on PVOs in the Foreign Assistance Program*, 120. See also Clark, *Democratizing Development*, 4, 125–98, and Barbara J. Bramble and Garth Porter, "Non-governmental Organizations and the Making of U.S. International Environmental Policy," in Andrew Hurrell and Benedict Kingsbury, eds., *The International Politics of the Environment: Actors, Interests and Institutions* (Oxford: Clarindon Press, 1992), 326.

91. Doug Siglin, "From Relief toward Development and Empowerment," in *Hunger 1994: Transforming the Politics of Hunger* (Silver Spring, Md.: Bread for the World Institute, 1993), 20–30; Smith, *More than Altruism*, 129.

92. Ibid., 125.

93. Robert J. Berg, *Non-Governmental Organizations: A New Force in Third World Development and Politics* (East Lansing: Michigan State University Center for Advanced Study in International Development, May 1987). Anthony Bebington and John Farrington, "Governments, NGOs and Agricultural Development: Perspectives on Changing Inter-Organizational Relationships," *Journal of Development Studies* 29 (January 1993): 199–219.

94. In its 1993 annual report, the Advisory Committee on Voluntary Foreign Aid expressed concern that the relationship between AID and the PVO community was evolving toward a customer-contractor relationship. Advisory Committee on Voluntary Foreign Aid, *International Development and Private Voluntarism: A Maturing Relationship* (Washington: US/AID, 1993).

95. I am indebted to Rolf Sartorius, Jr., for conducting a number of the interviews on which I draw in this section.

96. A 1977 assessment of the future of the Peace Corps recommended that it also be organized as a public nonprofit corporation. See Harlan Cleveland, *The Future of the Peace Corps* (Princeton, N.J.: Aspen Institute for Humanistic Studies, 1977). My excuse for not including the Peace Corps within the scope of this book is that I view it primarily as an investment in the education of American youth rather than an investment in the economic development of Third World countries. The periodic attempts to transform the Peace Corps into a technical assistance agency have, in my judgment, been misguided. It is somewhat surprising that I have not been able to identify a serious evaluation of the Peace Corps experience. For idealized histories of the Peace Corps, see Gerard T. Rice, *The Bold Experiment: JFK's Peace Corps* (Notre Dame: University of Notre Dame Press, 1985); Coates Redman, *Come as You Are: The Peace Corps Story* (New York: Harcourt Brace Jovanovich, 1986).

97. I am indebted to William D. Fuller and Allen C. Choate for comments on an earlier draft of this section.

98. U.S. Congress, Senate Committee on Foreign Relations, *The Asia Foundation: Past, Present, and Future* (Committee Print), 98th Cong., 1st sess. (Washington: US/GPO, February 1983), 1. This report is an exceedingly useful analysis of the evolution of the Asia Society since the mid-1970s. I have drawn on it extensively in this section.

99. The only detailed history of a country program with which I am familiar is the very useful report by Marcus Franda, *A History of the Asia Foundation in Thailand* (College Park: University of Maryland Office of International Affairs, 1986, mimeo).

100. The Asia Foundation-CIA connection did, however, affect attitudes toward other foundations working in Asia. When I worked for the Rockefeller Foundation at the International Rice Research Institute in the Philippines (1963–65) and later with the Agricultural Development Council (ADC) (1973–78), I was frequently told by Asian colleagues that they assumed that IRRI and ADC were CIA "fronts" and that we all had CIA connections. When I became president of the Agricultural Development Council in 1973, I made it a point to announce at each annual staff meeting that any staff member who made it a practice to accept opportunities for CIA "debriefings" would be immediately terminated. A somewhat amusing incident occurred when I returned to the University of Minnesota in 1978. I received a call from an ambiguous "office of the U.S. government" about the possibility of an appointment. The young man who came to my office inquired about my extensive foreign travel and asked if I would be willing to keep his office informed. My response was to ask "Why are you coming to see me now? During the time I was working in Asia, no one ever thought my work important enough to seek a debriefing." He responded to the effect that they now had a few more staff members in the St. Paul office. After a bit more discussion, I told him that, if his office would write me an official request, I would be glad to put it on my reprint mailing list. The request never came.

101. Senate Committee on Foreign Relations, *The Asia Foundation,* 2.

102. Ibid.

103. Ibid.

104. Ronald Reagan, "Address to Members of the British Parliament," Westminster, 8 June 1982, quoted in Senate Committee on Foreign Relations, *The Asia Foundation,* 11. It is of interest that this commitment represented an unacknowledged return to the political development thrust of the House Foreign Affairs Committee in the early and mid-1960s. See Chapter 4.

105. Senate Committee on Foreign Relations, *The Asia Foundation,* 12, 30, 47.

106. U.S. Agency for International Development, *Democracy and Governance* (Washington: US/AID, November 1991). To an outside observer both the AID policy paper and the Asia Society political development program seemed to represent a partial recycling of themes that had informed the political development literature of the 1960s. See Vernon W. Ruttan, "What Happened to Political Development," *Economic Development and Cultural Change* 39 (January 1991): 265–92.

107. For an introduction to the early history of the Inter-American Foundation, see the three promotional books commissioned by the foundation: *Inter-American Foundation, They Know How: An Experiment in Development Assistance* (Washington: USGPO, 1977); Eugene J. Meehan (with Charles Reilly and Thomas Raney), *In Partnership with*

People: An Alternative Development Strategy (Rosslyn, Va.: Inter-American Foundation, 1978), 8–14; Patrick Breslin, *Development and Dignity: Grassroots Development and the Inter-American Foundation, 1987* (Rosslyn, Va.: Inter-American Foundation, 1987. For a review of the same events, written from the perspective of the Republican Right, see Cleto D. Giovanni, Jr., *The Inter-American Foundation* (Washington: Heritage Foundation, 1981).

108. Rudolf A. Peterson, *U.S. Foreign Assistance in the 1970s: A New Approach*, Report to the President from the Task Force on International Development (Washington: USGPO, 4 March 1970). The Peterson commission also recommended the creation of a U.S. International Development Bank to make capital and technical assistance loans and an International Development Council to coordinate trade, financial, and investment policy—with the council chairman a presidential appointee located in the White House. The Peterson proposals were not acted on by Congress.

109. William P. Stedman, Jr., Peter L. Scanton, and Sidney Weintraub, *The Inter-American Foundation: Report of the Evaluation Group* (Washington: Inter-American Foundation, March 1984), 10.

110. The Social Progress Trust Fund (SPTF) was established on 19 June 1961 through an agreement between the U.S. government and the Inter-American Development Bank under which U.S. funding is made available to the bank to assist social development projects. Repayment is made in local currencies. In 1973 Congress authorized the IAF to draw on the local currency repayments.

111. U.S. Congress, House Committee on Foreign Affairs, Subcommittee on Inter-American Affairs, *Inter-American Foundation: First Year of Operations, Hearings,* 92d Cong., 2d sess., 25 April 1972 (Washington, USGPO, 1973), 28–35. During this hearing IAF was also asked to respond to the criticism that it was not "getting down to the grassroots level" but rather was working through intermediary organizations. See also U.S. Congress, House Committee on Foreign Affairs, Subcommittee on Inter-American Affairs, *Inter-American Foundation: Second Year of Operations, Hearings,* 93d Cong., 1st sess., 27 September 1973 (Washington, USGPO, 1973), 19–29.

112. U.S. General Accounting Office, *Social Development Activities in Latin America Promoted by the Inter-American Foundation, FY 1972* (Washington: Comptroller General of the United States, 1973).

113. Meehan characterized the relationship between the foundation and the IGA as "guerrilla warfare with IGA as aggressor . . . The opening round was fired by IGA in a report (issued in November 1974) sharply criticizing the records management system in the Foundation, the lack of contact between the IAF and the America development community, and the use made of Social Progress Trust Fund (SPTF)." Meehan, *In Partnership with People,* 27. The IGA criticisms were rejected both by the foundation board and by supporters in Congress.

114. Giovanni, *The Inter-American Foundation.* See also Peter D. Bell, *A Response to the Heritage Foundation Report on the Inter-American Foundation* (Washington: Inter-American Foundation, 13 November 1981). The Heritage Foundation report on the IAF is a rather curious document. It, as well as many other Heritage Foundation documents of this period, displays the symbols of objective scholarship (footnotes,

quotations from supposedly authoritative sources) but almost none of the substance of scholarship (such as careful weighing of the evidence). The most polite way to describe the report is as an exercise in persuasive discourse.

115. Ibid., 65, 66, 67.

116. The IAF has sponsored evaluation by well-known social scientists including Judith Tendler (with Kevin Healgard and Carol Michaels O'Laughlin), *What To Think about Cooperatives* (Rosslyn, Va.: Inter-American Foundation, 1983); Albert O. Hirschman, *Getting Ahead Collectively: Grassroots Experience in Latin America* (New York: Pergamon Press, 1984). The IAF also publishes articles on project experience in its journal, *Grassroots Development* (before 1982 *The Journal of the Inter-American Foundation*). In its publications, the IAF tends to emphasize quality of communication relative to documentation.

117. William P. Stedman, Jr., Peter L. Scanton, and Sidney Weintraub, *The Inter-American Foundation: Report of the Evaluation Group* (Washington: Inter-American Foundation, March 1984), 16, 6 (the Weintraub report).

118. Stedman, Scanton, and Weintraub, *The Inter-American Foundation,* 40–43, 55–57.

119. Vernon W. Ruttan, telephone interview with Deborah Szekley, 9 July 1993.

120. Stephen Hellinger, Douglas Hellinger, Fred M. O'Regan, *AID for Just Development* (Boulder: Lynne Rienner Publishers, 1988), 87.

121. Ibid., x, xi.

122. U.S. Congress, House Committee on Appropriations, *Foreign Operations, Export Financing and Related Programs Appropriations for 1990s, Hearings* (Washington: USGPO, 1989), 1120.

123. For an evaluation of the in-country service organizations, see Edward T. LaFarge, Thomas J. Scanlon, and Juan M. Gooden, *The ICS—Past and Future: A Management Review* (Washington: Inter-American Foundation, October 1991, mimeo).

124. Stedman, Scanton, and Weintraub, *Inter-American Foundation: Report of the Evaluation Group* (Washington: Inter-American Foundation, 1988) (the second Weintraub report), 10; Memo from Deborah Szekely, AIF President, to Victor Blanco, Chairman of the IAF Board of Directors dated 12 January 1989.

125. For background materials on the founding and early history of the African Development Foundation, see Hellinger, Hellinger, and O'Regan, *AID for Just Development,* 89–94; General Accounting Office, *Issues Affecting Appropriations for the African Development Foundation*, NSIAD-85-62 (Gaithersburg, Md.: GAO, 7 May 1985); U.S. Congress, Office of Technology Assessment, *Grassroots Development: The African Development Foundation*, OTA-F-387 (Washington: USGPO, June 1988); U.S. Congress, House Committee on International Relations, *To Establish an African Development Foundation: Hearings* (Washington: USGPO, 1978).

126. Appropriations of $4.5 million were made from 1981 through 1983. The funds were made available on a "no-year" basis and were carried over for future use.

127. GAO, *Issues Affecting Appropriations*, 4; Molly Sinclair, "Conflict-ridden Agency Has Provided No Funds for Grass-Roots of Africa," *Washington Post*, 4 May 1984, A-19.

128. OTA, *Grassroots Development: ADF,* 10; U.S. Congress, House Committee on

Foreign Affairs, *Foreign Assistance Legislation for Fiscal Years 1990–91 (Part 6), Hearings and Markup,* 101st Cong., 1st sess. (Washington: USGPO, 1990), 438–41.

129. African Development Foundation, *Framework for Progress: A Five-Year Plan, 1990–94* (Washington: ADF, 1990), 53–56. ADF also supported environmental, health, and fisheries projects during this period.

130. House Committee on Appropriations, Subcommittee on Foreign Operations and Related Agencies, *Foreign Assistance and Related Programs Appropriations for 1987*, ADF Congressional Presentation, Fiscal Year 1987 (Washington: USGPO, 1986), 1663–89.

131. Rolf Sartorius, Lynn Herbon-Gwinn interview, 2 March 1990, and Adwoa Dunn interview, 2 March 1990. Herbon-Gwinn was congressional liaison for ADF, and Adwoa Dunn was staff consultant, House Committee on Foreign Affairs, Subcommittee on Africa.

132. U.S. Congress, House Committee on Appropriations, *Foreign Operations, Export Financing and Related Programs Appropriations for 1990: Hearings* (Washington: USGPO, 1989), 25, 226.

133. Rolf Sartorius, Herbon-Gwinn interview, 2 March 1990.

134. OTA, *Grassroots Development: ADF,* 36. The government officials named were the under-secretary of state for African affairs and AID's assistant administrator for Africa. Four of the five representatives of the private sector were business people, none with African experience.

135. Sartorius, Herbon-Gwinn interview, 2 March 1990.

136. *Foreign Assistance Legislation for Fiscal Years 1990–91 (Part 6)*, 441–42.

137. Sartorius, Herbon-Gwinn interview, 2 March 1990.

138. An autonomous foundation-like institution to fund PVO activities overseas could be attractive to both the PVOs and AID. On 2 May 1989, Douglas Siglen, testifying before the Senate Foreign Relations Committee on behalf of the American Council on International Voluntary Action (InterAction), a coalition of PVOs engaged in humanitarian and development work overseas, commented that "some of us . . . have envisioned the day when cooperation between the government and the PVO's will be handled through a joint foundation like structure, more focused on meeting long term development problems and less dependent on the exigencies of lateral government-to-government relationships." U.S. Congress, Senate Committee on Foreign Relations, *Foreign Assistance Authorization for Fiscal Year 1990: Hearings,* 101st Cong., 1st sess. (Washington: USGPO, 1989), 101–273, 188. From the AID perspective such an arrangement could institutionalize the relationship with PVOs or, as one AID official commented, "We could pension them off and get them out of our hair" (personal communication, 1989).

Chapter 10 Economic Assistance for Strategic Objectives

1. I am indebted to Ragui Assad, Douglas C. Dacy, Thomas A. Dine, Paul Findlay, C. Patrick Quinlan, John Turner, Robert T. Holt, Larry Q. Nowels, Robert Pastor,

Yacov Tsur, Manuel Vanegas, and Robert White for comments on an earlier draft of this chapter.

2. Steven A. Hildreth, "Perceptions of U.S. Security Assistance, 1959–1983: The Public Record," in *U.S. Security Assistance*, ed. Ernest Graves and Steven A. Hildreth (Lexington, Mass.: Lexington Books, 1985), 83.

3. In this chapter I have focussed primarily on the major recipients of ESF resources. For a very useful discussion of U.S. policy toward several other ESF recipients, see Robert F. Zimmerman, *Dollars, Diplomacy, and Dependency: Dilemmas of U.S. Economic Aid* (Boulder: Lynne Rienner Publishers, 1983), 11–138. For discussion of assistance to the former Soviet Union, see the several excellent reports by Curt Tarnoff, *The Former Soviet Union and U.S. Foreign Assistance in 1992: The Role of Congress* (Washington: Library of Congress, Congressional Research Service, 12 October 1993); *U.S. and International Assistance to the Former Soviet Union* (Washington: Library of Congress, Congressional Research Service, 26 March 1994).

4. The prevailing view among development economists and political scientists is that the pursuit of strategic objectives by donors has typically reduced the effect of economic assistance when evaluated in terms of contribution to economic development. See, for example, Anne O. Krueger and Vernon W. Ruttan, "Assistance to Korea" and "Assistance to Turkey," in Krueger, Michalopoulos, and Ruttan, *Aid and Development*, 226–49, 250–68; Stanton H. Burnett, *Investing in Security: Economic Aid for Noneconomic Purposes* (Washington: Center for Strategic and International Studies, 1992).

5. In developing this chapter I have been confronted with a massive literature on the political and military aspects and a relative paucity of literature on the economic aspects of assistance to Vietnam. For an exceedingly useful documentation of U.S. policy toward Vietnam, see William Conrad Gibbons, *The U.S. Government and the Vietnam War, Executive and Legislative Rates and Relationships: Part I, 1945–60; Part II, 1961–64; Part III, January–July 1965* (Princeton: Princeton University Press, 1986, 1989). See also the US/AID Vietnam Terminal Report prepared under the direction of Robert V. Craig, *United States Economic Assistance to South Vietnam* (Washington: US/AID, 31 December 1975), vols. 1–3.

6. Paul M. Kattenburg, *The Vietnam Trauma in American Foreign Policy, 1945–75* (New Brunswick: Transaction Books, 1980), 195.

7. Patrick L. Hatcher, *The Suicide of an Elite: American Internationalists and Vietnam* (Stanford: Stanford University Press, 1990).

8. In this section I have drawn very heavily on the exceedingly useful discussion by Douglas C. Dacy, *Foreign Aid, War and Economic Development: South Vietnam, 1955–1975* (Cambridge: Cambridge University Press, 1966), 194–97. See also the discussion of the Commercial Import Program in John D. Montgomery, *The Politics of Foreign Aid: American Experience in Southeast Asia* (New York: Praeger, 1962), 85–93.

9. Franklin D. Roosevelt, quoted from Bernard B. Fall, *The Two Vietnams: A Political and Military Analysis* (New York: Praeger, 1963), 53.

10. Craig, *United States Economic Assistance*, 1:10.

11. John D. Montgomery, *The Politics of Foreign Aid* (New York: Praeger, 1962), 44–48.

12. For a more detailed discussion of the Vietminh, the Vietcong, and the Diem government land reforms, see Robert L. Sansom, *The Economics of Insurgency in the Mekong Delta* (Cambridge: MIT Press, 1970), 53–69. Also J. Price Gittinger, *Studies on Land Tenure in Vietnam: Terminal Report* (Saigon: U.S. Operations Mission to Vietnam, December 1959); Craig, *United States Economic Assistance,* 2(b):1–59.

13. For a useful case history of the Michigan State Civil Guard Project, see Montgomery, *The Politics of Foreign Aid*, 64–70. Montgomery also presents case studies of the Civic Action Development Program, the Land Development Program, and the Land Reform Program. These programs, like the Civil Guard Program, became sources of tensions between the Diem government and the USOM because of the conflicting interests of the two parties.

14. See Fall, *The Two Vietnams*, 326.

15. Frances Fitzgerald, *Fire in the Lake: The Vietnamese and the Americans in Vietnam* (Boston: Little, Brown, 1972), 103.

16. Dacy, *Foreign Aid,* 9, 12.

17. Craig, *United States Economic Assistance*, 1:24–26; see also the detailed reviews of sectoral programs in vol. 2.

18. Roy L. Posterman and Jeffrey M. Riedinger, *Land Reform and Democratic Development* (Baltimore: Johns Hopkins University Press, 1987), 113–41.

19. Kattenburg, *The Vietnam Trauma*, 143.

20. Dacy, *Foreign Aid,* 16–20.

21. Douglas Pike, "South Vietnam: Autopsy of a Compound Crisis," in *Friendly Tyrants: An American Dilemma*, ed. Daniel Pipes and Adam Garfunkle (New York: St. Martin's, 1991), 58.

22. George F. Kennan, *Russia and the West under Lenin and Stalin* (Boston: Little, Brown, 1961), 26 (quoted in Fall, *The Two Vietnams*, 268).

23. In this section I have drawn very heavily on Leslie H. Gelb (with Richard K. Betts), *The Irony of Vietnam: The System Worked* (Washington: Brookings Institution, 1979), 27–180, and Kattenburg, *The Vietnam Trauma*. The Gelb book is built around three propositions: (1) "US involvement in Vietnam is not mainly a story of inadvertent descent into unforseen quicksand but of why US leaders considered it vital not to lose Vietnam by force to communism . . . (2) The Presidents, Congress, public opinion, and the press all both reinforced the stakes against losing and introduced constraints against winning. (3) The presidents and most of their lieutenants were not deluded by reports of progress and were not deluded on the basis of optimism about winning a near term or even longer term military victory" (p. 25). I find myself less then fully persuaded by Gelb, particularly with respect to his third point.

24. Fall, *The Two Vietnams*, 225; Gelb, *The Irony of Vietnam*, 59.

25. Ibid., 68; Fall, *The Two Vietnams*, 331.

26. John F. Kennedy, quoted in George C. Herring, *America's Longest War: The United States and Vietnam, 1950–1975*, 2d ed. (New York: Alfred A. Knopf, 1986), 36; John F. Kennedy, "America's Stake in Vietnam," *Vital Speeches* 22 (August 1956): 617–19.

27. Herring, *America's Longest War*, 75–76. In 1961 the only major advocate within

the Kennedy administration to our backing of Vietnam was Under-Secretary of State Chester Bowles. He was regarded as too close to the liberal wing of the party and was replaced as under-secretary in November 1961. Gelb, *The Irony of Vietnam*, 74. By 1963 Robert Kennedy was arguing a political solution and U.S. withdrawal. Ibid., 92.

28. Herring, *America's Longest War*, 84–85.

29. Ibid.

30. King C. Chen, "Hanoi's Three Decisions and the Escalation of the Vietnam War," *Political Science Quarterly* 90 (Summer 1975): 254–55.

31. Frances Fitzgerald, *Fire in the Lake: The Vietnamese and the Americans in Vietnam* (Boston: Little, Brown, 1972), 75.

32. Herring, *America's Longest War*, 104. "With his administration sharply divided to the very end Kennedy stuck by his compromise policy. Harriman, Hillsman and others felt that Diem should go. Vice President Johnson, top CIA and Pentagon officials, and Harkins continued to insist that there was no real alternative and that Diem's removal would bring chaos to South Vietnam. Kennedy himself vacillated, adhering to a policy of not overtly supporting a coup but not discouraging one either." See also Gelb, *The Irony of Vietnam*, 81–86, 106, 107.

33. Ibid., 113.

34. Lyndon B. Johnson, quoted from Herring, *America's Longest War,* 122.

35. Ibid., 123.

36. Herring, *America's Longest War,* 145.

37. Ibid., 158; Fitzgerald, *Fire in the Lake*, 312.

38. Stanley Karnow, *Vietnam: A History* (New York: Penguin, 1984), 432; David M. Barnett, "The Mythology Surrounding Lyndon Johnson, His Advisors, and the 1965 Decision To Escalate the Vietnam War," *Political Science Quarterly* 103 (Winter 1989), 637–63.

39. George Ball, quoted from William Conrad Gibbons, *The U.S. Government and the Vietnam War: Executive and Legislative Roles and Relationships, Part II, 1961–1964* (Princeton: Princeton University Press, 1986), 362. See also Deborah Shapley, *Promise and Power: The Life and Times of Robert McNamara* (Boston: Little, Brown, 1993).

40. James C. Thompson, "Getting Out and Speaking Out," *Foreign Policy* 13 (Winter 1973–74): 49–69; Herring, *America's Longest War,* 179.

41. Ibid., 160.

42. Ibid., 189.

43. Ibid., 195.

44. The "Wise Men," officially the Senior Informal Advisory Group on Vietnam, had first met in November 1967. The group consisted of Dean Acheson, George Ball, McGeorge Bundy, Douglas Dillon, Cyrus Vance, Arthur Dean, John McCloy, Robert Murphy, Arthur Goldberg, Henry Cabot Lodge, Abe Fortas, and Generals Omar Bradley, Mathew Ridgeway, and Maxwell Taylor. Gelb, *The Irony of Vietnam*, 174–76.

45. Lyndon B. Johnson, quoted from Herring, *America's Longest War,* 206; David Halberstam, *The Best and the Brightest* (New York: Random House, 1972), 653.

46. Johnson, quoted from Herring, *America's Longest War,* 207.

47. Kissinger had indicated in an article published in January 1969, but written

before he was invited to join the Nixon administration, that it had been unwise for the United States to get involved in Vietnam in the first place—no vital U.S. national interests were involved—but that the United States could not simply cut its losses and withdraw without undermining U.S. "credibility" in other areas where national interests were involved. See Henry Kissinger, "The Viet Nam Negotiations," *Foreign Affairs* 47 (January 1969): 211–34.

48. Michael A. Genovese, *The Nixon Presidency: Power and Politics in Turbulent Times* (New York: Greenwood Press, 1990), 106; Walter Isaacson, *Kissinger: A Biography* (New York: Simon & Schuster, 1992), 235. Isaacson argued, somewhat prematurely, that 25 July 1969 ended the era of interventionisms that had begun in 1947 when President Truman had agreed to take over from Britain the burden of defending Greece and Turkey from communism (p. 239).

49. For a personal perspective see Henry Kissinger, *White House Years* (Boston: Little, Brown 1979), 226–30, 433–521, 968–1048, 1097–1123, 1301–1476; Kissinger, *Diplomacy*, 674–702.

50. Genovese, *The Nixon Presidency*, 116.

51. Herring, *America's Longest War*, 245.

52. Isaacson, *Kissinger*, 333–54.

53. Kattenburg, *The Vietnam Trauma*, 149–50.

54. Isaacson, *Kissinger*, 461–90.

55. Herring, *America's Longest War*, 257.

56. Gelb, *The Irony of Vietnam*, 190.

57. Kattenburg, *The Vietnam Trauma*, 222–37.

58. William J. Lederer and Eugene Burdick, *The Ugly American* (New York: Norton, 1958). For an interpretation that carried more weight with the American press corps in Vietnam, see Graham Greene, *The Quiet American* (London: Penguin, 1955).

59. Gelb, *The Irony of Vietnam*, 204.

60. Ibid., 204.

61. Fitzgerald, *Fire in the Lake*, 80–89; Robert Sheer and Warren Hinckle, "The Vietnam Lobby," in *The Viet-Nam Reader*, ed. Marcus G. Raskin and Gernard B. Fall (New York: Random House, 1965), 66–81 (reprinted from *Ramparts*, July 1965).

62. Montgomery, *The Politics of Foreign Aid*, 223, 224.

63. Herring, *America's Longest War*, 128, 133.

64. Herring, *America's Longest War*, 143.

65. Montgomery, *The Politics of Foreign Aid*, 232.

66. Herring, *America's Longest War*, 92.

67. Quoted in Herring, *America's Longest War*, 92.

68. "Charles Mohr . . . as early as 1962 was reporting from Saigon that the war in Vietnam was at best questionable and at worst a no-win proposition . . . His last file in the fall of 1963 began, 'The war in Vietnam is being lost.' . . . 'The story was entirely rewritten by my senior editor and then edited by Otto Fuerringer (the managing editor) to the point of saying the war was not only winnable, but that there was already light at the end of the tunnel.' Mohr quit and went to the *New York Times*." John Gregory Dunn, "Your Time Is My Time," *New York Review* 39 (23 April 1992): 49 (49–55).

69. I made trips to Vietnam, from the International Rice Research Institute in the Philippines, on 8–12 July and 15–16 July 1963, 21–23 March 1964, 16–19 June 1964, and 5–8 October 1964 to consult with USOM and GVN about rice price policy. It became clear to me very quickly that the GVN had little interest in policy changes that would improve production incentive to farmers as long as food aid continued. In my 5–8 October 1964 trip notes, I wrote that in Saigon "business is continuing as usual. All this seems to have little to do with what is really going on in the country. There is a power vacuum which no one seems able to fill. I don't know how long this can continue without the GVN evaporating." For insight into the reasons for the lack of success by the GVN military against the Vietcong, see David Halberstam, *The Making of a Quagmire: America and Vietnam during the Kennedy Era,* rev. ed. (New York: Alfred A. Knopf, 1988). For a discussion of the social and political strategies employed by the GVN and the Vietcong which led to the failure of the GVN in rural areas, see Jeffrey Race, *War Comes to Long An* (Berkeley: University of California Press, 1972).

70. John Mecklin, who served as public affairs officer in the U.S. mission in Saigon between 1961 and 1964, later wrote: "The root of the problem was the fact that much of what the newsmen took to be lies was exactly what the Mission genuinely believed and was reporting to Washington. The Mission itself was unaware of how badly the war was going." John Mecklin, *Mission in Torment: An Intimate Account of the U.S. Role in Vietnam* (Garden City, N.Y.: Doubleday, 1965), 100.

71. Fitzgerald, *Fire in the Lake,* 272.

72. Kattenburg, *The Vietnam Trauma*, 215. The political fall-out from the intellectual commitment of leading scholars to U.S. intervention in Vietnam contributed to substantial discrediting of the promising new field of political development. See Vernon W. Ruttan, "What Happened to Political Development," *Economic Development and Cultural Change* 39 (January 1991): 265–92.

73. Fitzgerald, *Fire in the Lake*, 360.

74. See Don Luce and John Sumner, *Viet-Nam—The Unheard Voices* (Ithaca: Cornell University Press, 1969), for a useful perspective on U.S. assistance from the field level.

75. Fitzgerald, *Fire in the Lake*, 361.

76. Montgomery, *The Politics of Foreign Aid*, 63.

77. Kattenburg, *The Vietnam Trauma*, 287–303.

78. This view is still disputed. Douglas Pike, who served in the U.S. embassy in Saigon between 1954 and 1974, has continued to insist on the strategic importance of Vietnam. See Douglas Pike, "South Vietnam: Autopsy of a Compound Crisis," in *Friendly Tyrants: An American Dilemma*, ed. Daniel Pipes and Adam Garfunkle (New York: St. Martin's, 1991), 41–61. Pike is, however, critical of the several U.S. administrations in failing to articulate effectively the geopolitical basis for U.S. involvement in Vietnam. "Beyond the general missionary intent of defeating communism worldwide, no lucid and stable geo-political purpose explained U.S. involvement in Vietnam." (p. 44).

79. I have not been able to identify a careful economic analysis of the flow of aid flows to Israel and Egypt comparable to the analysis by Douglas C. Dacy, *Foreign Aid,*

War and Economic Development, for Vietnam. See, however, the study by Larry Q. Nowles, *Economic Security Assistance as a Tool of American Foreign Policy: The Current Dilemma and Future Options* (Washington: National War College, 1987). On the sources of U.S. policy toward Israel and the Middle East, there are several very useful studies. See particularly Steven L. Spiegel, *The Other Arab-Israeli Conflict: Making America's Middle East Policy from Truman to Reagan* (Chicago: University of Chicago Press, 1985), and William B. Quandt, *Peace Process: American Diplomacy and the Arab-Israeli Conflict since 1967* (Washington: Brookings Institute; Berkeley: University of California Press, 1993). On the organization of pro-Israel and pro-Arab political action committees, see Richard H. Curtiss, *Stealth PACs: Lobbying Congress for Control of U.S. Middle East Policy* (Washington: American Educational Trust, 1990). For more personal accounts of U.S. domestic politics of policy in the Middle East, see Paul Findlay, *They Dare To Speak Out: People and Institutions Confront Israel's Lobby* (Westport, Conn.: Lawrence Hill, 1985; Chicago: Chicago Review Press, 1989); Edward Tivnan, *The Lobby: Jewish Political Power and American Foreign Policy* (New York: Simon & Schuster, 1987); George W. Ball and Douglas B. Ball, *The Passionate Attachment: America's Involvement with Israel, 1947 to the Present* (New York: Norton, 1992); and Thomas L. Friedman, *From Beirut to Jerusalem* (New York: Farrar, Straus, Giroux, 1989).

80. Clyde R. Mark, *Israel: U.S. Foreign Assistance* (Washington: Congressional Research Service, 23 March 1993), 23. Mark also discusses some of the other forms of assistance to Israel and some of the unique aspects of aid to Israel. The most important are provisions that allow Israel to receive all of its assistance in the first 30 days of the year rather than in four allotments, as is the case for other countries.

81. Nowles, *Economic Security Assistance*, 50, 51.

82. Bent Hansen, *The Political Economy of Poverty, Equity, and Growth: Egypt and Turkey* (Oxford: Oxford University Press, 1991), 16.

83. Steven L. Spiegel, *The Other Arab-Israeli Conflict: Making America's Middle East Policy, from Truman to Reagan* (Chicago: University of Chicago Press, 1985), 3–10; Robert D. Kaplan, *The Arabists: The Romance of an American Elite* (New York: Free Press, 1993).

84. Spiegel, *The Other Arab-Israeli Conflict*, 6.

85. Quoted from Spiegel, *The Other Arab-Israeli Conflict*, 171.

86. "The June War of 1967 altered the role of Israel in American Jewish thinking and action, and the distinction among the organizations became blurred. Israel became a main central concern and support for it intensified. American Jews suddenly became aware of the intensity of their feelings and their commitment to the survival and well-being of the Jewish state." Bernard Reich, *The United States and Israel: Influence in the Special Relationship* (New York: Praeger, 1984), 196.

87. Spiegel, *The Other Arab-Israeli Conflict*, 12.

88. For a detailed personal account of the role of Truman's foreign policy advisors and his personal staff in Truman's decision to recognize Israel, see Clark Clifford (with Richard Holbrooke), *Counsel to the President: A Memoir* (New York: Random House, 1991), 3–24; see also Spiegel, *The Other Arab-Israeli Conflict*, 16–39.

89. Spiegel, *The Other Arab-Israeli Conflict*, 55. For the domestic politics of U.S. policy toward the Middle East during the Eisenhower administration, see pp. 50–93.

90. For a detailed account, see Benny Morris, *Israel's Border Wars: 1949–1956* (Oxford: Oxford University Press, 1993), 227–62; also Ball and Ball, *The Passionate Attachment*, 28–33.

91. For a detailed discussion of the events leading up to the Suez crisis and the negotiations for Israeli withdrawal, see Spiegel, *The Other Arab-Israeli Conflict*, 71–82.

92. Ball and Ball, *The Passionate Attachment*, 50, 51. For greater detail on the Johnson plan, see Spiegel, *The Other Arab-Israeli Conflict*, 110–17. Also, see Tivnan, *The Lobby*, 58.

93. For discussion of the sources of U.S. policy toward Israel during the Johnson administration, see Spiegel, *The Other Arab-Israeli Conflict*, 118–65.

94. Tivnan, *The Lobby*, 64. For a history of the events leading to the war, see Walter Laqueor, *The Road to War: The Origin and Aftermath of the Arab-Israeli Conflict, 1967–8* (Baltimore: Penquin, 1968). For detail on the Israeli-U.S. discussions preceding June 5, see Quandt, *Peace Process*, 66.

95. Ball and Ball, *The Passionate Attachment*, 62.

96. Ibid., 62, 63; Quandt, *Peace Process*, 56.

97. Quandt, *Peace Process*, 66; Spiegel, *The Other Arab-Israeli Conflict*, 181–89. The issue of Vietnam was particularly difficult for many American Jewish leaders. Lyndon Johnson complained to Abba Eban, "A bunch of rabbis came here one day in 1967 to tell me that I ought not to send a single screwdriver to Vietnam, but on the other hand, should push all our aircraft carriers through the Strait of Tiran to help Israel." Spiegel, *The Other Arab-Israeli Conflict*, 130. Objecting to pressure from Israel that American Jewish organizations support President Nixon's Vietnam policy, Hertzberg told Golda Meir, "Madam Prime Minister, if you expect to put me as a Zionist between your version of Zionism and my children, you will lose." Quoted in Tivnan, *The Lobby*, 72. See also Arthur Hertzberg, *Jewish Polemics* (New York: Columbia University Press, 1992).

98. Tivnan, *The Lobby*, 78, 79.

99. Ball and Ball, *The Passionate Attachment*, 73–75; Quandt, *The Peace Process*, 148–82.

100. Spiegel argues, however, that the October war strengthened anti-Israeli sentiment in the business and policy-making communities. *The Other Arab-Israeli Conflict*, 220–22.

101. By the mid-1970s AIPAC had become the major pro-Israel lobby organization in the United States. I. L. (Si) Kenan, who headed AIPAC from 1954 to 1974, operated with a small staff and reliance on personal relationships. Findlay, *They Dare To Speak Out*, 25–49; Tivnan, *The Lobby*, 83.

102. For an excellent account of the U.S. role in the Yom Kippur war and Kissinger's shuttle diplomacy during 1973–75, see Isaacson, *Kissinger*, 511–72. For a highly personal account, see Edward R. F. Sheehan, *The Arabs, Israelis, and Kissinger: A Secret History of American Diplomacy in the Middle East* (New York: Thomas Y. Crowell, 1976). For Kissinger's own perspective on the same events, see Henry Kissinger, *Years of Upheaval* (Boston: Little, Brown, 1982), 799–853; 935–78; 1032–1110.

103. Tivnan, *The Lobby*, 88.

104. Ibid.

105. For the full text, see Edward R. F. Sheehan, *The Arabs, Israelis, and Kissinger* (New York: Readers Digest Press, 1976), 175.

106. Charles Mathias, "Ethnic Groups and Foreign Policy," *Foreign Affairs* (Summer 1981): 993 (975–98); Spiegel, *The Other Arab-Israeli Conflict*, 300.

107. See Zbigniew Brzezinski, "Recognizing the Crisis," *Foreign Policy* 17 (Summer 1974–75): 63–74; Brookings Middle East Study Group, *Toward Peace in the Middle East* (Washington: Brookings Institution, December 1975). "To Kissinger the key state in the Middle East was Egypt and the central problem facing American policy in the area was to block the Russians from a major role. To Brzezinski . . . the key state in the region is Saudi Arabia and the central problem, energy. Israel had a role to play in Kissinger's approach, but is of little value to the United States in Brzezinski's. Stephen L. Spiegel, "The United States and the Arab-Israeli Dispute," in *Eagle Entangled: U.S. Foreign Policy in Complex World*, ed. Kenneth A. Oye, Donald Rothchild, and Robert J. Lieber (New York: Longman, 1979), 352.

108. Tivnan, *The Lobby*, 101; *Weekly Compilation of Presidential Documents*, 21 March 1977, 361.

109. Tivnan, *The Lobby*, 104, 121.

110. Spiegel, *The Other Arab-Israeli Conflict*, 300.

111. Tivnan, *The Lobby*, 121.

112. Seth P. Tillman, *The United States in the Middle East: Interests and Obstacles* (Bloomington: Indiana University Press, 1982), 24–34; Spiegel, *The Other Arab-Israeli Conflict*, 353–73.

113. Quandt, *Peace Process*, 284–331; Tivnan, *The Lobby*, 131. For a discussion of the domestic political tensions in Israel after the Sadat visit to Israel and the Camp David negotiations, see Robert O. Freedman, "Moscow, Jerusalem, and Washington in the Begin Era," *Israel in the Begin Era* (New York: Praeger, 1982), 167–89.

114. The Ford administration's view, as expressed by Secretary of State Henry Kissinger to a group of Jewish leaders: "The strength of Israel is needed for its own survival but not to prevent the spread of Communism in the Arab world. So it doesn't necessarily help United States global interest as far as the Middle East is concerned. The survival of Israel has sentimental importance to the United States." Cited in Tivnan, *The Lobby*, 167. By the end of his administration, Carter was beginning to view Israel as a strategic asset. Quandt, *Peace Process*, 424.

115. Spiegel, *The Other Arab-Israeli Conflict*, 395–408.

116. Thomas A. Dine, "A Primer for Capital Hill," *New York Times*, 4 April 1975, 33; Tivnan, *The Lobby*, 138.

117. Tivnan, *The Lobby*, 140. For Secretary Haig's perspective on the AWACS controversy, see Alexander M. Haig, Jr., *Caveat: Realism, Reagan, and Foreign Policy* (New York: Macmillian, 1984), 167–93.

118. See George P. Schultz, *Turmoil and Triumph: My Years as Secretary of State* (New York: Charles Scribner's Sons, 1993), 104–14.

119. Nowles, *Economic Security Assistance*, 7. During the early and mid-1980s, support by AIPAC became essential for the passage of foreign aid appropriations. In

1983 AIPAC support had resulted in a $510 million increase in aid for Israel in spite of efforts by the administration to block the increase. "Except for a few humanitarian and church-related organizations, AIPAC serves as foreign aid's only domestic constituency. Without AIPAC foreign aid legislation would not be approved at the $7 billion plus level of 1973 and might have difficulty in surviving at all." Findlay, *They Dare To Speak Out*, 29.

120. Ball and Ball, *The Passionate Attachment*, 258–64, 280.

121. U.S. General Accounting Office, *U.S. Assistance to Israel* (Washington: GAO, 24 June 1983). For an earlier and much more critical draft of this report, see Mohammed El-Khawas and Samer Abed-Rabba, *American Aid to Israel* (Brattleboro, Vt.: Amana Books, 1984), 116–91. See also Assaf Razin, "U.S. Foreign Aid to Israel," *Jerusalem Quarterly* 29 (Fall 1983): 11–19; Stanly Fischer and Herbert Stein, "For Israel's Sake, Time for Economic Independence," *International Herald Tribune*, 14 October 1991, 4; Ball and Ball, *The Passionate Attachment*, 299–302; and Nadev Halevi, "Economic Implications of Peace: The Israeli Perspective," in *The Economics of Middle East Peace: Views from the Region*, ed. Stanley Fischer, Dani Rodrick, and Elias Tuma (Cambridge: MIT Press, 1993), 87–116.

122. For a review of this literature, see Tivnan, *The Lobby*, 216–40. It is of interest that essentially the same analysis of the effect of military and economic assistance on the economies of Egypt, Jordan, and Syria have been made by two Israeli economists. See Victor Lavy and Eliezer Sheffer, *Foreign Aid and Economic Development in the Middle East: Egypt, Syria and Jordan* (New York: Praeger, 1991).

123. For an excellent analysis see Assaf Razin and Efram Sadka, *The Economy of Modern Israel: Malaise and Promise* (Chicago: University of Chicago Press, 1993). In spite of Razin's earlier concern about the negative effect of U.S. assistance, the only reference to U.S. assistance in the Razin-Sadka book is to note that the intifada did not make much difference to the Israeli economy but that it "contributed to the political tension between Israel and the United States, thereby indirectly leading to a fall in the real value of U.S. aid to Israel." Ibid., 4. For a more critical assessment of post-1985 economic policy, see Nadev Halevi, "Economic Implications of Peace: The Israeli Perspective," in Fischer, Rodrick, and Tuma, *Economics of Middle East Peace,* 87–116.

124. Friedman, *From Beirut to Jerusalem*, 156–66, 480–90; Arthur Hertzberg, *Jewish Polemics* (New York: Columbia University Press, 1992), 120–36; Stuart E. Eizenstat, "Loving Israel—Warts and All," *Foreign Policy* 8 (Winter 1990–91): 87–105; Leon T. Hadar, "Reforming Israel—Before It Is Too Late," *Foreign Policy* 8 (Winter 1990–91): 106–27.

125. Findlay, *They Dare To Speak Out*, 2d ed., 334–40, 238–64.

126. Mark, *Israel: U.S. Foreign Assistance*, 4. Observers have argued that the political costs, at least at the presidential level, of support for policies that were opposed by Israel and the pro-Israel lobbies have been less than the critics have contended. See, for example, Steven L. Spiegel, "U.S. National Interests in the Middle East," in *The National Interests of the United States*, ed. Prosser Gifford (Washington: University Press of America, 1981), 117–29. I am less than fully convinced.

127. "Rabin Assails pro-Israel Lobbying Group in the U.S.," *Minneapolis Star*

Tribune, 17 August 1992. In November 1992, the president of AIPAC, David Steiner, resigned after assertions to a potential donor that AIPAC was negotiating with the Clinton campaign about key appointments. Charles Babcock, "Israel Lobby's Chief Quits after Insider Boasts to Caller Turn Up in Print," *Washington Post,* 5 November 1992, A6. In June 1993, Thomas A. Dine resigned as executive director of AIPAC after allegedly making remarks that were interpreted as insulting to ultra-Orthodox Jews. He was succeeded in February 1994 by Neal M. Scher, Director of the Justice Department Office of Special Investigations. *National Journal*, 10 February 1994, 439. Dine was nominated to be AID Assistant Administrator for the Europe and New Independent States Bureau and was approved by the Senate in February 1994.

128. In this section I have drawn heavily on Marvin G. Weinbaum, *Egypt and the Politics of U.S. Economic Aid* (Boulder: Westview Press, 1986). See also William J. Burns, *Economic Aid and American Policy toward Egypt, 1955–1981* (Albany: State University of New York Press, 1985); John Waterbury, *The Egypt of Nasser and Sadat: The Political Economy of Two Regimes* (Princeton: Princeton University Press, 1983); Robert F. Zimmerman, *Dollars, Diplomacy, and Dependency: Dilemmas of U.S. Economic Aid* (Boulder: Lynne Rienner Publishers, 1993), 81–110. For a personal account of U.S. involvement in Egyptian political affairs from the early 1950s through the June 1967 Arab-Israeli War, see Miles Copeland, *The Game of Nations: The Amorality of Power Politics* (London: Weidenfeld & Nicholson, 1969).

129. Weinbaum, *Egypt and U.S. Economic Aid*, 30, 31; Burns, *Economic Aid*, 11, 12.

130. For a detailed discussion of the events leading up to the purchase of military supplies and equipment from the USSR and Czechoslovakia, see Burns, *Economic Aid*, 13–33; for detailed discussion of the Aswan Dam negotiations, see Burns, *Economic Aid*, 36–100; for additional analysis of negotiations to finance the Aswan High Dam, see Edward S. Mason and Robert E. Asher, *The World Bank since Bretton Woods* (Washington: Brookings Institute, 1973), 627–41. See also John White, *The Politics of Foreign Aid* (New York: St. Martin's, 1974), 204, 205.

131. Mason and Asher, *World Bank since Bretton Woods*, 636, 639.

132. Burns, *Economic Aid*, 113.

133. For a personal perspective on United States–Egyptian relations during the Kennedy administration, see John S. Badeau, *The Middle East Remembered* (New York: Columbia University Middle East Institute, 1983); Burns, *Economic Aid*, 126.

134. For Sadat's own perception of the legacy he inherited from Nasser, see Anwar el-Sadat, *In Search of Identity: An Autobiography* (New York: Harper & Row, 1977).

135. Weinbaum, *Egypt and U.S. Economic Aid*, 32. See Chapter 8 for a discussion of the food aid considerations.

136. Ball and Ball, *The Passionate Attachment*, 268, 269; Heba Handoussa and Nemat Shafik, "The Economics of Peace: The Egyptian Case," in Fischer, Rodrik, and Tuma, *Economics of Middle East Peace*, 19–54.

137. Zimmerman, *Dollars, Diplomacy, and Dependency*, 86–89.

138. For a detailed analysis, see Olivia Cua Ke, "An Analysis of the Macroeconomic Effects of Foreign Aid: The Case of Egypt" (St. Paul: University of Minnesota, Department of Agricultural and Applied Economics, 2 June 1993, mimeo).

139. For greater detail on the content of the US/AID program in Egypt during 1974–84, see Weinbaum, *Egypt and U.S. Economic Aid*, 68–99; Burns, *Economic Aid*, 174–99. The Egyptian government has resented the differential oversight that US/AID exercised over assistance flows to Egypt and Israel. Egypt would like to receive its assistance in a lump sum payment, yet "offers by AID to exchange possible sector grants for policy economic reforms are also deeply resented in Egyptian government circles. Even the appearance of a deal creates apprehension lest it seem that basic policies are being dictated by the United States. The ministry of agriculture broke off negotiations with AID for a sector grant proposal to compensate the government for costs of raising prices to farmers when it became clear that AID had injected itself into a too politically sensitive area" (p. 96).

140. Ibid., 140.

141. Robert Holt and Terry Roe, "The Political Economy of Reform: Egypt in the 1980s" (Paper prepared for the Ford Foundation—Duke University Project on the Political Economy of Structural Adjustment, undated mimeo).

142. Robert F. Zimmerman, "The U.S.-Egypt Assistance Relationship: Success, Failure, and Prospects" (Washington: US/AID Asia and Near East Bureau, 10 September 1987, mimeo).

143. Clyde H. Farnsworth, "Egypt's Reward: Forgiven Debt," *New York Times*, 10 April 1991, D1, D10; Alan Richards, "The Political Economy of Dilatory Reform: Egypt in the 1980s" *World Development* 19, no. 12 (1991): 1721–30. In his critique of Egyptian economic policy, Richards notes: "Egypt's policy drift has been sustained both by the oil rents of petroleum exports and remittances from Egyptian workers in the Gulf and by the 'strategic rent' which Egypt has been able to extract from the United States and, to a lesser extent, from other Organization for Economic Cooperative and Development (OECD) countries and international agencies such as the International Monetary Fund (IMF). Such 'rents,' of course, derive from Egypt's contribution to U.S. foreign policy goals in the region" (p. 1721). As of 1994, both oil reserve and remittances had declined from the level of the late 1980s.

144. Zimmerman, *Dollars, Diplomacy and Dependency*, 106.

145. Ball and Ball note that, in its attachment to Israel and in its policies toward the Middle East, America has all but abandoned the principles of American exceptionalism—that it should conduct itself as "a light unto all nations." The passionate attachment has led America to follow a pattern of hypocrisy—"so long as our country keeps silent while a nation it subsidizes persistently disdains international principles, it makes a mockery of its claim to moral leadership." *The Passionate Attachment*, 294.

146. Robert A. Pastor, *Whirlpool: U.S. Foreign Policy toward Latin America and the Caribbean* (Princeton: Princeton University Press, 1992), 18.

147. Lars Schoultz, *National Security and United States Policy toward Latin America* (Princeton: Princeton University Press, 1987), 4–25.

148. Ronald Reagan, cited by Ronnie Dugger, *On Reagan: The Man and His Presidency* (New York: McGraw-Hill, 1983), 518–19.

149. In this section I draw very heavily on Robert A. Pastor, *Condemned to Repetition: The United States and Nicaragua* (Princeton: Princeton University Press, 1987).

See also Richard Millet, "The United States and Central America," in U.S. Congress Joint Economic Committee, Subcommittee on International Trade, Finance and Security Economics, *The Political Economy of the Western Hemisphere: Selected Issues for U.S. Policy* (Washington: USGPO, 1981), 11–44; Jeane J. Kirkpatrick, *Dictatorship and Double Standards: Rationalism and Realism in Politics* (New York: Simon & Schuster, 1982), 53–95; Walter La Feber, *Inevitable Revolutions: The United States in Central America* (New York: Norton, 1983); Raymond Bonner, *Weakness and Deceit: U.S. Policy and El Salvador* (New York: Times Books, 1984); and Howard J. Wiarda, *American Foreign Policy toward Latin America in the 80's and 90's: Issues and Controversies from Reagan to Bush* (New York: New York University Press, 1992).

150. Richard Millett, *Guardians of the Dynasty* (Maryknoll, N.Y.: Orbis Books, 1977).

151. "In September 1956, after receiving his party nomination to serve another presidential term, Antonio Somoza Garcia attended a Saturday night dance in León. There Rigoberto López Pérez, a young Nicaraguan poet, shot him five times before being killed by Somoza's bodyguards. With U.S. help, Somoza was flown for emergency treatment to the Canal Zone, but within a week he was dead." Pastor, *Condemned to Repetition*, 31.

152. Ibid., 28.

153. Ibid., 34.

154. Ibid., 43.

155. "On December 23, 1972 the streets of Managua were lifted by a powerful earthquake, then dropped, and finally burned by a storm of fire. When the streets settled and cooled, the city was a rubble, 8,000–10,000 people were dead, and hundreds of thousands of people were left homeless . . . Many members of the National Guard deserted either to help their families or to loot. Somoza . . . transformed a tragic national loss into a personal financial gain. He accomplished this by channeling aid through his companies and purchasing the parts of the city where he planned to undertake reconstruction. He also encouraged Guard leaders to profit from the foreign aid and the reconstruction efforts in the city." Pastor, *Condemned to Repetition*, 36.

156. Pastor, *Condemned to Repetition*, 38.

157. Ibid., 38, 39.

158. Ibid., 35.

159. "Soon after Christmas in 1974, José Mariá Chema Castillo Quant, a wealthy friend of Somoza and a former minister of agriculture, hosted a farewell for Ambassador Shelton . . . The Sandinistas had decided to do something to show they were a viable threat to the Somoza regime. Tomás Borge, who had received two years of military training in Cuba, prepared a small group of Sandinistas to capture prominent officials at an embassy reception, but when they heard about the Castillo party on the radio they changed their plans. Shelton had departed by the time the Sandinistas arrived, but many guests were still there . . . The Sandinistas killed Castillo, held the rest of his guests hostage and demanded that Archbishop Obando act as mediator." Pastor, *Condemned to Repetition*, 39.

160. Ibid., 54.

161. At the time of the assassination, it was assumed that Somoza was responsible. Chamorro's son was convinced that Somoza was not responsible. In 1981 the Sandinista government found a Miami-based Cuban exile guilty. Ibid., 59, 334.

162. For a personal account of the drafting of the letter, see ibid., 66–71.

163. Humberto Ortega, reported in ibid., 73.

164. Quoted in ibid., 74. For an argument that the fall of the Somoza regime and the "loss of Nicaragua" were a deliberate consequence of U.S. policy, see Kirkpatrick, *Dictatorship and Double Standards*, 69–79.

165. Kirkpatrick, *Dictatorship and Double Standards*, 77.

166. General Omar Torrijos, President of Panama, threatened to bomb President Somosa's bunker in Managua to galvanize U.S. action to force Somosa's departure. Pastor, *Condemned to Repetition*, 87–93.

167. Ibid., 119.

168. Ibid., 142.

169. Ibid., 187.

170. La Feber, *Inevitable Revolutions*, 238–40.

171. Schoultz, *National Security and U.S. Policy*, 47.

172. Pastor, *Condemned to Repetition*, 229.

173. Alexander M. Haig, Jr., *Caveat: Realism, Reagan, and Foreign Policy* (New York: Macmillan, 1984), 96–97. Haig's interest in Nicaragua and El Salvador reflected his broader concerns about the expansion of Soviet influence in the developing world rather than specific concerns in Central America and the Caribbean.

174. Pastor, *Condemned to Repetition*, 232.

175. The Reagan administration moved rapidly to remove Carter Foreign Service officers who had played active Central American policy roles from their responsibilities. See Schoultz, *National Security and U.S. Policy*, 9, 10.

176. Pastor, *Condemned to Repetition*, 234.

177. Ibid., 237. For detail on the struggle between State Department advocates of a political approach to events in Nicaragua and El Salvador and National Security Council advocates of use of force during the first two years of the Reagan administration, see Barry Rubin, "Reagan Administration Policy toward Central America," in *Central America: Anatomy of Conflict*, ed. Robert S. Leiken (New York: Pergamon Press, 1984), 299–318.

178. Pastor, *Condemned to Repetition*, 238.

179. William M. Leogrande, "The Contras and Congress," in *Reagan versus the Sandinistas: The Undeclared War on Nicaragua*, ed. Thomas W. Walker (Boulder: Westview Press, 1987), 202–27.

180. For further discussion of congressional opposition to administration support for the Contras, see I. M. Dester, "The Elusive Consensus, Congress and Central America," in Leiken, *Central America*, 319–35.

181. U.S. President's Special Review Board, *The Tower Commission Report* (New York: Times Books, 1987), 450.

182. Schoultz, *National Security and U.S. Policy*, 63; Pastor, *Condemned to Repetition*, 247.

183. Jack Spence, "The U.S. Media Covering (over) Nicaragua," in Walker, *Reagan versus the Sandinistas*, 182–201.

184. United States National Bipartisan Commission on Central America (the Kissinger commission), *Report of the President's National Bipartisan Commission on Central America* (New York: Macmillan, 1984), ii. For a critique see Larry Hufford, *The United States in Central America: An Analysis of the Kissinger Commission Report* (Lewiston, N.Y.: Edwin Mellen Press, 1987).

185. Kissinger commission, *Report*, 121, 122, 138; Pastor, *Condemned to Repetition*, 298.

186. Ronald Reagan, quoted from Pastor, *Condemned to Repetition*, 250.

187. The phrase had been inserted into a Reagan speech by Patrick Buchanan. Wiarda, *American Foreign Policy*, 8. Wiarda also notes that, although the administration was returning to the mainstream of American foreign policy during 1983–85, policy toward Central America remained an exception. He attributes this lack of interest in Central America to Secretary of State George Schultz and the replacement of foreign policy professionals (such as Thomas Enders) with neoconservative ideologists (such as Elliot Abrams) in the Bureau for Inter-American Affairs of the State Department. For a more positive perspective on the Contra opposition, see Roger Miranda and William Ratliff, *The Civil War in Nicaragua: Inside the Sandinistas* (New Brunswick, N.J.: Transaction Publishers, 1993).

188. Pastor, *Condemned to Repetition*, 252, 253.

189. When Alexander Haig was succeeded as secretary of state by George P. Shultz in July 1992, Shultz found that he was already "out of the loop" on efforts to destabilize the Sandinista regime. For a personal account, written from a somewhat self-serving perspective, of his efforts to recapture the foreign policy agenda for the State Department, see George P. Shultz, *Turmoil and Triumph: My Years as Secretary of State* (New York: Charles Scribner's Sons, 1993).

190. Pastor, *Condemned to Repetition*, 258. For additional detail on the breakdown of the national security decision and management processes that led to the Iran-Contra affair, see U.S. President's Special Review Board, *The Tower Commission Report* (New York: Bantam Books/Times Books, 1987).

191. Theodore Draper, "Iran-Contra: The Mystery Solved," *New York Review*, 10 June 1993, 53–59.

192. Pastor, *Whirlpool*, 236.

193. Ibid., 237; Miranda and Ratliff, *The Civil War in Nicaragua*, 273.

194. For greater detail on the organization of the election and the transition from FSLN to UNO rule, see ibid., 234–36.

195. Pastor argues that, if the Bush administration had not refused to demobilize the Contras before the election, as originally proposed by Ortega, Humberto Ortega would have retired. The Sandinistas were worried about the delay in negotiating the Contras' disarmament, and Chomorro felt compelled to appoint Ortega as chief of the army. Ortega's role as army chief was then used by the Bush administration and the right wing of the Republican Party in Congress as a reason for limiting economic assistance to Nicaragua. Pastor, *Whirlpool*, 244–46.

196. For a sense of the disparate views of the accomplishments of the Chomorro government by liberal supporters and conservative critics, see Subcommittee on Western Hemisphere Affairs, Committee on Foreign Affairs, House of Representatives, *Democracy and Reconciliation in Nicaragua: A Critical Assessment, Hearings* (Washington: USGPO, 4 February 1993).

197. Bonner, *Weakness and Deceit*, 11.

198. Ibid., 164, 165.

199. Schoultz, *National Security and U.S. Policy*, 41–43. For greater detail on the reforms, see Roy L. Prosterman and Jeffery M. Riedinger, *Land Reform and Democratic Development* (Baltimore: Johns Hopkins University Press, 1987), 143–73. Also Rupert W. Scofield, "Land Reform in Central America," in *Agrarian Reform and Grassroots Development: Ten Case Studies*, ed. Roy L. Posterman, Mary N. Temple, and Timothy M. Hanstad (Boulder: Lynne Rienner Publishers, 1990), 139–53.

200. A few days before the assassination, Roberto D'Aubuisson, who was later to form the Nationalist Republican Alliance (ARENA), is reported to have presided over a meeting of military personnel who drew straws for the "honor" of killing Archbishop Romero. Bonner, *Weakness and Deceit*, 178.

201. Ibid., 290–321.

202. Ibid., 354. Robert Pastor has argued, citing its efforts to prevent the rightists from monopolizing power, that there was more continuity in policy between the Carter and Reagan administrations than one might judge from the rhetoric of the Reagan administration. An important difference, however, was that the Carter support was conditional on implementing reforms and stopping repression. The Reagan administration, in contrast, provided the military unconditional support in their struggle against the Left. See "Continuity and Change in U.S. Foreign Policy: Carter and Reagan on El Salvador," *Journal of Policy Analysis and Management* 3 (2 November 1984): 175–90.

203. Joseph S. Tulchin and Gary Bland, eds., *Is There a Transition to Democracy in El Salvador?* (Boulder: Lynne Rienner Publishers, 1992), 2; George R. Vickers, "The Political Reality after Eleven Years of War," in Tulchin and Bland, *Is There a Transition?* 25–57.

204. Gary Bland, "Assessing the Transition to Democracy," in Tulchin and Bland, *Is There a Transition?* 172.

205. Vickers, "The Political Reality," 37; Randall B. Ripley and James M. Lindsay, *Congress Resurgent: Foreign and Defense Policy on Capitol Hill* (Ann Arbor: University of Michigan Press, 1993), 5.

206. Alvaro de Soto, "The Negotiations following the New York Agreement," in Tulchin and Bland, *Is There a Transition?* 139–59. The United States was sometimes less than helpful during the United Nations–sponsored negotiations. When in January 1991 an FMLN unit shot down a U.S. helicopter in rebel-controlled territory and executed two of the occupants, President Bush released the $42.5 million in military assistance that had been withheld by Congress, and General Colin Powell hinted at direct U.S. military intervention in El Salvador. At the same time, U.S. officials in the State Department leaked stories indicating displeasure with the work of the U.N.

representatives handling negotiations. Heather Foot, "Commentary," in Tulchin and Bland, *Is There a Transition?* 74, 75.

207. Cynthia J. Arnson, "Has There Been Progress?" in Tulchin and Bland, *Is There a Transition?* 59.

208. John McAwend, "Commentary," in Tulchin and Bland, *Is There a Transition?* 59; Gary Bland, "Assessing the Transition to Democracy," 164.

209. Cynthia Arnson, *As Bad as Ever: A Report on Human Rights in El Salvador* (New York: America's Watch Committee, 1984), 91.

210. Bruce L. R. Smith, ed., *Next Steps in Central America* (Washington: Brookings Institution, 1991), 3.

211. Ibid., 6.

212. Robert E. Harkavy, *Bases Abroad: The Global Foreign Military Presence* (Oxford: Oxford University Press, 1980). The Harkavy book contains a carefully detailed discussion of the policies and economics of foreign military bases. For a more critical discussion, see Joseph Gersona and Bruce Birchard, eds., *The Sun Never Sets: Confronting the Network of Foreign U.S Military Bases* (Boston: South End Press, 1991). For a listing of U.S. major bases and U.S. military personnel stationed abroad in the late 1980s, see "The Global Network of United States Military Bases," *Defense Monitor* 18 (1989): 1–8. See also "Department of Defense Worldwide Military Strength as of December 31, 1993" (Washington: Office of Assistant Secretary of Defense, Public Affairs, news release, 4 April 1994).

213. Harkavy, *Bases Abroad*, 5.

214. Ibid., 4.

215. Ibid., 4. See also House Committee on Armed Services, *Report of the Defense Burden Sharing Panel* (Washington: USGPO, August 1988), 53.

216. "These include signal intelligence (SIGNIT), space tracking (telescopes, laser sources, satellite control and data relay, ground terminal and data processing facilities for underwater cables, early-warning radars, seismological detection and others." Ibid., 6.

217. "Conversation between General of the Army MacArthur and Mr. George Kennan, 5 March 1948—Top Secret," in *Containment: Documents on American Policy and Strategy 1949–50*, ed. Thomas Etzvold and John Lewis Gaddis (New York: Colombia University Press, 1978), 229.

218. For a history of the negotiations between the United States and the government of the Philippines over base rights, see William E. Berry, Jr., *U.S. Bases in the Philippines: The Evolution of a Special Relationship* (Boulder: Westview Press, 1989).

219. Burnett, *Investing in Security*, 51–54.

220. Berry, *U.S. Bases in the Philippines,* 251.

221. George Bush, *New York Times,* 1 July 1981, 13. Quoted in Berry, *U.S. Bases in the Philippines,* 280.

222. Zimmerman, *Dollars, Diplomacy, and Dependency*, 112–17, 284, 285.

223. Berry, *U.S. Bases in the Philippines,* 293. For more detailed discussion of the 1991 base negotiations, see Ted Galen Carpenter, *A Search for Enemies: America's Alliances after the Cold War* (Washington: Cato Institute, 1992), 103–12.

224. Zimmerman, *Dollars, Diplomacy and Dependency*, 116.

225. Theodore A. Couioumbis, *The United States, Greece and Turkey: The Troubled Triage* (New York: Praeger, 1983).

226. Carol Migdalovitz, *Greece and Turkey: Current Foreign Aid Issues* (Washington: Library of Congress, Congressional Research Service, 23 July 1992); Monteagle Sterns, *Entangling Alliances: U.S. Policy toward Greece, Turkey and Cyprus* (New York: Council on Foreign Relations, 1992), 40–50; David Rogers, "Greek, Turkish Lobbyists Fear the New Winds in East Block May Dry Up U.S. Military Aid Pool," *Wall Street Journal*, 10 January 1990, A12.

227. Anne O. Krueger and Vernon W. Ruttan, "Assistance to Turkey," in Krueger, Michalopoulos, and Ruttan, *Aid and Development*, 250.

228. House Committee on Armed Forces, *Defense Burden Sharing Panel*, 53, 56.

229. In addition to the cases discussed in this chapter, see the long litany of cases in John Quigley, *The Ruses for War: American Interventionism since World War II* (Buffalo: Prometheas Books, 1992).

230. Joseph Kraft, quoted from Isaacson, *Kissinger*, 586; I. F. Stone, quoted from Jonathan Kwitny, *Endless Enemies: The Making of an Unfriendly World* (New York: Viking Penguin, 1984).

231. U.S. Presidents' Special Review Board, *The Tower Commission Report* (New York: Bantam Books/Times Books, 1987), x.

232. Stephen J. Stedman, "The New Interventionists," *Foreign Affairs* 72 (Winter 1993): 1–28.

Chapter 11 Policy toward the Multilateral Lending Institutions

1. The author is indebted to Robert Blake, José D. Epstein, Richard E. Feinberg, Anne O. Krueger, Raymond Mikesell, JoAnn Paulson, Rita M. Rodriguez, and Arnold H. Weiss for comments on an earlier draft of this chapter.

2. Organization for Economic Cooperation and Development, *Twenty-Five Years of Development Cooperation: A Review* (Paris: OECD, 1985), 140. The World Bank and the International Monetary Fund are officially U.N. specialized agencies. For a history of the early relationship between the bank and the United Nations, see Mason and Asher, *World Bank since Bretton Woods* (Washington: Brookings Institution, 1973), 550–76. In this chapter I do not discuss the development assistance role of the International Monetary Fund. Traditionally, the fund was responsible for short-term stability, whereas the bank took a long-term development perspective. Since the collapse of the Bretton Woods system of fixed exchange rates in 1973, there has been a gradual blurring of levels of responsibility between the two institutions. See Richard E. Feinberg, "The Changing Relationship between the World Bank and the International Monetary Fund," *International Organization* 42 (Summer 1988): 545–59.

3. William B. Dale, "The Role of the International Monetary Fund in Economic Development and Financial Integration," in *U.S. Policy towards the Bretton Woods Institutions*, ed. Alvin P. Drischler and M. P. Benjenk (Washington: Johns Hopkins University School of Advanced International Studies, 1988), 17.

4. Raymond F. Mikesell, *U.S. Private and Government Investment Abroad* (Eugene: University of Oregon Books, 1962), 464.

5. I do not, in this section, discuss the broader issue of coordination of the U.S. bilateral aid program with the programs of multilateral donors or other bilateral donors. The fora for such coordination includes the Development Assistance Committee of the OCED and the several country assistance consortia, such as the Aid India Consortium.

6. "The formal composition of the Council . . . includes the Secretary of the Treasury (Chairman), the Secretary of State, the Secretary of Commerce, the Chairman of the Board of Governors of the Federal Reserve System, and the President of the Export-Import Bank. In addition to these members provided by statute, representatives of other agencies participate on a regular basis in the work of the NAC. These include the U.S. executive directors for the International Monetary Fund, the International Bank for Reconstruction and Development, the International Finance Corporation, the Inter-American Development Bank, and the International Development Association, and their alternates, the Director of the Development Loan Fund (later AID), and representatives from the Department of Agriculture and the Bureau of Budget. Representatives of other agencies, including the Department of Defense and the Securities and Exchange Commission, participate from time to time when the Council considers matters pertaining to their interests or operations." Mikesell, *Private and Government Investment Abroad,* 464.

7. Jonathan E. Sanford, *U.S. Foreign Policy and Multilateral Development Banks* (Boulder: Westview Press, 1982), 95.

8. Ibid., 96.

9. The MDB boards are the places where member-government influence on bank policy is the strongest. U.S. influence on MDB policies has fluctuated with the competence and distinction of the U.S. representatives. Unfortunately, the Treasury practice of treating the U.S. executive directors as "messengers" rather than participants in the MDB policy process has often been an obstacle to strong U.S. representation.

10. J. N. Behrman, "U.S. Government Encouragement of Private Direct Investment Abroad," in Mikesell, *Private and Government Investment Abroad,* 191–229.

11. The Export-Import Bank "was originally organized under the authority of the National Industrial Recovery Act to facilitate trade between the United States and the USSR . . . Difficulties over the settlement of debts owed to the United States led to a postponement of financing of U.S. export to the Soviet Union by the new bank. Meanwhile, the government of Cuba requested a loan to finance the purchase of silver for minting into silver pesos . . . A second Export-Import Bank of Washington was created by Executive Order in March 1934; this institution made a loan of $4 million to the Republic of Cuba for the purchase of silver bullion. The following year the assets of the second bank were transferred to the original Export-Import Bank." Raymond F. Mikesell, "The Export-Import Bank of Washington," in Mikesell, *Private and Government Investment Abroad,* 459. See also the very useful article by Rita M. Rodriguez, "Exim's Mission and Accomplishments: 1934–84," in *The Export-Import Bank at Fifty: The International Environment and the Institution's Role,* ed. Rita M. Rodriguez (Lexington, Mass.: D. C. Heath, 1987), 1–23.

12. Mikesell, *Private and Government Investment Abroad,* 464.

13. "Less than one percent of the total value of the loans have taken the form of exporter credits . . . For example, during the fiscal year 1958, 141 out of a total of 191 credits extended by the Bank were to U.S. exporters (or financial institutions) for financing export transactions. However, the total value of these 141 credits come to only $17.4 million as against $838 million for the 50 credits authorized on request of overseas governments and firms." Ibid., 474, 475.

14. Ibid., 463.

15. Ibid., 301, 471.

16. Subsidized interest rates date from the late 1960s, when U.S. nominal interest rates began to rise above their historical 3–5 percent level. In the early 1980s, after U.S. inflation rates rose to double-digit levels, the subsidy on the typical Eximbank loan exceeded 4 percent. When Eximbank management tried to reduce the export subsidies, it was reminded by Congress that its primary function is to offer credit that is fully competitive with the funding available from other countries. Rodriguez, "Exim's Mission," 18–19.

17. David A. Stockman, *The Triumph of Politics: The Inside Story of the Reagan Revolution* (New York: Avon Books, 1987). "Cutting the Export-Import Bank was an initiative dear to my free market heart. Export subsidies are a mercantilist illusion based on the illogical proposition that the nation can raise its employment and GNP by giving away its goods for less than what it costs to make them . . . Moreover, in 1981, the Ex-Im's practice was to bestow about two-thirds of its subsidies on a handful of giant manufacturers, including Boeing Aircraft, General Electric, and Westinghouse" (p. 124).

18. U.S. Congress, House Committee on Appropriations, *Foreign Operations, Export Financing, and Related Programs Appropriations for 1990: Hearings,* 100th Cong., 1st sess. (Washington: USGPO, 1989), 119–63.

19. U.S. Congress, House Committee on Banking, Finance and Lending Affairs, *Future of the Export-Import Bank's Direct Lending Program,* 100th Cong., 1st sess. (Washington: USGPO, 10 May 1989), 13, 14.

20. Congressional Budget Office, *Budgeting for Eximbank: A Case Study of Credit Reform* (Washington: CBO, January 1990).

21. Mikesell, *Private and Government Investment Abroad,* 295.

22. Raymond F. Mikesell, *Public International Lending for Development* (New York: Random House, 1966), 92.

23. Ibid., 90. It should be noted, however, that the changes were largely cosmetic. The 10-year grace period and below-market rates imply a very large grant element in the "loans."

24. For an example of the confusion over the loans repayable in local currencies, see the dialogue between Vance Brand, Managing Director of the Development Loan Fund, and Senator Henry Dworshak (D-Idaho) in the hearings on the Mutual Security Appropriations for 1961. Senate Committee on Appropriations, *Mutual Security Appropriations for 1961,* 86th Cong., 2d sess. (Washington: USGPO, 1961), 174–76.

25. Quoted from Alan C. Brenglass, *The Overseas Private Investment Corporation:*

A Study in Political Risk (New York: Praeger, 1983), x. The Brenglass study contains an exceedingly careful review of the legislative history of the Overseas Private Investment Corporation.

26. "The statute delegated to OPIC the specific risk guarantee program of its immediate predecessor, the Agency for International Development, renamed investment insurance, affording protection against loss due to three specific types of political risk—inconvertibility, expropriation, and war; the former AID extended risk investment guarantee program renamed investment guarantees, permitting guarantees against business risks on loans and equity investments; the former Public Law 480 (Cooley) loan program, renamed direct investment, providing loans in U.S. dollars or local currencies on a reimbursable basis to firms privately owned or of mixed private and public ownership; and small reinvestment and technical assistance programs, together with a pilot agricultural credit and self-help community development institution program in Latin America. The program of political risk is the *sine qua non* of OPIC's existence." Ibid., x, xi. The direct loan program has remained small—amounting to less than $25 million in 1989. U.S. Congress, House Committee on Appropriations, *Foreign Operations, Export Financing and Related Programs Appropriations for 1990, Hearings*, 100th Cong., 1st sess. (Washington: USGPO, 1989), 55–117.

27. Benjamin A. Javits, *Peace by Investment* (New York: Funk & Wagnalls, 1950). See also Benjamin A. Javits and Leon H. Keyserling, *The Peace Investment Corporation* (Washington: International Committee for Peace by Investment, June 1961).

28. The next several paragraphs on the formation of PIC draw heavily on Brenglass, *The Overseas Private Investment Corporation*, 1–38.

29. Ibid., 201–4.

30. Ibid.

31. General Accounting Office, *Foreign Aid: Impact of Overseas Private Investment Corporation Activities on U.S. Employment* (Washington: GAO, May 1987); House Committee on Appropriations, *Foreign Operations, Export Financing Appropriations 1990*, 84–98.

32. House Committee on Appropriations, *Foreign Operations, Export Financing Appropriations 1990*, 207–12.

33. GAO, *Impact of Overseas Private Investment Corporation*; House Committee on Appropriations, *Foreign Operations, Export Financing Appropriations 1990*, 84–98; Arthur Young International, *A Study of the U.S. Effects of OPIC-assisted Private Investment Overseas* (Washington: Arthur Young International, December 1987).

34. Brenglass, *The Overseas Private Investment Corporation*, 217. Most of the major exporting countries also make political risk insurance available to their multinational firms. See Fariborz Ghadar, ed., *Financing Third World Development: A Survey of Official Project Finance Programs in OECD Countries* (Washington: International Law Institute, 1987); J. E. Austin, *Managing in Developing Countries* (New York: Free Press, 1990), 172–75. In April 1988 a group of 10 developed and 25 developing countries, with the assistance of the World Bank, established a new Multilateral Investment Guarantee Agency, which will also offer insurance against political and other noncommercial risk.

35. Rebecca M. Sammary and Larry J. Sammary, "The Overseas Private Investment Corporation and Developing Countries," *Economic Development and Cultural Change* 42 (July 1994): 816–27.

36. A third organization, an International Trade Organization, that would coordinate and enforce rules on international trade was also planned. After two years of negotiations, culminating in a U.N. Conference on Trade and Employment in Havana on 24 March 1948, the idea of a comprehensive agreement was shelved in favor of a more limited General Agreement on Tariffs and Trade.

37. Lord Keynes, quoted from Lars Schoultz, "Politics, Economics, and U.S. Participation in Multilateral Development Banks," *International Organization* 36 (Summer 1982): 538.

38. U.S. Department of State, *Proceedings and Documents of the United Nations Monetary and Financial Conference, Bretton Woods, New Hampshire, July 1–22, 1944* (Washington: USGPO, 1946), I:88.

39. Mason and Asher, *World Bank since Bretton Woods*, 1973. See also Catherine Gwin, *U.S. Relations with the World Bank, 1945–1992* (Washington: Brookings Institution, 1994).

40. Ibid., 463, 498.

41. Ibid., 500–501.

42. Simon G. Hanson, "The End of the Good Neighbor Policy," *Inter-American Economic Affairs* 7 (Autumn 1953): 21, 22.

43. Mason and Asher, *World Bank since Bretton Woods*, 502–3.

44. Ibid., 463, 504–5.

45. This discussion of the establishment of the International Finance Corporation and the International Development Association draws primarily on Mason and Asher, *World Bank since Bretton Woods,* 345–50, 380–96, and Jonathan E. Sanford, *U.S. Foreign Policy and Multilateral Development Banks* (Boulder: Westview Press, 1982), 44–48. See also B. E. Matecki, *Establishment of the IFC and United States Policy* (New York: Praeger, 1957); James H. Weaver, *The International Development Association: A New Approach to Foreign Aid* (New York: Praeger, 1965); James C. Baker, *International Business Expansion into Less-Developed Countries: The International Finance Corporation and Its Operations* (New York: International Business Press, 1993).

46. Sanford, *U.S. Foreign Policy*, 44.

47. Mason and Asher, *World Bank since Bretton Woods,* 380–81. See also Ronald T. Libby, "International Development Association: A Legal Fiction Designed To Secure an LDC Constituency," *International Organization* 29 (Fall 1975): 1065–72. Libby argues that the IDA clients have become an important bank political constituency in support of IDA replenishments. In the mid-1960s the Centre for Settlement of Investment Disputes (ICSID) became a fourth member of the World Bank Group. See Mason and Asher, *World Bank since Bretton Woods,* 82. See also Hassan M. Salim, *Development Assistance Policies and the Performance of Aid Agencies* (New York: St. Martin's, 1983), 276–338.

48. In this review of the establishment of the regional development banks, I draw primarily on John A. White, *Regional Development Banks: The Asian, African and*

Inter-American Development Banks (New York: Praeger, 1972); Mason and Asher, *World Bank since Bretton Woods,* 578–86; and Sanford, *U.S. Foreign Policy*, 48–57. See also Hassan M. Salim, *Development Assistance Policies and the Performance of Aid Agencies* (New York: St. Martin's, 1983), 276–338.

49. White, *Regional Development Banks,* 145.

50. Ibid, 146.

51. For greater detail see Po-Wen Huang, Jr., *The Asian Development Bank: Diplomacy and Development in Asia* (New York: Vintage Press, 1975), 11–58.

52. Lyndon B. Johnson, *New York Times,* 9 April 1965 (cited in White, *Regional Development Banks,* 45).

53. White reports that "the first round of voting failed to produce a conclusive result and it soon became clear that certain arrangements which had been made privately were breaking down. At this point, the entire conference was floated out into Manila Bay aboard the president's yacht. The yacht broke down (according to the folklore that has grown up around this incident, the breakdown was engineered), and the yacht stayed out in the bay until sufficient support had been mobilized for Manila's candidacy" (p. 49). This episode is not reported in Huang, *The Asian Development Bank.* Huang does emphasize the exceedingly effective political campaign by the government of the Philippines to have the ADB located in Manila. See pp. 92–97.

54. White, *Regional Development Banks,* 65.

55. Ibid., 91.

56. Robert Gardiner, quoted from White, *Regional Development Banks,* 92.

57. White, *Regional Development Banks,* 96, 99, 101.

58. For a personal account of the early years of the AfDB, see Kwame Donkoh Fordor, *The African Development Bank: Problems of International Cooperation* (New York: Pergamon Press, 1981). Dr. Fordor served as president of AfDB from 1976 to 1979. The book reviews the troubled history of AfDB governance during 1964–79. For a somewhat muted critique of more recent history, see Bo Jerlström, *Banking on Africa: An Evaluation of the African Development Bank* (Stockholm: Ministry of Foreign Affairs, 1990).

59. In testimony before the Senate Committee on Finance, *Implementation of the Brady Plan* (Washington: USGPO, 2 March 1990), J. Fred Bergston argued that "the new European Bank for Reconstruction and Development is a very sharp slap in the face of the United States . . . It is intended to give us a smaller share than that of the individual European countries. In part it is the chickens coming home to roost for our being niggardly with the World Bank and the IMF" (p. 31).

60. The U.S. role with respect to the multilateral banks during this period has been chronicled in considerable detail in Mason and Asher, *World Bank since Bretton Woods*, 406–13, and Sanford, *U.S. Foreign Policy*, 58–61.

61. Mason and Asher, *World Bank since Bretton Woods*, 416.

62. Sanford, *U.S. Foreign Policy*, 62.

63. National Advisory Council on International Monetary and Fiscal Policies, *Annual Report to the President and to the Congress* (Washington: USGPO, 1972), 12.

64. The "tilt" toward Pakistan in the United States and at the bank occurred as

Henry Kissinger, the national security advisor to President Nixon, was attempting to achieve an "opening" to China by working through General Yaha Khan, president of Pakistan. The NAC interagency policy coordination mechanism was completely bypassed in the policy discussions on the IDA credits. The political issues were simply too immediate to be resolved by normal bureaucratic processes. See Michael E. Akins, "United States Control over World Bank Group Decision-Making" (Ph.D. diss., University of Pennsylvania, 1981), 135–43.

65. Bartram S. Brown, *The United States and the Politicization of the World Bank* (London: Kegan Paul International, 1992), 157–70. In his campaign Allende had pledged that he would, if elected, refuse to deal with the International Monetary Fund. This gave the World Bank a reason to maintain that Chile was out of compliance with earlier fund agreements and thus had became noncreditworthy. The Allende government did submit a proposal to the World Bank, which the bank regarded as nonviable. Toward the end of the Allende regime, substantial progress was being made on the loan application, which was approved shortly after his death. José D. Epstein, letter, 4 June 1992.

66. Akins, "United States Control," 15.

67. Ibid., 68.

68. Myer Rasish, who served as under-secretary of state during 1981–82, commented: "It is no secret that the Reagan administration came to office . . . with a certain amount of intellectual and ideological baggage. Included was a suspicion of the World Banks' policies, a preference for bilateral assistance, and animosity toward the new International Economic Order and all its works, particularly the U.N. global negotiations." Myer Rasish, "The World Bank at a Crossroads: Some Observations," in *U.S. Policy toward the Bretton Woods Institutions*, ed. Alvin Paul Drischler and M. P. Benjenk (Washington: Johns Hopkins University School of Advanced International Studies, February 1988), 22.

69. "1980 Republican Party Platform Text," *Congressional Quarterly Almanac 1980* 36 (1980): 83-B.

70. For a more positive perspective on McNamara's tenure, see William Clark, "Robert McNamara at the World Bank," *Foreign Affairs* 60 (Fall 1981): 167–83. See also Robert L. Ayres, "Breaking the Bank," *Foreign Policy* (Summer 1981): 104–20.

71. The Clausen appointment had been speeded up to head off pressure from some member countries to name someone from a country other than the United States to the presidency. See Clyde H. Farnsworth, "Bank of America's Chief Chosen by Carter To Head World Bank," *New York Times,* 31 October 1980.

72. Sanford, *U.S. Foreign Policy*, 76.

73. Clyde H. Farnsworth, "U.S. Vote No at World Bank More Often under Reagan," *New York Times*, 26 November 1984, 30.

74. The issues of U.S. concern over MDB staff salaries had been a continuing source of tension since the early 1960s. The U.S. executive directors in the MDBs were under instructions to fight against any raises that would result in salary levels above the higher levels in the U.S. civil service pay scale. José D. Epstein, letter, 4 June 1992.

75. Department of the Treasury, *United States Participation in the Multilateral*

Development Banks in the 1980s (Washington: USGPO, 1982), 4–9. The bank also commissioned an external study by Raymond F. Mikesell, *The Economics of Foreign Aid and Self-Sustaining Development* (Boulder: Westview Press, 1983). Both the Treasury and the Mikesell reports were more supportive of the MDBs than Regan and Sprinkle had anticipated. The Treasury study was characterized by a former World Bank vice president for external relations as "a report of astonishing mediocrity and full of internal contradictions." M. P. Benjenk, "The United States and the Bretton Woods Organizations on the World Geopolitical Scene," in Drischler and Benjenk, *Policy toward Bretton Woods Institutions.* See also the more detailed criticisms by Morris B. Goldman, "The United States Treasury Review of the Multilateral Development Banks: An Economic Critique," *Journal of Monetary Economics* 13 (1984): 275–93. Goldman argues that an official report that would provide a thoroughgoing assessment of the MDBs and U.S. policy toward them was probably unattainable because internal administration politics required the production of a report that would appeal to supporters as well as critics of the MDBs. The result was a lack of internal consistency. "The World Bank has been publicizing the view that the merits of its programs have been vindicated by the Treasury's critical assessment, yet opponents of the MDBs note that the assessment's overall conclusion recommends reduced financial support for these institutions" (p. 292).

76. For a detailed account of the political processes within the U.S. government and between the U.S. government and the multinational and commercial banks involved in the Baker and Brady plans, see Raymond Vernon, Debora L. Spar, and Glen Tobin, *Iron Triangles and Revolving Doors: Cases in U.S. Foreign Economic Policy Making* (New York: Westview Press, 1991), 82–111. See also Jonathan E. Sanford, *Multilateral Development Banks: Issues for the 101st Congress* (Washington: Library of Congress Congressional Research Service, 16 April 1990); Rudiger Dornbusch, John H. Makin, and David Zlowe, eds., *Alternative Solutions to Developing Country Debt Problems* (Washington: American Enterprise Institute for Public Policy Research, 1989).

77. Vernon, Spar, and Tobin, *Iron Triangles and Revolving Doors*, 98.

78. For a more critical perspective on the Brady plan, see Jeffrey D. Sachs and C. Fred Bergsten in U.S. Congress, Senate Committee on Finance, *Implementation of the Brady Plan, Senate Hearing 101–108,* 100th Cong., 2d sess. (Washington: USGPO, 1990).

79. In this section I draw very heavily from Jonathan E. Sanford, "U.S. Policy toward the Multilateral Development Banks: The Role of Congress," *George Washington University Journal of International Law and Economics* 22 (November 1988): 1–115.

80. International Bank for Reconstruction and Development, Article IV, Section 10. Similar clauses are included in other multilateral bank charters. See Lars Schoultz, "Politics, Economics, and U.S. Participation in Multilateral Development Banks," *International Organization* 36 (Summer 1982): 537–74.

81. Sanford, *U.S. Foreign Policy,* 13–14.

82. Ibid., 157–58.

83. Ibid., 116.

84. Ibid., 21–22.

85. In 1987 the Senate version of the 1988 trade bill contained a Foreign Agricultural Investment Reform (FAIR) amendment that would have prohibited MDBs from borrowing in U.S. capital markets or using other dominated financial instruments to finance loans for the production of agricultural commodities competitive with U.S. exports—particularly wheat, soybeans, and cotton. The Senate proposal was omitted in the final legislation. Sanford, *U.S. Foreign Polity*, 54–55.

86. Ibid., 49–50.

87. Brown, *Politicization of the World Bank,* 190.

88. See, for example, the testimony presented by American commodity organizations in U.S. Congress, Joint Economic Committee, *Foreign Agriculture Investment Reform* (Washington: USGPO, 1987). The World Bank introduced structural adjustment lending in 1979 to assist member countries in dealing with the second oil shock by providing temporary balance-of-payment financing while the stabilization and structural reform efforts needed to deal with the oil shock were taking effect.

89. Sanford, *U.S. Foreign Policy,* 106.

90. James P. Houck, "Link between Agricultural Assistance and International Trade," *Agricultural Economics* 2 (1988): 154–66; Alain de Janvry and Elizabeth Sadoulet, "The Conditions of Harmony between Third World Agricultural Development and U.S. Farm Exports," *American Journal of Agricultural Economics* 68 (December 1986): 1340–46.

91. Robert S. McNamara, "Address to the Board of Governors" (Washington: International Bank for Reconstruction and Development, 1973). For a history of the evolution of the poverty-oriented rural development programs at the World Bank, see Robert L. Ayres, *Banking on the Poor: The World Bank and World Poverty* (Cambridge: MIT Press, 1983), 93–147.

92. Alan Hughy, "Is the World Bank Biting Off More Than It Can Chew?" *Forbes* (26 May 1980): 123.

93. This section draws on Philippe Le Prestre, *The World Bank and the Environmental Challenge* (Selinsgrove, Pa.: Susquehanna University Press; Cranbury, N.J.: Associated University Press, 1989); Raymond F. Mikesell and Larry Williams, *International Banks and the Environment: From Growth to Sustainability, An Unfinished Agenda* (San Francisco: Sierra Club Books, 1992); Gareth Porter and Janet Welsh Brown, *Global Environmental Politics* (Boulder: Westview Press, 1991); Barbara J. Bramble and Gareth Porter, "Non-governmental Organizations and the Making of U.S. International Environmental Policy," in Andrew Huwell and Benedict Kingsbury, eds., *The International Politics of the Environment: Actors, Interests and Institutions* (Oxford: Clarendon Press, 1992), 313–53; Bruce Rich, *Mortgaging the Earth: The World Bank, Environmental Impoverishment and the Crisis of Development* (Boston: Beacon Press, 1994); Paul J. Nelson, "The World Bank and Nongovernmental Organization" (Ph.D. diss., University of Wisconsin, 27 February 1991).

94. Robert McNamara, "Address to the United Nations Economic and Social Council" (Washington: World Bank, 1979, mimeo), 5 (quoted from Le Prestre, *World Bank and Environmental Challenge*, 17).

95. The unit was initially entitled the Office of Environmental and Health Affairs. It later was reorganized as the Office of Environmental Affairs and in the early 1980s as the Office of Environmental and Scientific Affairs (OESA).

96. See U.S. Congress, House Committee on Banking, Finance and Urban Affairs, *Environmental Impact of Multilateral Development Bank-funded Projects,* Hearings before the Subcommittee on International Development Institutions and Finance, 98th Cong., lat. sess., 1983; idem, *Draft Recommendations on the Multilateral Bank and the Environment,* Hearings before the Subcommittee on International Development Institutions and Finance, 98th Cong., 2d sess., 1984; U.S. Congress, House Committee on Foreign Affairs, *U.S. International Environmental Policy,* Hearings before the Subcommittee on Human Rights and International Organizations, 98th Cong., 2d sess., 1984.

97. Interaction between domestic and transnational activism remains something of a "black box" in both the political science and the sociology literature on social movements. See, however, Porter and Brown, *Global Environmental Politics,* 56–64; Margaret Keck and Kathryn Sikkink, "International Issue Networks in the Environmental Human Rights" (Paper presented at the International Congress of the Latin American Studies Association, Los Angeles, 24–27 September 1992); Allan Hunter, "Democracy Yes, Sovereignty No: An Explanation of Tensions between Domestic and Transnational Political Activism," Working Paper 11–1 (Minneapolis: University of Minnesota Institute of International Studies, MacArthur Program on Peace and International Cooperation, September 1994).

98. Mikesell and Williams, *International Banks and the Environment,* 18–27.

99. Constance Holdren, "The Greening of the World Bank," *Science* 240 (17 June 1988): 1610.

100. Pat Aufderheidel and Bruce Rich, "Environmental Reform and the Multilateral Banks," *World Policy Journal* (Spring 1988): 301–23; Bruce Rich, "The Emperor's New Clothes: The World Bank and Environmental Reform," *World Policy Journal* 7 (Spring 1990): 305–29; Rich, *Mortgaging the Earth,* 148–99. Bruce Rich is the senior attorney and director of the International Program at the Environmental Defense Fund.

101. Robert Winterbottom, *Taking Stock: The Tropical Forestry Action Plan after Five Years* (Washington: World Resources Institute, 1990); Ola Ullsten, Salleh Mohd Nor, and Montague Yudelman, *Tropical Forestry Action Plan: Report of the Independent Review* (Kuala Lumpur: Malaysia, May 1990); Mikesell and Williams, *International Banks and the Environment,* 131–34.

102. Bradford Morse and Thomas Berger, *Sandar Savouar: Report of the Independent Review* (Ottawa, Canada: Resource Futures International, 1992) (the Morse commission); Willi A. Wapenhans et al., *Report of the Portfolio Management Task Force* (Washington: World Bank, 1 July 1992, mimeo).

103. See the very useful discussion of the criticism from the Left and the Right in Roger C. Riddell, *Foreign Aid Reconsidered* (Baltimore: Johns Hopkins University Press, 1987), 129–75. For an official perspective see Department of the Treasury, *United States Participation in the Multilateral Development Banks in the 1980's* (Washington: USGPO, 1982), 153–94.

104. Peter T. Bauer, *Dissent on Development* (Cambridge: Harvard University Press, 1972); idem, *Equality, the Third World and Economic Delusion* (London: Weidenfled & Nickolson, 1981); idem, *Reality and Rhetoric: Studies in the Economics of Development* (Cambridge: Harvard University Press, 1984).

105. Doug Brandow, "What's Still Wrong with the World Bank?" *Orbus* 33 (Winter 1989): 76.

106. Cheryl Payer, *The World Bank: A Critical Analysis* (New York: Monthly Review Press, 1982), 20, 42. For a similar perspective, see Teresa Hayter, *Aid as Imperialism* (Baltimore: Penguin Books, 1971).

107. For a very useful review, see Don Babai, "The World Bank and the IMF: Rolling Back the State or Backing Its Role," in *The Promise of Prioritization: Challenge for U.S. Policy*, ed. Raymond Vernon (New York: Council on Foreign Relations, 1988), 254–84.

108. Mason and Asher, *World Bank since Bretton Woods,* 13.

109. For a review of these and other contributions, see Anne O. Krueger and Vernon W. Ruttan, "Toward a Theory of Development Assistance," in Krueger, Michalopoulas, and Ruttan, *Aid and Development*, 32–52.

110. Malcolm S. Tammen, "World Bank Snookers U.S. Congress Again," *Heritage Foundation Background,* no. 649 (23 May 1988): 1.

111. Ayres, *Banking on the Poor*, 93–147; Richard E. Feinberg, "An Open Letter to the World Bank's New President," in *Between Two Worlds: The World Bank's Next Decade* (New Brunswick, N.J.: Transaction Books, 1986), 3–30.

112. James W. Conrow, "Statement," Senate Committee on Appropriations, *Foreign Assistance and Related Programs Appropriations, Fiscal Year 1988, Hearings,* 100th Cong., 1st sess. (Washington: USGPO), 79.

113. Akins, "United States Control," 135–43.

114. Stephen D. Krasner, "Power Structures and Regional Development Banks," *International Organization* 35 (Spring 1981): 303–28, 321.

Chapter 12 Policy toward the Specialized Agencies and Voluntary Programs of the United Nations

1. In this chapter I draw heavily on Kelly Wesemann Seyid, "The United States and the United Nations Development Assistance: U.S. Participation in Specialized Agencies and Voluntary Programs Involved in Assistance to Developing Countries" (Master's thesis, University of Minnesota, 1992). I am indebted to Robert J. Berg, Betsey Baker, John J. Donohue, Walter Galenson, Howard Hjort, Mark Imber, Harold Jacobson, William Mashler, William H. Mansfield, Gayl Ness, and Joel S. Spiro for comments on an earlier draft of this chapter.

2. Donald J. Puchala, "American Interests and the United Nations," *Political Science Quarterly* 97 (Winter 1982–83): 256.

3. Juliana Geran Pilon, "International Organizations," in *Mandate for Leadership: Continuing the Conservative Revolution*, ed. Stuart M. Butler, Michael Sanera, and W. Bruce Weinrod (Washington: Heritage Foundation, 1984), 364.

4. For further discussion of the roles and merits of bilateral and multilateral assistance, see John White, *The Politics of Foreign Aid* (New York: St. Martin's, 1974), 35–67.

5. For a discussion of the proliferation of other economic and social programs funded by the regular U.N. budget and extrabudgetary resources, see K. D. Saksena, *Reforming the United Nations* (New Delhi: Sage Publications, 1993), 57–104.

6. The United Nations Commission for Latin America (CEPAL), under the intellectual leadership of the Argentine economist Raul Prebish, exerted a pervasive influence on the development of the intellectual rationalization for the import substitution policies adopted by most Latin American countries during the 1950s and 1960s. The ideas of the Latin American structuralist school were also largely responsible for the creation of the U.N. Conference on Trade and Development in 1964. The work of Prebish and his association was regarded as dangerously radical in U.S. official and right-wing circles. David Lehman, *Democracy and Development in Latin America* (Philadelphia: Temple University Press, 1990), 3–13. There has been growing disillusionment, even among supporters of the U.N. system, with the U.N. bodies set up to deal with issues of economic development. See Max Jacobson, *The United Nations in the 1990: A Second Chance?* (New York: Twentieth Century Fund, 1993), 149–54.

7. For a partial explanation see J. Martin Rochester, "The Rise and Fall of International Organization as a Field of Study," *International Organization* 40 (Autumn 1986): 777–813. Among the more useful introductions to research on international organization are Robert W. Cox and Harold K. Jacobson, eds., *The Anatomy of Influence: Decision Making in International Organizations* (New Haven: Yale University Press, 1993); Harold K. Jacobson, *Networks of Interdependence: International Organizations and the Global Political System* (New York: Alfred A. Knopf, 1984), 59–73; Gayl D. Ness and Steven R. Brechen, "Bridging the Gap: International Organizations as Organizations," *International Organization* 42 (Spring 1988): 245–73.

8. Mark F. Imber, *The USA, ILO, UNESCO and IAEA: Politicization and Withdrawal in the Specialized Agencies* (New York: St. Martin's, 1989), 4. See also pp. 13–27 for a more detailed discussion of functionalism and its critics.

9. For greater detail on the structure, governance, and administration of the specialized agencies and voluntary programs, see Patrick Demeongeat, "U.N. System Development Assistance," in *U.S. Foreign Assistance: Investment or Folly?* ed. John Wilhelm and Gerry Feinstein (New York: Praeger, 1984), 304–29, and Edward W. Erikson and Daniel A. Sumner, "The U.N. and Economic Development," in Burton Yale Pines, *A World without a U.N.: What Would Happen If the U.N. Shut Down?* (Washington: Heritage Foundation, 1984), 1–21.

10. Department of State, *United States Contributions to International Organizations: Report to the Congress for Fiscal Year 1990* (Washington: U.S. Department of State, 1991), xi; U.N. General Assembly, *Contributions Pledged or Paid at the 1990 United Nations Pledging Conference for Development Activities as of 30 June 1991*, GA Document A/Conf/154/2 (New York: United Nations, 2 October 1991).

11. Juliana Geran Pilon, "International Organizations," in *Mandate for Leadership: Continuing the Conservative Revolution*, ed. Stuart M. Butler, Michael Sanera, and W. Bruce Weinrod (Washington: Heritage Foundation, 1984), 364.

12. Paul Taylor, "The United Nations System under Stress: Financial Pressures and Their Consequences," *Review of International Studies,* 17, no. 4 (1991): 369; Mark F. Imber, *The USA, ILO, UNESCO and IAEA: Politicization and Withdrawal in the Specialized Agencies* (New York: St. Martin's, 1989), 121–36.

13. U.S. Government Accounting Office, *United Nations: Issues Related to Payment of U.S. Contributions* (Washington: GAO, November 1989), 7.

14. George Shultz, "Subject: U.S. Discussion Paper on Kassebaum Amendment and Gramm-Rudman-Hollings Legislation for Geneva Group Consultative Level Meeting, March 20–21, 1986" (Washington: 1986, unclassified telegram).

15. U.S. Congress, Senate Committee on Foreign Relations, Subcommittee on Terrorism, Narcotics, and International Operations, *Foreign Relations Authorization Act for Fiscal Years 1992–1993,* 102d Cong., 1st sess., 7, 12, and 21 March and 1 and 19 April 1991 (Washington: USGPO, 1991), 69.

16. Government Accounting Office, *United Nations: Payment of Contributions*, 7.

17. Ibid., 7.

18. Senate Committee on Foreign Relations, *Foreign Relations Authorization Act 1992–1993,* 69, 8.

19. Department of State, *United States Contributions to International Organizations,* July 1993; U.S. Congress, *Budget for Fiscal Year 1993,* House Document 102–178, 102d Cong., 2d sess., pt. 1, 250.

20. Douglas Williams, *The Specialized Agencies and the United Nations: The System in Crisis* (New York: St. Martin's, 1987), 83. The budgets of the specialized agencies are from the assessed contributions of their members, the subventions that agencies receive from UNDP, and various Funds in Trust that the agencies negotiate from various donors or that have been established for special purposes and are financed voluntarily by member governments of the United Nations.

21. C. V. Narasimhan, *The United Nations: An Inside View* (New Delhi: UNITAR and Vikas Publishing House, 1988), 151.

22. R. G. A. Jackson, *A Study of the Capacity of the United Nations Development System*, 2 vols. (Geneva: United Nations, 1969). For comments on the Jackson report, see Johan Kaufmann, "The Capacity of the United Nations Development Program: The Jackson Report," *International Organization* (1971): 938–49; Dharam P. Ghai, "The United Nations Capacity Study: An Evaluation of the Jackson Report," *Journal of World Trade Law* 4 (1978): 245–54.

23. Commission on International Development, *Partners in Development* (New York: Praeger, 1969) (the Pearson report).

24. Jackson, *A Study of the Capacity,* 1:13.

25. Lester B. Pearson, chairman, *Partners in Development: Report of the Commission on International Development* (New York: Praeger, 1969), 4.

26. U.S. Congress, House Committee on Foreign Affairs, *United States Role in the U.N. System*, 92d Cong., 1st sess. (Washington: USGPO, 13 and 14 October 1971), 5, 19.

27. Demeongeat, "U.N. System Development Assistance."

28. Dennis Goulet and Michael Hudson, *The Myth of Aid: The Hidden Agenda of the Development Reports* (New York: IDOC North America, 1971), 23. Critics con-

tended that the shift to multilateral aid through the banks was an attempt to mask bilateral as multilateral aid.

29. U.S. Senate, *U.S. Contributions to Multilateral Development Banks and International Organizations, Hearings*, 97th Cong., 1st sess. (Washington: USGPO, 21 April 1981), 27.

30. Erikson and Sumner, "The U.N. and Economic Development," 14–21; Christopher Whalen, "Unholy Alliance Global Bureaucrats Must Break the Socialist Ties That Bind," *Barron's,* 22 July 1991, 12; idem, "Reply to William Draper," *Barron's,* 26 August 1991, 22.

31. Amity Shales, "Quota King: How They Chose Top U.N. Man," *Wall Street Journal,* 25 November 1991, sec. A, 12.

32. Williams, *The Specialized Agencies*, 175.

33. See, for example, the review by David C. Korten, "Sustainable Development," *World Policy Journal* (Winter 1991–92): 158–90.

34. Sergio Marchisio and Antonietta Di Blase, *The Food and Agriculture Organization: The First 40 Years* (Dordrecht: Martinus Nijhoff, 1991), 205.

35. In this section I draw rather heavily on Gove Hambridge, *The Story of FAO* (New York: Van Nostrand, 1955); Ralph Phillips, *The FAO, Its Organization, Work and U.S. Participation* (Washington: USDA Foreign Agriculture Service, 1978); Hans Jorgen Kristensen, *The Future Role of FAO in the U.N. System* (Horsholm, Denmark: Institute for Food Studies and Agroindustrial Development, 1986); Food and Agriculture Organization, *FAO: The First 40 Years, 1945–1985* (Rome: FAO, 1986); Raymond F. Hopkins, "International Food Organizations and the United States: Drifting Leadership and Diverging Interests," in *The United States and Multilateral Institutions: Patterns of Changing Instrumentality and Influence,* ed. Margaret P. Karns and Karen A. Mingst (Boston: Unwin Hyman, 1990), 177–204; Ross B. Talbot, *The Four World Food Agencies in Rome* (Ames: Iowa State University Press, 1990); Marchisio and Di Blase, *The Food and Agriculture Organization*; John Abbott, *Politics and Poverty: A Critique of the Food and Agriculture Organization of the United Nations* (London: Routledge, 1992). In addition to the FAO, other international bodies (most of which are part of the U.N. system) deal with international food efforts. These include the World Food Program, the International Fund for Agricultural Development, the International Wheat Council, the Consultative Group on International Agricultural Research, and the World Food Council. See Chapter 8 for additional detail on the other organizations.

36. U.S. Department of State, *United States Contributions to International Organizations* (Washington: Department of State, 1990), 36.

37. For the effort to establish the linkage between food and health, see Marchisio and Di Blase, *The Food and Agriculture Organization*, 7–10; Abbott, *Politics and Poverty,* 2. For a more recent articulation, see David E. Bell, William C. Clark, and Vernon W. Ruttan, "Global Research Systems for Sustainable Development: Agriculture, Health, and Environment," in Vernon W. Ruttan, (ed.), *Agriculture, Environment and Health: Sustainable Development in the 21st Century* (Minneapolis: University of Minnesota Press, 1994), 358–80.

38. John Boyd Orr, *As I Recall* (London: MacGibbon & Kee, 1966), 160, 161.

39. Gove Hambridge, *The Story of FAO* (New York: Von Nostrand, 1955); Marchisio and Di Blase, *The Food and Agriculture Organization*, 10.

40. Boyd Orr, *As I Recall*, 163.

41. Ibid., 164.

42. Marchisio and Di Blase, *The Food and Agriculture Organization*, 16.

43. Ibid., 17; Boyd Orr, *As I Recall*, 194, 160; Marchisio and Di Blase, *The Food and Agriculture Organization*, 17, 18.

44. Abbott, *Politics and Poverty*, 34.

45. Phillips, *The FAO, Its Organization*, 23.

46. Ibid., 24.

47. For a personal account see B. R. Sen, *Towards a Newer World* (Dublin: Tycooly International, 1982), 137–59.

48. Ibid., 154, 159.

49. Ibid., 182–85, 197–202.

50. Comptroller General of the United States, *Report to the Senate Committee on Governmental Affairs* (Washington: USGPO, 1977), 7.

51. Marchisio and Di Blase, *The Food and Agriculture Organization*, 69–72; Warren Baum, *Partners against Hunger: The Consultative Group on International Agricultural Research* (Washington: World Bank, 1986), 34.

52. Marchisio and Di Blase, *The Food and Agriculture Organization*, 82.

53. Comptroller General of the United States, *Report to the Senate Committee on Governmental Affairs* (Washington: USGPO, 1977), 7.

54. Ibid., 11, 12.

55. Ibid., iii, 53–69.

56. Georges Fauriol, *The Food and Agriculture Organization: A Flawed Strategy in the War against Hunger* (Washington: Heritage Foundation, 1984); Georges Fauriol, "The U.N. and the World Food Supply," in *A World without a U.N.*, ed. Burton Yale Pines (Washington: Heritage Foundation, 1984), 73–92. For additional discussion of the Fauriol and related criticisms, see Talbot, *The Four World Food Agencies*, 34–39. One of the criticisms from the Right has been that the FAO programs have a strong anti–private sector bias. Yet the U.S. private sector suppliers of agricultural imports have been strong supporters of the FAO. Critics from the Left have often accused the FAO of excessively close relationships with the private sector input supply and forest industries.

57. Abbott, *Politics and Poverty*, 41.

58. The position of U.S. representative was raised to the level of ambassador to accommodate the appointment of Millicent Fenwick, formerly a Republican congresswoman from New Jersey, who had run unsuccessfully for the U.S. Senate. Fenwick established a warm personal relationship with Saouma. Her replacement, Fred J. Eckert, was also a defeated U.S. congressman from New York. Eckert's appointment coincided with an increasingly hard line by the Reagan administration toward the FAO. As Eckert became more familiar with FAO management and operations, he concluded, in a classified communication, that the problem was not with FAO but with the State Department International Organizations Bureau. Talbot, *The Four World Food Agencies*, 36–37, 134–35.

59. The program was supported by both Israel and the United States when progress was reported to the 1991 conference. Howard Hjort, letter, 8 August 1993.

60. U.S. Congress, House Committee on Foreign Affairs, *U.S. Policy toward the Food and Agriculture Organization* (Washington: USGPO, 10 October 1990), 42, 47, 27, 35.

61. In this section I have drawn heavily on James P. Sewell, *UNESCO and World Politics: Engaging in International Relations* (Princeton: Princeton University Press, 1975); Roger A. Coate, *Unilateralism, Ideology, and U.S. Foreign Policy: The United States in and out of UNESCO* (Boulder: Lynne Rienner Publishers, 1988); Roger A. Coate, "Changing Patterns of Conflict: The United States and UNESCO," in *The United States and Multilateral Institutions: Patterns of Changing Instrumentality and Influence*, ed. Margaret P. Karns and Karen A. Mingst (Boston: Unwin Hyman, 1990), 231–60; Mark Imber, *The USA, ILO, UNESCO and IAEA: Politicization and Withdrawal in the Specialized Agencies* (New York: St. Martin's, 1989); William Preston, Jr., Edward S. Herman, and Herbert I. Schiller, *Hope and Folly: The United States and UNESCO, 1945–1985* (Minneapolis: University of Minnesota Press, 1989); U.S. Congress, House Committee on Foreign Affairs, *U.S. Withdrawal from UNESCO* (Washington: USGPO, 1984).

62. Coate, *Unilateralism, Ideology, and Foreign Policy,* 49, 26.

63. Imber, *USA, ILO, UNESCO and IAEA*, 97.

64. Coate, *Unilateralism, Ideology, and Foreign Policy*, 40.

65. Imber, *USA, ILO, UNESCO and IAEA*, 100.

66. Ibid., 28. Biddle apparently was not supported within the State Department, where some resented what was seen as an overt act of patronage.

67. Ibid., 28. Also Cox and Jacobson, *Anatomy of Influence*, 155.

68. Imber, *USA, ILO, UNESCO and IAEA*, 28; Coate, "Changing Patters of Conflict," 235; Coate, *Unilateralism, Ideology, and Foreign Policy*, 29; James P. Sewell, "UNESCO: Pluralism Rampart," in Cox and Jacobson, *Anatomy of Influence*, 162–68; Karns and Mingst, *United States and Multilateral Institutions*, 235.

69. Karns and Mingst, *United States and Multilateral Institutions*, 236; Julien Behrstock, *The Eighth Case: Troubled Times in the United Nations* (New York: University Press of America, 1987), 51.

70. Vittorino Veronese resigned because of ill health in November 1961. Maheu was appointed acting director general and in November 1962 was elected to a six-year term by the General Conference. Maheu was the first UNESCO director-general to be appointed from within the organization. He was also, in retrospect, UNESCO's most effective director-general. His aggressive efforts to expand and strengthen the UNESCO program provoked considerable opposition. Sewell, *UNESCO and World Politics*, 266–75.

71. Karns and Mingst, *United States and Multilateral Institutions*, 237; Imber, *USA, ILO, UNESCO and IAEA*, 100.

72. Karns and Mingst, *United States and Multilateral Institutions*, 236.

73. Preston, Herman, and Schiller, *Hope and Folly*, 120–48.

74. Ibid., 213–81.

75. Leonard Sussman, "Statement," in House Committee on Foreign Affairs, *U.S. Withdrawal from UNESCO: Hearings, April 25, 26 and May 2* (Washington: USGPO, 1984), 205.

76. Coate, *Unilateralism, Ideology, and Foreign Policy*, 34; Coate, "Changing Patterns of Conflict," 240.

77. Imber, *USA, ILO, UNESCO and IAEA*, 103; U.S. Department of State, *U.S. Participation in the U.N.* (Washington: Department of State, 1976), 257.

78. Coate, *Unilateralism, Ideology, and Foreign Policy*, 9.

79. U.S. Department of State, *Perspectives on the U.S. Withdrawal from UNESCO* (Washington: Department of State, 31 October 1984); "Report to Congress on UNESCO Policies and Procedures with Respect to the Media Requested in Section 109 of Public Law 97–241" (Washington: Department of State, January 1984); *U.S./UNESCO Policy Review* (Washington: Department of State, 27 February 1984); U.S. Department of State, *U.S. Participation in the UN* (Washington: Department of State, 1983).

80. Department of State, *U.S. Participation in the UN*, 254. The MacBride commission, officially the International Commission for the Study of Communications, was chaired by Sean MacBride of Ireland. The commission was established to study measures to facilitate the free and balanced flow of information between the developed and developing countries. The United States supported the appointment of the commission to move debates away from ideological rhetoric and toward more substantive discussion. In 1980 UNESCO unanimously adopted the report of the commission. Coate, "Changing Patterns of Conflict," 239.

81. For a more extended discussion, see Coate, "Changing Patterns of Conflict," 243–47.

82. House Committee on Foreign Affairs, *U.S. Withdrawal from UNESCO*, 33.

83. See, for example, Thomas Gulick, *For UNESCO: A Failing Grade in Education* (Washington: Heritage Foundation, 21 October 1982), 221. For a vigorous, and often indignant, critique of the Heritage Foundation role in the U.S. withdrawal from UNESCO, see Preston, Herman, and Schiller, *Hope and Folly*, esp. 21.

84. Thomas Gulick, *UNESCO: Where Culture Becomes Propaganda* (Washington: Heritage Foundation, 13 December 1982), backgrounder 233.

85. Karns and Mingst, *United States and Multilateral Organizations*, 246; Coate, *Unilateralism, Ideology, and Foreign Policy*, 253; Imber, *USA, ILO, UNESCO and IAEA*, 118–20.

86. Coate, *Unilateralism, Ideology, and Foreign Policy*, 57–58.

87. *Structural/institutional* referred to (1) a perceived imbalance in authority between the secretariat and the delegate bodies and (2) the decline of the Western Group from a position of dominance to a status of automatic minority. *Political* referred to undue politicization in UNESCO delegate body debates (i.e., Arab-Israeli) and certain programs (NWICO, collective rights, peace and disarmament). *Program/administrative* referred to specific concerns in program planning, lack of program concentration and prioritization, program monitoring and evaluation, and budget management.

88. Coate, *Unilateralism, Ideology, and Foreign Policy*, 66.

89. Ibid., 253. Gregory Newell was a former campaign aid and Reagan White

House employee appointed assistant secretary of state for international organization affairs. He made UNESCO withdrawal his issue.

90. Ibid., 22; Imber, *USA, ILO, UNESCO and IAEA*, 119.

91. U.S. Department of State, *The Activities of UNESCO since U.S. Withdrawal: A Report by the Secretary of State* (Washington: USGPO, 17 April 1990). See also *The Activities after April 30, 1990 of the United Nations Educational, Scientific and Cultural Organization by the Secretary of State* (Washington: Department of State, 24 July 1992, mimeo).

92. American Panel on UNESCO, *Schooling for Democracy: Reinventing UNESCO for the Post–Cold War World* (New York: United Nations Association of the United States of America, 20 May 1993).

93. Imber, *USA, ILO, UNESCO and IAEA*, 43; Walter Galenson, *The International Labor Organization* (Madison: University of Wisconsin Press, 1981); David A. Morse, *The Origins and Evolution of the ILO and Its Role in the World Community* (Ithaca: W. F. Humphrey Press, 1969); Antony Alcock, *History of the International Labor Organization* (New York: Octagon Books, 1971), 17.

94. Morse, *Origins and Evolution of the ILO*, 21.

95. John Mainwaring, *The International Labor Organization: A Canadian View* (Ottawa: Canadian Government Publishing Center, 1986), 108.

96. Imber, *Unilateralism, Ideology, and Foreign Policy*, 44; Mainwaring, *ILO: A Canadian View*, 108.

97. For a more complete discussion, see Galenson, *The International Labor Organization*, 107–251.

98. Mainwaring, *ILO: A Canadian View*, 124.

99. For greater detail see Galenson, *The International Labor Organization*, 140–96.

100. International Labour Organization, *Bibliography of Published Research of the World Employment Programme*, 3d ed. (Geneva: International Labour Office, 1980), 3. See particularly *Towards Full Employment: A Programme for Colombia* (1970); *Matching Employment Opportunities and Expectations: A Programme of Action for Ceylon* (1971 and 1974); *Employment, Incomes and Equality: A Strategy for Increasing Productive Employment in Kenya* (1972 and 1977); and *Total Involvement: A Strategy for Development in Liberia* (1972).

101. Imber, *USA, ILO, UNESCO and IAEA*, 49–51.

102. Galenson, *The International Labor Organization*, 23–24.

103. Imber, *USA, ILO, UNESCO and IAEA*, 54.

104. Ibid., 55–56; U.S. Department of Labor, *The U.S. and the ILO: A Revitalized Relationship* (Washington: USGPO, 1983).

105. Ibid., 60; Lois McHugh, *International Labor Organization: Issues of U.S. Membership* (Washington: Congressional Research Service, 1984), 66.

106. Imber, *USA, ILO, UNESCO and IAEA*, 65, 67, 59.

107. U.S. Congress, Senate Committee on Labor and Human Resources, *The United States and the International Labor Organization*, 99th Cong., 1st sess. (Washington: USGPO, 11 September 1985), 43.

108. In this section I have relied heavily on Szeming Sze, *The Origins of the World*

Health Organization: A Personal Memoir, 1945–1948 (Boca Raton: LISZ Publications, 1982); Karen A. Mingst, "The United States and the World Health Organization," in Karns and Mingst, *United States and Multilateral Institutions*, 205–30; Leon Gordenker, "The World Health Organization: Sector Leader or Occasional Benefactor?" in *U.S. Policy and the Future of the United Nations*, ed. Roger A. Coate (New York: Twentieth Century Fund, 1994), 167–91.

109. Cox and Jacobson, *Anatomy of Influence*, 178.

110. The International Sanitary Bureau established in 1902 changed its name to the Pan American Sanitary Board (PASB) in 1923, to the Pan American Sanitary Organization in 1947, and to the Pan American Health Organization (PAHO) in 1958. The organization has served as the regional agency of the World Health Organization since 1947. *United States Contributions to International Organizations* (Washington: Department of State, 1990), 87–88. In 1990, the U.S. contributed $39 million in assessed contributions to PAHO after withholdings for deferral and tax equalization.

111. Sze, *Origins of World Health Organization*, 25.

112. Cox and Jacobson, *Anatomy of Influence*, 178–87.

113. In this section, I draw primarily on the definitive report by F. Fenner, D. A. Henderson, I. Arita, J. Jezek, and I. D. Ladnyi, *Smallpox and Its Eradication* (Geneva: World Health Organization, 1988), 365–419.

114. Cox and Jacobson, *Anatomy of Influence*, 182; Fenner et al., *Smallpox and Its Eradication*, vii.

115. Jean Martin, "La mise en oeuvre de soins de sante primaires," *International Development Review* 21, no. 2 (1979): 23–38.

116. For greater detail on the issue discussed below, see Mingst, "United States and World Health Organization," 216–18.

117. Gordenker, "The World Health Organization," 184.

118. For a history of UNICEF, see Maggie Black, *The Children and the Nations: The Story of UNICEF* (New York: UNICEF, 1986). See also U.S. Department of State, *U.S. Participation in the U.N.* (Washington: Department of State, 1989), 120; U.S. Department of State, *U.N. Children's Fund* (Washington: Department of State, July 1981).

119. Black, *The Children and the Nations*, 25.

120. Ibid., 30–34.

121. Judith M. Spiegelman, *We Are the Children: A Celebration of UNICEF's First Forty Years* (Boston: Atlantic Monthly Press, 1986).

122. U.S. Department of State, *Contributions to International Organizations* (Washington: Department of State, 1990), 6.

123. Black, *The Children and the Nations*, 66.

124. Ibid., 66.

125. U.S. Department of State, *United States Participation in the U.N.* (Washington: U.S. Department of State, 1961), 269.

126. Black, *The Children and the Nations*, 84.

127. Spiegelman, *We Are the Children.*

128. U.S. Department of State, *United States Participation in the U.N.* (Washington: U.S. Department of State, 1963), 231.

129. Black, *The Children and the Nations*, 209.

130. Ibid., 314; U.S. Congress, Senate Committee on Foreign Relations, *International Development Assistance Authorization and S. Res. 118*, 95th Cong., 2d sess., 23 March and 28 April 1978 (Washington: USGPO, 1978).

131. Senate Committee on Foreign Relations, *International Development Assistance Authorization and S. Res. 118*, 332.

132. James P. Grant, *Disparity Reduction Rates as Social Indicators: A Proposal for Measuring and Targeting Progress in Meeting Basic Needs*, monograph 11 (Washington: Overseas Development Council, 1978).

133. U.S. Department of State, *U.S. Participation in the U.N.* (Washington: Department of State, 1989), 121.

134. U.S. Government Accounting Office, *United Nations: Issues Related to Payment of U.S. Contributions* (Washington: GAO, 1989); GAO, *United Nations: U.S. Participation in the Children's Fund* (Washington: USGAO, 1989).

135. United Nations, *World Declaration on the Survival, Protection and Development of Children and Plan of Action for Implementing the World Declaration on the Survival, Protection and Development of Children in the 1990s* (New York: United Nations, 30 September 1990). See also United Nations Childrens Fund, *Progress Report on the Follow Up to the World Summit on Children* (New York: United Nations Economic and Social Council, 22 May 1992).

136. In writing this section I have drawn heavily on Wade Rowland, *The Plot To Save the World* (Toronto: Clark, Irwin, 1973); World Commission on Environment and Development, *Our Common Future* (Oxford: Oxford University Press, 1987) (Brundtland Commission report); and John McCormick, *Reclaiming Paradise: The Global Environmental Movement* (Bloomington: Indiana University Press, 1989), 88–124. I am indebted to William H. Mansfield for comment on an earlier draft of this section.

137. Lynton K. Caldwell, *Man and His Environment: Policy and Administration* (New York: Harper & Row, 1975); Mastafa Tolba, *Evolving Environmental Perceptions* (London: Butterworths, 1988), 3–8; Rowland, *Plot To Save the World*, 140–89.

138. Mary Lean, *UNEP Profile* (Nairobi: United Nations Environmental Program, 1990), 39.

139. Ibid., 37; U.N. General Assembly, "Contributions Pledged or Paid at the 1990 United Nations Pledging Conference for Development Activities as of 30 June 1991," AL Conf. 15412 (New York: United Nations, 2 October 1991), 48.

140. Peter Sand, "International Cooperation: The Environmental Experience," in Jessica Tuchman Matthews, ed., *Preserving the Global Environment* (New York: Norton, 1991), 239.

141. During the early 1970s Congress was able, in spite of opposition by the Nixon administration, to pass several important pieces of environmental legislation, including the Clean Air Act (1970), the Occupational Safety and Health Act (1970), the Alaska Native Claims Settlement Act (1971), and an act on pesticide control (1972). During the middle and late 1970s, the United States added to its environmental legislation law in areas such as coastal zone management; protection of wetlands; safe drinking water; water pollution control; chemical controls; protection of parks, wild-

life, and endangered species; curbs on acid rain; and protection of the stratospheric ozone layer. The Endangered Species Act (1973), Safe Drinking Water Act (1974), Federal Land Policy and Management Act (1976), Federal Mine Safety and Health Act (1977), and Surface Mining Control Act (1977) represented major landmarks during the mid-1970s.

142. Rowland, *Plot To Save the World*, 48–50. Another important influence was the book by Donella H. Meadows and Dennis L. Meadows with Jorgen Randers and William W. Behrens III, *The Limits to Growth* (London: Earth Island Press, 1972). The book, sponsored by the Club of Rome, was published just a few weeks before the Stockholm Conference.

143. U.S. Congress, House Committee on Foreign Affairs, *U.S. Policy toward the United Nations Conference on Environment and Development*, 17 April, 24 July, and 3 October 1991 (Washington: USGPO, 1991), 76; Tolba, *Evolving Environmental Perceptions*, 60.

144. The arrangements for the NGO conference by the Swedish government were specifically designed to limit the ability of the NGOs and the assorted other interest groups and activists to disrupt the official conference proceedings. See Caldwell, *Man and His Environment*, 131; Rowland, *Plot To Save the World*, 1, 2, 121–31.

145. Rowland, *Plot To Save the World*, 100.

146. For further discussion of the difficulties faced by UNEP during its first decade, see McCormick, *Reclaiming Paradise*, 106–24.

147. Garth Porter and Janet Welsh Brown, *Global Environmental Politics* (Boulder: Westview Press, 1991), 46–51. See also U.S. Congress, House Committee on Foreign Affairs, *International Environment: Briefing Book on Major Selected Issues* (Washington: USGPO, July 1993), 79–81.

148. George P. Smith, "The U.N. and the Environment," in *A World without a U.N.*, ed. Burton Yale Pines (Washington: Heritage Foundation, 1984), 37–56, 43; Lean, *UNEP Profile*, 36.

149. Lynton K. Caldwell, *U.S. Interests and the Global Environment*, occasional paper 35 (Muscatine, Iowa: Stanley Foundation, February 1985), 17, 22; Tolba, *Evolving Environmental Perceptions*, 9–10.

150. World Commission on Environment and Development, *Our Common Future* (New York: Oxford University Press, 1987), 43. For the evolution of thought on sustainable development, see Sharachandra M. Lele, "Sustainable Development: A Critical Review," *World Development* 19 (November 1991): 607–22.

151. World Commission on Environment and Development, *Our Common Future*, 317.

152. Ibid., 320.

153. U.S. Congress, House Committee on Foreign Affairs, *U.S. Policy toward the 1992 United Nations Conference on Environment and Development* (Washington: USGPO, 1992), 79–81.

154. The United States initially declined to make a direct financial contribution to the GEF and instead announced that it would make a contribution of $50 million in parallel financing through AID. However, in late February 1992, during negotiations on the climate change convection, the U.S. changed its position and announced that it

would make a direct contribution of $50 million to the GEF. U.S. Congress, Senate Committee on Foreign Relations and House Committee on Foreign Affairs, *Financing New International Environmental Commitment* (Washington: USGPO, 1992), 27–31.

155. Susan R. Fletcher, *Congress and International Environmental Policy* (Washington: Library of Congress, Congress and Research Service, 4 May 1993), 5. Some NGOs, involving over 20,000 people, came together in a parallel event, the Global Forum, held in Rio at the same time as the Earth Summit.

156. House Committee on Foreign Affairs, *U.S. Policy toward the 1992 United Nations Conference*, 30.

157. Fletcher, *Congress and International Environmental Policy*, 17. After the Earth Summit, President George Bush proposed an "Interim Biodiversity Survey, Inventory, and Data Organization Plan" that would involve "the formation of an international group of experts to promote World Wide information exchange, and to evaluate and recommend methodologies for use in efforts to survey, inventory, and manage biodiversity." *Diversity* 8, no. 3 (1992): 20.

158. Mark Imber, "Too Many Cooks? The Post-Rio Reform of the United Nationals," *International Affairs* 69, no. 1 (1993): 55–70.

159. Kathryn G. Sessions and E. Zell Steever, "The U.N. Commission on Sustainable Development: Building the Capacities for Change," in Coate, *Future of the United Nations*, 193–215. See also Porter and Brown, *Global Environmental Politics*, 48–57.

160. Coate, "Changing Patterns of Conflict," 235.

161. For a discussion of the coordination issues, see Roger A. Coate, "Increasing the Effectiveness of the UN System," in Coate, *Future of the United Nations*, 56–62.

162. Paul D. Martin, "U.S. Public Opinion and the U.N.," in Toby T. Gati, ed., *The U.S, the U.N. and the Management of Global Change* (New York: New York University Press, 1983), 285–302.

Chapter 13 Reforming U.S. Foreign Economic Assistance

1. The author is indebted to C. Stuart Callison, John R. Eriksson, Curtis Farrar, Lester E. Gordon, Frank B. Kimball, Erik Newsom, Ralph H. Smuckler, and John G. Stovall for comments on an earlier draft of this chapter.

2. For reviews of reorganization and reform proposals, see U.S. Congress, House Committee on Foreign Affairs, *The Reorganization of U.S. Development Aid: Comparison and Summary Analysis of Some Official and Unofficial Proposals* (Washington: USGPO, 1973; U.S. Congress, House Committee on Foreign Affairs, *Foreign Assistance Policy Studies: A Review of Major Reports and Recommendations* (Washington: USGPO, 1988); U.S. Agency for International Development, Bureau for Program and Policy Coordination, *The Future of Foreign Assistance: A Summary of Issues and Annotated Bibliography* (Washington: April 1989); U.S. Agency for International Development, *AID Operations Management and Organization: A Bibliography, 1989–1993* (Washington: USAID Center for Development Information and Evaluation, January 1993).

3. Charles William Maynes, "American Third World Hang-Ups," *Foreign Policy* 71 (Summer 1988): 117–40.

4. John White, *The Politics of Foreign Aid* (New York: St. Martin's, 1974), 215.

5. Jerome Levinson and Juan de Onis, *The Alliance That Lost Its Way: A Critical Report on the Alliance for Progress* (Chicago: Quadrangle Books, 1970), 34–58, 333–47.

6. Frank M. Coffin, *Witness for AID* (Boston: Houghton Mifflin, 1964), 85–87. See also President's Task Force on Foreign Economic Assistance, *An Act for International Development: A Summary Presentation* (Washington: USGPO, June 1961).

7. Ibid., 126.

8. Arthur M. Schlesinger, Jr., *A Thousand Days: John F. Kennedy in the White House* (Boston: Houghton Mifflin, 1965), 589–600. Hamilton had originally been under consideration for the directorship of CIA. Schlesinger characterized Hamilton as "a tough and brisk administrator, well fitted to carry through the job of reorganization; and this he did with expedition. The technical assistance specialists were dethroned." The perspective from inside the agency was quite different. Hamilton was more concerned with the perks of the office—what limousine he was assigned—than with implementing the new legislation. By the time he was replaced by Bell, much of the momentum for reform had been dissipated. One former associate commented that "David Bell knew more about AID the day he arrived than Fowler Hamilton knew the day he left."

9. Rostow, *Eisenhower, Kennedy, and Foreign Aid*, 172. It is rather remarkable that Rostow was able to discuss the implementation of the 1961 act without mentioning either Hamilton or Bell by name. After a disappointing interview with President Kennedy, Hamilton was given the AID appointment.

10. In the hearings on his nomination as AID administrator on 22 January 1963, David E. Bell defended the shift away from grants and toward loans and argued that it should be possible, over a reasonably short period, to change the terms of the loan so that they progressively approached market rates. Bell also commented that the most significant change in the 1962 reorganization was achieving greater program centralization in Washington under regional assistant administrators for the Far East, for the Near East and South Asia, for Africa, and for Latin America. He also indicated that since the reorganization many of the technical people in the field, such as the agriculture, industry, health, and education officers and their staffs, thought that they had lost influence within the agency. Many former AID staff date the decline in the AID capacity for technical assistance to the 1961 reorganization. One frequently encounters a comment to the effect that "the programmers and the money people began to dominate the scientists and technicians." For Bell's testimony, see U.S. Congress, Senate Committee on Foreign Relations, *Hearings on Nominations of Christian A. Herter, William T. Gossett, and David E. Bell* (Washington: USGPO, 22 January 1983).

11. Jerome Levinson and Juan de Onis, *The Alliance That Lost Its Way* (Chicago: Quadrangle Books, 1970), 59–73.

12. In 1961 the Kennedy administration had been successful in obtaining a substantial increase in the foreign assistance budget over the strong objections of Representa-

tive Otto Passman (D-La.), chairman of the Foreign Operations Subcommittee of the House Appropriations Committee (Chap. 3). AID's apparent failure to show significant results during its year of grace gave Passman a chance to return to the battle in 1962. He did this with undiminished zest, even keeping one hapless regional director on the stand for 100 hours of detailed and divisive interrogation. At the same time, Wayne Morse, Ernest Gruening, and other liberal Democrats in the Senate, alienated by the persisting emphasis on military aid, began to fight against the program. All of this produced a congressional mood that cut the president's 1962 request from $4.9 to $3.9 billion and reduced development loans by more than 20 percent. Schlesinger, *A Thousand Days,* 596.

13. Richard M. Nixon, "U.S. Foreign Policy for the 1970s, a New Strategy for Peace," Presidential Report to Congress, 18 February 1970, reprinted in *Public Papers of the Presidents of the United States: Richard Nixon, 1970* (Washington: USGPO, 1971), 116–90.

14. Robert A. Pastor, *Congress and the Politics of U.S. Foreign Economic Policy, 1929–1976* (Berkeley: University of California Press, 1980), 278.

15. Curtis Farrar, interview, 19 September 1989.

16. Lester E. Gordon, *An Assessment of Development Assistance Strategies: Interim Report* (Washington: Brookings Institution, 6 October 1977, mimeo): 27.

17. For a very useful review, see U.S. General Accounting Office, *Coordinating U.S. Development Assistance: Problems Facing the International Development Cooperation Agency,* ID-80-13 (Washington: USGAO, 1 February 1980). In this section I have drawn rather liberally on the language of the GAO report.

18. Jimmy Carter, *United States International Development Cooperation Agency: Message to Congress,* Transmitting Reorganization Plan No. 2 of 1979 (Washington: White House, 10 April 1979). See also *Message from the President of the United States Transmitting a Reorganization Plan To Consolidate Certain Foreign Assistance Activities of the United States Government Pursuant to 5 USC 903,* House Document 96-94, 96th Cong., 1st sess. (Washington: USGPO, 10 April 1979). Additional amendments were transmitted on House Document 96-127 on 21 May 1979.

19. See Senate Committee on Governmental Affairs, *Hearings on Reorganization Plan No. 2 of 1979* (Washington: USGPO, 1 May 1979); House Committee on Government Operations, *Hearings on Reorganization Plan No. 2 of 1979* (Washington: USGPO, 21 May 1979).

20. For a useful review, see William Colglazier and Paul Doty, "U.S. Debates a New Agency," *Bulletin of the Atomic Scientists* 36 (May 1980): 43–47. The ISTC initiative was strongly supported by Frank Press, the president's science advisor. However, all elements of the academic community were not equally enthusiastic about the establishment of an ISTC. Some land-grant universities thought that their interests had been met by the passage of Title XII of the Foreign Assistance Act of 1975, which established the Board on International Food and Agriculture for Development (see Chap. 7).

21. "Foreign Aid Appropriations, Conference Action, Scientific Institute," *Congressional Quarterly Almanac* 35 (1979): 268. The Carter administration had originally

proposed an ISTC budget of $96 million. This included $25 million of new money and a $71 million transfer of existing research from AID. The 1980 foreign aid authorization bill included the proposal to establish ISTC and authorized $23.75 million in new funds. The House version of the foreign aid appropriations bill (H.R. 4423) included funding for ISTC. However, the Senate bill eliminated ISTC funding. On the Senate floor Senator DeConcini successfully inserted an amendment prohibiting the use of any money for ISTC planning in fiscal 1980. The conference committee was unable to resolve the deadlock, and the fiscal 1980 foreign aid appropriations bill remained stalled in the House-Senate conference committee at the end of the 1979 congressional session. Ibid., 258–68.

22. Administrator Gilligan had a penchant for offhand comments that tended to produce negative feedback. On being appointed as AID administrator, he is reported to have commented, "The trouble with the AID staff is that they are over-age, over-paid, and over here."

23. For an excellent review of the evolution of U.S. economic security assistance, see Larry Q. Nowels, *Economic Security Assistance as a Tool of American Foreign Policy: The Current Dilemma and Future Options* (Washington: National War College, February 1987), quotation from p. 5.

24. John Felton, "Shultz Comes Up Short in Bid for Foreign Aid," *Congressional Quarterly* 17 (May 1986): 1101, quoted in Nowels, *Economic Security Assistance,* 1.

25. Commission on Security and Economic Assistance, *A Report to the Secretary of State* (Washington: USGPO, 1983) (the Carlucci commission). See also Richard Hough, *Economic Assistance and Security: Rethinking U.S. Policy* (Washington: National Defense University, 1982), 73.

26. David R. Obey and Carol Lancaster, "Funding Foreign Aid," *Foreign Policy* 71 (Summer 1988): 141–55.

27. Ibid., 153.

28. John W. Sewell and Christine E. Contee, "Foreign Aid and Gramm-Rudman," *Foreign Affairs* 65 (Summer 1987): 1015–36.

29. Ibid., 1019, 1027. See also the review of U.S. assistance to Turkey in Krueger, Michalopoulos, and Ruttan, *Aid and Development,* chap. 14. In Turkey, the United States repeatedly backed away from pressing for political and economic reform when policy dialogues appeared to represent an obstacle to cooperation on security issues.

30. Sewell and Contee, "Foreign Aid and Gramm-Rudman," 1028. Sewell and Contee point out that at present Israel is the only country whose entire aid program is delivered in the form of program aid. But they also call for reform of assistance to Israel. Since Israel has an annual per capita income of well above $5000, Sewell and Contee find it difficult to discover any rationale that can justify military and security assistance equivalent to $750 per capita. They argue that concessional aid be phased out and be replaced by lending at near commercial rates and a free trade arrangement.

31. Ibid., 1032.

32. Ralph H. Smuckler and Robert J. Berg (with David F. Gordon), *New Challenges, New Opportunities: U.S. Cooperation for International Growth and Development in the 1990s* (East Lansing: Michigan State University Center for Advanced

Study in International Development, 1988). Some of the papers commissioned as part of the Michigan State University project have been reproduced in Robert J. Berg and David F. Gordon, eds., *Cooperation for International Development: The United States and the Third World in the 1990s* (Boulder: Lynne Rienner Publishers, 1989).

33. Alan Woods, *Development and the National Interest: U.S. Economic Assistance into the 21st Century* (Washington: Agency for International Development, 17 February 1989). The Woods report had been circulating in Washington in prepublished form since mid-November 1988.

34. Ibid., 112, 120. The Woods report has been criticized by AID staff for its lack of appreciation (1) of the accomplishments of U.S. economic assistance and (2) of the technical and institutional requirements for effective response to macro- and sector-level policy reform. Public sector expenditures for health and education were regarded as unproductive "consumption activities." See C. Stuart Callison, "Development and the National Interest," *Foreign Service Journal* (January 1990): 28–33.

35. Secretary of State James A. Baker III and other officials did appeal to Congress to reduce the earmarking of spending levels. One knowledgeable observer commented that the administration felt no need to present its own reform agenda because the Hamilton-Gilman reforms reflected administration views on this issue. In general, the House committees with jurisdiction over foreign aid have been sympathetic to the reduction of earmarking while the Senate committees have been more aggressive about earmarking. John Felton, "Foreign Aid Measure Puts Hill Sharply at Odds with Bush," *Congressional Quarterly*, 18 November 1989, 3175–83. See also Alan Woods, statement, in U.S. Congress, Senate Committee on Foreign Relations, *Foreign Assistance Authorizations for Fiscal Year 1990* (Washington: USGPO, 1989), 4–35.

36. Lee Hamilton, Remarks, Washington, September 14 (mimeo).

37. Task Force on Foreign Assistance, *Report to the Committee on Foreign Affairs, U.S. House of Representatives* (Washington: USGPO, 1989).

38. Ibid., v, vi.

39. The task force noted that, in the 1989 fiscal year, Congress had earmarked specific spending levels for 92 percent of all military aid, 98 percent of the Economic Support Fund, and 49 percent of Development Assistance. It also noted that current law requires the administration to send Congress 288 separate reports on the foreign aid program.

40. Section 1201-e incorporated the language of a proposal, the Global Poverty Reduction Act, that had been introduced in the House and Senate in 1988 (H.R. 4277 and S. 2454). The bill was widely supported by the PVO community. The objectives of Section 1201-e were to (1) reduce under-five mortality rates by at least 50 percent of the 1980 levels, or to not more than 70 per thousand live births; (2) achieve universal primary education and at least 80 percent female literacy; and (3) reduce the proportion of the population living in poverty by at least 50 percent of that proportion in 1980. The spirit was similar to the basic human needs mandate of the 1973 Foreign Assistance Act, and the language drew directly on the basic needs proposals by the Overseas Development Council in the late 1970s. See James P. Grant, *Disparity Reduction Rates in Social Indicators: A Proposal for Measuring and Targeting Progress in*

Meeting Basic Needs (Washington: Overseas Development Council Monograph 11, September 1978).

41. "The unanimous committee vote appeared to signal not so much universal satisfaction with the bill as relief by committee members to be rid of it. Pell had called repeated mark up sessions starting on June 9 only to be frustrated by members refusals to show up." *Congressional Quarterly*, 13 July 1989, 1796.

42. The Senate, unlike the House, has no Rules Committee to control debate and limit the number of amendments. As a result, any bill has the potential to trigger an extended debate, numerous amendments, or even a filibuster.

43. Congress had enacted only two foreign aid authorization bills during the Reagan administration—in 1981 and 1985. *Congressional Quarterly*, 18 July 1989, 1705.

44. Congressman Obey expressed himself rather forcefully on this issue: "Last year we had a total bill before this committee of $14.3 billion . . . This year the administration has asked for . . . a budget of $14.7 billion . . . They are going to get $14.3 billion because . . . I have read Mr. Bush's lips in slow motion and I believe there are going to be no new taxes." U.S. Congress, House Committee on Appropriations, *Foreign Operations, Export Financing, and Related Programs Appropriations for 1990* (Washington: USGPO, 1989), 133.

45. John Felton, "Foreign Aid Deals Reached, but Veto Threat Remains," *Congressional Quarterly*, 11 November 1989, 3080–82.

46. After Roskens' appointment Edelman returned to his former position as deputy administrator. Differences between Edelman and Roskens led to Edelman's resignation from AID in the fall of 1992. When Edelman left the agency, he commented that, "in 25 years of government this is the worst bureaucracy I've ever worked with." Christopher Madison, "Rejiggering AID's Archaic Bureaucracy," *Government Executive* (October 1991): 10. Priscilla Del Bosque, vice president of the Foreign Service Association, asked in reply, "What have you done, Mr. Edelman, to improve the management of the organization? . . . Who is providing leadership and vision for the organization?" "From the Vice President," *ASFA News* (January 1992): 4.

47. C. Stuart Callison and John G. Stovall, "AID's Identity Crisis," *Foreign Science Journal* (January 1992): 32.

48. "The struggle for the soul of AID has been going on for some time. Congress attempted to capture it with the 1973 Foreign Assistance Act, known as the Basic Human Needs (BHN) mandate or 'New Directions' redirecting development assistance to the poor majority in developing countries. But in the late 1970's Congress and the Carter administration began to shift staff resources away from the BHN toward security interests and stressed the private sector as the key to development." Callison and Stovall, "AID's Identity Crisis," 32, 34.

49. During the consideration on the Foreign Assistance Act of 1991, the Senate Committee on Foreign Relations proposed greater emphasis on large infrastructure investment, supported by tied aid and mixed credits. The initiative, sponsored by Democratic Senators Boren, Bentson, Byrd, and Bacus and dubbed the "Killer B's bill," was first opposed and then supported by the administration. There were several versions of the bill. Its effect would have been to shift ESF resources to expenditures on

capital goods, primarily for infrastructure development, tied to U.S. procurement. The result would be to further decrease funding for programs and projects associated with the 1970s basic human needs mandate. The proposed increase would have to come from existing activities in the foreign assistance budget. *Congressional Quarterly,* 9 March 1991, 596.

50. Christopher Madison, "Rejiggering AID's Archaic Bureaucracy," *Government Executive* (October 1991): 10–12. In December 1991 Cable News Network (CNN) aired a series entitled "AID: Under Investigation." An AID fact sheet documented numerous inaccuracies in the CNN reports.

51. Christopher Madison, "Foreign Aid Follies," *National Journal* (1 June 1991): 1288–91.

52. Before his nomination as vice president, Senator Al Gore had called for a Global Marshall Plan for the environment—a "massive effort to design and then transfer to poor nations the new technologies needed for sustained economic progress, a world wide program to stabilize world population, and binding commitments by the industrial nations to accelerate their own transition to an environmentally responsible pattern of life." Al Gore, *Earth in the Balance: Ecology and the Human Spirit* (Boston: Houghton Mifflin, 1992), 297.

53. For brief summaries of a much broader set of reviews and proposals, see George Ingram, *Summaries of Reviews of U.S. Foreign Assistance* (Washington: House Committee on Foreign Affairs, 28 January 1993, mimeo).

54. John W. Sewell and Peter M. Storm, *United States Budget for a New World Order: Promoting National Security and Advancing America's Interests Abroad, Fiscal 1992* (Washington: Overseas Development Council, 1991), 3.

55. Environmental Energy Study Institute Task Force (Spaeth task force), *Partnership for Sustainable Development: A New U.S. Agenda for International Development and Environmental Security* (Washington: May 1991).

56. President's Commission on the Management of AID Programs, *Report to the President: An Action Plan* (Washington: The Commission, 16 April 1992); *A Progress Report* (Washington: USGPO, 29 September 1992); *Critical Underlying Issues—Further Analysis* (Washington: USGPO, 22 December 1992) (Ferris commission). The work of the Ferris commission was complemented by a series of General Accounting Office studies of AID management conducted in 1991 and 1992. The GAO was particularly critical of what it regarded as excessive decentralization and lack of accountability at the mission level for program results.

57. Senator Leahy was particularly disturbed by the lag between project initiation and the disbursement of funds. His concern was apparently stimulated by a visit to a "self-help" housing project in Egypt. During 1991 and 1992 these concerns were also stimulated by a series of press reports of corruption, or at least lax financial controls, in the agency both in Washington and in the field. On 19 August 1992 Senator Leahy wrote to President Bush urging that before the election the administration undertake an internal assessment of development assistance priorities and programs. In his letter Leahy noted that "it has become patently clear to me that our international assistance program is exhausted intellectually, conceptually and politically. It has no widely

understood and agreed upon set of goals, it lacks coherence and vision, and there is a very real question whether parts of it serve broadly accepted United States National interests any longer." Patrick Leahy, letter, 19 August 1992.

58. President's Commission on the Management of AID Programs, *Report to the President*, 5. The administration was not enthusiastic about the establishment of the Ferris commission. OMB attempted to deflect the anticipated findings of the commission by setting up a joint OMB/AID "SWAT" team to examine management problems and recommend solutions. See Office of Management and Budget, *Improving Management at the Agency for International Development* (Washington: USGPO, July 1992). It was reported in the press that Commission Chairman Ferris had difficulty arranging a meeting with Secretary of State James Baker to discuss the commission report. This situation changed in late September when AID came under intense public and congressional criticism for allegedly subsidizing the transfer of jobs abroad under the Caribbean Basin program. It then became very convenient for the administration to point to the Ferris report as evidence that it was already examining the management of AID programs. The life of the commission was extended to 31 December 1992, and access to the acting secretary of state, Lawrence Eagleburger, was facilitated.

59. The commission, drawing on the Congressional Research Service, identified 78 U.S. government agencies engaged in yielding benefits to foreign governments. The commission was particularly concerned with the 19 agencies with the largest programs. *Critical Underlying Issues*, 50. For a scholarly discussion see Raymond F. Hopkins, "The International Role of Domestic Bureaucracy," *International Organization* 30 (Summer 1976): 405–31.

60. As an example of lack of coordination, the Ferris commission noted that "program officials for the East European Assistance Program were not aware that specialists in the SEC [Securities Exchange Commission] were running a $25 million program to develop a stock exchange in Poland." *Critical Underlying Issues*, 52.

61. President's Commission on the Management of AID Programs, *Report to the President,* 11. A rather curious paper by James C. Chad and Roger D. Store, "New Mission for Foreign Aid," *Foreign Affairs* 7 (Winter 1993): 196–205, attempted to achieve some consistency between the Spaeth and Ferris reports by urging U.S. aid to advance sustainable development by subsidizing the U.S. export of environmental technology.

62. American Foreign Policy Council, *Modernizing Foreign Assistance: Resource Management as an Instrument of Foreign Policy* (Westport, Conn.: Praeger, 1992), 23.

63. Ibid., 68, 69.

64. Task Force on Development Assistance and Economic Growth, *International Cooperation for Sustainable Economic Growth: The US Interest and Proposals for Revitalization* (Washington: Board for International Food and Agricultural Development and International Cooperation, February 1992). See also the comment by D. Allen Bromley, director of the White House Office of Science and Technology Policy, "We have failed miserably in trying to convince our State Department that science and technology should be an integral part of foreign relations." Conversations with Allen Bromley, "Reflections on Exiting Center Stage," *Physics Today* (January 1993): 58 (53–59).

65. Task Force on Development Assistance and Economics Growth, *International Cooperation*, 73.

66. Carnegie Commission on Science, Technology, and Government, *Science and Technology in US International Affairs* (Washington: Carnegie Corporation of New York, January 1992), 84–91.

67. Callison and Stovall, "AID's Identity Crisis," 33; Jack Anderson and Dale Van Atta, "Checking Rolodexes of the State Department," *Washington Post*, 11 September 1990, 20. See also an unclassified State Department cable, "The Rolodex Test: Making Businesses the Business of AID Missions," Washington Agency for International Development Telecommunication Center, 30 June 1990. The authorship of the cable, which instructed AID staff to have more businesses than bureaucrat numbers and addresses on their Rolodexes, is attributed to then assistant administrator for Asia and the Near East, Carol Adelman.

68. Independent Group on the Future of US Development Cooperation, *Reinventing Foreign AID: White Paper on US Development Cooperation in a New Democratic Era* (Washington: Overseas Development Council, December 1992). The report emerged out of a series of informal seminars organized by the Rockefeller Foundation and the Overseas Development Council beginning in the spring of 1992.

69. Ibid., 9, 10. Before the 1980s sustainability was discussed primarily in reference to the sustainability of the natural resource base. After the publication of the Brundtland commission report in 1985, the concept was embraced by the development community and broadened to include the viability of both natural and human communities. "Sustainable development is development that meets the needs of the present without compromising the ability of future generations to meet their own needs." World Commission Environment and Development, *Our Common Future* (New York: Oxford University Press, 1987), 43.

70. Bread for the World Institute, *U.S. Foreign Aid: What Counts for Sustainable Development?* (Washington: 5 March 1993).

71. This was also the theme of a report by the American Foreign Policy Council, *Modernizing Foreign Assistance: Resource Management as an Instrument of Foreign Policy* (Westport, Conn.: Praeger, 1991).

72. Editorial, "Aid: Back to the Drawing Board," *Washington Post*, 1 April 1993, A-22.

73. U.S. Congress, House, Hearing before the Committee on Foreign Affairs, 26 July 1993, in *Foreign Aid Reform* (Washington: USGPO, 1993); Task Force To Reform A.I.D. and the International Affairs Budget, *Preventive Diplomacy: Revitalizing A.I.D. and Foreign Assistance for the Post–World War Era* (Washington: Department of State, September 1993, mimeo).

74. U.S. Agency for International Development, *Strategies for Sustainable Development* (Washington: US/AID, March 1984).

75. Editorial, "A Face Lift for Foreign Aid," *Washington Post*, 18 February 1994, A24.

76. Henry Kissinger and Cyrus Vance, "Bi-partisan Objectives for American Foreign Policy," *Foreign Affairs* 67 (Summer 1988): 910.

Chapter 14 Does AID Have a Future?

1. The author is indebted to Nancy Alexander, Richard E. Bissell, C. Stuart Callison, Robert Muscat, James Roumasset, and Clifton R. Wharton, Jr., for comments and suggestions on an earlier draft of this chapter.

2. In this chapter, I draw on material reprinted with permission from Vernon W. Ruttan, "Solving the Foreign Aid Vision Thing," *Challenge* (May/June 1991): 41–46; "An Emerging Vision of Global Futures," *Challenge* (May/June 1992): 51, 52; "Il Futuro dell' Assistenza delgi Stati Uniti," *Politica Internazionale* 21 (October/December 1993): 207–27.

3. World Commission on Environment and Development, *Our Common Future* (New York: Oxford University Press, 1987), 43 (the Brundtland commission); Al Gore, *Earth in the Balance: Ecology and the Human Spirit* (Boston: Houghton Mifflin, 1992); U.S. Agency for International Development, *Strategies for Sustainable Development* (Washington: US/AID, March 1994).

4. The Congressional Budget Office has estimated that implementation of programs along the lines outlined in the AID strategy document would cost the United States $12.5 billion a year above 1994 budget levels—an increase of approximately 150 percent in development assistance. Congressional Budget Office, *Enhancing U.S. Security through Foreign Aid* (Washington: CBO, April 1994).

5. U.S. Congress, House Committee Foreign Affairs, *U.S. Foreign Aid in a Changing World Order: Options for New Priorities* (Washington: USGPO, 1991).

6. Robert Zimmerman, *Dollars, Diplomacy, and Dependency: Dilemmas of U.S. Economic Aid* (Boulder: Lynne Rienner Publishers, 1993), 10–12; Nicholas Eberstadt, *Foreign Aid and America's Purpose* (Washington: American Enterprise Institute for Public Policy, 1988). Both Zimmerman and Eberstadt draw on the series of studies by John E. Reilly, *American Public Opinion and U.S. Foreign Policy* (Chicago: Chicago Council of Foreign Relations, 1983 and earlier).

7. William Schneider, "Public Opinion," in Joseph S. Nye, Jr., *The Making of America's Soviet Policy* (New York: Council on Foreign Relations, 1989), 12. The Schneider chapter contains a very useful review of elite and popular opinion in the area of foreign policy for the 1948–82 period.

8. Henry A. Kissinger, *Diplomacy* (New York: Simon & Schuster, 1994), 703–32.

9. Duane M. Oldfield and Aaron W. Wildavsky, "Reconsidering the Two Presidencies," *Society* (July/August 1989): 57.

10. This section draws on material discussed in greater detail in Krueger, Michalopoulos, and Ruttan, *Aid and Development*.

11. For more extensive discussion the reader is referred to the very useful reports on the effects of adjustment lending prepared by the World Bank. See particularly International Bank for Reconstruction and Development, Country Economics Department, *Report on Adjustment Lending* (Washington: IBRD, 1 August 1988), and idem, *Adjustment Lending Policies for Sustainable Growth*, Policy and Research Series No. 14 (Washington: IBRD, 1990). For an earlier report on U.S. bilateral policy-based lending experience, see Agency for International Development, *The Use of Program Loans To Influence Policy*, DDC/Evaluation Paper 1A (Washington: US/AID, March 1970).

12. Willis L. Peterson, "Rates of Return to Assistance Capital: An International Comparison," *Kyklos* 42, fasc. 2 (1989): 203–4.

13. Stanton H. Burnett, *Investing in Security: Economic Aid for Non-Economic Purposes* (Washington: Center for Strategic and International Studies, 1992); Robert F. Zimmerman, *Dollars, Diplomacy, and Dependency,* 139–185.

14. Vernon W. Ruttan, "What Happened to Political Development?" *Economic Development and Cultural Change* 39 (January 1991): 265–92. For a more iconoclastic perspective on the state of knowledge about political development, see Adam Przeworski and Fernando Limongi, "Political Regimes and Economic Growth," *Journal of Economic Perspectives* 7 (Summer 1993): 51–70.

15. For a more balanced approach, see Ronald I. McKinnon, *The Order of Economic Liberalization: Financial Control in the Transition to a Market Economy* (Baltimore: Johns Hopkins University Press, 1991), 4–10, 184–86. See also the International Finance Corporation Annual Lecture by the former deputy prime minister and finance minister of Poland, Leszek Balcerowicz, "Economic Transition in Central and Eastern Europe: Comparisons and Lessons" (Washington: International Finance Corporation, 1 December 1993).

16. This proposal calls for a broader mandate than the proposals for an autonomous Institute for Scientific and Technical Cooperation that were discussed in the late 1970s. It is similar to the proposal that has emerged from a series of recent workshops on the future of technical assistance. See G. Edward Schuh, "A Proposal To Establish a National Institute for International, Scientific and Technological Collaboration for Sustainable Economic Development" (Minneapolis: Hubert H. Humphrey Institute of Public Affairs, December 1990). If the capacity of AID to manage science and technology programs continues to erode, it is possible that ISTC responsibility should be located in another agency, such as the National Institute of Standards and Technology.

17. A Center for Voluntary Cooperation in Development was included in the International Economic Cooperation Act (H.R. 2655) passed by the House of Representatives on 29 June 1989. Its establishment was advanced by the PVO community. See the testimony by the president of the American Council for Voluntary International Action (InterAction), Peter J. Davies, "Statement," in U.S. Congress, House Select Committee on Hunger, *Role of Private Voluntary Organizations and the U.S. Foreign Assistance Program: Hearings* (Washington: USGPO, 1989), 14–20, 122–36.

18. See Bread for the World Institute, *U.S. Foreign Aid: What Counts for Sustainable Development?* (Washington: BWI, 18 March 1993), 53–59.

19. George F. Kennan, *The Cloud of Danger: Current Realities—an American Foreign Policy* (Boston: Little, Brown, 1977), 82. See also Strobe Talbott, "What To Do about Israel," *Time* 118 (7 September 1981): 18–20.

20. It will be objected that U.S. dependence on oil from the Persian Gulf gives the United States a vital security interest in the Middle East. There are several reasons to reassess this argument: (1) the collapse of the USSR removes what has in the past been viewed as a primary threat, (2) the dependence of the region on oil exports will remain regardless of the political configuration of the region, (3) the U.S. military cost of safeguarding access to the region exceeds any costs that cooperation among countries

in the region in the pricing of oil would be able to impose, (4) economic cooperation among the Arab (and other Islamic) states in the region would probably be more conducive of political stability in the region than would an interventionist U.S. policy. On the hidden costs of U.S. dependence on energy from the Persian Gulf region, see Harold M. Hubbard, "The Real Costs of Energy," *Scientific American* 264 (April 1991): 36–42. On prospects for a more open energy market, see Joseph Stanislaw and Daniel Yergin, "Oil: Reopening the Door," *Foreign Affairs* 72 (September/October 1993): 81–93.

21. Jeane J. Kirkpatrick, "Beyond the Cold War," *Foreign Affairs* 69 (1990): 1–16; Kissinger, *Diplomacy,* 19.

22. Thomas I. Friedman, "A New Kind of Foreign Policy," (Minneapolis) *Star-Tribune*, 3 October 1993, 26A.

23. For an effort to place a series of these new threats on the foreign policy agenda, see Graham Allison and Gregory F. Treverton, eds., *Rethinking America's Security: Beyond Cold War to New World Order* (New York: Norton, 1992). For a polemical attack on efforts to find new enemies to replace the Soviet Union, see Jonathan Kwitney, *Endless Enemies: The Making of an Unfriendly World* (New York: Viking Penguin, 1986).

24. Vernon W. Ruttan, ed., *Health and Sustainable Agricultural Development: Perspectives on Growth and Constraints* (Boulder: Westview Press, 1994).

25. Vernon W. Ruttan, "Sustainable Growth in Agricultural Production," in Vernon W. Ruttan, ed., *Agriculture, Environment and Health: Sustainable Development in the 21st Century* (Minneapolis: University of Minnesota Press, 1994), 3–20; Vernon W. Ruttan, "Constraints on the Design of Sustainable Systems of Agricultural Production," *Ecological Economics* 10 (1994): 209–19.

26. Harlan Cleveland, *Birth of a New World: An Open Moment for International Leadership* (San Francisco: Jossey-Bass Publishers, 1993), 77–104.

27. Martin van Creveld, *The Transformation of War* (New York: Free Press, 1991), 192–223.

Index

Library of Congress Cataloging-in-Publication Data

Ruttan, Vernon W.

United States development assistance policy : the domestic politics of foreign economic aid / Vernon W. Ruttan.

p. cm. — (The Johns Hopkins studies in development)

Includes index.

ISBN 0-8018-5051-7

1. Economic assistance, American—Developing countries—History—20th century. 2. Pressure groups—United States—History—20th century. 3. United States—Foreign relations. 4. United States—Politics and government. I. Title. II. Series.

HC60.R84 1996

338.9'17301724—dc20 95-6422